Don

W9-BUD-302

DK

ULTIMATE VISUAL DICTIONARY

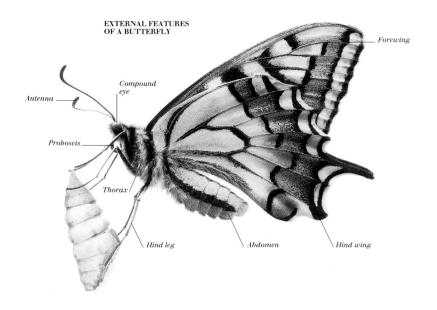

**EXTERNAL FEATURES
OF A BUTTERFLY**

Forewing

Antenna

Compound
eye

Proboscis

Thorax

Hind leg

Abdomen

Hind wing

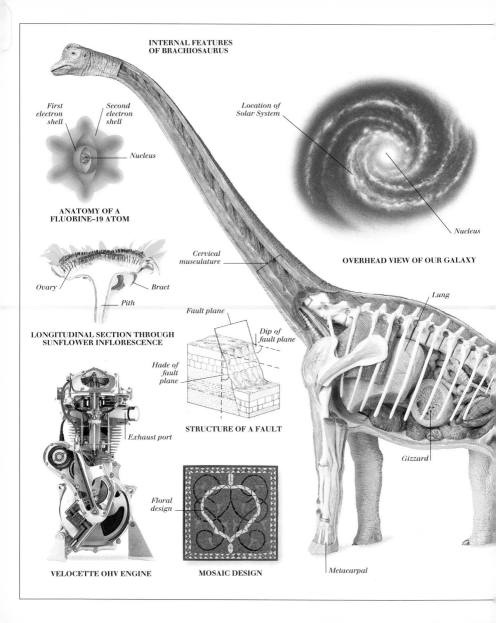

**INTERNAL FEATURES
OF BRACHIOSAURUS**

*First
electron
shell*

*Second
electron
shell*

Nucleus

**ANATOMY OF A
FLUORINE–19 ATOM**

*Location of
Solar System*

Nucleus

OVERHEAD VIEW OF OUR GALAXY

*Cervical
musculature*

Ovary

Bract

Pith

**LONGITUDINAL SECTION THROUGH
SUNFLOWER INFLORESCENCE**

Fault plane

*Dip of
fault plane*

*Hade of
fault
plane*

STRUCTURE OF A FAULT

Lung

Gizzard

Exhaust port

VELOCETTE OHV ENGINE

*Floral
design*

MOSAIC DESIGN

Metacarpal

DK

ULTIMATE VISUAL DICTIONARY

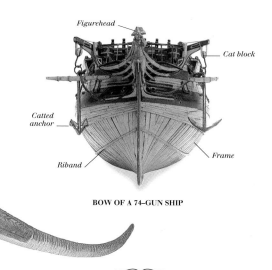

Figurehead

Cat block

Catted anchor

Riband

Frame

BOW OF A 74–GUN SHIP

Ankle joint

DK

DK PUBLISHING, INC

www.dk.com

A DK PUBLISHING BOOK

www.dk.com

PROJECT ART EDITORS HEATHER McCARRY, JOHNNY PAU, CHRIS WALKER, KEVIN WILLIAMS
DESIGNER SIMON MURRELL

PROJECT EDITORS LUISA CARUSO, PETER JONES, JANE MASON, GEOFFREY STALKER
EDITOR JO EVANS
US EDITOR JULEE BINDER

DTP DESIGNER ZIRRINIA AUSTIN
PICTURE RESEARCHER CHARLOTTE BUSH

MANAGING ART EDITOR TONI KAY
SENIOR EDITOR ROGER TRITTON
MANAGING EDITOR SEAN MOORE

PRODUCTION MANAGER HILARY STEPHENS

ANATOMICAL AND BOTANICAL MODELS SUPPLIED BY SOMSO MODELLE, COBURG, GERMANY

Sound hole

Hollow body

Headstock

Bridge

ACOUSTIC GUITAR

FIRST AMERICAN EDITION, 1994
FIRST PAPERBACK EDITION, 1998
4 6 8 10 9 7 5 3
PUBLISHED IN THE UNITED STATES BY DK PUBLISHING, INC.,
95 MADISON AVENUE,
NEW YORK, NEW YORK 10016

COPYRIGHT © 1994 DORLING KINDERSLEY LIMITED, LONDON

ALL RIGHTS RESERVED UNDER INTERNATIONAL AND PAN-AMERICAN COPYRIGHT CONVENTIONS.
NO PART OF THIS PUBLICATION MAY BE REPRODUCED, STORED IN A RETRIEVAL SYSTEM,
OR TRANSMITTED IN ANY FORM OR BY ANY MEANS, ELECTRONIC, MECHANICAL, PHOTOCOPYING,
RECORDING, OR OTHERWISE, WITHOUT THE PRIOR WRITTEN PERMISSION OF THE COPYRIGHT OWNER.
PUBLISHED IN GREAT BRITAIN BY DORLING KINDERSLEY LIMITED.

LIBRARY OF CONGRESS CATALOGING-IN-PUBLICATION DATA

Ultimate visual dictionary. - - 1st American ed.
 p.   cm.
 Includes index.
 ISBN 0–7894–2874–1 (alk. paper)
 1. Picture Dictionaries, English. I. DK Publishing, Inc.
 II. Title : ultimate visual dictionary.
PE1629.U48 1998   97–44408
423' . 1– –DC21   CIP

REPRODUCED BY COLOURSCAN, SINGAPORE

Printed in Singapore

Prosoma (cephalothorax) *Spinneret*

Leg

EXTERNAL FEATURES OF A SPIDER

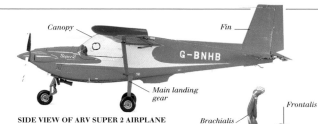

Canopy *Fin*

Main landing gear

SIDE VIEW OF ARV SUPER 2 AIRPLANE

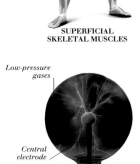

Frontalis

Brachialis

Deltoid

Rectus femoris

SUPERFICIAL SKELETAL MUSCLES

Barrel

Permanent black ink

FOUNTAIN PEN AND INK

CONTENTS

Architrave

Podium

TEMPLE OF VESTA, TIVOLI, ITALY, C. 80 BC

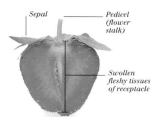

Sepal *Pedicel (flower stalk)*

Swollen fleshy tissues of receptacle

LONGITUDINAL SECTION THROUGH A STRAWBERRY

Low-pressure gases

Central electrode

BALL CONTAINING HIGH-TEMPERATURE GAS (PLASMA)

Nonbreakable plastic

Shock absorber

FOOTBALL HELMET

Introduction

THE ULTIMATE VISUAL DICTIONARY is a completely new kind of reference book. It provides a link between pictures and words in a way that no ordinary dictionary ever has. Most dictionaries simply tell you what a word means, but the *ULTIMATE VISUAL DICTIONARY* shows you — through a combination of detailed annotations, explicit photographs, and illustrations. In the *ULTIMATE VISUAL DICTIONARY*, pictures define the annotations around them. You do not read definitions of the annotated words, you see them. The highly accessible format of the *ULTIMATE VISUAL DICTIONARY*, the thoroughness of its annotations, and the range of its subject matter make it a unique and helpful reference tool.

How to use the ULTIMATE VISUAL DICTIONARY
You will find the *ULTIMATE VISUAL DICTIONARY* simple to use. It is divided by subject into 14 sections— THE UNIVERSE, PREHISTORIC EARTH, PLANTS, ANIMALS, THE HUMAN BODY, etc. Each section begins with a table of contents listing the major entries within that section. For example, THE VISUAL ARTS section contains entries on *Drawing, Tempera, Fresco, Oils, Watercolor, Pastels, Acrylics, Calligraphy, Printmaking, Mosaic,* and *Sculpture.* Every entry includes a short introduction explaining the purpose of the photographs and illustrations, and the significance of the annotations.

If you know what something looks like, but don't know its name, turn to the annotations surrounding the pictures; if you know a word, but don't know what it refers to, use the comprehensive index to direct you to the appropriate page.

Suppose you want to know what the bone at the end of your little finger is called. With a standard dictionary, you wouldn't know where to begin. But with the *ULTIMATE VISUAL DICTIONARY* you simply turn to the entry called *Hands*—within THE HUMAN BODY section—and you will find four fully annotated color photographs showing the skin, muscles, and bones

of the human hand. In this entry you will quickly find that the bone you are searching for is called the distal phalanx. In addition, you will discover that it is attached to the middle phalanx by the distal interphalangeal joint.

Perhaps you want to know what a catalytic converter looks like. If you look up "catalytic converter" in an ordinary dictionary, you will be told what it is and possibly what it does—but you will not be able to tell what shape it is or what it is made of. However, if you look up "catalytic converter" in the index of the *ULTIMATE VISUAL DICTIONARY*, you will be directed to the *Modern engines* entry on page 344—where the introduction gives you basic information about what a catalytic converter is—and to page 350—where there is a spectacular exploded-view photograph of the mechanics of a Renault Clio. From these pages you will find out not only what a catalytic converter looks like, but also that it is attached at one end to an exhaust downpipe and at the other to a silencer.

Whatever it is that you want to find a name for, or whatever name you want to find a picture for, you will find it quickly and easily in the *ULTIMATE VISUAL DICTIONARY.* Perhaps you need to know where the vamp on a shoe is; or how to tell obovate and lanceolate leaves apart; or what a spiral galaxy looks like; or whether birds have nostrils. With the *ULTIMATE VISUAL DICTIONARY* close by, the answers to each of these questions, and thousands more, are readily available.

The *ULTIMATE VISUAL DICTIONARY* does not just tell you what the names of the different parts of an object are. The photographs, illustrations, and annotations are all specially arranged to help you understand which parts relate to one another and how objects function.

With the *ULTIMATE VISUAL DICTIONARY*, in seconds you can find the words or pictures that you are looking for; or you can simply browse. The *ULTIMATE VISUAL DICTIONARY* is not intended to replace a standard dictionary or encyclopedia, but is instead a stimulating and valuable companion to ordinary reference volumes. Giving you access to the language that is used by astronomers and architects, musicians and mechanics, pilots and professional athletes, it is the ideal reference book for experts and novices of all ages.

***Sections of the* Ultimate Visual Dictionary**
The 14 sections of the *Ultimate Visual Dictionary* contain a total of more than 30,000 terms, encompassing a wide range of topics:

● In the first section, The Universe, spectacular photographs and illustrations are used to show the names of the stars and planets and to explain the structure of solar systems, galaxies, nebulae, comets, and black holes.

● Prehistoric Earth tells the story of how our own planet has evolved since its formation. It includes examples of prehistoric flora and fauna, and fascinating dinosaur models— some with parts of the body stripped away to show anatomical sections.

● Plants covers a huge range of species— from the familiar to the exotic. In addition to the color photographs of plants included in this section, there is a series of micrographic photographs illustrating plant details—such as pollen grains, spores, and cross-sections of stems and roots.

● In the Animals section, skeletons, anatomical diagrams, and different parts of animals' bodies have been meticulously annotated. This section provides a comprehensive guide to the vocabulary of zoological classification and animal physiology.

● The structure of the human body, its parts, and its systems are presented in The Human Body. The section includes lifelike, three-dimensional models and the latest false-color images. Clear and authoritative annotations indicate the correct anatomical terms.

● Geology, Geography, and Meteorology describes the structure of the Earth—from the inner core to the exosphere—and the physical phenomena, such as volcanoes, rivers, glaciers, and climate, that shape its surface.

● Physics and Chemistry is a visual journey through the fundamental principles underlying the physical universe, that provides the essential vocabulary of these sciences.

● In Rail and Road, a wide range of trains, trolleys and buses, cars, bicycles, and motorcycles are described. Exploded-view photographs show mechanical details with striking clarity.

● Sea and Air illustrates hundreds of parts of ships and airplanes. The section includes civil and fighting craft, both historical and modern.

● The Visual Arts shows the equipment and materials used by painters, sculptors, printers, and other artists. Well-known compositions have been chosen to illustrate specific artistic techniques and effects.

● Architecture includes photographs of exemplary architectural models and illustrates dozens of additional features such as columns, domes, and arches.

● Music provides a visual introduction to the special language of music and musical instruments. It includes clearly annotated photographs of each of the major groups of traditional instruments—brass, woodwind, strings, and percussion—together with modern electronic instruments.

● The Sports section is a guide to the playing areas, formations, equipment, and techniques needed for many of today's most popular sports.

● In Everyday Things, familiar objects, such as shoes, clocks, and toasters, are taken apart—down to the very last screw or length of thread—to show their inner workings and to give a special insight into the language that is used by their manufacturers.

THE UNIVERSE

Anatomy of the Universe

Fireball of rapidly expanding, extremely hot gas lasting about one million years

THE UNIVERSE CONTAINS EVERYTHING that exists, from the tiniest subatomic particles to galactic superclusters (the largest structures known). Nobody knows how big the Universe is, but astronomers estimate that it contains about 100 billion galaxies, each comprising an average of 100 billion stars. The most widely accepted theory about the origin of the Universe is the Big Bang theory, which states that the Universe came into being in a huge explosion—the Big Bang—that took place between 10 and 20 billion years ago. The Universe initially consisted of a very hot, dense fireball of expanding, cooling gas. After about one million years, the gas probably began to condense into localized clumps called protogalaxies. During the next five billion years, the protogalaxies continued condensing, forming galaxies in which stars were being born. Today, billions of years later, the Universe as a whole is still expanding, although there are localized areas in which objects are held together by gravity; for example, many galaxies are found in clusters. The Big Bang theory is supported by the discovery of faint, cool background radiation coming evenly from all directions. This radiation is believed to be the remnant of the radiation produced by the Big Bang. Small "ripples" in the temperature of the cosmic background radiation are thought to be evidence of slight fluctuations in the density of the early Universe, which resulted in the formation of galaxies. Astronomers do not yet know if the Universe is "closed," which means it will eventually stop expanding and begin to contract, or if it is "open," which means it will continue expanding forever.

COMPUTER-ENHANCED MICROWAVE MAP OF COSMIC BACKGROUND RADIATION

Pink indicates "warm ripples" in background radiation

Pale blue indicates "cool ripples" in background radiation

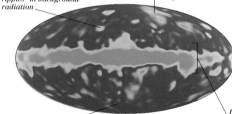

Deep blue indicates background radiation corresponding to -454.5°F (remnant of the Big Bang)

Red and pink band indicates radiation from our galaxy

Low-energy microwave radiation corresponding to about -454°F

High-energy gamma radiation corresponding to about 5,400°F

ORIGIN AND EXPANSION OF THE UNIVERSE

Quasar (probably the center
of a galaxy containing a
massive black hole)

Universe one to five
billion years after
Big Bang

Protogalaxy
(condensing gas cloud)

Galaxy spinning and
flattening to become
spiral shaped

Dark cloud
(dust and gas
condensing
to form a
protogalaxy)

Elliptical
galaxy in
which stars
form rapidly

Universe today
(10–20 billion years
after Big Bang)

Cluster of
galaxies held
together by gravity

Elliptical galaxy
containing old stars
and little gas and dust

Irregular galaxy

Spiral galaxy
containing gas,
dust, and young stars

OBJECTS IN THE UNIVERSE

**CLUSTER OF
GALAXIES IN VIRGO**

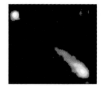

**COLOR-ENHANCED IMAGE
OF 3C273 (QUASAR)**

**NGC 4406
(ELLIPTICAL GALAXY)**

**NGC 5236
(SPIRAL GALAXY)**

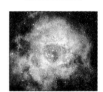

**NGC 6822
(IRREGULAR GALAXY)**

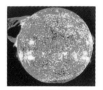

**THE ROSETTE NEBULA
(EMISSION NEBULA)**

**THE JEWEL BOX
(STAR CLUSTER)**

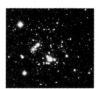

**THE SUN
(MAIN SEQUENCE STAR)**

EARTH

THE MOON

Galaxies

SOMBRERO,
A SPIRAL GALAXY

A GALAXY IS A HUGE MASS OF STARS, nebulae, and interstellar material. The smallest galaxies contain about 100,000 stars, while the largest contain up to 3,000 billion stars. There are three main types of galaxy, classified according to their shape: elliptical, which are oval shaped; spiral, which have arms spiraling outward from a central bulge; and irregular, which have no obvious shape. Sometimes, the shape of a galaxy is distorted by a collision with another galaxy. Quasars (quasi-stellar objects) are thought to be galactic nuclei but are so far away that their exact nature is still uncertain. They are compact, highly luminous objects in the outer reaches of the known Universe; while the farthest known "ordinary" galaxies are about 10 billion light-years away, the farthest known quasar is about 15 billion light-years away. Active galaxies, such as Seyfert galaxies and radio galaxies, emit intense radiation. In a Seyfert galaxy, this radiation comes from the galactic nucleus; in a radio galaxy, it also comes from huge lobes on either side of the galaxy. The radiation from active galaxies and quasars is thought to be caused by black holes (see pp. 28-29).

OPTICAL IMAGE OF NGC 4486 (ELLIPTICAL GALAXY)

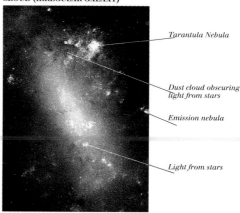

Globular cluster containing very old red giants

Central region containing old red giants

Less densely populated region

Neighboring galaxy

OPTICAL IMAGE OF LARGE MAGELLANIC CLOUD (IRREGULAR GALAXY)

Tarantula Nebula

Dust cloud obscuring light from stars

Emission nebula

Light from stars

OPTICAL IMAGE OF NGC 2997 (SPIRAL GALAXY)

Glowing nebula in spiral arm

Spiral arm containing young stars

Galactic nucleus containing old stars

Dust in spiral arm reflecting blue light from hot young stars

Hot, ionized hydrogen gas emitting red light

Dust lane

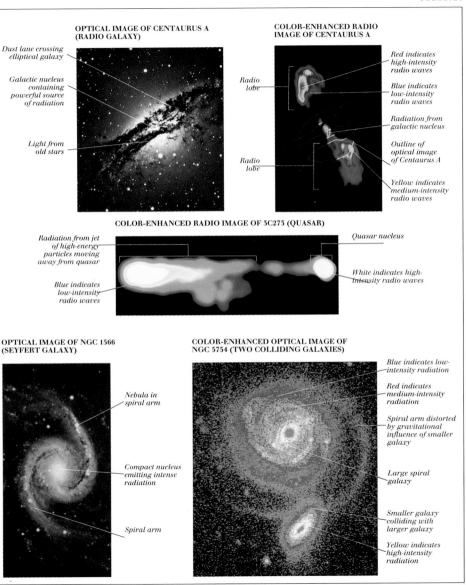

OPTICAL IMAGE OF CENTAURUS A (RADIO GALAXY)

Dust lane crossing elliptical galaxy

Galactic nucleus containing powerful source of radiation

Light from old stars

COLOR-ENHANCED RADIO IMAGE OF CENTAURUS A

Red indicates high-intensity radio waves

Blue indicates low-intensity radio waves

Radio lobe

Radiation from galactic nucleus

Outline of optical image of Centaurus A

Radio lobe

Yellow indicates medium-intensity radio waves

COLOR-ENHANCED RADIO IMAGE OF 3C273 (QUASAR)

Radiation from jet of high-energy particles moving away from quasar

Quasar nucleus

Blue indicates low-intensity radio waves

White indicates high-intensity radio waves

OPTICAL IMAGE OF NGC 1566 (SEYFERT GALAXY)

Nebula in spiral arm

Compact nucleus emitting intense radiation

Spiral arm

COLOR-ENHANCED OPTICAL IMAGE OF NGC 5754 (TWO COLLIDING GALAXIES)

Blue indicates low-intensity radiation

Red indicates medium-intensity radiation

Spiral arm distorted by gravitational influence of smaller galaxy

Large spiral galaxy

Smaller galaxy colliding with larger galaxy

Yellow indicates high-intensity radiation

The Milky Way

VIEW TOWARD GALACTIC CENTER

THE MILKY WAY IS THE NAME GIVEN TO THE FAINT BAND OF LIGHT that stretches across the night sky. This light comes from stars and nebulae in our galaxy, known as the Milky Way Galaxy or simply as "the Galaxy." The Galaxy is shaped like a spiral, with a dense central bulge that is encircled by four arms spiraling outward and surrounded by a less dense halo. We cannot see the spiral shape because our Solar System is in one of the spiral arms, the Orion Arm (also called the Local Arm). From our position, the center of the Galaxy is completely obscured by dust clouds; as a result, optical maps give only a limited view of the Galaxy. However, a more complete picture can be obtained by studying radio, infrared, and other radiation. The central bulge of the Galaxy is a relatively small, dense sphere that contains mainly older red and yellow stars. The halo is a less dense region in which the oldest stars are situated; some of these stars may be as old as the Galaxy itself (possibly 15 billion years). The spiral arms contain mainly hot, young, blue stars, as well as nebulae (clouds of dust and gas, inside which stars are born). The Galaxy is vast—about 100,000 light-years across (a light-year is about 5,879 billion miles); in comparison, the Solar System seems small, at about 12 light-hours across (about 8 billion miles). The entire Galaxy is rotating in space, although the inner stars travel faster than those further out. The Sun, which is about two-thirds out from the center, completes one lap of the Galaxy about every 220 million years.

PANORAMIC OPTICAL MAP OF OUR GALAXY AND NEARBY GALAXIES

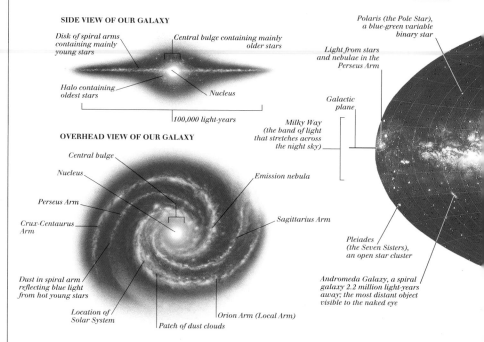

SIDE VIEW OF OUR GALAXY

Disk of spiral arms containing mainly young stars

Central bulge containing mainly older stars

Halo containing oldest stars

Nucleus

100,000 light-years

OVERHEAD VIEW OF OUR GALAXY

Central bulge

Nucleus

Perseus Arm

Crux-Centaurus Arm

Emission nebula

Sagittarius Arm

Dust in spiral arm reflecting blue light from hot young stars

Location of Solar System

Patch of dust clouds

Orion Arm (Local Arm)

Polaris (the Pole Star), a blue-green variable binary star

Light from stars and nebulae in the Perseus Arm

Galactic plane

Milky Way (the band of light that stretches across the night sky)

Pleiades (the Seven Sisters), an open star cluster

Andromeda Galaxy, a spiral galaxy 2.2 million light-years away; the most distant object visible to the naked eye

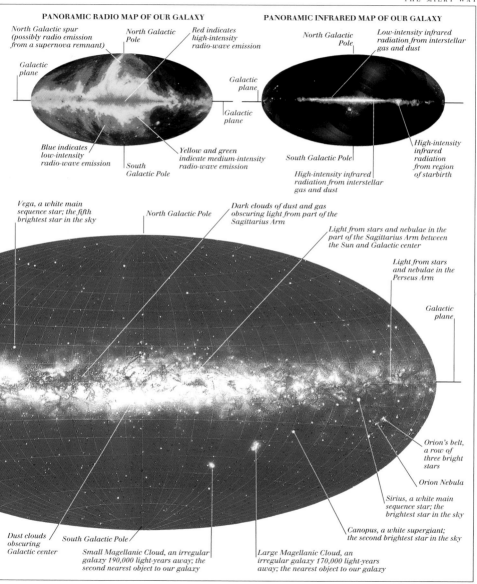

PANORAMIC RADIO MAP OF OUR GALAXY

North Galactic spur
(possibly radio emission
from a supernova remnant)

North Galactic
Pole

Red indicates
high-intensity
radio-wave emission

Galactic
plane

Blue indicates
low-intensity
radio-wave emission

South
Galactic Pole

Yellow and green
indicate medium-intensity
radio-wave emission

PANORAMIC INFRARED MAP OF OUR GALAXY

North Galactic
Pole

Low-intensity infrared
radiation from interstellar
gas and dust

Galactic
plane

Galactic
plane

South Galactic Pole

High-intensity
infrared
radiation
from region
of starbirth

High-intensity infrared
radiation from interstellar
gas and dust

Vega, a white main
sequence star; the fifth
brightest star in the sky

North Galactic Pole

Dark clouds of dust and gas
obscuring light from part of the
Sagittarius Arm

Light from stars and nebulae in the
part of the Sagittarius Arm between
the Sun and Galactic center

Light from stars
and nebulae in the
Perseus Arm

Galactic
plane

Dust clouds
obscuring
Galactic center

South Galactic Pole

Small Magellanic Cloud, an irregular
galaxy 190,000 light-years away; the
second nearest object to our galaxy

Large Magellanic Cloud, an
irregular galaxy 170,000 light-years
away; the nearest object to our galaxy

Canopus, a white supergiant;
the second brightest star in the sky

Sirius, a white main
sequence star; the
brightest star in the sky

Orion Nebula

Orion's belt,
a row of
three bright
stars

Nebulae and star clusters

HODGE 11, A
GLOBULAR CLUSTER

A NEBULA IS A CLOUD OF DUST AND GAS inside a galaxy. Nebulae become visible if the gas glows or if the cloud reflects starlight or obscures light from more distant objects. Emission nebulae shine because their gas emits light when it is stimulated by radiation from hot young stars. Reflection nebulae shine because their dust reflects light from stars in or around the nebula. Dark nebulae appear as silhouettes because they block light from shining nebulae or stars behind them. Two types of nebula are associated with dying stars: planetary nebulae and supernova remnants. Both consist of expanding shells of gas that were once the outer layers of a star. A planetary nebula is a gas shell drifting away from a dying stellar core. A supernova remnant is a gas shell moving away from a stellar core at great speed following a violent explosion called a supernova (see pp. 26-27). Stars are often found in groups known as clusters. Open clusters are loose groups of a few thousand young stars that were born in the same cloud and are drifting apart. Globular clusters are densely packed, roughly spherical groups of hundreds of thousands of older stars.

TRIFID NEBULA (EMISSION NEBULA)

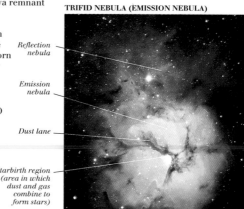

Reflection nebula

Emission nebula

Dust lane

Starbirth region (area in which dust and gas combine to form stars)

PLEIADES (OPEN STAR CLUSTER) WITH A REFLECTION NEBULA

Wisps of dust and hydrogen gas remaining from cloud in which stars formed

Young star in an open cluster of 300–500 stars

Reflection nebula

HORSEHEAD NEBULA (DARK NEBULA)

Glowing filament of hot, ionized hydrogen gas

Alnitak (star in Orion's belt)

Dust lane

Emission nebula

Star near southern end of Orion's belt

Emission nebula

Horsehead Nebula

Reflection nebula

Dark nebula obscuring light from distant stars

ORION NEBULA (DIFFUSE EMISSION NEBULA)

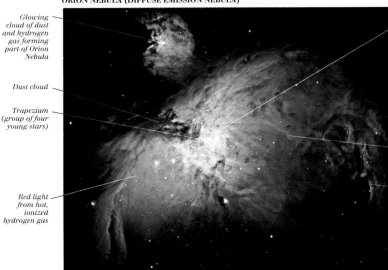

Glowing cloud of dust and hydrogen gas forming part of Orion Nebula

Dust cloud

Trapezium (group of four young stars)

Red light from hot, ionized hydrogen gas

Gas cloud emitting light because of ultraviolet radiation from the four young Trapezium stars

Green light from hot, ionized oxygen gas

Glowing filament of hot, ionized hydrogen gas

VELA SUPERNOVA REMNANT

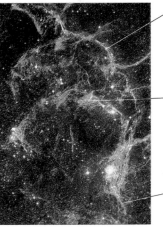

Supernova remnant (gas shell consisting of outer layers of star thrown off in supernova explosion)

Hydrogen gas emitting red light due to being heated by supernova explosion

Glowing filament of hot, ionized hydrogen gas

HELIX NEBULA (PLANETARY NEBULA)

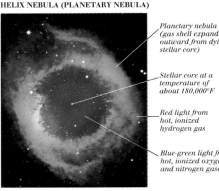

Planetary nebula (gas shell expanding outward from dying stellar core)

Stellar core at a temperature of about 180,000°F

Red light from hot, ionized hydrogen gas

Blue-green light from hot, ionized oxygen and nitrogen gases

Stars of northern skies

WHEN YOU LOOK AT THE NORTHERN SKY, you look away from the densely populated Galactic center, so the northern sky generally appears less bright than the southern sky (see pp. 20-21). Among the best-known sights in the northern sky are the constellations Ursa Major (the Great Bear) and Orion. Some ancient civilizations believed that the stars were fixed to a celestial sphere surrounding the Earth, and modern maps of the sky are based on a similar idea. The North and South Poles of this imaginary celestial sphere are directly above the North and South Poles of the Earth, at the points where the Earth's axis of rotation intersects the sphere. The celestial North Pole is at the center of the map shown here, and Polaris (the Pole Star) lies very close to it. The celestial equator marks a projection of the Earth's equator on the sphere. The ecliptic marks the path of the Sun across the sky as the Earth orbits the Sun. The Moon and planets move against the background of the stars because the stars are much more distant; the nearest star outside the Solar System (Proxima Centauri) is more than 50,000 times farther away than the planet Jupiter.

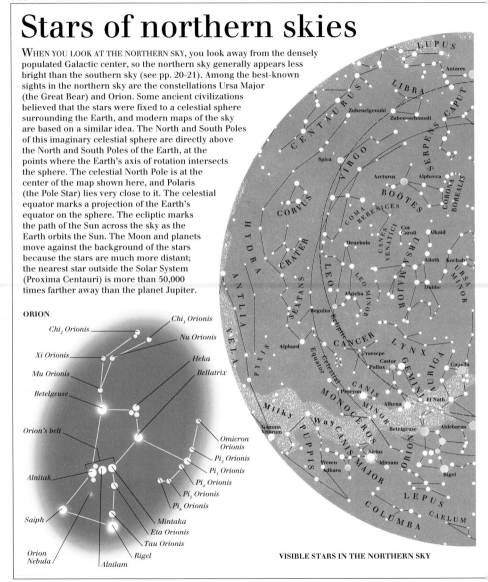

ORION

Chi$_2$ Orionis
Chi$_1$ Orionis
Nu Orionis
Xi Orionis
Heka
Mu Orionis
Bellatrix
Betelgeuse
Orion's belt
Omicron Orionis
Pi$_2$ Orionis
Pi$_3$ Orionis
Alnitak
Pi$_4$ Orionis
Pi$_5$ Orionis
Pi$_6$ Orionis
Saiph
Mintaka
Eta Orionis
Tau Orionis
Orion Nebula
Rigel
Alnilam

VISIBLE STARS IN THE NORTHERN SKY

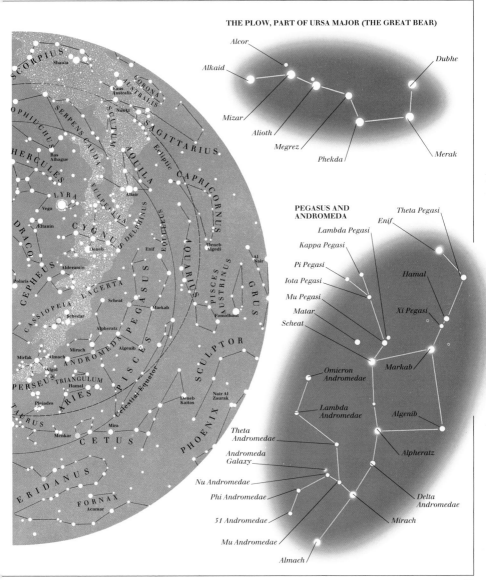

THE PLOW, PART OF URSA MAJOR (THE GREAT BEAR)

Alcor
Alkaid
Dubhe
Mizar
Alioth
Megrez
Phekda
Merak

PEGASUS AND ANDROMEDA

Theta Pegasi
Enif
Lambda Pegasi
Kappa Pegasi
Pi Pegasi
Hamal
Iota Pegasi
Mu Pegasi
Xi Pegasi
Matar
Scheat
Omicron Andromedae
Markab
Lambda Andromedae
Algenib
Theta Andromedae
Alpheratz
Andromeda Galaxy
Nu Andromedae
Phi Andromedae
Delta Andromedae
51 Andromedae
Mirach
Mu Andromedae
Almach

Stars of southern skies

WHEN YOU LOOK AT THE SOUTHERN SKY, you look toward the Galactic center, which has a huge population of stars. As a result, the Milky Way appears brighter in the southern sky than in the northern sky (see pp. 18-19). The southern sky is rich in nebulae and star clusters. It contains the Large and Small Magellanic Clouds, which are the two nearest galaxies to our own. Stars make fixed patterns in the sky called constellations. The constellations, however, are only apparent groupings of stars, because the distances to the stars in a constellation may vary enormously. The shapes of constellations may change over many thousands of years because of the relative motions of stars. The apparent movement of entire constellations across the sky is due to the Earth's motion in space. The daily rotation of the Earth causes the constellations to move across the sky from east to west, and the orbit of the Earth around the Sun causes different areas of sky to be visible in different seasons. The visibility of areas of sky also depends on the location of the observer. For instance, stars near the celestial equator may be seen from either hemisphere at some time during the year, while stars close to the celestial poles (the celestial South Pole is at the center of the map shown here) can never be seen from the opposite hemisphere.

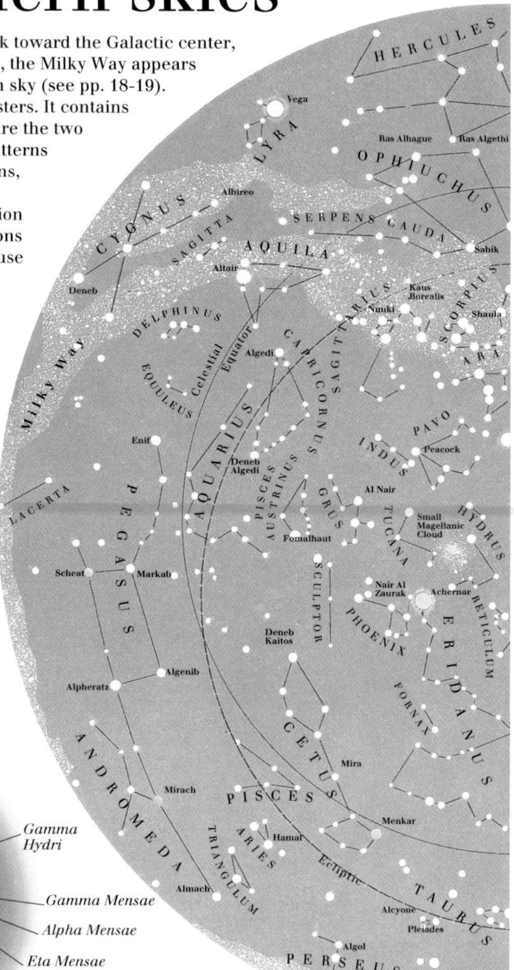

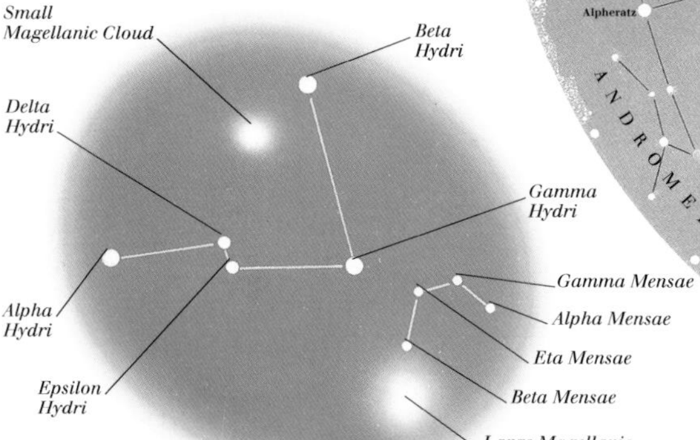

Small Magellanic Cloud

Beta Hydri

Delta Hydri

Gamma Hydri

Gamma Mensae

Alpha Mensae

Eta Mensae

Beta Mensae

Alpha Hydri

Epsilon Hydri

Large Magellanic Cloud

HYDRUS (THE WATER SNAKE) AND MENSA (THE TABLE)

HERCULES
Vega
LIRA
Ras Alhague   Ras Algethi
OPHIUCHUS
Albireo
CYGNUS
SERPENS CAUDA
SAGITTA
AQUILA
Sobik
Deneb
Altair
RIUS
Katus Borealis
Nunki
SCORPIUS
Shaula
DELPHINUS
Celestial Equator
CAPRICORNUS
ARA
EQUULEUS
Algedi
Enif
AQUARIUS
Deneb Algedi
INDUS
Peacock
PAVO
MILKY WAY
LACERTA
PISCES AUSTRINUS
GRUS
Al Nair
TUCANA
Small Magellanic Cloud
HYDRUS
PEGASUS
Scheat
Markab
SCULPTOR
Nair Al Zaurak
Achernar
RETICULUM
Fomalhaut
PHOENIX
ERIDANUS
Deneb Kaitos
Alpherata
Algenib
Mira
FORNAX
ANDROMEDA
Mirach
CETUS
Menkar
PISCES
Hamal
TRIANGULUM
ARIES
Almach
Ecliptic
TAURUS
Alcyone
Pleiades
PERSEUS
Algol
Mirfak

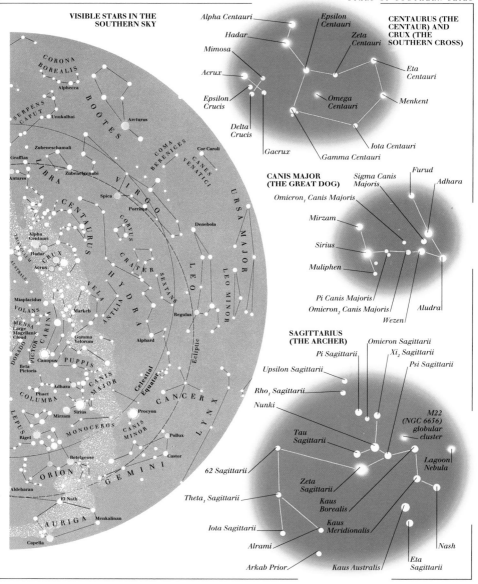

VISIBLE STARS IN THE SOUTHERN SKY

CENTAURUS (THE CENTAUR) AND CRUX (THE SOUTHERN CROSS)

Alpha Centauri
Hadar
Mimosa
Acrux
Epsilon Crucis
Delta Crucis
Gacrux
Epsilon Centauri
Zeta Centauri
Eta Centauri
Menkent
Omega Centauri
Iota Centauri
Gamma Centauri

CANIS MAJOR (THE GREAT DOG)

Sigma Canis Majoris
Furud
Adhara
Omicron₁ Canis Majoris
Mirzam
Sirius
Muliphen
Pi Canis Majoris
Omicron₂ Canis Majoris
Wezen
Aludra

SAGITTARIUS (THE ARCHER)

Omicron Sagittarii
Pi Sagittarii
Xi₂ Sagittarii
Psi Sagittarii
Upsilon Sagittarii
Rho₁ Sagittarii
Nunki
Tau Sagittarii
62 Sagittarii
Zeta Sagittarii
Theta₁ Sagittarii
Kaus Borealis
Iota Sagittarii
Kaus Meridionalis
Alrami
Arkab Prior
Kaus Australis
Eta Sagittarii
Nash
Lagoon Nebula
M22 (NGC 6656) globular cluster

CORONA BOREALIS
Alphecca
SERPENS CAPUT
BOOTES
Unukalhai
Zubeneschamali
Graffias
Zubenelgenubi
Antares
LIBRA
Arcturus
COMA BERENICES
CANES VENATICI
Cor Caroli
Spica
VIRGO
Porrima
URSA MAJOR
Denebola
CENTAURUS
CORVUS
CRATER
SEXTANS
LEO
LEO MINOR
Alpha Centauri
CRUX
Hadar
HYDRA
VELA
ANTLIA
Acrux
Regulus
TRIANGULUM AUSTRALE
Markeb
Alphard
Miaplacidus
VOLANS
MENSA
Large Magellanic Cloud
CARINA
PICTOR
Gamma Velorum
DORADO
Canopus
PUPPIS
Beta Pictoris
COLUMBA
Phact
Adhara
CANIS MAJOR
Mirzam
Sirius
Procyon
CANIS MINOR
Celestial Equator
LEPUS
Rigel
MONOCEROS
CANCER
Pollux
LYNX
Castor
Betelgeuse
GEMINI
ORION
Ecliptic
Aldebaran
El Nath
TAURUS
Menkalinan
AURIGA
Capella

Stars

OPEN STAR CLUSTER AND DUST CLOUD

Sᴛᴀʀs ᴀʀᴇ ʙᴏᴅɪᴇs of hot glowing gas that are born in nebulae (see pp. 24-27). They vary enormously in size, mass, and temperature: diameters range from about 450 times smaller to over 1,000 times bigger than that of the Sun; masses range from about a twentieth to over 50 solar masses; and surface temperatures range from about 5,500°F to over 90,000°F. The color of a star is determined by its temperature: the hottest stars are blue and the coolest are red. The Sun, with a surface temperature of 10,000°F, is between these extremes and appears yellow. The energy emitted by a shining star is produced by nuclear fusion in the star's core. The brightness of a star is measured in magnitudes—the brighter the star, the lower its magnitude. There are two types of magnitude: apparent magnitude, which is the brightness seen from Earth, and absolute magnitude, which is the brightness that would be seen from a standard distance of 10 parsecs (32.6 light-years). The light emitted by a star may be split to form a spectrum containing a series of dark lines (absorption lines). The patterns of lines indicate the presence of particular chemical elements, enabling astronomers to deduce the composition of the star's atmosphere. The magnitude and spectral type (color) of stars may be plotted on a graph called a Hertzsprung-Russell diagram, which shows that stars tend to fall into several well-defined groups. The principal groups are main sequence stars (those which are fusing hydrogen to form helium), giants, supergiants, and white dwarfs.

STAR SIZES

Red giant (diameters between about 10 million and 100 million miles)

The Sun (main sequence star with diameter about 870,000 miles)

White dwarf (diameters between about 2,000 and 30,000 miles)

ENERGY EMISSION FROM THE SUN

Nuclear fusion in core produces gamma rays and neutrinos

Neutrinos travel to Earth directly from Sun's core in about 8 minutes

Lower-energy radiation travels to Earth in about 8 minutes

Earth

Lower-energy radiation (mainly ultraviolet, infrared, and light rays) leaves surface

Sun

High-energy radiation (gamma rays) loses energy while traveling to surface over 2 million years

STAR MAGNITUDES

APPARENT MAGNITUDE   **ABSOLUTE MAGNITUDE**

Brighter stars

-9

Rigel: absolute magnitude of -7.1

Sirius: apparent magnitude of -1.46

Rigel: apparent magnitude of +0.12

0

Sirius: absolute magnitude of +1.4

Objects of magnitude higher than about +5.5 cannot be seen by the naked eye

+9

Fainter stars

NUCLEAR FUSION IN MAIN SEQUENCE STARS LIKE THE SUN

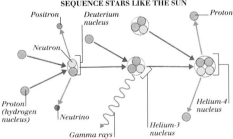

Positron

Deuterium nucleus

Proton

Neutron

Proton (hydrogen nucleus)

Neutrino

Gamma rays

Helium-3 nucleus

Helium-4 nucleus

HERTZSPRUNG-RUSSELL DIAGRAM

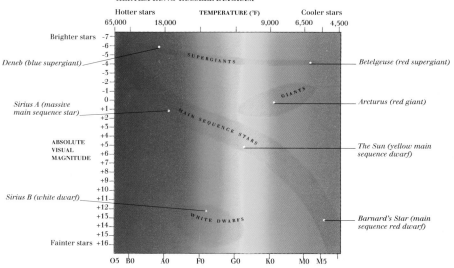

Hotter stars   **TEMPERATURE (°F)**   Cooler stars

Brighter stars

Deneb (blue supergiant)

SUPERGIANTS

Betelgeuse (red supergiant)

GIANTS

Sirius A (massive main sequence star)

MAIN SEQUENCE STARS

Arcturus (red giant)

The Sun (yellow main sequence dwarf)

ABSOLUTE VISUAL MAGNITUDE

Sirius B (white dwarf)

WHITE DWARFS

Barnard's Star (main sequence red dwarf)

Fainter stars

O5   B0   A0   F0   G0   K0   M0   M5

SPECTRAL TYPE

STELLAR SPECTRAL ABSORPTION LINES

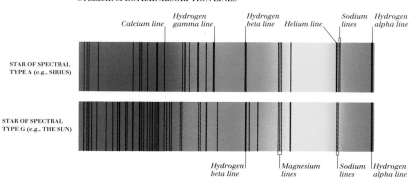

Calcium line   *Hydrogen gamma line*   *Hydrogen beta line*   *Helium line*   *Sodium lines*   *Hydrogen alpha line*

STAR OF SPECTRAL TYPE A (e.g., SIRIUS)

STAR OF SPECTRAL TYPE G (e.g., THE SUN)

Hydrogen beta line   *Magnesium lines*   *Sodium lines*   *Hydrogen alpha line*

Small stars

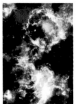

REGION OF STAR FORMATION IN ORION

SMALL STARS HAVE A MASS of up to about one and a half times that of the Sun. They begin to form when a region of higher density in a nebula condenses into a huge globule of gas and dust that contracts under its own gravity. Within a globule, regions of condensing matter heat up and begin to glow, forming protostars. If a protostar contains enough matter, the central temperature reaches about 27 million °F. At this temperature, nuclear reactions in which hydrogen fuses to form helium can start. This process releases energy, which prevents the star from contracting further, and also causes it to shine; it is now a main sequence star. A star of about one solar mass remains in the main sequence for about 10 billion years, until the hydrogen in the star's core has been converted into helium. The helium core then contracts again, and nuclear reactions continue in a shell around the core. The core becomes hot enough for helium to fuse to form carbon, while the outer layers of the star expand, cool, and shine less brightly. The expanding star is known as a red giant. When the helium in the core runs out, the outer layers of the star may drift off as an expanding gas shell called a planetary nebula. The remaining core (about 80 percent of the original star) is now in its final stages. It becomes a white dwarf star that gradually cools and dims. When it finally stops shining altogether, the dead star will become a black dwarf.

STRUCTURE OF A MAIN SEQUENCE STAR

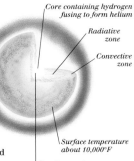

Core containing hydrogen fusing to form helium

Radiative zone

Convective zone

Surface temperature about 10,000°F

Core temperature about 27 million °F

STRUCTURE OF A NEBULA

Young main sequence star

Dense region of dust and gas (mainly hydrogen) condensing under gravity to form globules

Hot, ionized hydrogen gas emitting red light due to stimulation by radiation from hot young stars

Dark globule of dust and gas (mainly hydrogen) contracting to form protostars

LIFE OF A SMALL STAR OF ABOUT ONE SOLAR MASS

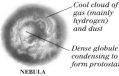

Cool cloud of gas (mainly hydrogen) and dust

Dense globule condensing to form protostars

NEBULA

Glowing ball of gas (mainly hydrogen)

Natal cocoon (shell of dust blown away by radiation from protostar)

PROTOSTAR
Duration: 50 million years

About 870,000 miles

Star producing energy by nuclear fusion in core

MAIN SEQUENCE STAR
Duration: 10 billion years

STRUCTURE OF A RED GIANT

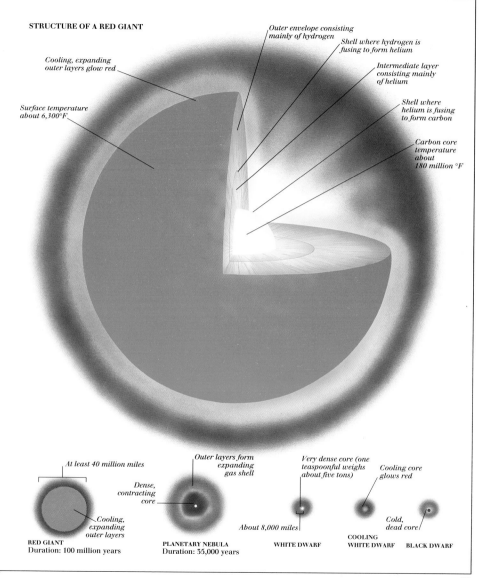

Cooling, expanding
outer layers glow red

Surface temperature
about 6,300°F

Outer envelope consisting
mainly of hydrogen

Shell where hydrogen is
fusing to form helium

Intermediate layer
consisting mainly
of helium

Shell where
helium is fusing
to form carbon

Carbon core
temperature
about
180 million °F

At least 40 million miles

*Cooling,
expanding
outer layers*

RED GIANT
Duration: 100 million years

*Outer layers form
expanding
gas shell*

*Dense,
contracting
core*

PLANETARY NEBULA
Duration: 35,000 years

*Very dense core (one
teaspoonful weighs
about five tons)*

About 8,000 miles

WHITE DWARF

*Cooling core
glows red*

*Cold,
dead core*

**COOLING
WHITE DWARF**

BLACK DWARF

Massive stars

MASSIVE STARS HAVE A MASS AT LEAST THREE TIMES that of the Sun, and some stars are as massive as about 50 Suns. A massive star evolves in a similar way to a small star until it reaches the main sequence stage (see pp. 24-25). During the main sequence, a star shines steadily until the hydrogen in its core has fused to form helium. This process takes billions of years in a small star, but only millions of years in a massive star. A massive star then becomes a red supergiant, which initially consists of a helium core surrounded by outer layers of cooling, expanding gas. Over the next few million years, a series of nuclear reactions form different elements in shells around an iron core. The core eventually collapses in less than a second, causing a massive explosion called a supernova, in which a shock wave blows away the outer layers of the star. Supernovae shine brighter than an entire galaxy for a short time. Sometimes, the core survives the supernova explosion. If the surviving core is between about one and a half and three solar masses, it contracts to become a tiny, dense neutron star. If the core is considerably greater than three solar masses, it contracts to become a black hole (see pp. 28-29).

SUPERNOVA

TARANTULA NEBULA BEFORE SUPERNOVA

STRUCTURE OF A RED SUPERGIANT

Outer envelope consisting mainly of hydrogen

Layer consisting mainly of helium

Layer consisting mainly of carbon

Layer consisting mainly of oxygen

Layer consisting mainly of silicon

Shell of hydrogen fusing to form helium

Shell of helium fusing to form carbon

Shell of carbon fusing to form oxygen

Shell of oxygen fusing to form silicon

Shell of silicon fusing to form iron core

Surface temperature about 5,500°F

Cooling, expanding outer layers glow red

Core of mainly iron at a temperature of 5.4–9 billion °F

LIFE OF A MASSIVE STAR OF ABOUT 10 SOLAR MASSES

Dense globule condensing to form protostars

Cool cloud of gas (mainly hydrogen) and dust

NEBULA

Glowing ball of gas (mainly hydrogen)

Natal cocoon (shell of dust blown away by radiation from protostar)

PROTOSTAR
Duration: a few hundred thousand years

About 2 million miles

Star producing energy by nuclear fusion in core

MAIN SEQUENCE STAR
Duration: 10 million years

FEATURES OF A SUPERNOVA

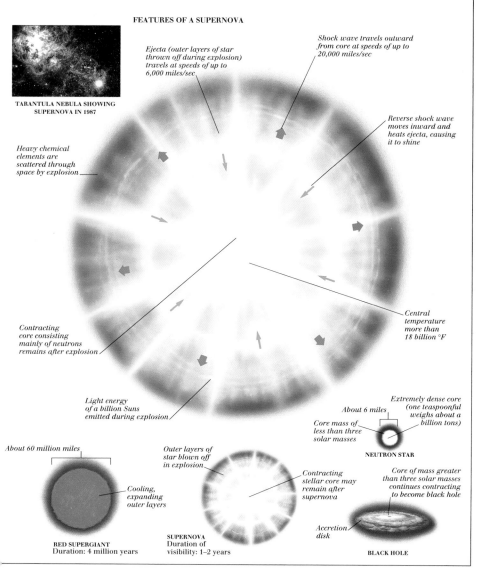

TARANTULA NEBULA SHOWING
SUPERNOVA IN 1987

Ejecta (outer layers of star
thrown off during explosion)
travels at speeds of up to
6,000 miles/sec

Shock wave travels outward
from core at speeds of up to
20,000 miles/sec

Reverse shock wave
moves inward and
heats ejecta, causing
it to shine

Heavy chemical
elements are
scattered through
space by explosion

Contracting
core consisting
mainly of neutrons
remains after explosion

Central
temperature
more than
18 billion °F

Light energy
of a billion Suns
emitted during explosion

Extremely dense core
(one teaspoonful
weighs about a
billion tons)

About 6 miles

Core mass of
less than three
solar masses

NEUTRON STAR

About 60 million miles

Cooling,
expanding
outer layers

Outer layers of
star blown off
in explosion

Contracting
stellar core may
remain after
supernova

Core of mass greater
than three solar masses
continues contracting
to become black hole

Accretion
disk

RED SUPERGIANT
Duration: 4 million years

SUPERNOVA
Duration of
visibility: 1–2 years

BLACK HOLE

27

Neutron stars and black holes

NEUTRON STARS AND BLACK HOLES form from the stellar cores that remain after stars have exploded as supernovae (see pp. 26-27). If the remaining core is between about one and a half and three solar masses, it contracts to form a neutron star. If the remaining core is considerably greater than about three solar masses, it contracts to form a black hole. Neutron stars are typically only about six miles in diameter and consist almost entirely of subatomic particles called neutrons. These stars are so dense that a teaspoonful would weigh about a billion tons. Neutron stars are observed as pulsars, so-called because they rotate rapidly and emit two beams of radio waves, which sweep across the sky and are detected as short pulses. Black holes are characterized by their extremely strong gravity, which is so powerful that not even light can escape; as a result, black holes are invisible. However, they may be detected if they have a close companion star. The gravity of the black hole pulls gas from the other star, forming an accretion disk that spirals around the black hole at high speed, heating up and emitting radiation. Eventually, the matter spirals in to cross the event horizon (the boundary of the black hole), finally disappearing from the visible Universe.

X-ray emission from pulsar (neutron star rotating 30 times each second)

X-ray emission from center of nebula

X-RAY IMAGE OF THE CRAB NEBULA (SUPERNOVA REMNANT)

PULSAR (ROTATING NEUTRON STAR)

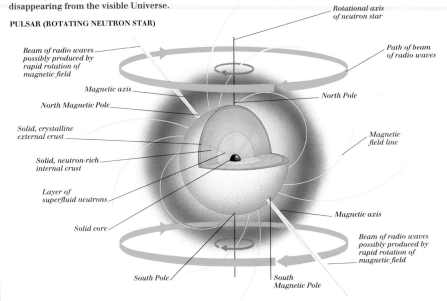

Rotational axis of neutron star

Beam of radio waves possibly produced by rapid rotation of magnetic field

Path of beam of radio waves

Magnetic axis

North Magnetic Pole

North Pole

Solid, crystalline external crust

Magnetic field line

Solid, neutron-rich internal crust

Layer of superfluid neutrons

Solid core

Magnetic axis

Beam of radio waves possibly produced by rapid rotation of magnetic field

South Pole

South Magnetic Pole

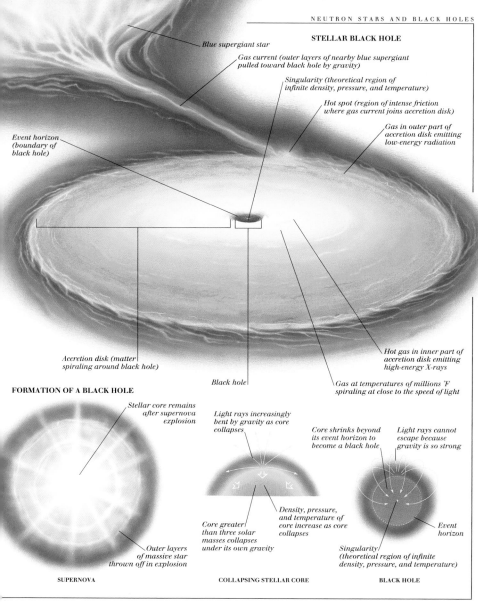

STELLAR BLACK HOLE

Blue supergiant star

Gas current (outer layers of nearby blue supergiant pulled toward black hole by gravity)

Singularity (theoretical region of infinite density, pressure, and temperature)

Hot spot (region of intense friction where gas current joins accretion disk)

Gas in outer part of accretion disk emitting low-energy radiation

Event horizon (boundary of black hole)

Accretion disk (matter spiraling around black hole)

Black hole

Hot gas in inner part of accretion disk emitting high-energy X-rays

Gas at temperatures of millions °F spiraling at close to the speed of light

FORMATION OF A BLACK HOLE

Stellar core remains after supernova explosion

Light rays increasingly bent by gravity as core collapses

Core shrinks beyond its event horizon to become a black hole

Light rays cannot escape because gravity is so strong

Outer layers of massive star thrown off in explosion

Core greater than three solar masses collapses under its own gravity

Density, pressure, and temperature of core increase as core collapses

Singularity (theoretical region of infinite density, pressure, and temperature)

Event horizon

SUPERNOVA

COLLAPSING STELLAR CORE

BLACK HOLE

The Solar System

THE SUN

THE SOLAR SYSTEM consists of a central star (the Sun) and the bodies that orbit it. These bodies include nine planets and their 61 known moons, asteroids, comets, and meteoroids. The Solar System also contains interplanetary gas and dust. Most of the planets fall into two groups: four small rocky planets near the Sun (Mercury, Venus, Earth, and Mars), and four planets farther out, the gas giants (Jupiter, Saturn, Uranus, and Neptune). Pluto belongs to neither group—it is very small, solid, and icy. Pluto is the outermost planet, except when it passes briefly inside Neptune's orbit. Between the rocky planets and gas giants is the asteroid belt, which contains thousands of chunks of rock orbiting the Sun. Most of the bodies in the Solar System move around the Sun in elliptical orbits located in a thin disk around the Sun's equator. All the planets orbit the Sun in the same direction (counterclockwise when viewed from above) and all but Venus, Uranus, and Pluto also spin around their axes in this direction. Moons also spin as they, in turn, orbit their planets. The entire Solar System orbits the center of our galaxy, the Milky Way (see pp. 14-15).

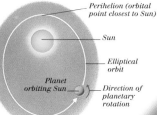

Perihelion (orbital point closest to Sun)

Sun

Elliptical orbit

Planet orbiting Sun

Direction of planetary rotation

Aphelion (orbital point farthest from Sun)

Aphelion of Neptune: 2,819 million miles

ORBITS OF INNER PLANETS

Average orbital speed of Venus: 21.8 miles/sec

Average orbital speed of Mercury: 29.8 miles/sec

Average orbital speed of Earth: 18.5 miles/sec

Average orbital speed of Mars: 15 miles/sec

Mercury

Perihelion of Mercury: 28.5 million miles

Perihelion of Venus: 66.7 million miles

Perihelion of Earth: 91.4 million miles

Perihelion of Mars: 128.4 million miles

Mars

Earth

Venus

Sun

Aphelion of Mercury: 43.3 million miles

Asteroid belt

Aphelion of Venus: 67.7 million miles

Aphelion of Earth: 94.5 million miles

Aphelion of Mars: 154.8 million miles

Aphelion of Pluto: 4,583 million miles

MERCURY
Year: 87.97 Earth days
Mass: 0.055 Earth masses
Diameter: 3,031 miles

VENUS
Year: 224.7 Earth days
Mass: 0.81 Earth masses
Diameter: 7,521 miles

EARTH
Year: 365.26 days
Mass: 1 Earth mass
Diameter: 7,926 miles

MARS
Year: 1.88 Earth years
Mass: 0.11 Earth masses
Diameter: 4,217 miles

JUPITER
Year: 11.86 Earth years
Mass: 318 Earth masses
Diameter: 88,850 miles

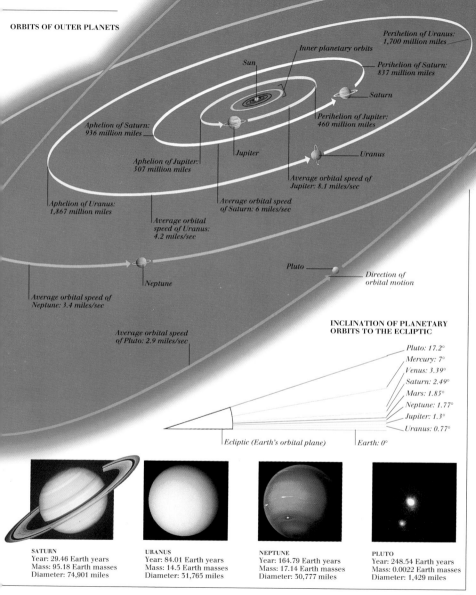

ORBITS OF OUTER PLANETS

Inner planetary orbits

Perihelion of Uranus: 1,700 million miles

Sun

Perihelion of Saturn: 837 million miles

Saturn

Aphelion of Saturn: 936 million miles

Perihelion of Jupiter: 460 million miles

Aphelion of Jupiter: 507 million miles

Jupiter

Uranus

Average orbital speed of Jupiter: 8.1 miles/sec

Aphelion of Uranus: 1,867 million miles

Average orbital speed of Saturn: 6 miles/sec

Average orbital speed of Uranus: 4.2 miles/sec

Neptune

Pluto

Direction of orbital motion

Average orbital speed of Neptune: 3.4 miles/sec

Average orbital speed of Pluto: 2.9 miles/sec

INCLINATION OF PLANETARY ORBITS TO THE ECLIPTIC

Pluto: 17.2°
Mercury: 7°
Venus: 3.39°
Saturn: 2.49°
Mars: 1.85°
Neptune: 1.77°
Jupiter: 1.3°
Uranus: 0.77°

Ecliptic (Earth's orbital plane)   *Earth: 0°*

SATURN
Year: 29.46 Earth years
Mass: 95.18 Earth masses
Diameter: 74,901 miles

URANUS
Year: 84.01 Earth years
Mass: 14.5 Earth masses
Diameter: 31,765 miles

NEPTUNE
Year: 164.79 Earth years
Mass: 17.14 Earth masses
Diameter: 30,777 miles

PLUTO
Year: 248.54 Earth years
Mass: 0.0022 Earth masses
Diameter: 1,429 miles

The Sun

SOLAR PHOTOSPHERE

THE SUN IS THE STAR AT THE CENTER of our Solar System. It is about five billion years old and will probably continue to shine as it does now for about another five billion years. The Sun is a yellow main sequence star (see pp. 22-23) about 870,000 miles in diameter. It consists almost entirely of hydrogen and helium. In the Sun's core, hydrogen is converted to helium by nuclear fusion, releasing energy in the process. The energy travels from the core through the radiative and convective zones to the photosphere (visible surface), where it leaves the Sun in the form of heat and light. On the photosphere there are often dark, relatively cool areas called sunspots. These usually appear in pairs or groups and are thought to be caused by magnetic fields. Other types of solar activity are flares, which are usually associated with sunspots, and prominences. Flares are sudden discharges of high-energy radiation and atomic particles. Prominences are huge loops or filaments of gas extending into the solar atmosphere; some last for hours, others for months. Beyond the photosphere is the chromosphere (inner atmosphere) and the extremely rarified corona (outer atmosphere), which extends millions of miles into space. Tiny particles that escape from the corona give rise to the solar wind, which streams through space at hundreds of miles per second. The chromosphere and corona can be seen from Earth when the Sun is totally eclipsed by the Moon.

HOW A SOLAR ECLIPSE OCCURS

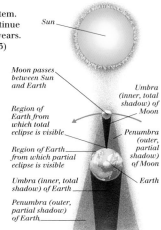

Sun

Moon passes between Sun and Earth

Umbra (inner, total shadow) of Moon

Region of Earth from which total eclipse is visible

Penumbra (outer, partial shadow) of Moon

Region of Earth from which partial eclipse is visible

Earth

Umbra (inner, total shadow) of Earth

Penumbra (outer, partial shadow) of Earth

SURFACE FEATURES

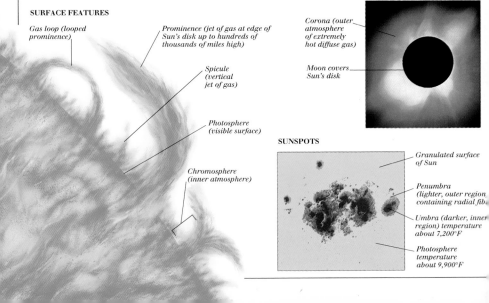

Gas loop (looped prominence)

Prominence (jet of gas at edge of Sun's disk up to hundreds of thousands of miles high)

Spicule (vertical jet of gas)

Photosphere (visible surface)

Chromosphere (inner atmosphere)

TOTAL SOLAR ECLIPSE

Corona (outer atmosphere of extremely hot diffuse gas)

Moon covers Sun's disk

SUNSPOTS

Granulated surface of Sun

Penumbra (lighter, outer region containing radial fib.

Umbra (darker, inner region) temperature about 7,200°F

Photosphere temperature about 9,900°F

**EXTERNAL FEATURES AND
INTERNAL STRUCTURE OF THE SUN**

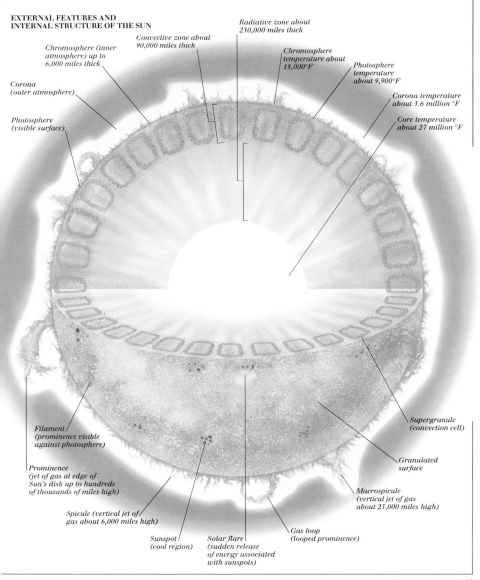

Radiative zone about
230,000 miles thick

Convective zone about
90,000 miles thick

Chromosphere (inner
atmosphere) up to
6,000 miles thick

Chromosphere
temperature about
18,000°F

Photosphere
temperature
about 9,900°F

Corona
(outer atmosphere)

Corona temperature
about 3.6 million °F

Core temperature
about 27 million °F

Photosphere
(visible surface)

Filament
(prominence visible
against photosphere)

Prominence
(jet of gas at edge of
Sun's disk up to hundreds
of thousands of miles high)

Spicule (vertical jet of
gas about 6,000 miles high)

Sunspot
(cool region)

Solar flare
(sudden release
of energy associated
with sunspots)

Gas loop
(looped prominence)

Macrospicule
(vertical jet of gas
about 25,000 miles high)

Granulated
surface

Supergranule
(convection cell)

Mercury

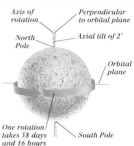

Axis of rotation

Perpendicular to orbital plane

North Pole

Axial tilt of 2°

Orbital plane

One rotation takes 58 days and 16 hours

South Pole

MERCURY

MERCURY IS THE NEAREST PLANET to the Sun, orbiting at an average distance of about 36 million miles. Because Mercury is the closest planet to the Sun, it moves faster than any other planet, traveling at an average speed of nearly 30 miles per second and completing an orbit in just under 88 days. Mercury is very small (only Pluto is smaller) and rocky. Most of the surface has been heavily cratered by the impact of meteorites, although there are also smooth, sparsely cratered plains. The Caloris Basin is the largest crater, measuring about 800 miles across. It is thought to have been formed when a rock the size of an asteroid hit the planet and is surrounded by concentric rings of mountains thrown up by the impact. The surface also has many ridges, called rupes, that are thought to have been formed when the hot core of the young planet cooled and shrank about four billion years ago, buckling the planet's surface in the process. The planet rotates about its axis very slowly, taking nearly 59 Earth days to complete one rotation. As a result, a solar day (sunrise to sunrise) on Mercury is about 176 Earth days—twice as long as the 88-day Mercurian year. Mercury has extreme surface temperatures, ranging from a maximum of 800°F on the sunlit side to -270°F on the dark side. At nightfall, the temperature drops very quickly because the planet's atmosphere is almost nonexistent. It consists only of minute amounts of helium and hydrogen captured from the solar wind, plus traces of other gases.

DEGAS AND BRONTË (RAY CRATERS)

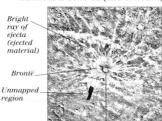

Bright ray of ejecta (ejected material)

Brontë

Unmapped region

Degas with central peak

FORMATION OF A RAY CRATER

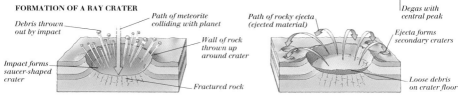

Debris thrown out by impact

Path of meteorite colliding with planet

Wall of rock thrown up around crater

Impact forms saucer-shaped crater

Fractured rock

METEORITE IMPACT

Path of rocky ejecta (ejected material)

Ejecta forms secondary craters

Loose debris on crater floor

SECONDARY CRATERING

Wall of rock forms ring of mountains

Ray of ejecta (ejected material)

Small secondary crater

Loose ejected rock

Central mountain rings form if floor of large crater recoils from meteorite impact

Falling debris forms ridges on side of wall

RAY CRATER

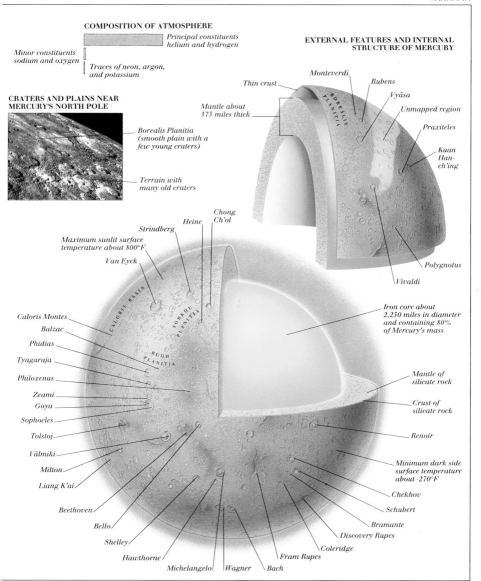

COMPOSITION OF ATMOSPHERE

*Principal constituents
helium and hydrogen*

*Minor constituents
sodium and oxygen*

*Traces of neon, argon,
and potassium*

**EXTERNAL FEATURES AND INTERNAL
STRUCTURE OF MERCURY**

Thin crust

Monteverdi
Rubens
Vyāsa
Unmapped region
Praxiteles
Kuan Han-ch'ing

BOREALIS PLANITIA

Mantle about
375 miles thick

Polygnotus

Vivaldi

**CRATERS AND PLAINS NEAR
MERCURY'S NORTH POLE**

Borealis Planitia
(smooth plain with a
few young craters)

Terrain with
many old craters

Chong Ch'ol
Heine
Strindberg

Maximum sunlit surface
temperature about 800°F

Van Eyck

CALORIS BASIN
SOBKOU PLANITIA

Caloris Montes
Balzac
Phidias
Tyagaraja
Philoxenus
Zeami
Goya
Sophocles
Tolstoj
Vālmiki
Milton
Liang K'ai
Beethoven
Bello
Shelley
Hawthorne
Michelangelo
Wagner
Bach

BUDH PLANITIA

Iron core about
2,250 miles in diameter
and containing 80%
of Mercury's mass

Mantle of
silicate rock

Crust of
silicate rock

Renoir

Minimum dark side
surface temperature
about -270°F

Chekhov
Schubert
Bramante
Discovery Rupes
Coleridge
Fram Rupes

35

Venus

VENUS IS A ROCKY PLANET and the second planet from the Sun. Venus spins slowly backward as it orbits the Sun, causing its rotational period to be the longest in the Solar System, at about 243 Earth days. It is slightly smaller than Earth and probably has a similar internal structure, consisting of a semisolid metal core surrounded by a rocky mantle and crust. Venus is the brightest object in the sky after the Sun and Moon because its atmosphere reflects sunlight strongly. The main component of the atmosphere is carbon dioxide, which traps heat in a greenhouse effect far stronger than that on Earth. As a result, Venus is the hottest planet, with a maximum surface temperature of about 900°F. The thick cloud layers contain droplets of sulfuric acid and are driven around the planet by winds at speeds of up to 220 miles per hour. Although the planet takes 243 Earth days to rotate once, the high-speed winds cause the clouds to circle the planet in only four Earth days. The high temperature, acidic clouds, and enormous atmospheric pressure (about 90 times greater at the surface than that on Earth) make the environment extremely hostile. However, orbiting satellites have managed to land on Venus and photograph its dry, dusty surface. The Venusian surface has also been mapped by probes with radar equipment that can "see" through the cloud layers. Such radar maps reveal a terrain with craters, mountains, volcanoes, and areas where craters have been covered by plains of solidified volcanic lava. There are two large highland regions called Aphrodite Terra and Ishtar Terra.

RADAR IMAGE OF VENUS

Axis of rotation
Perpendicular to orbital plane
North Pole
Axial tilt of 2°
Orbital plane
One rotation takes 243 days and 14 minutes
South Pole

CLOUD FEATURES

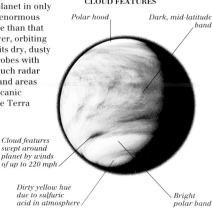

Polar hood
Dark, mid-latitude band
Cloud features swept around planet by winds of up to 220 mph
Dirty yellow hue due to sulfuric acid in atmosphere
Bright polar band

VENUSIAN CRATERS

Danilova
Ejecta (ejected material)
Central peak
Howe

COMPUTER-ENHANCED RADAR MAP OF THE SURFACE OF VENUS

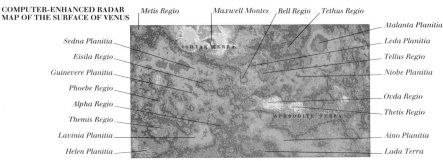

Metis Regio
Maxwell Montes
Bell Regio
Tethus Regio
Atalanta Planitia
Sedna Planitia
ISHTAR TERRA
Leda Planitia
Eisila Regio
Tellus Regio
Guinevere Planitia
Niobe Planitia
Phoebe Regio
Alpha Regio
Ovda Regio
Themis Regio
Thetis Regio
APHRODITE TERRA
Lavinia Planitia
Aino Planitia
Helen Planitia
Lada Terra

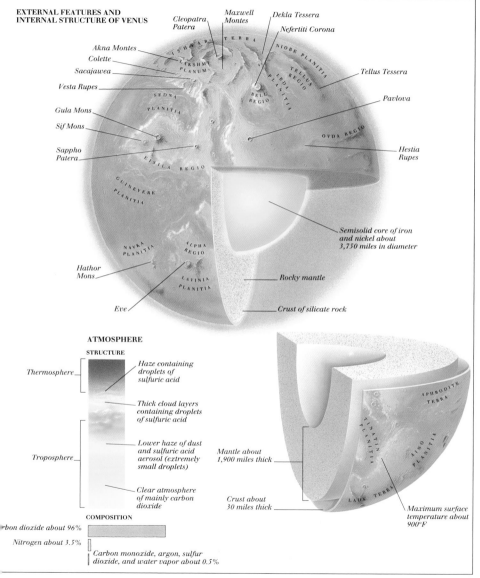

**EXTERNAL FEATURES AND
INTERNAL STRUCTURE OF VENUS**

Cleopatra Patera

Maxwell Montes

Dekla Tessera

Nefertiti Corona

ISHTAR TERRA

NIOBE PLANITIA

Akna Montes

LAKSHMI PLANUM

Colette

Sacajawea

Vesta Rupes

SEDNA PLANITIA

TELLUS REGIO

LEDA PLANITIA

BETA REGIO

Tellus Tessera

Gula Mons

Sif Mons

Sappho Patera

Pavlova

OVDA REGIO

EISILA REGIO

Hestia Rupes

GUINEVERE PLANITIA

NAVKA PLANITIA

ALPHA REGIO

Semisolid core of iron and nickel about 3,750 miles in diameter

Hathor Mons

LAVINIA PLANITIA

Eve

Rocky mantle

Crust of silicate rock

ATMOSPHERE

STRUCTURE

Thermosphere

Haze containing droplets of sulfuric acid

Thick cloud layers containing droplets of sulfuric acid

Troposphere

Lower haze of dust and sulfuric acid aerosol (extremely small droplets)

Clear atmosphere of mainly carbon dioxide

APHRODITE TERRA

TINATIN PLANITIA

AINO PLANITIA

LADA TERRA

Mantle about 1,900 miles thick

Crust about 30 miles thick

Maximum surface temperature about 900°F

COMPOSITION

Carbon dioxide about 96%

Nitrogen about 3.5%

Carbon monoxide, argon, sulfur dioxide, and water vapor about 0.5%

The Earth

TILT AND ROTATION OF THE EARTH

THE EARTH

THE EARTH IS THE THIRD of the nine planets that orbit the Sun. It is the largest and densest rocky planet, and the only one known to support life. About 70 percent of the Earth's surface is covered by water, which is not found in liquid form on the surface of any other planet. There are four main layers: the inner core, the outer core, the mantle, and the crust. At the heart of the planet the solid inner core has a temperature of about 7,230°F. The heat from this inner core causes material in the molten outer core and mantle to circulate in convection currents. It is thought that these convection currents generate the Earth's magnetic field, which extends into space as the magnetosphere. The Earth's atmosphere helps screen out some of the harmful radiation from the Sun, stops meteorites from reaching the planet's surface, and traps enough heat to prevent extremes of cold. The Earth has one natural satellite, the Moon, which is large enough for both bodies to be considered a double-planet system.

Axis of rotation

Axial tilt of 23.4°

North Pole

Orbital plane

South Pole

One rotation takes 23 hours and 56 minutes

Perpendicular to orbital plane

THE FORMATION OF THE EARTH

The heat of the collisions caused the planet to glow red

The cloud broke up into particles of ice and rock, which stuck together to form planets

Microorganisms began to photosynthesize, creating a supply of oxygen

4,600 YEARS AGO, THE SOLAR SYSTEM FORMED FROM A CLOUD OF GAS AND DUST

THE EARTH WAS FORMED FROM COLLIDING ROCKS

4,500 YEARS AGO THE SURFACE COOLED TO FORM THE CRUST

THE CONTINENTS BROKE UP AND REFORMED, GRADUALLY TAKING THEIR PRESENT POSITIONS

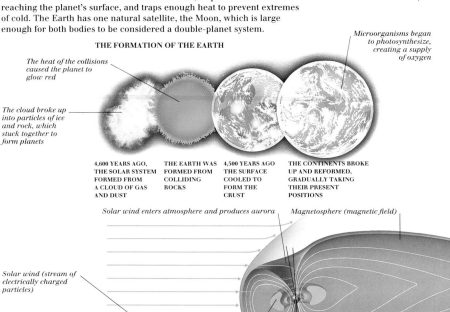

Solar wind enters atmosphere and produces aurora

Magnetosphere (magnetic field)

Solar wind (stream of electrically charged particles)

THE EARTH'S MAGNETOSPHERE

Axis of geographic poles

Van Allen radiation belt

Earth

Axis of magnetic poles

EXTERNAL FEATURES AND INTERNAL STRUCTURE OF THE EARTH

COMPOSITION OF THE EARTH

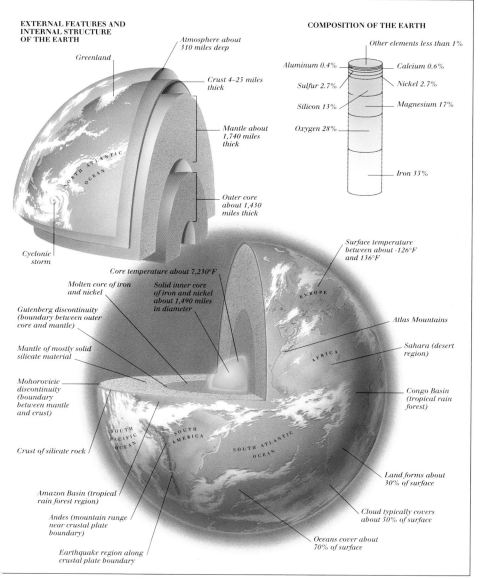

Greenland

Atmosphere about 310 miles deep

Crust 4–25 miles thick

Mantle about 1,740 miles thick

Outer core about 1,430 miles thick

Cyclonic storm

Other elements less than 1%

Aluminum 0.4%

Calcium 0.6%

Sulfur 2.7%

Nickel 2.7%

Silicon 13%

Magnesium 17%

Oxygen 28%

Iron 35%

Surface temperature between about -126°F and 136°F

Core temperature about 7,230°F

Molten core of iron and nickel

Solid inner core of iron and nickel about 1,490 miles in diameter

Gutenberg discontinuity (boundary between outer core and mantle)

Mantle of mostly solid silicate material

Atlas Mountains

Sahara (desert region)

Mohorovicic discontinuity (boundary between mantle and crust)

Congo Basin (tropical rain forest)

Crust of silicate rock

Amazon Basin (tropical rain forest region)

Andes (mountain range near crustal plate boundary)

Earthquake region along crustal plate boundary

Land forms about 30% of surface

Cloud typically covers about 50% of surface

Oceans cover about 70% of surface

NORTH ATLANTIC OCEAN

EUROPE

AFRICA

SOUTH PACIFIC OCEAN

SOUTH AMERICA

SOUTH ATLANTIC OCEAN

The Moon

THE MOON IS THE EARTH'S only natural satellite. It is relatively large for a moon, with a diameter of about 2,155 miles—just over a quarter that of the Earth. The Moon takes the same time to rotate on its axis as it takes to orbit the Earth (27.3 days), and so the same side (the near side) always faces us. However, the amount of the surface we can see—the phase of the Moon—depends on how much of the near side is in sunlight. The Moon is dry and barren, with no atmosphere or water. It consists mainly of solid rock, although its core may contain molten rock or iron. The surface is dusty, with highlands covered in craters caused by meteorite impacts, and lowlands in which large craters have been filled by solidified lava to form dark areas called maria or "seas." Maria occur mainly on the near side, which has a thinner crust than the far side. Many of the craters are rimmed by mountain ranges that form the crater walls and can be thousands of feet high.

TILT AND ROTATION OF THE MOON

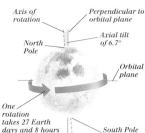

Axis of rotation
Perpendicular to orbital plane
Axial tilt of 6.7°
North Pole
Orbital plane
One rotation takes 27 Earth days and 8 hours
South Pole

CRATERS ON OCEANUS PROCELLARUM

Aristarchus
Cobra Head (head of Schröter's Valley)
Herodotus

NEAR SIDE OF THE MOON

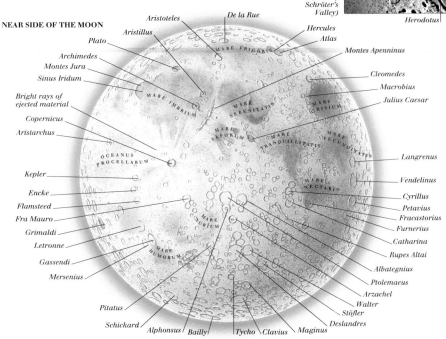

Aristoteles
De la Rue
Aristillus
Plato
Archimedes
Montes Jura
Sinus Iridum
Bright rays of ejected material
Copernicus
Aristarchus
Kepler
Encke
Flamsteed
Fra Mauro
Grimaldi
Letronne
Gassendi
Mersenius
Pitatus
Schickard
Alphonsus
Bailly
Tycho
Clavius
Maginus
Deslandres
Stöfler
Walter
Arzachel
Ptolemaeus
Albategnius
Rupes Altai
Catharina
Furnerius
Fracastorius
Petavius
Cyrillus
Vendelinus
Langrenus
Julius Caesar
Macrobius
Cleomedes
Montes Apenninus
Atlas
Hercules

MARE FRIGORIS
MARE IMBRIUM
MARE SERENITATIS
MARE CRISIUM
MARE VAPORUM
MARE TRANQUILLITATIS
MARE FECUNDITATIS
OCEANUS PROCELLARUM
MARE NECTARIS
MARE NUBIUM
MARE HUMORUM

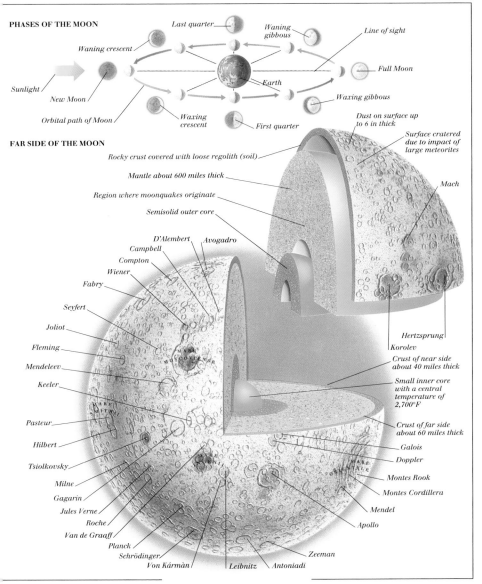

PHASES OF THE MOON

Last quarter

Waning gibbous

Line of sight

Waning crescent

Sunlight

Full Moon

New Moon

Earth

Orbital path of Moon

Waxing gibbous

Waxing crescent

First quarter

FAR SIDE OF THE MOON

Dust on surface up to 6 in thick

Surface cratered due to impact of large meteorites

Rocky crust covered with loose regolith (soil)

Mantle about 600 miles thick

Mach

Region where moonquakes originate

Semisolid outer core

D'Alembert

Avogadro

Campbell

Compton

Wiener

Fabry

Seyfert

Joliot

Fleming

Mendeleev

Keeler

Pasteur

Hilbert

Tsiolkovsky

Milne

Gagarin

Jules Verne

Roche

Van de Graaff

Planck

Schrödinger

Von Kármàn

Leibnitz

Antoniadi

Zeeman

Apollo

Mendel

Montes Cordillera

Montes Rook

Doppler

Galois

Crust of far side about 60 miles thick

Small inner core with a central temperature of 2,700°F

Crust of near side about 40 miles thick

Korolev

Hertzsprung

MARE MOSCOVIENSE

MARE SMYTHII

Mars

MARS

TILT AND ROTATION OF MARS

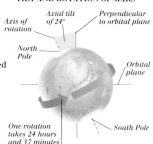

Axis of rotation

Axial tilt of 24°

Perpendicular to orbital plane

North Pole

Orbital plane

One rotation takes 24 hours and 37 minutes

South Pole

MARS, KNOWN AS THE RED PLANET, is the fourth planet from the Sun and the outermost rocky planet. In the 19th century, astronomers first observed what were thought to be signs of life on Mars. These signs included apparent canal-like markings on the surface, and dark patches that were thought to be vegetation. It is now known that the canals are an optical illusion and the dark patches are areas where the red dust that covers most of the planet has blown away. The fine dust particles are often whipped up by winds into dust storms that occasionally obscure almost all Mars's surface. Residual dust in the atmosphere gives the Martian sky a pinkish hue. The northern hemisphere of Mars has many large plains formed of solidified volcanic lava, while the southern hemisphere has many craters and large impact basins. There are also several huge, extinct volcanoes, including Olympus Mons, which at 370 miles wide and 15 miles high is the largest known volcano in the Solar System. The surface also has many canyons and branching channels. The canyons were formed by movements of the surface crust, but the channels are thought to have been formed by flowing water that has now vaporized almost completely and escaped from the atmosphere. The Martian atmosphere is much thinner than Earth's, with only a few clouds and morning mists. Mars has two tiny irregularly shaped moons, Phobos and Deimos. Their small size indicates that they may be asteroids that have been captured by the gravity of Mars.

SURFACE FEATURES OF MARS

Bright water-ice fog

Fog in canyon about 12 miles wide at end of Valles Marineris

Syria Planum

NOCTIS LABYRINTHUS (CANYON SYSTEM)

Summit caldera consisting of overlapping collapsed volcanic craters

Crater

Gentle slope produced by lava flow

Cloud formation

OLYMPUS MONS (EXTINCT SHIELD VOLCANO)

THE SURFACE OF MARS

Dark area where dust has been blown away by wind

South polar ice cap

Surface covered with red-colored iron oxide dust

MOONS OF MARS

PHOBOS
Average diameter: 14 miles
Average distance from planet: 5,800 miles

DEIMOS
Average diameter: 8 miles
Average distance from planet: 14,600 miles

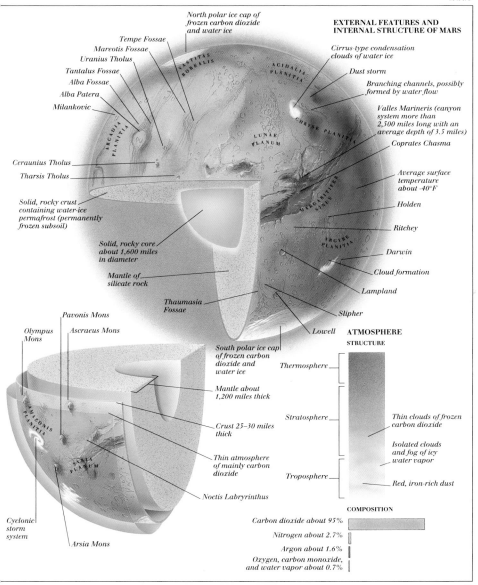

EXTERNAL FEATURES AND INTERNAL STRUCTURE OF MARS

North polar ice cap of frozen carbon dioxide and water ice

Tempe Fossae
Mareotis Fossae
Uranius Tholus
Tantalus Fossae
Alba Fossae
Alba Patera
Milankovic

Cirrus-type condensation clouds of water ice

Dust storm

Branching channels, possibly formed by water flow

Valles Marineris (canyon system more than 2,500 miles long with an average depth of 3.5 miles)

Coprates Chasma

Ceraunius Tholus
Tharsis Tholus

Average surface temperature about -40°F

Solid, rocky crust containing water-ice permafrost (permanently frozen subsoil)

Holden

Solid, rocky core about 1,600 miles in diameter

Ritchey

Mantle of silicate rock

Darwin

Cloud formation

Thaumasia Fossae

Lampland

Slipher

Lowell

Pavonis Mons
Ascraeus Mons

Olympus Mons

ATMOSPHERE
STRUCTURE

South polar ice cap of frozen carbon dioxide and water ice

Thermosphere

Mantle about 1,200 miles thick

Thin clouds of frozen carbon dioxide

Stratosphere

Crust 25–30 miles thick

Isolated clouds and fog of icy water vapor

Thin atmosphere of mainly carbon dioxide

Troposphere

Red, iron-rich dust

Noctis Labryrinthus

COMPOSITION

Cyclonic storm system

Carbon dioxide about 95%
Nitrogen about 2.7%
Argon about 1.6%
Oxygen, carbon monoxide, and water vapor about 0.7%

Arsia Mons

43

Jupiter

JUPITER

JUPITER IS THE FIFTH PLANET from the Sun and the first of the four gas giants. It is the largest and the most massive planet, with a diameter about 11 times that of the Earth and a mass about 2.5 times the combined mass of the eight other planets. Jupiter is thought to have a small rocky core surrounded by an inner mantle of metallic hydrogen (liquid hydrogen that acts like a metal). Outside the inner mantle is an outer mantle of liquid hydrogen and helium that merges into the gaseous atmosphere. Jupiter's rapid rate of rotation causes the clouds in its atmosphere to form belts and zones that encircle the planet parallel to the equator. Belts are dark, low-lying, relatively warm cloud layers. Zones are bright, high-altitude, cooler cloud layers. Within the belts and zones, turbulence causes the formation of cloud features such as white ovals and red spots, both of which are huge storm systems. The most prominent cloud feature is a storm called the Great Red Spot, which consists of a spiraling column of clouds three times wider than the Earth that rises about five miles above the upper cloud layer. Jupiter has one thin, faint, main ring, inside of which is a halo ring of tiny particles extending toward the planet. There are 16 known Jovian moons. The four largest moons (called the Galileans) are Ganymede, Callisto, Io, and Europa. Ganymede and Callisto are cratered and probably icy. Europa is smooth and icy and may contain water. Io is covered in bright red, orange, and yellow splotches. This coloring is caused by sulfurous material from active volcanoes that shoot plumes of lava hundreds of miles above the surface.

TILT AND ROTATION OF JUPITER

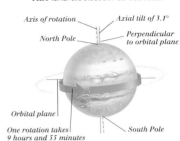

Axis of rotation
Axial tilt of 3.1°
North Pole
Perpendicular to orbital plane
Orbital plane
One rotation takes 9 hours and 55 minutes
South Pole

GREAT RED SPOT AND WHITE OVAL

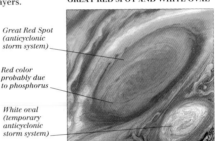

Great Red Spot (anticyclonic storm system)

Red color probably due to phosphorus

White oval (temporary anticyclonic storm system)

RINGS OF JUPITER

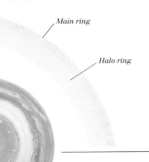

Main ring

Halo ring

GALILEAN MOONS OF JUPITER

EUROPA
Diameter: 1,950 miles
Average distance from planet: 416,900 miles

CALLISTO
Diameter: 2,983 miles
Average distance from planet: 1,168,200 miles

GANYMEDE
Diameter: 3,270 miles
Average distance from planet: 664,900 miles

IO
Diameter: 2,263 miles
Average distance from planet: 262,100 miles

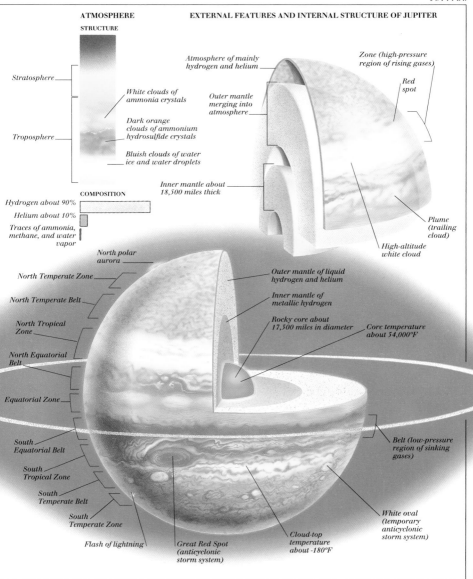

ATMOSPHERE

EXTERNAL FEATURES AND INTERNAL STRUCTURE OF JUPITER

STRUCTURE

Stratosphere

Troposphere

White clouds of ammonia crystals

Dark orange clouds of ammonium hydrosulfide crystals

Bluish clouds of water ice and water droplets

COMPOSITION

Hydrogen about 90%

Helium about 10%

Traces of ammonia, methane, and water vapor

Atmosphere of mainly hydrogen and helium

Outer mantle merging into atmosphere

Inner mantle about 18,500 miles thick

Zone (high-pressure region of rising gases)

Red spot

Plume (trailing cloud)

High-altitude white cloud

North polar aurora

North Temperate Zone

North Temperate Belt

North Tropical Zone

North Equatorial Belt

Equatorial Zone

South Equatorial Belt

South Tropical Zone

South Temperate Belt

South Temperate Zone

Flash of lightning

Great Red Spot (anticyclonic storm system)

Outer mantle of liquid hydrogen and helium

Inner mantle of metallic hydrogen

Rocky core about 17,500 miles in diameter

Core temperature about 34,000°F

Belt (low-pressure region of sinking gases)

White oval (temporary anticyclonic storm system)

Cloud-top temperature about -180°F

45

Saturn

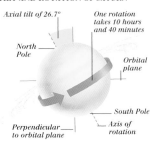

SATURN IS THE SIXTH PLANET from the Sun. It is a gas giant almost as big as Jupiter, with an equatorial diameter of about 74,900 miles. Saturn is thought to consist of a small core of rock and ice surrounded by an inner mantle of metallic hydrogen (liquid hydrogen that acts like a metal). Outside the inner mantle is an outer mantle of liquid hydrogen that merges into a gaseous atmosphere. Saturn's clouds form belts and zones similar to those on

COLOR-ENHANCED IMAGE OF SATURN

Jupiter, but obscured by overlying haze. Storms and eddies, seen as red or white ovals, occur in the clouds. Saturn has an extremely thin but wide system of rings that is less than one mile thick but extends outward to about 260,000 miles from the planet's surface. The main rings comprise thousands of narrow ringlets, each made of icy lumps that range in size from tiny particles to chunks several yards across. The D, E, and G rings are very faint, the F ring is brighter, and the A, B, and C rings are bright enough to be seen from Earth with binoculars. Saturn has 18 known moons, some of which orbit inside the rings and are thought to exert a gravitational influence on the shapes of the rings. Unusually, seven of the moons are co-orbital—they share an orbit with another moon. Astronomers believe that such co-orbital moons may have originated from a single satellite that broke up.

TILT AND ROTATION OF SATURN

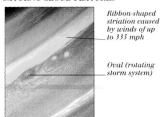

Axial tilt of 26.7°

One rotation takes 10 hours and 40 minutes

North Pole

Orbital plane

South Pole

Perpendicular to orbital plane

Axis of rotation

COLOR-ENHANCED IMAGE OF SATURN'S CLOUD FEATURES

Ribbon-shaped striation caused by winds of up to 335 mph

Oval (rotating storm system)

INNER RINGS OF SATURN

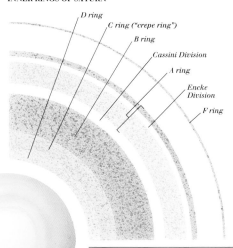

D ring

C ring ("crepe ring")

B ring

Cassini Division

A ring

Encke Division

F ring

MOONS OF SATURN

ENCELADUS
Diameter: 309 miles
Average distance from planet: 148,000 miles

TETHYS
Diameter: 652 miles
Average distance from planet: 183,000 miles

DIONE
Diameter: 695 miles
Average distance from planet: 234,000 miles

MIMAS
Diameter: 247 miles
Average distance from planet: 115,600 miles

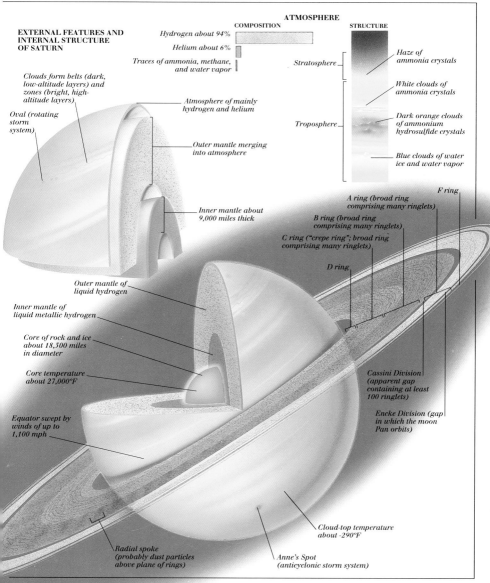

EXTERNAL FEATURES AND INTERNAL STRUCTURE OF SATURN

ATMOSPHERE

COMPOSITION

Hydrogen about 94%

Helium about 6%

Traces of ammonia, methane, and water vapor

STRUCTURE

Stratosphere

Troposphere

Haze of ammonia crystals

White clouds of ammonia crystals

Dark orange clouds of ammonium hydrosulfide crystals

Blue clouds of water ice and water vapor

Clouds form belts (dark, low-altitude layers) and zones (bright, high-altitude layers)

Oval (rotating storm system)

Atmosphere of mainly hydrogen and helium

Outer mantle merging into atmosphere

Inner mantle about 9,000 miles thick

Outer mantle of liquid hydrogen

Inner mantle of liquid metallic hydrogen

Core of rock and ice about 18,500 miles in diameter

Core temperature about 27,000°F

Equator swept by winds of up to 1,100 mph

A ring (broad ring comprising many ringlets)

B ring (broad ring comprising many ringlets)

C ring ("crepe ring"; broad ring comprising many ringlets)

D ring

F ring

Cassini Division (apparent gap containing at least 100 ringlets)

Encke Division (gap in which the moon Pan orbits)

Cloud-top temperature about -290°F

Radial spoke (probably dust particles above plane of rings)

Anne's Spot (anticyclonic storm system)

Uranus

COLOR-ENHANCED
IMAGE OF URANUS

URANUS IS THE SEVENTH PLANET from the Sun and the third largest, with a diameter of about 32,000 miles. It is thought to consist of a dense mixture of different types of ice and gas around a solid core. Its atmosphere contains traces of methane, giving the planet a blue-green hue, and the temperature at the cloud tops is about -350°F. Uranus is the most featureless planet to have been closely observed: only a few icy clouds of methane have been seen so far. Uranus is unique among the planets in that its axis of rotation lies close to its orbital plane. As a result of its strongly tilted rotational axis, Uranus rolls on its side along its orbital path around the Sun, while other planets spin more or less upright. Uranus is encircled by 11 rings that consist of rocks interspersed with dust lanes. The rings contain some of the darkest matter in the Solar System. They are extremely narrow, making them difficult to detect: nine of them are less than six miles wide, whereas most of Saturn's rings are thousands of miles in width. There are 15 known Uranian moons, all of which are icy and most of which are farther out than the rings. The 10 inner moons are small and dark, with diameters of less than 100 miles, and the five outer moons are between about 290 and 1,000 miles in diameter. The outer moons have a wide variety of surface features. Miranda has the most varied surface, with cratered areas broken up by huge ridges and cliffs 12 miles high.

TILT AND ROTATION OF URANUS

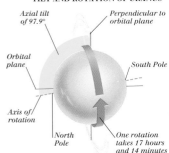

Axial tilt of 97.9°

Perpendicular to orbital plane

Orbital plane

South Pole

Axis of rotation

North Pole

One rotation takes 17 hours and 14 minutes

OUTER MOONS

MIRANDA
Diameter: 293 miles
Average distance from planet: 80,700 miles

RINGS OF URANUS

Epsilon ring

Ring 1986 U1R

Delta ring

Gamma ring

Eta ring

Beta ring

Alpha ring

Rings 4 and 5

Ring 6

Ring 1986 U2R

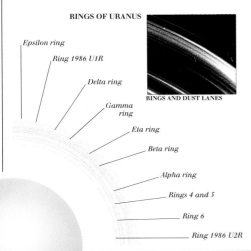

RINGS AND DUST LANES

ARIEL
Diameter: 720 miles
Average distance from planet: 118,800 miles

UMBRIEL
Diameter: 726 miles
Average distance from planet: 165,300 miles

TITANIA
Diameter: 981 miles
Average distance from planet: 270,900 miles

OBERON
Diameter: 946 miles
Average distance from planet: 362,000 miles

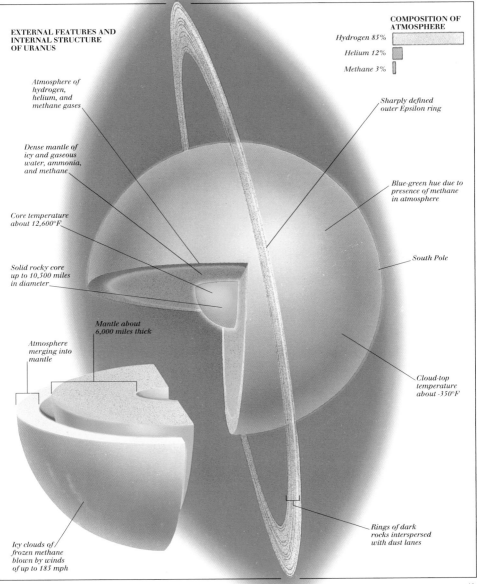

EXTERNAL FEATURES AND
INTERNAL STRUCTURE
OF URANUS

COMPOSITION OF
ATMOSPHERE

Hydrogen 85%

Helium 12%

Methane 3%

Atmosphere of
hydrogen,
helium, and
methane gases

Sharply defined
outer Epsilon ring

Dense mantle of
icy and gaseous
water, ammonia,
and methane

Blue-green hue due to
presence of methane
in atmosphere

Core temperature
about 12,600°F

Solid rocky core
up to 10,500 miles
in diameter

South Pole

Mantle about
6,000 miles thick

Atmosphere
merging into
mantle

Cloud-top
temperature
about -350°F

Icy clouds of
frozen methane
blown by winds
of up to 185 mph

Rings of dark
rocks interspersed
with dust lanes

Neptune and Pluto

COLOR-ENHANCED IMAGE OF NEPTUNE

NEPTUNE AND PLUTO are the two farthest planets from the Sun, at an average distance of about 2,800 million miles and 3,700 million miles, respectively. Neptune is a gas giant and is thought to consist of a small rocky core surrounded by a mixture of liquids and gases. The atmosphere contains several prominent cloud features. The largest of these are the Great Dark Spot, which is as wide as the Earth, the Small Dark Spot, and the Scooter. The Great and Small Dark Spots are huge storms that are swept around the planet by winds of about 1,200 miles per hour. The Scooter is a large area of cirrus cloud. Neptune has four tenuous rings and eight known moons. Triton is the largest Neptunian moon and the coldest object in the Solar System, with a temperature of -391°F. Unlike most moons in the Solar System, Triton orbits its mother planet in the opposite direction to the planet's rotation. Pluto is usually the outermost planet, but its elliptical orbit causes it to pass inside the orbit of Neptune for 20 years of its 248-year orbit. Pluto is so small and distant that little is known about it. It is a rocky planet, probably covered with ice and frozen methane. Pluto's only known moon, Charon, is large for a moon, at half the size of its parent planet. Because of the small difference in their sizes, Pluto and Charon are sometimes considered to be a double-planet system.

TILT AND ROTATION OF NEPTUNE

Axis of rotation

Axial tilt of 28.8°

Perpendicular to orbital plane

North Pole

Orbital plane

South Pole

One rotation takes 16 hours and 7 minutes

CLOUD FEATURES OF NEPTUNE

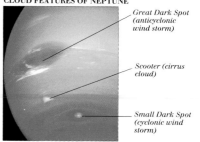

Great Dark Spot (anticyclonic wind storm)

Scooter (cirrus cloud)

Small Dark Spot (cyclonic wind storm)

RINGS OF NEPTUNE

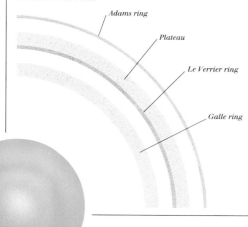

Adams ring

Plateau

Le Verrier ring

Galle ring

HIGH-ALTITUDE CLOUDS

Methane cirrus clouds 25 miles above main cloud deck

Cloud shadow

Main cloud deck blown by winds at speeds of about 1,200 mph

MOONS OF NEPTUNE

TRITON
Diameter: 1,681 miles
Average distance from planet: 220,500 miles

PROTEUS
Diameter: 259 miles
Average distance from planet: 73,100 miles

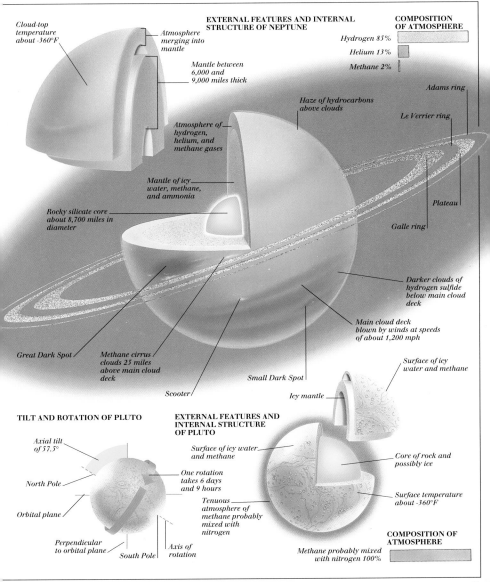

EXTERNAL FEATURES AND INTERNAL STRUCTURE OF NEPTUNE

Cloud-top temperature about -360°F

Atmosphere merging into mantle

Mantle between 6,000 and 9,000 miles thick

COMPOSITION OF ATMOSPHERE

Hydrogen 85%

Helium 13%

Methane 2%

Haze of hydrocarbons above clouds

Atmosphere of hydrogen, helium, and methane gases

Mantle of icy water, methane, and ammonia

Rocky silicate core about 8,700 miles in diameter

Adams ring

Le Verrier ring

Plateau

Galle ring

Darker clouds of hydrogen sulfide below main cloud deck

Main cloud deck blown by winds at speeds of about 1,200 mph

Great Dark Spot

Methane cirrus clouds 25 miles above main cloud deck

Scooter

Small Dark Spot

Surface of icy water and methane

Icy mantle

TILT AND ROTATION OF PLUTO

Axial tilt of 57.5°

North Pole

Orbital plane

Perpendicular to orbital plane

South Pole

Axis of rotation

EXTERNAL FEATURES AND INTERNAL STRUCTURE OF PLUTO

Surface of icy water and methane

One rotation takes 6 days and 9 hours

Tenuous atmosphere of methane probably mixed with nitrogen

Core of rock and possibly ice

Surface temperature about -360°F

COMPOSITION OF ATMOSPHERE

Methane probably mixed with nitrogen 100%

Asteroids, comets, and meteoroids

ASTEROID 951 GASPRA

ASTEROIDS, COMETS, AND METEOROIDS are all debris remaining from the nebula in which the Solar System formed 4.6 billion years ago. Asteroids are rocky bodies up to several hundred miles in diameter, although most are much smaller. Most of them orbit the Sun in the asteroid belt, which lies between the orbits of Mars and Jupiter. Comets may originate in a huge cloud, called the Oort Cloud, that is thought to surround the Solar System. They are made of frozen gases and dust, and are a few miles in diameter. Occasionally, a comet is deflected from the Oort Cloud to orbit the Sun in a long, elliptical path. As the comet approaches the Sun, the comet's surface starts to vaporize in the heat, producing a brightly shining coma (a huge sphere of gas and dust around the nucleus), a gas tail, and a dust tail. Meteoroids are small chunks of stone or stone and iron, some of which are fragments of asteroids or comets. Meteoroids range in size from tiny dust particles to objects tens of yards across. If a meteoroid enters the Earth's atmosphere, it is heated by friction and appears as a glowing streak of light called a meteor (also known as a shooting star). Meteor showers occur when the Earth passes through the trail of dust particles left by a comet. Most meteors burn up in the atmosphere. The few that are large enough to reach the Earth's surface are termed meteorites.

COLOR-ENHANCED IMAGE OF HALLEY'S COMET

High-intensity light emission

Nucleus

Medium-intensity light emission

Low-intensity light emission

COLOR-ENHANCED IMAGE OF A LEONID METEOR SHOWER

METEORITES

STONY METEORITE

Fusion crust formed when passing through atmosphere

Olivine and pyroxene mineral interior

STONY-IRON METEORITE

Iron

Stone (olivine)

DEVELOPMENT OF COMET TAILS

Dust tail deflected by photons in sunlight and curved due to comet's motion

Gas tail pushed away from Sun by charged particles in solar wind

Tails lengthen as comet nears Sun

Sun

Direction of comet's orbital motion

Coma surrounding nucleus

Tails behind nucleus

Tails in front of nucleus

Nucleus vaporized by Sun's heat, forming a coma with two tails

Gas tail

Dust tail

Coma and tails fade as comet moves away from Sun

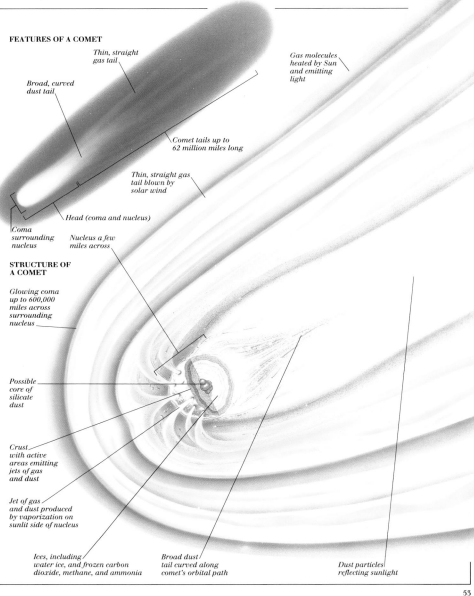

FEATURES OF A COMET

Thin, straight
gas tail

Broad, curved
dust tail

Gas molecules
heated by Sun
and emitting
light

Comet tails up to
62 million miles long

Thin, straight gas
tail blown by
solar wind

Head (coma and nucleus)

Coma
surrounding
nucleus

Nucleus a few
miles across

**STRUCTURE OF
A COMET**

Glowing coma
up to 600,000
miles across
surrounding
nucleus

Possible
core of
silicate
dust

Crust
with active
areas emitting
jets of gas
and dust

Jet of gas
and dust produced
by vaporization on
sunlit side of nucleus

Ices, including
water ice, and frozen carbon
dioxide, methane, and ammonia

Broad dust
tail curved along
comet's orbital path

Dust particles
reflecting sunlight

PREHISTORIC EARTH

The changing Earth

THE EARTH FORMED FROM A CLOUD OF DUST and gas drifting through space about 4,600 million years ago. Dense minerals sank to the center while lighter ones formed a thin rocky crust. However, the first known life forms—bacteria and blue-green algae—did not appear until about 3,400 million years ago, and it was only about 700 million years ago that more complex plants and animals began to develop. Since then, thousands of animal and plant species have evolved. Some, such as the dinosaurs, survived for millions of years, while others died out quickly. The Earth itself is continually changing. Although continents neared their present locations about 50 million years ago, they are still drifting slowly over the planet's surface, and mountain ranges such as the Himalayas—which began to form 40 million years ago—are continually being built up and worn away. Climate is also subject to change: the Earth has undergone a series of ice ages interspersed with warmer periods (the most recent ice age was at its height about 20,000 years ago).

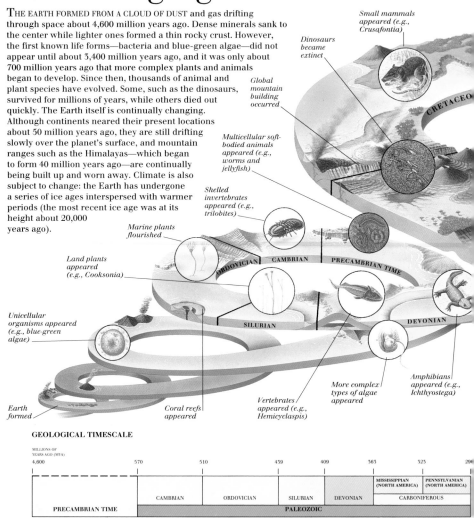

Small mammals appeared (e.g., Crusafontia)

Dinosaurs became extinct

Global mountain building occurred

Multicellular soft-bodied animals appeared (e.g., worms and jellyfish)

Shelled invertebrates appeared (e.g., trilobites)

Marine plants flourished

Land plants appeared (e.g., Cooksonia)

Unicellular organisms appeared (e.g., blue-green algae)

Earth formed

Coral reefs appeared

Vertebrates appeared (e.g., Hemicyclaspis)

More complex types of algae appeared

Amphibians appeared (e.g., Ichthyostega)

CRETACEOUS

ORDOVICIAN CAMBRIAN PRECAMBRIAN TIME

SILURIAN

DEVONIAN

GEOLOGICAL TIMESCALE

MILLIONS OF
YEARS AGO (MYA)

4,600	570	510	439	409	363	325	290

	CAMBRIAN	ORDOVICIAN	SILURIAN	DEVONIAN	MISSISSIPPIAN (NORTH AMERICA)	PENNSYLVANIAN (NORTH AMERICA)
PRECAMBRIAN TIME					CARBONIFEROUS	
		PALEOZOIC				

EVOLUTION OF THE EARTH

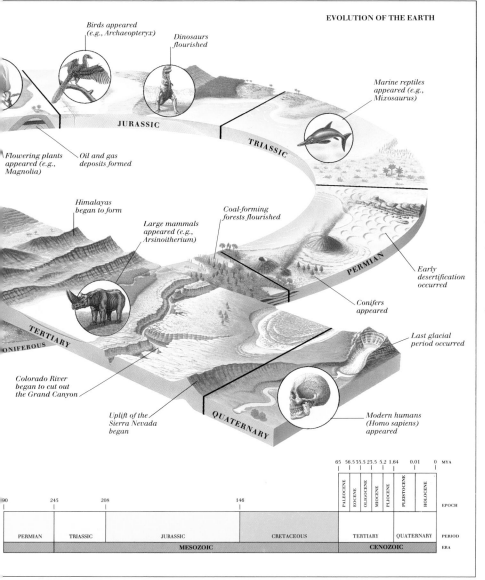

Birds appeared
(e.g., Archaeopteryx)

Dinosaurs
flourished

Marine reptiles
appeared (e.g.,
Mixosaurus)

JURASSIC

TRIASSIC

Flowering plants
appeared (e.g.,
Magnolia)

Oil and gas
deposits formed

Himalayas
began to form

Large mammals
appeared (e.g.,
Arsinoitherium)

Coal-forming
forests flourished

PERMIAN

Early
desertification
occurred

Conifers
appeared

TERTIARY

ONIFEROUS

Last glacial
period occurred

Colorado River
began to cut out
the Grand Canyon

Uplift of the
Sierra Nevada
began

QUATERNARY

Modern humans
(Homo sapiens)
appeared

		65	56.5	55.5	23.5	5.2	1.64		0.01		0 MYA
			PALEOCENE	EOCENE	OLIGOCENE	MIOCENE	PLIOCENE	PLEISTOCENE		HOLOCENE	EPOCH
90	245	208			146						
PERMIAN	TRIASSIC	JURASSIC		CRETACEOUS		TERTIARY			QUATERNARY		PERIOD
		MESOZOIC				CENOZOIC					ERA

The Earth's crust

THE EARTH'S CRUST IS THE SOLID outer shell of the Earth. It includes continental crust (about 25 miles thick) and oceanic crust (about four miles thick). The crust and the topmost layer of the mantle form the lithosphere. The lithosphere consists of semi-rigid plates that move relative to each other on the underlying asthenosphere (a partly molten layer of the mantle). This movement is known as plate tectonics and helps explain continental drift. Where two plates move apart, there are rifts in the crust. In mid-ocean, this movement results in seafloor spreading and the formation of ocean ridges; on continents, crustal spreading can form rift valleys. When plates move toward each other, one may be subducted beneath (forced under) the other. In mid-ocean, this causes ocean trenches, seismic activity, and arcs of volcanic islands. Where oceanic crust is subducted beneath continental crust or where continents collide, land may be uplifted and mountains formed (see pp. 62–63). Plates may also slide past each other—along the San Andreas fault, for example. Crustal movement on continents may result in earthquakes, while movement under the seabed can lead to tidal waves.

ELEMENTS IN THE EARTH'S CRUST

Other elements 2%
Potassium 2.6%
Calcium 3.6%
Aluminum 8%
Magnesium 2%
Sodium 2.8%
Iron 5%
Silicon 28%
Oxygen 46%

FEATURES OF PLATE MOVEMENTS

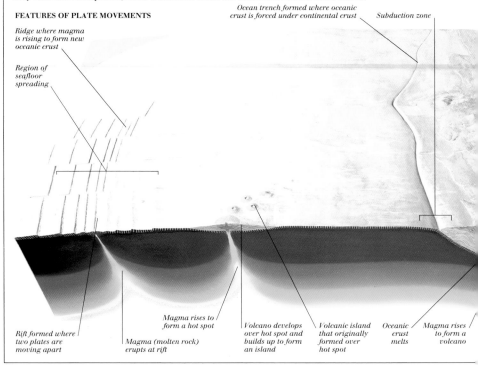

Ocean trench formed where oceanic crust is forced under continental crust

Subduction zone

Ridge where magma is rising to form new oceanic crust

Region of seafloor spreading

Rift formed where two plates are moving apart

Magma rises to form a hot spot

Magma (molten rock) erupts at rift

Volcano develops over hot spot and builds up to form an island

Volcanic island that originally formed over hot spot

Oceanic crust melts

Magma rises to form a volcano

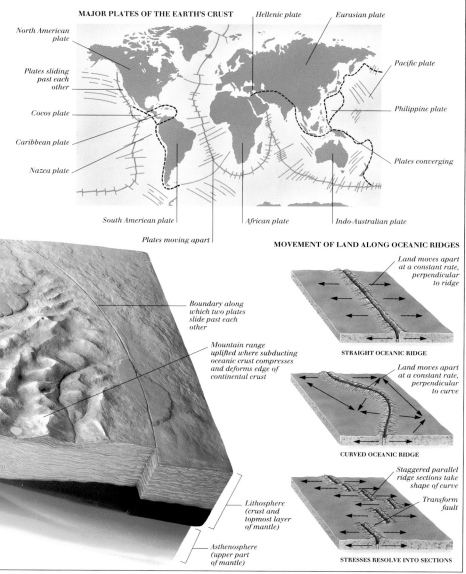

MAJOR PLATES OF THE EARTH'S CRUST

Hellenic plate

Eurasian plate

North American plate

Pacific plate

Plates sliding past each other

Philippine plate

Cocos plate

Caribbean plate

Nazca plate

Plates converging

South American plate

African plate

Indo-Australian plate

Plates moving apart

MOVEMENT OF LAND ALONG OCEANIC RIDGES

Boundary along which two plates slide past each other

Mountain range uplifted where subducting oceanic crust compresses and deforms edge of continental crust

Land moves apart at a constant rate, perpendicular to ridge

STRAIGHT OCEANIC RIDGE

Land moves apart at a constant rate, perpendicular to curve

CURVED OCEANIC RIDGE

Lithosphere (crust and topmost layer of mantle)

Staggered parallel ridge sections take shape of curve

Transform fault

Asthenosphere (upper part of mantle)

STRESSES RESOLVE INTO SECTIONS

Faults and folds

THE CONTINUOUS MOVEMENT of the Earth's crustal plates (see pp. 58–59) can squeeze, stretch, or break rock strata, deforming them and producing faults and folds. A fault is a fracture in a rock along which there is movement of one side relative to the other. The movement can be vertical, horizontal, or oblique (vertical and horizontal). Faults develop when rocks are subjected to compression or tension. They tend to occur in hard, rigid rocks, which are more likely to break than bend. The smallest faults occur in single mineral crystals and are microscopically small, while the largest —the Great Rift Valley in Africa, which formed between 5 million and 100,000 years ago—is more than 6,000 miles long. A fold is a bend in a rock layer caused by compression. Folds occur in elastic rocks, which tend to bend rather than break. The two main types of fold are anticlines (upfolds) and synclines (downfolds). Folds vary in size from a few millimeters long to folded mountain ranges hundreds of miles long, such as the Himalayas (see pp. 62–63) and the Alps, which are repeatedly folding. In addition to faults and folds, other features associated with rock deformations include boudins, mullions, and *en échelon* fractures.

STRUCTURE OF A FOLD

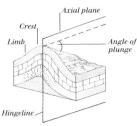

Axial plane

Crest

Limb

Angle of plunge

Hingeline

STRUCTURE OF A FAULT

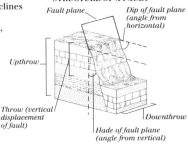

Fault plane

Dip of fault plane (angle from horizontal)

Upthrow

Throw (vertical displacement of fault)

Downthrow

Hade of fault plane (angle from vertical)

STRUCTURE OF A SLOPE

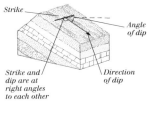

Strike

Angle of dip

Strike and dip are at right angles to each other

Direction of dip

FOLDED ROCK

Crest of anticline

Steeply dipping limbs

Plunge

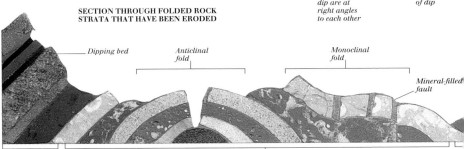

SECTION THROUGH FOLDED ROCK STRATA THAT HAVE BEEN ERODED

Dipping bed

Anticlinal fold

Monoclinal fold

Mineral-filled fault

Upper Carboniferous Millstone Grit

Lower Carboniferous Limestone

EXAMPLES OF FOLDS

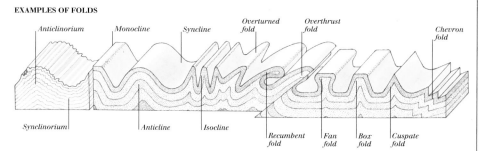

Anticlinorium · Monocline · Syncline · Overturned fold · Overthrust fold · Chevron fold · Synclinorium · Anticline · Isocline · Recumbent fold · Fan fold · Box fold · Cuspate fold

EXAMPLES OF FAULTS

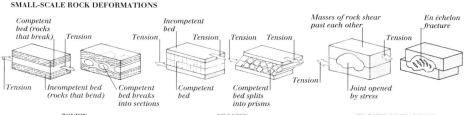

Sinistral strike-slip (lateral) fault · Dextral strike-slip (lateral) fault · Horst · Tear fault · Normal dip-slip fault · Reverse dip-slip fault · Thrust fault · Oblique-slip fault · Graben · Cylindrical fault

SMALL-SCALE ROCK DEFORMATIONS

Competent bed (rocks that break) · Tension · Tension · Incompetent bed · Tension · Tension · Tension · Masses of rock shear past each other · Tension · En échelon fracture

Tension · Incompetent bed (rocks that bend) · Competent bed breaks into sections · Competent bed · Competent bed splits into prisms · Joint opened by stress

BOUDIN · **MULLION** · **EN ECHELON FRACTURE**

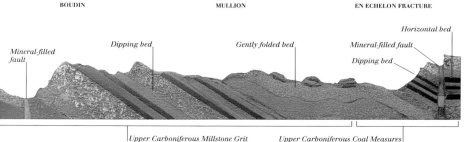

Mineral-filled fault · Dipping bed · Gently folded bed · Horizontal bed · Mineral-filled fault · Dipping bed

Upper Carboniferous Millstone Grit · Upper Carboniferous Coal Measures

Mountain building

THE PROCESSES INVOLVED in mountain building—termed orogenesis—occur as a result of the movement of the Earth's crustal plates (see pp. 58-59). There are three main types of mountains: volcanic mountains, fold mountains, and block mountains. Most volcanic mountains have been formed along plate boundaries where plates have come together or moved apart and lava and other debris have been ejected onto the Earth's surface. The lava and debris may have built up to form a dome around the vent of a volcano. Fold mountains are formed where plates push together and cause the rock to buckle upward. Where oceanic crust meets less dense continental crust, the oceanic crust is forced under the continental crust. The continental crust is buckled by the impact. This is how folded mountain ranges, such as the Appalachian Mountains in North America, were formed. Fold mountains are also formed where two areas of continental crust meet. The Himalayas, for example, began to form when India collided with Asia, buckling the sediments and parts of the oceanic crust between them. Block mountains are formed when a block of land is uplifted between two faults as a result of compression or tension in the Earth's crust (see pp. 60-61). Often, the movement along faults has taken place gradually over millions of years. However, two plates may cause an earthquake by suddenly sliding past each other along a faultline.

Asia

Himalayas formed by buckling of sediment and part of the oceanic crust between two colliding continents

BHAGIRATHI PARBAT, HIMALAYAS

India moves north

India collides with Asia about 40 million years ago

EXAMPLES OF MOUNTAINS

Active volcano

Vent

Extinct volcano

Layers of lava and ash build up to form volcanic mountain

VOLCANIC MOUNTAIN

Compression

Layers of rock buckled by compression to form syncline

Layers of rock buckled by compression to form anticline

Compressio

FOLD MOUNTAIN

Block uplifted to form mountain range

Fault

Tension

Tension

Block forced down

BLOCK-FAULT MOUNTAIN

Block uplifted to form mountain range

Fault

Fault

Block forced down

Block forced down

UPLIFTED BLOCK-FAULT MOUNTAIN

STAGES IN THE FORMATION OF THE HIMALAYAS

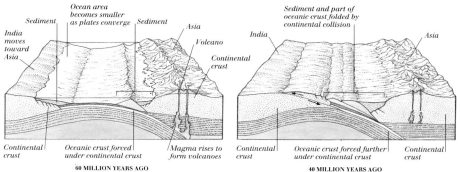

Ocean area
becomes smaller
as plates converge

Sediment

Sediment

Asia

India
moves
toward
Asia

Volcano

Continental
crust

Continental
crust

Oceanic crust forced
under continental crust

Magma rises to
form volcanoes

60 MILLION YEARS AGO

Sediment and part of
oceanic crust folded by
continental collision

India

Asia

Continental
crust

Oceanic crust forced further
under continental crust

Continental
crust

40 MILLION YEARS AGO

Ganges
plain

Sediment and part of
oceanic crust folded
and uplifted

India

Asia

Continental
crust

Continental
crust

20 MILLION YEARS AGO

Sediment and part of
oceanic crust further
folded and uplifted
to form Himalayas

Ripple effect of collision
forms mountains and
plateau of Tibet

Ganges
plain

India

Asia

Continental
crust

Continental
crust

TODAY

SAN ANDREAS FAULT

EARTHQUAKES

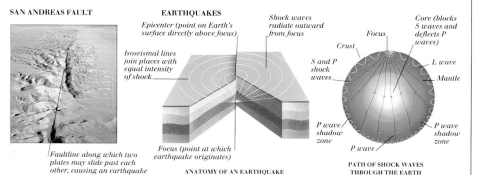

Epicenter (point on Earth's
surface directly above focus)

Shock waves
radiate outward
from focus

Core (blocks
S waves and
deflects P
waves)

Focus

Isoseismal lines
join places with
equal intensity
of shock

Crust

S and P
shock
waves

L wave

Mantle

P wave
shadow
zone

P wave
shadow
zone

P wave

Faultline along which two
plates may slide past each
other, causing an earthquake

Focus (point at which
earthquake originates)

ANATOMY OF AN EARTHQUAKE

**PATH OF SHOCK WAVES
THROUGH THE EARTH**

Precambrian to Devonian periods

MIDDLE ORDOVICIAN POSITIONS OF PRESENT-DAY LANDMASSES

WHEN THE EARTH FORMED about 4,600 million years ago, its atmosphere consisted of volcanic gases with little oxygen, making it hostile to most forms of life. One large supercontinent, Gondwanaland, was situated over the southern polar region, while other smaller continents were spread over the rest of the world. Constant movement of the earth's crustal plates carried continents across the earth's surface. The first primitive life-forms emerged around 3,400 million years ago in shallow, warm seas. The build up of oxygen began to form a shield of ozone around the earth, protecting living organisms from the sun's harmful rays and helping to establish an atmosphere in which life could sustain itself. The first vertebrates appeared about 470 million years ago, during the Ordovician period (510–439 million years ago), the first land plants appeared around 400 million years ago during the Devonian period (409–363 million years ago), and the first land animals about 30 million years later.

EXAMPLES OF PRECAMBRIAN TO DEVONIAN PLANT GROUPS

A PRESENT-DAY CLUBMOSS
(*Lycopodium sp.*)

A PRESENT-DAY LAND PLANT
(*Asparagus setaceous*)

FOSSIL OF AN EXTINCT LAND PLANT
(*Cooksonia hemisphaerica*)

FOSSIL OF AN EXTINCT SWAMP PLANT
(*Zosterophyllum llanoveranum*)

EXAMPLES OF PRECAMBRIAN TO DEVONIAN TRILOBITES

ACADAGNOSTUS
Family: Agnostidae
Length: $\frac{1}{3}$ in (8 mm)

PHACOPS
Family: Phacopidae
Length: $1\frac{3}{4}$ in (4.5 cm)

OLENELLUS
Family: Olenellidae
Length: $2\frac{1}{2}$ in (6 cm)

ELRATHIA
Family: Ptychopariidae
Length: $\frac{3}{4}$ in (2 cm)

THE EARTH DURING THE MIDDLE ORDOVICIAN PERIOD

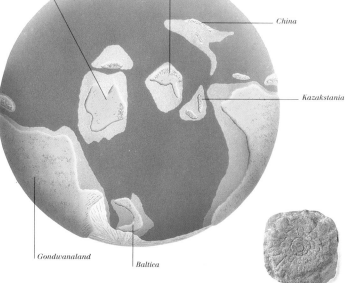

Siberia

Laurentia

China

Kazakstania

Gondwanaland

Baltica

FOSSIL NAUTILOID
*(Estonioceras
perforatum)*

FOSSIL BRACHIOPOD
(Dicoelosia bilobata)

TRACE FOSSIL
(Mawsonites spriggi)

FOSSIL GRAPTOLITE
*(Monograptus
convolutus)*

EXAMPLES OF DEVONIAN FISH

RHAMPHODOPSIS
Family: Ptyctodontidae
Length: 6 in (15 cm)

PTERASPIS
Family: Pteraspidae
Length: 10 in (25 cm)

COCCOSTEUS
Family: Coccosteidae
Length: 14 in (35 cm)

BOTHRIOLEPIS
Family: Bothriolepidae
Length: 16 in (40 cm)

CHEIRACANTHUS
Family: Acanthodidae
Length: 12 in (30 cm)

PTERICHTHYODES
Family: Asterolepidae
Length: 6 in (15 cm)

CHEIROLEPIS
Family: Cheirolepidae
Length: 6 $\frac{3}{4}$ in (17 cm)

CEPHALASPIS
Family: Cephalaspidae
Length: 8 $\frac{1}{4}$ in (22 cm)

65

Carboniferous to Permian periods

LATE CARBONIFEROUS POSITIONS
OF PRESENT-DAY LANDMASSES

LATE CARBONIFEROUS POSITIONS
OF PRESENT-DAY LANDMASSES

THE CARBONIFEROUS PERIOD (363–290 million years ago) takes its name from the thick, carbon-rich layers—now coal—that were produced during this period when swampy tropical forests were repeatedly drowned by shallow seas. The humid climate across northern and equatorial continents throughout Carboniferous times produced the first dense plant cover on Earth. During the early part of this period, the first reptiles appeared. Their development of a waterproof egg with a protective internal structure ended animal life's dependence on an aquatic environment. Toward the end of Carboniferous times, the earth's continents Laurussia and Gondwanaland collided, resulting in the huge landmass of Pangaea. Glaciers smothered much of the southern hemisphere during the Permian period (290–245 million years ago), covering Antarctica, parts of Australia, and much of South America, Africa, and India. Ice locked up much of the world's water and large areas of the northern hemisphere experienced a drop in sea-level. Away from the poles, deserts and a hot dry climate predominated. As a result of these conditions, the Permian period ended with the greatest mass extinction of life on earth ever.

EXAMPLES OF CARBONIFEROUS AND PERMIAN PLANT GROUPS

A PRESENT-DAY FIR
(Abies concolor)

FOSSIL OF AN EXTINCT FERN
(Zeilleria frenzlii)

FOSSIL OF AN
EXTINCT HORSETAIL
(Equisetites sp.)

FOSSIL OF AN
EXTINCT CLUBMOSS
(Lepidodendron sp.)

EXAMPLES OF CARBONIFEROUS AND PERMIAN TREES

PECOPTERIS
Family: Marattiaceae
Height: 13 ft (4 m)

PARIPTERIS
Family: Medullosaceae
Height: 16 ft 6 in (5 m)

MARIOPTERIS
Family: Unclassified
Height: 16 ft 6 in (5 m)

MEDULLOSA
Family: Medullosaceae
Height: 16 ft 6 in (5 m)

THE EARTH DURING THE LATE CARBONIFEROUS PERIOD

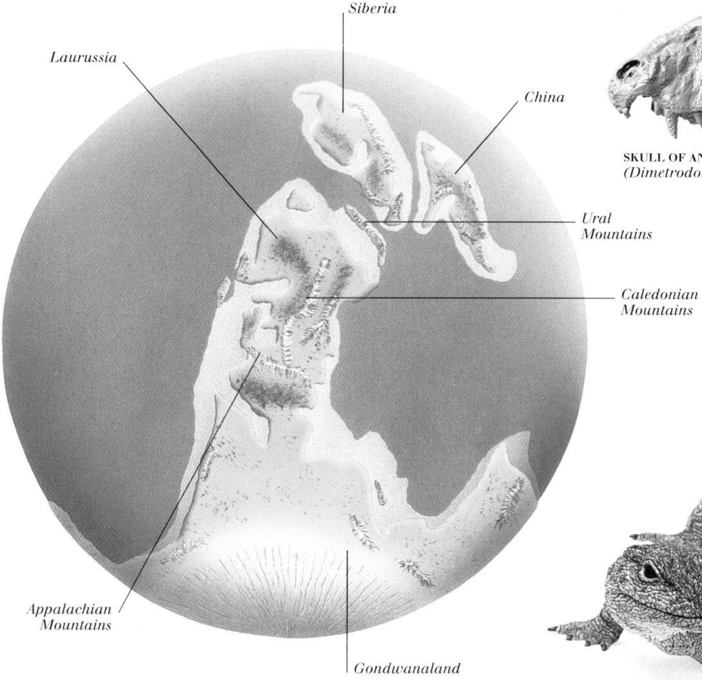

Siberia

Laurussia

China

Ural Mountains

Caledonian Mountains

Appalachian Mountains

Gondwanaland

EXAMPLES OF CARBONIFEROUS AND PERMIAN ANIMALS

SKULL OF AN EXTINCT SYNAPSID REPTILE
(Dimetrodon loomisi)

**FOSSIL TEETH OF
AN EXTINCT SHARK**
(Helicoprion bessonowi)

**MODEL OF AN EXTINCT
CARBONIFEROUS REPTILE**
(Westlothiana lizziae)

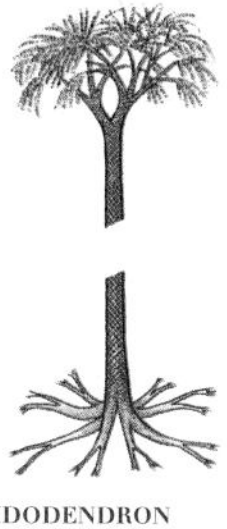

LEPIDODENDRON
Family: Lepidodendraceae
Height: 100 ft (30 m)

CORDAITES
Family: Cordaitacea
Height: 33 ft (10 m)

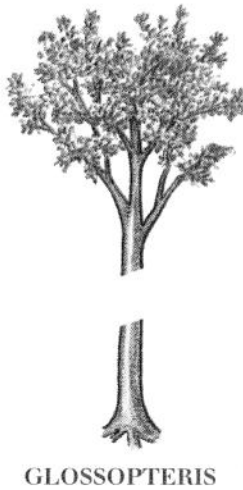

GLOSSOPTERIS
Family: Glossopteridaceae
Height: 26 ft (8 m)

ALETHOPTERIS
Family Medullosaceae
Height: 16 ft 6 in (5 m)

Triassic period

TRIASSIC POSITIONS OF
PRESENT-DAY LANDMASSES

North
America   Europe   Asia

South
America

Africa   Australia

Antarctica   India

THE TRIASSIC PERIOD (245–208 million years ago) marked the beginning
of what is known as the Age of the Dinosaurs (the Mesozoic era).
During this period, the present-day continents were massed together,
forming one huge continent known as Pangaea. This landmass
experienced extremes of climate, with lush green areas around
the coast or by lakes and rivers, and arid deserts in the interior.
The only forms of plant life were nonflowering plants, such
as conifers, ferns, cycads, and ginkgos; flowering plants had
not yet evolved. The principal forms of animal life included
primitive amphibians, rhynchosaurs ("beaked lizards"),
and primitive crocodilians. Dinosaurs first appeared about
250 million years ago, at the beginning of the Late Triassic
period. The earliest known dinosaurs were the carnivorous
(flesh-eating) herrerasaurids and staurikosaurids, such as
Herrerasaurus and *Staurikosaurus*. Early herbivorous (plant-eating)
dinosaurs first appeared in Late Triassic times and included *Plateosaurus*
and *Technosaurus*. By the end of the Triassic period, dinosaurs dominated
Pangaea, possibly contributing to the extinction of many other reptiles.

**EXAMPLES OF TRIASSIC
PLANT GROUPS**

A PRESENT-DAY
CYCAD
(*Cycas revoluta*)

A PRESENT-DAY GINKGO
(*Ginkgo biloba*)

A PRESENT-DAY CONIFER
(*Araucaria araucana*)

FOSSIL OF AN
EXTINCT FERN
(*Pachypteris* sp.)

FOSSIL LEAF OF AN
EXTINCT CYCAD
(*Cycas* sp.)

EXAMPLES OF TRIASSIC DINOSAURS

MELANOROSAURUS
A melanorosaurid
Length: 40 ft (12.2 m)

MUSSAURUS
A plateosaurid
Length: 6 ft 6 in–10 ft (2–3 m)

HERRERASAURUS
A herrerasaurid
Length: 10 ft (3 m)

PISANOSAURUS
A primitive ornithischian
Length: 3 ft (90 cm)

THE EARTH DURING THE TRIASSIC PERIOD

EXAMPLES OF TRIASSIC ANIMALS

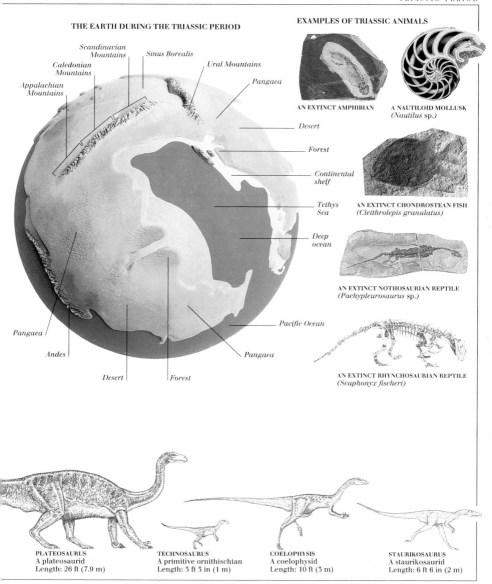

Scandinavian Mountains

Caledonian Mountains

Sinus Borealis

Ural Mountains

Pangaea

Appalachian Mountains

Desert

Forest

Continental shelf

Tethys Sea

Deep ocean

Pangaea

Andes

Pacific Ocean

Pangaea

Desert

Forest

AN EXTINCT AMPHIBIAN

A NAUTILOID MOLLUSK
(Nautilus sp.)

AN EXTINCT CHONDROSTEAN FISH
(Cleithrolepis granulatus)

AN EXTINCT NOTHOSAURIAN REPTILE
(Pachypleurosaurus sp.)

AN EXTINCT RHYNCHOSAURIAN REPTILE
(Scaphonyx fischeri)

PLATEOSAURUS
A plateosaurid
Length: 26 ft (7.9 m)

TECHNOSAURUS
A primitive ornithischian
Length: 3 ft 3 in (1 m)

COELOPHYSIS
A coelophysid
Length: 10 ft (3 m)

STAURIKOSAURUS
A staurikosaurid
Length: 6 ft 6 in (2 m)

Jurassic period

THE JURASSIC PERIOD, the middle part of the Mesozoic era, lasted from 208 to 146 million years ago. During the Jurassic period, the landmass of Pangaea broke up into the continents of Gondwanaland and Laurasia, and sea-levels rose, flooding areas of lower land. The Jurassic climate was warm and moist. Plants such as ginkgos, horsetails, and conifers thrived, and giant redwood trees appeared, as did the first flowering plants. The abundance of plant food coincided with the proliferation of herbivorous (plant-eating) dinosaurs, such as the large sauropods (e.g., *Diplodocus*) and stegosaurs (e.g., *Stegosaurus*). Carnivorous (flesh-eating) dinosaurs, such as *Compsognathus* and *Allosaurus,* also flourished by hunting the many animals that existed—among them other dinosaurs. Further Jurassic animals included shrewlike mammals, and pterosaurs (flying reptiles), as well as plesiosaurs and ichthyosaurs (both marine reptiles).

EXAMPLES OF JURASSIC PLANT GROUPS

A PRESENT-DAY FERN
(Dicksonia antarctica)

A PRESENT-DAY HORSETAIL
(Equisetum arvense)

A PRESENT-DAY CONIFER
(Taxus baccata)

**FOSSIL LEAF OF AN
EXTINCT CONIFER**
(Taxus sp.)

**FOSSIL LEAF OF AN
EXTINCT REDWOOD**
(Sequoiadendron affinis)

EXAMPLES OF JURASSIC DINOSAURS

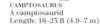

DIPLODOCUS
A diplodocid
Length: 88 ft (26.8 m)

CAMPTOSAURUS
A camptosaurid
Length: 16–23 ft (4.9–7 m)

DRYOSAURUS
A dryosaurid
Length: 10–13 ft (3–4 m)

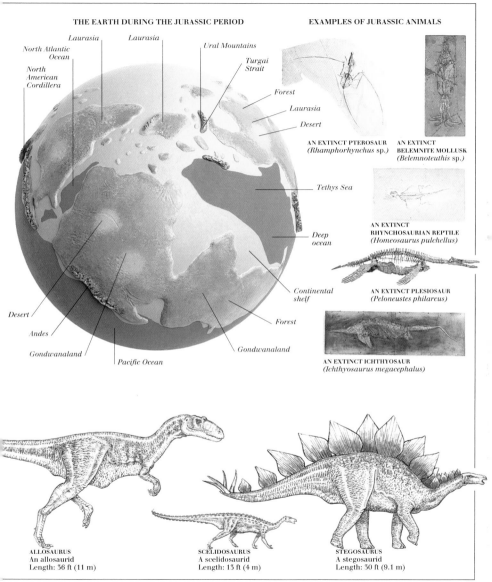

THE EARTH DURING THE JURASSIC PERIOD

Laurasia

Laurasia

North Atlantic Ocean

North American Cordillera

Ural Mountains

Turgai Strait

Forest

Laurasia

Desert

Tethys Sea

Deep ocean

Continental shelf

Desert

Andes

Gondwanaland

Pacific Ocean

Forest

Gondwanaland

EXAMPLES OF JURASSIC ANIMALS

AN EXTINCT PTEROSAUR
(Rhamphorhynchus sp.)

AN EXTINCT BELEMNITE MOLLUSK
(Belemnoteuthis sp.)

AN EXTINCT RHYNCHOSAURIAN REPTILE
(Homeosaurus pulchellus)

AN EXTINCT PLESIOSAUR
(Peloneustes philarcus)

AN EXTINCT ICHTHYOSAUR
(Ichthyosaurus megacephalus)

ALLOSAURUS
An allosaurid
Length: 36 ft (11 m)

SCELIDOSAURUS
A scelidosaurid
Length: 13 ft (4 m)

STEGOSAURUS
A stegosaurid
Length: 30 ft (9.1 m)

Cretaceous period

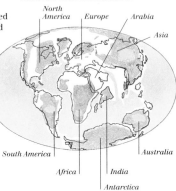

North
America   Europe   Arabia

Asia

South America   Australia

Africa   India

Antarctica

THE MESOZOIC ERA ENDED WITH the Cretaceous period, which lasted from 146 to 65 million years ago. During this period, Gondwanaland and Laurasia were breaking up into smaller landmasses that more closely resembled those of the modern continents. The climate remained mild and moist, but the seasons became more marked. Flowering plants, including deciduous trees, replaced many cycads, seed ferns, and conifers. Animal species became more varied, with the evolution of new mammals, insects, fish, crustaceans, and turtles. Dinosaurs evolved into a wide variety of species during Cretaceous times; more than half of all known dinosaurs—including *Iguanodon, Deinonychus, Tyrannosaurus,* and *Hypsilophodon* —lived during this period. At the end of the Cretaceous period, however, large dinosaurs became extinct. The reason for this mass extinction is unknown but it is thought to have been caused by climatic changes due to either a catastrophic meteor impact with the Earth or extensive volcanic eruptions.

EXAMPLES OF CRETACEOUS PLANT GROUPS

A PRESENT-DAY CONIFER
(Pinus muricata)

**A PRESENT-DAY
DECIDUOUS TREE**
(Magnolia sp.)

**FOSSIL OF AN
EXTINCT FERN**
(Sphenopteris latiloba)

**FOSSIL OF AN
EXTINCT GINKGO**
(Ginkgo pluripartita)

**FOSSIL LEAVES
OF AN EXTINCT
DECIDUOUS TREE**
(Cercidyphyllum sp.)

EXAMPLES OF
CRETACEOUS DINOSAURS

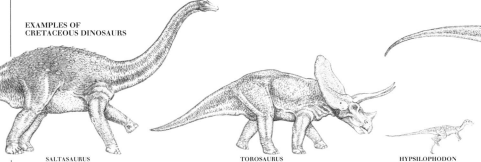

SALTASAURUS
A titanosaurid
Length: 40 ft (12.2 m)

TOROSAURUS
A ceratopsid
Length: 25 ft (7.6 m)

HYPSILOPHODON
A hypsilophodontid
Length: 4 ft 6 in–7 ft 6 in (1.4–2.3 m)

THE EARTH DURING THE CRETACEOUS PERIOD

EXAMPLES OF CRETACEOUS ANIMALS

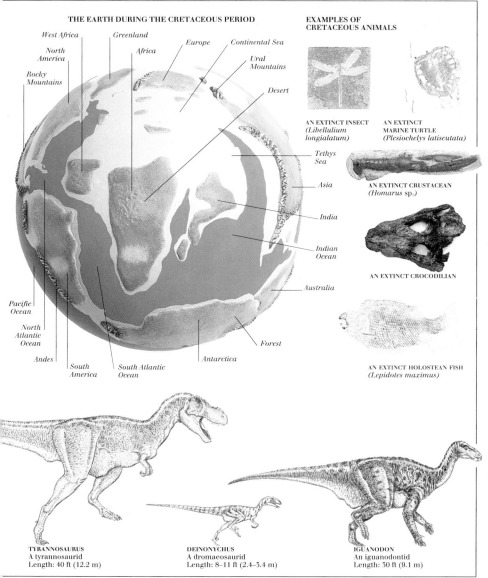

West Africa

Greenland

Europe

Continental Sea

North America

Africa

Ural Mountains

Rocky Mountains

Desert

Tethys Sea

Asia

India

Indian Ocean

Pacific Ocean

North Atlantic Ocean

Andes

South America

South Atlantic Ocean

Antarctica

Australia

Forest

AN EXTINCT INSECT
(*Libellulium longialatum*)

AN EXTINCT MARINE TURTLE
(*Plesiochelys latiscutata*)

AN EXTINCT CRUSTACEAN
(*Homarus* sp.)

AN EXTINCT CROCODILIAN

AN EXTINCT HOLOSTEAN FISH
(*Lepidotes maximus*)

TYRANNOSAURUS
A tyrannosaurid
Length: 40 ft (12.2 m)

DEINONYCHUS
A dromaeosaurid
Length: 8–11 ft (2.4–3.4 m)

IGUANODON
An iguanodontid
Length: 30 ft (9.1 m)

Tertiary period

North America

Europe

Asia

South America

Africa

Australia

Antarctica

FOLLOWING THE DEMISE OF THE DINOSAURS at the end of the Cretaceous period, the Tertiary period (65–1.6 million years ago), which formed the first part of the Cenozoic era (65 million years ago–present), was characterized by a huge expansion of mammal life. Placental mammals nourish and maintain their young in the mother's uterus; only three orders of placental mammals existed during Cretaceous times, compared with 25 orders during the Tertiary period. One of these 25 included the first hominid (see pp.108–109), *Australopithecus*, which appeared in Africa. By the beginning of the Tertiary period, the continents had almost reached their present position. The Tethys Sea, which had separated the northern continents from Africa and India, began to close up, forming the Mediterranean Sea and allowing the migration of terrestrial animals between Africa and western Europe. India's collision with Asia led to the formation of the Himalayas. During the middle part of the Tertiary period, the forest-dwelling and browsing mammals were replaced by mammals such as the horse, better suited to grazing the open savannahs that began to dominate. Repeated cool periods throughout the Tertiary period established the Antarctic as an icy island continent.

EXAMPLES OF TERTIARY PLANT GROUPS

A PRESENT-DAY OAK
(*Quercus palustris*)

A PRESENT-DAY BIRCH
(*Betula grossa*)

**FOSSIL LEAF OF AN
EXTINCT BIRCH**
(*Betulites sp.*)

**FOSSIL STEM OF AN
EXTINCT PALM**
(*Palmoxylon*)

EXAMPLES OF TERTIARY
ANIMAL GROUPS

HYAENODON
An hyaenodontid
Length: 6 ft 6 in (2 m)

TITANOHYRAX
A pliohyracid
Length: 6 ft 6 in (2 m)

PHORUSRHACUS
A phorusrhacid
Length: 5 ft (1.5 m)

SAMOTHERIUM
A giraffid
Length: 10 ft (3 m)

THE EARTH DURING THE TERTIARY PERIOD

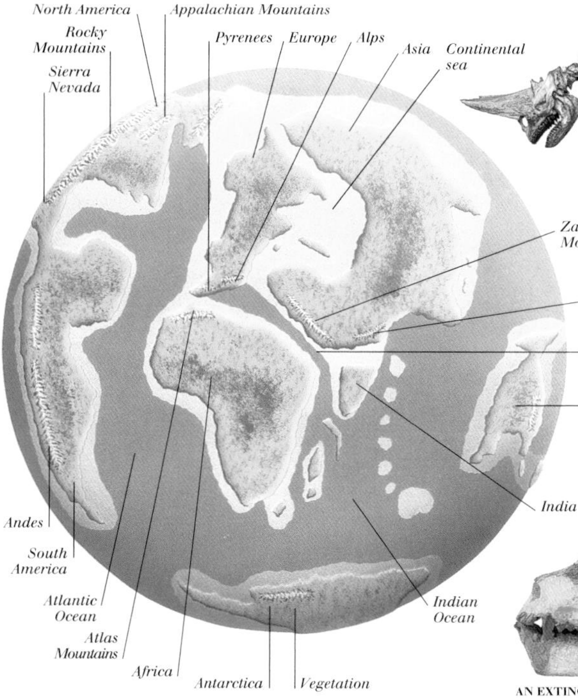

North America
Rocky Mountains
Sierra Nevada
Appalachian Mountains
Pyrenees
Europe
Alps
Asia
Continental sea
Zagros Mountains
Himalayas
Tethys Sea
Australia
India
Andes
South America
Atlantic Ocean
Atlas Mountains
Africa
Antarctica
Vegetation
Indian Ocean

EXAMPLES OF TERTIARY ANIMALS

AN EXTINCT MAMMAL
(Arsinoitherium sp.)

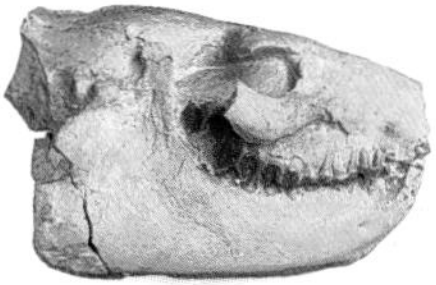

AN EXTINCT MAMMAL
(Merycoidodon culbertsonii)

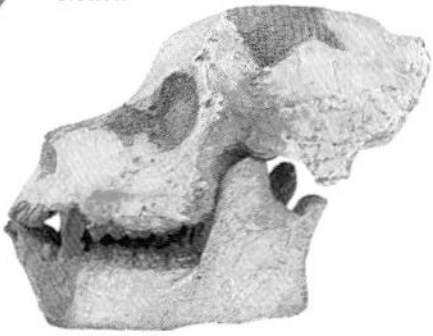

AN EXTINCT HOMINID
(Aegyptopithecus sp.)

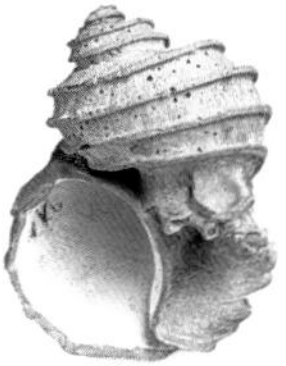

AN EXTINCT GASTROPOD MOLLUSC
(Ecphora quadricostata)

MAMMUT
A mammutid
Length: 8 ft (2.5 m)

TETRALOPHODON
A gomphotheriid
Length: 8 ft (2.5 m)

75

Quaternary period

THE QUATERNARY PERIOD (1.6 million years ago–present) forms the second part of the Cenozoic era (65 million years ago–present): it has been characterized by alternating cold (glacial) and warm (interglacial) periods. During cold periods, ice sheets and glaciers have formed repeatedly on northern and southern continents. The cold environments in North America and Eurasia, and to a lesser extent in southern South America and parts of Australia, have caused the migration of many life forms toward the Equator. Only the specialized ice-age mammals such as *Mammuthus* and *Coelodonta*, with their thick wool and fat insulation, were suited to life in very cold climates. Humans developed throughout the Pleistocene period (1.6 million–10,000 years ago) in Africa and migrated northward into Europe and Asia. Modern humans, *Homo sapiens*, lived on the cold European continent 30,000 years ago and hunted mammals. The end of the last ice age and the climatic changes that occurred about 10,000 years ago brought extinction to many Pleistocene mammals, but enabled humans to flourish.

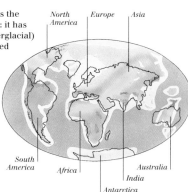

North America Europe Asia South America Africa Australia India Antarctica

EXAMPLES OF QUATERNARY PLANT GROUPS

A PRESENT-DAY BIRCH
(*Betula lenta*)

A PRESENT-DAY SWEETGUM
(*Liquidambar styraciflua*)

FOSSIL LEAF OF A SWEETGUM
(*Liquidambar europeanum*)

FOSSIL LEAF OF A BIRCH
(*Betula sp.*)

EXAMPLES OF QUATERNARY ANIMAL GROUPS

PROCOPTODON
A macropodid
Length: 10 ft (3 m)

DIPROTODON
A diprotodontid
Length: 10 ft (3 m)

TOXODON
A toxodontid
Length: 10 ft (3 m)

MAMMUTHUS
An elephantid
Length: 10 ft (3 m)

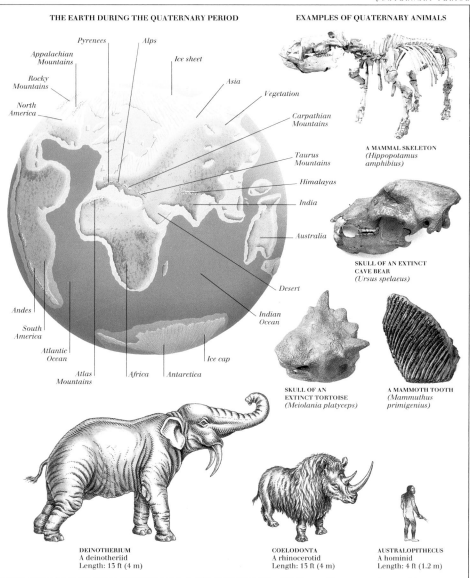

THE EARTH DURING THE QUATERNARY PERIOD

EXAMPLES OF QUATERNARY ANIMALS

Pyrenees

Alps

Appalachian
Mountains

Ice sheet

Rocky
Mountains

Asia

North
America

Vegetation

Carpathian
Mountains

Taurus
Mountains

Himalayas

India

Australia

Andes

South
America

Atlantic
Ocean

Desert

Indian
Ocean

Atlas
Mountains

Africa

Antarctica

Ice cap

A MAMMAL SKELETON
(*Hippopotamus
amphibius*)

**SKULL OF AN EXTINCT
CAVE BEAR**
(*Ursus spelaeus*)

**SKULL OF AN
EXTINCT TORTOISE**
(*Meiolania platyceps*)

A MAMMOTH TOOTH
(*Mammuthus
primigenius*)

DEINOTHERIUM
A deinotheriid
Length: 13 ft (4 m)

COELODONTA
A rhinocerotid
Length: 13 ft (4 m)

AUSTRALOPITHECUS
A hominid
Length: 4 ft (1.2 m)

Early signs of life

FOR ALMOST A THOUSAND MILLION YEARS after its formation, there was no known life on Earth. The first simple, sea-dwelling organic structures appeared about 3,400 years ago; they may have formed when certain chemical molecules joined together. Prokaryotes, single-celled micro-organisms such as blue-green algae, were able to photosynthesize (see pp. 138–139), and thus produce oxygen. A thousand million years later, sufficient oxygen had built up in the earth's atmosphere to allow multicellular organisms to proliferate in the Precambrian seas (before 570 million years ago). Soft-bodied jellyfish, corals, and seaworms flourished about 700 million years ago. Trilobites, the first animals with hard body frames, developed during the Cambrian period (570–510 million years ago). However, it was not until the beginning of the Devonian period (409–363 million years ago) that early land plants, such as *Asteroxylon*, formed a water-retaining cuticle, which ended their dependence on an aquatic environment. About 363 million years ago, the first amphibians (see pp. 80–81) crawled onto the land, although they still returned to the water to lay their soft eggs. Not until the emergence of the first reptiles would animals appear that were not dependent on water in this way.

STROMATOLITIC LIMESTONE

Layered structure

Alternate layers of mud and sand

Layers bound by algae

Limestone

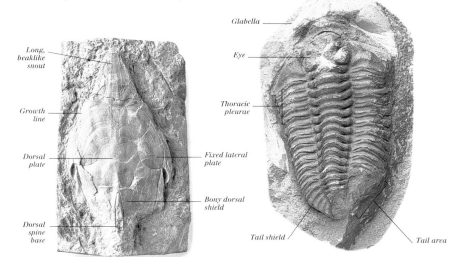

Long, beaklike snout

Growth line

Dorsal plate

Dorsal spine base

Glabella

Eye

Thoracic pleurae

Fixed lateral plate

Bony dorsal shield

Tail shield

Tail area

FOSSILIZED JAWLESS FISH

FOSSILIZED TRILOBITE

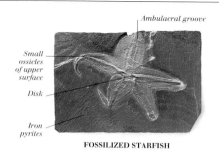

Ambulacral groove

Small ossicles of upper surface

Disk

Iron pyrites

FOSSILIZED STARFISH

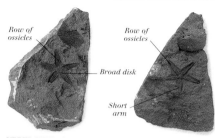

Row of ossicles

Row of ossicles

Broad disk

Short arm

UPPER SURFACE OF FOSSILIZED STARFISH

LOWER SURFACE OF FOSSILIZED STARFISH

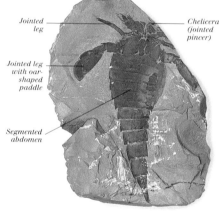

Jointed leg

Chelicera (jointed pincer)

Jointed leg with oar-shaped paddle

Segmented abdomen

UNDERSIDE OF FOSSILIZED EURYPTERID

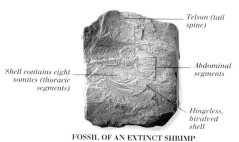

Telson (tail spine)

Abdominal segments

Shell contains eight somites (thoracic segments)

Hingeless, bivalved shell

FOSSIL OF AN EXTINCT SHRIMP

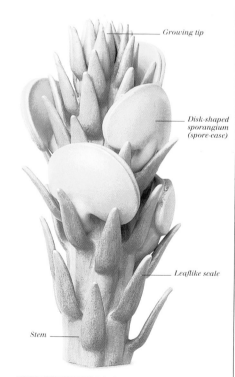

Growing tip

Disk-shaped sporangium (spore-case)

Leaflike scale

Stem

RECONSTRUCTION OF ASTEROXYLON

Amphibians and reptiles

THE EARLIEST KNOWN AMPHIBIANS, such as *Acanthostega* and *Ichthyostega*, lived about 363 million years ago at the end of the Devonian period (409–363 million years ago). Their limbs may have evolved from the muscular fins of lungfish. These fish can use their fins to push themselves along the bottom of lakes and some can breathe at the water's surface. While amphibians (see pp. 182–183) can exist on land, they are dependent on a wet environment because their skin does not retain moisture and they must return to the water to lay their eggs. Evolving from amphibians, reptiles (see pp. 184–187) first appeared during the Carboniferous period (363–290 million years ago): *Westlothiana*, the earliest known reptile, lived on land 338 million years ago. The development of the amniotic egg, with an embryo enclosed in its own wet environment (the amnion) and protected by a waterproof shell, freed reptiles from the amphibian's dependence on a wet habitat. A scaly skin protected the reptile from desiccation on land and enabled it to exploit ways of life closed to its amphibian ancestors. Reptiles include the dinosaurs, which came to dominate life on land during the Mesozoic era (245–65 million years ago).

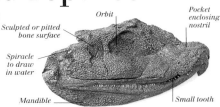

FOSSIL SKULL OF ACANTHOSTEGA

Orbit

Pocket enclosing nostril

Sculpted or pitted bone surface

Spiracle to draw in water

Mandible

Small tooth

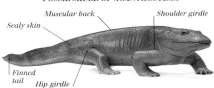

MODEL OF ICHTHYOSTEGA

Muscular back

Shoulder girdle

Scaly skin

Finned tail

Hip girdle

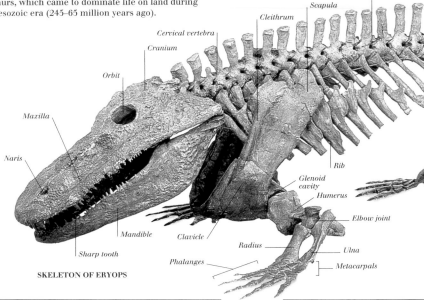

SKELETON OF ERYOPS

Dorsal vertebra

Scapula

Cleithrum

Cervical vertebra

Cranium

Orbit

Maxilla

Naris

Mandible

Clavicle

Sharp tooth

Phalanges

Radius

Rib

Glenoid cavity

Humerus

Elbow joint

Ulna

Metacarpals

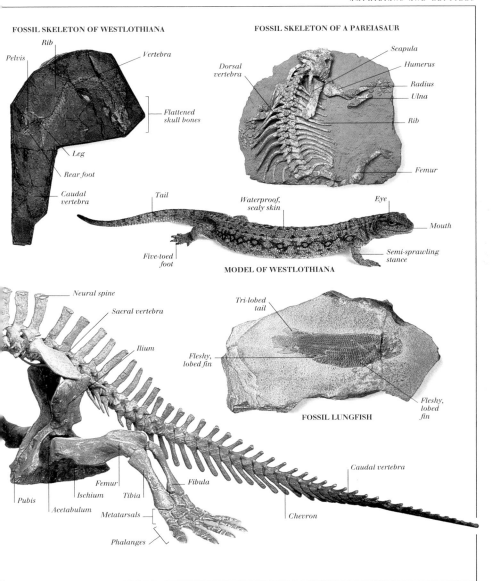

FOSSIL SKELETON OF WESTLOTHIANA

Rib

Pelvis

Vertebra

Flattened
skull bones

Leg

Rear foot

Caudal
vertebra

FOSSIL SKELETON OF A PAREIASAUR

Scapula

Humerus

Radius

Ulna

Dorsal
vertebra

Rib

Femur

Tail

Waterproof,
scaly skin

Eye

Mouth

Five-toed
foot

Semi-sprawling
stance

MODEL OF WESTLOTHIANA

Neural spine

Sacral vertebra

Ilium

Tri-lobed
tail

Fleshy,
lobed fin

Fleshy,
lobed
fin

FOSSIL LUNGFISH

Femur

Fibula

Caudal vertebra

Pubis

Ischium

Tibia

Acetabulum

Metatarsals

Chevron

Phalanges

The dinosaurs

STRUCTURE OF SAURISCHIAN PELVIS

THE DINOSAURS WERE A LARGE GROUP of reptiles that were the dominant land vertebrates (animals with backbones) for most of the Mesozoic era (245–65 million years ago). They appeared some 230 million years ago and were distinguished from other scaly, egg-laying reptiles by an important feature: dinosaurs had an erect limb stance. This enabled them to keep their bodies well above the ground, unlike the sprawling and semi-sprawling stance of other reptiles. The head of the dinosaur's femur (thighbone) fits into a socket in its pelvis (hipbone), producing efficient and mobile locomotion. Dinosaurs are categorized into two groups according to the structure of their pelvis: saurischian (lizard-hipped) and ornithischian (bird-hipped) dinosaurs. In the case of most saurischians, the pubis (part of the pelvis) jutted forward, while in ornithischians it slanted back, parallel to the ischium (another part of the pelvis). The enormous variety of dinosaur species equals that of mammals. The Dinosauria were the most successful land vertebrates ever, and survived for 165 million years, until their extinction 65 million years ago.

Ilium
Postacetabular process
Ilio-ischial joint
Ischium
Hook of preacetabular process
Ilio-pubic joint
Acetabulum
Pubis
Pubic foot

GALLIMIMUS
A saurischian dinosaur

POSITION OF PELVIS IN A SAURISCHIAN DINOSAUR

STRUCTURE OF ORNITHISCHIAN PELVIS

Ilium
Postacetabular process
Ilio-ischial joint
Preacetabular process
Ilio-pubic joint
Prepubis
Acetabulum
Pubis
Ischium

HYPSILOPHODON
An ornithischian dinosaur

POSITION OF PELVIS IN AN ORNITHISCHIAN DINOSAUR

BAROSAURUS
A saurischian dinosaur

COMPARISON OF ANIMAL STANCES

SPRAWLING STANCE
The thighs and upper arms project straight out from the body so that the knees and elbows are bent at right angles.

COMMON IGUANA
(*Iguana iguana*)
A present-day reptile

ERECT STANCE
The thighs and upper arms project straight down from the body so that the knees and elbows are straight.

SEMI-SPRAWLING STANCE
The thighs and upper arms project downward and outward so that the knees and elbows are slightly bent.

DWARF CROCODILE
(*Osteolaemus tetraspis*)
A present-day reptile

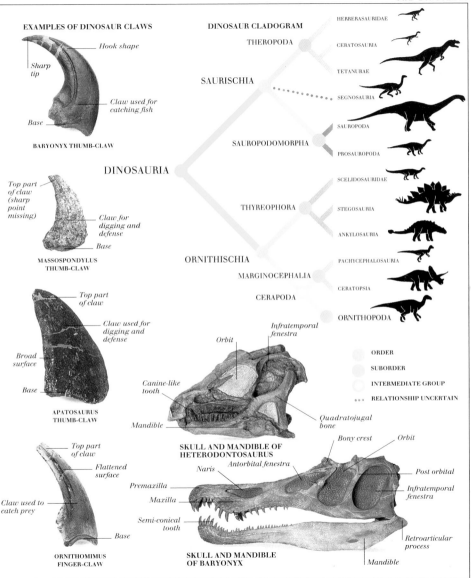

EXAMPLES OF DINOSAUR CLAWS

Hook shape

Sharp tip

Claw used for catching fish

Base

BARYONYX THUMB-CLAW

Top part of claw (sharp point missing)

Claw for digging and defense

Base

MASSOSPONDYLUS THUMB-CLAW

Top part of claw

Claw used for digging and defense

Broad surface

Base

APATOSAURUS THUMB-CLAW

Top part of claw

Flattened surface

Claw used to catch prey

Base

ORNITHOMIMUS FINGER-CLAW

DINOSAUR CLADOGRAM

THEROPODA

SAURISCHIA

SAUROPODOMORPHA

DINOSAURIA

THYREOPHORA

ORNITHISCHIA

MARGINOCEPHALIA

CERAPODA

ORNITHOPODA

HERRERASAURIDAE

CERATOSAURIA

TETANURAE

SEGNOSAURIA

SAUROPODA

PROSAUROPODA

SCELIDOSAURIDAE

STEGOSAURIA

ANKYLOSAURIA

PACHYCEPHALOSAURIA

CERATOPSIA

● ORDER
● SUBORDER
● INTERMEDIATE GROUP
••• RELATIONSHIP UNCERTAIN

Orbit

Infratemporal fenestra

Canine-like tooth

Quadratojugal bone

Mandible

SKULL AND MANDIBLE OF HETERODONTOSAURUS

Bony crest

Orbit

Antorbital fenestra

Post orbital

Naris

Infratemporal fenestra

Premaxilla

Maxilla

Semi-conical tooth

Retroarticular process

SKULL AND MANDIBLE OF BARYONYX

Mandible

Theropods 1

AN ENORMOUSLY SUCCESSFUL SUBORDER of the Saurischia, the bipedal (two-footed) theropods ("beast feet") emerged 230 million years ago in Late Triassic times; the oldest known example comes from South America. Theropods spanned the whole of the Age of the Dinosaurs (230–65 million years ago) and included most known predatory dinosaurs. The typical theropod had small arms with sharp, clawed fingers; powerful jaws lined with sharp teeth; an S-shaped neck; long, muscular hind limbs; and clawed, usually four-toed feet. Many theropods may have been warm-blooded; most were exclusively carnivorous. Theropods ranged from animals no larger than a chicken to huge creatures, such as *Tyrannosaurus* and *Baryonyx*. The group also included ostrichlike omnivores and herbivores with toothless beaks, such as *Struthiomimus* and *Gallimimus*. Many scientists believe that birds are the closest living relatives to the dinosaurs, and share a common ancestor with the theropods. *Archaeopteryx*, small and feathered, was the first known bird and lived alongside its dinosaur relatives.

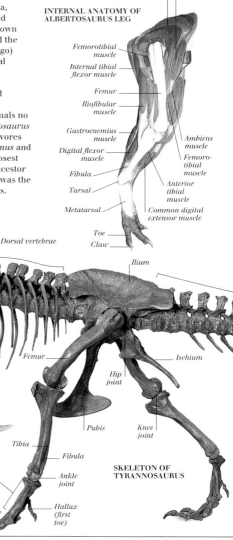

INTERNAL ANATOMY OF ALBERTOSAURUS LEG

Iliotibial muscle
Iliofemoral muscle
Femorotibial muscle
Internal tibial flexor muscle
Femur
Iliofibular muscle
Gastrocnemius muscle
Digital flexor muscle
Fibula
Tarsal
Metatarsal
Ambiens muscle
Femoro-tibial muscle
Anterior tibial muscle
Common digital extensor muscle
Toe
Claw

Cranium
Supraoccipital crest
Orbit
Naris
Cervical vertebrae
Dorsal vertebrae
Ilium
Cervical rib
Scapula
Shoulder joint
Ulna
Mandible
Phalanges
Metacarpals
Serrated tooth
Wrist joint
Elbow joint
Coracoid
Rib
Humerus
Femur
Ischium
Hip joint
Naris
Eye
Thigh
Scaly skin
Tail
Pubis
Knee joint
Hand
Forelimb
Knee
Ankle
Foot
Tibia
Fibula
Metatarsals
Ankle joint
SKELETON OF TYRANNOSAURUS
Hind limb
Toe
Phalanges
Hallux (first toe)
Claw
EXTERNAL FEATURES OF TYRANNOSAURUS

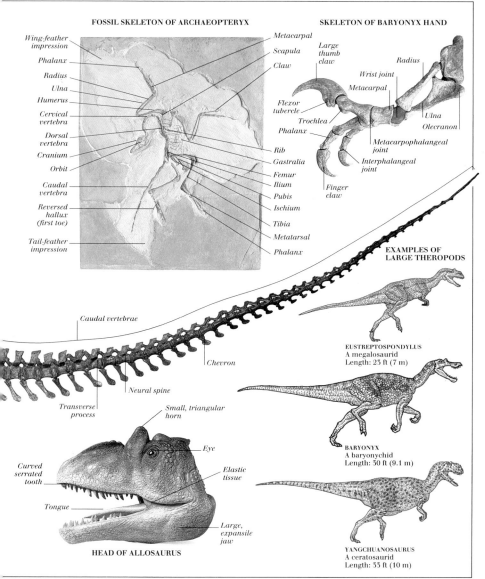

FOSSIL SKELETON OF ARCHAEOPTERYX

Wing-feather impression
Phalanx
Radius
Ulna
Humerus
Cervical vertebra
Dorsal vertebra
Cranium
Orbit
Caudal vertebra
Reversed hallux (first toe)
Tail-feather impression

Metacarpal
Scapula
Claw

Rib
Gastralia
Femur
Ilium
Pubis
Ischium
Tibia
Metatarsal
Phalanx

SKELETON OF BARYONYX HAND

Large thumb claw
Flexor tubercle
Trochlea
Phalanx
Finger claw
Radius
Wrist joint
Metacarpal
Ulna
Olecranon
Metacarpophalangeal joint
Interphalangeal joint

Caudal vertebrae
Chevron
Neural spine
Transverse process

EXAMPLES OF LARGE THEROPODS

EUSTREPTOSPONDYLUS
A megalosaurid
Length: 23 ft (7 m)

BARYONYX
A baryonychid
Length: 30 ft (9.1 m)

YANGCHUANOSAURUS
A ceratosaurid
Length: 33 ft (10 m)

Small, triangular horn
Eye
Curved serrated tooth
Elastic tissue
Tongue
Large, expansile jaw

HEAD OF ALLOSAURUS

85

Theropods 2

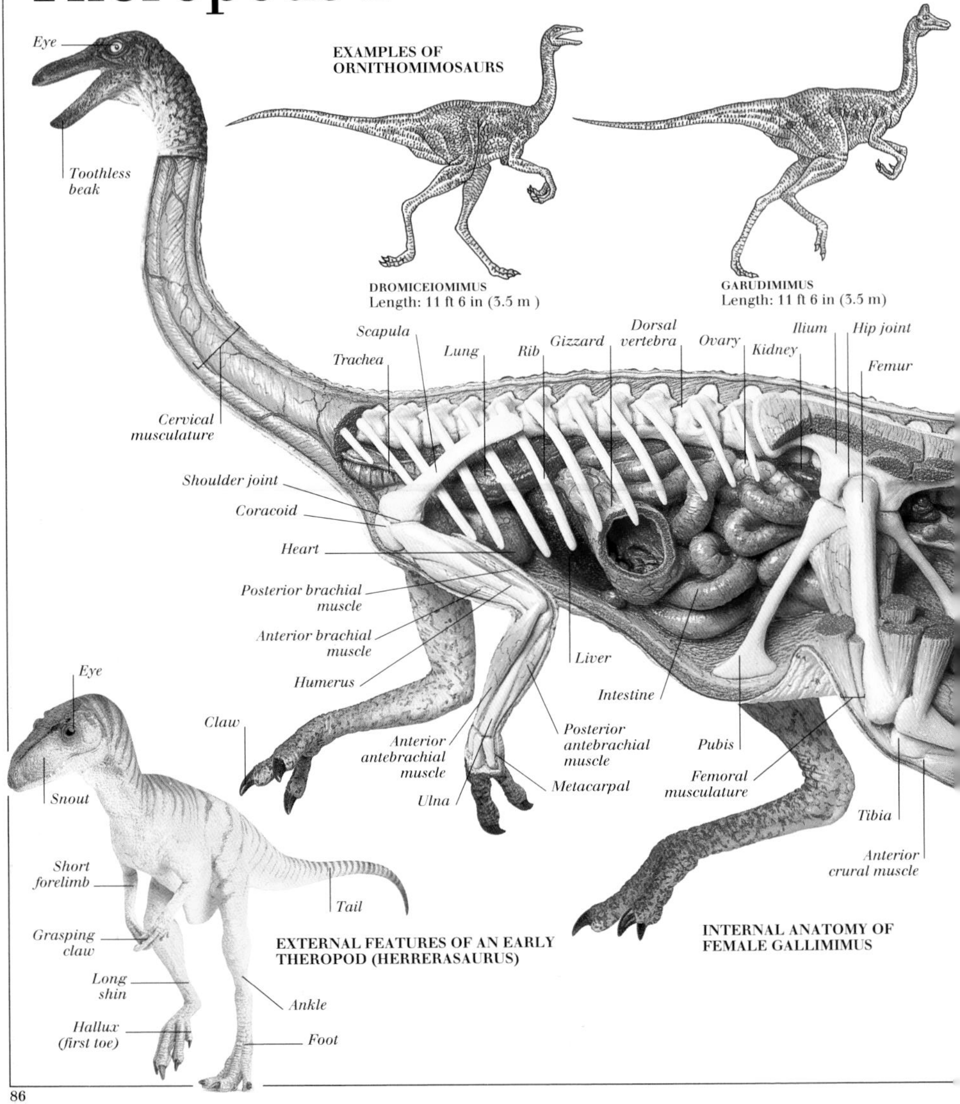

Eye

Toothless beak

EXAMPLES OF ORNITHOMIMOSAURS

DROMICEIOMIMUS
Length: 11 ft 6 in (3.5 m)

GARUDIMIMUS
Length: 11 ft 6 in (3.5 m)

Cervical musculature

Scapula

Trachea

Lung

Rib

Gizzard

Dorsal vertebra

Ovary

Kidney

Ilium

Hip joint

Femur

Shoulder joint

Coracoid

Heart

Posterior brachial muscle

Anterior brachial muscle

Humerus

Claw

Eye

Snout

Short forelimb

Grasping claw

Long shin

Hallux (first toe)

Anterior antebrachial muscle

Ulna

Tail

Ankle

Foot

Liver

Intestine

Posterior antebrachial muscle

Metacarpal

Pubis

Femoral musculature

Tibia

Anterior crural muscle

EXTERNAL FEATURES OF AN EARLY THEROPOD (HERRERASAURUS)

INTERNAL ANATOMY OF FEMALE GALLIMIMUS

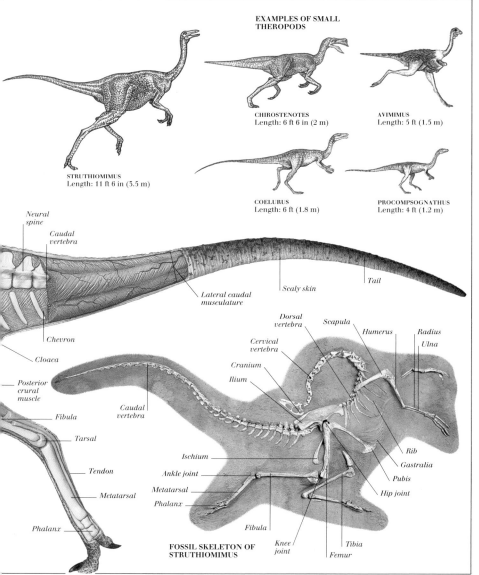

EXAMPLES OF SMALL THEROPODS

CHIROSTENOTES
Length: 6 ft 6 in (2 m)

AVIMIMUS
Length: 5 ft (1.5 m)

STRUTHIOMIMUS
Length: 11 ft 6 in (3.5 m)

COELURUS
Length: 6 ft (1.8 m)

PROCOMPSOGNATHUS
Length: 4 ft (1.2 m)

Neural spine

Caudal vertebra

Lateral caudal musculature

Scaly skin

Tail

Chevron

Cloaca

Posterior crural muscle

Fibula

Tarsal

Tendon

Metatarsal

Phalanx

Caudal vertebra

Dorsal vertebra

Cervical vertebra

Cranium

Ilium

Scapula

Humerus

Radius

Ulna

Ischium

Ankle joint

Metatarsal

Phalanx

Rib

Gastralia

Pubis

Hip joint

Fibula

Knee joint

Tibia

Femur

FOSSIL SKELETON OF STRUTHIOMIMUS

Sauropodomorphs 1

THE SAUROPODOMORPHA ("lizard-feet forms")
were herbivorous, usually quadrupedal (four-footed)
dinosaurs. A suborder of the Saurischia, they
were characterized by small heads, bulky bodies,
and long necks and tails. There were two
infraorders: prosauropods and sauropods.

THECODONTOSAURUS

Prosauropods lived from Late Triassic to Early
Jurassic times (225–180 million years ago) and included beasts such
as the small *Anchisaurus* and one of the first very large dinosaurs,
Melanosaurus. By Middle Jurassic times (about 165 million years ago),
sauropods had replaced prosauropods and spread worldwide. They
included the heaviest and longest land animals ever, such as *Diplodocus*
and *Brachiosaurus*. Sauropods persisted to the end of the Cretaceous
period (65 million years ago). Many of these dinosaurs moved in herds,
protected from predatory theropods by their huge bulk and powerful
tails, which they could use to lash out at attackers. Sauropodomorphs
were the most common large herbivores until Late Jurassic
times (about 145 million years ago), and appear to
have survived in southern continents
long after they had disappeared
from the north.

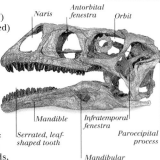

SKULL AND MANDIBLE OF PLATEOSAURUS

Naris — *Antorbital fenestra* — *Orbit*

Mandible — *Infratemporal fenestra* — *Paroccipital process*

Serrated, leaf-shaped tooth

Mandibular fenestra

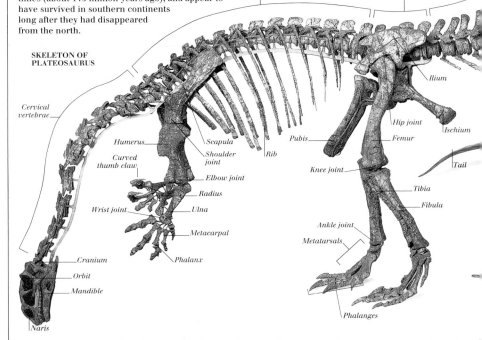

SKELETON OF PLATEOSAURUS

Dorsal vertebrae — *Sacral vertebrae*

Ilium

Cervical vertebrae

Hip joint — *Ischium*

Humerus — *Scapula* — *Pubis* — *Femur*

Curved thumb claw — *Shoulder joint* — *Rib*

Tail

Elbow joint — *Knee joint*

Radius — *Tibia*

Wrist joint — *Ulna* — *Fibula*

Metacarpal

Ankle joint

Metatarsals

Cranium

Orbit

Phalanx

Mandible

Phalanges

Naris

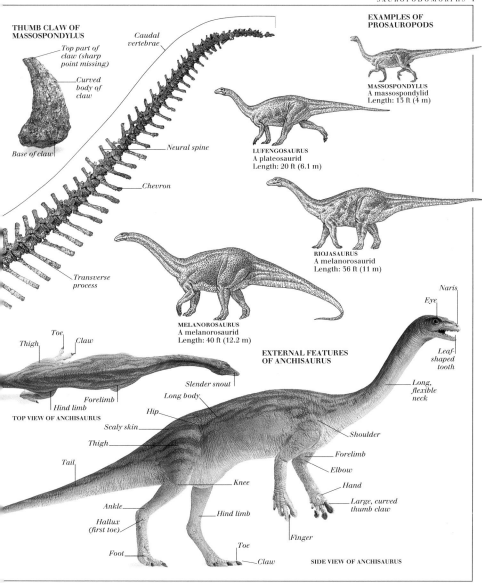

THUMB CLAW OF MASSOSPONDYLUS

Top part of claw (sharp point missing)

Curved body of claw

Base of claw

Caudal vertebrae

Neural spine

Chevron

Transverse process

EXAMPLES OF PROSAUROPODS

MASSOSPONDYLUS
A massospondylid
Length: 13 ft (4 m)

LUFENGOSAURUS
A plateosaurid
Length: 20 ft (6.1 m)

RIOJASAURUS
A melanorosaurid
Length: 36 ft (11 m)

MELANOROSAURUS
A melanorosaurid
Length: 40 ft (12.2 m)

EXTERNAL FEATURES OF ANCHISAURUS

Naris

Eye

Leaf-shaped tooth

Long, flexible neck

Slender snout

Long body

Hip

Shoulder

Scaly skin

Forelimb

Thigh

Elbow

Hand

Large, curved thumb claw

Tail

Knee

Ankle

Hind limb

Hallux (first toe)

Finger

Foot

Toe

Claw

SIDE VIEW OF ANCHISAURUS

Thigh

Toe

Claw

Forelimb

Hind limb

TOP VIEW OF ANCHISAURUS

Sauropodomorphs 2

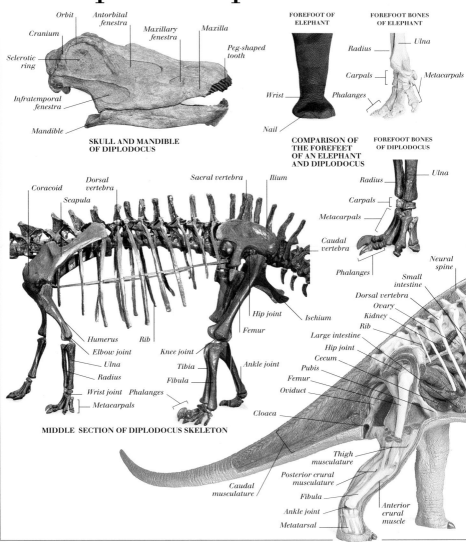

Orbit
Antorbital fenestra
Cranium
Maxillary fenestra
Maxilla
Sclerotic ring
Peg-shaped tooth
Infratemporal fenestra
Mandible

SKULL AND MANDIBLE OF DIPLODOCUS

FOREFOOT OF ELEPHANT

Wrist
Nail

FOREFOOT BONES OF ELEPHANT

Radius
Ulna
Carpals
Metacarpals
Phalanges

COMPARISON OF THE FOREFEET OF AN ELEPHANT AND DIPLODOCUS

FOREFOOT BONES OF DIPLODOCUS

Radius
Ulna
Carpals
Metacarpals
Phalanges

Coracoid
Dorsal vertebra
Scapula
Sacral vertebra
Ilium
Caudal vertebra
Hip joint
Ischium
Femur
Humerus
Rib
Elbow joint
Knee joint
Ulna
Tibia
Ankle joint
Radius
Fibula
Wrist joint
Phalanges
Metacarpals

MIDDLE SECTION OF DIPLODOCUS SKELETON

Neural spine
Small intestine
Dorsal vertebra
Ovary
Kidney
Rib
Large intestine
Hip joint
Cecum
Pubis
Femur
Oviduct
Cloaca
Thigh musculature
Posterior crural musculature
Caudal musculature
Fibula
Ankle joint
Anterior crural muscle
Metatarsal

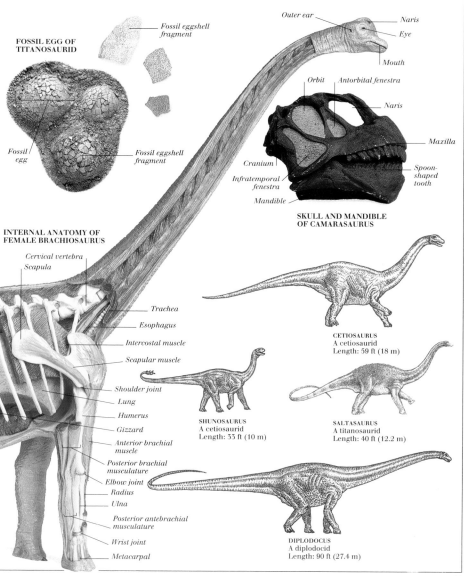

FOSSIL EGG OF TITANOSAURID

Fossil eggshell fragment

Fossil egg

Fossil eggshell fragment

Outer ear

Naris

Eye

Mouth

Orbit

Antorbital fenestra

Naris

Maxilla

Cranium

Infratemporal fenestra

Mandible

Spoon-shaped tooth

SKULL AND MANDIBLE OF CAMARASAURUS

INTERNAL ANATOMY OF FEMALE BRACHIOSAURUS

Cervical vertebra

Scapula

Trachea

Esophagus

Intercostal muscle

Scapular muscle

Shoulder joint

Lung

Humerus

Gizzard

Anterior brachial muscle

Posterior brachial musculature

Elbow joint

Radius

Ulna

Posterior antebrachial musculature

Wrist joint

Metacarpal

CETIOSAURUS
A cetiosaurid
Length: 59 ft (18 m)

SHUNOSAURUS
A cetiosaurid
Length: 33 ft (10 m)

SALTASAURUS
A titanosaurid
Length: 40 ft (12.2 m)

DIPLODOCUS
A diplodocid
Length: 90 ft (27.4 m)

91

Thyreophorans 1

THYREOPHORANS ("SHIELD BEARERS") were a group
of quadrupedal armored dinosaurs. A suborder of the
Ornithischia (bird-hipped dinosaurs), they were characterized
by rows of bony studs, plates, or spikes along the back, which
protected some from predators and may have helped others regulate
body temperature. Up to 30ft (9m) long, with a small head and small cheek
teeth, Thyreophorans had shorter forelimbs than hind limbs and probably
browsed on low-level vegetation. The earliest thyreophorans were
small and lived in Early Jurassic times (about 200 million
years ago) in Europe, North America, and
China. Stegosaurs, such as *Stegosaurus*
and *Kentrosaurus*, replaced these older
forms. The earliest stegosaur remains
come from England and China. Several genera
of stegosaurs survived into the Early Cretaceous period
(146–100 million years ago), but only in India did they persist
into Late Cretaceous times (97–65 million years ago).
Ankylosaurs, with their toothless beaks and cheek
teeth adapted for cropping vegetation,
appeared later than stegosaurs.
They originated in the Late
Jurassic period (155 million
years ago) and in North
America survived until the
extinction of the dinosaurs,
65 million years ago.

TUOJIANGOSAURUS
A stegosaurid
Length: 23 ft (7 m)

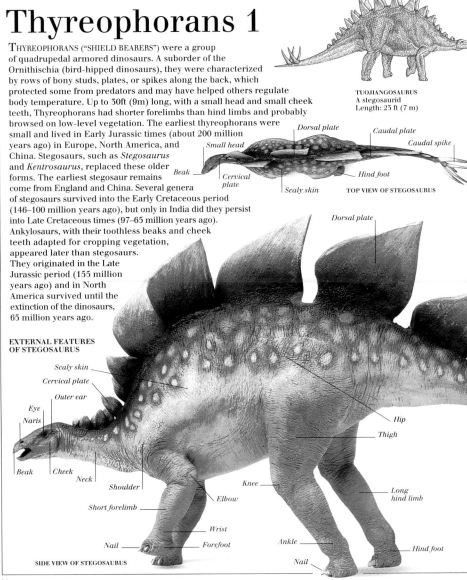

Dorsal plate

Caudal plate

Caudal spike

Small head

Beak

Cervical plate

Scaly skin

Hind foot

TOP VIEW OF STEGOSAURUS

Dorsal plate

**EXTERNAL FEATURES
OF STEGOSAURUS**

Scaly skin

Cervical plate

Outer ear

Eye

Naris

Beak

Cheek

Neck

Shoulder

Elbow

Short forelimb

Wrist

Nail

Forefoot

Knee

Hip

Thigh

Long
hind limb

Ankle

Hind foot

Nail

SIDE VIEW OF STEGOSAURUS

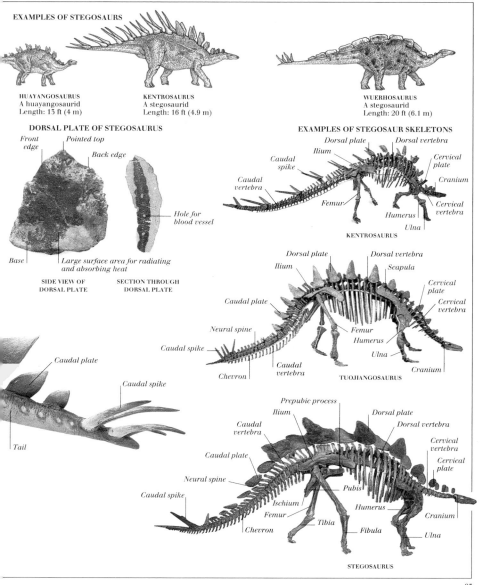

EXAMPLES OF STEGOSAURS

HUAYANGOSAURUS
A huayangosaurid
Length: 13 ft (4 m)

KENTROSAURUS
A stegosaurid
Length: 16 ft (4.9 m)

WUERHOSAURUS
A stegosaurid
Length: 20 ft (6.1 m)

DORSAL PLATE OF STEGOSAURUS

Front edge
Pointed top
Back edge
Hole for blood vessel
Base
Large surface area for radiating and absorbing heat

SIDE VIEW OF DORSAL PLATE

SECTION THROUGH DORSAL PLATE

Caudal plate
Caudal spike
Tail

EXAMPLES OF STEGOSAUR SKELETONS

Dorsal plate
Ilium
Dorsal vertebra
Caudal spike
Cervical plate
Caudal vertebra
Cranium
Femur
Humerus
Cervical vertebra
Ulna

KENTROSAURUS

Dorsal plate
Ilium
Dorsal vertebra
Scapula
Caudal plate
Cervical plate
Neural spine
Cervical vertebra
Caudal spike
Femur
Humerus
Chevron
Caudal vertebra
Ulna
Cranium

TUOJIANGOSAURUS

Prepubic process
Ilium
Dorsal plate
Caudal vertebra
Dorsal vertebra
Caudal plate
Cervical vertebra
Cervical plate
Neural spine
Caudal spike
Pubis
Ischium
Humerus
Femur
Cranium
Chevron
Tibia
Fibula
Ulna

STEGOSAURUS

93

Thyreophorans 2

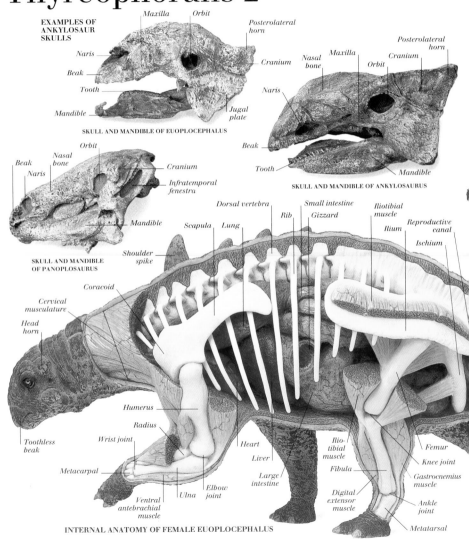

EXAMPLES OF ANKYLOSAUR SKULLS

Maxilla
Orbit
Posterolateral horn
Naris
Cranium
Beak
Tooth
Mandible
Jugal plate

SKULL AND MANDIBLE OF EUOPLOCEPHALUS

Posterolateral horn
Nasal bone
Maxilla
Orbit
Cranium
Naris
Beak
Tooth
Mandible

SKULL AND MANDIBLE OF ANKYLOSAURUS

Orbit
Beak
Nasal bone
Naris
Cranium
Infratemporal fenestra
Mandible

SKULL AND MANDIBLE OF PANOPLOSAURUS

Dorsal vertebra
Small intestine
Iliotibial muscle
Lung
Rib
Gizzard
Ilium
Reproductive canal
Scapula
Ischium
Shoulder spike
Coracoid
Cervical musculature
Head horn
Humerus
Radius
Wrist joint
Heart
Toothless beak
Metacarpal
Liver
Iliotibial muscle
Femur
Knee joint
Gastrocnemius muscle
Ventral antebrachial muscle
Ulna
Elbow joint
Large intestine
Fibula
Digital extensor muscle
Ankle joint
Metatarsal

INTERNAL ANATOMY OF FEMALE EUOPLOCEPHALUS

EXTERNAL FEATURES OF EDMONTONIA

EXAMPLES OF ANKYLOSAURS

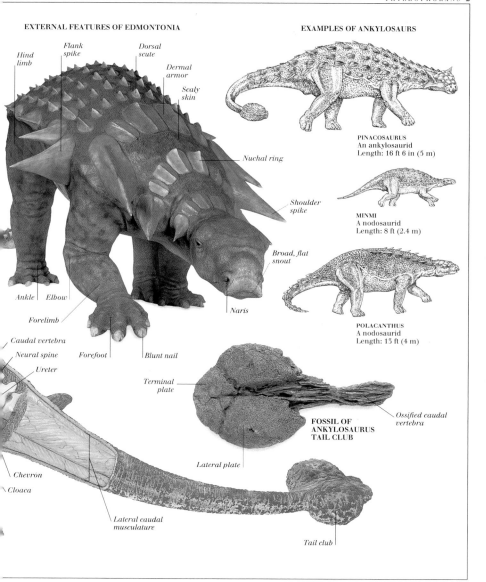

Hind
limb

Flank
spike

Dorsal
scute

Dermal
armor

Scaly
skin

Nuchal ring

Shoulder
spike

Broad, flat
snout

Ankle   Elbow

Forelimb

Naris

Caudal vertebra

Neural spine

Ureter

Forefoot   Blunt nail

Terminal
plate

Chevron

Cloaca

Lateral caudal
musculature

Lateral plate

Tail club

PINACOSAURUS
An ankylosaurid
Length: 16 ft 6 in (5 m)

MINMI
A nodosaurid
Length: 8 ft (2.4 m)

POLACANTHUS
A nodosaurid
Length: 13 ft (4 m)

Ossified caudal
vertebra

**FOSSIL OF
ANKYLOSAURUS
TAIL CLUB**

Ornithopods 1

IGUANODON TOOTH

ORNITHOPODS ("BIRD FEET") were a group of ornithischian ("bird-hipped") dinosaurs. These bipedal and quadrupedal herbivores had a horny beak, plant-cutting or grinding cheek teeth, and a pelvic and tail region stiffened by bony tendons. They evolved teeth and jaws adapted to pulping vegetation and flourished from the Middle Jurassic to the Late Cretaceous period (165–65 million years ago) in North America, Europe, Africa, China, Australia, and Antarctica. Some ornithopods were no larger than a dog, while others were immense creatures up to 49 ft (15 m) long. Iguanodonts, an ornithopod group, had a broad, toothless beak at the end of a long snout, large jaws with long rows of ridged, closely packed teeth for grinding vegetation, a bulky body, and a heavy tail. *Iguanodon* and some other iguanodonts had large thumb-spikes that were strong enough to stab attackers. Another group, the hadrosaurs, such as *Gryposaurus* and *Hadrosaurus*, lived in Late Cretaceous times (97–65 million years ago) and with their broad beaks are sometimes known as "duckbills." They were characterized by their deep skulls and closely packed rows of teeth, while some, such as *Corythosaurus* and *Lambeosaurus*, had tall, hollow, bony head crests.

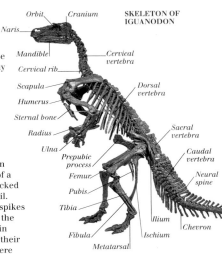

SKELETON OF IGUANODON

Orbit · Cranium · Naris · Mandible · Cervical vertebra · Cervical rib · Scapula · Dorsal vertebra · Humerus · Sternal bone · Radius · Sacral vertebra · Ulna · Prepubic process · Caudal vertebra · Femur · Neural spine · Pubis · Tibia · Ilium · Chevron · Fibula · Ischium · Metatarsal

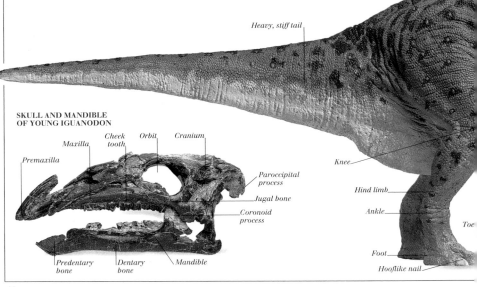

Thigh

Heavy, stiff tail

SKULL AND MANDIBLE OF YOUNG IGUANODON

Cheek tooth · Maxilla · Orbit · Cranium · Premaxilla · Paroccipital process · Jugal bone · Coronoid process · Predentary bone · Dentary bone · Mandible

Knee · Hind limb · Ankle · Toe · Foot · Hooflike nail

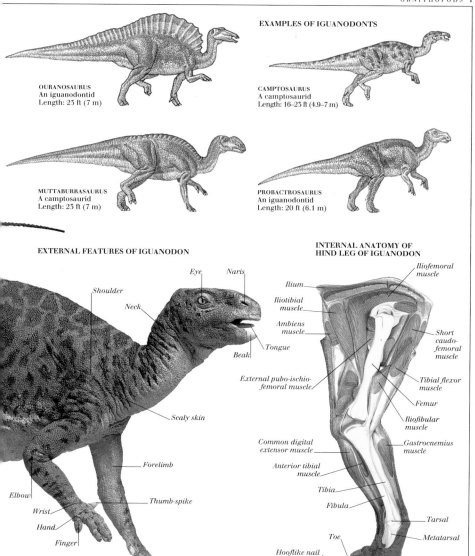

EXAMPLES OF IGUANODONTS

OURANOSAURUS
An iguanodontid
Length: 23 ft (7 m)

CAMPTOSAURUS
A camptosaurid
Length: 16–23 ft (4.9–7 m)

MUTTABURRASAURUS
A camptosaurid
Length: 23 ft (7 m)

PROBACTROSAURUS
An iguanodontid
Length: 20 ft (6.1 m)

EXTERNAL FEATURES OF IGUANODON

Eye

Naris

Shoulder

Neck

Tongue

Beak

Scaly skin

Forelimb

Elbow

Wrist

Hand

Thumb-spike

Finger

Hooflike nail

**INTERNAL ANATOMY OF
HIND LEG OF IGUANODON**

Iliofemoral
muscle

Ilium

Iliotibial
muscle

Ambiens
muscle

Short
caudo-
femoral
muscle

External pubo-ischio-
femoral muscle

Tibial flexor
muscle

Femur

Iliofibular
muscle

Common digital
extensor muscle

Gastrocnemius
muscle

Anterior tibial
muscle

Tibia

Fibula

Tarsal

Toe

Metatarsal

Hooflike nail

Ornithopods 2

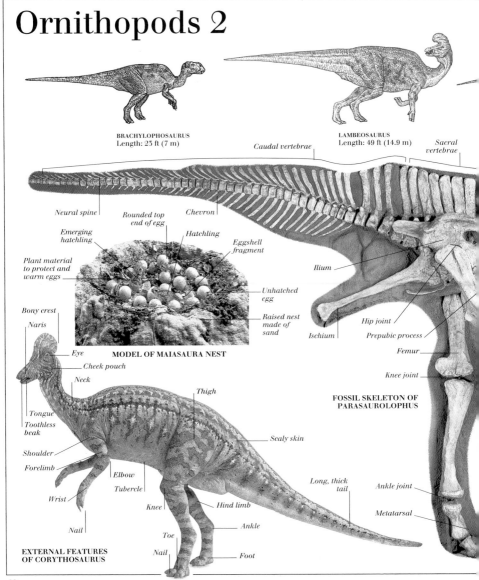

BRACHYLOPHOSAURUS
Length: 25 ft (7 m)

LAMBEOSAURUS
Length: 49 ft (14.9 m)

Caudal vertebrae

Sacral vertebrae

Neural spine

Rounded top end of egg

Chevron

Emerging hatchling

Hatchling

Eggshell fragment

Plant material to protect and warm eggs

Ilium

Bony crest

Unhatched egg

Naris

Raised nest made of sand

Hip joint

Ischium

Prepubic process

Eye

MODEL OF MAIASAURA NEST

Femur

Cheek pouch

Neck

Thigh

Knee joint

FOSSIL SKELETON OF PARASAUROLOPHUS

Tongue

Toothless beak

Scaly skin

Shoulder

Forelimb

Elbow

Tubercle

Long, thick tail

Ankle joint

Wrist

Knee

Hind limb

Metatarsal

Nail

Ankle

Toe

EXTERNAL FEATURES OF CORYTHOSAURUS

Nail

Foot

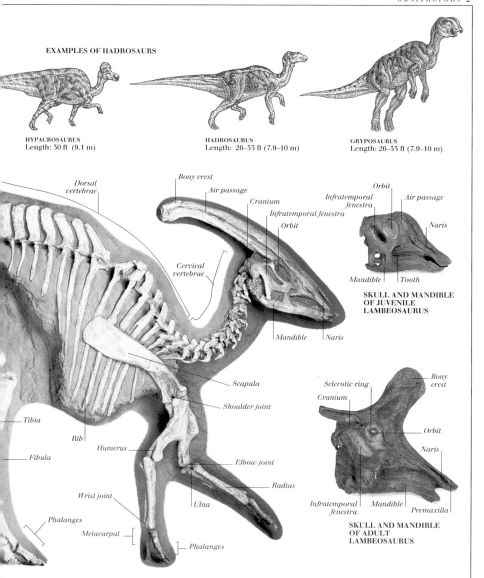

EXAMPLES OF HADROSAURS

HYPACROSAURUS
Length: 30 ft (9.1 m)

HADROSAURUS
Length: 26–33 ft (7.9–10 m)

GRYPOSAURUS
Length: 26–33 ft (7.9–10 m)

Dorsal vertebrae

Bony crest

Air passage

Cranium

Infratemporal fenestra

Orbit

Cervical vertebrae

Mandible

Naris

Orbit

Infratemporal fenestra

Air passage

Naris

Mandible

Tooth

**SKULL AND MANDIBLE
OF JUVENILE
LAMBEOSAURUS**

Scapula

Shoulder joint

Tibia

Rib

Humerus

Fibula

Elbow joint

Radius

Wrist joint

Ulna

Phalanges

Metacarpal

Phalanges

Sclerotic ring

Cranium

Bony crest

Orbit

Naris

Infratemporal fenestra

Mandible

Premaxilla

**SKULL AND MANDIBLE
OF ADULT
LAMBEOSAURUS**

Marginocephalians 1

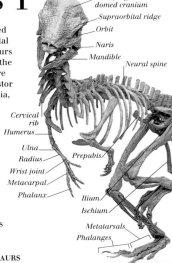

Thick, high-domed cranium
Supraorbital ridge
Orbit
Naris
Mandible
Neural spine

HEAD-BUTTING PRENOCEPHALES

MARGINOCEPHALIA ("margined heads") were a group of bipedal and quadrupedal ornithischian dinosaurs with a narrow shelf or deep, bony frill at the back of the skull. Marginocephalians were probably descended from the same ancestor as the ornithopods and lived in what are now North America, Africa, Asia, and Europe during the Cretaceous period (146–65 million years ago). They were divided into two infraorders: Pachycephalosauria ("thick-headed lizards"), such as *Pachycephalosaurus* and *Stegoceras*, and Ceratopsia ("horned faces"), such as *Triceratops* and *Psittacosaurus*. The thick skulls of Pachycephalosauria protected their brains during head-butting contests fought to win territory and mates; their hips and spines were also strengthened to withstand the shock. The bony frill of Ceratopsia would have added to their frightening appearance when charging; the neck was strengthened for impact and to support the huge head, with its snipping beak and powerful slicing toothed jaws. A charging ceratops would have been a formidable opponent for even the largest predators. Ceratopsia were among the most abundant herbivorous dinosaurs of the Late Cretaceous period (97–65 million years ago).

Cervical rib
Humerus
Ulna
Radius
Prepubis
Wrist joint
Metacarpal
Phalanx
Ilium
Ischium
Metatarsals
Phalanges

EXAMPLES OF SKULLS OF PACHYCEPHALOSAURS

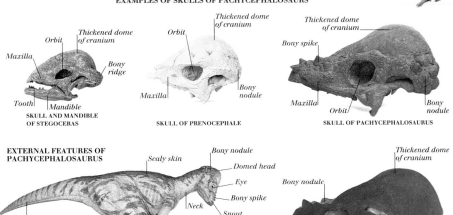

Orbit
Thickened dome of cranium
Maxilla
Bony ridge
Tooth
Mandible
SKULL AND MANDIBLE OF STEGOCERAS

Thickened dome of cranium
Orbit
Maxilla
Bony nodule
SKULL OF PRENOCEPHALE

Thickened dome of cranium
Bony spike
Maxilla
Orbit
Bony nodule
SKULL OF PACHYCEPHALOSAURUS

EXTERNAL FEATURES OF PACHYCEPHALOSAURUS

Scaly skin
Bony nodule
Domed head
Eye
Bony spike
Neck
Snout
Tail
Knee
Forelimb
Hind limb
Finger
Ankle
Hand
Foot
Claw
Toe

Thickened dome of cranium
Bony nodule
Buccal cavity
Brain cavity
SECTION THROUGH SKULL OF PACHYCEPHALOSAURUS

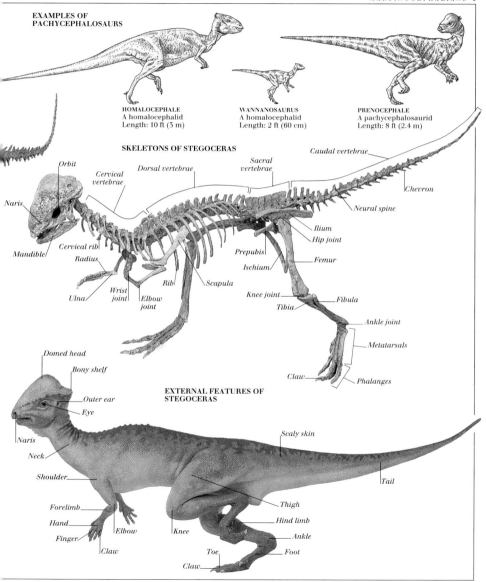

EXAMPLES OF PACHYCEPHALOSAURS

HOMALOCEPHALE
A homalocephalid
Length: 10 ft (3 m)

WANNANOSAURUS
A homalocephalid
Length: 2 ft (60 cm)

PRENOCEPHALE
A pachycephalosaurid
Length: 8 ft (2.4 m)

SKELETONS OF STEGOCERAS

Orbit

Cervical
vertebrae

Dorsal vertebrae

Sacral
vertebrae

Caudal vertebrae

Chevron

Naris

Neural spine

Mandible

Cervical rib

Ilium

Hip joint

Radius

Prepubis

Femur

Ischium

Wrist
joint

Rib

Scapula

Ulna

Elbow
joint

Knee joint

Fibula

Tibia

Ankle joint

Metatarsals

Claw

Phalanges

Domed head

Bony shelf

**EXTERNAL FEATURES OF
STEGOCERAS**

Outer ear

Eye

Naris

Scaly skin

Neck

Shoulder

Tail

Forelimb

Hand

Thigh

Hind limb

Finger

Elbow

Knee

Ankle

Claw

Toe

Foot

Claw

Marginocephalians 2

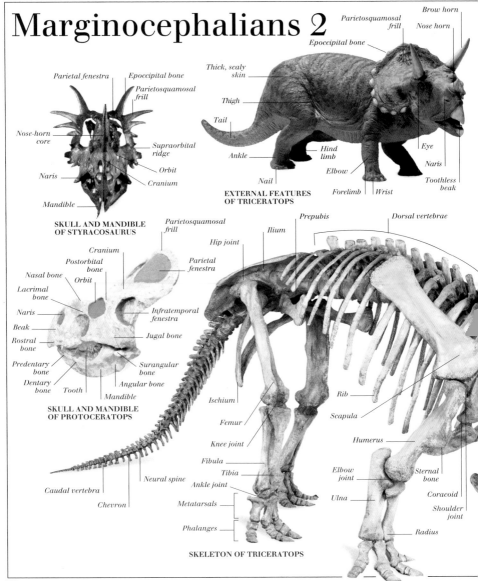

Parietosquamosal frill

Brow horn

Nose horn

Epoccipital bone

Parietal fenestra

Epoccipital bone

Parietosquamosal frill

Thick, scaly skin

Nose-horn core

Thigh

Supraorbital ridge

Tail

Orbit

Naris

Cranium

Ankle

Eye

Mandible

Nail

Hind limb

Naris

Elbow

Toothless beak

SKULL AND MANDIBLE OF STYRACOSAURUS

Forelimb

Wrist

EXTERNAL FEATURES OF TRICERATOPS

Parietosquamosal frill

Prepubis

Dorsal vertebrae

Cranium

Hip joint

Ilium

Postorbital bone

Parietal fenestra

Nasal bone

Orbit

Lacrimal bone

Infratemporal fenestra

Naris

Beak

Jugal bone

Rostral bone

Predentary bone

Surangular bone

Dentary bone

Angular bone

Tooth

Mandible

Ischium

Rib

SKULL AND MANDIBLE OF PROTOCERATOPS

Femur

Scapula

Knee joint

Humerus

Fibula

Tibia

Elbow joint

Sternal bone

Caudal vertebra

Neural spine

Ankle joint

Ulna

Coracoid

Chevron

Metatarsals

Shoulder joint

Phalanges

Radius

SKELETON OF TRICERATOPS

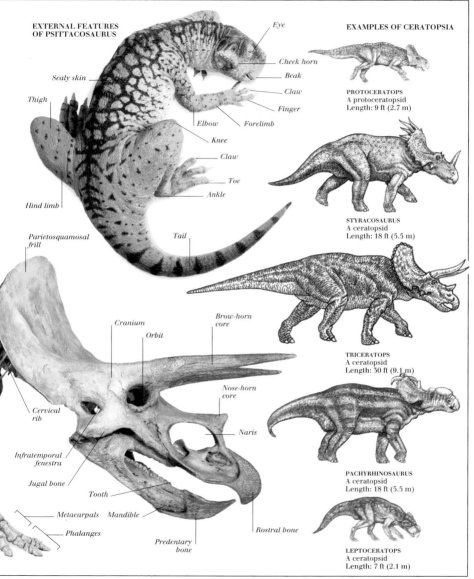

EXTERNAL FEATURES OF PSITTACOSAURUS

Eye

Cheek horn

Beak

Claw

Finger

Scaly skin

Thigh

Elbow

Forelimb

Knee

Claw

Toe

Ankle

Hind limb

Parietosquamosal frill

Tail

Cranium

Orbit

Brow-horn core

Nose-horn core

Cervical rib

Naris

Infratemporal fenestra

Jugal bone

Tooth

Metacarpals *Mandible*

Phalanges

Predentary bone

Rostral bone

EXAMPLES OF CERATOPSIA

PROTOCERATOPS
A protoceratopsid
Length: 9 ft (2.7 m)

STYRACOSAURUS
A ceratopsid
Length: 18 ft (5.5 m)

TRICERATOPS
A ceratopsid
Length: 30 ft (9.1 m)

PACHYRHINOSAURUS
A ceratopsid
Length: 18 ft (5.5 m)

LEPTOCERATOPS
A ceratopsid
Length: 7 ft (2.1 m)

Mammals 1

TETRALOPHODON
CHEEK TEETH

SINCE THE EXTINCTION of the dinosaurs 65 million years ago, mammals have been the dominant vertebrates on Earth and include terrestrial, aerial, and aquatic forms. Having developed from the reptilian Therapsids, the first true mammals—small, nocturnal, rodentlike creatures, such as *Megazostrodon*—appeared over 200 million years ago during the Triassic period (245–208 million years ago). Mammals had several features that improved on those of their reptilian ancestors: an efficient four-chambered heart allowed these warm-blooded animals to sustain high levels of activity; a covering of hair helped them maintain a constant body temperature; an improved limb structure gave them more efficient locomotion; and the birth of live young and the immediate supply of food from the mother's milk aided their rapid growth. Since the end of the Mesozoic era (65 million years ago), the number of different mammal orders and the abundance of species in each order have varied dramatically. For example, the Perissodactyla (the order that includes *Coelodonta* and modern horses) was the most common group during the Early Tertiary period (about 54 million years ago). Today, the mammalian orders with the most populous species are the Rodentia (rats and mice), the Carnivora (bears, cats, and dogs), and the Artiodactyla (cattle, deer, and pigs), while the Proboscidea order, which included many genera, such as *Phiomia, Moeritherium, Tetralophodon,* and *Mammuthus*, now has only one member: the modern elephant. In Australia and South America, millions of years of continental isolation led to the development of the marsupials, a group of mammals distinct from the placentals (see p. 74) that existed elsewhere.

MODEL OF A
MEGAZOSTRODON

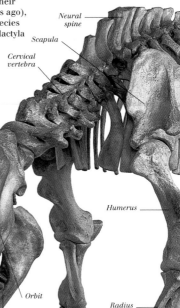

Long tail aids
balance

Insulating
hair

Neural
spine

Scapula

Cervical
vertebra

Humerus

Nasal horn

Naris

Orbit

Predentary
bone

Mandible

Radius

Chisel-edged
molar

Ulna

Metacarpal

Phalanx

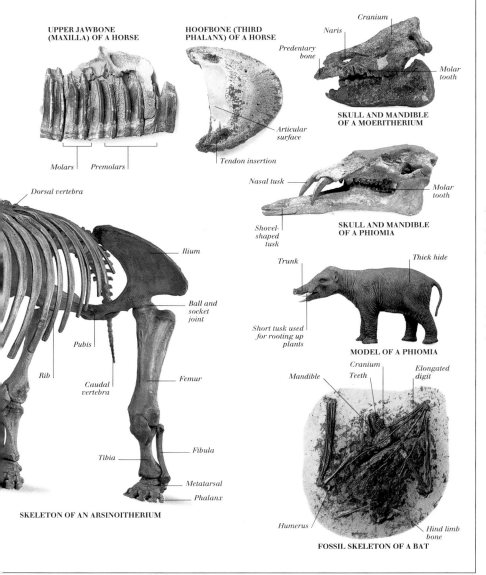

UPPER JAWBONE (MAXILLA) OF A HORSE

Molars

Premolars

HOOFBONE (THIRD PHALANX) OF A HORSE

Articular surface

Tendon insertion

Cranium

Naris

Predentary bone

Molar tooth

SKULL AND MANDIBLE OF A MOERITHERIUM

Nasal tusk

Molar tooth

Shovel-shaped tusk

SKULL AND MANDIBLE OF A PHIOMIA

Dorsal vertebra

Ilium

Ball and socket joint

Pubis

Rib

Caudal vertebra

Femur

Tibia

Fibula

Metatarsal

Phalanx

SKELETON OF AN ARSINOITHERIUM

Trunk

Thick hide

Short tusk used for rooting up plants

MODEL OF A PHIOMIA

Cranium

Teeth

Elongated digit

Mandible

Humerus

Hind limb bone

FOSSIL SKELETON OF A BAT

Mammals 2

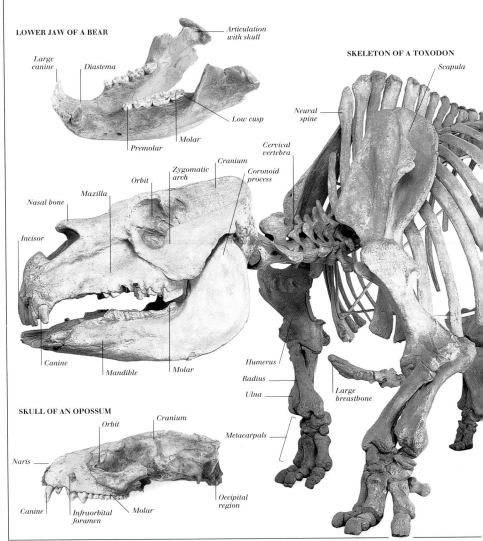

LOWER JAW OF A BEAR

Articulation with skull

Large canine

Diastema

Low cusp

Premolar

Molar

SKELETON OF A TOXODON

Scapula

Neural spine

Cervical vertebra

Cranium

Coronoid process

Orbit

Zygomatic arch

Maxilla

Nasal bone

Incisor

Canine

Mandible

Molar

Humerus

Radius

Ulna

Large breastbone

Metacarpals

SKULL OF AN OPOSSUM

Orbit

Cranium

Naris

Canine

Infraorbital foramen

Molar

Occipital region

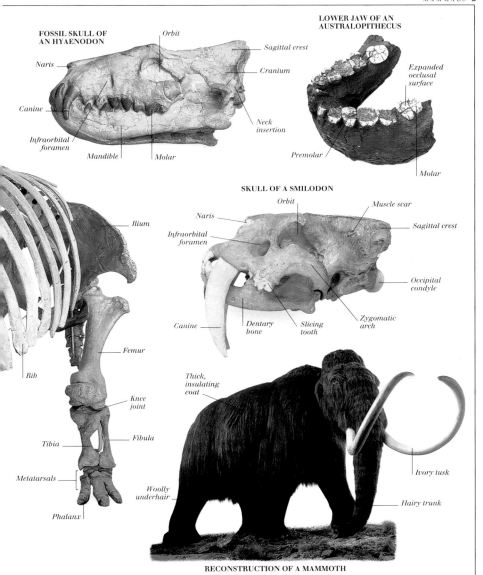

FOSSIL SKULL OF AN HYAENODON

Orbit

Naris

Canine

Infraorbital foramen

Mandible

Molar

Sagittal crest

Cranium

Neck insertion

LOWER JAW OF AN AUSTRALOPITHECUS

Expanded occlusal surface

Premolar

Molar

Ilium

Rib

Femur

Knee joint

Tibia

Fibula

Metatarsals

Phalanx

SKULL OF A SMILODON

Orbit

Naris

Infraorbital foramen

Canine

Dentary bone

Slicing tooth

Muscle scar

Sagittal crest

Occipital condyle

Zygomatic arch

Thick, insulating coat

Woolly underhair

Ivory tusk

Hairy trunk

RECONSTRUCTION OF A MAMMOTH

The first hominids

JAWBONE OF AUSTRALOPITHECUS
(SOUTHERN APE)

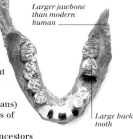

Larger jawbone
than modern
human

Large back
tooth

MODERN HUMANS BELONG TO THE MAMMALIAN order of primates
(see pp. 202–203), which originated about 55 million years ago; they
comprise the only extant hominid species. The earliest hominid was
Australopithecus ("southern ape"), a small-brained intermediate between
apes and humans that was capable of standing and walking upright. *Homo
habilis*, the first known human appeared at least 2 million years ago. This
larger-brained "handy man" began making tools for hunting. *Homo erectus*
first appeared in Africa about 1.8 million years ago and spread into Asia about
800,000 years later. Smaller toothed than *Homo habilis*, it developed fire as a
tool, which enabled it to cook food. Neanderthals, a near relative of modern
humans, originated about 200,000 years ago, and *Homo sapiens* (modern humans)
appeared in Africa about 100,000 years later. The two coexisted for thousands of
years, but by 30,000 years ago, *Homo sapiens* had become dominant and the
Neanderthals had died out. Classification of *Homo sapiens* in relation to its ancestors
is enormously problematic: modern humans must be classified not only by bone structure,
but also by specific behavior—the ability to plan future action; to follow traditions;
and to use symbolic communication, including complex language and the
ability to use and recognize symbols.

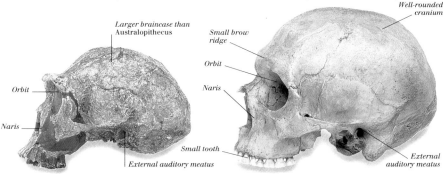

Jutting brow
ridge

Cranium

Orbit

Naris

Jutting
jawbone

SKULL OF AUSTRALOPITHECUS
(SOUTHERN APE)

Orbit

Naris

SKULL OF HOMO HABILIS
(FIRST KNOWN HUMAN)

Well-rounded
cranium

Larger braincase than
Australopithecus

Small brow
ridge

Orbit

Orbit

Naris

Naris

Small tooth

External
auditory meatus

External auditory meatus

SKULL OF HOMO ERECTUS (UPRIGHT MAN)

SKULL OF HOMO SAPIENS (MODERN HUMAN)

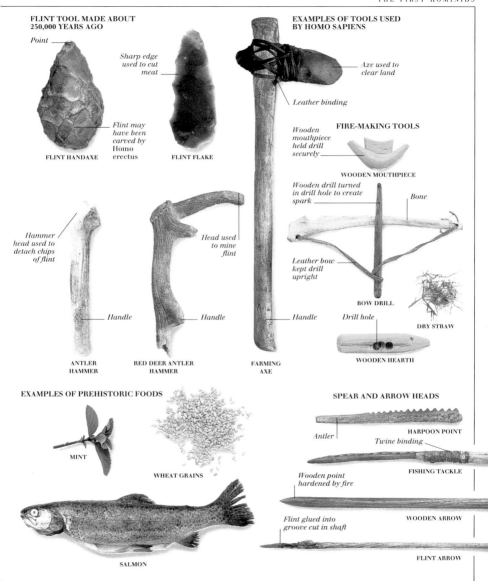

FLINT TOOL MADE ABOUT 250,000 YEARS AGO

Point

Sharp edge used to cut meat

Flint may have been carved by Homo erectus

FLINT HANDAXE

FLINT FLAKE

Hammer head used to detach chips of flint

Head used to mine flint

Handle

Handle

ANTLER HAMMER

RED DEER ANTLER HAMMER

EXAMPLES OF TOOLS USED BY HOMO SAPIENS

Axe used to clear land

Leather binding

FIRE-MAKING TOOLS

Wooden mouthpiece held drill securely

WOODEN MOUTHPIECE

Wooden drill turned in drill hole to create spark

Bone

Leather bow kept drill upright

BOW DRILL

DRY STRAW

Drill hole

WOODEN HEARTH

Handle

FARMING AXE

EXAMPLES OF PREHISTORIC FOODS

MINT

WHEAT GRAINS

SALMON

SPEAR AND ARROW HEADS

Antler

HARPOON POINT

Twine binding

FISHING TACKLE

Wooden point hardened by fire

WOODEN ARROW

Flint glued into groove cut in shaft

FLINT ARROW

PLANTS

Plant varieties

Leaf

THERE ARE MORE THAN 300,000 SPECIES of plants. They
show a wide diversity of forms, ranging from delicate liverworts, adapted for life
in a damp habitat, to cacti, capable of surviving in the desert. The plant kingdom includes
herbaceous plants, such as corn, which completes its life cycle in one year, to the giant redwood tree, which
can live for thousands of years. This diversity reflects the adaptations of plants to survive in a wide range of
habitats. This is seen most clearly in the flowering plants (phylum Angiospermophyta), which are the most
numerous, with over 250,000 species. They are also the most widespread, being found from the tropics to the
arctic. Despite their diversity, plants share certain characteristics. Typically, plants are green, and make their
food by photosynthesis. Most plants live in or on a substrate, such as soil, and do not actively move. Algae
(kingdom Protista) and fungi (kingdom Fungi) have some plantlike characteristics and are
often studied alongside plants, although they are not true plants.

GREEN ALGA
Micrograph of desmid
(*Micrasterias sp.*)

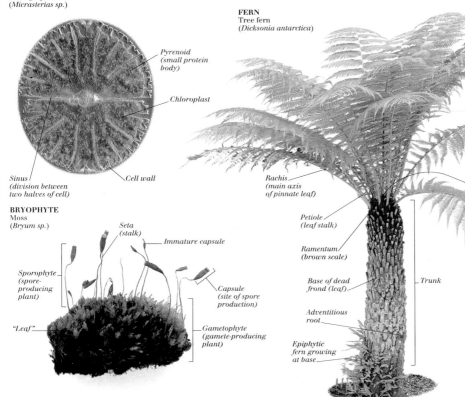

*Pyrenoid
(small protein
body)*

Chloroplast

*Sinus
(division between
two halves of cell)*

Cell wall

FERN
Tree fern
(*Dicksonia antarctica*)

*Rachis
(main axis
of pinnate leaf)*

*Petiole
(leaf stalk)*

*Ramentum
(brown scale)*

*Base of dead
frond (leaf)*

Trunk

*Adventitious
root*

*Epiphytic
fern growing
at base*

BRYOPHYTE
Moss
(*Bryum sp.*)

*Seta
(stalk)*

Immature capsule

*Sporophyte
(spore-
producing
plant)*

"Leaf"

*Capsule
(site of spore
production)*

*Gametophyte
(gamete-producing
plant)*

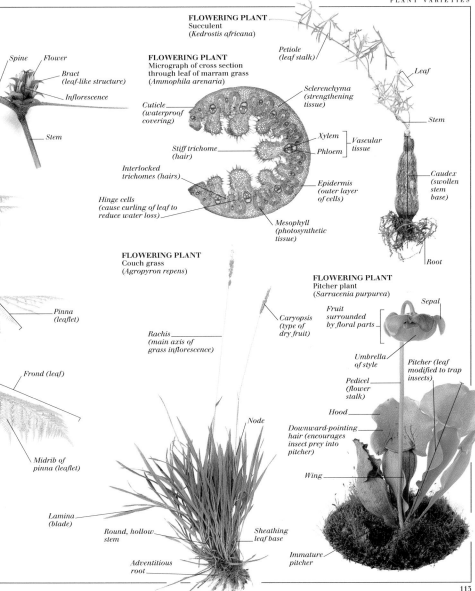

FLOWERING PLANT
Succulent
(*Kedrostis africana*)

*Petiole
(leaf stalk)*

Leaf

Stem

*Caudex
(swollen
stem
base)*

Root

Spine *Flower*

*Bract
(leaf-like structure)*

Inflorescence

Stem

FLOWERING PLANT
Micrograph of cross section
through leaf of marram grass
(*Ammophila arenaria*)

*Sclerenchyma
(strengthening
tissue)*

*Cuticle
(waterproof
covering)*

Xylem
Phloem } *Vascular
tissue*

*Stiff trichome
(hair)*

*Interlocked
trichomes (hairs)*

*Epidermis
(outer layer
of cells)*

*Hinge cells
(cause curling of leaf to
reduce water loss)*

*Mesophyll
(photosynthetic
tissue)*

FLOWERING PLANT
Couch grass
(*Agropyron repens*)

*Pinna
(leaflet)*

Frond (leaf)

*Midrib of
pinna (leaflet)*

*Rachis
(main axis of
grass inflorescence)*

*Caryopsis
(type of
dry fruit)*

Node

*Lamina
(blade)*

*Round, hollow
stem*

*Adventitious
root*

*Sheathing
leaf base*

FLOWERING PLANT
Pitcher plant
(*Sarracenia purpurea*)

Sepal

*Fruit
surrounded
by floral parts*

*Umbrella
of style*

*Pitcher (leaf
modified to trap
insects)*

*Pedicel
(flower
stalk)*

Hood

*Downward-pointing
hair (encourages
insect prey into
pitcher)*

Wing

*Immature
pitcher*

Fungi and lichens

FUNGI WERE ONCE THOUGHT OF AS PLANTS but are now classified as a separate kingdom. This kingdom includes not only the familiar mushrooms, puffballs, stinkhorns, and molds, but also yeasts, smuts, rusts, and lichens. Most fungi are multicellular, consisting of a mass of thread-like hyphae that together form a mycelium. However, the simpler fungi, like yeasts, are microscopic, single-celled organisms. Typically, fungi reproduce by means of spores. Most fungi feed on dead or decaying matter or on living organisms. A few fungi obtain their food from plants or algae, with which they have a symbiotic (mutually advantageous) relationship. Lichens are a symbiotic partnership between algae and fungi. Of the six types of lichens the three most common are crustose (flat and crusty), foliose (leafy), and fruticose (shrub-like). Some lichens (such as *Cladonia floerkeana*) are a combination of types. Lichens reproduce by means of spores or soredia (powdery vegetative fragments).

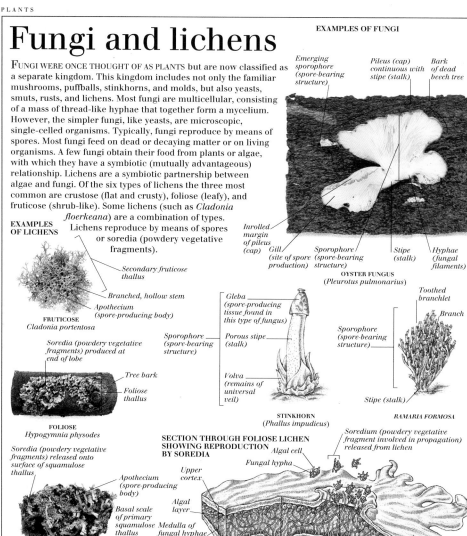

EXAMPLES OF LICHENS

Secondary fruticose thallus

Branched, hollow stem

Apothecium (spore-producing body)

FRUTICOSE
Cladonia portentosa

Soredia (powdery vegetative fragments) produced at end of lobe

Tree bark

Foliose thallus

FOLIOSE
Hypogymnia physodes

Soredia (powdery vegetative fragments) released onto surface of squamulose thallus

Apothecium (spore-producing body)

Basal scale of primary squamulose thallus

Podetium (granular stalk) of secondary fruticose thallus

Moss

SQUAMULOSE (SCALY) AND FRUTICOSE THALLUS
Cladonia floerkeana

Emerging sporophore (spore-bearing structure)

Pileus (cap) continuous with stipe (stalk)

Bark of dead beech tree

Inrolled margin of pileus (cap)

Gill (site of spore production)

Sporophore (spore-bearing structure)

Stipe (stalk)

Hyphae (fungal filaments)

OYSTER FUNGUS
(Pleurotus pulmonarius)

Gleba (spore-producing tissue found in this type of fungus)

Sporophore (spore-bearing structure)

Porous stipe (stalk)

Volva (remains of universal veil)

STINKHORN
(Phallus impudicus)

Toothed branchlet

Branch

Sporophore (spore-bearing structure)

Stipe (stalk)

RAMARIA FORMOSA

SECTION THROUGH FOLIOSE LICHEN SHOWING REPRODUCTION BY SOREDIA

Algal cell

Fungal hypha

Soredium (powdery vegetative fragment involved in propagation) released from lichen

Upper cortex

Algal layer

Medulla of fungal hyphae (mycelium)

Lower cortex

Rhizine (bundle of absorptive hyphae)

Soralium (pore in upper surface of thallus)

Upper surface of thallus

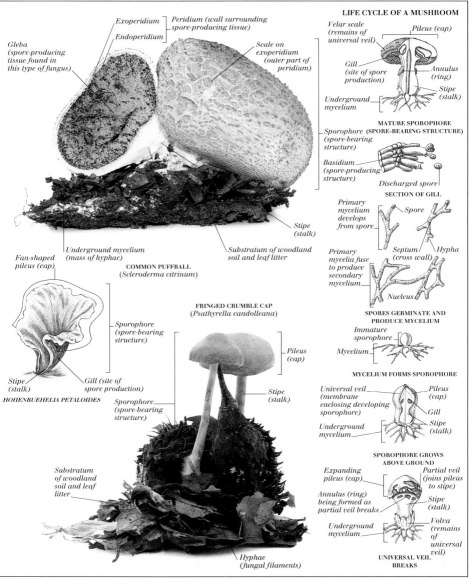

Exoperidium

Endoperidium

Peridium (wall surrounding spore-producing tissue)

Gleba (spore-producing tissue found in this type of fungus)

Scale on exoperidium (outer part of peridium)

Stipe (stalk)

Underground mycelium (mass of hyphae)

Substratum of woodland soil and leaf litter

COMMON PUFFBALL (Scleroderma citrinum)

Fan-shaped pileus (cap)

Sporophore (spore-bearing structure)

Stipe (stalk)

Gill (site of spore production)

HOHENBUEHELIA PETALOIDES

FRINGED CRUMBLE CAP (Psathyrella candolleana)

Pileus (cap)

Stipe (stalk)

Sporophore (spore-bearing structure)

Substratum of woodland soil and leaf litter

Hyphae (fungal filaments)

LIFE CYCLE OF A MUSHROOM

Velar scale (remains of universal veil)

Pileus (cap)

Gill (site of spore production)

Annulus (ring)

Stipe (stalk)

Underground mycelium

MATURE SPOROPHORE

Sporophore (SPORE-BEARING STRUCTURE) (spore-bearing structure)

Basidium (spore-producing structure)

Discharged spore

SECTION OF GILL

Primary mycelium develops from spore

Spore

Septum (cross wall)

Hypha

Primary mycelia fuse to produce secondary mycelium

Nucleus

SPORES GERMINATE AND PRODUCE MYCELIUM

Immature sporophore

Mycelium

MYCELIUM FORMS SPOROPHORE

Universal veil (membrane enclosing developing sporophore)

Pileus (cap)

Gill

Underground mycelium

Stipe (stalk)

SPOROPHORE GROWS ABOVE GROUND

Expanding pileus (cap)

Partial veil (joins pileus to stipe)

Annulus (ring) being formed as partial veil breaks

Stipe (stalk)

Underground mycelium

Volva (remains of universal veil)

UNIVERSAL VEIL BREAKS

Algae and seaweed

ALGAE ARE NOT TRUE PLANTS. They form a diverse group of plantlike organisms that belong to the kingdom Protista. Like plants, algae possess the green pigment chlorophyll and make their own food by photosynthesis (see pp. 138-139). Many algae also possess other pigments by which they can be classified. For example, the brown pigment fucoxanthin is found in brown algae. Some of the ten phyla of algae are exclusively unicellular (single-celled); others also contain aggregates of cells in filaments or colonies. Three phyla—the Chlorophyta (green algae), Rhodophyta (red algae), and Phaeophyta (brown algae)—contain larger, multicellular, thalloid (flat), marine organisms commonly known as seaweed.

Most algae can reproduce sexually. For example, in brown seaweed *Fucus vesiculosus*, gametes (sex cells) are produced in conceptacles (chambers) in the receptacles (fertile tips of fronds); after their release into the sea, antherozoids (male gametes) and oospheres (female gametes) fuse. The resulting zygote settles on a rock and develops into a new seaweed.

BROWN SEAWEED
Channeled wrack
(*Pelvetia canaliculata*)

Receptacle (fertile tip of frond)

Thallus (plant body)

Apical notch

Margin of lamina (blade) rolled inwards to form channel

Hapteron (holdfast)

BROWN SEAWEED
Spiral wrack
(*Fucus spiralis*)

Apical notch

Conceptacle (chamber)

Receptacle (fertile tip of frond)

Thallus (plant body)

Lamina (blade)

Smooth margin

Midrib

Hapteron (holdfast)

Apical notch

Receptacle (fertile tip of frond)

Conceptacle (chamber) containing reproductive structures

Lamina (blade)

Midrib

RECEPTACLE
Spiral wrack
(*Fucus spiralis*)

EXAMPLES OF ALGAE

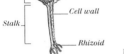

Reproductive chamber

Cap

Sterile whorl

Cell wall

Stalk

Rhizoid

GREEN ALGA
Acetabularia sp.

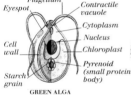

Flagellum

Eyespot

Contractile vacuole

Cytoplasm

Nucleus

Chloroplast

Cell wall

Pyrenoid (small protein body)

Starch grain

GREEN ALGA
Chlamydomonas sp.

Coenobium (colony of cells)

Daughter coenobium

Girdle

Gelatinous sheath

Nucleus

Biflagellate cell

GREEN ALGA
Volvox sp.

Spine

Cytoplasm

Vacuole

Plastid (photosynthetic organelle)

DIATOM
Thalassiosira sp.

BROWN SEAWEED
Oarweed
(*Laminaria digitata*)

Thallus (plant body)

Lamina (blade) palmately divided

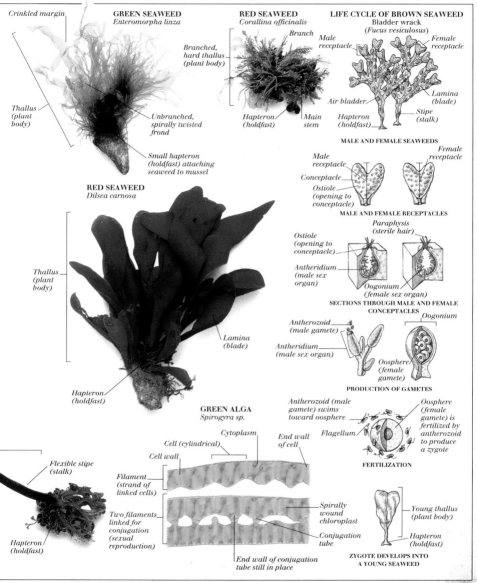

GREEN SEAWEED
Enteromorpha linza

Crinkled margin

Thallus (plant body)

Unbranched, spirally twisted frond

Small hapteron (holdfast) attaching seaweed to mussel

RED SEAWEED
Corallina officinalis

Branch

Branched, hard thallus (plant body)

Hapteron (holdfast)

Main stem

LIFE CYCLE OF BROWN SEAWEED
Bladder wrack
(*Fucus vesiculosus*)

Male receptacle

Female receptacle

Air bladder

Lamina (blade)

Hapteron (holdfast)

Stipe (stalk)

MALE AND FEMALE SEAWEEDS

Male receptacle

Female receptacle

Conceptacle

Ostiole (opening to conceptacle)

MALE AND FEMALE RECEPTACLES

Paraphysis (sterile hair)

Ostiole (opening to conceptacle)

Antheridium (male sex organ)

Oogonium (female sex organ)

SECTIONS THROUGH MALE AND FEMALE CONCEPTACLES

Antherozoid (male gamete)

Oogonium

Antheridium (male sex organ)

Oosphere (female gamete)

PRODUCTION OF GAMETES

RED SEAWEED
Dilsea carnosa

Thallus (plant body)

Lamina (blade)

Hapteron (holdfast)

Antherozoid (male gamete) swims toward oosphere

Flagellum

Oosphere (female gamete) is fertilized by antherozoid to produce a zygote

FERTILIZATION

GREEN ALGA
Spirogyra sp.

Flexible stipe (stalk)

Hapteron (holdfast)

Cytoplasm

Cell (cylindrical)

Cell wall

Filament (strand of linked cells)

Two filaments linked for conjugation (sexual reproduction)

End wall of cell

Spirally wound chloroplast

Conjugation tube

End wall of conjugation tube still in place

Young thallus (plant body)

Hapteron (holdfast)

ZYGOTE DEVELOPS INTO A YOUNG SEAWEED

Liverworts and mosses

"Stem"

"Leaf"

Rhizoid

LIVERWORTS AND MOSSES ARE SMALL, LOW-GROWING PLANTS that belong to the phylum Bryophyta. Bryophytes do not have true stems, leaves, or roots (they are anchored to the ground by rhizoids), nor do they have the vascular tissues (xylem and phloem) that transport water and nutrients in higher plants. With no outer, waterproof cuticle, bryophytes are susceptible to dehydration, and most grow in moist habitats. The bryophyte life cycle has two stages. In stage one, the green plant (gametophyte) produces male and female gametes (sex cells), which fuse to form a zygote. In stage two, the zygote develops into a sporophyte that remains attached to the gametophyte. The sporophyte produces spores, which are released and germinate into new green plants. Liverworts (class Hepaticae) grow horizontally and may be thalloid (flat and ribbon-like) or "leafy." Mosses (class Musci) typically have an upright "stem" with spirally arranged "leaves."

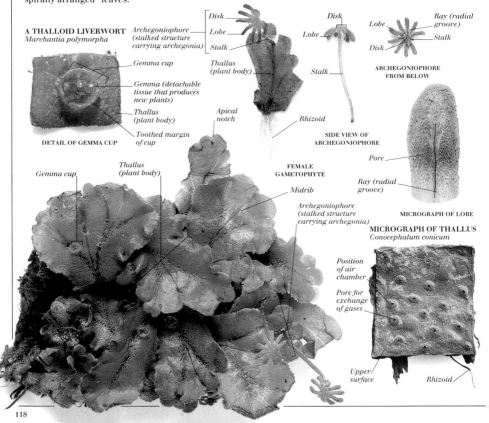

A THALLOID LIVERWORT
Marchantia polymorpha

Archegoniophore (stalked structure carrying archegonia)

Lobe

Stalk

Thallus (plant body)

Disk

Disk

Lobe

Stalk

Lobe

Ray (radial groove)

Stalk

Disk

ARCHEGONIOPHORE FROM BELOW

Gemma cup

Gemma (detachable tissue that produces new plants)

Thallus (plant body)

Toothed margin of cup

DETAIL OF GEMMA CUP

Apical notch

Rhizoid

SIDE VIEW OF ARCHEGONIOPHORE

Pore

Ray (radial groove)

MICROGRAPH OF LOBE

FEMALE GAMETOPHYTE

Gemma cup

Thallus (plant body)

Midrib

Archegoniophore (stalked structure carrying archegonia)

MICROGRAPH OF THALLUS
Conocephalum conicum

Position of air chamber

Pore for exchange of gases

Upper surface

Rhizoid

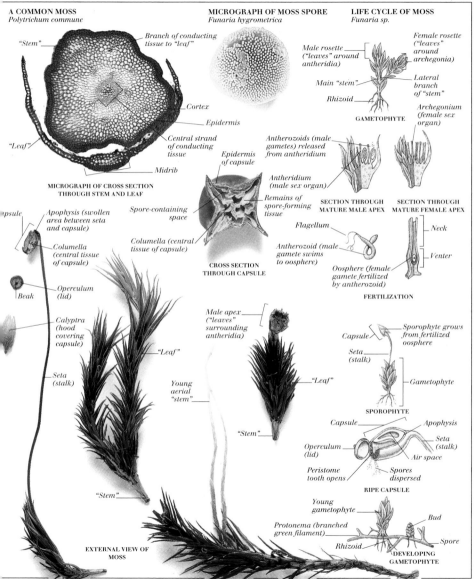

A COMMON MOSS
Polytrichum commune

"Stem"

Branch of conducting
tissue to "leaf"

Cortex

Epidermis

Central strand
of conducting
tissue

"Leaf"

Midrib

**MICROGRAPH OF CROSS SECTION
THROUGH STEM AND LEAF**

MICROGRAPH OF MOSS SPORE
Funaria hygrometrica

Epidermis
of capsule

Spore-containing
space

Columella (central
tissue of capsule)

**CROSS SECTION
THROUGH CAPSULE**

LIFE CYCLE OF MOSS
Funaria sp.

Male rosette
("leaves" around
antheridia)

Main "stem"

Rhizoid

Female rosette
("leaves"
around
archegonia)

Lateral
branch
of "stem"

GAMETOPHYTE

Archegonium
(female sex
organ)

Antherozoids (male
gametes) released
from antheridium

Antheridium
(male sex organ)

Remains of
spore-forming
tissue

**SECTION THROUGH
MATURE MALE APEX**

Neck

Venter

**SECTION THROUGH
MATURE FEMALE APEX**

Flagellum

Antherozoid (male
gamete swims
to oosphere)

Oosphere (female
gamete fertilized
by antherozoid)

FERTILIZATION

psule

Apophysis (swollen
area between seta
and capsule)

Columella
(central tissue
of capsule)

Operculum
(lid)

Beak

Calyptra
(hood
covering
capsule)

Seta
(stalk)

"Leaf"

Young
aerial
"stem"

"Stem"

Male apex
("leaves" surrounding
antheridia)

"Leaf"

"Stem"

Capsule

Seta
(stalk)

Sporophyte grows
from fertilized
oosphere

Gametophyte

SPOROPHYTE

Capsule

Operculum
(lid)

Peristome
tooth opens

Apophysis

Seta
(stalk)

Air space

Spores
dispersed

RIPE CAPSULE

Young
gametophyte

Protonema (branched
green filament)

Rhizoid

Bud

Spore

**DEVELOPING
GAMETOPHYTE**

"Stem"

**EXTERNAL VIEW OF
MOSS**

Horsetails, club mosses, and ferns

HORSETAILS, CLUB MOSSES, AND FERNS are primitive land plants, which, like higher plants, have stems, roots, leaves, and vascular systems that transport water, minerals, and food. Unlike higher plants, however, they do not produce seeds when reproducing. Their life cycles involve two stages. In stage one, the sporophyte (green plant) produces spores in sporangia. In stage two, the spores germinate, developing into small, short-lived gametophyte plants that produce male and female gametes (sex cells). The gametes fuse to form a zygote from which a new sporophyte plant develops. Horsetails (phylum Sphenophyta) have erect green stems with branches arranged in whorls. Some stems are fertile and have a single spore-producing strobilus (group of sporangia) at the tip. Club mosses (phylum Lycopodophyta) typically have small leaves arranged spirally around the stem, with spore-producing strobili at the tip of some stems. Ferns (phylum Filicinophyta) usually have large, pinnate leaves called fronds. Sporangia, grouped together in sori, develop on the underside of fertile fronds.

FROND
Male fern
(*Dryopteris filix-mas*)

CLUB MOSS
Lycopodium sp.

Stem with spirally arranged leaves

Branch

Strobilus (group of sporangia)

CLUB MOSS
Selaginella sp.

Epidermis (outer layer of cells)

Vascular tissue — Phloem / Xylem

Lacuna (air space)

MICROGRAPH OF CROSS SECTION THROUGH CLUB MOSS STEM

Cortex (layer between epidermis and vascular tissue)

Shoot apex

Branch

Rhizophore (leafless branch)

Root

Creeping stem with spirally arranged leaves

HORSETAIL
Common horsetail
(*Equisetum arvense*)

Apex of sterile shoot

Sporangiophore (structure carrying sporangia)

Strobilus (group of sporangia)

Non-photosynthetic fertile stem

Collar of small brown leaves

Young shoot

Lateral branch

Photosynthetic sterile stem

Node

Internode

Node

Tuber

Rhizome

Adventitious root

Endodermis (inner layer of cortex)

Vascular tissue

Sclerenchyma (strengthening tissue)

Epidermis (outer layer of cells)

Chlorenchyma (photosynthetic tissue)

Cortex (layer between epidermis and vascular tissue)

Parenchyma (packing tissue)

Hollow pith cavity

Vallecular canal (longitudinal channel)

Carinal canal (longitudinal channel)

MICROGRAPH OF CROSS SECTION THROUGH HORSETAIL STEM

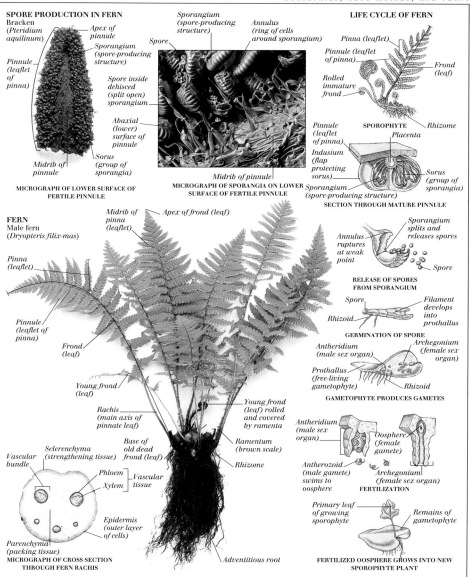

SPORE PRODUCTION IN FERN

Bracken
(*Pteridium aquilinum*)

Apex of pinnule

Sporangium (spore-producing structure)

Pinnule (leaflet of pinna)

Spore inside dehisced (split open) sporangium

Abaxial (lower) surface of pinnule

Midrib of pinnule

Sorus (group of sporangia)

MICROGRAPH OF LOWER SURFACE OF FERTILE PINNULE

Sporangium (spore-producing structure)

Spore

Annulus (ring of cells around sporangium)

Midrib of pinnule

MICROGRAPH OF SPORANGIA ON LOWER SURFACE OF FERTILE PINNULE

LIFE CYCLE OF FERN

Pinna (leaflet)

Pinnule (leaflet of pinna)

Frond (leaf)

Rolled immature frond

Rhizome

SPOROPHYTE

Pinnule (leaflet of pinna)

Indusium (flap protecting sorus)

Sporangium (spore-producing structure)

Placenta

Sorus (group of sporangia)

SECTION THROUGH MATURE PINNULE

Sporangium splits and releases spores

Annulus ruptures at weak point

Spore

RELEASE OF SPORES FROM SPORANGIUM

Spore

Rhizoid

Filament develops into prothallus

GERMINATION OF SPORE

Antheridium (male sex organ)

Prothallus (free-living gametophyte)

Archegonium (female sex organ)

Rhizoid

GAMETOPHYTE PRODUCES GAMETES

Antheridium (male sex organ)

Antherozoid (male gamete) swims to oosphere

Oosphere (female gamete)

Archegonium (female sex organ)

FERTILIZATION

Primary leaf of growing sporophyte

Remains of gametophyte

FERTILIZED OOSPHERE GROWS INTO NEW SPOROPHYTE PLANT

FERN

Male fern
(*Dryopteris filix-mas*)

Midrib of pinna (leaflet)

Apex of frond (leaf)

Pinna (leaflet)

Pinnule (leaflet of pinna)

Frond (leaf)

Young frond (leaf)

Rachis (main axis of pinnate leaf)

Base of old dead frond (leaf)

Young frond (leaf) rolled and covered by ramenta

Ramentum (brown scale)

Rhizome

Vascular bundle

Sclerenchyma (strengthening tissue)

Phloem

Xylem

Vascular tissue

Epidermis (outer layer of cells)

Parenchyma (packing tissue)

MICROGRAPH OF CROSS SECTION THROUGH FERN RACHIS

Adventitious root

Gymnosperms 1

THE GYMNOSPERMS ARE FOUR RELATED PHYLA of seed-producing plants: Their seeds, however, lack the protective outer covering which surrounds the seeds of flowering plants. Typically, gymnosperms are woody, perennial shrubs or trees, with stems, leaves, roots, and a well-developed vascular (transport) system. The reproductive structures in most gymnosperms are cones. Male cones produce microspores in which male gametes (sex cells) develop; female cones produce megaspores in which female gametes develop. Microspores are blown by the wind to female cones, male and female gametes fuse during fertilization, and a seed develops. The four gymnosperm phyla are the conifers (phylum Coniferophyta), mostly tall trees; cycads (phylum Cycadophyta), small palm-like trees; the ginkgo or maidenhair tree (phylum Ginkgophyta), a tall tree with bilobed leaves; and gnetophytes (phylum Gnetophyta), a diverse group of plants, mainly shrubs, but also including the horizontally growing welwitschia.

LIFE CYCLE OF SCOTS PINE
(*Pinus sylvestris*)

Needle (foliage leaf)

Cone

Ovuliferous scale (ovule-/seed-bearing structure)

MALE CONES **YOUNG FEMALE CONE**

Pollen grain in micropyle (entrance to ovule) *Ovuliferous scale*

Pollen grain

Nucleus

Air sac

Ovule (contains female gamete)

POLLINATION

Integument (outer part of ovule)

Archegonium (containing female gamete)

Pollen tube (carries male gamete from pollen grain to ovum)

FERTILIZATION

Seed

Ovuliferous scale (ovule-/seed-bearing structure)

Seed

Wing

MATURE FEMALE CONE AND WINGED SEED

SCALE AND SEEDS
Pine
(*Pinus sp.*)

Ovuliferous scale (ovule-/seed-bearing structure)

Wing of seed derived from ovuliferous scale

Seed

Point of attachment to axis of cone

Wing scar

Seed

Seed scar

OVULIFEROUS SCALE FROM THIRD-YEAR FEMALE CONE

Microsporangium (structure in which pollen grains are formed)

Microsporophyll (modified leaf carrying microsporangia)

Scale leaf

Axis of cone

Ovuliferous scale (ovule-/seed-bearing structure)

MICROGRAPH OF LONGITUDINAL SECTION THROUGH YOUNG MALE CONE

Ovule (contains female gametes)

Bract scale

Axis of cone

MICROGRAPH OF LONGITUDINAL SECTION THROUGH SECOND-YEAR FEMALE CONE

Plumule (embryonic shoot)

Cotyledon (seed leaf)

Root

GERMINATION OF PINE SEEDLING

WELWITSCHIA
(*Welwitschia mirabilis*)

Frayed end of leaf

SMOOTH CYPRESS
(*Cupressus glabra*)

Immature female cone

Ovuliferous scale (ovule-/seed-bearing structure)

Scalelike leaf

Mature female cone

Immature male cone

Ovuliferous scale

Ovule (contains female gamete)

CROSS SECTION THROUGH IMMATURE CONE

Ovuliferous scale (ovule-/seed-bearing structure)

Seed

CROSS SECTION THROUGH MATURE CONE

Woody scale

Opening between woody scales through which seeds are released

DISCARDED CONE

YEW
(*Taxus baccata*)

Single ovule (contains female gamete)

Female "cone"

Scale

Scale

Developing seed

Scale

FEMALE "CONES" AT VARIOUS STAGES OF DEVELOPMENT

Seed

Aril (fleshy outgrowth from seed)

Stem

Needle (foliage leaf)

CYCAD
Sago palm
(*Cycas revoluta*)

Pinna (leaflet)

Pinnate leaf

Scale leaf

Old leaf base

Stem covered by scale leaves

GINKGO
(*Ginkgo biloba*)

Stem

Girdle scar

Petiole (leaf stalk)

Bilobed leaf

Continuously growing leaf

Site of cone growth

Adaxial (upper) surface of leaf

Abaxial (lower) surface of leaf

Frayed end of leaf

Immature cone

Stalk scar

Woody stem

Gymnosperms 2

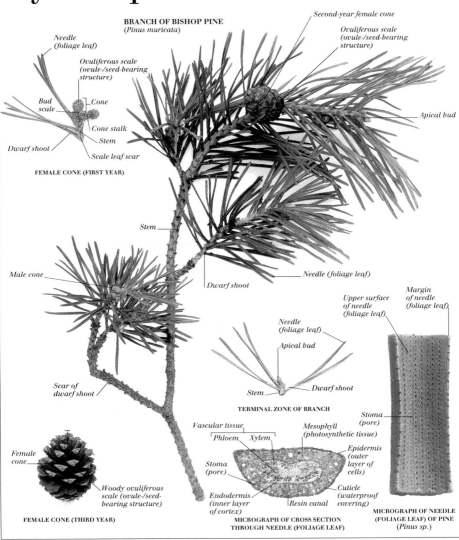

BRANCH OF BISHOP PINE
(*Pinus muricata*)

*Needle
(foliage leaf)*

*Ovuliferous scale
(ovule-/seed-bearing
structure)*

*Bud
scale*

Cone

Cone stalk

Stem

Dwarf shoot

Scale leaf scar

FEMALE CONE (FIRST YEAR)

Second-year female cone

*Ovuliferous scale
(ovule-/seed-bearing
structure)*

Apical bud

Stem

Male cone

Needle (foliage leaf)

Dwarf shoot

*Scar of
dwarf shoot*

*Female
cone*

*Woody ovuliferous
scale (ovule-/seed-
bearing structure)*

FEMALE CONE (THIRD YEAR)

*Needle
(foliage leaf)*

Apical bud

Stem

Dwarf shoot

TERMINAL ZONE OF BRANCH

*Upper surface
of needle
(foliage leaf)*

*Margin
of needle
(foliage leaf)*

*Stoma
(pore)*

**MICROGRAPH OF NEEDLE
(FOLIAGE LEAF) OF PINE**
(*Pinus sp.*)

Vascular tissue

Phloem *Xylem*

*Mesophyll
(photosynthetic tissue)*

*Stoma
(pore)*

*Epidermis
(outer
layer of
cells)*

*Endodermis
(inner layer
of cortex)*

Resin canal

*Cuticle
(waterproof
covering)*

**MICROGRAPH OF CROSS SECTION
THROUGH NEEDLE (FOLIAGE LEAF)**

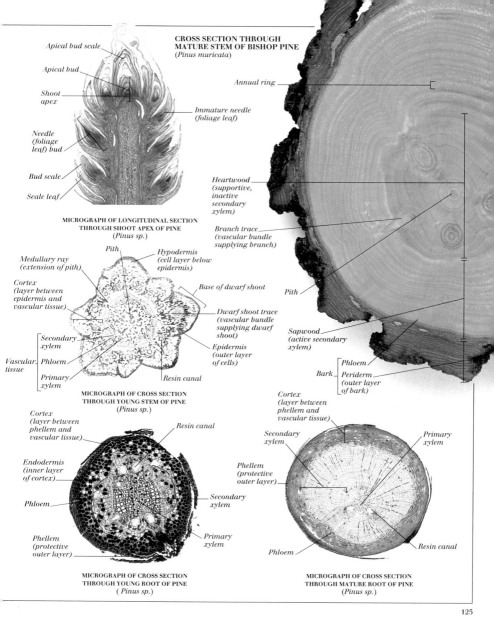

CROSS SECTION THROUGH MATURE STEM OF BISHOP PINE
(*Pinus muricata*)

Apical bud scale

Apical bud

Shoot apex

Needle (foliage leaf) bud

Bud scale

Scale leaf

Immature needle (foliage leaf)

MICROGRAPH OF LONGITUDINAL SECTION THROUGH SHOOT APEX OF PINE
(*Pinus sp.*)

Annual ring

Heartwood (supportive, inactive secondary xylem)

Branch trace (vascular bundle supplying branch)

Pith

Sapwood (active secondary xylem)

Phloem

Bark — Periderm (outer layer of bark)

Medullary ray (extension of pith)

Cortex (layer between epidermis and vascular tissue)

Secondary xylem

Vascular tissue — Phloem

Primary xylem

Pith

Hypodermis (cell layer below epidermis)

Base of dwarf shoot

Dwarf shoot trace (vascular bundle supplying dwarf shoot)

Epidermis (outer layer of cells)

Resin canal

MICROGRAPH OF CROSS SECTION THROUGH YOUNG STEM OF PINE
(*Pinus sp.*)

Cortex (layer between phellem and vascular tissue)

Endodermis (inner layer of cortex)

Phloem

Phellem (protective outer layer)

Resin canal

Secondary xylem

Primary xylem

MICROGRAPH OF CROSS SECTION THROUGH YOUNG ROOT OF PINE
(*Pinus sp.*)

Cortex (layer between phellem and vascular tissue)

Secondary xylem

Phellem (protective outer layer)

Phloem

Primary xylem

Resin canal

MICROGRAPH OF CROSS SECTION THROUGH MATURE ROOT OF PINE
(*Pinus sp.*)

Monocotyledons and dicotyledons

FLOWERING PLANTS (PHYLUM ANGIOSPERMOPHYTA) are divided into two classes: monocotyledons (class Monocotyledoneae) and dicotyledons (class Dicotyledoneae). Typically, monocotyledons have seeds with one cotyledon (seed leaf); their foliage leaves are narrow with parallel veins; the flower components occur in multiples of three; sepals and petals are indistinguishable and are known as tepals; vascular (transport) tissues are scattered in random bundles throughout the stem; and, because they lack stem cambium (actively dividing cells that produce wood), most monocotyledons are herbaceous (see pp. 128-129). Dicotyledons have seeds with two cotyledons; leaves are broad with a central midrib and branched veins; flower parts occur in multiples of four or five; sepals are generally small and green; petals are large and colorful; vascular bundles are arranged in a ring around the edge of the stem; and, because many dicotyledons possess wood-producing stem cambium, there are woody forms (see pp. 130-131) as well as herbaceous ones.

CROSS SECTION THROUGH MONOCOTYLEDONOUS LEAF BASES

Vein (parallel venation)
Leaflet
Petiole (leaf stalk)
Emerging leaf
Leaf base
Adventitious root

A MONOCOTYLEDON
Paradise palm
(Howea forsteriana)

Water-absorbing parenchyma (packing tissue)
Mesophyll (photosynthetic tissue)
Xylem
Phloem
Vascular tissue
Vein
Sunken stoma (pore)
Cuticle (waterproof covering)
Sclerenchyma (strengthening tissue)
Epidermis (outer layer of cells)

MICROGRAPH OF CROSS SECTION THROUGH A MONOCOTYLEDONOUS LEAF
Yucca (Yucca sp.)

Palisade mesophyll (tightly packed photosynthetic tissue)
Spongy mesophyll (loosely packed photosynthetic tissue)
Vascular tissue
Xylem
Phloem
Collenchyma (supporting tissue)
Vein
Epidermis (outer layer of cells)
Parenchyma (packing tissue)
Midrib

MICROGRAPH OF CROSS SECTION THROUGH A DICOTYLEDONOUS LEAF
Crab apple (Malus sp.)

Outer tepal (monocotyledonous sepal)
Lateral, inner tepal (monocotyledonous petal)
Stamen
Filament
Anther
Pollen on anther
Column (stamens and style)
Guide hair
Labellum (lip) forming landing area for pollinator
Funnel guide for bird pollinators' beak
Stigma
Petal

A MONOCOTYLEDONOUS FLOWER
Orchid
(Phalaenopsis sp.)

A DICOTYLEDONOUS FLOWER
Hibiscus
(Hibiscus rosa-sinensis)

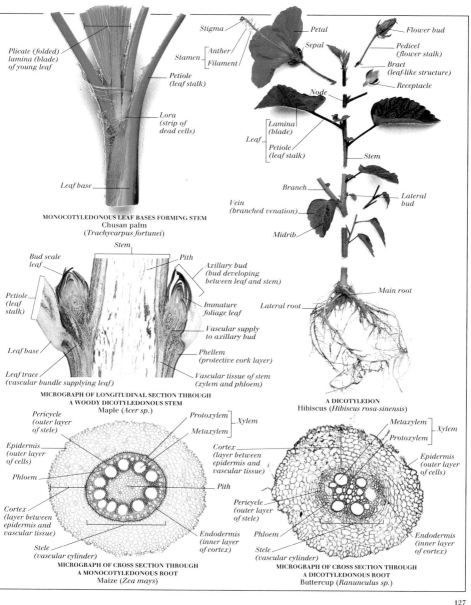

Plicate (folded) lamina (blade) of young leaf

Petiole (leaf stalk)

Lora (strip of dead cells)

Leaf base

MONOCOTYLEDONOUS LEAF BASES FORMING STEM
Chusan palm
(*Trachycarpus fortunei*)

Stigma

Stamen {
Anther
Filament

Petal

Sepal

Flower bud

Pedicel (flower stalk)

Bract (leaf-like structure)

Receptacle

Node

Leaf {
Lamina (blade)
Petiole (leaf stalk)

Stem

Branch

Vein (branched venation)

Midrib

Lateral bud

A DICOTYLEDON
Hibiscus (*Hibiscus rosa-sinensis*)

Stem

Bud scale leaf

Pith

Petiole (leaf stalk)

Axillary bud (bud developing between leaf and stem)

Immature foliage leaf

Vascular supply to axillary bud

Leaf base

Leaf trace (vascular bundle supplying leaf)

Phellem (protective cork layer)

Vascular tissue of stem (xylem and phloem)

MICROGRAPH OF LONGITUDINAL SECTION THROUGH A WOODY DICOTYLEDONOUS STEM
Maple (*Acer sp.*)

Main root

Lateral root

Pericycle (outer layer of stele)

Protoxylem } Xylem
Metaxylem

Epidermis (outer layer of cells)

Phloem

Cortex (layer between epidermis and vascular tissue)

Pith

Cortex (layer between epidermis and vascular tissue)

Stele (vascular cylinder)

Endodermis (inner layer of cortex)

MICROGRAPH OF CROSS SECTION THROUGH A MONOCOTYLEDONOUS ROOT
Maize (*Zea mays*)

Metaxylem } Xylem
Protoxylem

Epidermis (outer layer of cells)

Pericycle (outer layer of stele)

Phloem

Stele (vascular cylinder)

Endodermis (inner layer of cortex)

MICROGRAPH OF CROSS SECTION THROUGH A DICOTYLEDONOUS ROOT
Buttercup (*Ranunculus sp.*)

Herbaceous flowering plants

HERBACEOUS FLOWERING PLANTS TYPICALLY HAVE GREEN NON-WOODY STEMS, and tend to be relatively short-lived. Many herbaceous plants live for only one or two years. Annuals (such as sweet peas) grow from seed, produce flowers and then seeds, and die within a single year. Biennials (like carrots) have a two-year life cycle. In the first year, seeds grow into plants, which produce leaves and store food in underground storage organs; the stems and foliage then die in winter. In the second year, new stems grow from the storage organs, produce leaves, flowers, and seeds, and then die. Some herbaceous plants (such as potatoes) are perennial. They grow back year after year, producing shoots and flowers in spring, storing food in underground tubers or rhizomes during summer, dying in autumn, and surviving underground during winter.

Young plant forming

Petiole (stalk) of young leaf

Lateral root

Stipule (structure at base of leaf)

Trifoliate leaf

Node

Simple ovate leaflet

Root nodule

Main root

SWEET PEA
(*Lathyrus odoratus*)

STRAWBERRY
(*Fragaria* x *ananassa*)

Runner (creeping stem)

Lateral root scar

Remains of leaves

Leaf scar

Stem

Rib

Lateral root

Tap root

CARROT
(*Daucus carota*)

Leaf scar

Leaf base

Petiole (leaf stalk)

Spine (modified leaf)

Slender rhizome

Stem tuber

Adventitious root

Stem

Narrow, succulent leaf

Simple deltoid leaf

POTATO
(*Solanum tuberosum*)

ROCK STONECROP
(*Sedum rupestre*)

Adventitious root

PARTS OF HERBACEOUS FLOWERING PLANTS

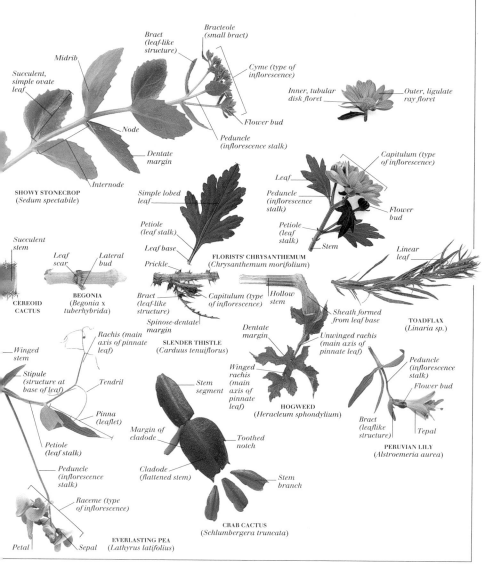

Midrib

Bract
(leaf-like
structure)

Bracteole
(small bract)

Succulent,
simple ovate
leaf

Cyme (type of
inflorescence)

Inner, tubular
disk floret

Outer, ligulate
ray floret

Node

Flower bud

Dentate
margin

Peduncle
(inflorescence stalk)

Capitulum (type
of inflorescence)

Leaf

Internode

Peduncle
(inflorescence
stalk)

SHOWY STONECROP
(Sedum spectabile)

Simple lobed
leaf

Flower
bud

Petiole
(leaf stalk)

Petiole
(leaf
stalk)

Stem

Linear
leaf

Succulent
stem

Leaf base

Leaf
scar

Lateral
bud

Petiole
(leaf stalk)

Prickle

FLORISTS' CHRYSANTHEMUM
(Chrysanthemum morifolium)

**CEREOID
CACTUS**

BEGONIA
*(Begonia x
tuberhybrida)*

Bract
(leaf-like
structure)

Capitulum (type
of inflorescence)

Hollow
stem

Sheath formed
from leaf base

TOADFLAX
(Linaria sp.)

Spinose-dentate
margin

Dentate
margin

Unwinged rachis
(main axis of
pinnate leaf)

Rachis (main
axis of pinnate
leaf)

SLENDER THISTLE
(Carduus tenuiflorus)

Winged
stem

Stipule
(structure at
base of leaf)

Tendril

Stem
segment

Winged
rachis
(main
axis of
pinnate
leaf)

Peduncle
(inflorescence
stalk)

Flower bud

Pinna
(leaflet)

HOGWEED
(Heracleum sphondylium)

Bract
(leaflike
structure)

Tepal

Petiole
(leaf stalk)

Margin of
cladode

PERUVIAN LILY
(Alstroemeria aurea)

Peduncle
(inflorescence
stalk)

Toothed
notch

Raceme (type
of inflorescence)

Cladode
(flattened stem)

Stem
branch

Petal

Sepal

CRAB CACTUS
(Schlumbergera truncata)

EVERLASTING PEA
(Lathyrus latifolius)

Woody flowering plants

Woody flowering plants are perennial: They continue to grow and reproduce for many years. They have one or more permanent stems above ground and numerous smaller branches. The stems and branches have a strong woody core that supports the plant and contains vascular tissue for transporting water and nutrients. Outside the woody core is a layer of tough, protective bark, which has lenticels (tiny pores) to allow gases to pass through. Woody flowering plants may be shrubs, which have several stems rising from the soil; bushes, which are shrubs with dense branching and foliage; or trees, which typically have a single upright stem (the trunk) that bears branches. Deciduous woody plants (like roses) shed all their leaves once a year and remain leafless during winter. Evergreen woody plants (such as holly) shed their leaves gradually, so they retain full leaf cover throughout the year.

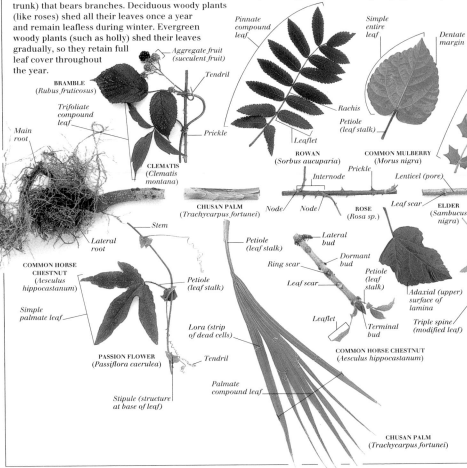

Aggregate fruit (succulent fruit)

Tendril

BRAMBLE
(Rubus fruticosus)

Trifoliate compound leaf

Main root

Prickle

CLEMATIS
(Clematis montana)

Pinnate compound leaf

Rachis

Petiole (leaf stalk)

Leaflet

ROWAN
(Sorbus aucuparia)

Simple entire leaf

Dentate margin

COMMON MULBERRY
(Morus nigra)

Prickle

Internode

Node

Node

Lenticel (pore)

Leaf scar

ELDER
(Sambucus nigra)

ROSE
(Rosa sp.)

CHUSAN PALM
(Trachycarpus fortunei)

Stem

Lateral root

COMMON HORSE CHESTNUT
(Aesculus hippocastanum)

Simple palmate leaf

Petiole (leaf stalk)

PASSION FLOWER
(Passiflora caerulea)

Tendril

Stipule (structure at base of leaf)

Petiole (leaf stalk)

Ring scar

Leaf scar

Lateral bud

Dormant bud

Petiole (leaf stalk)

Leaflet

Terminal bud

Palmate compound leaf

Adaxial (upper) surface of lamina

Triple spine (modified leaf)

COMMON HORSE CHESTNUT
(Aesculus hippocastanum)

CHUSAN PALM
(Trachycarpus fortunei)

Lora (strip of dead cells)

PARTS OF WOODY FLOWERING PLANTS

DURMAST OAK
(*Quercus petraea*)

Simple lobed obovate leaf

Midrib

Pinnate compound leaf

Remains of bracts

Nut (dry fruit)

Immature acorn

Spine

Pinna (leaflet)

MAHONIA
(*Mahonia lomariifolia*)

Flower bud

Sepal

Receptacle

Pedicel (flower stalk)

Stamen

Petal

Sepal

Ovary

ROSE
(*Rosa sp.*)

Axillary bud

Pedicel (flower stalk)

Peduncle (inflorescence stalk)

Bract

Variegated lamina (blade)

Pome (succulent fruit)

Stipule (structure at base of leaf)

Leaflet

Adventitious root

Remains of style

Stem

ROSE
(*Rosa sp.*)

COMMON ENGLISH IVY
(*Hedera helix* 'Goldheart')

MOUNTAIN ASH
(*Sorbus aucuparia*)

Lateral bud

Sepal

Node

Ring scar

Petiole (leaf stalk)

Culm (jointed stem)

BAMBOO
(*Arundinaria nitida*)

MOUNTAIN ASH
(*Sorbus aucuparia*)

Flower bud

Pedicel (flower stalk)

Petiole (leaf stalk)

Vein

Adaxial (upper) surface of lamina (blade)

Stem

Petiole (leaf stalk)

Simple lanceolate leaf

CLEMATIS
(*Clematis sp.*)

Peduncle (inflorescence stalk)

TREE MALLOW
(*Lavatera arborea*)

Stem

Leaf

Pedicel (flower stalk)

Double samara (winged dry fruit)

Peduncle (inflorescence stalk)

Drupe (succulent fruit)

Pedicel (flower stalk)

Wing

Pericarp (fruit wall) enclosing seed

SYCAMORE MAPLE
(*Acer pseudoplatanus*)

PEACH
(*Prunus persica*)

Triple spine (modified leaf)

Compound inflorescence (panicle)

BARBERRY
(*Berberis sp.*)

SILVER LACE VINE
(*Polygonum baldschuanicum*)

Roots

ROOTS ARE THE UNDERGROUND PARTS OF PLANTS. They have three main functions. First, they anchor the plant in the soil. Second, they absorb water and minerals from the spaces between soil particles. The roots' absorptive properties are increased by root hairs, which grow behind the root tip, allowing maximum absorption of vital substances. Third, the root is part of the plant's transport system. Xylem carries water and minerals from the roots to the stem and leaves, and phloem carries nutrients from the leaves to all parts of the root system. In addition, some roots (like carrots) are food stores. Roots have an outer epidermis covering a cortex of parenchyma (packing tissue), and a central cylinder of vascular tissue. This arrangement helps the roots resist the forces of compression as they grow through the soil.

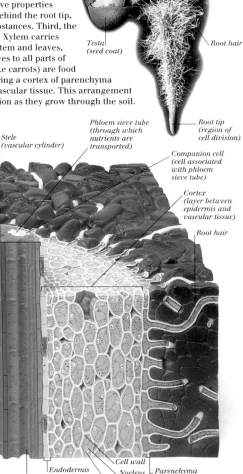

Split in testa
as seed
germinates

Cotyledon
(seed leaf)

Primary root

Testa
(seed coat)

Root hair

Root tip
(region of
cell division)

CARROT
(*Daucus carota*)

FEATURES OF A TYPICAL ROOT
Buttercup
(*Ranunculus sp.*)

Stele
(vascular cylinder)

Phloem sieve tube
(through which
nutrients are
transported)

Companion cell
(cell associated
with phloem
sieve tube)

Pericycle
(outer layer
of stele)

Root hair

Air space
(allowing gas
diffusion in
the root)

Cortex
(layer between
epidermis and
vascular tissue)

Root hair

Epidermis
(outer layer
of cells)

Xylem vessel
(through which water
and minerals are transported)

Endodermis
(inner layer
of cortex)

Cell wall

Nucleus

Cytoplasm

Parenchyma
(packing) cell

PRIMARY ROOT AND MICROGRAPHS OF SECTIONS THROUGH ROOTS

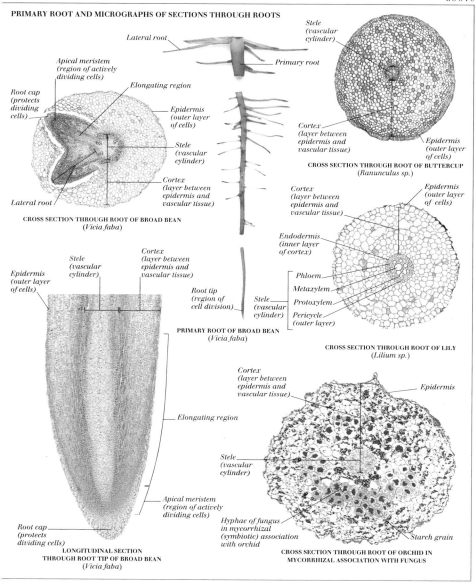

Lateral root

Primary root

Apical meristem
(region of actively
dividing cells)

Elongating region

Root cap
(protects
dividing
cells)

Epidermis
(outer layer
of cells)

Stele
(vascular
cylinder)

Cortex
(layer between
epidermis and
vascular tissue)

Lateral root

CROSS SECTION THROUGH ROOT OF BROAD BEAN
(Vicia faba)

Stele
(vascular
cylinder)

Cortex
(layer between
epidermis and
vascular tissue)

Epidermis
(outer layer
of cells)

CROSS SECTION THROUGH ROOT OF BUTTERCUP
(Ranunculus sp.)

Cortex
(layer between
epidermis and
vascular tissue)

Epidermis
(outer layer
of cells)

Endodermis
(inner layer
of cortex)

Phloem

Metaxylem

Protoxylem

Pericycle
(outer layer)

Stele
(vascular
cylinder)

CROSS SECTION THROUGH ROOT OF LILY
(Lilium sp.)

Stele
(vascular
cylinder)

Cortex
(layer between
epidermis and
vascular tissue)

Epidermis
(outer layer
of cells)

Root tip
(region of
cell division)

Stele
(vascular
cylinder)

PRIMARY ROOT OF BROAD BEAN
(Vicia faba)

Elongating region

Apical meristem
(region of actively
dividing cells)

Root cap
(protects
dividing cells)

LONGITUDINAL SECTION
THROUGH ROOT TIP OF BROAD BEAN
(Vicia faba)

Cortex
(layer between
epidermis and
vascular tissue)

Epidermis

Stele
(vascular
cylinder)

Hyphae of fungus
in mycorrhizal
(symbiotic) association
with orchid

Starch grain

CROSS SECTION THROUGH ROOT OF ORCHID IN
MYCORRHIZAL ASSOCIATION WITH FUNGUS

Stems

THE STEM IS THE MAIN SUPPORTIVE PART OF A PLANT that grows above ground. Stems bear leaves (organs of photosynthesis), which grow at nodes; buds (shoots covered by protective scales), which grow at the stem tip (apical or terminal buds) and in the angle between a leaf and the stem (axillary or lateral buds); and flowers (reproductive structures). The stem forms part of the plant's transport system. Xylem tissue in the stem transports water and minerals from the roots to the aerial parts of the plant, and phloem tissue transports nutrients manufactured in the leaves to other parts of the plant. Stem tissues are also used for storing water and food. Herbaceous (nonwoody) stems have an outer protective epidermis covering a cortex that consists mainly of parenchyma (packing tissue) but also has some collenchyma (supporting tissue). The vascular tissue of such stems is arranged in bundles, each of which consists of xylem, phloem, and sclerenchyma (strengthening tissue). Woody stems have an outer protective layer of tough bark, which is perforated with lenticels (pores) to allow gas exchange. Inside the bark is a ring of secondary phloem, which surrounds an inner core of secondary xylem.

MICROGRAPH OF LONGITUDINAL SECTION THROUGH APEX OF STEM
Coleus sp.

Apical meristem (region of actively dividing cells)

Procambial strand (cells that produce vascular tissue)

Leaf primordium (developing leaf)

Developing bud

Cortex (layer between epidermis and vascular tissue)

Vascular tissue

Pith

Epidermis (outer layer of cells)

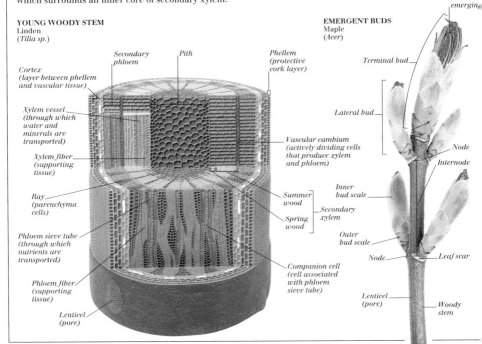

YOUNG WOODY STEM
Linden
(Tilia sp.)

Secondary phloem

Pith

Phellem (protective cork layer)

Cortex (layer between phellem and vascular tissue)

Xylem vessel (through which water and minerals are transported)

Xylem fiber (supporting tissue)

Ray (parenchyma cells)

Phloem sieve tube (through which nutrients are transported)

Phloem fiber (supporting tissue)

Lenticel (pore)

Vascular cambium (actively dividing cells that produce xylem and phloem)

Summer wood

Spring wood

Secondary xylem

Companion cell (cell associated with phloem sieve tube)

EMERGENT BUDS
Maple
(Acer)

Young leaves emerging

Terminal bud

Lateral bud

Node

Internode

Inner bud scale

Outer bud scale

Node

Leaf scar

Lenticel (pore)

Woody stem

MICROGRAPHS OF CROSS SECTIONS THROUGH VARIOUS STEMS

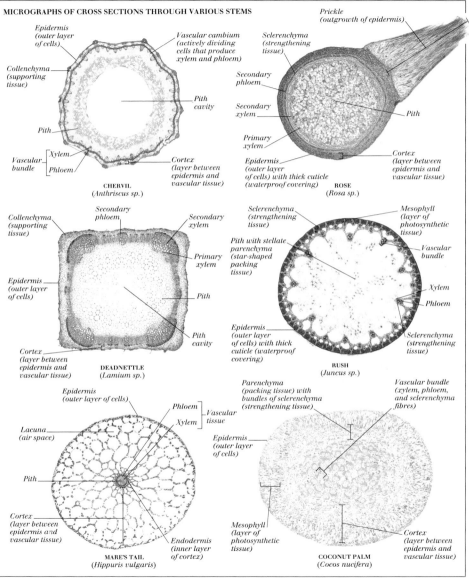

Epidermis (outer layer of cells)

Collenchyma (supporting tissue)

Pith

Vascular bundle { *Xylem* / *Phloem* }

Vascular cambium (actively dividing cells that produce xylem and phloem)

Pith cavity

Cortex (layer between epidermis and vascular tissue)

CHERVIL (*Anthriscus sp.*)

Prickle (outgrowth of epidermis)

Sclerenchyma (strengthening tissue)

Secondary phloem

Secondary xylem

Primary xylem

Epidermis (outer layer of cells) with thick cuticle (waterproof covering)

Pith

Cortex (layer between epidermis and vascular tissue)

ROSE (*Rosa sp.*)

Collenchyma (supporting tissue)

Epidermis (outer layer of cells)

Cortex (layer between epidermis and vascular tissue)

Secondary phloem

Secondary xylem

Primary xylem

Pith

Pith cavity

DEADNETTLE (*Lamium sp.*)

Sclerenchyma (strengthening tissue)

Pith with stellate parenchyma (star-shaped packing tissue)

Epidermis (outer layer of cells) with thick cuticle (waterproof covering)

Mesophyll (layer of photosynthetic tissue)

Vascular bundle

Xylem

Phloem

Sclerenchyma (strengthening tissue)

RUSH (*Juncus sp.*)

Epidermis (outer layer of cells)

Lacuna (air space)

Pith

Cortex (layer between epidermis and vascular tissue)

Phloem / *Xylem* } *Vascular tissue*

Endodermis (inner layer of cortex)

MARE'S TAIL (*Hippuris vulgaris*)

Parenchyma (packing tissue) with bundles of sclerenchyma (strengthening tissue)

Epidermis (outer layer of cells)

Mesophyll (layer of photosynthetic tissue)

Vascular bundle (xylem, phloem, and sclerenchyma fibres)

Cortex (layer between epidermis and vascular tissue)

COCONUT PALM (*Cocos nucifera*)

135

Leaves

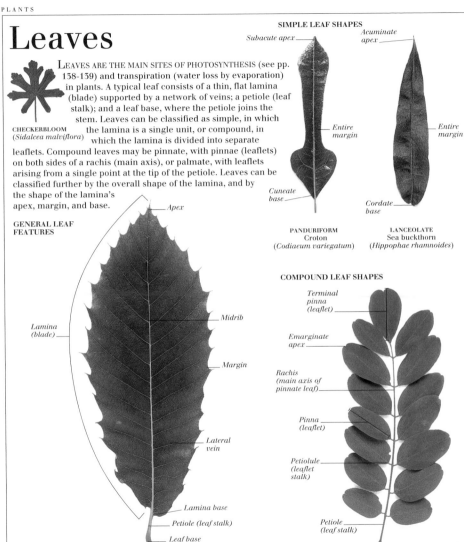

LEAVES ARE THE MAIN SITES OF PHOTOSYNTHESIS (see pp. 138-139) and transpiration (water loss by evaporation) in plants. A typical leaf consists of a thin, flat lamina (blade) supported by a network of veins; a petiole (leaf stalk); and a leaf base, where the petiole joins the stem. Leaves can be classified as simple, in which the lamina is a single unit, or compound, in which the lamina is divided into separate leaflets. Compound leaves may be pinnate, with pinnae (leaflets) on both sides of a rachis (main axis), or palmate, with leaflets arising from a single point at the tip of the petiole. Leaves can be classified further by the overall shape of the lamina, and by the shape of the lamina's apex, margin, and base.

CHECKERBLOOM
(*Sidalcea malviflora*)

GENERAL LEAF FEATURES

Apex

Lamina (blade)

Midrib

Margin

Lateral vein

Lamina base

Petiole (leaf stalk)

Leaf base

Spanish chestnut
(*Castanea sativa*)

SIMPLE LEAF SHAPES

Subacute apex

Acuminate apex

Entire margin

Entire margin

Cuneate base

Cordate base

PANDURIFORM
Croton
(*Codiaeum variegatum*)

LANCEOLATE
Sea buckthorn
(*Hippophae rhamnoides*)

COMPOUND LEAF SHAPES

Terminal pinna (leaflet)

Emarginate apex

Rachis (main axis of pinnate leaf)

Pinna (leaflet)

Petiolule (leaflet stalk)

Petiole (leaf stalk)

ODD PINNATE
Black locust
(*Robinia pseudoacacia*)

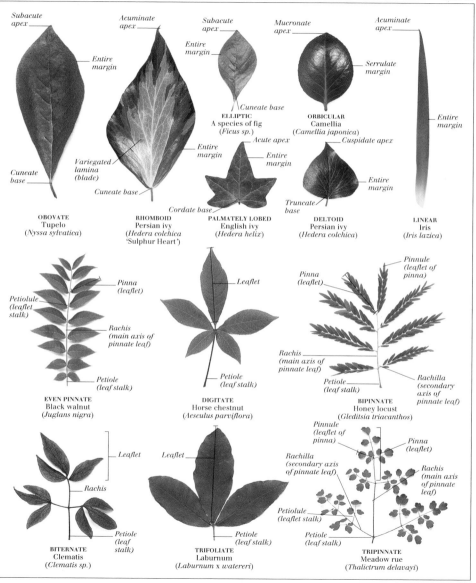

Subacute apex

Entire margin

Cuneate base

OBOVATE
Tupelo
(*Nyssa sylvatica*)

Acuminate apex

Variegated lamina (blade)

Entire margin

Cuneate base

RHOMBOID
Persian ivy
(*Hedera colchica*
'Sulphur Heart')

Subacute apex

Entire margin

Cuneate base

ELLIPTIC
A species of fig
(*Ficus sp.*)

Acute apex

Entire margin

Cordate base

PALMATELY LOBED
English ivy
(*Hedera helix*)

Mucronate apex

Serrulate margin

ORBICULAR
Camellia
(*Camellia japonica*)

Cuspidate apex

Entire margin

Truncate base

DELTOID
Persian ivy
(*Hedera colchica*)

Acuminate apex

Entire margin

LINEAR
Iris
(*Iris lazica*)

Pinna (leaflet)

Petiolule (leaflet stalk)

Rachis (main axis of pinnate leaf)

Petiole (leaf stalk)

EVEN PINNATE
Black walnut
(*Juglans nigra*)

Leaflet

Petiole (leaf stalk)

DIGITATE
Horse chestnut
(*Aesculus parviflora*)

Pinnule (leaflet of pinna)

Pinna (leaflet)

Rachis (main axis of pinnate leaf)

Petiole (leaf stalk)

Rachilla (secondary axis of pinnate leaf)

BIPINNATE
Honey locust
(*Gleditsia triacanthos*)

Leaflet

Rachis

Petiole (leaf stalk)

BITERNATE
Clematis
(*Clematis sp.*)

Leaflet

Petiole (leaf stalk)

TRIFOLIATE
Laburnum
(*Laburnum x watereri*)

Pinnule (leaflet of pinna)

Pinna (leaflet)

Rachilla (secondary axis of pinnate leaf)

Rachis (main axis of pinnate leaf)

Petiolule (leaflet stalk)

Petiole (leaf stalk)

TRIPINNATE
Meadow rue
(*Thalictrum delavayi*)

Photosynthesis

PHOTOSYNTHESIS IS THE PROCESS by which plants make their food using sunlight, water, and carbon dioxide. It takes place inside special structures in leaf cells called chloroplasts. The chloroplasts contain chlorophyll, a green pigment that absorbs energy from sunlight. During photosynthesis, the absorbed energy is used to join together carbon dioxide and water to form the sugar glucose, which is the energy source for the whole plant. Oxygen, a waste product, is released into the air. Leaves are the main sites of photosynthesis and have various adaptations for that purpose. Flat laminae (blades) provide a large surface for absorbing sunlight; stomata (pores) in the lower surface of the laminae allow gases (carbon dioxide and oxygen) to pass into and out of the leaves; and an extensive network of veins brings water into the leaves and transports the glucose produced by photosynthesis to the rest of the plant.

MICROGRAPH OF LEAF
Lily (*Lilium sp.*)

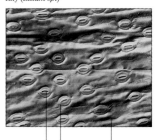

Stoma (pore) | *Guard cell (controls opening and closing of stoma)* | *Lower surface of lamina (blade)*

THE PROCESS OF PHOTOSYNTHESIS

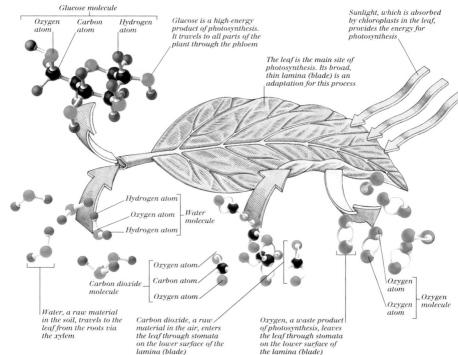

Glucose molecule

Oxygen atom | Carbon atom | Hydrogen atom

Glucose is a high-energy product of photosynthesis. It travels to all parts of the plant through the phloem

Sunlight, which is absorbed by chloroplasts in the leaf, provides the energy for photosynthesis

The leaf is the main site of photosynthesis. Its broad, thin lamina (blade) is an adaptation for this process

Hydrogen atom
Oxygen atom — Water molecule
Hydrogen atom

Oxygen atom
Carbon atom
Oxygen atom

Oxygen atom
Oxygen atom — Oxygen molecule

Carbon dioxide molecule

Water, a raw material in the soil, travels to the leaf from the roots via the xylem

Carbon dioxide, a raw material in the air, enters the leaf through stomata on the lower surface of the lamina (blade)

Oxygen, a waste product of photosynthesis, leaves the leaf through stomata on the lower surface of the lamina (blade)

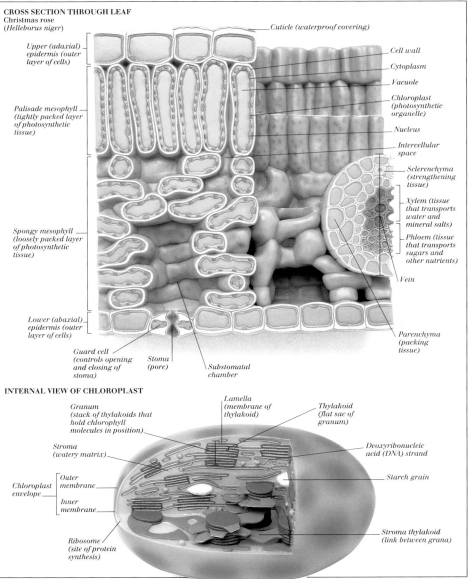

CROSS SECTION THROUGH LEAF
Christmas rose
(*Helleborus niger*)

Cuticle (waterproof covering)

Upper (adaxial) epidermis (outer layer of cells)

Cell wall

Cytoplasm

Vacuole

Chloroplast (photosynthetic organelle)

Nucleus

Palisade mesophyll (tightly packed layer of photosynthetic tissue)

Intercellular space

Sclerenchyma (strengthening tissue)

Xylem (tissue that transports water and mineral salts)

Phloem (tissue that transports sugars and other nutrients)

Spongy mesophyll (loosely packed layer of photosynthetic tissue)

Vein

Lower (abaxial) epidermis (outer layer of cells)

Parenchyma (packing tissue)

Guard cell (controls opening and closing of stoma)

Stoma (pore)

Substomatal chamber

INTERNAL VIEW OF CHLOROPLAST

Lamella (membrane of thylakoid)

Thylakoid (flat sac of granum)

Granum (stack of thylakoids that hold chlorophyll molecules in position)

Stroma (watery matrix)

Deoxyribonucleic acid (DNA) strand

Chloroplast envelope — Outer membrane — Inner membrane

Starch grain

Ribosome (site of protein synthesis)

Stroma thylakoid (link between grana)

Flowers 1

FLOWERS ARE THE SITES OF SEXUAL REPRODUCTION in flowering plants. Their component parts are arranged in whorls around the receptacle (tip of the flower stalk). The sepals (collectively called the calyx) are outermost; typically small and green, they protect the developing flower. The petals (collectively called the corolla) are typically large and brightly colored; they are found inside the sepals. In monocotyledonous flowers (see pp. 126-127), sepals and petals are indistinguishable; individually they are called tepals (collectively called the perianth). The petals surround the male and female reproductive structures (androecium and gynoecium). The androecium consists of stamens (male organs); each stamen is made up of a filament (stalk) and anther. The gynoecium has one or more carpels (female organs); each carpel consists of an ovary, style, and stigma. Some flowers (like the lily) occur singly on a pedicel (flower stalk); others (such as elder, sunflower) are arranged in a group (inflorescence) on a peduncle (inflorescence stalk).

Inner tepal (monocotyledonous petal)

Honey guide

Groove secreting nectar

Style

Filament

Outer tepal (monocotyledonous sepal)

Stigma

Anther

EXTERNAL VIEW

A MONOCOTYLEDONOUS FLOWER
Lily
(*Lilium sp.*)

Ovary

Syncarpous (fused carpels) gynoecium

Stigma

Style

Inner tepal (monocotyledonous petal)

Honey guide

Outer tepal (monocotyledonous sepal)

Tepal scar

Stamen

Anther

Filament

Receptacle

Ovary wall

Ovule

Pollen on anther

Pedicel (flower stalk)

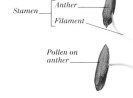

Papilla (fleshy hair)

Outer tepal sheath

Style

Folded inner tepal (monocotyledonous petal)

Stigma

Ovary

Receptacle

Anther

Pedicel (flower stalk)

Filament

LONGITUDINAL SECTION THROUGH FLOWER BUD

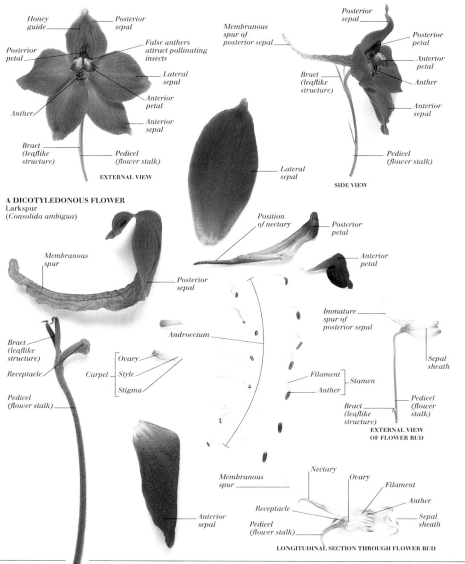

EXTERNAL VIEW

Honey guide

Posterior sepal

False anthers attract pollinating insects

Lateral sepal

Posterior petal

Anterior petal

Anterior sepal

Anther

Bract (leaflike structure)

Pedicel (flower stalk)

SIDE VIEW

Posterior sepal

Membranous spur of posterior sepal

Posterior petal

Anterior petal

Anther

Bract (leaflike structure)

Anterior sepal

Pedicel (flower stalk)

Lateral sepal

A DICOTYLEDONOUS FLOWER
Larkspur
(Consolida ambigua)

Membranous spur

Posterior sepal

Position of nectary

Posterior petal

Anterior petal

Bract (leaflike structure)

Receptacle

Pedicel (flower stalk)

Androecium

Immature spur of posterior sepal

Sepal sheath

Carpel — Ovary / Style / Stigma

Filament ⎤ Stamen
Anther ⎦

Bract (leaflike structure)

Pedicel (flower stalk)

EXTERNAL VIEW OF FLOWER BUD

Anterior sepal

Membranous spur

Nectary

Ovary

Filament

Anther

Receptacle

Sepal sheath

Pedicel (flower stalk)

LONGITUDINAL SECTION THROUGH FLOWER BUD

Flowers 2

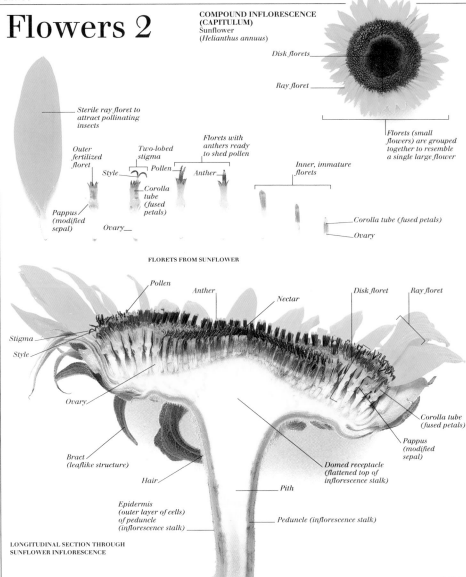

COMPOUND INFLORESCENCE (CAPITULUM)
Sunflower
(*Helianthus annuus*)

Disk florets

Ray floret

Florets (small flowers) are grouped together to resemble a single large flower

Sterile ray floret to attract pollinating insects

Outer fertilized floret

Two-lobed stigma

Florets with anthers ready to shed pollen

Inner, immature florets

Style

Pollen

Anther

Corolla tube (fused petals)

Pappus (modified sepal)

Ovary

Corolla tube (fused petals)

Ovary

FLORETS FROM SUNFLOWER

Pollen

Anther

Nectar

Disk floret

Ray floret

Stigma

Style

Ovary

Corolla tube (fused petals)

Pappus (modified sepal)

Bract (leaflike structure)

Hair

Domed receptacle (flattened top of inflorescence stalk)

Pith

Epidermis (outer layer of cells) of peduncle (inflorescence stalk)

Peduncle (inflorescence stalk)

LONGITUDINAL SECTION THROUGH SUNFLOWER INFLORESCENCE

ARRANGEMENT OF FLOWERS ON STEM

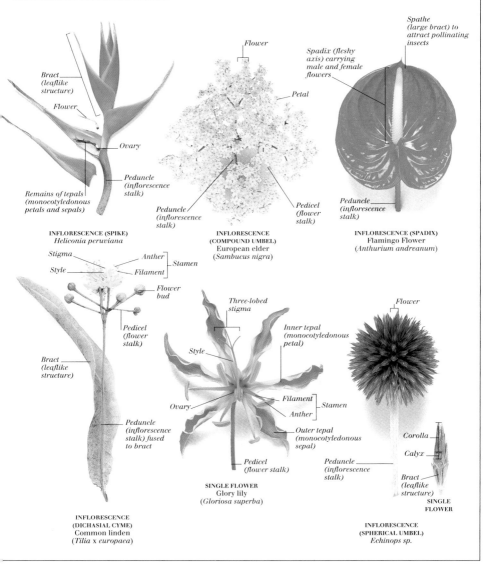

Bract (leaflike structure)

Flower

Ovary

Peduncle (inflorescence stalk)

Remains of tepals (monocotyledonous petals and sepals)

INFLORESCENCE (SPIKE)
Heliconia peruviana

Flower

Petal

Peduncle (inflorescence stalk)

Pedicel (flower stalk)

INFLORESCENCE (COMPOUND UMBEL)
European elder
(*Sambucus nigra*)

Spathe (large bract) to attract pollinating insects

Spadix (fleshy axis) carrying male and female flowers

Peduncle (inflorescence stalk)

INFLORESCENCE (SPADIX)
Flamingo Flower
(*Anthurium andreanum*)

Stigma

Style

Anther
Filament } Stamen

Flower bud

Pedicel (flower stalk)

Bract (leaflike structure)

Peduncle (inflorescence stalk) fused to bract

INFLORESCENCE (DICHASIAL CYME)
Common linden
(*Tilia x europaea*)

Three-lobed stigma

Style

Inner tepal (monocotyledonous petal)

Ovary

Filament
Anther } Stamen

Outer tepal (monocotyledonous sepal)

Pedicel (flower stalk)

SINGLE FLOWER
Glory lily
(*Gloriosa superba*)

Flower

Peduncle (inflorescence stalk)

Corolla

Calyx

Bract (leaflike structure)

SINGLE FLOWER

INFLORESCENCE (SPHERICAL UMBEL)
Echinops sp.

Pollination

POLLINATION IS THE TRANSFER OF POLLEN (which contains the male sex cells) from an anther (part of the male reproductive organ) to a stigma (part of the female reproductive organ). This process precedes fertilization (see pp. 146-147). Pollination may occur within the same flower (self-pollination), or between flowers on separate plants of the same species (cross-pollination). In most plants, pollination is carried out either by insects (entomophilous pollination) or by the wind (anemophilous pollination). Less commonly, birds, bats, or water are the agents of pollination. Insect-pollinated flowers are typically scented and brightly colored. They also produce nectar, on which insects feed. Such flowers also tend to have patterns that are visible only in ultraviolet light, which many insects can see but which humans cannot. These features attract insects, which become covered with the sticky pollen grains when they visit one flower, and then transfer the pollen to the next flower they visit. Wind-pollinated flowers are generally small, relatively inconspicuous, and unscented. They produce large quantities of light pollen grains that are easily blown by the wind to other flowers.

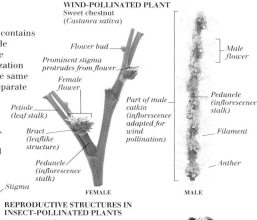

REPRODUCTIVE STRUCTURES IN WIND-POLLINATED PLANT
Sweet chestnut
(*Castanea sativa*)

Flower bud

Prominent stigma protrudes from flower

Female flower

Petiole (leaf stalk)

Bract (leaflike structure)

Peduncle (inflorescence stalk)

Stigma

Male flower

Part of male catkin (inflorescence adapted for wind pollination)

Peduncle (inflorescence stalk)

Filament

Anther

FEMALE

MALE

REPRODUCTIVE STRUCTURES IN INSECT-POLLINATED PLANTS

Style

Dehisced (split open) pollen sac

Boundary between two fused carpels (each carpel consists of a stigma, style, and ovary)

Ovary

Endothecium (pollen sac wall)

Pollen grain

Anther

Filament

Stamen

Calyx (whorl of sepals)

MICROGRAPHS OF POLLEN GRAINS

Exine (outer coat of pollen grain)

Pore

Colpus (furrow-shaped aperture)

Exine (outer coat of pollen grain)

EUROPEAN FIELD ELM
(*Ulmus minor*)

JUSTICIA AUREA

MICROGRAPH OF CARPELS (FEMALE ORGANS)
Yellow-wort
(*Blackstonia perfoliata*)

Exine (outer coat of pollen grain)

Pore

Exine (outer coat of pollen grain)

Baculum (rod-shaped structure)

MEADOW CRANESBILL
(*Geranium pratense*)

MICROGRAPH OF STAMENS (MALE ORGANS)
Common centaury
(*Centaurium erythraea*)

Colpus (furrow-shaped aperture)

Exine (outer coat of pollen grain)

Equatorial furrow

BOX-LEAVED MILKWORT
(*Polygala chamaebuxus*)

INSECT POLLINATION OF MEADOW SAGE

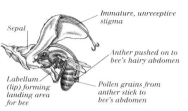

Sepal

Immature, unreceptive stigma

Anther pushed on to bee's hairy abdomen

Labellum (lip) forming landing area for bee

Pollen grains from anther stick to bee's abdomen

1. BEE VISITS FLOWER WITH MATURE ANTHERS BUT IMMATURE STIGMA

Pollen grains attached to hairy abdomen

2. BEE FLIES TO OTHER FLOWERS

Long style curves downward when bee enters flower

Sepal

Mature, receptive stigma touches bee's abdomen, picking up pollen

Labellum (lip) forming landing area for bee

5. BEE VISITS FLOWER WHERE THE ANTHERS HAVE WITHERED AND THE STIGMA IS MATURE

SUNFLOWER UNDER NORMAL AND ULTRAVIOLET LIGHT

Central area of disc florets

Ray floret

NORMAL LIGHT

Petal

Ovary

Stamen — *Filament*
Anther

Stigma

NORMAL LIGHT

ST JOHN'S WORT UNDER NORMAL AND ULTRAVIOLET LIGHT

Honey guide directs insects to dark, central part of flower

Lighter, outer part of ray floret

Darker, inner part of ray floret

Insects attracted to darkest, central part of flower, which contains nectaries, anthers, and stigmas

Dark central area containing nectaries, anthers, and stigmas

ULTRAVIOLET LIGHT

ULTRAVIOLET LIGHT

Pore

Exine (outer coat of pollen grain)

Trilete mark (development scar)

Columella (small column-shaped structure)

Colpus (furrow-shaped aperture)

Exine (outer coat of pollen grain)

Exine (outer coat of pollen grain)

Exine (outer coat of pollen grain)

Tricolpate (three colpae) pollen grain

MIMULOPSIS SOLMSH

THESIUM ALPINIUM

RUELLIA GRANDIFLORA

CROSSANDRA NILOTICA

Fertilization

FERTILIZATION IS THE FUSION of male and female gametes (sex cells) to produce a zygote (embryo). Following pollination (see pp. 144-145), the pollen grains that contain the male gametes are on the stigma, some distance from the female gamete (ovum) inside the ovule. To enable the gametes to meet, the pollen grain germinates and produces a pollen tube, which grows down and enters the embryo sac (the inner part of the ovule that contains the ovum). Two male gametes, traveling at the tip of the pollen tube, enter the embryo sac. One gamete fuses with the ovum to produce a zygote that will develop into an embryo plant. The other male gamete fuses with two polar nuclei to produce the endosperm, which acts as a food supply for the developing embryo. Fertilization also initiates other changes: the integument (outer part of ovule) forms a testa (seed coat) around the embryo and endosperm; the petals fall off; the stigma and style wither; and the ovary wall forms a layer (called the pericarp) around the seed. Together, the pericarp and seed form the fruit, which may be succulent (see pp. 148-149) or dry (see pp. 150-151). In some species (such as blackberry), apomixis can occur: The seed develops without fertilization of the ovum by a male gamete, but endosperm formation and fruit development take place as in other species.

BANANA
(*Musa 'Lacatan'*)

Petal

Stamen
- Filament
- Anther

Carpel
- Ovary
- Stigma
- Style

**1. FLOWER IN FULL BLOOM
ATTRACTS POLLINATORS**

Endocarp (inner layer of pericarp)

Mesocarp (middle layer of pericarp)

Exocarp (outer layer of pericarp)

Sepal

Abortive seed

Remains of style

Carpel

Receptacle

Remains of stamen

Pedicel (flower stalk)

**4. PERICARP FORMS
FLESH, SKIN, AND A HARD INNER
LAYER (SHOWN IN CROSS SECTION)**

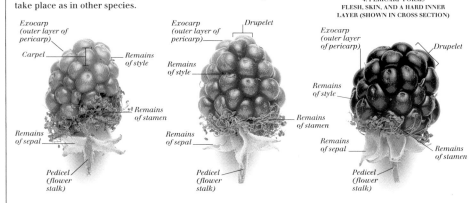

Exocarp (outer layer of pericarp)

Carpel

Remains of style

Remains of stamen

Remains of sepal

Pedicel (flower stalk)

**7. MESOCARP (FLESHY PART OF PERICARP)
OF EACH CARPEL STARTS TO
CHANGE COLOR**

Exocarp (outer layer of pericarp)

Drupelet

Remains of style

Remains of stamen

Remains of sepal

Pedicel (flower stalk)

**8. CARPELS MATURE INTO DRUPELETS
(SMALL FLESHY FRUITS WITH SINGLE SEEDS
SURROUNDED BY HARD ENDOCARP)**

Exocarp (outer layer of pericarp)

Drupelet

Remains of style

Remains of stamen

Remains of sepal

Pedicel (flower stalk)

**9. MESOCARP OF DRUPELET BECOMES
DARKER AND SWEETER**

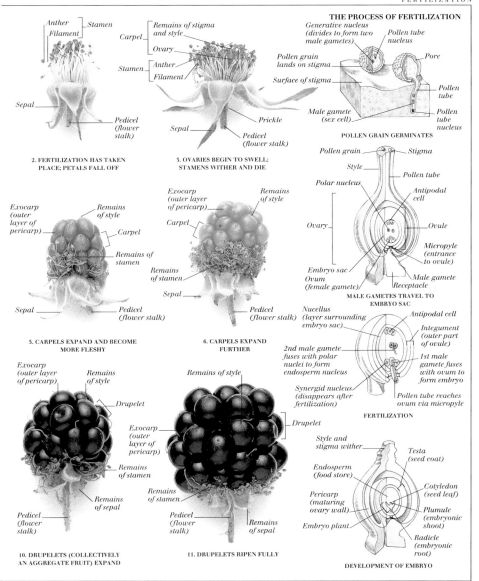

Anther — Stamen
Filament

Sepal

Pedicel
(flower
stalk)

2. FERTILIZATION HAS TAKEN PLACE; PETALS FALL OFF

Remains of stigma
and style

Carpel

Ovary

Stamen — Anther
Filament

Sepal

Prickle

Pedicel
(flower stalk)

5. OVARIES BEGIN TO SWELL; STAMENS WITHER AND DIE

THE PROCESS OF FERTILIZATION

Generative nucleus
(divides to form two
male gametes)

Pollen tube
nucleus

Pollen grain
lands on stigma

Pore

Surface of stigma

Pollen
tube

Male gamete
(sex cell)

Pollen
tube
nucleus

POLLEN GRAIN GERMINATES

Exocarp
(outer
layer of
pericarp)

Remains
of style

Carpel

Remains of
stamen

Sepal

Pedicel
(flower stalk)

5. CARPELS EXPAND AND BECOME MORE FLESHY

Exocarp
(outer layer
of pericarp)

Remains
of style

Carpel

Remains
of stamen

Sepal

Pedicel
(flower stalk)

6. CARPELS EXPAND FURTHER

Pollen grain — Stigma

Style — Pollen tube

Polar nucleus

Antipodal
cell

Ovary — Ovule

Micropyle
(entrance
to ovule)

Embryo sac
Ovum
(female gamete)

Male gamete

Receptacle

MALE GAMETES TRAVEL TO EMBRYO SAC

Nucellus
(layer surrounding
embryo sac)

Antipodal cell

Integument
(outer part
of ovule)

2nd male gamete
fuses with polar
nuclei to form
endosperm nucleus

1st male
gamete fuses
with ovum to
form embryo

Synergid nucleus
(disappears after
fertilization)

Pollen tube reaches
ovum via micropyle

FERTILIZATION

Exocarp
(outer layer
of pericarp)

Remains
of style

Drupelet

Remains of
stamen

Remains
of sepal

Pedicel
(flower
stalk)

10. DRUPELETS (COLLECTIVELY AN AGGREGATE FRUIT) EXPAND

Remains of style

Exocarp
(outer
layer
of
pericarp)

Drupelet

Remains
of stamen

Pedicel
(flower
stalk)

Remains
of sepal

11. DRUPELETS RIPEN FULLY

Style and
stigma wither

Testa
(seed coat)

Endosperm
(food store)

Cotyledon
(seed leaf)

Pericarp
(maturing
ovary wall)

Plumule
(embryonic
shoot)

Embryo plant

Radicle
(embryonic
root)

DEVELOPMENT OF EMBRYO

Succulent fruits

A FRUIT IS A FULLY DEVELOPED and ripened ovary—the seed-producing part of a plant's female reproductive organs. Fruits may be succulent or dry (see pp. 150-151). Succulent fruits are fleshy and brightly colored, making them attractive to animals, which eat them and disperse the seeds away from the parent plant. The wall (pericarp) of a succulent fruit has three layers: an outer exocarp, a middle mesocarp, and an inner endocarp. These three layers vary in thickness and texture in different types of fruits and may blend into each other. Succulent fruits can be classed as simple (derived from one ovary) or compound (derived from several ovaries). Simple succulent fruits include berries, which typically have many seeds, and drupes, which typically have a single stone or pit (such as cherry and peach). Compound succulent fruits include aggregate fruits, which are formed from many ovaries in one flower, and multiple fruits, which develop from the ovaries of many flowers. Some fruits, known as false fruits or pseudocarps, develop from parts of the flower in addition to the ovaries. For example, the flesh of the apple is formed from the receptacle (the upper end of the flower stalk).

BERRY
Cocoa
(*Theobroma cacao*)

HESPERIDIUM (A TYPE OF BERRY)
Lemon
(*Citrus limon*)

Pedicel (flower stalk)

Endocarp

Pedicel (flower stalk)

Exocarp

Mesocarp

Leathery exocarp

Seed

Vesicle (juice sac)

Oil gland

Placenta

Remains of style

Remains of style

EXTERNAL VIEW OF FRUIT

LONGITUDINAL SECTION THROUGH FRUIT

Hilum (point of attachment to ovary)

Embryo

Seed

Carpel wall

Carpel

Testa (seed coat)

Cotyledon (seed leaf)

Placenta

EXTERNAL VIEW AND SECTION THROUGH SEED

CROSS SECTION THROUGH FRUIT

SYCONIUM (A TYPE OF FALSE FRUIT)
Fig
(*Ficus carica*)

Remains of female flowers

Fleshy infolded receptacle

Remains of male flowers

Peduncle (inflorescence stalk)

Pit (seed surrounded by endocarp)

Skin

Pore closed by scales

EXTERNAL VIEW OF FRUIT

LONGITUDINAL SECTION THROUGH FRUIT

FRUIT WITH FLESHY ARIL
Lychee
(*Litchi chinensis*)

Pedicel (flower stalk)

Pedicel (flower stalk)

Seed

Aril (fleshy outgrowth from seed stalk)

Pericarp (fruit wall)

Pericarp (fruit wall)

Remains of style

Endocarp

EXTERNAL VIEW AND SECTION THROUGH PIT

Drupelet

Pit

Endocarp

Pedicel (flower stalk)

Embryo

Testa (seed coat)

Cotyledon (seed leaf)

EXTERNAL VIEW OF FRUIT

LONGITUDINAL SECTION THROUGH FRUIT

REMAINS OF A SINGLE FEMALE FLOWER

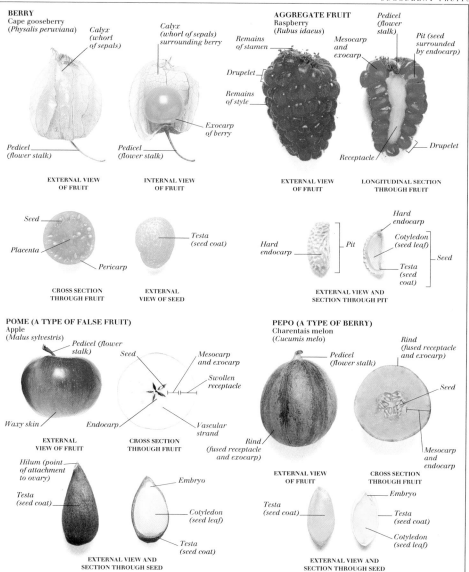

BERRY
Cape gooseberry
(Physalis peruviana)

Calyx (whorl of sepals)

Calyx (whorl of sepals) surrounding berry

Remains of stamen

Pedicel (flower stalk)

Exocarp of berry

Pedicel (flower stalk)

EXTERNAL VIEW OF FRUIT

INTERNAL VIEW OF FRUIT

AGGREGATE FRUIT
Raspberry
(Rubus idaeus)

Pedicel (flower stalk)

Mesocarp and exocarp

Pit (seed surrounded by endocarp)

Drupelet

Remains of style

Receptacle

Drupelet

EXTERNAL VIEW OF FRUIT

LONGITUDINAL SECTION THROUGH FRUIT

Seed

Placenta

Pericarp

Testa (seed coat)

Hard endocarp

Hard endocarp

Cotyledon (seed leaf)

Testa (seed coat)

Pit

Seed

CROSS SECTION THROUGH FRUIT

EXTERNAL VIEW OF SEED

EXTERNAL VIEW AND SECTION THROUGH PIT

POME (A TYPE OF FALSE FRUIT)
Apple
(Malus sylvestris)

Pedicel (flower stalk)

Seed

Mesocarp and exocarp

Swollen receptacle

Waxy skin

Endocarp

Vascular strand

EXTERNAL VIEW OF FRUIT

CROSS SECTION THROUGH FRUIT

Hilum (point of attachment to ovary)

Testa (seed coat)

Embryo

Cotyledon (seed leaf)

Testa (seed coat)

EXTERNAL VIEW AND SECTION THROUGH SEED

PEPO (A TYPE OF BERRY)
Charentais melon
(Cucumis melo)

Rind (fused receptacle and exocarp)

Pedicel (flower stalk)

Seed

Rind (fused receptacle and exocarp)

Mesocarp and endocarp

EXTERNAL VIEW OF FRUIT

CROSS SECTION THROUGH FRUIT

Testa (seed coat)

Embryo

Testa (seed coat)

Cotyledon (seed leaf)

EXTERNAL VIEW AND SECTION THROUGH SEED

Dry fruits

DRY FRUITS HAVE A HARD, DRY PERICARP (fruit wall) around their seeds, unlike succulent fruits, which have fleshy pericarps (see pp. 148-149). Dry fruits are divided into three types: dehiscent, in which the pericarp splits open to release the seeds; indehiscent, which do not split open; and schizocarpic, in which the fruit splits but the seeds are not exposed. Dehiscent dry fruits include capsules (for example, love-in-a-mist), follicles (delphinium), legumes (pea), and silicles (honesty). Typically, the seeds of dehiscent fruits are dispersed by the wind. Indehiscent dry fruits include nuts (sweet chestnut), nutlets (goose grass), achenes (strawberry), caryopses (wheat), samaras (elm), and cypselas (dandelion). Some indehiscent dry fruits are dispersed by the wind, assisted by "wings" (elm) or "parachutes" (dandelion); others (goose grass) have hooked pericarps to aid dispersal on animals' fur. Schizocarpic dry fruits include cremocarps (hogweed), and double samaras (sycamore maple); these are dispersed by the wind.

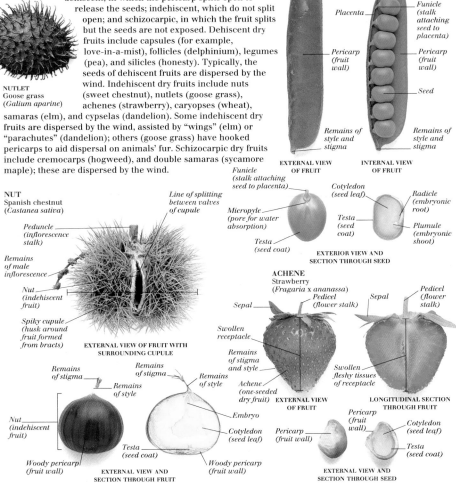

NUTLET
Goose grass
(*Galium aparine*)

LEGUME
Pea
(*Pisum sativum*)

Pedicel (flower stalk)
Receptacle
Remains of sepal
Remains of stamen
Placenta
Pericarp (fruit wall)
Remains of style and stigma

EXTERNAL VIEW OF FRUIT

Pedicel (flower stalk)
Receptacle
Remains of sepal
Funicle (stalk attaching seed to placenta)
Pericarp (fruit wall)
Seed
Remains of style and stigma

INTERNAL VIEW OF FRUIT

NUT
Spanish chestnut
(*Castanea sativa*)

Line of splitting between valves of cupule

Peduncle (inflorescence stalk)
Remains of male inflorescence
Nut (indehiscent fruit)
Spiky cupule (husk around fruit formed from bracts)

EXTERNAL VIEW OF FRUIT WITH SURROUNDING CUPULE

Remains of stigma
Remains of style
Nut (indehiscent fruit)
Woody pericarp (fruit wall)

Remains of stigma
Remains of style
Embryo
Cotyledon (seed leaf)
Testa (seed coat)
Woody pericarp (fruit wall)

EXTERNAL VIEW AND SECTION THROUGH FRUIT

Funicle (stalk attaching seed to placenta)
Micropyle (pore for water absorption)
Testa (seed coat)

Cotyledon (seed leaf)
Radicle (embryonic root)
Testa (seed coat)
Plumule (embryonic shoot)

EXTERIOR VIEW AND SECTION THROUGH SEED

ACHENE
Strawberry
(*Fragaria* x *ananassa*)

Sepal
Pedicel (flower stalk)
Swollen receptacle
Remains of stigma and style
Achene (one-seeded dry fruit)

EXTERNAL VIEW OF FRUIT

Sepal
Pedicel (flower stalk)
Swollen fleshy tissues of receptacle

LONGITUDINAL SECTION THROUGH FRUIT

Pericarp (fruit wall)
Pericarp (fruit wall)
Cotyledon (seed leaf)
Testa (seed coat)

EXTERNAL VIEW AND SECTION THROUGH SEED

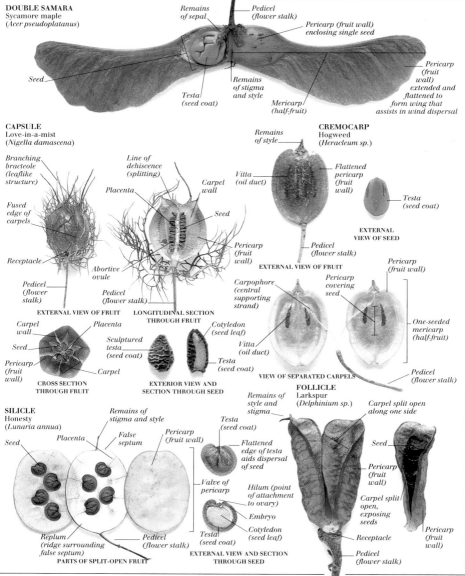

DOUBLE SAMARA
Sycamore maple
(*Acer pseudoplatanus*)

Remains of sepal

Pedicel (flower stalk)

Pericarp (fruit wall) enclosing single seed

Seed

Remains of stigma and style

Testa (seed coat)

Mericarp (half-fruit)

Pericarp (fruit wall) extended and flattened to form wing that assists in wind dispersal

CAPSULE
Love-in-a-mist
(*Nigella damascena*)

Branching bracteole (leaflike structure)

Line of dehiscence (splitting)

Placenta

Carpel wall

Seed

Fused edge of carpels

Receptacle

Abortive ovule

Pericarp (fruit wall)

Pedicel (flower stalk)

Pedicel (flower stalk)

EXTERNAL VIEW OF FRUIT

LONGITUDINAL SECTION THROUGH FRUIT

Carpel wall

Placenta

Seed

Sculptured testa (seed coat)

Cotyledon (seed leaf)

Pericarp (fruit wall)

Carpel

Testa (seed coat)

CROSS SECTION THROUGH FRUIT

EXTERIOR VIEW AND SECTION THROUGH SEED

CREMOCARP
Hogweed
(*Heracleum sp.*)

Remains of style

Vitta (oil duct)

Flattened pericarp (fruit wall)

Testa (seed coat)

EXTERNAL VIEW OF SEED

Pedicel (flower stalk)

EXTERNAL VIEW OF FRUIT

Carpophore (central supporting strand)

Pericarp (fruit wall)

Pericarp covering seed

Vitta (oil duct)

One-seeded mericarp (half-fruit)

Pedicel (flower stalk)

VIEW OF SEPARATED CARPELS

SILICLE
Honesty
(*Lunaria annua*)

Remains of stigma and style

Seed

Placenta

False septum

Pericarp (fruit wall)

Testa (seed coat)

Flattened edge of testa aids dispersal of seed

Valve of pericarp

Hilum (point of attachment to ovary)

Embryo

Cotyledon (seed leaf)

Testa (seed coat)

Replum (ridge surrounding false septum)

Pedicel (flower stalk)

PARTS OF SPLIT-OPEN FRUIT

EXTERNAL VIEW AND SECTION THROUGH SEED

FOLLICLE
Larkspur
(*Delphinium sp.*)

Remains of style and stigma

Carpel split open along one side

Seed

Pericarp (fruit wall)

Carpel split open, exposing seeds

Pericarp (fruit wall)

Receptacle

Pedicel (flower stalk)

Germination

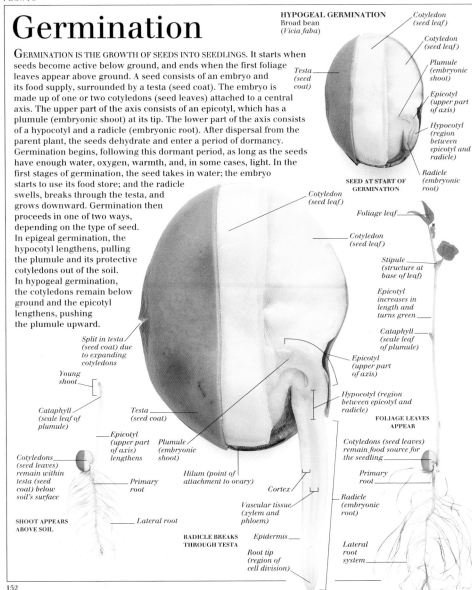

GERMINATION IS THE GROWTH OF SEEDS INTO SEEDLINGS. It starts when seeds become active below ground, and ends when the first foliage leaves appear above ground. A seed consists of an embryo and its food supply, surrounded by a testa (seed coat). The embryo is made up of one or two cotyledons (seed leaves) attached to a central axis. The upper part of the axis consists of an epicotyl, which has a plumule (embryonic shoot) at its tip. The lower part of the axis consists of a hypocotyl and a radicle (embryonic root). After dispersal from the parent plant, the seeds dehydrate and enter a period of dormancy. Germination begins, following this dormant period, as long as the seeds have enough water, oxygen, warmth, and, in some cases, light. In the first stages of germination, the seed takes in water; the embryo starts to use its food store; and the radicle swells, breaks through the testa, and grows downward. Germination then proceeds in one of two ways, depending on the type of seed. In epigeal germination, the hypocotyl lengthens, pulling the plumule and its protective cotyledons out of the soil. In hypogeal germination, the cotyledons remain below ground and the epicotyl lengthens, pushing the plumule upward.

HYPOGEAL GERMINATION
Broad bean
(*Vicia faba*)

Cotyledon
(seed leaf)

Cotyledon
(seed leaf)

Plumule
(embryonic
shoot)

Testa
(seed
coat)

Epicotyl
(upper part
of axis)

Hypocotyl
(region
between
epicotyl and
radicle)

Radicle
(embryonic
root)

**SEED AT START OF
GERMINATION**

Cotyledon
(seed leaf)

Foliage leaf

Cotyledon
(seed leaf)

Stipule
(structure at
base of leaf)

Epicotyl
increases in
length and
turns green

Cataphyll
(scale leaf
of plumule)

Epicotyl
(upper part
of axis)

Hypocotyl (region
between epicotyl and
radicle)

**FOLIAGE LEAVES
APPEAR**

Cotyledons (seed leaves)
remain food source for
the seedling

Primary
root

Radicle
(embryonic
root)

Lateral
root
system

Split in testa
(seed coat) due
to expanding
cotyledons

Young
shoot

Cataphyll
(scale leaf of
plumule)

Testa
(seed coat)

Epicotyl
(upper part
of axis)
lengthens

Plumule
(embryonic
shoot)

Hilum (point of
attachment to ovary)

Cortex

Vascular tissue
(xylem and
phloem)

Cotyledons
(seed leaves)
remain within
testa (seed
coat) below
soil's surface

Primary
root

**SHOOT APPEARS
ABOVE SOIL**

Lateral root

**RADICLE BREAKS
THROUGH TESTA**

Epidermis

Root tip
(region of
cell division)

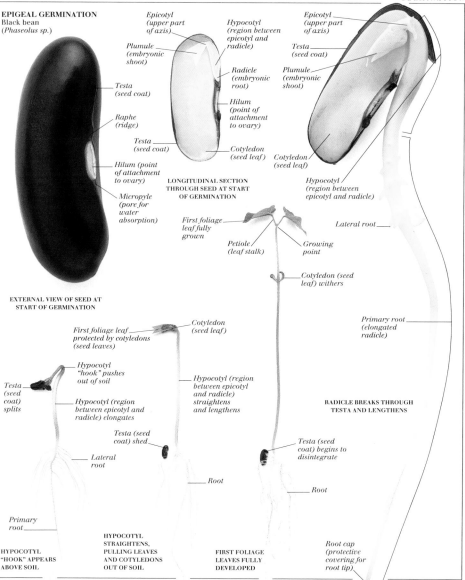

EPIGEAL GERMINATION
Black bean
(*Phaseolus sp.*)

Epicotyl (upper part of axis)

Plumule (embryonic shoot)

Hypocotyl (region between epicotyl and radicle)

Epicotyl (upper part of axis)

Testa (seed coat)

Radicle (embryonic root)

Plumule (embryonic shoot)

Testa (seed coat)

Hilum (point of attachment to ovary)

Raphe (ridge)

Testa (seed coat)

Cotyledon (seed leaf)

Cotyledon (seed leaf)

Hilum (point of attachment to ovary)

Hypocotyl (region between epicotyl and radicle)

Micropyle (pore for water absorption)

LONGITUDINAL SECTION THROUGH SEED AT START OF GERMINATION

First foliage leaf fully grown

Lateral root

Petiole (leaf stalk)

Growing point

EXTERNAL VIEW OF SEED AT START OF GERMINATION

Cotyledon (seed leaf) withers

First foliage leaf protected by cotyledons (seed leaves)

Cotyledon (seed leaf)

Primary root (elongated radicle)

Hypocotyl "hook" pushes out of soil

Testa (seed coat) splits

Hypocotyl (region between epicotyl and radicle) elongates

Hypocotyl (region between epicotyl and radicle) straightens and lengthens

RADICLE BREAKS THROUGH TESTA AND LENGTHENS

Testa (seed coat) shed

Lateral root

Testa (seed coat) begins to disintegrate

Root

Root

Primary root

HYPOCOTYL "HOOK" APPEARS ABOVE SOIL

HYPOCOTYL STRAIGHTENS, PULLING LEAVES AND COTYLEDONS OUT OF SOIL

FIRST FOLIAGE LEAVES FULLY DEVELOPED

Root cap (protective covering for root tip)

Vegetative reproduction

MANY PLANTS CAN PROPAGATE THEMSELVES by vegetative reproduction. In this process, part of a plant separates, takes root, and grows into a new plant. Vegetative reproduction is a type of asexual reproduction; it involves only one parent and there is no fusion of gametes (sex cells). Plants use various structures to reproduce vegetatively. Some plants use underground storage organs. Such organs include rhizomes (horizontal, underground stems), the branches of which produce new plants; bulbs (swollen leaf bases) and corms (swollen stems), which produce daughter bulbs or corms that separate from the parent; and stem tubers (thickened underground stems) and root tubers (swollen adventitious roots), which also separate from the parent. Other propagative structures include runners and stolons, creeping horizontal stems that take root and produce new plants; bulbils, small bulbs that develop on the stem or in the place of flowers, and then drop off and grow into new plants; and adventitious buds, miniature plants that form on leaf margins before dropping to the ground and growing into mature plants.

CORM
Gladiolus
(*Gladiolus sp.*)

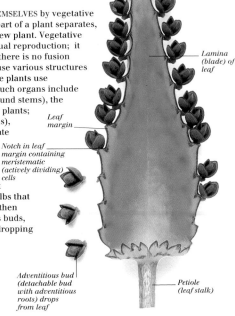

ADVENTITIOUS BUD
Mexican hat plant
(*Kalanchoe daigremontiana*)

Apex of leaf

Lamina (blade) of leaf

Leaf margin

Notch in leaf margin containing meristematic (actively dividing) cells

Adventitious bud (detachable bud with adventitious roots) drops from leaf

Petiole (leaf stalk)

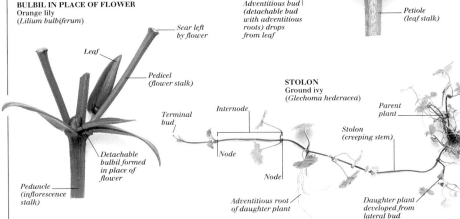

BULBIL IN PLACE OF FLOWER
Orange lily
(*Lilium bulbiferum*)

Scar left by flower

Leaf

Pedicel (flower stalk)

Terminal bud

Detachable bulbil formed in place of flower

Peduncle (inflorescence stalk)

STOLON
Ground ivy
(*Glechoma hederacea*)

Internode

Node

Node

Parent plant

Stolon (creeping stem)

Adventitious root of daughter plant

Daughter plant developed from lateral bud

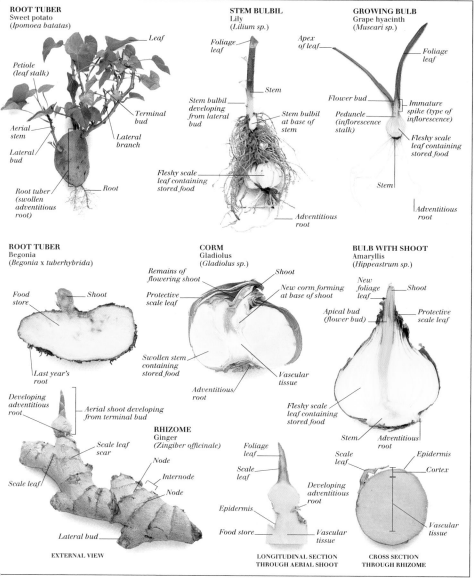

ROOT TUBER
Sweet potato
(*Ipomoea batatas*)

Leaf

Petiole
(leaf stalk)

Terminal
bud

Aerial
stem

Lateral
branch

Lateral
bud

Root tuber
(swollen
adventitious
root)

Root

STEM BULBIL
Lily
(*Lilium sp.*)

Foliage
leaf

Stem

Stem bulbil
developing
from lateral
bud

Stem bulbil
at base of
stem

Fleshy scale
leaf containing
stored food

Adventitious
root

GROWING BULB
Grape hyacinth
(*Muscari sp.*)

Apex
of leaf

Foliage
leaf

Flower bud

Immature
spike (type of
inflorescence)

Peduncle
(inflorescence
stalk)

Fleshy scale
leaf containing
stored food

Stem

Adventitious
root

ROOT TUBER
Begonia
(*Begonia* x *tuberhybrida*)

Food
store

Shoot

Last year's
root

CORM
Gladiolus
(*Gladiolus sp.*)

Remains of
flowering shoot

Shoot

Protective
scale leaf

New corm forming
at base of shoot

Swollen stem
containing
stored food

Vascular
tissue

Adventitious
root

BULB WITH SHOOT
Amaryllis
(*Hippeastrum sp.*)

New
foliage
leaf

Shoot

Apical bud
(flower bud)

Protective
scale leaf

Fleshy scale
leaf containing
stored food

Stem

Adventitious
root

Developing
adventitious
root

Aerial shoot developing
from terminal bud

Scale leaf
scar

Scale leaf

Node

Internode

Node

Lateral bud

EXTERNAL VIEW

RHIZOME
Ginger
(*Zingiber officinale*)

Foliage
leaf

Scale
leaf

Epidermis

Developing
adventitious
root

Food store

Vascular
tissue

**LONGITUDINAL SECTION
THROUGH AERIAL SHOOT**

Scale
leaf

Epidermis

Cortex

Vascular
tissue

**CROSS SECTION
THROUGH RHIZOME**

Dryland plants

LEAF SUCCULENT
Lithops sp.

DRYLAND PLANTS (XEROPHYTES) are able to survive in unfavorable habitats. All are found in places where little water is available; some live in high temperatures that cause excessive loss of water from the leaves. Xerophytes show a number of adaptations to dry conditions. These include reduced leaf area, rolled leaves, sunken stomata, hairs, spines, and thick cuticles. One group, succulent plants, stores water in specially enlarged spongy tissues found in leaves, roots, or stems. Leaf succulents have enlarged, fleshy, water-storing leaves. Root succulents have a large underground water-storage organ with short-lived stems and leaves above ground. Stem succulents are represented by the cacti (family Cactaceae). Cacti stems are fleshy, green, and photosynthetic. They are typically ribbed or covered by tubercles in rows, with leaves being reduced to spines or entirely absent.

STEM SUCCULENT
Golden barrel cactus
(*Echinocactus grusonii*)

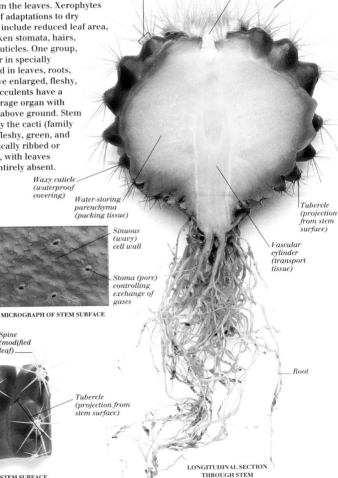

Areole (modified lateral shoot)

Trichome (hair)

Spine (modified leaf)

Waxy cuticle (waterproof covering)

Water-storing parenchyma (packing tissue)

Sinuous (wavy) cell wall

Stoma (pore) controlling exchange of gases

Tubercle (projection from stem surface)

Vascular cylinder (transport tissue)

Spine (modified leaf)

Tubercle (projection from stem surface)

Root

EXTERNAL VIEW

MICROGRAPH OF STEM SURFACE

Root

Spine (modified leaf)

Areole (modified lateral shoot)

Tubercle (projection from stem surface)

Waxy cuticle (waterproof covering)

DETAIL OF STEM SURFACE

LONGITUDINAL SECTION THROUGH STEM

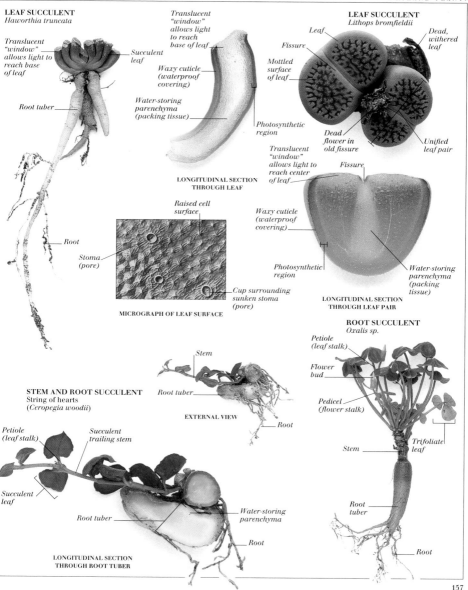

LEAF SUCCULENT
Haworthia truncata

Translucent "window" allows light to reach base of leaf

Succulent leaf

Root tuber

Root

Translucent "window" allows light to reach base of leaf

Waxy cuticle (waterproof covering)

Water-storing parenchyma (packing tissue)

Photosynthetic region

LONGITUDINAL SECTION THROUGH LEAF

LEAF SUCCULENT
Lithops bromfieldii

Leaf

Fissure

Mottled surface of leaf

Dead, withered leaf

Dead flower in old fissure

Unified leaf pair

Translucent "window" allows light to reach center of leaf

Fissure

Waxy cuticle (waterproof covering)

Photosynthetic region

Water-storing parenchyma (packing tissue)

LONGITUDINAL SECTION THROUGH LEAF PAIR

Raised cell surface

Stoma (pore)

Cup surrounding sunken stoma (pore)

MICROGRAPH OF LEAF SURFACE

ROOT SUCCULENT
Oxalis sp.

Petiole (leaf stalk)

Flower bud

Pedicel (flower stalk)

Stem

Trifoliate leaf

Root tuber

Root

Stem

Root tuber

Root

EXTERNAL VIEW

STEM AND ROOT SUCCULENT
String of hearts
(*Ceropegia woodii*)

Petiole (leaf stalk)

Succulent trailing stem

Succulent leaf

Root tuber

Water-storing parenchyma

Root

LONGITUDINAL SECTION THROUGH ROOT TUBER

Wetland plants

WETLAND PLANTS GROW SUBMERGED IN WATER, either partially, like the water hyacinth, or completely, like the pondweeds, and show various adaptations to this habitat. Typically, there are numerous air spaces inside the stems, leaves, and roots; these aid gas exchange and buoyancy. Submerged parts generally have no cuticle (waterproof covering), allowing the plants to absorb minerals and gases directly from the water. Also, because they are supported by the water, wetland plants need little of the supportive tissue found in land plants. Stomata, the gas exchange pores, are absent from plants that are completely submerged. In partially submerged plants with floating leaves, such as water lilies, stomata are found on the upper leaf surfaces, where they cannot be flooded.

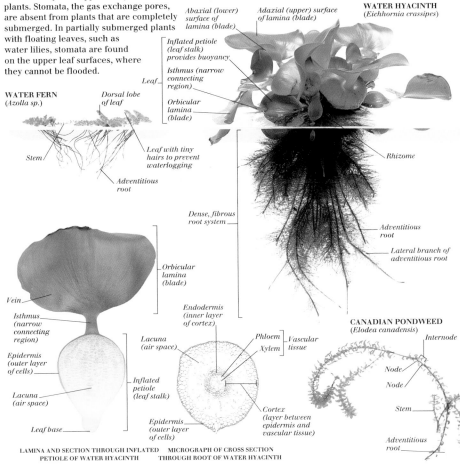

Abaxial (lower) surface of lamina (blade)

Adaxial (upper) surface of lamina (blade)

WATER HYACINTH
(Eichhornia crassipes)

Inflated petiole (leaf stalk) provides buoyancy

Isthmus (narrow connecting region)

Leaf

Orbicular lamina (blade)

WATER FERN
(Azolla sp.)

Dorsal lobe of leaf

Stem

Leaf with tiny hairs to prevent waterlogging

Adventitious root

Rhizome

Dense, fibrous root system

Adventitious root

Lateral branch of adventitious root

Orbicular lamina (blade)

Vein

Isthmus (narrow connecting region)

Epidermis (outer layer of cells)

Lacuna (air space)

Leaf base

Endodermis (inner layer of cortex)

Lacuna (air space)

Inflated petiole (leaf stalk)

Epidermis (outer layer of cells)

Phloem

Xylem

Vascular tissue

Cortex (layer between epidermis and vascular tissue)

CANADIAN PONDWEED
(Elodea canadensis)

Internode

Node

Node

Stem

Adventitious root

LAMINA AND SECTION THROUGH INFLATED PETIOLE OF WATER HYACINTH

MICROGRAPH OF CROSS SECTION THROUGH ROOT OF WATER HYACINTH

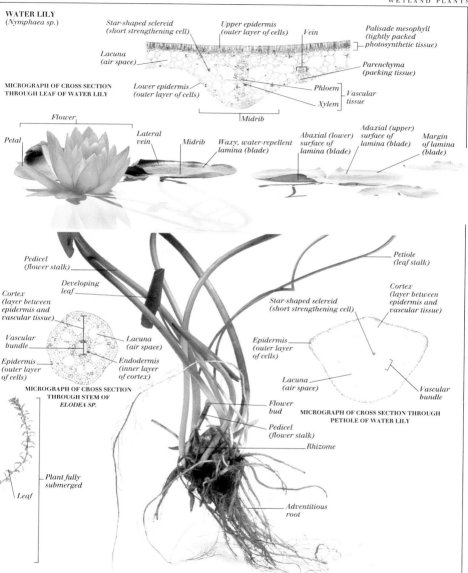

WATER LILY
(Nymphaea sp.)

*Star-shaped sclereid
(short strengthening cell)*

*Upper epidermis
(outer layer of cells)*

Vein

*Palisade mesophyll
(tightly packed
photosynthetic tissue)*

*Lacuna
(air space)*

**MICROGRAPH OF CROSS SECTION
THROUGH LEAF OF WATER LILY**

*Lower epidermis
(outer layer of cells)*

*Parenchyma
(packing tissue)*

Phloem

Xylem

*Vascular
tissue*

Midrib

Flower

Petal

*Lateral
vein*

Midrib

*Waxy, water-repellent
lamina (blade)*

*Abaxial (lower)
surface of
lamina (blade)*

*Adaxial (upper)
surface of
lamina (blade)*

*Margin
of lamina
(blade)*

*Pedicel
(flower stalk)*

*Petiole
(leaf stalk)*

*Developing
leaf*

*Cortex
(layer between
epidermis and
vascular tissue)*

*Star-shaped sclereid
(short strengthening cell)*

*Cortex
(layer between
epidermis and
vascular tissue)*

*Vascular
bundle*

*Lacuna
(air space)*

*Epidermis
(outer layer
of cells)*

*Epidermis
(outer layer
of cells)*

*Endodermis
(inner layer
of cortex)*

*Lacuna
(air space)*

*Vascular
bundle*

**MICROGRAPH OF CROSS SECTION
THROUGH STEM OF
ELODEA SP.**

**MICROGRAPH OF CROSS SECTION THROUGH
PETIOLE OF WATER LILY**

*Flower
bud*

*Pedicel
(flower stalk)*

Rhizome

*Plant fully
submerged*

Leaf

*Adventitious
root*

Carnivorous plants

Areola ("window" of transparent tissue)

Fishtail nectary

Wing

Hood

Pitcher

Tubular petiole (leaf stalk)

Areola ("window" of transparent tissue)

CARNIVOROUS (INSECTIVOROUS) PLANTS FEED ON INSECTS and other small animals in addition to producing food in their leaves by photosynthesis. The nutrients absorbed from trapped insects allow carnivorous plants to thrive in acid, boggy soils that lack essential minerals, especially nitrates, where most other plants could not survive.

All carnivorous plants have some leaves modified as traps. Many use bright colors and scented nectar to attract prey, and most use enzymes to digest the prey. There are three types of traps. Pitcher plants, such as the monkey cup and cobra lily, have leaves modified as pitcher-shaped pitfall traps, half-filled with water. Once lured inside the mouth of the trap, insects lose their footing on the slippery surface, fall into the liquid, and either decompose or are digested. Venus flytraps use a spring-trap mechanism; when an insect touches trigger hairs on the inner surfaces of the leaves, the two lobes of the trap snap shut. Butterworts and sundews entangle prey by sticky droplets on the leaf surface, while the edges of the leaves slowly curl over to envelop and digest the prey.

Dome-shaped hood develops

Fishtail nectary appears

Immature pitcher

Smooth surface

Nectar roll

Mouth

Wing

Downward-pointing hair

DEVELOPMENT OF MODIFIED LEAF IN COBRA LILY

Immature trap

Interlocked teeth

Closed trap

Red color of trap attracts insects

VENUS FLYTRAP
(*Dionaea muscipula*)

Phyllode (flattened petiole)

Summer petiole (leaf stalk)

Nectary zone (glands secrete nectar)

Digestive zone (glands secrete digestive enzymes)

Tooth

Lobe of trap

Midrib (hinge of trap)

Trigger hair

Trap (twin-lobed leaf blade)

Spring petiole (leaf stalk)

Inner surface of trap

Sensory hinge

Trigger hair

Digestive gland

MICROGRAPH OF LOBE OF VENUS FLYTRAP

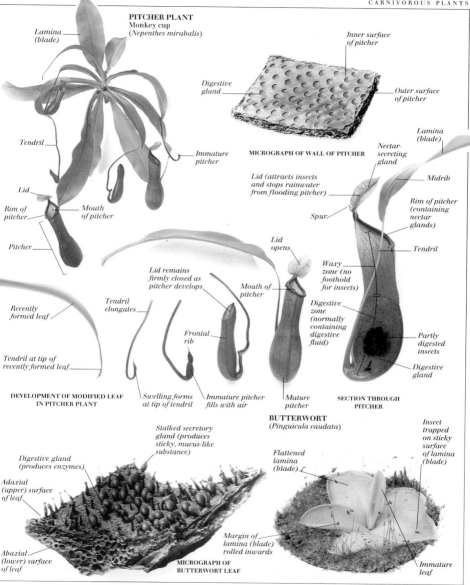

PITCHER PLANT
Monkey cup
(*Nepenthes mirabilis*)

Lamina (blade)

Tendril

Lid

Rim of pitcher

Pitcher

Immature pitcher

Mouth of pitcher

Inner surface of pitcher

Digestive gland

Outer surface of pitcher

MICROGRAPH OF WALL OF PITCHER

Nectar-secreting gland

Lamina (blade)

Midrib

Lid (attracts insects and stops rainwater from flooding pitcher)

Spur

Rim of pitcher (containing nectar glands)

Tendril

Recently formed leaf

Tendril at tip of recently formed leaf

Tendril elongates

Lid remains firmly closed as pitcher develops

Frontal rib

Lid opens

Mouth of pitcher

Waxy zone (no foothold for insects)

Digestive zone (normally containing digestive fluid)

Partly digested insects

Digestive gland

DEVELOPMENT OF MODIFIED LEAF IN PITCHER PLANT

Swelling forms at tip of tendril

Immature pitcher fills with air

Mature pitcher

SECTION THROUGH PITCHER

BUTTERWORT
(*Pinguicula caudata*)

Stalked secretory gland (produces sticky, mucus-like substance)

Digestive gland (produces enzymes)

Adaxial (upper) surface of leaf

Abaxial (lower) surface of leaf

MICROGRAPH OF BUTTERWORT LEAF

Insect trapped on sticky surface of lamina (blade)

Flattened lamina (blade)

Margin of lamina (blade) rolled inwards

Immature leaf

Epiphytic and parasitic plants

EPIPHYTIC AND PARASITIC PLANTS GROW ON OTHER LIVING PLANTS. Typically, epiphytic plants are not rooted in the soil. Instead, they live above ground level on the stems and branches of other plants. Epiphytes obtain water from trapped rainwater and from moisture in the air. They obtain minerals from organic matter that has accumulated on the surface of the plant on which they are growing. Like other green plants, epiphytes produce their food by photosynthesis. Epiphytes include tropical orchids and bromeliads (air plants) and some mosses that live in temperate regions. Parasitic plants obtain all their nutrient requirements from the host plants on which they grow. The parasites produce haustoria, root-like organs that penetrate the stem or roots of the host and grow inward to merge with the host's vascular tissue. These extract water, minerals, and manufactured nutrients. Because they have no need to produce their own food, parasitic plants lack chlorophyll, the green photosynthetic pigment, and they have no foliage leaves. Partial parasitic plants, like mistletoe, obtain water and minerals from the host plant but have green leaves and stems and are therefore able to produce their own food by photosynthesis.

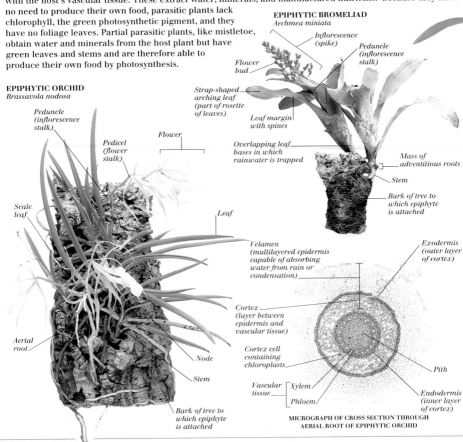

EPIPHYTIC BROMELIAD
Aechmea miniata

Inflorescence (spike)

Peduncle (inflorescence stalk)

Flower bud

Mass of adventitious roots

Stem

Bark of tree to which epiphyte is attached

EPIPHYTIC ORCHID
Brassavola nodosa

Strap-shaped arching leaf (part of rosette of leaves)

Leaf margin with spines

Overlapping leaf bases in which rainwater is trapped

Peduncle (inflorescence stalk)

Pedicel (flower stalk)

Flower

Scale leaf

Leaf

Velamen (multilayered epidermis capable of absorbing water from rain or condensation)

Exodermis (outer layer of cortex)

Cortex (layer between epidermis and vascular tissue)

Cortex cell containing chloroplasts

Vascular tissue — Xylem / Phloem

Pith

Endodermis (inner layer of cortex)

Aerial root

Node

Stem

Bark of tree to which epiphyte is attached

MICROGRAPH OF CROSS SECTION THROUGH AERIAL ROOT OF EPIPHYTIC ORCHID

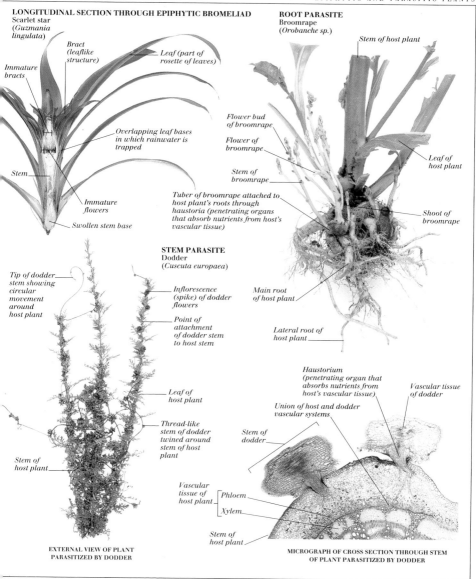

LONGITUDINAL SECTION THROUGH EPIPHYTIC BROMELIAD
Scarlet star
(*Guzmania lingulata*)

Immature bracts

Bract (leaflike structure)

Leaf (part of rosette of leaves)

Overlapping leaf bases in which rainwater is trapped

Stem

Immature flowers

Swollen stem base

ROOT PARASITE
Broomrape
(*Orobanche* sp.)

Stem of host plant

Flower bud of broomrape

Flower of broomrape

Stem of broomrape

Leaf of host plant

Tuber of broomrape attached to host plant's roots through haustoria (penetrating organs that absorb nutrients from host's vascular tissue)

Shoot of broomrape

Main root of host plant

Lateral root of host plant

STEM PARASITE
Dodder
(*Cuscuta europaea*)

Tip of dodder stem showing circular movement around host plant

Inflorescence (spike) of dodder flowers

Point of attachment of dodder stem to host stem

Leaf of host plant

Thread-like stem of dodder twined around stem of host plant

Stem of host plant

EXTERNAL VIEW OF PLANT PARASITIZED BY DODDER

Haustorium (penetrating organ that absorbs nutrients from host's vascular tissue)

Union of host and dodder vascular systems

Vascular tissue of dodder

Stem of dodder

Vascular tissue of host plant

Phloem

Xylem

Stem of host plant

MICROGRAPH OF CROSS SECTION THROUGH STEM OF PLANT PARASITIZED BY DODDER

ANIMALS

Sponges, jellyfish, and sea anemones

INTERNAL ANATOMY OF A SPONGE

SPONGES ARE MAINLY MARINE animals that make up the phylum Porifera. They are among the simplest of all animals, having no tissues or organs. Their bodies consist of two layers of cells separated by a jelly-like layer (mesohyal) that is strengthened by mineral spicules or protein fibers. The body is perforated by a system of pores and water channels called the aquiferous system. Special cells (choanocytes) with whip-like structures (flagella) draw water through the aquiferous system, thereby bringing tiny food particles to the sponge's cells. Jellyfish (class Scyphozoa), sea anemones (class Anthozoa), and corals (also class Anthozoa) belong to the phylum Cnidaria, also known as Coelenterata. More complex than sponges, coelenterates have simple tissues, such as nervous tissue; a radially symmetrical body; and a mouth surrounded by tentacles with unique stinging cells (cnidocytes).

Amebocyte

Osculum (excurrent pore)

Choanocyte (collar cell)

Ostium (incurrent pore)

Porocyte (pore cell)

Mesohyal

Spongocoel (atrium; paragaster)

Spicule

Pinacocyte (epidermal cell)

Ostium (incurrent pore)

SKELETON OF A SPONGE

Protein matrix

Pore

EXTERNAL FEATURES OF A SEA ANEMONE

Tentacle

EXAMPLES OF SEA ANEMONES

JEWEL ANEMONE
(Corynactis viridis)

PARASITIC ANEMONE
(Calliactis parasitica)

PLUMOSE ANEMONE
(Metridium senile)

MEDITERRANEAN SEA ANEMONE
(Condylactis sp.)

GREEN SNAKELOCK ANEMONE
(Anemonia viridis)

BEADLET ANEMONE
(Actinia equina)

GHOST ANEMONE
(Actinothoe sphyrodeta)

Sagartia elegans

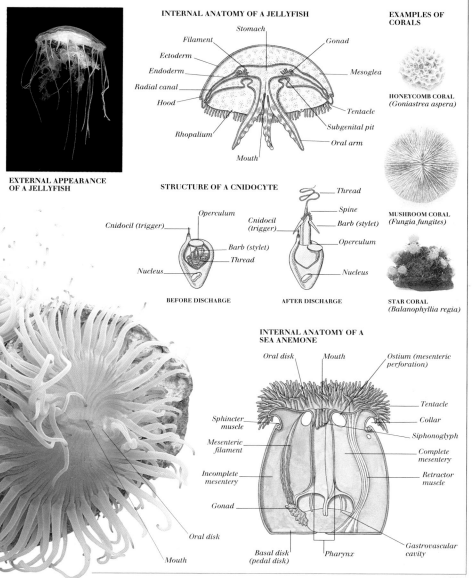

INTERNAL ANATOMY OF A JELLYFISH

Stomach

Filament

Gonad

Ectoderm

Endoderm

Mesoglea

Radial canal

Hood

Tentacle

Rhopalium

Subgenital pit

Oral arm

Mouth

**EXTERNAL APPEARANCE
OF A JELLYFISH**

**EXAMPLES OF
CORALS**

HONEYCOMB CORAL
(Goniastrea aspera)

MUSHROOM CORAL
(Fungia fungites)

STAR CORAL
(Balanophyllia regia)

STRUCTURE OF A CNIDOCYTE

Thread

Spine

Operculum

Barb (stylet)

Cnidocil (trigger)

Cnidocil
(trigger)

Operculum

Barb (stylet)

Thread

Nucleus

Nucleus

BEFORE DISCHARGE

AFTER DISCHARGE

**INTERNAL ANATOMY OF A
SEA ANEMONE**

Oral disk

Mouth

Ostium (mesenteric
perforation)

Tentacle

Sphincter
muscle

Collar

Siphonoglyph

Mesenteric
filament

Complete
mesentery

Incomplete
mesentery

Retractor
muscle

Gonad

Oral disk

Mouth

Basal disk
(pedal disk)

Pharynx

Gastrovascular
cavity

167

Insects

PUPA
(CHRYSALIS)

THE WORD INSECT REFERS to small invertebrate creatures, especially those with bodies divided into sections. Insects, including beetles, ants, bees, butterflies, and moths, belong to various orders in the class Insecta, which is a division of the phylum Arthropoda. Features common to all insects are an exoskeleton (external skeleton); three pairs of jointed legs; three body sections (head, thorax, and abdomen); and one pair of sensory antennae. Beetles (order Coleoptera) are the biggest group of insects, with about 300,000 species (about 30 percent of all known insects). They have a pair of hard elytra (wing cases), which are modified front wings. The principal function of the elytra is to protect the hind wings, which are used for flying. Ants, together with bees and wasps, form the order Hymenoptera, which contains about 200,000 species. This group is characterized by a marked narrowing between the thorax and abdomen. Butterflies and moths form the order Lepidoptera, which has about 150,000 species. They have wings covered with tiny scales, hence the name of their order (Lepidoptera means "scale wings"). The separation of lepidopterans into butterflies and moths is largely artificial as there are no features that categorically distinguish one group from the other. In general, however, most butterflies fly by day, whereas most moths are night flyers. Some insects, including butterflies and moths, undergo complete metamorphosis (transformation) during their life cycle. A butterfly metamorphoses from an egg to a larva (caterpillar), then to a pupa (chrysalis), and finally to an imago (adult).

EXAMPLES OF INSECTS

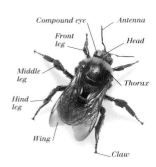

BUMBLEBEE

DAMSELFLY

EXTERNAL FEATURES OF A BEETLE

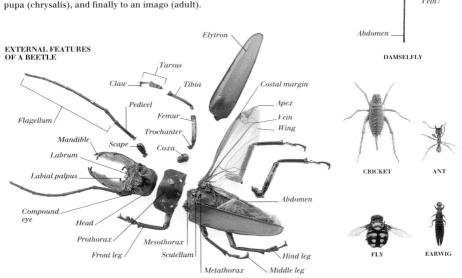

CRICKET

ANT

FLY

EARWIG

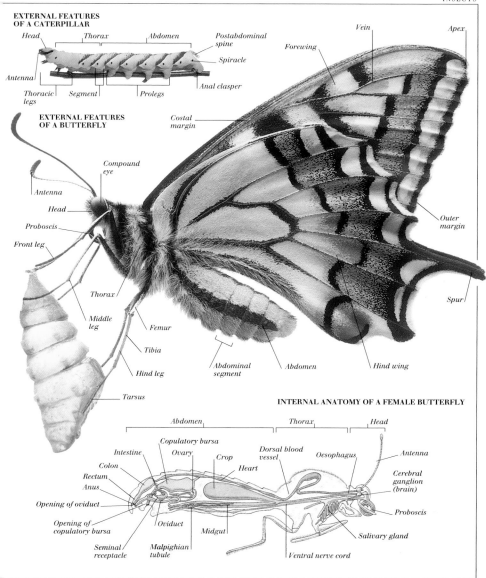

**EXTERNAL FEATURES
OF A CATERPILLAR**

Head
Thorax
Abdomen
Postabdominal
spine
Spiracle
Antenna
Thoracic
legs
Segment
Prolegs
Anal clasper

**EXTERNAL FEATURES
OF A BUTTERFLY**

Vein
Apex
Forewing
Costal
margin

Compound
eye
Antenna
Head
Proboscis
Front leg
Thorax
Middle
leg
Femur
Tibia
Hind leg
Tarsus
Abdominal
segment
Abdomen
Hind wing
Outer
margin
Spur

INTERNAL ANATOMY OF A FEMALE BUTTERFLY

Abdomen
Thorax
Head
Copulatory bursa
Intestine
Ovary
Crop
Dorsal blood
vessel
Oesophagus
Antenna
Colon
Heart
Cerebral
ganglion
(brain)
Rectum
Anus
Opening of oviduct
Proboscis
Opening of
copulatory bursa
Oviduct
Midgut
Salivary gland
Seminal
receptacle
Malpighian
tubule
Ventral nerve cord

Arachnids

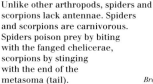

THE CLASS ARACHNIDA INCLUDES SPIDERS (order Araneae) and scorpions (order Scorpiones). The class is part of the phylum Arthropoda, which also includes insects and crustaceans.
Spiders and scorpions are characterized by having four pairs of walking legs; a pair of pincer-like mouthparts called chelicerae; another pair of frontal appendages called pedipalps, which are sensory in spiders but used for grasping in scorpions; and a body divided into two sections (a combined head and thorax called a cephalothorax, or prosoma, and an abdomen, or opisthosoma). Unlike other arthropods, spiders and scorpions lack antennae. Spiders and scorpions are carnivorous. Spiders poison prey by biting with the fanged chelicerae, scorpions by stinging with the end of the metasoma (tail).

MEXICAN TRUE RED-LEGGED TARANTULA
(Euathlus emilia)

INTERNAL ANATOMY OF A FEMALE SPIDER

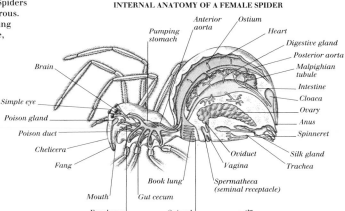

Anterior aorta · Ostium · Heart · Digestive gland · Posterior aorta · Malpighian tubule · Intestine · Cloaca · Ovary · Anus · Spinneret · Silk gland · Trachea · Spermatheca (seminal receptacle) · Spiracle · Vagina · Oviduct · Book lung · Gut cecum · Esophagus · Mouth · Fang · Chelicera · Poison duct · Poison gland · Simple eye · Brain · Pumping stomach

EXTERNAL FEATURES OF A SCORPION

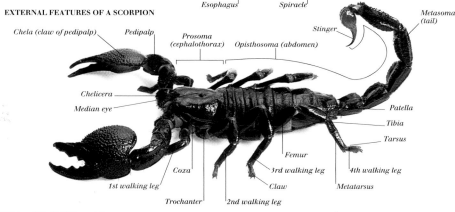

Chela (claw of pedipalp) · Pedipalp · Prosoma (cephalothorax) · Opisthosoma (abdomen) · Stinger · Metasoma (tail) · Chelicera · Median eye · Patella · Tibia · Tarsus · Coxa · Femur · 3rd walking leg · 4th walking leg · Metatarsus · 1st walking leg · Trochanter · 2nd walking leg · Claw

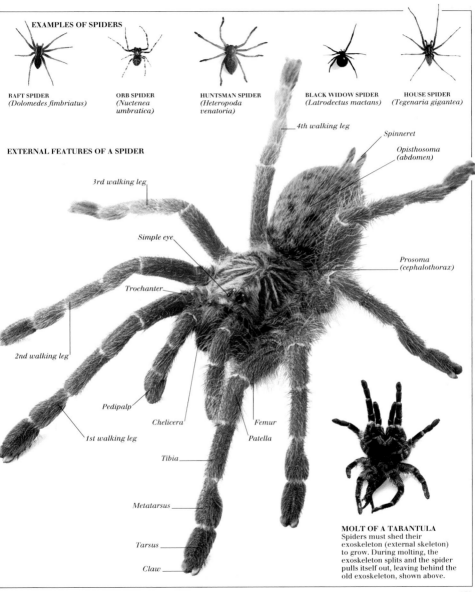

EXAMPLES OF SPIDERS

RAFT SPIDER
(Dolomedes fimbriatus)

ORB SPIDER
(Nuctenea umbratica)

HUNTSMAN SPIDER
(Heteropoda venatoria)

BLACK WIDOW SPIDER
(Latrodectus mactans)

HOUSE SPIDER
(Tegenaria gigantea)

EXTERNAL FEATURES OF A SPIDER

4th walking leg

Spinneret

Opisthosoma (abdomen)

3rd walking leg

Simple eye

Prosoma (cephalothorax)

Trochanter

2nd walking leg

Pedipalp

Chelicera

Femur

Patella

1st walking leg

Tibia

Metatarsus

Tarsus

Claw

MOLT OF A TARANTULA
Spiders must shed their exoskeleton (external skeleton) to grow. During molting, the exoskeleton splits and the spider pulls itself out, leaving behind the old exoskeleton, shown above.

Crustaceans

THE SUBPHYLUM CRUSTACEA is one of the largest groups
in the phylum Arthropoda. The subphylum is divided
into several classes, the most important of which
are Malacostraca and Cirripedia. The class
Malacostraca includes crayfish, crabs,
lobsters, and shrimps. Typical features of
malacostracans include a body divided
into two sections (a combined head
and thorax called a cephalothorax,
and an abdomen); an exoskeleton
(external skeleton) with a large
plate (carapace) covering the
cephalothorax; stalked,
compound eyes; and two
pairs of antennae. The class
Cirripedia includes barnacles,
which, unlike other
crustaceans, spend their
adult lives attached to a
surface, such as a rock. Other
characteristics of cirripedes
include an exoskeleton of
overlapping calcareous plates;
a body consisting almost entirely
of thorax (the abdomen and head
are minute); and six pairs of thoracic
appendages (cirri) used for filter feeding.

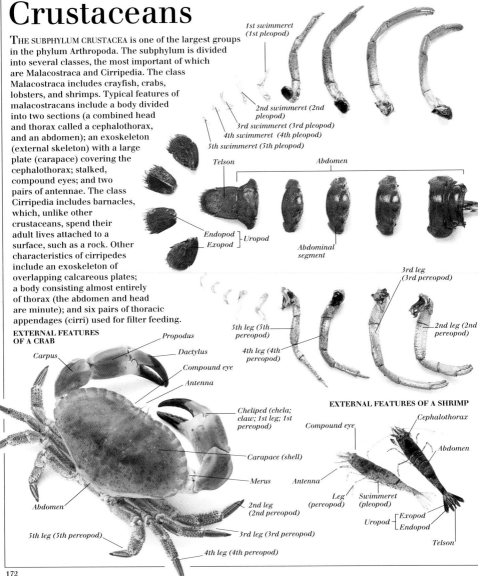

1st swimmeret
(1st pleopod)

2nd swimmeret (2nd
pleopod)

3rd swimmeret (3rd pleopod)

4th swimmeret (4th pleopod)

5th swimmeret (5th pleopod)

Telson

Abdomen

Endopod
Exopod — Uropod

Abdominal
segment

3rd leg
(3rd pereopod)

5th leg (5th
pereopod)

4th leg (4th
pereopod)

2nd leg (2nd
pereopod)

**EXTERNAL FEATURES
OF A CRAB**

Propodus

Carpus

Dactylus

Compound eye

Antenna

Cheliped (chela;
claw; 1st leg; 1st
pereopod)

Carapace (shell)

Merus

Antenna

Abdomen

5th leg (5th pereopod)

2nd leg
(2nd pereopod)

3rd leg (3rd pereopod)

4th leg (4th pereopod)

EXTERNAL FEATURES OF A SHRIMP

Compound eye

Cephalothorax

Abdomen

Leg
(pereopod)

Swimmeret
(pleopod)

Uropod — Exopod
Endopod

Telson

172

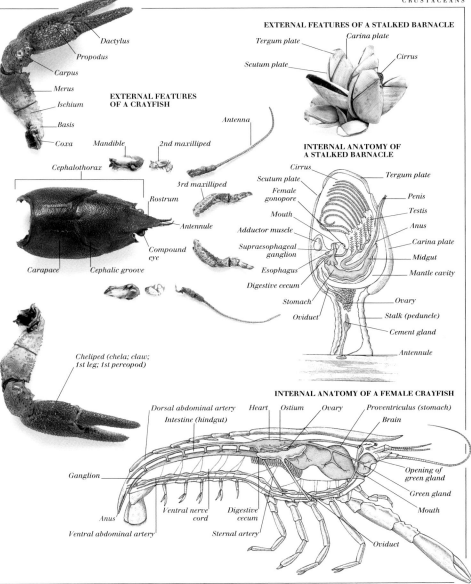

EXTERNAL FEATURES OF A STALKED BARNACLE

Tergum plate
Carina plate
Cirrus
Scutum plate

Dactylus
Propodus
Carpus
Merus
Ischium
Basis
Coxa

**EXTERNAL FEATURES
OF A CRAYFISH**

Mandible
2nd maxilliped
Antenna

Cephalothorax
Rostrum
3rd maxilliped

Antennule
Compound
eye

Carapace
Cephalic groove

INTERNAL ANATOMY OF
A STALKED BARNACLE

Cirrus
Scutum plate
Female
gonopore
Mouth
Adductor muscle
Supraesophageal
ganglion
Esophagus
Digestive cecum
Stomach
Oviduct

Tergum plate
Penis
Testis
Anus
Carina plate
Midgut
Mantle cavity

Ovary
Stalk (peduncle)
Cement gland
Antennule

Cheliped (chela; claw;
1st leg; 1st pereopod)

INTERNAL ANATOMY OF A FEMALE CRAYFISH

Dorsal abdominal artery
Intestine (hindgut)
Heart
Ostium
Ovary
Proventriculus (stomach)
Brain

Ganglion

Opening of
green gland
Green gland
Mouth

Anus
Ventral nerve
cord
Digestive
cecum
Sternal artery
Oviduct
Ventral abdominal artery

Starfish and sea urchins

STARFISH, SEA URCHINS, AND THEIR relatives (including
feather stars, brittle stars, basket stars, sea daisies,
sea lilies, and sea cucumbers) make up the phylum
Echinodermata. A unique feature of echinoderms is the water
vascular system, which consists of a series of water-filled canals
from which protrude thousands of tiny tube feet. The tube feet
may be used for movement, feeding, or respiration. Other features
include pentaradiate symmetry (that is, the body can be divided into
five parts radiating from the center); no head; a diffuse, decentralized
nervous system that lacks a brain; and no excretory organs. Typically,
echinoderms also have an endoskeleton (internal skeleton)
consisting of hard calcite ossicles embedded in the
body wall and often bearing protruding spines or
tubercles. The ossicles may fit together to
form a test (as in sea urchins) or
remain separate (as in
sea cucumbers).

**EXTERNAL FEATURES OF
A STARFISH (UPPER, OR
ABORAL, SURFACE)**

Disk

Madreporite

Spine

Arm

Tube foot

**INTERNAL ANATOMY
OF A STARFISH**

Rectum

Pyloric stomach

Madreporite

Stone canal

Anus

Rectal cecum

Ring canal

Lateral canal

Radial canal

Ampulla

Cardiac stomach

Pyloric duct

Pyloric cecum

Mouth

Esophagus

Gonad

Gonopore

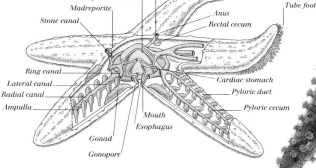

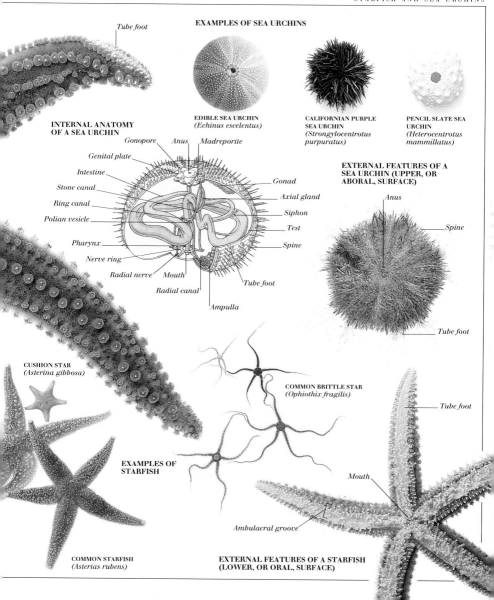

Tube foot

EXAMPLES OF SEA URCHINS

EDIBLE SEA URCHIN
(*Echinus escelentus*)

CALIFORNIAN PURPLE SEA URCHIN
(*Strongylocentrotus purpuratus*)

PENCIL SLATE SEA URCHIN
(*Heterocentrotus mammillatus*)

INTERNAL ANATOMY OF A SEA URCHIN

Gonopore
Anus
Madreporite
Genital plate
Intestine
Stone canal
Ring canal
Polian vesicle
Pharynx
Nerve ring
Radial nerve
Mouth
Radial canal
Ampulla
Gonad
Axial gland
Siphon
Test
Spine
Tube foot

EXTERNAL FEATURES OF A SEA URCHIN (UPPER, OR ABORAL, SURFACE)

Anus
Spine
Tube foot

CUSHION STAR
(*Asterina gibbosa*)

COMMON BRITTLE STAR
(*Ophiothix fragilis*)

Tube foot

EXAMPLES OF STARFISH

Mouth

Ambulacral groove

COMMON STARFISH
(*Asterias rubens*)

EXTERNAL FEATURES OF A STARFISH (LOWER, OR ORAL, SURFACE)

Mollusks

THE PHYLUM MOLLUSCA (MOLLUSKS) is a large group of animals that includes octopuses, snails, and scallops. Octopuses and their relatives —including squid and cuttlefish—form the class Cephalopoda. Cephalopods typically have a head with a radula (a file-like feeding organ) and beak; a well-developed nervous system; sucker-bearing tentacles; a muscular mantle (part of the body wall) that can expel water through the siphon, enabling movement by jet propulsion; and a small shell or no shell. Snails and their relatives—including slugs, limpets, and abalones—make up the class Gastropoda. Gastropods typically have a coiled external shell, although some, such as slugs, have a small internal shell or no shell; a flat foot; and a head with tentacles and a radula. Scallops and their relatives—including clams, mussels, and oysters—make up the class Bivalvia (also called Pelecypoda). Features of bivalves include a shell with two halves (valves); large gills that are used for breathing and filter feeding; and no radula.

EXTERNAL FEATURES OF A SCALLOP

Upper valve (shell)　Mantle　Ocellus (eye)

Lower valve (shell)　Shell rib　Sensory tentacle

Sensory tentacle　Ventral margin of shell　Shell rib

Anterior wing of shell

Umbo　Posterior wing of shell

Dorsal margin of shell

INTERNAL ANATOMY OF AN OCTOPUS

Cephalic vein
Poison gland
Skull
Crop
Brain
Digestive cecum
Siphon (funnel)
Dorsal mantle cavity
Buccal mass
Mantle muscles
Beak
Shell rudiment
Stomach
Cecum
Gonad
Systemic heart
Kidney
Branchial heart
Anus
Ctenidium
Muscular septum
Ink sac

Tentacle

Sucker

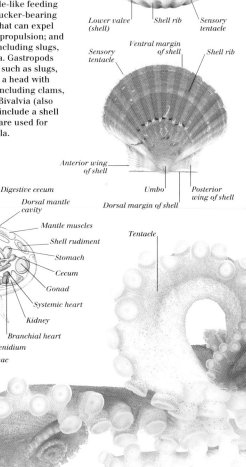

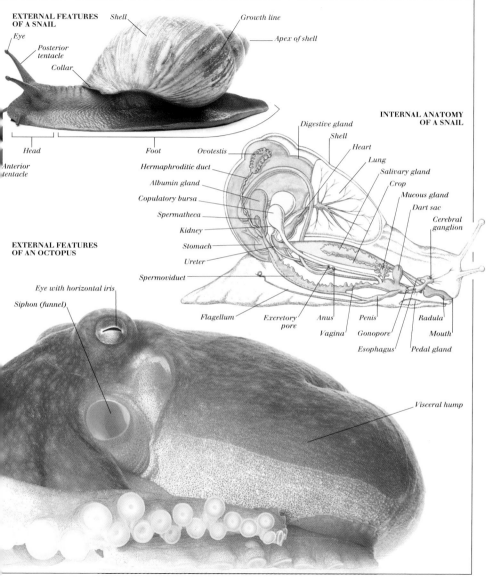

EXTERNAL FEATURES OF A SNAIL

Eye
Posterior tentacle
Collar
Shell
Growth line
Apex of shell
Head
Foot
Anterior tentacle

INTERNAL ANATOMY OF A SNAIL

Digestive gland
Shell
Heart
Lung
Salivary gland
Crop
Mucous gland
Dart sac
Cerebral ganglion
Ovotestis
Hermaphroditic duct
Albumin gland
Copulatory bursa
Spermatheca
Kidney
Stomach
Ureter
Spermoviduct
Flagellum
Excretory pore
Anus
Penis
Radula
Vagina
Gonopore
Mouth
Esophagus
Pedal gland

EXTERNAL FEATURES OF AN OCTOPUS

Eye with horizontal iris
Siphon (funnel)
Visceral hump

177

Sharks and jawless fish

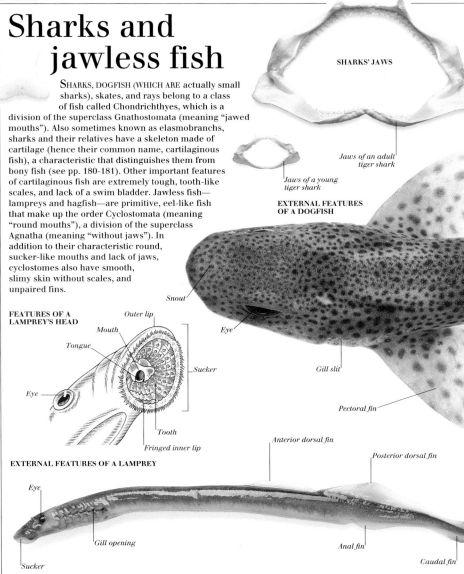

SHARKS' JAWS

SHARKS, DOGFISH (WHICH ARE actually small sharks), skates, and rays belong to a class of fish called Chondrichthyes, which is a division of the superclass Gnathostomata (meaning "jawed mouths"). Also sometimes known as elasmobranchs, sharks and their relatives have a skeleton made of cartilage (hence their common name, cartilaginous fish), a characteristic that distinguishes them from bony fish (see pp. 180-181). Other important features of cartilaginous fish are extremely tough, tooth-like scales, and lack of a swim bladder. Jawless fish— lampreys and hagfish—are primitive, eel-like fish that make up the order Cyclostomata (meaning "round mouths"), a division of the superclass Agnatha (meaning "without jaws"). In addition to their characteristic round, sucker-like mouths and lack of jaws, cyclostomes also have smooth, slimy skin without scales, and unpaired fins.

Jaws of an adult tiger shark

Jaws of a young tiger shark

EXTERNAL FEATURES OF A DOGFISH

Snout

Eye

Gill slit

Pectoral fin

FEATURES OF A LAMPREY'S HEAD

Outer lip

Mouth

Tongue

Eye

Sucker

Tooth

Fringed inner lip

EXTERNAL FEATURES OF A LAMPREY

Anterior dorsal fin

Posterior dorsal fin

Eye

Gill opening

Anal fin

Caudal fin

Sucker

178

EXAMPLES OF CARTILAGINOUS FISH

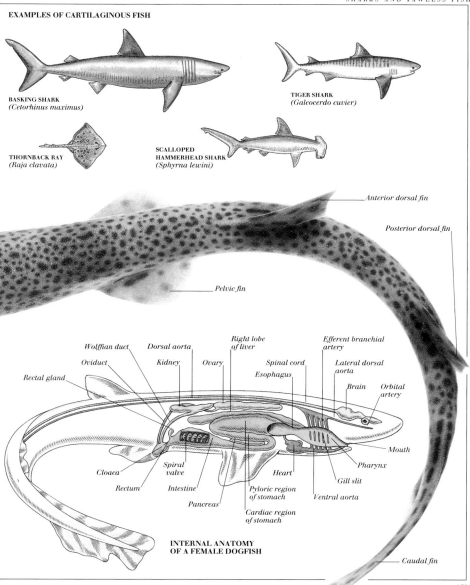

BASKING SHARK
(Cetorhinus maximus)

TIGER SHARK
(Galeocerdo cuvier)

THORNBACK RAY
(Raja clavata)

**SCALLOPED
HAMMERHEAD SHARK**
(Sphyrna lewini)

Anterior dorsal fin

Posterior dorsal fin

Pelvic fin

Wolffian duct

Dorsal aorta

*Right lobe
of liver*

*Efferent branchial
artery*

Oviduct

Kidney

Ovary

Spinal cord

*Lateral dorsal
aorta*

Esophagus

Rectal gland

Brain

*Orbital
artery*

Mouth

Pharynx

Cloaca

*Spiral
valve*

Heart

Gill slit

Rectum

Intestine

*Pyloric region
of stomach*

Ventral aorta

Pancreas

*Cardiac region
of stomach*

**INTERNAL ANATOMY
OF A FEMALE DOGFISH**

Caudal fin

Bony fish

BONY FISH, SUCH AS CARP, TROUT, SALMON, perch, and cod, are by far the best known and largest group of fish, with more than 20,000 species (over 95 percent of all known fish). As their name suggests, bony fish have skeletons made of bone, in contrast to the cartilaginous skeletons of sharks, jawless fish, and their relatives (see pp. 178-179). Other typical features of bony fish include a swim bladder, which functions as a variable-buoyancy organ, enabling a fish to remain effortlessly at whatever depth it is swimming; relatively thin, bone-like scales; a flap (called an operculum) covering the gills; and paired pelvic and pectoral fins. Scientifically, bony fish belong to the class Osteichthyes, which is a division of the superclass Gnathostomata (meaning "jawed mouths").

HOW FISH BREATHE

Fish "breathe" by extracting oxygen from water through their gills. Water is sucked in through the mouth; simultaneously, the opercula close to prevent the water from escaping. The mouth is then closed, and muscles in the walls of the mouth, pharynx, and opercular cavity contract to pump the water inside over the gills and out through the opercula. Some fish rely on swimming with their mouths open to keep water flowing over the gills.

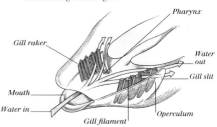

Gill raker

Pharynx

Water out

Gill slit

Mouth

Water in

Gill filament

Operculum

EXAMPLES OF BONY FISH

MANDARINFISH
(*Synchiropus splendidus*)

ANGLERFISH
(*Caulophryne jordani*)

LIONFISH
(*Pterois volitans*)

OCEANIC SEAHORSE
(*Hippocampus kuda*)

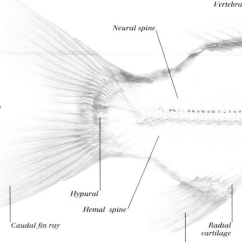

Vertebra

Neural spine

Hypural

Hemal spine

Caudal fin ray

Anal fin ray

Radial cartilage

STURGEON
(*Acipenser sturio*)

SNOWFLAKE MORAY EEL
(*Echidna nebulosa*)

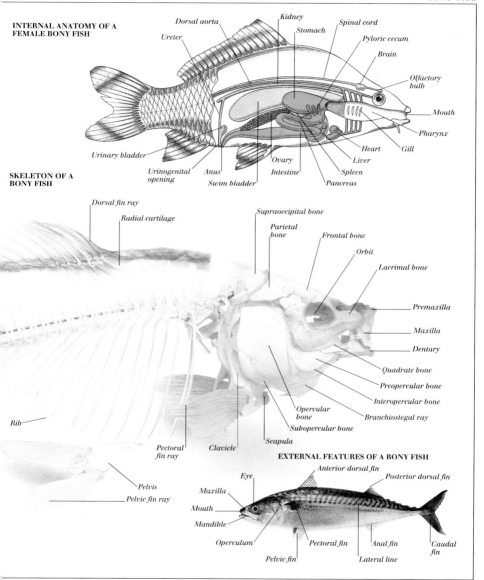

**INTERNAL ANATOMY OF A
FEMALE BONY FISH**

Dorsal aorta
Kidney
Ureter
Stomach
Spinal cord
Pyloric cecum
Brain
Olfactory
bulb
Mouth
Pharynx
Gill
Heart
Liver
Spleen
Pancreas
Urinary bladder
Ovary
Intestine
Urinogenital
opening
Anus
Swim bladder

**SKELETON OF A
BONY FISH**

Dorsal fin ray
Radial cartilage
Supraoccipital bone
Parietal
bone
Frontal bone
Orbit
Lacrimal bone
Premaxilla
Maxilla
Dentary
Quadrate bone
Preopercular bone
Interopercular bone
Branchiostegal ray
Opercular
bone
Subopercular bone
Scapula
Pectoral
fin ray
Clavicle
Rib
Pelvis
Pelvic fin ray

EXTERNAL FEATURES OF A BONY FISH

Eye
Anterior dorsal fin
Posterior dorsal fin
Maxilla
Mouth
Mandible
Operculum
Pectoral fin
Anal fin
Caudal
fin
Pelvic fin
Lateral line

Amphibians

THE CLASS AMPHIBIA INCLUDES FROGS and toads (which make
up the order Anura) and newts and salamanders (which make
up the order Urodela). Amphibians typically have moist,
scaleless, hairless skin; lungs; and are cold-blooded. They
also undergo complete metamorphosis, from eggs
laid in water through various water-living larval
stages (such as the tadpole stage) to land-living
adults. Typical features of adult frogs and toads
include a squat body with no tail; long, powerful
hind legs; and large, often bulging, eyes. Adult
newts and salamanders typically have a long
body with a well-developed tail; and relatively
short legs of equal size. However, newts and
salamanders show considerable variation;
for example, in some species the adults
have minute legs, external gills rather
than lungs, and spend their entire
lives in water.

**INTERNAL ANATOMY
OF A FEMALE FROG**

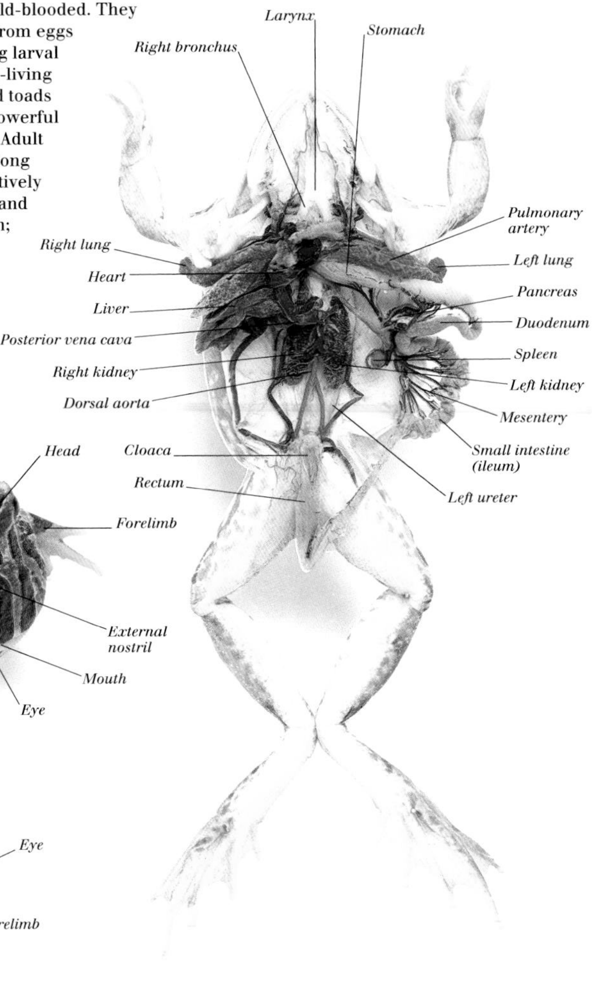

Larynx
Right bronchus
Stomach
Pulmonary artery
Right lung
Left lung
Heart
Pancreas
Liver
Duodenum
Posterior vena cava
Spleen
Right kidney
Left kidney
Dorsal aorta
Mesentery
Small intestine (ileum)
Cloaca
Rectum
Left ureter

**EXTERNAL FEATURES
OF A FROG**

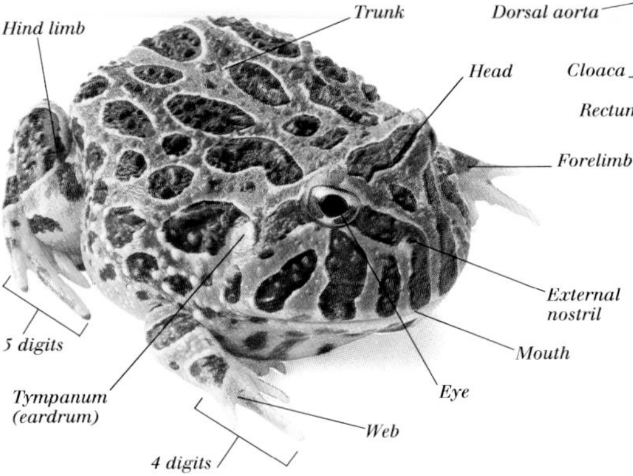

Trunk
Hind limb
Head
Forelimb
External nostril
Mouth
5 digits
Eye
Tympanum (eardrum)
Web
4 digits

**EXTERNAL FEATURES OF A
SALAMANDER**

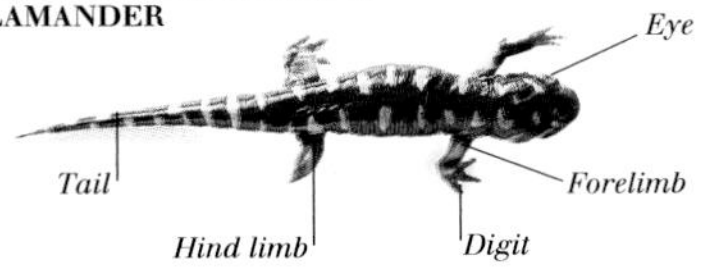

Eye
Tail
Forelimb
Hind limb
Digit

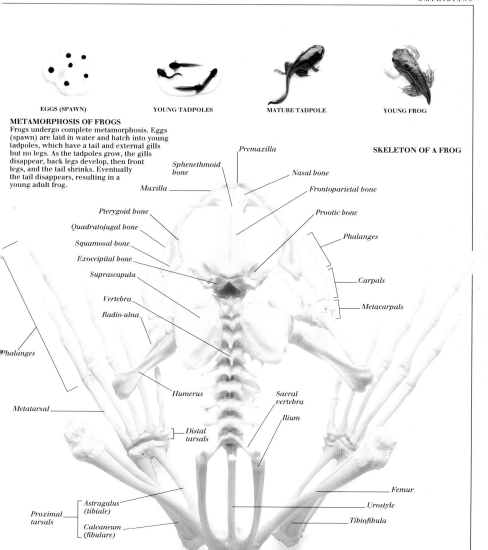

EGGS (SPAWN)

YOUNG TADPOLES

MATURE TADPOLE

YOUNG FROG

METAMORPHOSIS OF FROGS
Frogs undergo complete metamorphosis. Eggs
(spawn) are laid in water and hatch into young
tadpoles, which have a tail and external gills
but no legs. As the tadpoles grow, the gills
disappear, back legs develop, then front
legs, and the tail shrinks. Eventually
the tail disappears, resulting in a
young adult frog.

SKELETON OF A FROG

Premaxilla

Sphenethmoid
bone

Nasal bone

Frontoparietal bone

Maxilla

Pterygoid bone

Prootic bone

Quadratojugal bone

Phalanges

Squamosal bone

Exoccipital bone

Carpals

Suprascapula

Metacarpals

Vertebra

Radio-ulna

Phalanges

Humerus

Metatarsal

Sacral
vertebra

Ilium

Distal
tarsals

Femur

Proximal
tarsals

Astragalus
(tibiale)

Urostyle

Tibiofibula

Calcaneum
(fibulare)

Ischium

183

Lizards and snakes

LIZARDS AND SNAKES BELONG to the order Squamata, a division of the class Reptilia. Characteristic reptilian features include scaly skin, lungs, and cold-bloodedness. Most reptiles lay leathery-shelled eggs, although some hatch the eggs inside their bodies and give birth to live young. Lizards belong to the suborder Lacertilia. Typically, they have long tails, and shed their skin in several pieces. Many lizards can regenerate a tail if it is lost; some can change color; and some are limbless. Snakes make up the suborder Ophidia (also called Serpentes). All snakes have long, limbless bodies; can dislocate their lower jaw to swallow large prey; and have eyelids that are joined together to form a single transparent covering over the front of the eye. Most snakes shed their skin in a single piece. Constrictor snakes kill their prey by squeezing; venomous snakes poison their prey.

EXAMPLES OF SNAKES

MEXICAN MOUNTAIN KING SNAKE (*Lampropeltis triangulum annulata*)

BANDED MILK SNAKE (*Lampropeltis ruthveni*)

EXTERNAL FEATURES OF A LIZARD

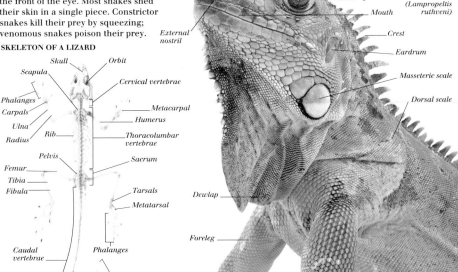

- Eye
- Mouth
- Crest
- Eardrum
- Masseteric scale
- Dorsal scale
- External nostril
- Dewlap
- Foreleg
- Belly
- Ventral scale

SKELETON OF A LIZARD

- Skull
- Orbit
- Scapula
- Cervical vertebrae
- Phalanges
- Carpals
- Metacarpal
- Humerus
- Ulna
- Radius
- Rib
- Thoracolumbar vertebrae
- Pelvis
- Femur
- Sacrum
- Tibia
- Fibula
- Tarsals
- Metatarsal
- Caudal vertebrae
- Phalanges
- Toe
- Claw

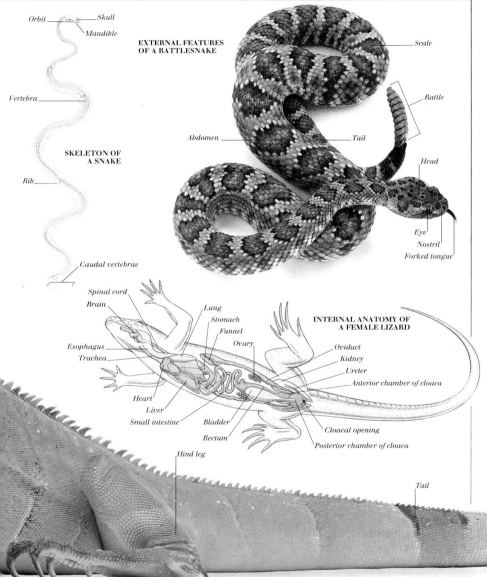

Orbit — *Skull*
Mandible

**EXTERNAL FEATURES
OF A RATTLESNAKE**

Scale

Vertebra

Rattle

**SKELETON OF
A SNAKE**

Abdomen — *Tail*

Head

Rib

Eye
Nostril
Forked tongue

Caudal vertebrae

Spinal cord
Brain
Lung
Stomach
Funnel
Ovary
**INTERNAL ANATOMY OF
A FEMALE LIZARD**
Esophagus
Trachea
Oviduct
Kidney
Ureter
Anterior chamber of cloaca
Heart
Liver
Small intestine
Bladder
Rectum
Cloacal opening
Posterior chamber of cloaca
Hind leg

Tail

Crocodilians and turtles

CROCODILIANS AND TURTLES BELONG to different orders in the class Reptilia. The order Crocodilia includes crocodiles, alligators, caimans, and gharials. Typically, crocodilians are carnivores (flesh-eaters), and have a long snout, sharp teeth for gripping prey, and hard, square scales. All crocodilians are adapted to living on land and in water: they have four strong legs for moving on land; a powerful tail for swimming; and their eyes and nostrils are high on the head so that they stay above water while the rest of the body is submerged. The order Chelonia includes marine turtles, freshwater turtles (terrapins), and land turtles (tortoises). Characteristically, chelonians have a short, broad body encased in a bony shell with an outer horny covering, into which the head and limbs can be withdrawn; and a horny beak instead of teeth.

GHARIAL
(Gavialis gangeticus)

NILE CROCODILE
(Crocodylus niloticus)

MISSISSIPPI ALLIGATOR
(Alligator mississippiensis)

SKELETON OF A CROCODILE

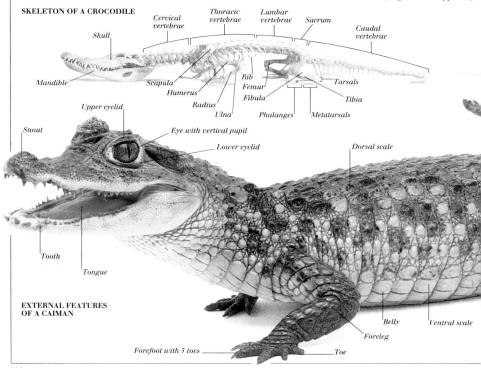

Cervical vertebrae
Thoracic vertebrae
Lumbar vertebrae
Sacrum
Caudal vertebrae
Skull
Mandible
Scapula
Humerus
Radius
Ulna
Rib
Femur
Fibula
Phalanges
Metatarsals
Tarsals
Tibia

Upper eyelid
Snout
Eye with vertical pupil
Lower eyelid
Dorsal scale
Tooth
Tongue

EXTERNAL FEATURES OF A CAIMAN

Belly
Ventral scale
Foreleg
Forefoot with 5 toes
Toe

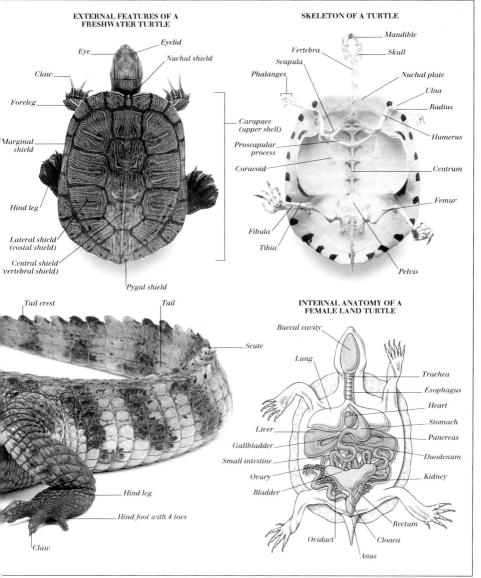

**EXTERNAL FEATURES OF A
FRESHWATER TURTLE**

Eyelid

Eye

Nuchal shield

Claw

Foreleg

Marginal
shield

Hind leg

Lateral shield
(costal shield)

Central shield
(vertebral shield)

Pygal shield

Carapace
(upper shell)

SKELETON OF A TURTLE

Mandible

Vertebra

Skull

Scapula

Phalanges

Nuchal plate

Ulna

Radius

Humerus

Proscapular
process

Coracoid

Centrum

Femur

Fibula

Tibia

Pelvis

Tail crest

Tail

Scute

Hind leg

Hind foot with 4 toes

Claw

**INTERNAL ANATOMY OF A
FEMALE LAND TURTLE**

Buccal cavity

Lung

Trachea

Esophagus

Heart

Stomach

Pancreas

Liver

Gallbladder

Duodenum

Small intestine

Kidney

Ovary

Bladder

Rectum

Oviduct

Cloaca

Anus

Birds 1

BIRDS MAKE UP THE CLASS AVES. There are more than 9,000 species, almost all of which can fly (the only flightless birds are penguins, ostriches, rheas, cassowaries, and kiwis). The ability to fly is reflected in the typical bird features: forelimbs modified as wings, a streamlined body, and hollow bones to reduce weight. All birds lay hard-shelled eggs, which the parents incubate. Birds' beaks and feet vary according to diet and way of life. Beaks range from general purpose types suitable for a mixed diet (those of thrushes, for example), to types specialized for particular foods (such as the large, curved, sieving beaks of flamingos). Feet range from the webbed "paddles" of ducks, to the talons of birds of prey. Plumage also varies widely, and in many species the male is brightly colored for courtship display whereas the female is drab.

EXTERNAL FEATURES OF A BIRD

Forehead

Eye

Crown

Nostril

Nape

Upper mandible

Beak

Lower mandible

Chin

Throat

EXAMPLES OF BIRDS

Minor coverts

Lesser wing coverts

Median wing coverts

MALE TUFTED DUCK
(*Aythya fuligula*)

Greater wing coverts (major coverts)

Secondary flight feathers (secondary remiges)

Breast

Primary flight feathers (primary remiges)

WHITE STORK
(*Ciconia ciconia*)

Belly

Flank

Thigh

Under tail coverts

Claw

Tarsus

Toe

Tail feathers (retrices)

MALE OSTRICH
(*Struthio camelus*)

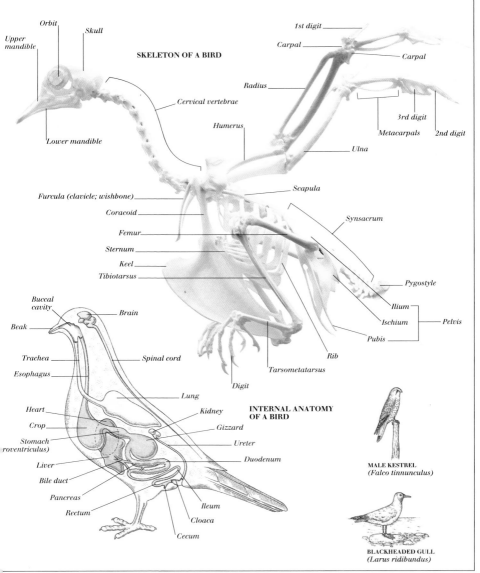

SKELETON OF A BIRD

Orbit

Skull

Upper mandible

1st digit

Carpal

Carpal

Radius

Cervical vertebrae

Humerus

3rd digit

Metacarpals

2nd digit

Lower mandible

Ulna

Scapula

Furcula (clavicle; wishbone)

Synsacrum

Coracoid

Femur

Sternum

Keel

Tibiotarsus

Pygostyle

Ilium

Ischium

Pelvis

Pubis

Rib

Tarsometatarsus

Digit

Buccal cavity

Brain

Beak

Trachea

Spinal cord

Esophagus

Lung

INTERNAL ANATOMY OF A BIRD

Heart

Kidney

Crop

Gizzard

Stomach (proventriculus)

Ureter

Liver

Duodenum

Bile duct

Pancreas

Rectum

Ileum

Cloaca

Cecum

MALE KESTREL
(Falco tinnunculus)

BLACKHEADED GULL
(Larus ridibundus)

Birds 2

EXAMPLES OF BIRDS' FEET

KITTIWAKE
(Rissa tridactyla)
The webbed feet are
adapted for paddling
through water.

LITTLE GREBE
(Tachybaptus ruficollis)
The lobed, flattened feet
are adapted for swimming
underwater.

TAWNY OWL
(Strix aluco)
The clawed feet are adapted
for gripping prey.

EXAMPLES OF BIRDS' BEAKS

KING VULTURE
(Sarcorhamphus papa)
The hooked beak is adapted
for pulling apart flesh.

GREATER FLAMINGO
(Phoenicopterus ruber)
In the living bird, the large,
curved beak contains a
cartilaginous "sieve" for
filtering food particles
from water.

MAVIS, OR MISTLE THRUSH
(Turdus viscivorus)
The all-purpose beak is suitable
for gathering a wide range of
animal and plant foods.

BLUE-AND-YELLOW MACAW
(Ara ararauna)
The broad, powerful, hooked beak
is adapted for crushing seeds and
eating fruit.

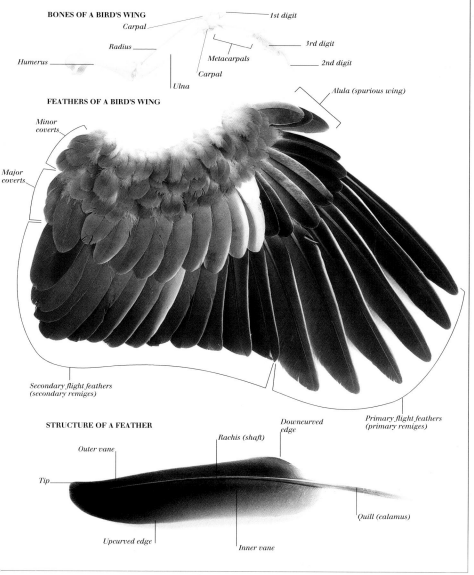

BONES OF A BIRD'S WING

1st digit

Carpal

Radius

3rd digit

Humerus

Metacarpals

2nd digit

Carpal

Ulna

Alula (spurious wing)

FEATHERS OF A BIRD'S WING

Minor coverts

Major coverts

Secondary flight feathers (secondary remiges)

Primary flight feathers (primary remiges)

STRUCTURE OF A FEATHER

Downcurved edge

Rachis (shaft)

Outer vane

Tip

Quill (calamus)

Upcurved edge

Inner vane

Eggs

AN EGG IS A SINGLE CELL, produced by the female, with the capacity to develop into a new individual. Development may take place inside the mother's body (as in most mammals) or outside, in which case the egg has a protective covering such as a shell. Egg yolk nourishes the growing young. Eggs developing inside the mother generally have little yolk, because the young are nourished from her body. Eggs developing outside may also have little yolk if they are produced by animals whose young go through a larval stage (such as a caterpillar) that feeds itself while developing into the adult form. The shelled eggs of birds and reptiles contain enough yolk to sustain the young until it hatches into a juvenile version of the adult.

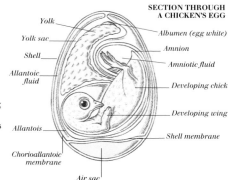

SECTION THROUGH A CHICKEN'S EGG

Yolk

Yolk sac

Shell

Allantoic fluid

Allantois

Chorioallantoic membrane

Air sac

Albumen (egg white)

Amnion

Amniotic fluid

Developing chick

Developing wing

Shell membrane

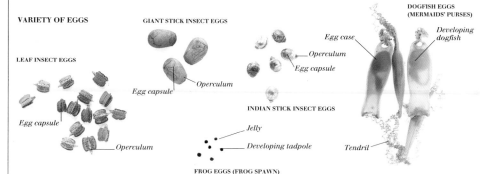

VARIETY OF EGGS

LEAF INSECT EGGS

Egg capsule

Operculum

GIANT STICK INSECT EGGS

Egg capsule

Operculum

INDIAN STICK INSECT EGGS

Operculum

Egg capsule

FROG EGGS (FROG SPAWN)

Jelly

Developing tadpole

DOGFISH EGGS (MERMAIDS' PURSES)

Egg case

Developing dogfish

Tendril

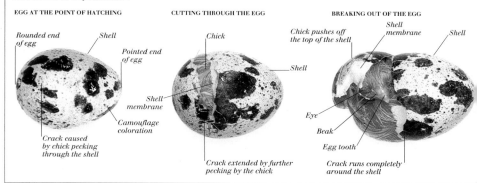

HATCHING OF A QUAIL'S EGG

EGG AT THE POINT OF HATCHING

Rounded end of egg

Shell

Pointed end of egg

Shell membrane

Camouflage coloration

Crack caused by chick pecking through the shell

CUTTING THROUGH THE EGG

Chick

Shell

Shell membrane

Crack extended by further pecking by the chick

BREAKING OUT OF THE EGG

Chick pushes off the top of the shell

Shell membrane

Shell

Eye

Beak

Egg tooth

Crack runs completely around the shell

EXAMPLES OF BIRDS' EGGS

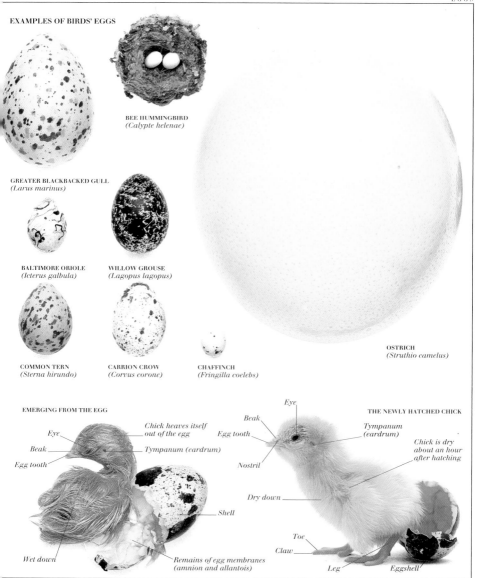

BEE HUMMINGBIRD
(Calypte helenae)

GREATER BLACKBACKED GULL
(Larus marinus)

BALTIMORE ORIOLE
(Icterus galbula)

WILLOW GROUSE
(Lagopus lagopus)

COMMON TERN
(Sterna hirundo)

CARRION CROW
(Corvus corone)

CHAFFINCH
(Fringilla coelebs)

OSTRICH
(Struthio camelus)

EMERGING FROM THE EGG

Chick heaves itself out of the egg

Eye

Beak

Egg tooth

Tympanum (eardrum)

Shell

Remains of egg membranes (amnion and allantois)

Wet down

THE NEWLY HATCHED CHICK

Eye

Beak

Egg tooth

Nostril

Tympanum (eardrum)

Chick is dry about an hour after hatching

Dry down

Toe

Claw

Leg

Eggshell

Carnivores

THE MAMMALIAN ORDER CARNIVORA includes cats, dogs, bears, raccoons, pandas, weasels, badgers, skunks, otters, civets, mongooses, and hyenas. The order's name is derived from the fact that most of its members are carnivores (flesh-eaters). Typical carnivore features therefore reflect a hunting lifestyle: speed and agility; sharp claws and well-developed canine teeth for holding and killing prey; carnassial teeth (cheek teeth) for cutting flesh; and forward-facing eyes for good distance judgment. However, some members of the order—bears, badgers, and foxes, for example—have a more mixed diet, and a few are entirely herbivorous (plant-eating), notably pandas. Such animals have no carnassial teeth and tend to be slower-moving than pure flesh-eaters.

EXTERNAL FEATURES OF A MALE LION

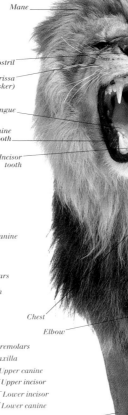

Nose
Eye
Mane
Nostril
Vibrissa (whisker)
Tongue
Canine tooth
Incisor tooth
Chest
Elbow
Lower arm
Toe

SKULL OF A LION

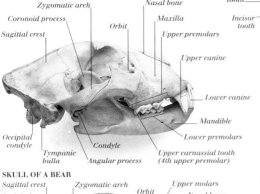

Zygomatic arch
Coronoid process
Nasal bone
Orbit
Maxilla
Sagittal crest
Upper premolars
Upper canine
Lower canine
Mandible
Lower premolars
Occipital condyle
Tympanic bulla
Condyle
Angular process
Upper carnassial tooth (4th upper premolar)

SKULL OF A BEAR

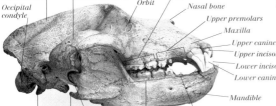

Sagittal crest
Zygomatic arch
Orbit
Upper molars
Occipital condyle
Nasal bone
Upper premolars
Maxilla
Upper canine
Upper incisor
Lower incisor
Lower canine
Mandible
Tympanic bulla
Angular process
Condyle
Lower premolars
Lower molars

EXAMPLES OF CARNIVORES

GERMAN SHEPHERD DOG
(Canis familiaris)

MANED WOLF
(Chrysocyon brachyurus)

RACCOON
(Procyon lotor)

AMERICAN BLACK BEAR
(Ursus americanus)

SKELETON OF A DOMESTIC CAT

Back

Rump

Hip

Rib cage

Caudal vertebrae

Sacrum

Lumbar vertebrae

Thoracic vertebrae

Cervical vertebrae

Skull

Pelvis

Femur

Scapula

Sternum

Humerus

Patella

Rib

Fibula

Ulna

Tibia

Radius

Carpals

Tarsals

Metatarsals

Metacarpals

Belly

Thigh

Phalanges

Knee

INTERNAL ANATOMY OF A MALE DOMESTIC CAT

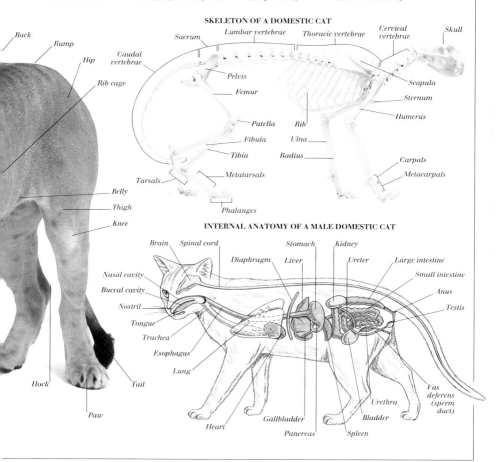

Brain

Spinal cord

Stomach

Kidney

Diaphragm

Liver

Ureter

Large intestine

Nasal cavity

Small intestine

Buccal cavity

Anus

Nostril

Testis

Tongue

Trachea

Esophagus

Lung

Hock

Tail

Vas deferens (sperm duct)

Paw

Urethra

Heart

Gallbladder

Bladder

Pancreas

Spleen

Rabbits and rodents

ALTHOUGH RABBITS AND RODENTS belong to different orders of mammals, they have some features in common. These features include chisel-shaped incisor teeth that grow continually, and eating their feces to extract more nutrients from their plant diet. Rabbits and hares belong to the order Lagomorpha. Characteristically, they have four incisors in the upper jaw and two in the lower jaw; powerful hind legs for jumping; forelimbs adapted for burrowing; long ears; and a small tail. Rodents make up the order Rodentia. This is the largest order of mammals, with more than 1,700 species, including squirrels, beavers, chipmunks, gophers, rats, mice, lemmings, gerbils, porcupines, cavies, and the capybara. Typical rodent features include two incisors in each jaw; short forelimbs for manipulating food; and cheek pouches for storing food.

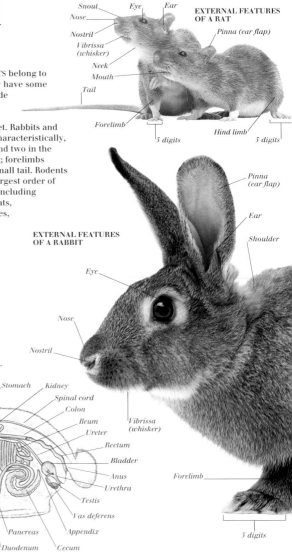

EXTERNAL FEATURES OF A RAT

Snout
Eye
Ear
Nose
Nostril
Vibrissa (whisker)
Neck
Mouth
Tail
Pinna (ear flap)
Forelimb
5 digits
Hind limb
5 digits

EXTERNAL FEATURES OF A RABBIT

Pinna (ear flap)
Ear
Shoulder
Eye
Nose
Nostril
Vibrissa (whisker)
Forelimb
5 digits

INTERNAL ANATOMY OF A MALE RABBIT

Gallbladder
Brain
Liver
Stomach
Kidney
Spinal cord
Colon
Ileum
Ureter
Rectum
Bladder
Anus
Urethra
Testis
Vas deferens
Appendix
Cecum
Duodenum
Pancreas
Heart
Diaphragm
Trachea
Lung
Esophagus
Tongue
Buccal cavity
Mouth
Nasal cavity

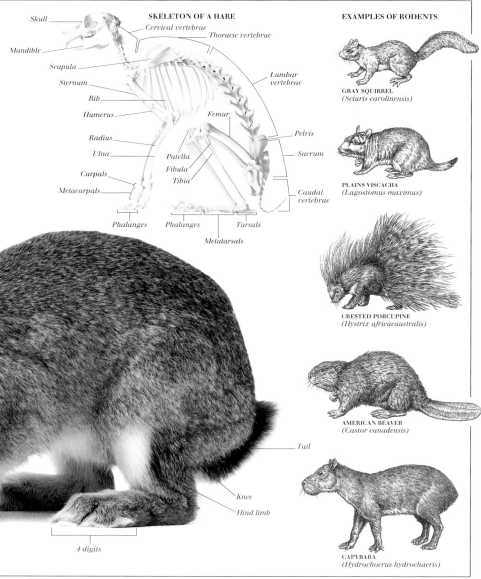

SKELETON OF A HARE

Skull

Mandible

Cervical vertebrae

Thoracic vertebrae

Scapula

Lumbar vertebrae

Sternum

Rib

Humerus

Femur

Radius

Pelvis

Ulna

Sacrum

Patella

Carpals

Fibula

Metacarpals

Tibia

Caudal vertebrae

Phalanges

Phalanges

Tarsals

Metatarsals

Tail

Knee

Hind limb

4 digits

EXAMPLES OF RODENTS

GRAY SQUIRREL
(*Sciuris carolinensis*)

PLAINS VISCACHA
(*Lagostomus maximus*)

CRESTED PORCUPINE
(*Hystrix africaeaustralis*)

AMERICAN BEAVER
(*Castor canadensis*)

CAPYBARA
(*Hydrochoerus hydrochaeris*)

Ungulates

UNGULATES IS A GENERAL TERM FOR a large, varied group of mammals that includes horses, cattle, and their relatives. The ungulates are divided into two orders on the basis of the number of toes. Members of the order Perissodactyla (odd-toed ungulates) have one or three toes. Perissodactyls include horses, asses, and zebras (all of which are one-toed), and rhinoceroses and tapirs (which are three-toed). Members of the order Artiodactyla (even-toed ungulates) have two or four toes. Most artiodactyls have two toes, which are typically encased in hooves to give the so-called cloven hoof. Two-toed, cloven-hoofed artiodactyls include cows and other cattle, sheep, goats, antelopes, deer, and giraffes. The other main two-toed artiodactyls are camels and llamas. Most two-toed artiodactyls are ruminants; that is, they have a four-chambered stomach and chew the cud. The principal four-toed artiodactyls are hogs and hippopotamuses.

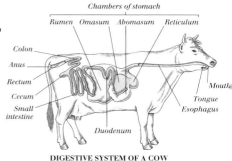

Chambers of stomach

Rumen   Omasum   Abomasum   Reticulum

Colon

Anus

Rectum   Mouth

Cecum   Tongue

Small   Esophagus
intestine

Duodenum

DIGESTIVE SYSTEM OF A COW

**COMPARISON OF THE FRONT FEET
OF A HORSE AND A COW**

SKELETON OF THE LEFT
FRONT FOOT OF A HORSE

SKELETON OF THE RIGHT
FRONT FOOT OF A COW

2nd metacarpal
(splint bone)

3rd metacarpal
(cannon bone)

Fused 3rd and
4th metacarpals

Sesamoid
bone

Sesamoid
bone

Phalanges of
3rd digit

Phalanges of
3rd digit

Hoof bone

Phalanges
of 4th digit

Hoof bone of 3rd digit

Hoof bone of
4th digit

Croup   Back

Loin

Root of tail

Buttock

Tail

Thigh

Flank

Stifle   Belly

Gaskin

Hock

Shannon bone
(cannon bone)

Coronet

Pastern

Heel   Hoof

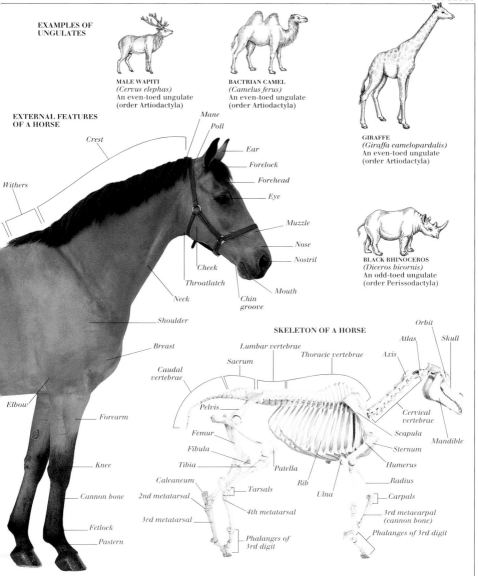

**EXAMPLES OF
UNGULATES**

MALE WAPITI
(Cervus elephas)
An even-toed ungulate
(order Artiodactyla)

BACTRIAN CAMEL
(Camelus ferus)
An even-toed ungulate
(order Artiodactyla)

GIRAFFE
(Giraffa camelopardalis)
An even-toed ungulate
(order Artiodactyla)

**EXTERNAL FEATURES
OF A HORSE**

Mane

Poll

Crest

Ear

Forelock

Forehead

Withers

Eye

Muzzle

Nose

Nostril

Cheek

Throatlatch

Neck

Chin
groove

Mouth

Shoulder

BLACK RHINOCEROS
(Diceros bicornis)
An odd-toed ungulate
(order Perissodactyla)

Breast

Elbow

Forearm

Knee

Cannon bone

Fetlock

Pastern

SKELETON OF A HORSE

Orbit

Atlas

Skull

Lumbar vertebrae

Thoracic vertebrae

Axis

Sacrum

Caudal
vertebrae

Cervical
vertebrae

Pelvis

Mandible

Femur

Scapula

Fibula

Sternum

Tibia

Patella

Humerus

Calcaneum

Radius

2nd metatarsal

Tarsals

Rib

Ulna

Carpals

4th metatarsal

3rd metatarsal

3rd metacarpal
(cannon bone)

Phalanges of
3rd digit

Phalanges of 3rd digit

Elephants

THE TWO SPECIES OF elephants—African and Asian—are the only members of the mammalian order Proboscidea. The bigger African elephant is the largest land animal: a fully grown male may be up to 13 ft (4m) tall and weigh as much as 7.7 tons (7 tonnes). A fully grown male Asian elephant may be 11 ft (3.3 m) tall and weigh 6 tons (5.4 tonnes). The muscular trunk—an extension of the nose and upper lip—is the elephant's most obvious feature. It is used for manipulating and lifting, feeding, drinking and spraying water, smelling, touching, and producing trumpeting sounds. Other characteristic features of this mighty plant-eater include a pair of ivory tusks, used for defense and for crushing vegetation; thick, pillar-like legs and broad feet to support the massive body; and large ear flaps that act as radiators to keep the elephant cool.

DIFFERENCES BETWEEN AFRICAN AND ASIAN ELEPHANTS

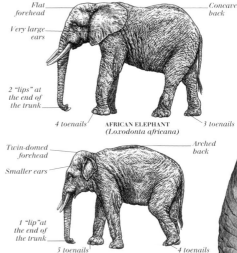

Flat forehead
Very large ears
2 "lips" at the end of the trunk
4 toenails

AFRICAN ELEPHANT
(*Loxodonta africana*)

Concave back
3 toenails

Twin-domed forehead
Smaller ears
1 "lip" at the end of the trunk
5 toenails

Arched back
4 toenails

ASIAN ELEPHANT
(*Elephas maximus*)

INTERNAL ANATOMY OF A FEMALE ELEPHANT

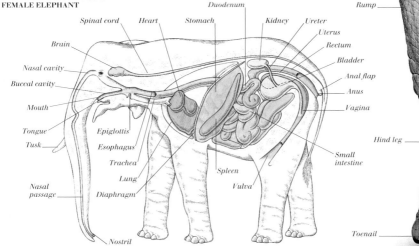

Spinal cord
Heart
Stomach
Duodenum
Kidney
Ureter
Rump

Brain
Uterus
Rectum

Nasal cavity
Bladder

Buccal cavity
Anal flap
Anus

Mouth
Vagina

Tongue
Tusk
Epiglottis
Esophagus
Trachea
Lung
Diaphragm
Hind leg
Spleen
Small intestine
Vulva

Nasal passage

Nostril

Toenail

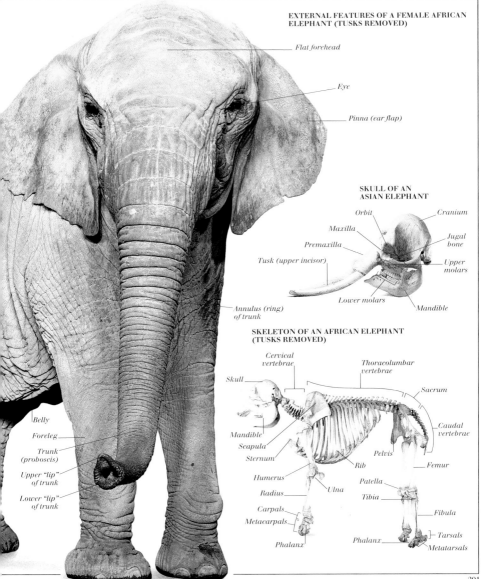

EXTERNAL FEATURES OF A FEMALE AFRICAN ELEPHANT (TUSKS REMOVED)

Flat forehead

Eye

Pinna (ear flap)

Belly

Foreleg

Trunk (proboscis)

Upper "lip" of trunk

Lower "lip" of trunk

Annulus (ring) of trunk

SKULL OF AN ASIAN ELEPHANT

Orbit

Cranium

Maxilla

Jugal bone

Premaxilla

Upper molars

Tusk (upper incisor)

Lower molars

Mandible

SKELETON OF AN AFRICAN ELEPHANT (TUSKS REMOVED)

Cervical vertebrae

Thoracolumbar vertebrae

Skull

Sacrum

Mandible

Caudal vertebrae

Scapula

Sternum

Pelvis

Rib

Femur

Humerus

Patella

Radius

Ulna

Tibia

Carpals

Fibula

Metacarpals

Tarsals

Phalanx

Metatarsals

Phalanx

201

Primates

THE MAMMALIAN ORDER PRIMATES consists of monkeys, apes, and their relatives (including humans). There are two suborders of primates: Prosimii, the primitive primates, which include lemurs, tarsiers, and lorises; and Anthropoidea, the advanced primates, which include monkeys, apes, and humans. The anthropoids are divided into New World monkeys, Old World monkeys, and hominids. New World monkeys typically have widespread nostrils that open to the side; and long tails, which are prehensile (grasping) in some species. This group of monkeys lives in South America, and includes marmosets, tamarins, and howler monkeys. Old World monkeys typically have close-set nostrils that open forward or downward and nonprehensile tails. This group of monkeys lives in Africa and Asia, and includes langurs, mandrills, macaques, and baboons. Hominids typically have large brains and no tail. This group includes the apes—chimpanzees, gibbons, gorillas, and orangutans—and humans.

INTERNAL ANATOMY OF A FEMALE CHIMPANZEE

- Buccal cavity
- Brain
- Nasal cavity
- Tongue
- Spinal cord
- Trachea
- Esophagus
- Lung
- Heart
- Liver
- Diaphragm
- Stomach
- Pancreas
- Spleen
- Small intestine
- Large intestine
- Cecum
- Rectum
- Appendix
- Bladder
- Ovary
- Urethra
- Uterus
- Vagina

SKELETON OF A RHESUS MONKEY

- Skull
- Orbit
- Cervical vertebrae
- Thoracic vertebrae
- Mandible
- Clavicle
- Scapula
- Rib
- Humerus
- Lumbar vertebrae
- Radius
- Ulna
- Femur
- Sacrum
- Patella
- Tibia
- Carpals
- Metacarpals
- Fibula
- Pelvis
- Caudal vertebrae
- Tarsals
- Metatarsals
- Phalanges
- Phalanges

SKULL OF A CHIMPANZEE

- Temporal bone
- Suture
- Frontal bone
- Parietal bone
- Supraorbital ridge
- Orbit
- Occipital bone
- Maxilla
- Premaxilla
- Auditory meatus
- Incisor tooth
- Zygomatic arch
- Canine tooth
- Mandible
- Molar tooth
- Premolar tooth

EXAMPLES OF PRIMATES

RING-TAILED LEMUR
(Lemur catta)
A prosimian

MALE RED HOWLER MONKEY
(Alouatta seniculus)
A New World monkey

MALE MANDRILL
(Mandrillus sphinx)
An Old World monkey

CHIMPANZEE
(Pan troglodytes)
An ape

**EXTERNAL FEATURES OF
A YOUNG GORILLA**

GOLDEN LION TAMARIN
(Leontopithecus rosalia)
A New World monkey

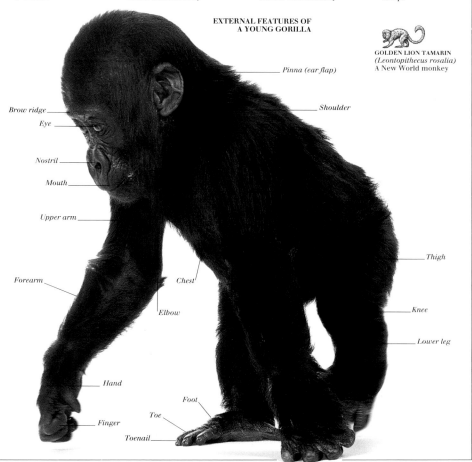

Pinna (ear flap)

Brow ridge

Shoulder

Eye

Nostril

Mouth

Upper arm

Thigh

Forearm

Chest

Knee

Elbow

Lower leg

Hand

Foot

Toe

Finger

Toenail

Dolphins, whales, and seals

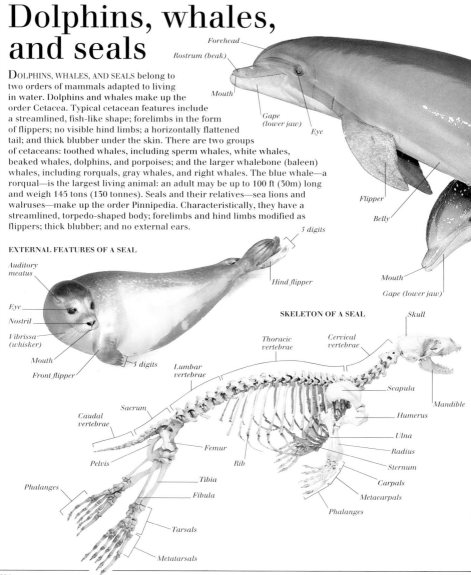

DOLPHINS, WHALES, AND SEALS belong to two orders of mammals adapted to living in water. Dolphins and whales make up the order Cetacea. Typical cetacean features include a streamlined, fish-like shape; forelimbs in the form of flippers; no visible hind limbs; a horizontally flattened tail; and thick blubber under the skin. There are two groups of cetaceans: toothed whales, including sperm whales, white whales, beaked whales, dolphins, and porpoises; and the larger whalebone (baleen) whales, including rorquals, gray whales, and right whales. The blue whale—a rorqual—is the largest living animal: an adult may be up to 100 ft (30m) long and weigh 145 tons (130 tonnes). Seals and their relatives—sea lions and walruses—make up the order Pinnipedia. Characteristically, they have a streamlined, torpedo-shaped body; forelimbs and hind limbs modified as flippers; thick blubber; and no external ears.

Forehead
Rostrum (beak)
Mouth
Gape (lower jaw)
Eye
Flipper
Belly
Mouth
Gape (lower jaw)

EXTERNAL FEATURES OF A SEAL

5 digits
Auditory meatus
Hind flipper
Eye
Nostril
Vibrissa (whisker)
Mouth
Front flipper
5 digits

SKELETON OF A SEAL

Skull
Thoracic vertebrae
Cervical vertebrae
Lumbar vertebrae
Scapula
Mandible
Caudal vertebrae
Humerus
Sacrum
Ulna
Femur
Radius
Pelvis
Rib
Sternum
Phalanges
Carpals
Tibia
Metacarpals
Fibula
Phalanges
Tarsals
Metatarsals

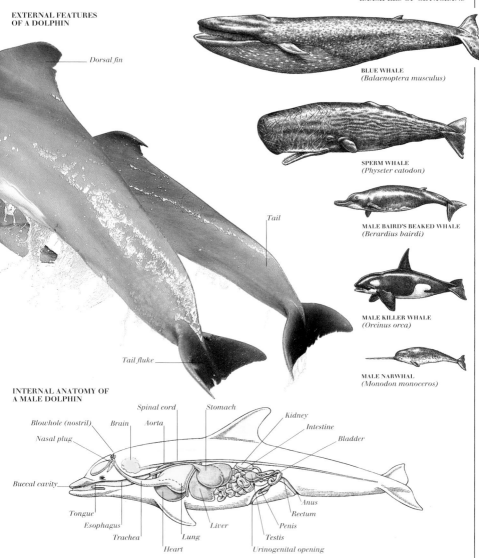

EXAMPLES OF CETACEANS

BLUE WHALE
(Balaenoptera musculus)

SPERM WHALE
(Physeter catodon)

MALE BAIRD'S BEAKED WHALE
(Berardius bairdi)

MALE KILLER WHALE
(Orcinus orca)

MALE NARWHAL
(Monodon monoceros)

EXTERNAL FEATURES OF A DOLPHIN

Dorsal fin

Tail

Tail fluke

INTERNAL ANATOMY OF A MALE DOLPHIN

Spinal cord

Stomach

Kidney

Blowhole (nostril)

Brain

Aorta

Intestine

Nasal plug

Bladder

Buccal cavity

Anus

Rectum

Tongue

Penis

Esophagus

Testis

Trachea

Urinogenital opening

Heart

Lung

Liver

Marsupials and Monotremes

MARSUPIALS AND MONOTREMES are two orders of mammals that differ from other mammalian groups in the ways that their young develop. The order Marsupalia, the pouched mammals, is made up of kangaroos and their relatives. Typically, marsupials give birth to their young at a very early stage of development. The young then crawls to the mother's pouch (which is on the outside of her abdomen), where it attaches itself to a nipple and remains until fully developed. Most marsupials live in Australia, although the opossums—which are classified as marsupials despite not having a pouch—live in the Americas. The order Monotremata is made up of the platypus and its relatives (the echidnas, or spiny anteaters). The monotremes are primitive mammals that lay eggs, which the mother incubates. The monotremes are found only in Australia and New Guinea.

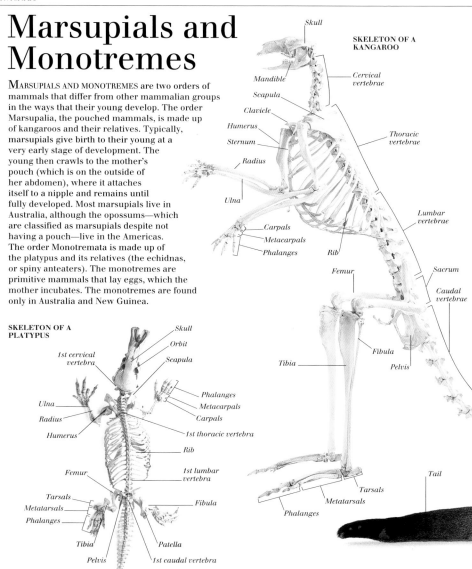

SKELETON OF A KANGAROO

Skull
Mandible
Cervical vertebrae
Scapula
Clavicle
Humerus
Sternum
Radius
Thoracic vertebrae
Ulna
Lumbar vertebrae
Carpals
Metacarpals
Phalanges
Rib
Femur
Sacrum
Caudal vertebrae
Fibula
Tibia
Pelvis
Tarsals
Metatarsals
Phalanges
Tail

SKELETON OF A PLATYPUS

Skull
Orbit
1st cervical vertebra
Scapula
Phalanges
Metacarpals
Carpals
Ulna
Radius
1st thoracic vertebra
Humerus
Rib
Femur
1st lumbar vertebra
Tarsals
Metatarsals
Fibula
Phalanges
Tibia
Patella
Pelvis
1st caudal vertebra

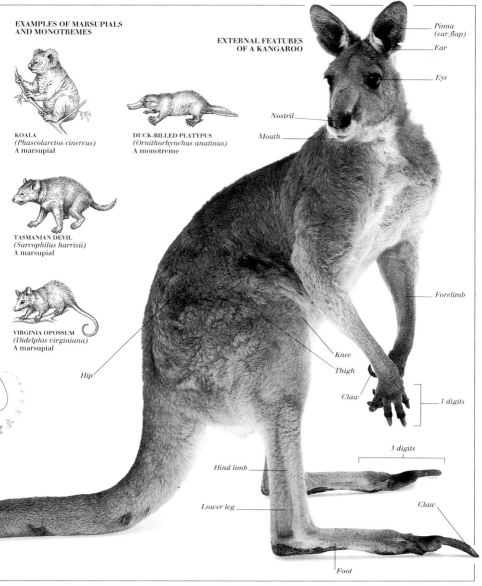

**EXAMPLES OF MARSUPIALS
AND MONOTREMES**

**EXTERNAL FEATURES
OF A KANGAROO**

KOALA
(Phascolarctos cinereus)
A marsupial

DUCK-BILLED PLATYPUS
(Ornithorhynchus anatinus)
A monotreme

TASMANIAN DEVIL
(Sarcophilus harrisii)
A marsupial

VIRGINIA OPOSSUM
(Didelphis virginiana)
A marsupial

Pinna
(ear flap)

Ear

Eye

Nostril

Mouth

Forelimb

Knee

Thigh

Claw

5 digits

3 digits

Hip

Hind limb

Lower leg

Claw

Foot

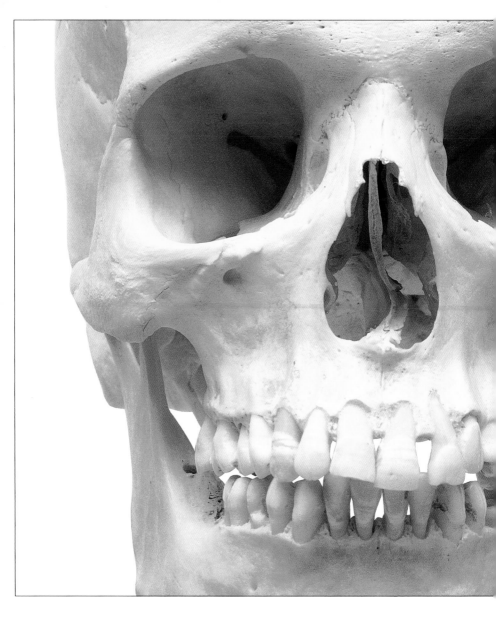

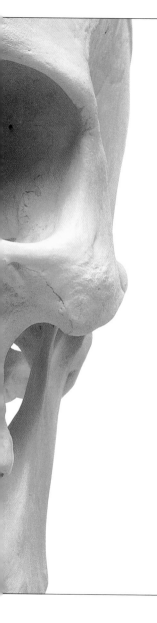

THE HUMAN BODY

Body features

ALTHOUGH THERE IS enormous variation between the external appearances of humans, all bodies contain the same basic features. The outward form of the human body depends on the size of the skeleton, the shape of the muscles, the thickness of the fat layer beneath the skin, the elasticity or sagginess of the skin, and the person's age and gender. Males tend to be taller than females, with broader shoulders, more body hair, and a different pattern of fat deposits under the skin; the female body tends to be less muscular and has a shallower and wider pelvis to allow for childbirth.

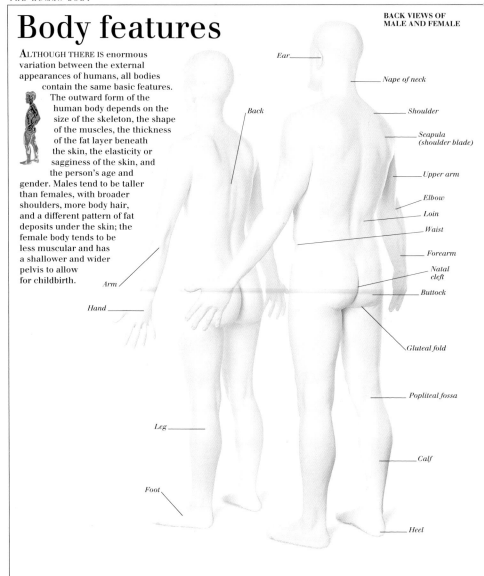

Ear

Nape of neck

Shoulder

Scapula
(shoulder blade)

Upper arm

Elbow

Loin

Waist

Forearm

Natal
cleft

Buttock

Back

Arm

Hand

Gluteal fold

Popliteal fossa

Leg

Calf

Foot

Heel

**FRONT VIEWS OF
MALE AND FEMALE**

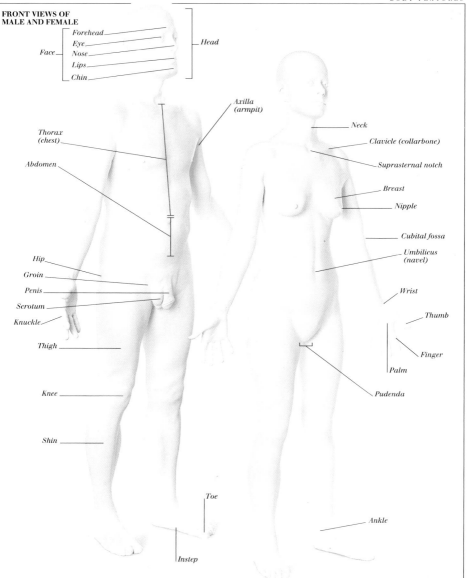

Head

Face — Forehead
Eye
Nose
Lips
Chin

Axilla
(armpit)

Thorax
(chest)

Abdomen

Hip

Groin

Penis

Scrotum

Knuckle

Thigh

Knee

Shin

Toe

Instep

Neck

Clavicle (collarbone)

Suprasternal notch

Breast

Nipple

Cubital fossa

Umbilicus
(navel)

Wrist

Thumb

Finger

Palm

Pudenda

Ankle

Head

IN A NEWBORN BABY, the head accounts for one quarter of the total body length; by adulthood, the proportion has reduced to one eighth. Contained in the head are the body's main sense organs: eyes, ears, olfactory nerves that detect smells, and the taste buds of the tongue. Signals from these organs pass to the body's great coordination center: the brain, housed in the protective, bony dome of the skull. Hair on the head insulates against heat loss, and adult males also grow thick facial hair. The face has three important openings: two nostrils through which air passes, and the mouth, which takes in nourishment and helps form speech. Although all heads are basically similar, differences in the size, shape, and color of features produce an infinite variety of appearances.

SIDE VIEW OF EXTERNAL FEATURES OF HEAD

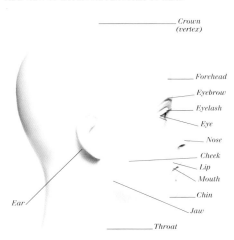

Crown (vertex)

Forehead

Eyebrow

Eyelash

Eye

Nose

Cheek

Lip

Mouth

Chin

Jaw

Ear

Throat

SECTION THROUGH HEAD

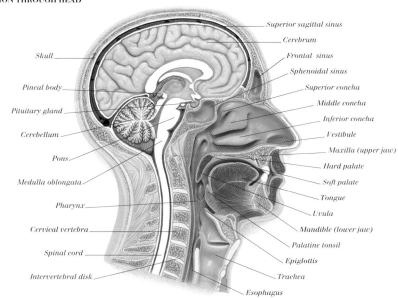

Skull

Pineal body

Pituitary gland

Cerebellum

Pons

Medulla oblongata

Pharynx

Cervical vertebra

Spinal cord

Intervertebral disk

Superior sagittal sinus

Cerebrum

Frontal sinus

Sphenoidal sinus

Superior concha

Middle concha

Inferior concha

Vestibule

Maxilla (upper jaw)

Hard palate

Soft palate

Tongue

Uvula

Mandible (lower jaw)

Palatine tonsil

Epiglottis

Trachea

Esophagus

**FRONT VIEW OF EXTERNAL
FEATURES OF HEAD**

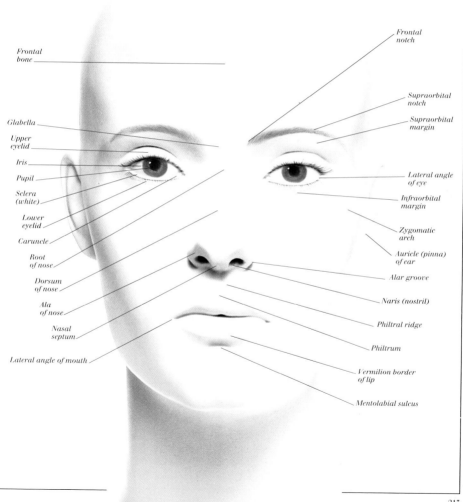

Frontal
notch

Frontal
bone

Supraorbital
notch

Supraorbital
margin

Glabella

Upper
eyelid

Iris

Pupil

Lateral angle
of eye

Sclera
(white)

Infraorbital
margin

Lower
eyelid

Zygomatic
arch

Caruncle

Auricle (pinna)
of ear

Root
of nose

Alar groove

Dorsum
of nose

Naris (nostril)

Ala
of nose

Philtral ridge

Nasal
septum

Philtrum

Lateral angle of mouth

Vermilion border
of lip

Mentolabial sulcus

Body organs

ALL THE VITAL BODY ORGANS except for the brain are enclosed within the trunk or torso (the body apart from the head and limbs). The trunk contains two large cavities separated by a muscular sheet called the diaphragm. The upper cavity, known as the thorax or chest cavity, contains the heart and lungs. The lower cavity, called the abdominal cavity, contains the stomach, intestines, liver, and pancreas, which all play a role in digesting food. Also within the trunk are the kidneys and bladder, which are part of the urinary system, and the reproductive organs, which hold the seeds of new human life. Modern imaging techniques, such as contrast X-rays and different types of scans, make it possible to see and study body organs without the need to cut through their protective coverings of skin, fat, muscle, and bone.

MAJOR INTERNAL STRUCTURES

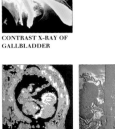

Thyroid gland

Larynx

Heart

Right lung

Left lung

Diaphragm

Liver

Stomach

Large intestine

Small intestine

Greater omentum

IMAGING THE BODY

SCINTIGRAM OF HEART CHAMBERS

ANGIOGRAM OF RIGHT LUNG

CONTRAST X-RAY OF GALLBLADDER

SCINTIGRAM OF NERVOUS SYSTEM

DOUBLE CONTRAST X-RAY OF COLON

ULTRASOUND SCAN OF TWINS IN UTERUS

ANGIOGRAM OF KIDNEYS

ANGIOGRAM OF ARTERIES OF HEAD

CT SCAN THROUGH FEMALE CHEST

THERMOGRAM OF CHEST REGION

ANGIOGRAM OF ARTERIES OF HEART

MRI SCAN THROUGH HEAD AT EYE LEVEL

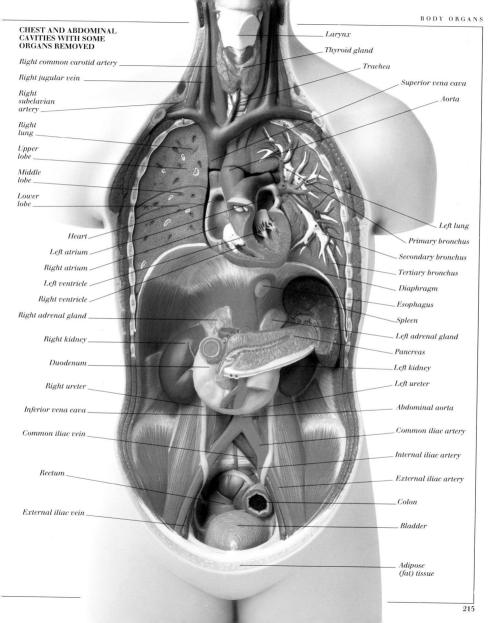

CHEST AND ABDOMINAL CAVITIES WITH SOME ORGANS REMOVED

Right common carotid artery

Right jugular vein

Right subclavian artery

Right lung

Upper lobe

Middle lobe

Lower lobe

Heart

Left atrium

Right atrium

Left ventricle

Right ventricle

Right adrenal gland

Right kidney

Duodenum

Right ureter

Inferior vena cava

Common iliac vein

Rectum

External iliac vein

Larynx

Thyroid gland

Trachea

Superior vena cava

Aorta

Left lung

Primary bronchus

Secondary bronchus

Tertiary bronchus

Diaphragm

Esophagus

Spleen

Left adrenal gland

Pancreas

Left kidney

Left ureter

Abdominal aorta

Common iliac artery

Internal iliac artery

External iliac artery

Colon

Bladder

Adipose (fat) tissue

Body cells

EVERYONE IS MADE UP OF BILLIONS OF CELLS, which are the basic structural units of the body. Bones, muscles, nerves, skin, blood, and all other body tissues are formed from different types of cells. Each cell has a specific function but works with other types of cells to perform the enormous number of tasks needed to sustain life. Most body cells have a similar basic structure. Each cell has an outer layer (called the cell membrane) and contains a fluid material (cytoplasm). Within the cytoplasm are many specialized structures (organelles). The most important organelle is the nucleus, which contains vital genetic material and acts as the cell's control center.

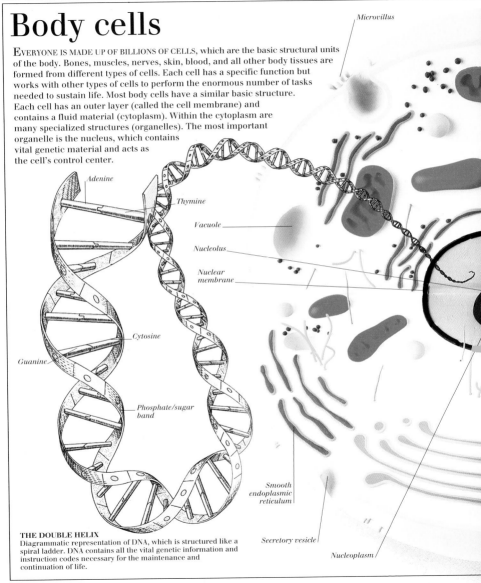

Microvillus

Adenine

Thymine

Vacuole

Nucleolus

Nuclear membrane

Cytosine

Guanine

Phosphate/sugar band

Smooth endoplasmic reticulum

Secretory vesicle

Nucleoplasm

THE DOUBLE HELIX
Diagrammatic representation of DNA, which is structured like a spiral ladder. DNA contains all the vital genetic information and instruction codes necessary for the maintenance and continuation of life.

GENERALIZED HUMAN CELL

Cytoplasm

Lysosome

Cell membrane

Mitochondrial crista

Nucleus

Rough endoplasmic reticulum

Microfilament

Pore of nuclear membrane

Ribosome

Centriole

Mitochondrion

Microtubule

Peroxisome

Pinocytotic vesicle

Golgi complex (Golgi apparatus; Golgi body)

TYPES OF CELLS

BONE-FORMING CELL

NERVE CELLS IN SPINAL CORD

SPERM CELLS IN SEMEN

SECRETORY THYROID GLAND CELLS

ACID-SECRETING STOMACH CELLS

CONNECTIVE TISSUE CELLS

MUCUS-SECRETING DUODENAL CELLS

RED AND TWO WHITE BLOOD CELLS

FAT CELLS IN ADIPOSE TISSUE

EPITHELIAL CELLS IN CHEEK

Skeleton

THE SKELETON IS A MOBILE FRAMEWORK made up of 206 bones, approximately half of which are in the hands and feet. Although individual bones are rigid, the skeleton as a whole is remarkably flexible and allows the human body a huge range of movement. The skeleton serves as an anchorage for the skeletal muscles, and as a protective cage for the body's internal organs. Female bones are usually smaller and lighter than male bones, and the female pelvis is shallower and has a wider cavity.

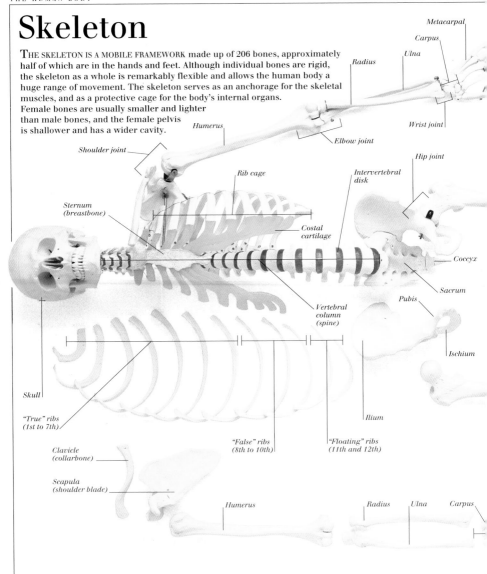

Metacarpal

Carpus

Ulna

Radius

Humerus

Shoulder joint

Elbow joint

Wrist joint

Hip joint

Rib cage

Intervertebral disk

Sternum (breastbone)

Costal cartilage

Coccyx

Sacrum

Pubis

Vertebral column (spine)

Ischium

Skull

Ilium

"True" ribs (1st to 7th)

"False" ribs (8th to 10th)

"Floating" ribs (11th and 12th)

Clavicle (collarbone)

Scapula (shoulder blade)

Humerus

Radius

Ulna

Carpus

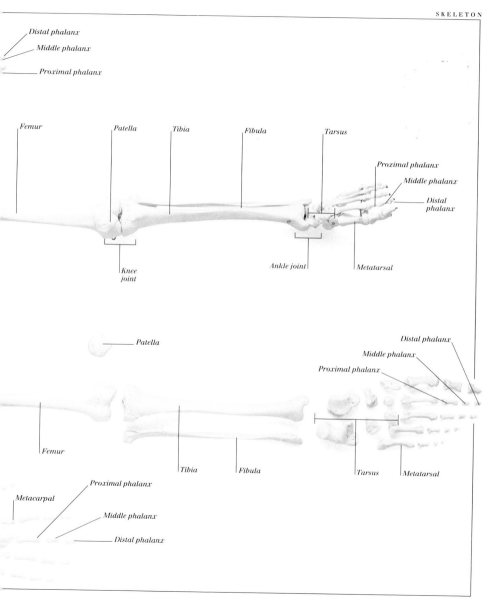

Distal phalanx

Middle phalanx

Proximal phalanx

Femur

Patella

Tibia

Fibula

Tarsus

Proximal phalanx

Middle phalanx

Distal phalanx

Knee joint

Ankle joint

Metatarsal

Patella

Distal phalanx

Middle phalanx

Proximal phalanx

Femur

Tibia

Fibula

Tarsus

Metatarsal

Metacarpal

Proximal phalanx

Middle phalanx

Distal phalanx

Skull

THE SKULL is the most complicated bony structure of the body—but every feature serves a purpose. Internally, the main hollow chamber of the skull has three levels that support the brain, with every bump and hollow corresponding to the shape of the brain. Underneath and toward the back of the skull is a large round hole, called the foramen magnum, through which the spinal cord passes. To the front of this are many smaller openings through which nerves, arteries, and veins pass to and from the brain. The roof of the skull is formed from four thin, curved bones that are firmly fixed together from the age of about two years. At the front of the skull are two orbits, which contain the eyeballs, and a central hole for the airway of the nose. The jawbone hinges on either side of the skull at ear level.

RIGHT SIDE VIEW OF A FETAL SKULL

Anterior fontanelle

Parietal bone

Coronal suture

Frontal bone

Nasal bone

Mental symphysis

Lambdoid suture

Occipital bone

Sphenoidal fontanelle

Mastoid fontanelle

External auditory meatus

RIGHT SIDE VIEW OF SKULL

Coronal suture

Frontal bone

Greater wing of sphenoid bone

Frontozygomatic suture

Parietal bone

Supraorbital margin

Squamous suture

Orbital cavity

Nasal bone

Anterior nasal spine

Maxilla (upper jaw)

Lambdoid suture

Occipital bone

Mandible (lower jaw)

Temporal bone

External auditory meatus

Condyle

Mastoid process

Coronoid process

Zygomatic bone

Mental foramen

VIEW OF SKULL FROM BELOW

External occipital crest

Foramen magnum

Occipital condyle

Carotid canal

Mastoid process

Pharyngeal tubercle

Pterygoid plate

Pterygoid hamulus

Greater palatine foramen

Styloid process

Zygomatic arch

Posterior border of vomer

Concha

Posterior nasal aperture

Mandible (lower jaw)

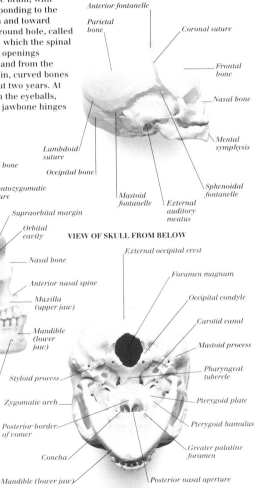

FRONT VIEW OF SKULL

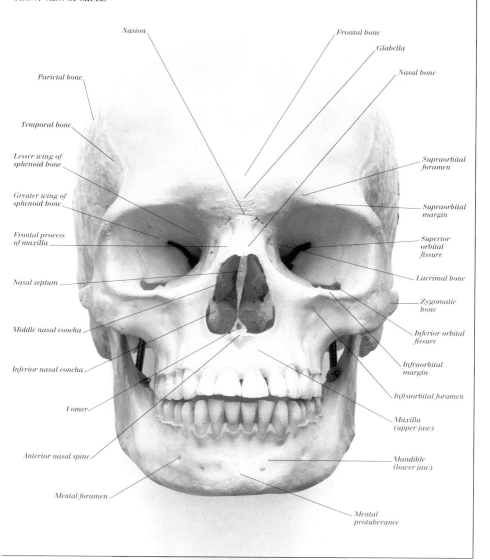

Nasion

Frontal bone

Glabella

Nasal bone

Parietal bone

Temporal bone

Lesser wing of
sphenoid bone

Greater wing of
sphenoid bone

Frontal process
of maxilla

Nasal septum

Middle nasal concha

Inferior nasal concha

Vomer

Anterior nasal spine

Mental foramen

Supraorbital
foramen

Supraorbital
margin

Superior
orbital
fissure

Lacrimal bone

Zygomatic
bone

Inferior orbital
fissure

Infraorbital
margin

Infraorbital foramen

Maxilla
(upper jaw)

Mandible
(lower jaw)

Mental
protuberance

Spine

THE SPINE (OR VERTEBRAL COLUMN) has two main functions: it serves as a protective surrounding for the delicate spinal cord and forms the supporting back bone of the skeleton. The spine consists of 24 separate differently shaped bones (vertebrae) with a curved, triangular bone (the sacrum) at the bottom. The sacrum is made up of fused vertebrae; at its lower end is a small tail-like structure made up of tiny bones collectively called the coccyx. Between each pair of vertebrae is a disc of cartilage that cushions the bones during movement. The top two vertebrae differ in appearance from the others and work as a pair: the first, called the atlas, rotates around a stout vertical peg on the second, the axis. This arrangement allows the skull to move freely up and down, and from side to side.

SPINE DIVIDED INTO VERTEBRAL SECTIONS   FRONT

- Cervical vertebrae
- Thoracic vertebrae
- Lumbar vertebrae
- Sacral vertebrae
- Coccygeal vertebrae

TYPES OF VERTEBRAE (VIEWED FROM ABOVE)

ATLAS
- Lateral mass with superior articular facet
- Anterior arch
- Posterior arch
- Anterior tubercle
- Posterior tubercle
- Vertebral foramen
- Transverse foramen
- Transverse process

AXIS
- Vertebral foramen
- Facet
- Dens
- Spinous process
- Lamina
- Transverse process and foramen

CERVICAL VERTEBRA
- Body
- Superior articular process
- Anterior tubercle
- Spinous process
- Posterior tubercle
- Vertebral foramen
- Transverse foramen

SKULL AND SPINE

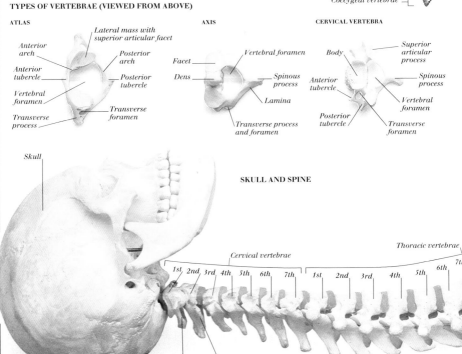

- Skull
- Cervical vertebrae
- Thoracic vertebrae
- 1st, 2nd, 3rd, 4th, 5th, 6th, 7th (Cervical vertebrae)
- 1st, 2nd, 3rd, 4th, 5th, 6th, 7th (Thoracic vertebrae)
- Atlas
- Axis

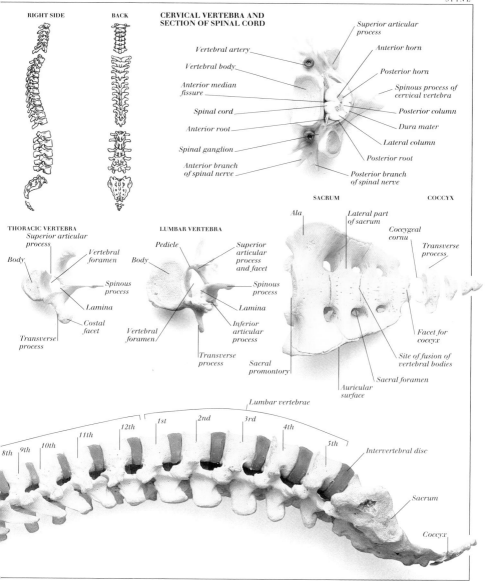

RIGHT SIDE

BACK

CERVICAL VERTEBRA AND SECTION OF SPINAL CORD

Vertebral artery

Vertebral body

Anterior median fissure

Spinal cord

Anterior root

Spinal ganglion

Anterior branch of spinal nerve

Superior articular process

Anterior horn

Posterior horn

Spinous process of cervical vertebra

Posterior column

Dura mater

Lateral column

Posterior root

Posterior branch of spinal nerve

SACRUM

COCCYX

Ala

Lateral part of sacrum

Coccygeal cornu

Transverse process

THORACIC VERTEBRA

Superior articular process

Vertebral foramen

Body

Spinous process

Lamina

Costal facet

Transverse process

LUMBAR VERTEBRA

Pedicle

Body

Superior articular process and facet

Spinous process

Lamina

Inferior articular process

Vertebral foramen

Transverse process

Sacral promontory

Auricular surface

Facet for coccyx

Site of fusion of vertebral bodies

Sacral foramen

Lumbar vertebrae

8th 9th 10th 11th 12th 1st 2nd 3rd 4th 5th

Intervertebral disc

Sacrum

Coccyx

Bones and joints

BONES FORM the body's hard, strong skeletal framework. Each bone has a hard, compact exterior surrounding a spongy, lighter interior. The long bones of the arms and legs, such as the femur (thigh bone), have a central cavity containing bone marrow. Bones are composed chiefly of calcium, phosphorus, and a fibrous substance known as collagen. Bones meet at joints, which are of several different types. For example, the hip is a ball-and-socket joint that allows the femur a wide range of movement, whereas finger joints are simple hinge joints that allow only bending and straightening. Joints are held in place by bands of tissue called ligaments. Movement of joints is facilitated by the smooth hyaline cartilage that covers the bone ends and by the synovial membrane that lines and lubricates the joint.

LIGAMENTS SURROUNDING HIP JOINT

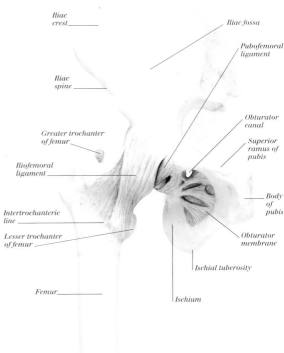

Iliac crest

Iliac fossa

Pubofemoral ligament

Iliac spine

Greater trochanter of femur

Obturator canal

Superior ramus of pubis

Iliofemoral ligament

Body of pubis

Intertrochanteric line

Lesser trochanter of femur

Obturator membrane

Ischial tuberosity

Femur

Ischium

SECTION THROUGH LEFT FEMUR

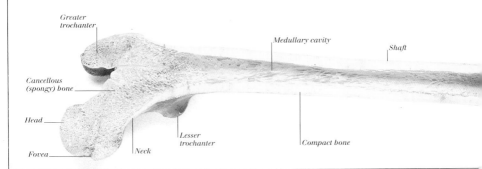

Greater trochanter

Medullary cavity

Shaft

Cancellous (spongy) bone

Head

Lesser trochanter

Compact bone

Fovea

Neck

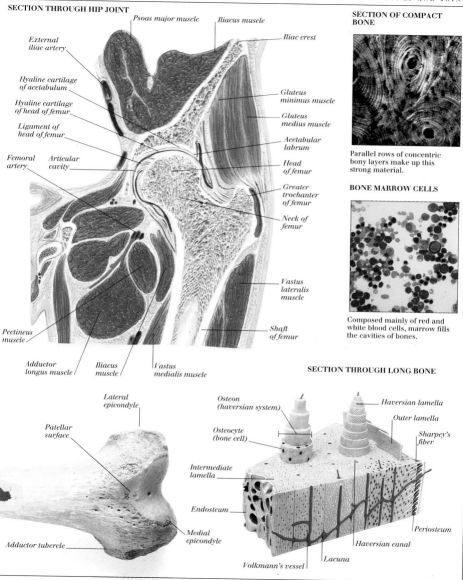

SECTION THROUGH HIP JOINT

Psoas major muscle

Iliacus muscle

External iliac artery

Iliac crest

Hyaline cartilage of acetabulum

Hyaline cartilage of head of femur

Ligament of head of femur

Gluteus minimus muscle

Gluteus medius muscle

Acetabular labrum

Femoral artery

Articular cavity

Head of femur

Greater trochanter of femur

Neck of femur

Vastus lateralis muscle

Pectineus muscle

Shaft of femur

Adductor longus muscle

Iliacus muscle

Vastus medialis muscle

SECTION OF COMPACT BONE

Parallel rows of concentric bony layers make up this strong material.

BONE MARROW CELLS

Composed mainly of red and white blood cells, marrow fills the cavities of bones.

SECTION THROUGH LONG BONE

Lateral epicondyle

Patellar surface

Medial epicondyle

Adductor tubercle

Osteon (haversian system)

Osteocyte (bone cell)

Intermediate lamella

Endosteum

Haversian lamella

Outer lamella

Sharpey's fiber

Periosteum

Haversian canal

Lacuna

Volkmann's vessel

225

Muscles 1

THERE ARE THREE MAIN TYPES OF MUSCLE: skeletal muscle (also called voluntary muscle because it can be consciously controlled); smooth muscle (also called involuntary muscle because it is not under voluntary control); and the specialized muscle tissue of the heart. Humans have more than 600 skeletal muscles, which differ in size and shape according to the jobs they do. Skeletal muscles are attached either directly or indirectly (via tendons) to bones, and work in opposing pairs (one muscle in the pair contracts while the other relaxes) to produce body movements as diverse as walking, threading a needle, and an array of facial expressions. Smooth muscles occur in the walls of internal body organs and perform actions such as forcing food through the intestines, contracting the uterus (womb) in childbirth, and pumping blood through the blood vessels.

SOME OTHER MUSCLES IN THE BODY

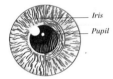

Iris
Pupil

IRIS
The muscle fibers contract and dilate (expand) to alter pupil size.

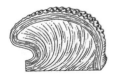

TONGUE
Interlacing layers of muscle allow great mobility.

ILEUM
Opposing muscle layers transport semidigested food.

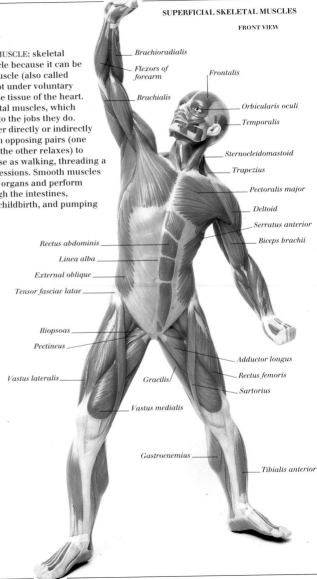

SUPERFICIAL SKELETAL MUSCLES

FRONT VIEW

Brachioradialis
Flexors of forearm
Frontalis
Brachialis
Orbicularis oculi
Temporalis
Sternocleidomastoid
Trapezius
Pectoralis major
Deltoid
Serratus anterior
Biceps brachii
Rectus abdominis
Linea alba
External oblique
Tensor fasciae latae
Iliopsoas
Pectineus
Adductor longus
Rectus femoris
Sartorius
Vastus lateralis
Gracilis
Vastus medialis
Gastrocnemius
Tibialis anterior

226

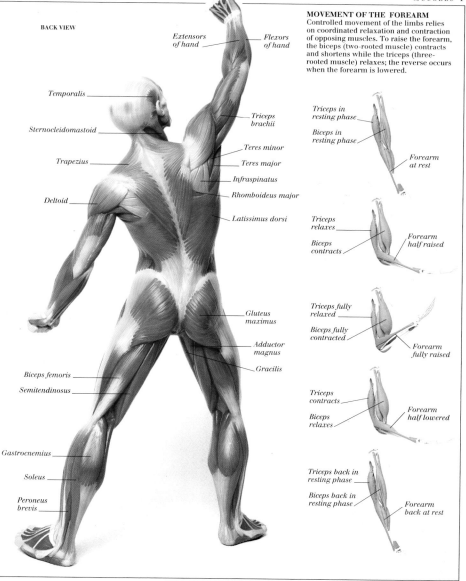

BACK VIEW

Extensors
of hand

Flexors
of hand

Temporalis

Sternocleidomastoid

Trapezius

Deltoid

Triceps
brachii

Teres minor

Teres major

Infraspinatus

Rhomboideus major

Latissimus dorsi

Gluteus
maximus

Adductor
magnus

Gracilis

Biceps femoris

Semitendinosus

Gastrocnemius

Soleus

Peroneus
brevis

MOVEMENT OF THE FOREARM
Controlled movement of the limbs relies
on coordinated relaxation and contraction
of opposing muscles. To raise the forearm,
the biceps (two-rooted muscle) contracts
and shortens while the triceps (three-
rooted muscle) relaxes; the reverse occurs
when the forearm is lowered.

Triceps in
resting phase

Biceps in
resting phase

Forearm
at rest

Triceps
relaxes

Biceps
contracts

Forearm
half raised

Triceps fully
relaxed

Biceps fully
contracted

Forearm
fully raised

Triceps
contracts

Biceps
relaxes

Forearm
half lowered

Triceps back in
resting phase

Biceps back in
resting phase

Forearm
back at rest

Muscles 2

SKELETAL MUSCLE FIBER

Myofibril

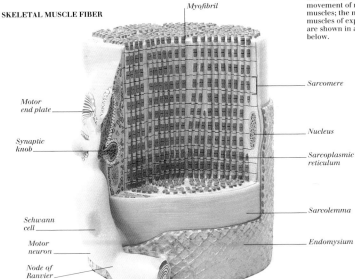

Motor end plate

Synaptic knob

Schwann cell

Motor neuron

Node of Ranvier

Sarcomere

Nucleus

Sarcoplasmic reticulum

Sarcolemma

Endomysium

MUSCLES OF FACIAL EXPRESSION
A single expression is the result of movement of many muscles; the main muscles of expression are shown in action below.

FRONTALIS

CORRUGATOR SUPERCILII

ORBICULARIS ORIS

ZYGOMATICUS MAJOR

DEPRESSOR ANGULI ORIS

TYPES OF MUSCLE

CARDIAC MUSCLE

SKELETAL MUSCLE

SMOOTH MUSCLE

CONTRACTION OF SKELETAL MUSCLE

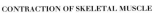

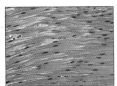

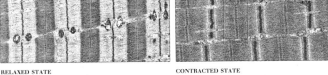

RELAXED STATE

CONTRACTED STATE

**MUSCLES OF
HEAD AND NECK**

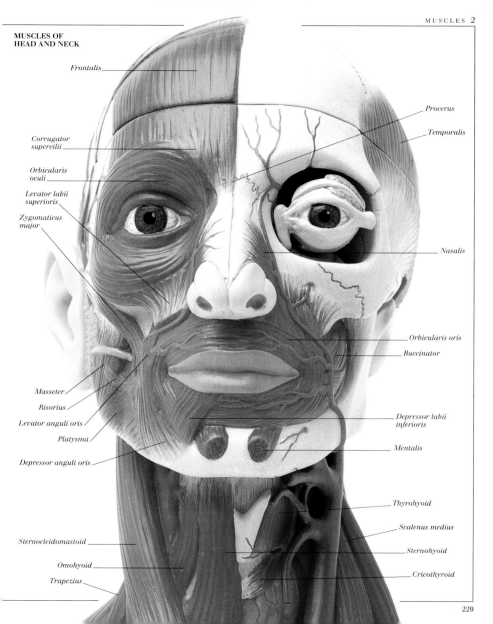

Frontalis

Procerus

Temporalis

Corrugator
supercilii

Orbicularis
oculi

Levator labii
superioris

Zygomaticus
major

Nasalis

Orbicularis oris

Buccinator

Masseter

Risorius

Levator anguli oris

Platysma

Depressor anguli oris

Depressor labii
inferioris

Mentalis

Thyrohyoid

Scalenus medius

Sternocleidomastoid

Omohyoid

Trapezius

Sternohyoid

Cricothyroid

Hands

THE HUMAN HAND is an extremely versatile tool, capable of delicate manipulation as well as powerful gripping actions. The arrangement of its 27 small bones, moved by 37 skeletal muscles that are connected to the bones by tendons, allows a wide range of movements. Our ability to bring the tips of our thumbs and fingers together, combined with the extraordinary sensitivity of our fingertips due to their rich supply of nerve endings, makes our hands uniquely dextrous.

X-RAY OF LEFT HAND OF A YOUNG CHILD

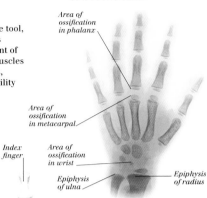

Area of ossification in phalanx

Area of ossification in metacarpal

Area of ossification in wrist

Epiphysis of ulna

Epiphysis of radius

Areas of cartilage in the wrist and at the ends of the finger bones are the sites of growth and have still to ossify.

BONES OF HAND

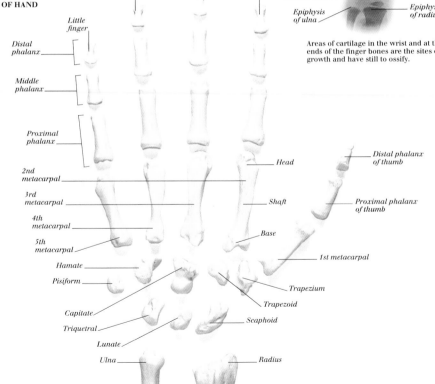

Ring finger

Middle finger

Index finger

Little finger

Distal phalanx

Middle phalanx

Proximal phalanx

2nd metacarpal

3rd metacarpal

4th metacarpal

5th metacarpal

Hamate

Pisiform

Capitate

Triquetral

Lunate

Ulna

Head

Shaft

Base

Trapezium

Trapezoid

Scaphoid

Radius

Distal phalanx of thumb

Proximal phalanx of thumb

1st metacarpal

**STRUCTURES UNDERLYING SKIN
OF PALM OF HAND**

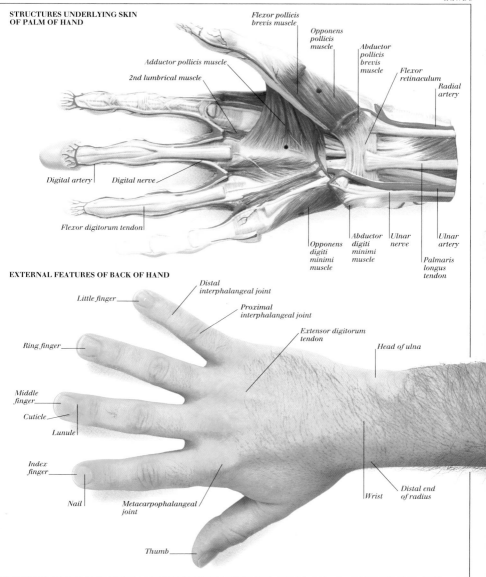

*Flexor pollicis
brevis muscle*

*Opponens
pollicis
muscle*

*Abductor
pollicis
brevis
muscle*

*Flexor
retinaculum*

*Radial
artery*

Adductor pollicis muscle

2nd lumbrical muscle

Digital artery   *Digital nerve*

Flexor digitorum tendon

*Opponens
digiti
minimi
muscle*

*Abductor
digiti
minimi
muscle*

*Ulnar
nerve*

*Ulnar
artery*

*Palmaris
longus
tendon*

EXTERNAL FEATURES OF BACK OF HAND

*Distal
interphalangeal joint*

Little finger

*Proximal
interphalangeal joint*

*Extensor digitorum
tendon*

Head of ulna

Ring finger

*Middle
finger*

Cuticle

Lunule

*Index
finger*

Nail

*Metacarpophalangeal
joint*

Wrist

*Distal end
of radius*

Thumb

Feet

THE FEET AND TOES are essential elements in body movement. They bear and propel the weight of the body during walking and running, and also help to maintain balance during changes of body position. Each foot has 26 bones, more than 100 ligaments, and 33 muscles, some of which are attached to the lower leg. The heel pad and the arch of the foot act as shock absorbers, providing a cushion against the jolts that occur with every step.

LIGAMENTS OF FOOT

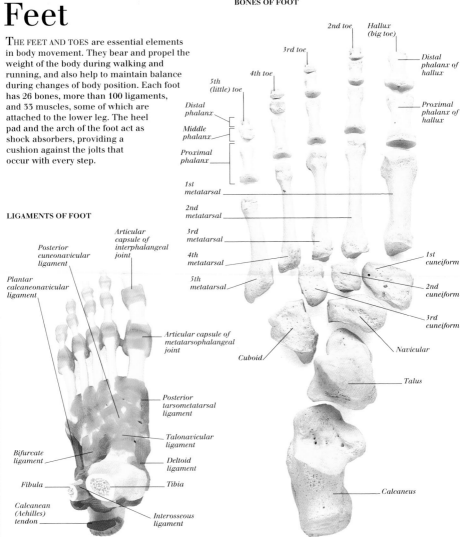

2nd toe

Hallux (big toe)

3rd toe

4th toe

5th (little) toe

Distal phalanx of hallux

Distal phalanx

Proximal phalanx of hallux

Middle phalanx

Proximal phalanx

1st metatarsal

2nd metatarsal

3rd metatarsal

4th metatarsal

5th metatarsal

1st cuneiform

2nd cuneiform

3rd cuneiform

Navicular

Cuboid

Talus

Calcaneus

Articular capsule of interphalangeal joint

Posterior cuneonavicular ligament

Plantar calcaneonavicular ligament

Articular capsule of metatarsophalangeal joint

Posterior tarsometatarsal ligament

Talonavicular ligament

Bifurcate ligament

Deltoid ligament

Fibula

Tibia

Calcanean (Achilles) tendon

Interosseous ligament

STRUCTURES UNDERLYING SKIN OF FOOT

Extensor hallucis
longus tendon

1st dorsal
interosseous muscle

Inferior extensor
retinaculum

Medial
malleolus

Tibialis
anterior muscle

Flexor hallucis
longus muscle

Flexor digitorum
longus muscle

Tibia

Soleus
muscle

Calcanean
(Achilles)
tendon

Extensor
digitorum
longus tendon

Abductor digiti
minimi muscle

Extensor hallucis
brevis muscle

Extensor digitorum
brevis muscle

Lateral
malleolus

Peroneus brevis tendon

Tibialis
posterior muscle

Peroneus
brevis muscle

Fibula

Peroneus
longus muscle

EXTERNAL FEATURES OF FOOT

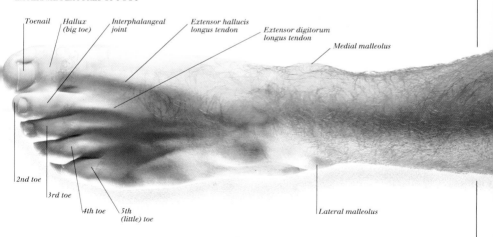

Toenail

Hallux
(big toe)

Interphalangeal
joint

Extensor hallucis
longus tendon

Extensor digitorum
longus tendon

Medial malleolus

2nd toe

3rd toe

4th toe

5th
(little) toe

Lateral malleolus

Skin and hair

SKIN IS THE BODY'S LARGEST ORGAN, a waterproof barrier that protects the internal organs against infection, injury, and harmful sun rays. The skin is also an important sensory organ and helps to control body temperature. The outer layer of the skin, known as the epidermis, is coated with keratin, a tough, horny protein that is also the chief constituent of hair and nails. Dead cells are shed from the skin's surface and are replaced by new cells from the base of the epidermis, the region that also produces the skin pigment, melanin. The dermis contains most of the skin's living structures, and includes nerve endings, blood vessels, elastic fibers, sweat glands that cool the skin, and sebaceous glands that produce oil to keep the skin supple. Beneath the dermis lies the subcutaneous tissue (hypodermis), which is rich in fat and blood vessels. Hair shafts grow from hair follicles situated in the dermis and subcutaneous tissue. Hair grows on every part of the skin apart from the palms of the hands and soles of the feet.

SECTION OF HAIR

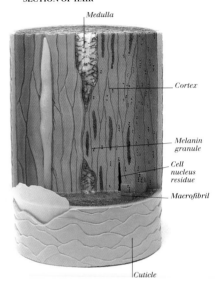

Medulla

Cortex

Melanin granule

Cell nucleus residue

Macrofibril

Cuticle

SECTIONS OF DIFFERENT TYPES OF SKIN

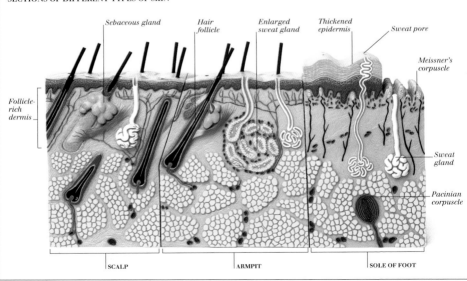

Sebaceous gland

Hair follicle

Enlarged sweat gland

Thickened epidermis

Sweat pore

Meissner's corpuscle

Follicle-rich dermis

Sweat gland

Pacinian corpuscle

SCALP

ARMPIT

SOLE OF FOOT

SECTION OF SKIN

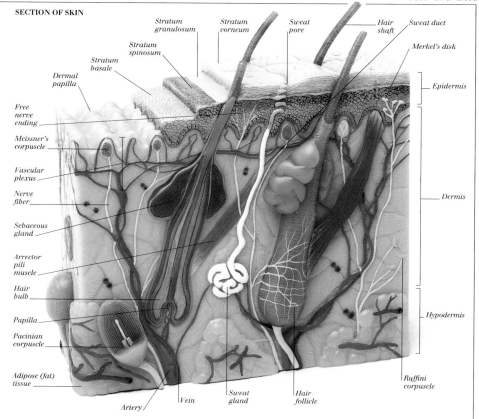

Stratum granulosum
Stratum corneum
Sweat pore
Hair shaft
Sweat duct
Stratum spinosum
Merkel's disk
Stratum basale
Dermal papilla
Epidermis
Free nerve ending
Meissner's corpuscle
Vascular plexus
Nerve fiber
Sebaceous gland
Arrector pili muscle
Hair bulb
Papilla
Pacinian corpuscle
Dermis
Adipose (fat) tissue
Hypodermis
Artery
Vein
Sweat gland
Hair follicle
Ruffini corpuscle

PHOTOMICROGRAPHS OF SKIN AND HAIR

SECTION OF SKIN
The flaky cells at the skin's surface are shed continuously.

SWEAT PORE
This allows loss of fluid as part of temperature control.

SKIN HAIR
Two hairs pushing through the outer layer of skin.

HEAD HAIR
The root and part of the shaft of a hair from the scalp.

235

Brain

THE BRAIN IS THE MAJOR ORGAN of the central nervous
system and the control center for all the body's voluntary
and involuntary activities. It is also responsible for the
complexities of thought, memory, emotion, and language.
In adults, this complex organ is a mere 3 lb (1.4 kg) in weight,
containing over 10 thousand million nerve cells. Three distinct
regions can easily be seen—the brainstem, the cerebellum, and
the large cerebrum. The brainstem controls vital body
functions, such as breathing and digestion. The cerebellum's
main functions are the maintenance of posture and the
coordination of body movements. The cerebrum, which
consists of the right and left cerebral hemispheres joined by
the corpus callosum, is the site of most conscious and
intelligent activities.

**MRI SCAN OF TRANSVERSE
SECTION THROUGH BRAIN**

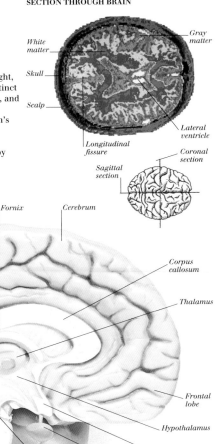

Gray
matter

White
matter

Skull

Scalp

Longitudinal
fissure

Lateral
ventricle

Coronal
section

Sagittal
section

**SAGITTAL SECTION
THROUGH BRAIN**

Central sulcus

Fornix

Cerebrum

Parietal lobe

Corpus
callosum

Parieto-occipital
sulcus

Thalamus

Pineal
body

Occipital
lobe

Frontal
lobe

Aqueduct

Hypothalamus

Cerebellum

Optic
chiasma

4th ventricle

Pituitary gland

Mesencephalon
(midbrain)

Pons

Brainstem

Spinal cord

Medulla
oblongata

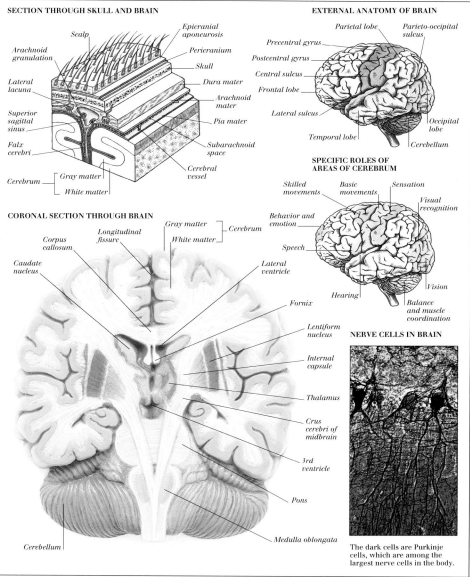

SECTION THROUGH SKULL AND BRAIN

Scalp
Epicranial aponeurosis
Arachnoid granulation
Pericranium
Skull
Dura mater
Lateral lacuna
Arachnoid mater
Superior sagittal sinus
Pia mater
Falx cerebri
Subarachnoid space
Cerebral vessel

Cerebrum { Gray matter / White matter

EXTERNAL ANATOMY OF BRAIN

Parietal lobe
Parieto-occipital sulcus
Precentral gyrus
Postcentral gyrus
Central sulcus
Frontal lobe
Lateral sulcus
Occipital lobe
Temporal lobe
Cerebellum

CORONAL SECTION THROUGH BRAIN

Gray matter } Cerebrum
White matter

Corpus callosum
Longitudinal fissure
Caudate nucleus
Lateral ventricle
Fornix
Lentiform nucleus
Internal capsule
Thalamus
Crus cerebri of midbrain
3rd ventricle
Pons
Medulla oblongata
Cerebellum

SPECIFIC ROLES OF AREAS OF CEREBRUM

Skilled movements
Basic movements
Sensation
Visual recognition
Behavior and emotion
Speech
Vision
Hearing
Balance and muscle coordination

NERVE CELLS IN BRAIN

The dark cells are Purkinje cells, which are among the largest nerve cells in the body.

Nervous system

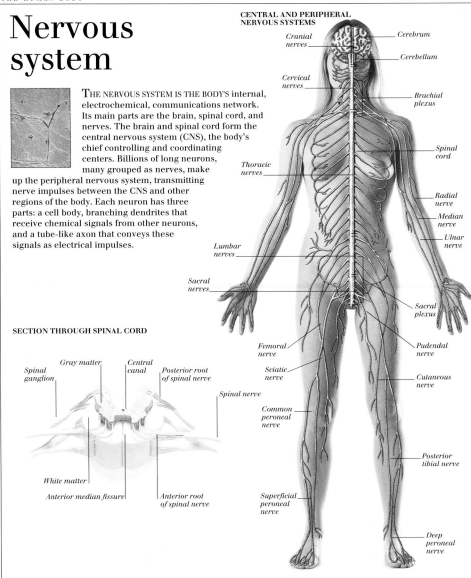

THE NERVOUS SYSTEM IS THE BODY'S internal, electrochemical, communications network. Its main parts are the brain, spinal cord, and nerves. The brain and spinal cord form the central nervous system (CNS), the body's chief controlling and coordinating centers. Billions of long neurons, many grouped as nerves, make up the peripheral nervous system, transmitting nerve impulses between the CNS and other regions of the body. Each neuron has three parts: a cell body, branching dendrites that receive chemical signals from other neurons, and a tube-like axon that conveys these signals as electrical impulses.

CENTRAL AND PERIPHERAL NERVOUS SYSTEMS

Cranial nerves

Cerebrum

Cerebellum

Cervical nerves

Brachial plexus

Spinal cord

Thoracic nerves

Radial nerve

Median nerve

Ulnar nerve

Lumbar nerves

Sacral nerves

Sacral plexus

Femoral nerve

Pudendal nerve

Sciatic nerve

Cutaneous nerve

Common peroneal nerve

Posterior tibial nerve

Superficial peroneal nerve

Deep peroneal nerve

SECTION THROUGH SPINAL CORD

Spinal ganglion

Gray matter

Central canal

Posterior root of spinal nerve

Spinal nerve

White matter

Anterior median fissure

Anterior root of spinal nerve

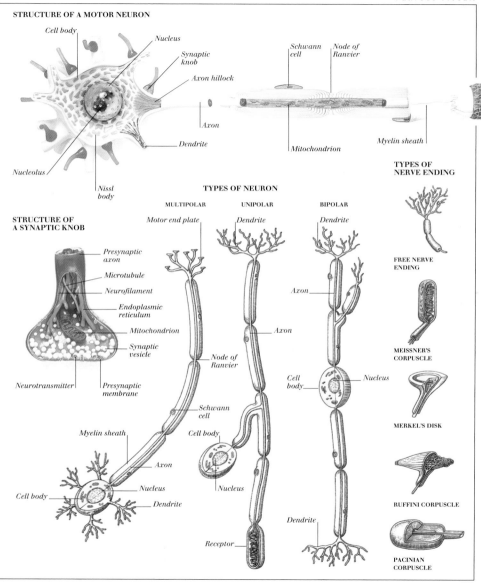

STRUCTURE OF A MOTOR NEURON

Cell body

Nucleus

Synaptic knob

Axon hillock

Axon

Dendrite

Nucleolus

Nissl body

Schwann cell

Node of Ranvier

Mitochondrion

Myelin sheath

TYPES OF NERVE ENDING

FREE NERVE ENDING

MEISSNER'S CORPUSCLE

MERKEL'S DISK

RUFFINI CORPUSCLE

PACINIAN CORPUSCLE

STRUCTURE OF A SYNAPTIC KNOB

Presynaptic axon

Microtubule

Neurofilament

Endoplasmic reticulum

Mitochondrion

Synaptic vesicle

Neurotransmitter

Presynaptic membrane

TYPES OF NEURON

MULTIPOLAR

Motor end plate

Node of Ranvier

Schwann cell

Myelin sheath

Axon

Cell body

Nucleus

Dendrite

UNIPOLAR

Dendrite

Axon

Cell body

Nucleus

Receptor

BIPOLAR

Dendrite

Axon

Cell body

Nucleus

Dendrite

Eye

THE EYE IS THE ORGAN OF SIGHT. The two eyeballs, protected within bony sockets called orbits and on the outside by the eyelids, eyebrows, and tear film, are directly connected to the brain by the optic nerves. Each eye is moved by six muscles, which are attached around the eyeball. Light rays entering the eye through the pupil are focused by the cornea and lens to form an image on the retina. The retina contains millions of light-sensitive cells, called rods and cones, which convert the image into a pattern of nerve impulses. These impulses are transmitted along the optic nerve to the brain. Information from the two optic nerves is processed in the brain to produce a single coordinated image.

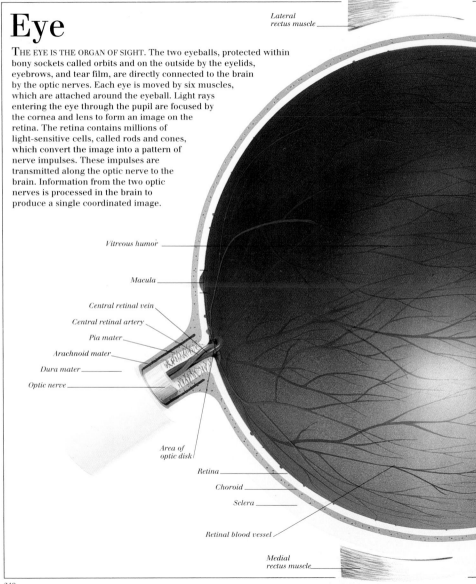

Lateral rectus muscle

Vitreous humor

Macula

Central retinal vein

Central retinal artery

Pia mater

Arachnoid mater

Dura mater

Optic nerve

Area of optic disk

Retina

Choroid

Sclera

Retinal blood vessel

Medial rectus muscle

SECTION THROUGH LEFT EYE

LACRIMAL (TEAR-PRODUCING) APPARATUS

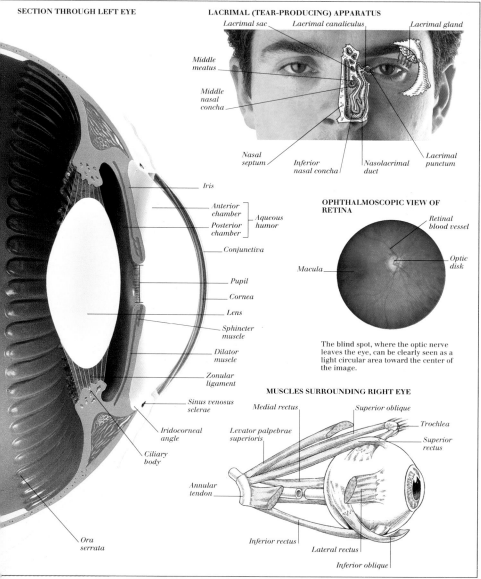

Lacrimal sac

Lacrimal canaliculus

Lacrimal gland

Middle meatus

Middle nasal concha

Nasal septum

Inferior nasal concha

Nasolacrimal duct

Lacrimal punctum

Iris

Anterior chamber

Posterior chamber

Aqueous humor

Conjunctiva

Pupil

Cornea

Lens

Sphincter muscle

Dilator muscle

Zonular ligament

Sinus venosus sclerae

Iridocorneal angle

Ciliary body

Ora serrata

OPHTHALMOSCOPIC VIEW OF RETINA

Retinal blood vessel

Optic disk

Macula

The blind spot, where the optic nerve leaves the eye, can be clearly seen as a light circular area toward the center of the image.

MUSCLES SURROUNDING RIGHT EYE

Medial rectus

Superior oblique

Trochlea

Superior rectus

Levator palpebrae superioris

Annular tendon

Inferior rectus

Lateral rectus

Inferior oblique

Ear

THE EAR IS THE ORGAN OF HEARING AND BALANCE. The outer ear consists of a flap called the auricle or pinna and the auditory canal. The main functional parts—the middle and inner ears—are enclosed within the skull. The middle ear consists of three tiny bones, known as auditory ossicles, and the eustachian tube, which links the ear to the back of the nose. The inner ear consists of the spiral-shaped cochlea, and also the semicircular canals and the vestibule, which are the organs of balance. Sound waves entering the ear travel through the auditory canal to the tympanic membrane (eardrum), where they are converted to vibrations that are transmitted via the ossicles to the cochlea. Here, the vibrations are converted by millions of microscopic hairs into electrical nerve signals to be interpreted by the brain.

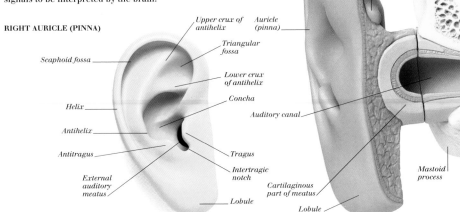

RIGHT AURICLE (PINNA)

Scaphoid fossa

Upper crux of antihelix

Auricle (pinna)

Triangular fossa

Lower crux of antihelix

Concha

Helix

Antihelix

Antitragus

Tragus

Intertragic notch

External auditory meatus

Lobule

Cartilaginous part of meatus

Lobule

Auditory canal

Temporal bone

Cartilage of auricle

Mastoid process

OSSICLES OF MIDDLE EAR

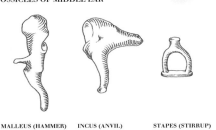

MALLEUS (HAMMER)   INCUS (ANVIL)   STAPES (STIRRUP)

These three tiny bones connect to form a bridge between the tympanic membrane and the oval window. With a system of membranes they convey sound vibrations to the inner ear.

INTERNAL STRUCTURE OF AMPULLA

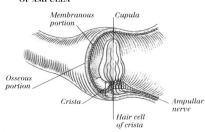

Membranous portion

Cupula

Osseous portion

Crista

Hair cell of crista

Ampullar nerve

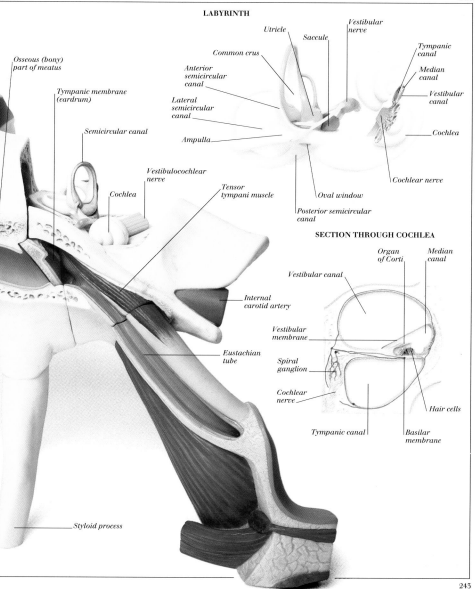

LABYRINTH

Utricle

Saccule

Vestibular nerve

Common crus

Anterior semicircular canal

Tympanic canal

Median canal

Vestibular canal

Lateral semicircular canal

Osseous (bony) part of meatus

Tympanic membrane (eardrum)

Semicircular canal

Ampulla

Cochlea

Vestibulocochlear nerve

Cochlea

Tensor tympani muscle

Cochlear nerve

Oval window

Posterior semicircular canal

Internal carotid artery

SECTION THROUGH COCHLEA

Organ of Corti

Median canal

Vestibular canal

Vestibular membrane

Spiral ganglion

Eustachian tube

Cochlear nerve

Hair cells

Tympanic canal

Basilar membrane

Styloid process

243

Nose, mouth, and throat

WITH EVERY BREATH, air passes through the nasal cavity down the pharynx (throat), larynx ("voice box"), and trachea (windpipe) to the lungs. The nasal cavity warms and moistens air, and the tiny layers in its lining protect the airway against damage by foreign bodies. During swallowing, the tongue moves up and back, the larynx rises, the epiglottis closes off the entrance to the trachea, and the soft palate separates the nasal cavity from the pharynx. Saliva, secreted from three pairs of salivary glands, lubricates food to make swallowing easier; it also begins the chemical breakdown of food, and helps to produce taste. The senses of taste and smell are closely linked. Both depend on the detection of dissolved molecules by sensory receptors in the olfactory nerve endings of the nose and in the taste buds of the tongue.

STRUCTURE OF TONGUE

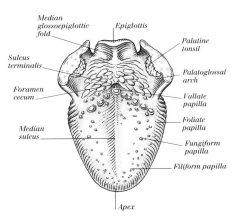

Median glossoepiglottic fold
Epiglottis
Palatine tonsil
Sulcus terminalis
Palatoglossal arch
Foramen cecum
Vallate papilla
Median sulcus
Foliate papilla
Fungiform papilla
Filiform papilla
Apex

STRUCTURES SURROUNDING PHARYNX

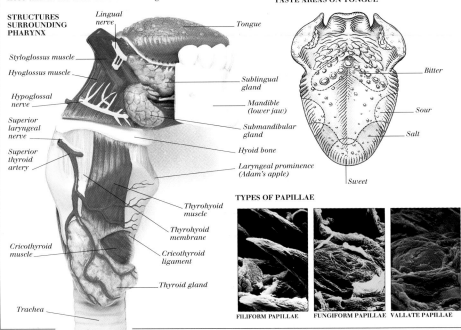

Lingual nerve
Tongue
Styloglossus muscle
Hyoglossus muscle
Sublingual gland
Hypoglossal nerve
Mandible (lower jaw)
Superior laryngeal nerve
Submandibular gland
Superior thyroid artery
Hyoid bone
Laryngeal prominence (Adam's apple)
Thyrohyoid muscle
Thyrohyoid membrane
Cricothyroid muscle
Cricothyroid ligament
Thyroid gland
Trachea

TASTE AREAS ON TONGUE

Bitter
Sour
Salt
Sweet

TYPES OF PAPILLAE

FILIFORM PAPILLAE   FUNGIFORM PAPILLAE   VALLATE PAPILLAE

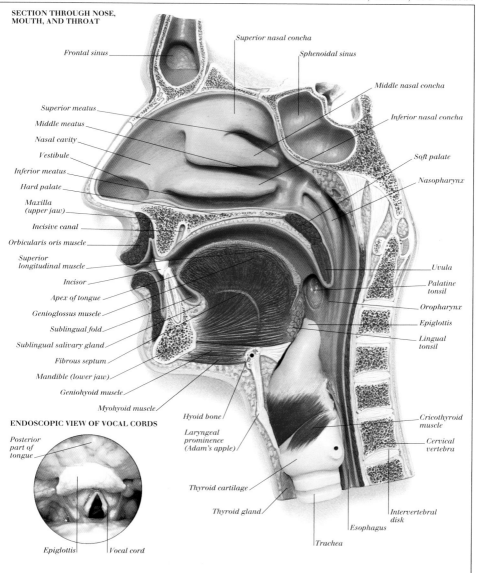

SECTION THROUGH NOSE, MOUTH, AND THROAT

Frontal sinus

Superior nasal concha

Sphenoidal sinus

Middle nasal concha

Superior meatus

Inferior nasal concha

Middle meatus

Nasal cavity

Soft palate

Vestibule

Nasopharynx

Inferior meatus

Hard palate

Maxilla
(upper jaw)

Incisive canal

Orbicularis oris muscle

Superior
longitudinal muscle

Uvula

Palatine
tonsil

Incisor

Apex of tongue

Oropharynx

Genioglossus muscle

Epiglottis

Sublingual fold

Lingual
tonsil

Sublingual salivary gland

Fibrous septum

Mandible (lower jaw)

Geniohyoid muscle

Myohyoid muscle

Hyoid bone

Cricothyroid
muscle

Cervical
vertebra

ENDOSCOPIC VIEW OF VOCAL CORDS

Laryngeal
prominence
(Adam's apple)

Posterior
part of
tongue

Thyroid cartilage

Intervertebral
disk

Thyroid gland

Epiglottis

Vocal cord

Trachea

Esophagus

Teeth

THE 20 PRIMARY TEETH (also called deciduous or milk teeth) usually begin to erupt when a baby is about six months old. They start to be replaced by the permanent teeth when the child is about six years old. By the age of 20, most adults have a full set of 32 teeth although the third molars (commonly called wisdom teeth) may never erupt. While teeth help people to speak clearly and give shape to the face, their main function is the chewing of food. Incisors and canines shear and tear the food into pieces; premolars and molars crush and grind it further. Although tooth enamel is the hardest substance in the body, it tends to be eroded and destroyed by acid produced in the mouth during the breakdown of food.

DEVELOPMENT OF TEETH IN A FETUS

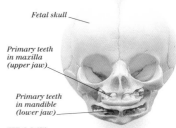

Fetal skull

Primary teeth in maxilla (upper jaw)

Primary teeth in mandible (lower jaw)

FETAL JAWS
By the sixth week of embryonic development areas of thickening occur in each jaw; these areas give rise to tooth buds. By the time the fetus is six months old, enamel has formed on the tooth buds.

DEVELOPMENT OF JAW AND TEETH

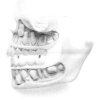

Maxilla (upper jaw)

Mandible (lower jaw)

A NEWBORN BABY'S JAWS
The primary teeth can be seen developing in the jawbones; they begin to erupt around the age of six months.

A FIVE-YEAR-OLD CHILD'S TEETH
There is a full set of 20 erupted primary teeth; the permanent teeth can be seen developing in the upper and lower jaws.

A NINE-YEAR-OLD CHILD'S TEETH
Most of the teeth are primary teeth but the permanent incisors and first molars have now emerged.

AN ADULT'S TEETH
By the age of 20, the full set of 32 permanent teeth (including the wisdom teeth) should be in position.

THE PERMANENT TEETH

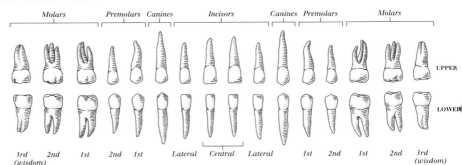

Molars   Premolars   Canines   Incisors   Canines   Premolars   Molars

UPPER

LOWER

3rd (wisdom)   *2nd*   *1st*   *2nd*   *1st*   *Lateral*   *Central*   *Lateral*   *1st*   *2nd*   *1st*   *2nd*   *3rd (wisdom)*

STRUCTURE OF A TOOTH

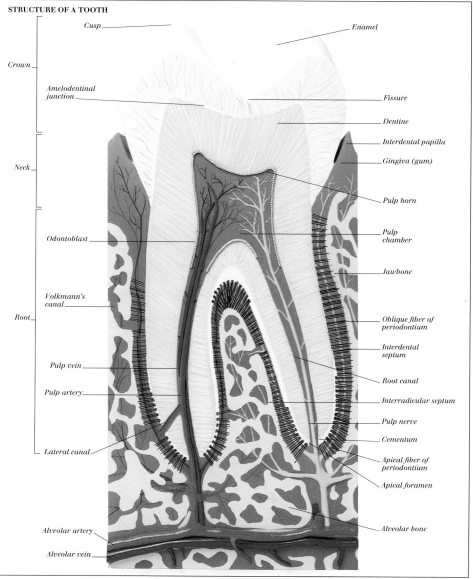

Cusp

Enamel

Crown

Ameledentinal
junction

Fissure

Dentine

Neck

Interdental papilla

Gingiva (gum)

Pulp horn

Odontoblast

Pulp
chamber

Jawbone

Volkmann's
canal

Root

Oblique fiber of
periodontium

Interdental
septum

Pulp vein

Root canal

Pulp artery

Interradicular septum

Pulp nerve

Cementum

Lateral canal

Apical fiber of
periodontium

Apical foramen

Alveolar artery

Alveolar bone

Alveolar vein

Digestive system

THE DIGESTIVE SYSTEM BREAKS DOWN FOOD into particles so tiny that blood can take nourishment to all parts of the body. The system's main part is a 30-foot (9 m) tube from mouth to rectum; muscles in this alimentary canal force food along. Chewed food first travels through the esophagus to the stomach, which churns and liquidizes food before it passes through the duodenum, jejunum, and ileum—the three parts of the long, convoluted small intestine. Here, digestive juices from the gallbladder and pancreas break down food particles; many filter out into the blood through tiny fingerlike villi that line the small intestine's inner wall. Undigested food in the colon forms feces that leave the body through the anus.

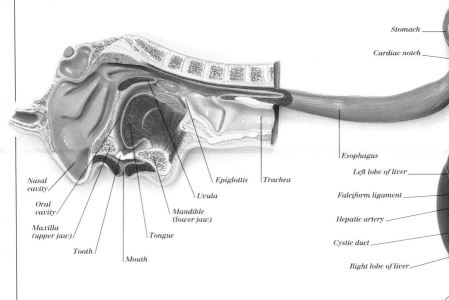

Stomach

Cardiac notch

Esophagus

Left lobe of liver

Falciform ligament

Hepatic artery

Cystic duct

Right lobe of liver

Gallbladder

Nasal cavity

Oral cavity

Maxilla (upper jaw)

Tooth

Mouth

Tongue

Mandible (lower jaw)

Uvula

Epiglottis

Trachea

ENDOSCOPIC VIEWS INSIDE ALIMENTARY CANAL

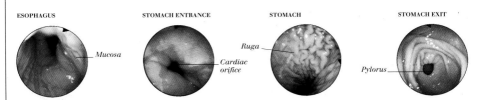

ESOPHAGUS

Mucosa

STOMACH ENTRANCE

Cardiac orifice

STOMACH

Ruga

STOMACH EXIT

Pylorus

ALIMENTARY CANAL

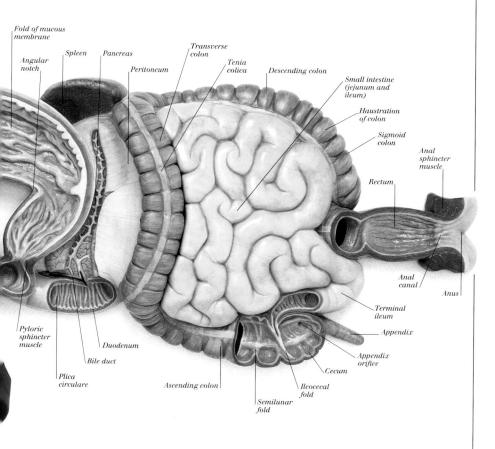

Fold of mucous membrane

Angular notch

Spleen

Pancreas

Peritoneum

Transverse colon

Tenia colica

Descending colon

Small intestine (jejunum and ileum)

Haustration of colon

Sigmoid colon

Anal sphincter muscle

Rectum

Anal canal

Anus

Terminal ileum

Appendix

Appendix orifice

Cecum

Ileocecal fold

Semilunar fold

Ascending colon

Plica circulare

Bile duct

Duodenum

Pyloric sphincter muscle

DUODENUM

Plica circulare

ILEUM

Villi of mucosa

COLON

Semilunar fold

Blood vessel

RECTUM

Mucosa

Heart

THE HEART IS A HOLLOW MUSCLE in the middle of the chest that pumps blood around the body, supplying cells with oxygen and nutrients. A muscular wall, called the septum, divides the heart lengthwise into left and right sides. A valve divides each side into two chambers: an upper atrium and a lower ventricle. When the heart muscle contracts, it squeezes blood through the atria and then through the ventricles. Oxygenated blood from the lungs flows from the pulmonary veins into the left atrium, through the left ventricle, and then out via the aorta to all parts of the body. Deoxygenated blood returning from the body flows from the vena cava into the right atrium, through the right ventricle, and then out via the pulmonary artery to the lungs for reoxygenation. At rest the heart beats between 60 and 80 times a minute; during exercise or at times of stress or excitement the rate may increase to 200 beats a minute.

ARTERIES AND VEINS SURROUNDING HEART

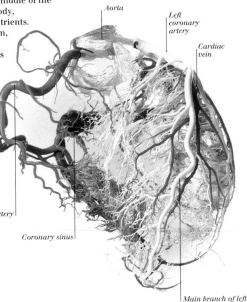

Aorta

Left coronary artery

Cardiac vein

Right coronary artery

Coronary sinus

Main branch of left coronary artery

SECTION THROUGH HEART WALL

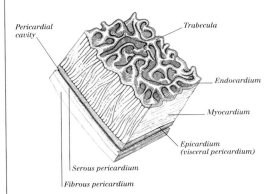

Pericardial cavity

Trabecula

Endocardium

Myocardium

Epicardium (visceral pericardium)

Serous pericardium

Fibrous pericardium

HEARTBEAT SEQUENCE

ATRIAL DIASTOLE

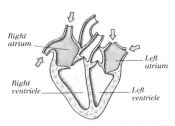

Right atrium

Left atrium

Right ventricle

Left ventricle

Deoxygenated blood enters the right atrium while the left atrium receives oxygenated blood.

STRUCTURE OF HEART

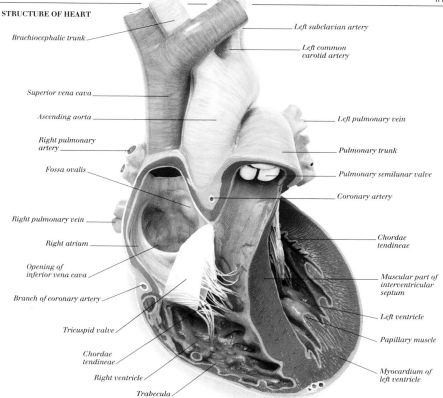

Brachiocephalic trunk

Left subclavian artery

Left common carotid artery

Superior vena cava

Ascending aorta

Left pulmonary vein

Right pulmonary artery

Pulmonary trunk

Fossa ovalis

Pulmonary semilunar valve

Coronary artery

Right pulmonary vein

Right atrium

Chordae tendineae

Opening of inferior vena cava

Muscular part of interventricular septum

Branch of coronary artery

Left ventricle

Papillary muscle

Tricuspid valve

Chordae tendineae

Myocardium of left ventricle

Right ventricle

Trabecula

ATRIAL SYSTOLE (VENTRICULAR DIASTOLE)

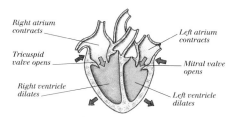

Right atrium contracts

Left atrium contracts

Tricuspid valve opens

Mitral valve opens

Right ventricle dilates

Left ventricle dilates

Left and right atria contract, forcing blood into the relaxed ventricles.

VENTRICULAR SYSTOLE

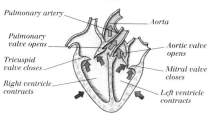

Pulmonary artery

Aorta

Pulmonary valve opens

Aortic valve opens

Tricuspid valve closes

Mitral valve closes

Right ventricle contracts

Left ventricle contracts

Ventricles contract and force blood to the lungs for oxygenation and via the aorta to the rest of the body.

Circulatory system

THE CIRCULATORY SYSTEM consists of the heart and blood vessels, which together maintain a continuous flow of blood around the body. The heart pumps oxygen-rich blood from the lungs to all parts of the body through a network of tubes called arteries, and smaller branches called arterioles. Blood returns to the heart via small vessels called venules, which lead in turn into larger tubes called veins. Arterioles and venules are linked by a network of tiny vessels called capillaries, where the exchange of oxygen and carbon dioxide between blood and body cells takes place. Blood has four main components: red blood cells, white blood cells, platelets, and liquid plasma.

ARTERIAL SYSTEM OF BRAIN

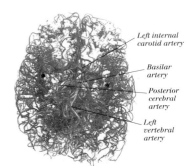

Left internal carotid artery

Basilar artery

Posterior cerebral artery

Left vertebral artery

CIRCULATORY SYSTEM OF HEART AND LUNGS

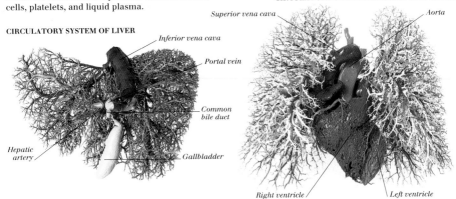

Superior vena cava

Aorta

Right ventricle

Left ventricle

CIRCULATORY SYSTEM OF LIVER

Inferior vena cava

Portal vein

Common bile duct

Hepatic artery

Gallbladder

SECTION OF MAIN ARTERY

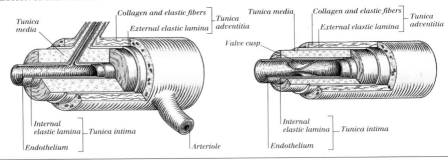

Tunica media

Collagen and elastic fibers

External elastic lamina

Tunica adventitia

Internal elastic lamina

Tunica intima

Endothelium

Arteriole

SECTION OF MAIN VEIN

Tunica media

Collagen and elastic fibers

External elastic lamina

Tunica adventitia

Valve cusp

Internal elastic lamina

Tunica intima

Endothelium

PRINCIPAL ARTERIES AND VEINS OF CIRCULATORY SYSTEM

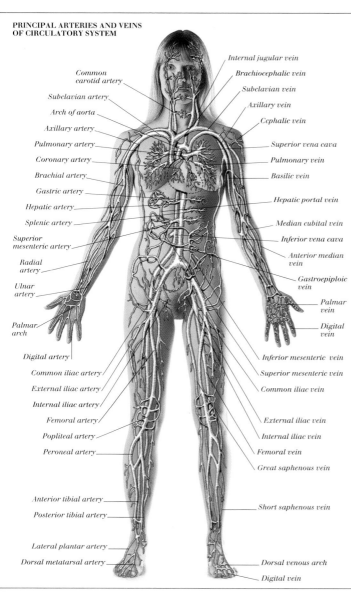

Internal jugular vein

Brachiocephalic vein

Subclavian vein

Axillary vein

Cephalic vein

Common carotid artery

Subclavian artery

Arch of aorta

Axillary artery

Pulmonary artery

Coronary artery

Brachial artery

Gastric artery

Hepatic artery

Splenic artery

Superior mesenteric artery

Radial artery

Ulnar artery

Palmar arch

Digital artery

Common iliac artery

External iliac artery

Internal iliac artery

Femoral artery

Popliteal artery

Peroneal artery

Anterior tibial artery

Posterior tibial artery

Lateral plantar artery

Dorsal metatarsal artery

Superior vena cava

Pulmonary vein

Basilic vein

Hepatic portal vein

Median cubital vein

Inferior vena cava

Anterior median vein

Gastroepiploic vein

Palmar vein

Digital vein

Inferior mesenteric vein

Superior mesenteric vein

Common iliac vein

External iliac vein

Internal iliac vein

Femoral vein

Great saphenous vein

Short saphenous vein

Dorsal venous arch

Digital vein

TYPES OF BLOOD CELLS

RED BLOOD CELLS
These cells are biconcave in shape to maximize their oxygen-carrying capacity.

WHITE BLOOD CELLS
Lymphocytes are the smallest white blood cells; they form antibodies against disease.

PLATELETS
Tiny cells that are activated whenever blood clotting or repair to vessels is necessary.

BLOOD CLOTTING

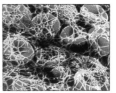

Filaments of fibrin enmesh red blood cells as part of the process of blood clotting.

Respiratory system

THE RESPIRATORY SYSTEM supplies the oxygen needed by body cells and carries off their carbon dioxide waste. Inhaled air passes via the trachea (windpipe) through two narrower tubes, the bronchi, to the lungs. Each lung comprises many fine, branching tubes called bronchioles that end in tiny clustered chambers called alveoli. Gases cross the thin alveolar walls to and from a network of tiny blood vessels. Intercostal (rib) muscles and the muscular diaphragm below the lungs operate the lungs like bellows, drawing air in and forcing it out at regular intervals.

BRONCHIOLE AND ALVEOLI

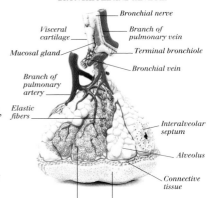

Bronchial nerve
Visceral cartilage
Branch of pulmonary vein
Mucosal gland
Terminal bronchiole
Bronchial vein
Branch of pulmonary artery
Elastic fibers
Interalveolar septum
Alveolus
Connective tissue
Capillary network
Epithelium

SEGMENTS OF BRONCHIAL TREE

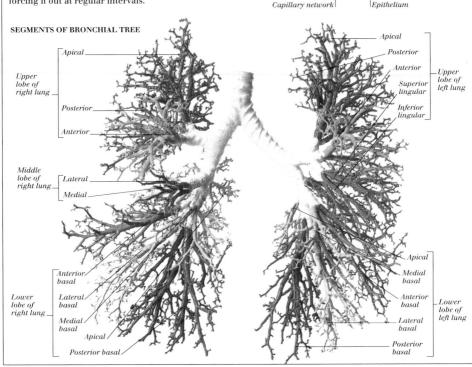

Apical

Upper lobe of right lung
Apical
Posterior
Anterior

Middle lobe of right lung
Lateral
Medial

Lower lobe of right lung
Anterior basal
Lateral basal
Medial basal
Apical
Posterior basal

Apical
Posterior
Anterior
Superior lingular
Inferior lingular
Upper lobe of left lung

Apical
Medial basal
Anterior basal
Lateral basal
Posterior basal
Lower lobe of left lung

STRUCTURES OF THORACIC CAVITY

GASEOUS EXCHANGE IN ALVEOLUS

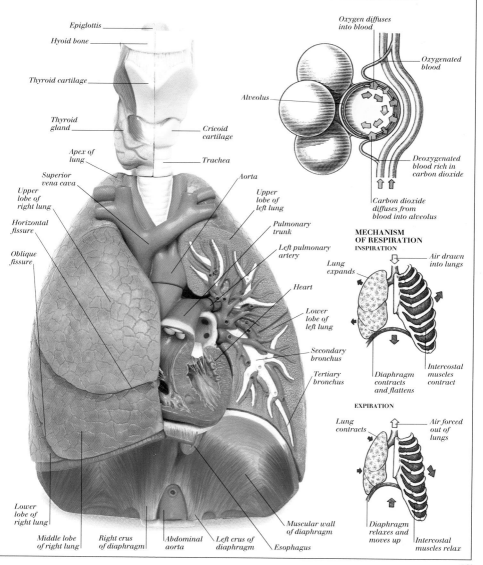

Epiglottis

Hyoid bone

Thyroid cartilage

Thyroid gland

Apex of lung

Superior vena cava

Upper lobe of right lung

Horizontal fissure

Oblique fissure

Cricoid cartilage

Trachea

Aorta

Upper lobe of left lung

Pulmonary trunk

Left pulmonary artery

Heart

Lower lobe of left lung

Secondary bronchus

Tertiary bronchus

Lower lobe of right lung

Middle lobe of right lung

Right crus of diaphragm

Abdominal aorta

Left crus of diaphragm

Esophagus

Muscular wall of diaphragm

Oxygen diffuses into blood

Oxygenated blood

Alveolus

Deoxygenated blood rich in carbon dioxide

Carbon dioxide diffuses from blood into alveolus

MECHANISM OF RESPIRATION
INSPIRATION

Air drawn into lungs

Lung expands

Diaphragm contracts and flattens

Intercostal muscles contract

EXPIRATION

Air forced out of lungs

Lung contracts

Diaphragm relaxes and moves up

Intercostal muscles relax

Urinary system

THE URINARY SYSTEM FILTERS WASTE PRODUCTS from the blood and removes them from the body via a system of tubes. Blood is filtered in the two kidneys, which are fist-sized, bean-shaped organs. The renal arteries carry blood to the kidneys; the renal veins remove blood after filtering. Each kidney contains about one million tiny units called nephrons. Each nephron is made up of a tubule and a filtering unit called a glomerulus, which consists of a collection of tiny blood vessels surrounded by the hollow Bowman's capsule. The filtering process produces a watery fluid that leaves the kidney as urine. The urine is carried via two tubes called ureters to the bladder, where it is stored until its release from the body through another tube called the urethra.

ARTERIAL SYSTEM OF KIDNEYS

- Aorta
- Celiac trunk
- Superior mesenteric artery
- Right renal artery
- Left renal artery
- Right ureter
- Left ureter

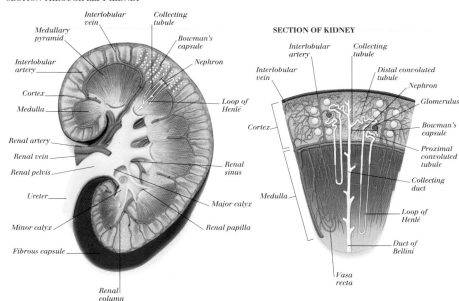

SECTION THROUGH LEFT KIDNEY

- Interlobular vein
- Collecting tubule
- Medullary pyramid
- Bowman's capsule
- Interlobular artery
- Nephron
- Cortex
- Medulla
- Loop of Henlé
- Renal artery
- Renal vein
- Renal pelvis
- Renal sinus
- Ureter
- Major calyx
- Minor calyx
- Renal papilla
- Fibrous capsule
- Renal column

SECTION OF KIDNEY

- Interlobular artery
- Collecting tubule
- Interlobular vein
- Distal convoluted tubule
- Cortex
- Nephron
- Glomerulus
- Bowman's capsule
- Proximal convoluted tubule
- Medulla
- Collecting duct
- Loop of Henlé
- Duct of Bellini
- Vasa recta

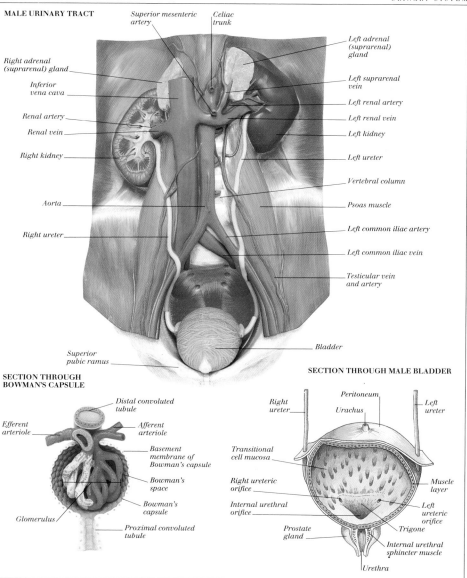

MALE URINARY TRACT

Superior mesenteric artery

Celiac trunk

Left adrenal (suprarenal) gland

Right adrenal (suprarenal) gland

Left suprarenal vein

Inferior vena cava

Left renal artery

Renal artery

Left renal vein

Renal vein

Left kidney

Right kidney

Left ureter

Vertebral column

Aorta

Psoas muscle

Right ureter

Left common iliac artery

Left common iliac vein

Testicular vein and artery

Bladder

Superior pubic ramus

SECTION THROUGH BOWMAN'S CAPSULE

Distal convoluted tubule

Efferent arteriole

Afferent arteriole

Basement membrane of Bowman's capsule

Bowman's space

Bowman's capsule

Glomerulus

Proximal convoluted tubule

SECTION THROUGH MALE BLADDER

Right ureter

Peritoneum

Urachus

Left ureter

Transitional cell mucosa

Right ureteric orifice

Muscle layer

Internal urethral orifice

Left ureteric orifice

Prostate gland

Trigone

Internal urethral sphincter muscle

Urethra

Reproductive system

SEX ORGANS LOCATED IN THE PELVIS create new human lives. Each month a ripe egg is released from one of the female's ovaries into a fallopian tube leading to the uterus (womb), a muscular pear-sized organ. A male produces minute tadpole-like sperm in two oval glands called testes. When the male is ready to release sperm into the female's vagina, many millions pass into his urethra and leave his body through the fleshy penis. The sperm travel up through the vagina into the uterus and one sperm may enter and fertilize an egg. The fertilized egg becomes embedded in the uterus wall and starts to grow into a new human being.

SECTION THROUGH OVARY

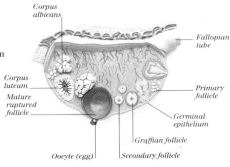

Corpus albicans

Fallopian tube

Corpus luteum

Mature ruptured follicle

Primary follicle

Germinal epithelium

Graffian follicle

Oocyte (egg)

Secondary follicle

SECTION THROUGH FEMALE PELVIC REGION

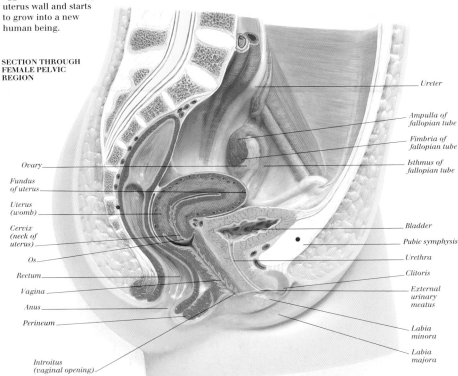

Ureter

Ampulla of fallopian tube

Fimbria of fallopian tube

Isthmus of fallopian tube

Ovary

Fundus of uterus

Uterus (womb)

Cervix (neck of uterus)

Os

Rectum

Vagina

Anus

Perineum

Bladder

Pubic symphysis

Urethra

Clitoris

External urinary meatus

Labia minora

Labia majora

Introitus (vaginal opening)

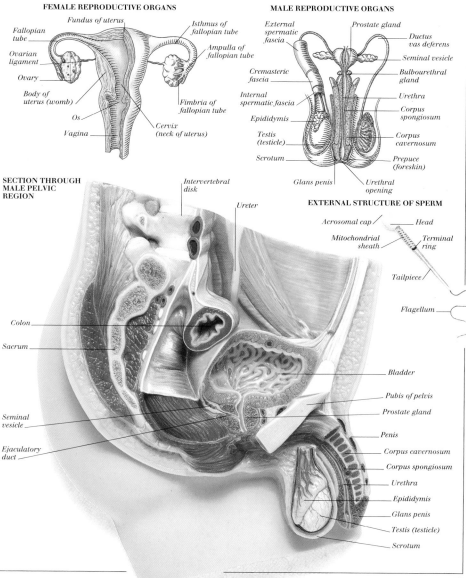

FEMALE REPRODUCTIVE ORGANS

Fallopian tube
Fundus of uterus
Isthmus of fallopian tube
Ovarian ligament
Ampulla of fallopian tube
Ovary
Body of uterus (womb)
Fimbria of fallopian tube
Os
Cervix (neck of uterus)
Vagina

MALE REPRODUCTIVE ORGANS

External spermatic fascia
Prostate gland
Ductus vas deferens
Seminal vesicle
Cremasteric fascia
Bulbourethral gland
Internal spermatic fascia
Urethra
Corpus spongiosum
Epididymis
Corpus cavernosum
Testis (testicle)
Scrotum
Prepuce (foreskin)
Glans penis
Urethral opening

SECTION THROUGH MALE PELVIC REGION

Intervertebral disk
Ureter

EXTERNAL STRUCTURE OF SPERM

Acrosomal cap
Head
Mitochondrial sheath
Terminal ring
Tailpiece
Flagellum

Colon
Sacrum
Bladder
Pubis of pelvis
Prostate gland
Seminal vesicle
Penis
Corpus cavernosum
Corpus spongiosum
Ejaculatory duct
Urethra
Epididymis
Glans penis
Testis (testicle)
Scrotum

Development of a baby

A FERTILIZED EGG IS NOURISHED AND PROTECTED as it develops into an embryo and then a fetus during the 40 weeks of pregnancy. The placenta, a mass of blood vessels implanted in the uterus lining, delivers nourishment and oxygen, and removes waste through the umbilical cord. Meanwhile, the fetus lies snugly in its amniotic sac, a bag of fluid that protects it against any sudden jolts. In the last weeks of the pregnancy, the rapidly growing fetus turns head down: a baby ready to be born.

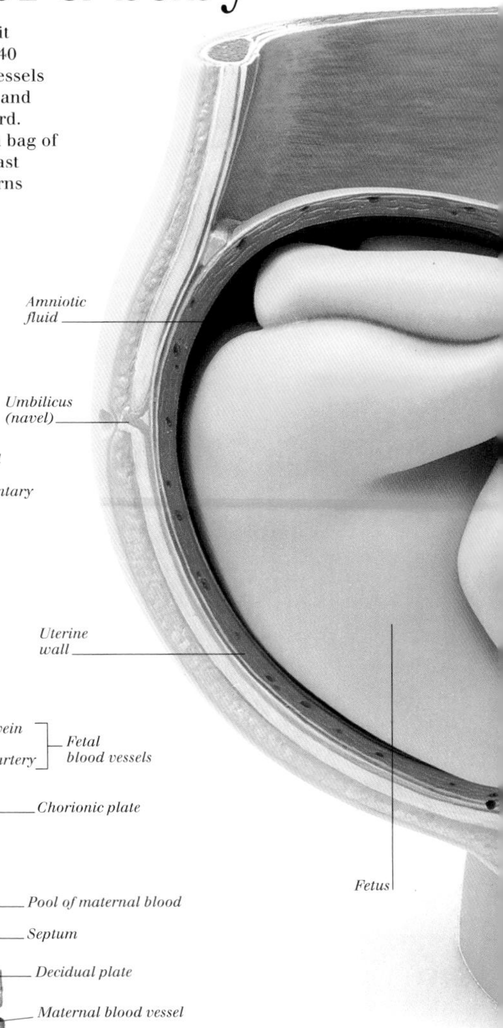

EMBRYO AT FIVE WEEKS

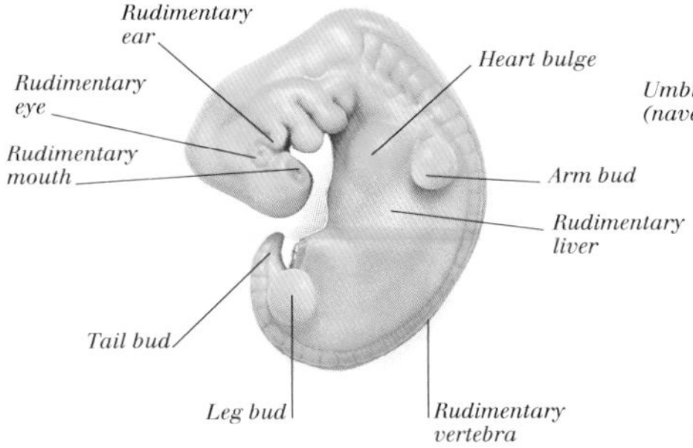

Rudimentary ear

Rudimentary eye

Rudimentary mouth

Heart bulge

Arm bud

Rudimentary liver

Tail bud

Leg bud

Rudimentary vertebra

Amniotic fluid

Umbilicus (navel)

Uterine wall

Fetus

SECTION THROUGH PLACENTA

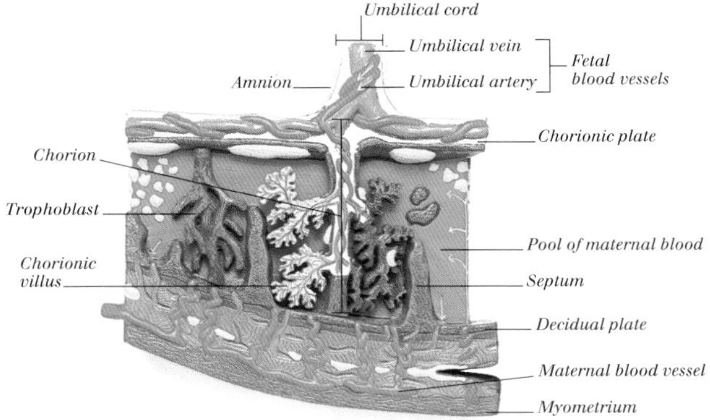

Umbilical cord

Umbilical vein

Umbilical artery

Fetal blood vessels

Amnion

Chorionic plate

Chorion

Trophoblast

Pool of maternal blood

Chorionic villus

Septum

Decidual plate

Maternal blood vessel

Myometrium

**SECTION THROUGH PELVIS IN
NINTH MONTH OF PREGNANCY**

THE DEVELOPING FETUS

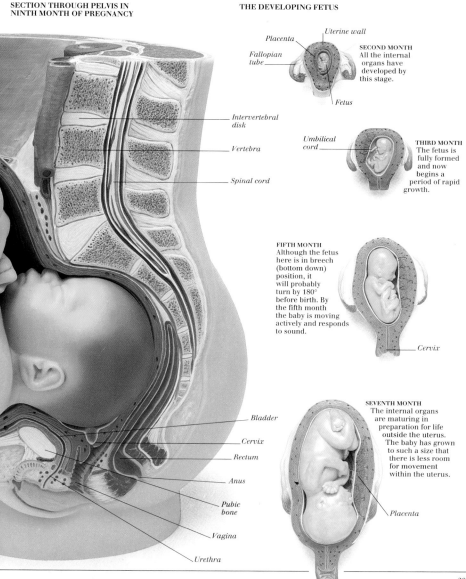

Placenta

Uterine wall

*Fallopian
tube*

SECOND MONTH
All the internal
organs have
developed by
this stage.

Fetus

*Umbilical
cord*

THIRD MONTH
The fetus is
fully formed
and now
begins a
period of rapid
growth.

*Intervertebral
disk*

Vertebra

Spinal cord

FIFTH MONTH
Although the fetus
here is in breech
(bottom down)
position, it
will probably
turn by 180°
before birth. By
the fifth month
the baby is moving
actively and responds
to sound.

Cervix

Bladder

Cervix

Rectum

Anus

SEVENTH MONTH
The internal organs
are maturing in
preparation for
life outside the uterus.
The baby has grown
to such a size that
there is less room
for movement
within the uterus.

*Pubic
bone*

Vagina

Placenta

Urethra

GEOLOGY, GEOGRAPHY, AND METEOROLGY

Earth's physical features

MOST OF THE EARTH'S SURFACE (about 70 percent) is covered with water. The largest single body of water, the Pacific Ocean, alone covers about 30 percent of the surface. Most of the land is distributed as seven continents; these are (from largest to smallest) Asia, Africa, North America, South America, Antarctica, Europe, and Australasia. The physical features of the land are remarkably varied. Among the most notable are mountain ranges, rivers, and deserts. The largest mountain ranges—the Himalayas in Asia and the Andes in South America—extend for thousands of miles. The Himalayas include the world's highest mountain, Mount Everest (29,029 feet). The longest rivers are the River Nile in Africa (4,160 miles) and the Amazon River in South America (4,000 miles). Deserts cover about 20 percent of the total land area. The largest is the Sahara, which covers nearly a third of Africa. The Earth's surface features can be represented in various ways. Only a globe can correctly represent areas, shapes, sizes, and directions, because there is always distortion when a spherical surface like the Earth's is projected onto the flat surface of a map. Each map projection is therefore a compromise: some aspects of global features are shown accurately by allowing others to be distorted. Even satellite mapping does not produce completely accurate maps, although they can show physical features with great clarity.

EXAMPLES OF MAP PROJECTIONS

CYLINDRICAL PROJECTION

CYLINDRICAL-PROJECTION MAP

180° 160° 120° 80°

Great Slave Lake
Great Bear Lake
Lake Superior
Greenland
Mackenzie-Peace River
Bering Sea
Hudson Bay
Baffin Island
NORTH AMERICA
Rocky Mountains
Mississippi-Missouri River
Lake Huron
Lake Ontario
Lake Erie
Lake Michigan
Sonoran Desert
Sierra Madre
Gulf of Mexico
Appalachian Mountains
ATLANTIC OCEAN
Chihuahuan Desert
Caribbean Sea
Guiana Highlands
Amazon River
Brazilian Highlar
PACIFIC OCEAN
SOUTH AMERICA
Andes
Atacama Desert
Gran Chaco
Mato Grosso
Parana River
Pampas
Patagonia
120° 80°

WEST OF GREENWICH MERIDIAN
180° 160°

SATELLITE MAPPING OF THE EARTH

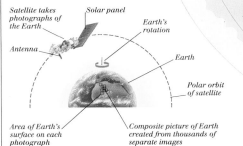

Satellite takes photographs of the Earth

Solar panel

Earth's rotation

Antenna

Earth

Polar orbit of satellite

Area of Earth's surface on each photograph

Composite picture of Earth created from thousands of separate images

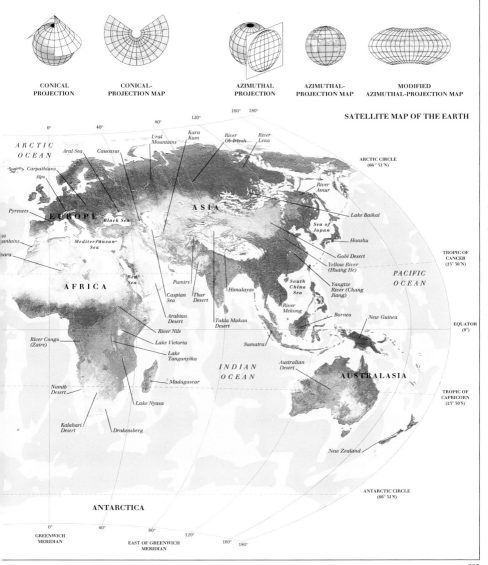

CONICAL
PROJECTION

CONICAL-
PROJECTION MAP

AZIMUTHAL
PROJECTION

AZIMUTHAL-
PROJECTION MAP

MODIFIED
AZIMUTHAL-PROJECTION MAP

SATELLITE MAP OF THE EARTH

160° 180°

120°

0° 40° 80°

*ARCTIC
OCEAN*

*Ural
Mountains*

*Kara
Kum*

*River
Ob-Irtysh*

*River
Lena*

Aral Sea

Caucasus

Carpathians

Alps

ARCTIC CIRCLE
(66° 52'N)

*River
Amur*

Pyrenees

E U R O P E

Black Sea

A S I A

Lake Baikal

*...
...ntains*

*Mediterranean
Sea*

*Sea of
Japan*

...sara

Honshu

*Red
Sea*

Pamirs

A F R I C A

*Caspian
Sea*

*Thar
Desert*

Himalayas

Gobi Desert

*Yellow River
(Huang He)*

TROPIC OF
CANCER
(25° 50'N)

*South
China
Sea*

PACIFIC
OCEAN

*Yangtze
River (Chang
Jiang)*

*Arabian
Desert*

*River
Mekong*

River Nile

*Takla Makan
Desert*

Borneo

New Guinea

EQUATOR
(0°)

*River Congo
(Zaire)*

Lake Victoria

Sumatra

*Lake
Tanganyika*

INDIAN
OCEAN

*Australian
Desert*

AUSTRALASIA

*Namib
Desert*

Madagascar

TROPIC OF
CAPRICORN
(25° 50'S)

Lake Nyasa

*Kalahari
Desert*

Drakensberg

New Zealand

ANTARCTIC CIRCLE
(66° 52'S)

ANTARCTICA

0° 40° 80° 120° 160° 180°

GREENWICH
MERIDIAN

EAST OF GREENWICH
MERIDIAN

The rock cycle

THE ROCK CYCLE IS A CONTINUOUS PROCESS through which old rocks are transformed into new ones. Rocks can be divided into three main groups: igneous, sedimentary, and metamorphic. Igneous rocks are formed when magma (molten rock) from the Earth's interior cools and solidifies (see pp. 274-275). Sedimentary rocks are formed when sediment (rock particles, for example) becomes compressed and cemented together in a process known as lithification (see pp. 276-277). Metamorphic rocks are formed when igneous, sedimentary, or other metamorphic rocks are changed by heat or pressure (see pp. 274-275). Rocks are added to the Earth's surface by crustal movements and volcanic activity. Once exposed on the surface, the rocks are broken down into rock particles by weathering (see pp. 282-283). The particles are then transported by glaciers, rivers, and wind and are deposited as sediment in lakes, deltas, deserts, and on the ocean floor. Some of this sediment undergoes lithification and forms sedimentary rock. This rock may be thrust back to the surface by crustal movements or forced deeper into the Earth's interior, where heat and pressure transform it into metamorphic rock. The metamorphic rock in turn may be pushed up to the surface or may be melted to form magma. Eventually, the magma cools and solidifies—below or on the surface—forming igneous rock. When the sedimentary, igneous, and metamorphic rocks are exposed once more on the Earth's surface, the cycle begins again.

HEXAGONAL BASALT
COLUMNS, ICELAND

THE ROCK CYCLE

Igneous
rock

Weathering, transport,
and deposition → Sediment

Cooling and solidification (crystallization)

Heat and pressure (metamorphism)

Weathering, transport, and deposition

Weathering, transport, and deposition

Compression and cementation (lithification)

Magma

Melting

Metamorphic
rock

Heat and pressure
(metamorphism)

Sedimentary
rock

STAGES IN THE ROCK CYCLE

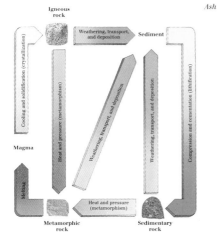

Magma extruded as lava, which solidifies to form igneous rock

Lava flow

Vent

Main conduit

Secondary conduit

Lava

Ash

Rock surrounding magma changed by heat to form metamorphic rock

Intense heat of rising magma melts some of the surrounding rock

Sedimentary rock crushed and folded to form metamorphic rock

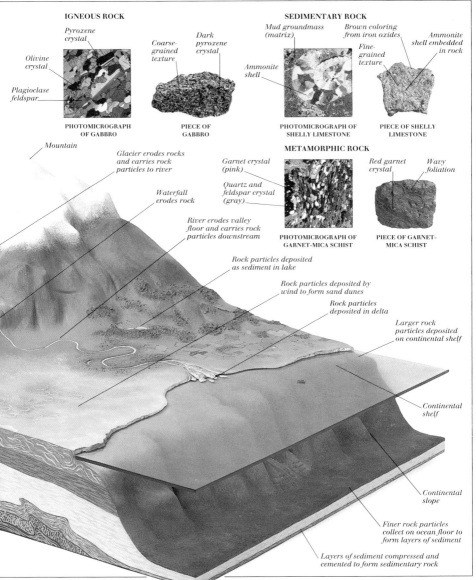

IGNEOUS ROCK

Pyroxene crystal

Olivine crystal

Plagioclase feldspar

Coarse-grained texture

Dark pyroxene crystal

PHOTOMICROGRAPH OF GABBRO

PIECE OF GABBRO

SEDIMENTARY ROCK

Mud groundmass (matrix)

Ammonite shell

Brown coloring from iron oxides

Fine-grained texture

Ammonite shell embedded in rock

PHOTOMICROGRAPH OF SHELLY LIMESTONE

PIECE OF SHELLY LIMESTONE

METAMORPHIC ROCK

Garnet crystal (pink)

Quartz and feldspar crystal (gray)

Red garnet crystal

Wavy foliation

PHOTOMICROGRAPH OF GARNET-MICA SCHIST

PIECE OF GARNET-MICA SCHIST

Mountain

Glacier erodes rocks and carries rock particles to river

Waterfall erodes rock

River erodes valley floor and carries rock particles downstream

Rock particles deposited as sediment in lake

Rock particles deposited by wind to form sand dunes

Rock particles deposited in delta

Larger rock particles deposited on continental shelf

Continental shelf

Continental slope

Finer rock particles collect on ocean floor to form layers of sediment

Layers of sediment compressed and cemented to form sedimentary rock

Minerals

A MINERAL IS A NATURALLY OCCURRING SUBSTANCE that has a characteristic chemical composition and specific physical properties, such as habit and streak (see pp. 270-271). A rock, by comparison, is an aggregate of minerals and need not have a specific chemical composition. Minerals are made up of elements (substances that cannot be broken down chemically into simpler substances), each of which can be represented by a chemical symbol. Minerals can be divided into two main groups: native elements and compounds. Native elements are made up of a pure element. Examples include gold (chemical symbol Au), silver (Ag), copper (Cu), and carbon (C); carbon occurs as a native element in two forms, diamond and graphite. Compounds are combinations of two or more elements. For example, sulfides are compounds of sulfur (S) and one or more other elements, such as lead (Pb) in the mineral galena, or antimony (Sb) in the mineral stibnite.

NATIVE ELEMENTS

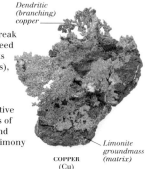

Dendritic (branching) copper

Limonite groundmass (matrix)

COPPER
(Cu)

SULFIDES

Cubic galena crystal

GALENA
(PbS)

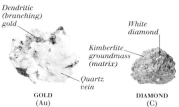

Dendritic (branching) gold

Quartz vein

GOLD
(Au)

Kimberlite groundmass (matrix)

White diamond

DIAMOND
(C)

Hexagonal graphite crystal

GRAPHITE
(C)

Prismatic stibnite crystal

Quartz groundmass (matrix)

STIBNITE
(Sb₂S₃)

OXIDES/HYDROXIDES

Milky quartz groundmass (matrix)

Smoky quartz crystal

SMOKY QUARTZ
(SiO₂)

Rounded bauxite grains in groundmass (matrix)

BAUXITE
(FeO(OH) and Al₂O₃.2H₂O)

Mass of specular hematite crystals

SPECULAR HEMATITE
(Fe₂O₃)

Perfect octahedral pyrites crystal

Quartz crystal

PYRITES
(FeS₂)

Parallel bands of onyx

ONYX
(SiO₂)

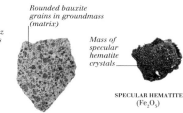

Kidney ore hematite

Specular crystals of hematite

KIDNEY ORE HEMATITE
(Fe₂O₃)

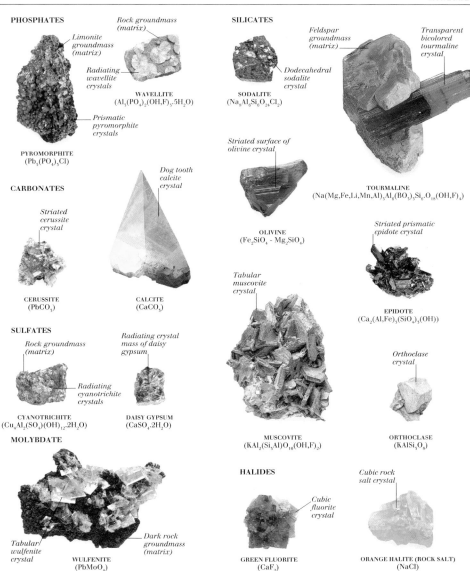

PHOSPHATES

Limonite groundmass (matrix)

Rock groundmass (matrix)

Radiating wavellite crystals

Prismatic pyromorphite crystals

WAVELLITE
$(Al_3(PO_4)_2(OH,F)_3.5H_2O)$

PYROMORPHITE
$(Pb_5(PO_4)_3Cl)$

CARBONATES

Striated cerussite crystal

Dog tooth calcite crystal

CERUSSITE
$(PbCO_3)$

CALCITE
$(CaCO_3)$

SULFATES

Rock groundmass (matrix)

Radiating crystal mass of daisy gypsum

Radiating cyanotrichite crystals

CYANOTRICHITE
$(Cu_4Al_2(SO_4)(OH)_{12}.2H_2O)$

DAISY GYPSUM
$(CaSO_4.2H_2O)$

MOLYBDATE

Tabular wulfenite crystal

Dark rock groundmass (matrix)

WULFENITE
$(PbMoO_4)$

SILICATES

Feldspar groundmass (matrix)

Transparent bicolored tourmaline crystal

Dodecahedral sodalite crystal

SODALITE
$(Na_8Al_6Si_6O_{24}Cl_2)$

Striated surface of olivine crystal

TOURMALINE
$(Na(Mg,Fe,Li,Mn,Al)_3Al_6(BO_3)_3Si_6.O_{18}(OH,F)_4)$

OLIVINE
$(Fe_2SiO_4 - Mg_2SiO_4)$

Striated prismatic epidote crystal

Tabular muscovite crystal

EPIDOTE
$(Ca_2(Al,Fe)_3(SiO_4)_3(OH))$

Orthoclase crystal

MUSCOVITE
$(KAl_2(Si_3Al)O_{10}(OH,F)_2)$

ORTHOCLASE
$(KAlSi_3O_8)$

HALIDES

Cubic fluorite crystal

Cubic rock salt crystal

GREEN FLUORITE
(CaF_2)

ORANGE HALITE (ROCK SALT)
$(NaCl)$

Mineral features

MINERALS CAN BE IDENTIFIED BY STUDYING features such as fracture, cleavage, crystal system, habit, hardness, color, and streak. Minerals can break in different ways. If a mineral breaks in an irregular way, leaving rough surfaces, it possesses fracture. If a mineral breaks along well-defined planes of weakness, it possesses cleavage. Specific minerals have distinctive patterns of cleavage. For example, mica cleaves along one plane. Most minerals form crystals that can be categorized into crystal systems according to their symmetry and number of faces. Within each system, several different but related forms of crystal are possible; for example, a cubic crystal can have six, eight, or twelve sides. A mineral's habit is the typical form taken by an aggregate of its crystals. Examples of habit include botryoidal (like a bunch of grapes) and massive (no definite form). The relative hardness of a mineral may be assessed by testing its resistance to scratching. This property is usually measured using Mohs' scale, which increases in hardness from 1 (talc) to 10 (diamond). The color of a mineral is not a dependable guide to its identity as some minerals have a range of colors. Streak (the color the powdered mineral makes when rubbed across an unglazed tile) is a more reliable indicator.

CLEAVAGE

Cleavage in one direction

CLEAVAGE ALONG ONE PLANE

Cleavage in three directions, forming a block cube

CLEAVAGE ALONG THREE PLANES

Horizontal cleavage

Vertical cleavage

CLEAVAGE ALONG TWO PLANES

Cleavage in four directions, forming a double-pyramid crystal

CLEAVAGE ALONG FOUR PLANES

CRYSTAL SYSTEMS

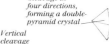

Cubic iron pyrites crystal

Tetragonal idocrase crystal

Representation of tetragonal system

TETRAGONAL SYSTEM

CUBIC SYSTEM

Representation of cubic system

Hexagonal beryl crystal

Representation of hexagonal/trigonal system

HEXAGONAL/TRIGONAL SYSTEM

Orthorhombic barite crystal

Representation of orthorhombic system

ORTHORHOMBIC SYSTEM

Monoclinic selenite crystal

Representation of monoclinic system

Triclinic axinite crystal

Representation of triclinic system

MONOCLINIC SYSTEM

TRICLINIC SYSTEM

FRACTURE

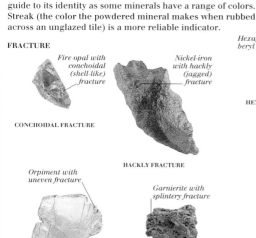

Fire opal with conchoidal (shell-like) fracture

CONCHOIDAL FRACTURE

Nickel-iron with hackly (jagged) fracture

HACKLY FRACTURE

Orpiment with uneven fracture

Garnierite with splintery fracture

UNEVEN FRACTURE

SPLINTERY FRACTURE

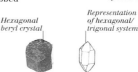

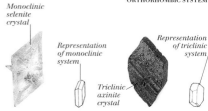

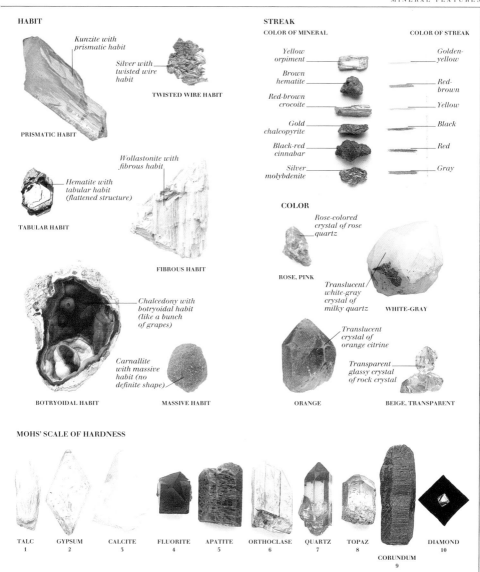

HABIT

Kunzite with prismatic habit

Silver with twisted wire habit

TWISTED WIRE HABIT

PRISMATIC HABIT

Wollastonite with fibrous habit

Hematite with tabular habit (flattened structure)

TABULAR HABIT

FIBROUS HABIT

Chalcedony with botryoidal habit (like a bunch of grapes)

Carnallite with massive habit (no definite shape)

BOTRYOIDAL HABIT   **MASSIVE HABIT**

STREAK

COLOR OF MINERAL   **COLOR OF STREAK**

Yellow orpiment   *Golden-yellow*

Brown hematite   *Red-brown*

Red-brown crocoite   *Yellow*

Gold chalcopyrite   *Black*

Black-red cinnabar   *Red*

Silver molybdenite   *Gray*

COLOR

Rose-colored crystal of rose quartz

ROSE, PINK

Translucent white-gray crystal of milky quartz   **WHITE-GRAY**

Translucent crystal of orange citrine

Transparent glassy crystal of rock crystal

ORANGE   **BEIGE, TRANSPARENT**

MOHS' SCALE OF HARDNESS

| TALC | GYPSUM | CALCITE | FLUORITE | APATITE | ORTHOCLASE | QUARTZ | TOPAZ | CORUNDUM | DIAMOND |
| 1 | 2 | 3 | 4 | 5 | 6 | 7 | 8 | 9 | 10 |

Volcanoes

VOLCANOES ARE VENTS OR FISSURES IN THE EARTH'S crust through which magma (molten rock that originates from deep beneath the crust) is forced onto the surface as lava. They occur most commonly along the boundaries of crustal plates; most volcanoes lie in a belt called the "Ring of Fire," which runs along the edge of the Pacific Ocean. Volcanoes can be classified according to the violence and frequency of their eruptions.

Nonexplosive volcanic eruptions generally occur where crustal plates pull apart. These eruptions produce runny basaltic lava that spreads quickly over a wide area to form relatively flat cones. The most violent eruptions take place where plates collide. Such eruptions produce thick rhyolitic lava and may also blast out clouds of dust and pyroclasts (lava fragments). The lava does not flow far before cooling and therefore builds up steep-sided, conical volcanoes. Some volcanoes produce lava and ash eruptions, which build up composite volcanic cones. Volcanoes that erupt frequently are described as active, those that erupt rarely are termed dormant, and those that have stopped erupting altogether are termed extinct. Besides the volcanoes themselves, other features associated with volcanic regions include geysers, hot mineral springs, solfataras, fumaroles, and bubbling mud pools.

Folded, rope-
like surface

PAHOEHOE
(ROPY LAVA)

HORU GEYSER,
NEW ZEALAND

VOLCANO TYPES

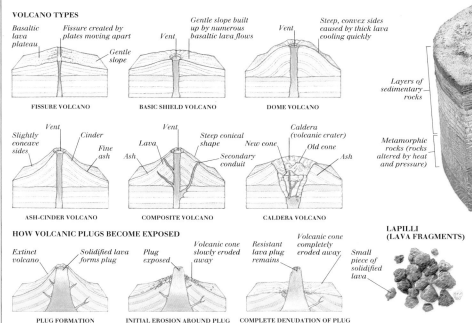

Basaltic
lava
plateau

Fissure created by
plates moving apart

Gentle
slope

FISSURE VOLCANO

Gentle slope built
up by numerous
basaltic lava flows

Vent

BASIC SHIELD VOLCANO

Vent

Steep, convex sides
caused by thick lava
cooling quickly

DOME VOLCANO

Layers of
sedimentary
rocks

Metamorphic
rocks (rocks
altered by heat
and pressure)

Slightly
concave
sides

Vent

Cinder

Fine
ash

ASH-CINDER VOLCANO

Vent

Lava

Ash

Steep conical
shape

Secondary
conduit

COMPOSITE VOLCANO

Caldera
(volcanic crater)

New cone

Old cone

Ash

CALDERA VOLCANO

LAPILLI
(LAVA FRAGMENTS)

HOW VOLCANIC PLUGS BECOME EXPOSED

Extinct
volcano

Solidified lava
forms plug

PLUG FORMATION

Plug
exposed

Volcanic cone
slowly eroded
away

INITIAL EROSION AROUND PLUG

Resistant
lava plug
remains

Volcanic cone
completely
eroded away

Small
piece of
solidified
lava

COMPLETE DENUDATION OF PLUG

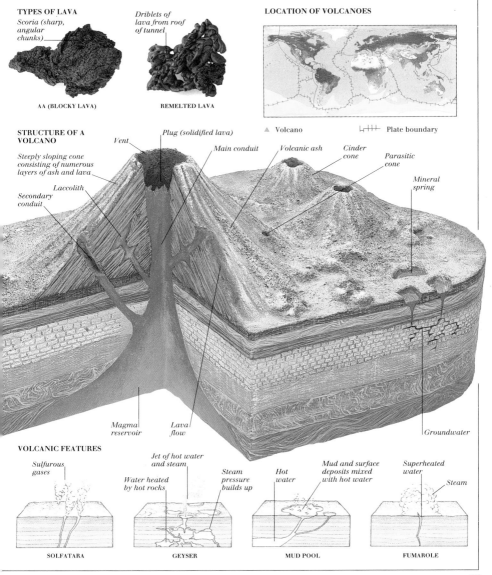

TYPES OF LAVA

Scoria (sharp, angular chunks)

AA (BLOCKY LAVA)

Driblets of lava from roof of tunnel

REMELTED LAVA

LOCATION OF VOLCANOES

▲ Volcano   ⊢╫╫┤ Plate boundary

STRUCTURE OF A VOLCANO

Steeply sloping cone consisting of numerous layers of ash and lava

Vent

Plug (solidified lava)

Main conduit

Volcanic ash

Cinder cone

Parasitic cone

Mineral spring

Laccolith

Secondary conduit

Magma reservoir

Lava flow

Groundwater

VOLCANIC FEATURES

Sulfurous gases

Jet of hot water and steam

Water heated by hot rocks

Steam pressure builds up

Hot water

Mud and surface deposits mixed with hot water

Superheated water

Steam

SOLFATARA

GEYSER

MUD POOL

FUMAROLE

Igneous and metamorphic rocks

BASALT COLUMNS

IGNEOUS ROCKS ARE FORMED WHEN MAGMA (molten rock that originates from deep beneath the Earth's crust) cools and solidifies. There are two main types of igneous rock: intrusive and extrusive. Intrusive rocks are formed deep underground, where magma is forced into cracks or between rock layers to form structures including sills, dikes, and batholiths. The magma cools slowly to form coarse-grained rocks such as gabbro and pegmatite. Extrusive rocks are formed above the Earth's surface from lava (magma that has been ejected in a volcanic eruption). The molten lava cools quickly, producing fine-grained rocks such as rhyolite and basalt. Metamorphic rocks are those that have been altered by intense heat (contact metamorphism) or extreme pressure (regional metamorphism). Contact metamorphism occurs when rocks are changed by heat from, for example, an igneous intrusion or lava flow. Regional metamorphism occurs when rock is crushed in the middle of a folding mountain range. Metamorphic rocks can be formed from igneous rocks, sedimentary rocks, or even other metamorphic rocks.

Cinder cone

Large eroded lava flow

Cedar tree laccolith

Butte

Plug

Cone sheet

Ring dike

Batholith

Dike

Sill

Dike swarm

Lopolith

IGNEOUS ROCK STRUCTURES

CONTACT METAMORPHISM

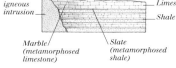

Metamorphic aureole (region where contact metamorphism occurs)

Hot igneous intrusion

Limestone

Shale

Marble (metamorphosed limestone)

Slate (metamorphosed shale)

REGIONAL METAMORPHISM

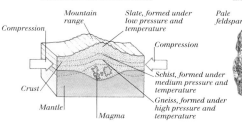

Mountain range

Slate, formed under low pressure and temperature

Compression

Compression

Crust

Schist, formed under medium pressure and temperature

Mantle

Gneiss, formed under high pressure and temperature

Magma

EXAMPLES OF METAMORPHIC ROCKS

Pale feldspar

Dark mica

Dark mineral band

Pale calcite

GNEISS

FOLDED SCHIST

SKARN

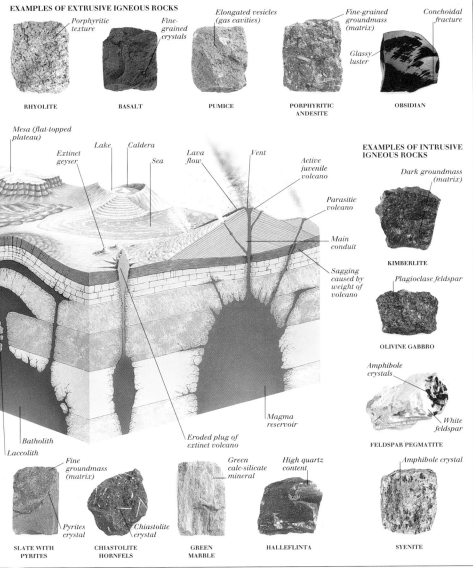

EXAMPLES OF EXTRUSIVE IGNEOUS ROCKS

Porphyritic texture

Fine-grained crystals

Elongated vesicles (gas cavities)

Fine-grained groundmass (matrix)

Conchoidal fracture

Glassy luster

RHYOLITE

BASALT

PUMICE

PORPHYRITIC ANDESITE

OBSIDIAN

Mesa (flat-topped plateau)

Extinct geyser

Lake

Caldera

Sea

Lava flow

Vent

Active juvenile volcano

Parasitic volcano

Main conduit

Sagging caused by weight of volcano

Magma reservoir

Eroded plug of extinct volcano

Batholith

Laccolith

EXAMPLES OF INTRUSIVE IGNEOUS ROCKS

Dark groundmass (matrix)

KIMBERLITE

Plagioclase feldspar

OLIVINE GABBRO

Amphibole crystals

White feldspar

FELDSPAR PEGMATITE

Amphibole crystal

SYENITE

Fine groundmass (matrix)

Pyrites crystal

SLATE WITH PYRITES

Chiastolite crystal

CHIASTOLITE HORNFELS

Green calc-silicate mineral

GREEN MARBLE

High quartz content

HALLEFLINTA

Sedimentary rocks

SEDIMENTARY ROCKS ARE FORMED BY THE ACCUMULATION and consolidation of sediments (see pp. 266-267). There are three main types of sedimentary rock: clastic sedimentary rocks, such as breccia or sandstone, are formed from other rocks that have been broken down into fragments by weathering (see pp. 282-283), which have then been transported and deposited elsewhere; organic sedimentary rocks, such as coal (see pp. 280-281), are derived from plant and animal remains; and chemical sedimentary rocks are formed by chemical processes. For example, rock salt is formed when salt dissolved in water is deposited as the water evaporates. Sedimentary rocks are laid down in layers called beds, or strata. Each new layer is laid down horizontally over older ones. There are usually some gaps in the sequence, called unconformities. These represent periods in which no new sediments were being laid down, or when earlier sedimentary layers were raised above sea level and eroded away.

THE GRAND CANYON, U.S.A.

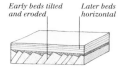

Early beds tilted and eroded

Later beds horizontal

ANGULAR UNCONFORMITY

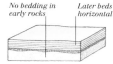

No bedding in early rocks

Later beds horizontal

NONCONFORMITY

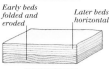

Early beds folded and eroded

Later beds horizontal

DISCONFORMITY

SEDIMENTARY LAYERS OF THE GRAND CANYON REGION

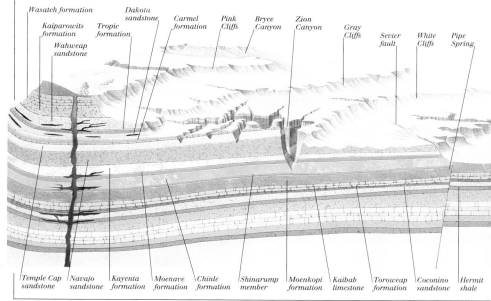

Wasatch formation
Kaiparowits formation
Wahweap sandstone
Tropic formation
Dakota sandstone
Carmel formation
Pink Cliffs
Bryce Canyon
Zion Canyon
Gray Cliffs
Sevier fault
White Cliffs
Pipe Spring

Temple Cap sandstone
Navajo sandstone
Kayenta formation
Moenave formation
Chinle formation
Shinarump member
Moenkopi formation
Kaibab limestone
Toroweap formation
Coconino sandstone
Hermit shale

EXAMPLES OF SEDIMENTARY ROCKS

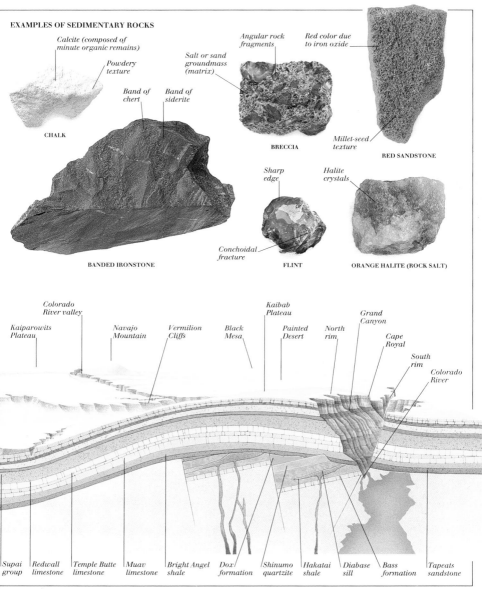

Calcite (composed of minute organic remains)

Powdery texture

CHALK

Band of chert

Band of siderite

BANDED IRONSTONE

Angular rock fragments

Salt or sand groundmass (matrix)

BRECCIA

Red color due to iron oxide

Millet-seed texture

RED SANDSTONE

Sharp edge

Conchoidal fracture

FLINT

Halite crystals

ORANGE HALITE (ROCK SALT)

Colorado River valley

Kaiparowits Plateau

Navajo Mountain

Vermilion Cliffs

Black Mesa

Kaibab Plateau

Painted Desert

North rim

Grand Canyon

Cape Royal

South rim

Colorado River

Supai group

Redwall limestone

Temple Butte limestone

Muav limestone

Bright Angel shale

Dox formation

Shinumo quartzite

Hakatai shale

Diabase sill

Bass formation

Tapeats sandstone

Fossils

FOSSILS ARE THE REMAINS of plants and animals that have been preserved in rock. A fossil may be the preserved remains of an organism itself, an impression of it in rock, or preserved traces (known as trace fossils) left by an organism while it was alive, such as organic carbon outlines, fossilized footprints, or droppings. Most dead organisms soon rot away or are eaten by scavengers. For fossilization to occur, rapid burial by sediment is necessary. The organism decays, but the harder parts—bones, teeth, and shells, for example—may be preserved and hardened by minerals from the surrounding sediment. Fossilization may also occur even when the hard parts of an organism are dissolved away to leave an impression called a mold. The mold is filled by minerals, thereby creating a cast of the organism. The study of fossils (paleontology) not only can show how living things have evolved, but can also help reveal the Earth's geological history—for example, by aiding in the dating of rock strata.

PROCESS OF FOSSILIZATION

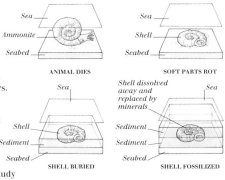

ANIMAL DIES

SOFT PARTS ROT

SHELL BURIED

SHELL FOSSILIZED

EXAMPLES OF FOSSILS

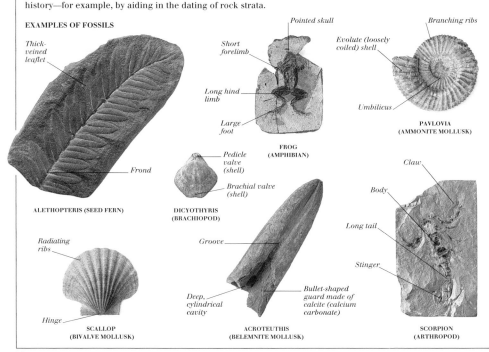

Thick-veined leaflet

Frond

ALETHOPTERIS (SEED FERN)

Short forelimb

Long hind limb

Large foot

Pointed skull

FROG
(AMPHIBIAN)

Evolute (loosely coiled) shell

Branching ribs

Umbilicus

PAVLOVIA
(AMMONITE MOLLUSK)

Pedicle valve (shell)

Brachial valve (shell)

DICYOTHYRIS
(BRACHIOPOD)

Radiating ribs

Hinge

SCALLOP
(BIVALVE MOLLUSK)

Groove

Deep, cylindrical cavity

Bullet-shaped guard made of calcite (calcium carbonate)

ACROTEUTHIS
(BELEMNITE MOLLUSK)

Claw

Body

Long tail

Stinger

SCORPION
(ARTHROPOD)

THE FOSSIL RECORD

Precambrian time

Proterozoic eon

Palaeozoic era

Phanerozoic eon

Mesozoic era

Cenozoic era

570 / 570 — Cambrian period

510 — Ordovician period

439 — Silurian period

409 — Devonian period

Trilobite

363 — Carboniferous period

290 — Permian period

245 / 245 — Triassic period

Ammonites and Belemnites

208 — Jurassic period

Seed ferns

146 — Cretaceous period

Dinosaurs

65 / 65

VERTEBRATES
Fish
Amphibians
Birds
Reptiles
Mammals
Primates

INVERTEBRATES
Echinoderms
Brachiopods
Chelicerates
Insectans
Crustaceans
Bivalves
Gastropods
Cephalopods
Worms
Corals and jellyfish
Bryozoans
Sponges
Foraminiferans

PLANTS
Algae
Vascular plants
Sphenopsids
Ferns
Cycads
Angiosperms
Ginkgos
Conifers

56.5 — Palaeocene epoch

35.5 — Eocene epoch

23.5 — Oligocene epoch

Tertiary period

5.2 — Miocene epoch

1.64 — Pliocene epoch

0.01 — Pleistocene epoch

Holocene epoch

Quaternary period

MILLIONS OF YEARS AGO (MYA)

Ambulacral area

Turreted spire

Ribs

Large body whorl

Aperture

STRUTHIOLARIA (GASTROPOD MOLLUSK)

Large, elevated eye

Spiny, segmented body

Wide head

Spiny tail

LEONASPIS (TRILOBITE)

Claw

Carapace

MUD CRAB (CRUSTACEAN)

Tiny tubercle

Genital pore

CLYPEASTER (ECHINODERM)

279

Mineral resources

Stalk   *Leaf*

PLANT MATTER

MINERAL RESOURCES CAN BE DEFINED AS naturally occurring substances that can be extracted from the Earth and are useful as fuels and raw materials. Coal, oil, and gas—collectively called fossil fuels—are commonly included in this group, but are not strictly minerals, because they are of organic origin. Coal formation begins when vegetation is buried and partly decomposed to form peat. Overlying sediments compress the peat and transform it into lignite (soft brown coal). As the overlying sediments accumulate,

Decayed plant matter

OIL RIG, NORTH SEA

increasing pressure and temperature eventually transform the lignite into bituminous and hard anthracite coals. Oil and gas are usually formed from organic molecules that were deposited in marine sediments. Under the effects of heat and pressure, the compressed organic molecules undergo complex chemical changes to form oil and gas. The oil and gas percolate upward through water-saturated permeable rocks. They may rise to the Earth's surface, or accumulate below an impermeable layer of rock that has been folded or faulted to form a trap—an anticline (upfold) trap, for example. Minerals are inorganic substances that may consist of a single chemical element, such as gold, silver, or copper, or combinations of elements (see pp. 268-269). Some minerals are concentrated in mineralization zones in rock associated with crustal movements or volcanic activity. Others may be found in sediments as placer deposits—accumulations of high-density minerals that have been weathered out of rocks, transported, and deposited (on riverbeds, for example).

About 60% carbon   PEAT   *About 70% carbon*

Crumbly texture   LIGNITE (BROWN COAL)   *Powdery texture*

About 80% carbon

HOW COAL IS FORMED

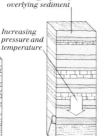

Increasing layers of overlying sediment

Vegetation

Increasing layers of overlying sediment

Increasing pressure and temperature

Increasing pressure and temperature

Peat (about 60% carbon)

PEAT

Lignite (about 70% carbon)

LIGNITE (BROWN COAL)

Bituminous coal (about 80% carbon)

BITUMINOUS COAL

Shiny surface   BITUMINOUS COAL   *About 95% carbon*

ANTHRACITE COAL

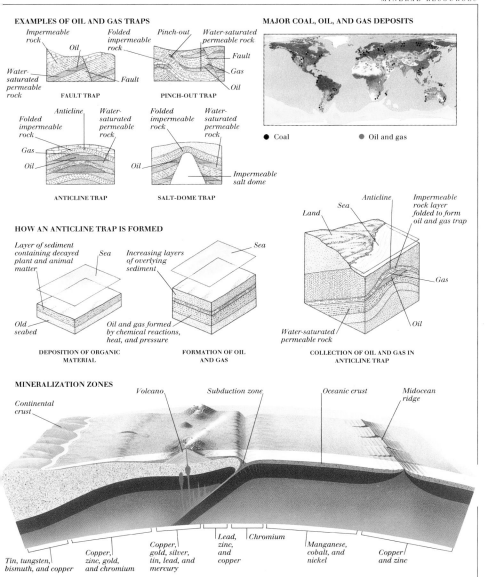

EXAMPLES OF OIL AND GAS TRAPS

Impermeable rock

Oil

Folded impermeable rock

Water-saturated permeable rock

Fault

FAULT TRAP

Pinch-out

Water-saturated permeable rock

Fault

Gas

Oil

PINCH-OUT TRAP

Anticline

Water-saturated permeable rock

Folded impermeable rock

Gas

Oil

ANTICLINE TRAP

Folded impermeable rock

Water-saturated permeable rock

Oil

Impermeable salt dome

SALT-DOME TRAP

MAJOR COAL, OIL, AND GAS DEPOSITS

● Coal   ● Oil and gas

Anticline

Sea

Land

Impermeable rock layer folded to form oil and gas trap

Gas

Oil

Water-saturated permeable rock

COLLECTION OF OIL AND GAS IN ANTICLINE TRAP

HOW AN ANTICLINE TRAP IS FORMED

Layer of sediment containing decayed plant and animal matter

Sea

Old seabed

DEPOSITION OF ORGANIC MATERIAL

Increasing layers of overlying sediment

Sea

Oil and gas formed by chemical reactions, heat, and pressure

FORMATION OF OIL AND GAS

MINERALIZATION ZONES

Continental crust

Volcano

Subduction zone

Oceanic crust

Midocean ridge

Tin, tungsten, bismuth, and copper

Copper, zinc, gold, and chromium

Copper, gold, silver, tin, lead, and mercury

Lead, zinc, and copper

Chromium

Manganese, cobalt, and nickel

Copper and zinc

281

Weathering and erosion

WEATHERING IS THE BREAKING DOWN of rocks on the Earth's surface. There are two main types: physical (or mechanical), and chemical. Physical weathering may be caused by temperature changes, such as freezing and thawing, or by abrasion from material carried by winds, rivers, or glaciers. Rocks may also be broken down by the actions of animals and plants, such as the burrowing of animals and the growth of roots. Chemical weathering causes rocks to decompose by changing their chemical composition. For example, rainwater may dissolve certain minerals in a rock. Erosion is the wearing away and removal of land surfaces by water, wind, or ice. It is greatest in areas of little or no surface vegetation, such as deserts, where sand dunes may form.

FORMATION OF A ROCK PAVEMENT (HAMADA)

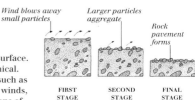

Wind blows away small particles

Larger particles aggregate

Rock pavement forms

FIRST STAGE   SECOND STAGE   FINAL STAGE

FEATURES OF WEATHERING AND EROSION

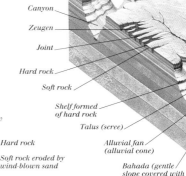

Mesa (flat-topped plateau)

Canyon

Zeugen

Joint

Hard rock

Soft rock

Shelf formed of hard rock

Talus (scree)

Alluvial fan (alluvial cone)

Bahada (gentle slope covered with loose rock)

Bolson (alluvium-filled basin)

FEATURES PRODUCED BY WIND ACTION

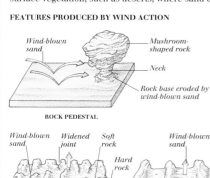

Wind-blown sand

Mushroom-shaped rock

Neck

Rock base eroded by wind-blown sand

ROCK PEDESTAL

Wind-blown sand   Widened joint   Soft rock   Hard rock

ZEUGEN

Wind-blown sand   Furrow

Hard rock

Soft rock eroded by wind-blown sand

YARDANG

EXAMPLES OF PHYSICAL WEATHERING PROCESSES

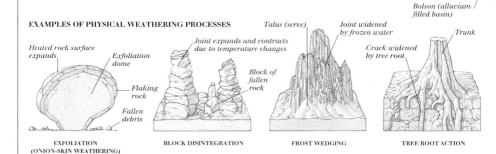

Heated rock surface expands

Exfoliation dome

Flaking rock

Fallen debris

EXFOLIATION (ONION-SKIN WEATHERING)

Joint expands and contracts due to temperature changes

Block of fallen rock

BLOCK DISINTEGRATION

Talus (scree)

Joint widened by frozen water

FROST WEDGING

Crack widened by tree root

Trunk

TREE ROOT ACTION

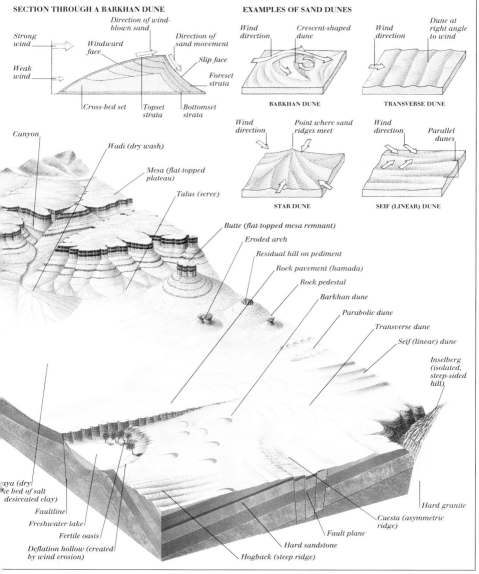

SECTION THROUGH A BARKHAN DUNE

Strong wind

Weak wind

Direction of wind-blown sand

Windward face

Direction of sand movement

Slip face

Foreset strata

Cross-bed set

Topset strata

Bottomset strata

EXAMPLES OF SAND DUNES

Wind direction

Crescent-shaped dune

BARKHAN DUNE

Wind direction

Dune at right angle to wind

TRANSVERSE DUNE

Wind direction

Point where sand ridges meet

STAR DUNE

Wind direction

Parallel dunes

SEIF (LINEAR) DUNE

Canyon

Wadi (dry wash)

Mesa (flat-topped plateau)

Talus (scree)

Butte (flat-topped mesa remnant)

Eroded arch

Residual hill on pediment

Rock pavement (hamada)

Rock pedestal

Barkhan dune

Parabolic dune

Transverse dune

Seif (linear) dune

Inselberg (isolated, steep-sided hill)

Playa (dry lake bed of salt desiccated clay)

Faultline

Freshwater lake

Fertile oasis

Deflation hollow (created by wind erosion)

Hogback (steep ridge)

Hard sandstone

Fault plane

Cuesta (asymmetric ridge)

Hard granite

283

Caves

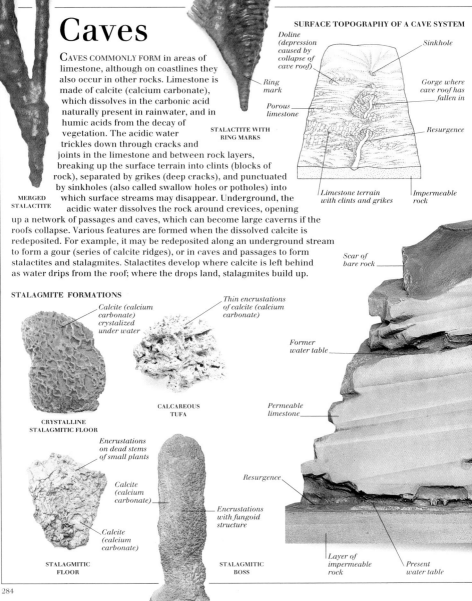

CAVES COMMONLY FORM in areas of limestone, although on coastlines they also occur in other rocks. Limestone is made of calcite (calcium carbonate), which dissolves in the carbonic acid naturally present in rainwater, and in humic acids from the decay of vegetation. The acidic water trickles down through cracks and joints in the limestone and between rock layers, breaking up the surface terrain into clints (blocks of rock), separated by grikes (deep cracks), and punctuated by sinkholes (also called swallow holes or potholes) into which surface streams may disappear. Underground, the acidic water dissolves the rock around crevices, opening up a network of passages and caves, which can become large caverns if the roofs collapse. Various features are formed when the dissolved calcite is redeposited. For example, it may be redeposited along an underground stream to form a gour (series of calcite ridges), or in caves and passages to form stalactites and stalagmites. Stalactites develop where calcite is left behind as water drips from the roof; where the drops land, stalagmites build up.

STALACTITE WITH RING MARKS

Ring mark

Porous limestone

MERGED STALACTITE

SURFACE TOPOGRAPHY OF A CAVE SYSTEM

Doline (depression caused by collapse of cave roof)

Sinkhole

Gorge where cave roof has fallen in

Resurgence

Limestone terrain with clints and grikes

Impermeable rock

STALAGMITE FORMATIONS

Calcite (calcium carbonate) crystalized under water

Thin encrustations of calcite (calcium carbonate)

CRYSTALLINE STALAGMITIC FLOOR

CALCAREOUS TUFA

Scar of bare rock

Former water table

Permeable limestone

Encrustations on dead stems of small plants

Calcite (calcium carbonate)

Calcite (calcium carbonate)

STALAGMITIC FLOOR

Encrustations with fungoid structure

STALAGMITIC BOSS

Resurgence

Layer of impermeable rock

Present water table

DEVELOPMENT OF A CAVE SYSTEM

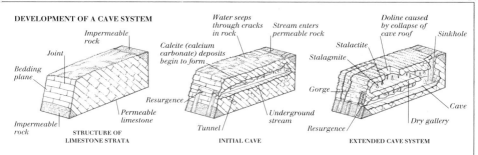

Impermeable rock

Joint

Bedding plane

Impermeable rock

Permeable limestone

STRUCTURE OF LIMESTONE STRATA

Water seeps through cracks in rock

Stream enters permeable rock

Calcite (calcium carbonate) deposits begin to form

Resurgence

Tunnel

Underground stream

INITIAL CAVE

Doline caused by collapse of cave roof

Sinkhole

Stalactite

Stalagmite

Gorge

Resurgence

Cave

Dry gallery

EXTENDED CAVE SYSTEM

INTERCONNECTED CAVE SYSTEM

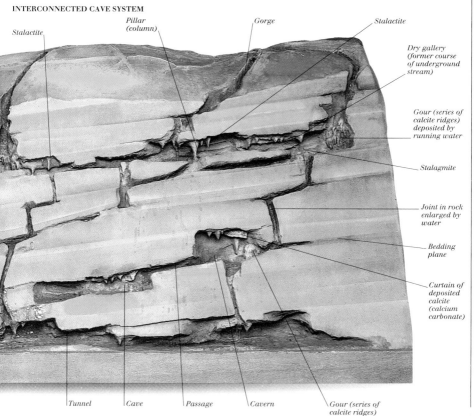

Stalactite

Pillar (column)

Gorge

Stalactite

Dry gallery (former course of underground stream)

Gour (series of calcite ridges) deposited by running water

Stalagmite

Joint in rock enlarged by water

Bedding plane

Curtain of deposited calcite (calcium carbonate)

Tunnel

Cave

Passage

Cavern

Gour (series of calcite ridges)

285

Glaciers

GLACIER BAY, ALASKA

A VALLEY GLACIER IS A LARGE MASS OF ICE that forms on land and moves slowly downhill under its own weight. It is formed from snow that collects in cirques (mountain hollows also known as corries), compressing into ice as more and more snow accumulates. The cirque is deepened by frost wedging and abrasion (see pp. 282-283), and arêtes (sharp ridges) develop between adjacent cirques. Eventually, so much ice builds up that the glacier begins to flow. As the glacier moves it collects moraine (debris), which may range in size from particles of dust to large boulders. The rocks at the base of the glacier erode the glacial valley, giving it a U-shaped cross section. Under the glacier, *roches moutonnées* (eroded outcrops of hard rock) and drumlins (rounded mounds of rock and clay) are left behind on the valley floor. The glacier ends at a terminus (the snout), where the ice melts as fast as it arrives. If the temperature increases, the ice melts faster than it arrives, and the glacier retreats. The retreating glacier leaves behind its moraine and also erratics (isolated single boulders). Glacial streams from the melting glacier deposit eskers and kames (ridges and mounds of sand and gravel) but carry away the finer sediment to form a stratified outwash plain. Lumps of ice carried on to this plain melt, creating holes called kettles.

VALLEY GLACIER

Lateral moraine
Meltwater pool
Medial moraine
Suspended erratic
Horn
Medial moraine
Englacial stream
Cave
Arête (ridge)
Hanging valley
Suspended erratic
Melting glacier
Stream
Ice margin lake
Snout
Terminal moraine
Waterfall
Braided stream
Steep side of U-shaped valley
Boulder clay
Terminal lake
Meltwater stream
Roche moutonnée
Lake
Push moraine

POST-GLACIAL VALLEY

Collapsed sediment
Drumlin
Exposed valley floor
Roche moutonnée
Horn of mountain
Kame terrace
Esker
Erratic
Arête (ridge)
Lacustrine terrace
Post-glacial stream
Kame delta
Kettle
Terminal moraine
Kettle lake
Terminal moraine
Outwash terrace
Boulder clay
Kame
Roche moutonnée
Outwash fan
Steep side of U-shaped valley
Roche moutonnée

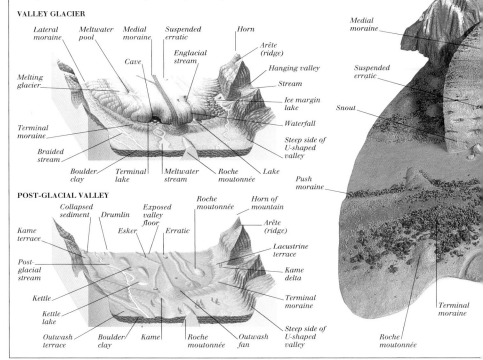

FEATURES OF A GLACIER

Firn (compressed snow)

Tributary glacier

Moving ice

U-shaped valley

Medial moraine

Lateral moraine

Cirque (corrie)

Arête (ridge)

Tributary moraine joins medial moraine

Subglacial stream

Rock being eroded by ice

Brittle surface ice

Viscous flowing ice

Englacial moraine

Crevasse

Ribbon lake

Outwash plain

Meltwater

Stream

Sediment deposited by meltwater

ICE-FALL

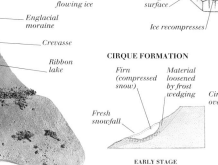

Slope flattens

Steep slope

Gentle slope

Smooth surface

Rougher surface

Crevasse deepens and widens

Ice recompresses

Ice block tilts and twists

Ice breaks into blocks

CIRQUE FORMATION

Firn (compressed snow)

Material loosened by frost wedging

Fresh snowfall

EARLY STAGE

Moraine pulled from ground

Steep back wall

Glacier

Base of cirque eroded by glacier's pivoting action

Rock lip

LATER STAGE

U-SHAPED VALLEY FORMATION

Arête (ridge)

Horn

Cirque overspills

Glacier

DURING GLACIATION

Deepened cirque

Deep U-shaped valley

Hanging valley

Tarn

AFTER GLACIATION

Rivers

RIVERS FORM PART of the water cycle—the continuous circulation of water between the land, sea, and atmosphere. The source of a river may be a mountain spring, or lake, or a melting glacier. The course that the river subsequently takes depends on the slope of the terrain and on the rock types and formations over which it flows. In its early, upland stages, a river tumbles steeply over rocks and boulders and cuts a steep-sided V-shaped valley. Farther downstream, it flows smoothly over sediments and forms winding meanders, eroding sideways to create broad valleys and plains. On reaching the coast, the river may deposit sediment, forming an estuary or delta (see pp. 290-291).

RIVER CAPTURE

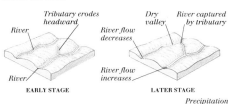

Tributary erodes headward
River
River flow decreases
Dry valley
River captured by tributary
River
River flow increases

EARLY STAGE   LATER STAGE

THE WATER CYCLE

Precipitation falls on high ground
Wind
Water carried downstream by river
Water vapor released into atmosphere by trees and other plants
Wind
Water vapor forms clouds
Water evaporates from sea
Water stored in sea
River flows into sea
Water seeps underground and flows to sea
Water evaporates from lake
Water seeps underground and flows to sea

SATELLITE IMAGE OF GANGES RIVER DELTA, BANGLADESH

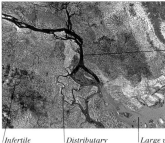

River Ganges

Ganges delta

Infertile swampland   Distributary   Large volume of sediment

Seabed
Sea

RIVER DRAINAGE PATTERNS

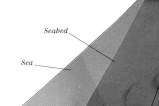

RADIAL   CENTRIPETAL   PARALLEL   DENDRITIC

DERANGED   TRELLISED   ANNULAR   RECTANGULAR

Sediment layers

STAGES IN A RIVER'S DEVELOPMENT

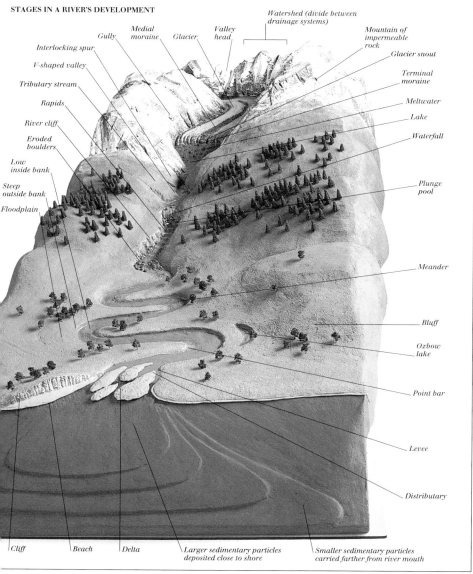

Watershed (divide between drainage systems)

Gully

Medial moraine

Glacier

Valley head

Mountain of impermeable rock

Glacier snout

Interlocking spur

Terminal moraine

V-shaped valley

Meltwater

Tributary stream

Lake

Rapids

Waterfall

River cliff

Eroded boulders

Plunge pool

Low inside bank

Steep outside bank

Floodplain

Meander

Bluff

Oxbow lake

Point bar

Levee

Distributary

Cliff

Beach

Delta

Larger sedimentary particles deposited close to shore

Smaller sedimentary particles carried farther from river mouth

River features

RIVERS ARE ONE OF THE MAJOR FORCES that shape the landscape. Near its source, a river is steep (see pp. 288-289). It erodes downward, carving out V-shaped valleys and deep gorges. Waterfalls and rapids are formed where the river flows from hard rock to softer, more easily eroded rock. Farther downstream, meanders may form and there is greater sideways erosion, resulting in a broad river valley. The river sometimes erodes through the neck of a meander to form an oxbow lake. Sediment deposited on the valley floor by meandering rivers and during floods helps to create a floodplain. Floods may also deposit sediment on the banks of the river to form levees. As a river spills into the sea or a lake, it deposits large amounts of sediment, and may form a delta. A delta is an area of sand bars, swamps and lagoons through which the river flows in several channels called distributaries—the Mississippi delta, for example. Often, a rise in sea level may have flooded the river mouth to form a broad estuary, a tidal section where seawater mixes with fresh water.

HOW WATERFALLS AND RAPIDS ARE FORMED

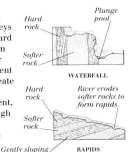

Hard rock
Softer rock
Plunge pool

WATERFALL

Hard rock
Softer rock
River erodes softer rocks to form rapids
Gently sloping rock strata

RAPIDS

A RIVER VALLEY DRAINAGE SYSTEM

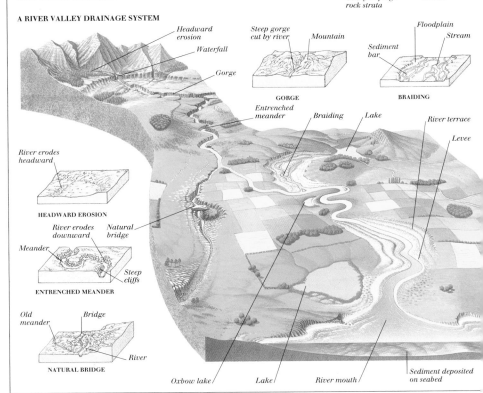

Headward erosion

Waterfall

Gorge

Steep gorge cut by river   *Mountain*

GORGE

Floodplain
Stream
Sediment bar

BRAIDING

Entrenched meander   *Braiding*   *Lake*

River terrace

Levee

River erodes headward

HEADWARD EROSION

River erodes downward   *Natural bridge*

Meander

Steep cliffs

ENTRENCHED MEANDER

Old meander   *Bridge*

River

NATURAL BRIDGE

Oxbow lake   *Lake*   *River mouth*   *Sediment deposited on seabed*

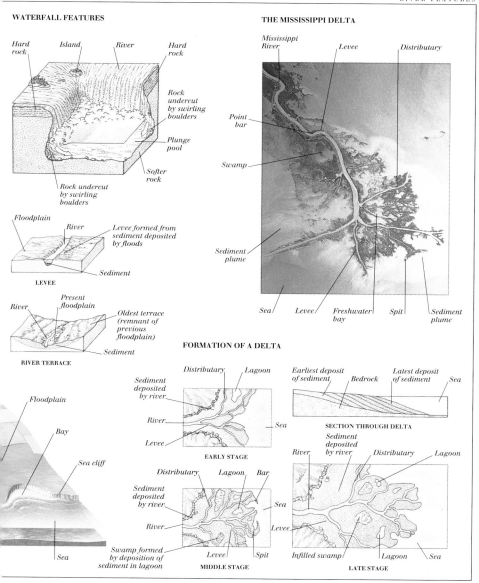

WATERFALL FEATURES

Hard rock

Island

River

Hard rock

Rock undercut by swirling boulders

Plunge pool

Softer rock

Rock undercut by swirling boulders

Floodplain

River

Levee formed from sediment deposited by floods

Sediment

LEVEE

River

Present floodplain

Oldest terrace (remnant of previous floodplain)

Sediment

RIVER TERRACE

Floodplain

Bay

Sea cliff

Sea

THE MISSISSIPPI DELTA

Mississippi River

Levee

Distributary

Point bar

Swamp

Sediment plume

Sea

Levee

Freshwater bay

Spit

Sediment plume

FORMATION OF A DELTA

Distributary

Lagoon

Sediment deposited by river

River

Levee

Sea

EARLY STAGE

Earliest deposit of sediment

Bedrock

Latest deposit of sediment

Sea

SECTION THROUGH DELTA

Distributary

Lagoon

Bar

Sediment deposited by river

River

Sea

Swamp formed by deposition of sediment in lagoon

Levee

Spit

MIDDLE STAGE

Sediment deposited by river

River

Distributary

Lagoon

Levee

Infilled swamp

Lagoon

Sea

LATE STAGE

Lakes and groundwater

NATURAL LAKES OCCUR WHERE a large quantity of water collects in a hollow in impermeable rock or is prevented from draining away by a barrier, such as moraine (glacial deposits) or solidified lava. Lakes are often relatively short-lived landscape features, because they tend to become silted up by sediment from the streams and rivers that feed them. Some of the more long-lasting lakes are found in deep rift valleys formed by vertical movements of the Earth's crust (see pp. 58-59)—for example, Lake Baikal in Russia, the world's largest freshwater lake, and the Dead Sea in the Middle East, one of the world's saltiest lakes. Where water is able to drain away, it sinks into the ground until it reaches a layer of impermeable rock, then accumulates in the permeable rock above it. This water-saturated permeable rock is called an aquifer. The saturated zone varies in depth according to seasonal and climatic changes. In wet conditions, the water stored underground builds up, while in dry periods it becomes depleted. Where the upper edge of the saturated zone—the water table—meets the ground surface, water emerges as springs. In an artesian basin, where the aquifer is below an aquiclude (layer of impermeable rock), the water table throughout the basin is determined by its height at the rim. At the center of such a basin, the water table is above ground level. The water in the basin is thus trapped below the water table and can rise under its own pressure along fault lines or well shafts.

LAKE BAIKAL, RUSSIA

EXAMPLES OF SPRINGS

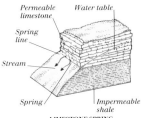

Permeable limestone
Water table
Spring line
Stream
Spring
Impermeable shale

LIMESTONE SPRING

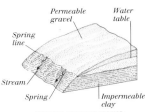

Permeable gravel
Water table
Spring line
Stream
Spring
Impermeable clay

COASTAL (VALLEY) SPRING

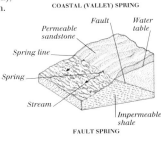

Fault
Water table
Permeable sandstone
Spring line
Spring
Stream
Impermeable shale

FAULT SPRING

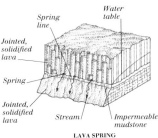

Water table
Spring line
Jointed, solidified lava
Spring
Jointed, solidified lava
Stream
Impermeable mudstone

LAVA SPRING

STRUCTURE OF AN ARTESIAN BASIN

Recharge area

Water table

Height of water table in recharge area

Artesian spring

Aquiclude (impermeable rock)

Artesian spring

Fault

Artesian well

Aquifer (saturated rock)

Aquiclude (impermeable rock)

FEATURES OF A GROUNDWATER SYSTEM

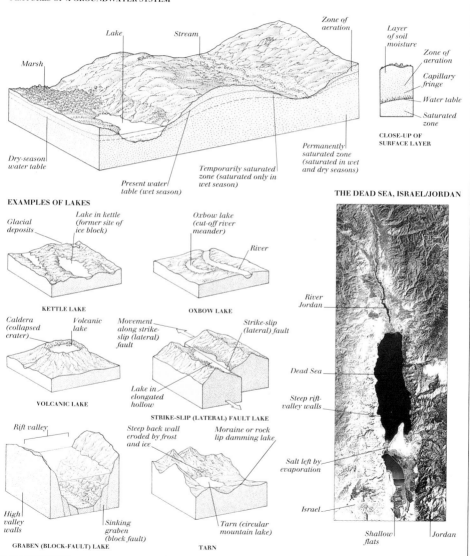

Zone of aeration

Lake

Stream

Marsh

Layer of soil moisture

Zone of aeration

Capillary fringe

Water table

Saturated zone

Dry-season water table

Present water table (wet season)

Temporarily saturated zone (saturated only in wet season)

Permanently saturated zone (saturated in wet and dry seasons)

CLOSE-UP OF SURFACE LAYER

EXAMPLES OF LAKES

Glacial deposits

Lake in kettle (former site of ice block)

KETTLE LAKE

Oxbow lake (cut-off river meander)

River

OXBOW LAKE

Caldera (collapsed crater)

Volcanic lake

VOLCANIC LAKE

Movement along strike-slip (lateral) fault

Strike-slip (lateral) fault

Lake in elongated hollow

STRIKE-SLIP (LATERAL) FAULT LAKE

Rift valley

High valley walls

Sinking graben (block fault)

GRABEN (BLOCK-FAULT) LAKE

Steep back wall eroded by frost and ice

Moraine or rock lip damming lake

Tarn (circular mountain lake)

TARN

THE DEAD SEA, ISRAEL/JORDAN

River Jordan

Dead Sea

Steep rift-valley walls

Salt left by evaporation

Israel

Shallow flats

Jordan

293

Coastlines

COASTLINES ARE AMONG THE MOST RAPIDLY changing landscape features. Some are eroded by waves, wind, and rain, causing cliffs to be undercut and caves to be hollowed out of solid rock. Others are built up by waves transporting sand and small rocks in a process known as longshore drift and by rivers depositing sediment in deltas. Additional influences include the activities of living organisms such as coral, crustal movements, and sea-level variations due to climatic changes. Rising land or a drop in sea level creates an emergent coastline, with cliffs and beaches standing above the new shoreline. Sinking land or a rise in sea level produces a drowned coastline, typified by fjords (submerged glacial valleys) or submerged river valleys.

FEATURES OF A SEA CLIFF

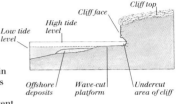

Cliff top
Cliff face
High tide level
Low tide level
Offshore deposits
Wave-cut platform
Undercut area of cliff

FEATURES OF WAVES

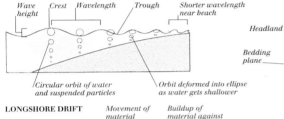

Wave height
Crest
Wavelength
Trough
Shorter wavelength near beach
Circular orbit of water and suspended particles
Orbit deformed into ellipse as water gets shallower

LONGSHORE DRIFT

Pebble
Backwash
Movement of material along beach
Buildup of material against groyne
Beach
Groyne
Waves approaching shore at an oblique angle
Swash zone
Swash

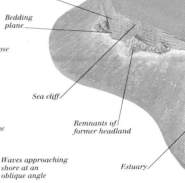

Mature river
Headland
Bedding plane
Sea cliff
Remnants of former headland
Estuary

DEPOSITIONAL FEATURES OF COASTLINES

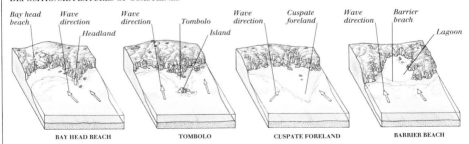

Bay head beach
Wave direction
Headland
Wave direction
Tombolo
Island
Wave direction
Cuspate foreland
Wave direction
Barrier beach
Lagoon

BAY HEAD BEACH
TOMBOLO
CUSPATE FORELAND
BARRIER BEACH

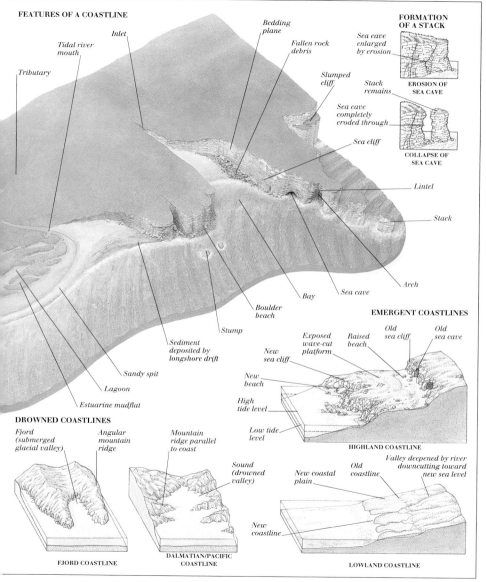

FEATURES OF A COASTLINE

Tributary

Tidal river mouth

Inlet

Bedding plane

Fallen rock debris

Slumped cliff

FORMATION OF A STACK

Sea cave enlarged by erosion

EROSION OF SEA CAVE

Stack remains

Sea cave completely eroded through

COLLAPSE OF SEA CAVE

Sea cliff

Lintel

Stack

Arch

Sea cave

Bay

Boulder beach

Stump

Sediment deposited by longshore drift

Sandy spit

Lagoon

Estuarine mudflat

EMERGENT COASTLINES

Exposed wave-cut platform

Old sea cliff

Old sea cave

Raised beach

New sea cliff

New beach

High tide level

Low tide level

HIGHLAND COASTLINE

DROWNED COASTLINES

Fjord (submerged glacial valley)

Angular mountain ridge

Mountain ridge parallel to coast

Sound (drowned valley)

FJORD COASTLINE

DALMATIAN/PACIFIC COASTLINE

Valley deepened by river downcutting toward new sea level

New coastal plain

Old coastline

New coastline

LOWLAND COASTLINE

Oceans and seas

OCEANS AND SEAS COVER ABOUT 70 PERCENT of the Earth's surface and account for about 97 percent of its total water. These oceans and seas play a crucial role in regulating temperature variations and determining climate. Their waters absorb heat from the Sun, especially in tropical regions, and the surface currents distribute it around the Earth, warming overlying air masses and neighboring land in winter and cooling them in summer. The oceans are never still. Differences in temperature and salinity drive deep current systems, while surface currents are generated by winds blowing over the oceans. All currents are deflected—to the right in the Northern Hemisphere, to the left in the Southern Hemisphere—as a result of the Earth's rotation. This deflective factor is known as the Coriolis force. A current that begins on the surface is immediately deflected. This current in turn generates a current in the layer of water beneath, which is also deflected. As the movement is transmitted downward, the deflections form an Ekman spiral. The waters of the oceans and seas are also moved by the constant ebb and flow of tides. These are caused by the gravitational pull of the Moon and Sun. The highest tides (Spring tides) occur at full and new Moon; the lowest tides (neap tides) occur at first and last quarter.

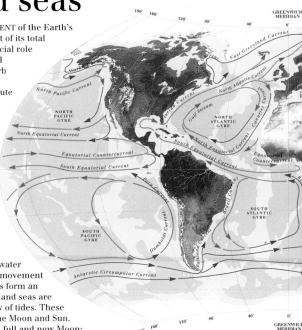

OFFSHORE CURRENTS

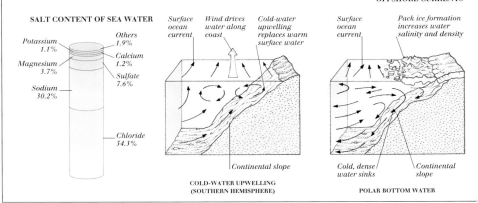

SALT CONTENT OF SEA WATER

Others 1.9%
Potassium 1.1%
Magnesium 3.7%
Sodium 30.2%
Calcium 1.2%
Sulfate 7.6%
Chloride 54.3%

Surface ocean current
Wind drives water along coast
Cold-water upwelling replaces warm surface water
Continental slope

COLD-WATER UPWELLING (SOUTHERN HEMISPHERE)

Surface ocean current
Pack ice formation increases water salinity and density
Cold, dense water sinks
Continental slope

POLAR BOTTOM WATER

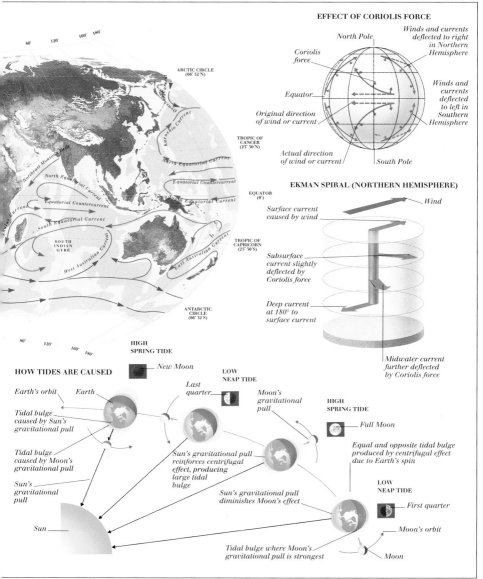

EFFECT OF CORIOLIS FORCE

Winds and currents deflected to right in Northern Hemisphere

North Pole

Coriolis force

Equator

Winds and currents deflected to left in Southern Hemisphere

Original direction of wind or current

Actual direction of wind or current

South Pole

EKMAN SPIRAL (NORTHERN HEMISPHERE)

EQUATOR (0°)

Wind

Surface current caused by wind

Subsurface current slightly deflected by Coriolis force

Deep current at 180° to surface current

TROPIC OF CANCER (23° 30'N)

TROPIC OF CAPRICORN (23° 30'S)

Midwater current further deflected by Coriolis force

ARCTIC CIRCLE (66° 32'N)

ANTARCTIC CIRCLE (66° 32'S)

North Equatorial Current
Equatorial Countercurrent
South Equatorial Current
Equatorial Countercurrent
South Equatorial Current
SOUTH INDIAN GYRE
West Australia Current
East Australian Current
Kuroshio Current
Northeast Monsoon Drift
North Equatorial Current

HIGH SPRING TIDE
New Moon

LOW NEAP TIDE
Last quarter

HIGH SPRING TIDE
Full Moon

LOW NEAP TIDE
First quarter

HOW TIDES ARE CAUSED

Earth's orbit — Earth

Tidal bulge caused by Sun's gravitational pull

Tidal bulge caused by Moon's gravitational pull

Sun's gravitational pull

Sun

Moon's gravitational pull

Sun's gravitational pull reinforces centrifugal effect, producing large tidal bulge

Sun's gravitational pull diminishes Moon's effect

Equal and opposite tidal bulge produced by centrifugal effect due to Earth's spin

Moon's orbit

Tidal bulge where Moon's gravitational pull is strongest

Moon

297

The ocean floor

THE OCEAN FLOOR INCLUDES TWO SECTIONS: the continental shelf and slope, and the deep-ocean floor. The continental shelf and slope are part of the continental crust, but may extend far into the ocean. Sloping quite gently to a depth of about 460 feet, the continental shelf is covered in sandy deposits shaped by waves and tidal currents. At the edge of the continental shelf, the seabed slopes down to the abyssal plain, which lies at an average depth of about 12,500 feet. On this deep-ocean floor is a layer of sediment made up of clays, fine oozes formed from the remains of tiny sea creatures, and occasional mineral-rich deposits. Echo-sounding and remote sensing from satellites has revealed that the abyssal plain is divided by a world-circling system of mountain ranges, far bigger than any on land—the midocean ridge. Here, magma (molten rock) wells up from the Earth's interior and solidifies, widening the ocean floor (see pp. 58-59). As the ocean floor spreads, volcanoes that have formed over hot spots in the crust move away from their magma source; they become extinct and are increasingly submerged and eroded. Volcanoes eroded below sea level remain as seamounts (underwater mountains). In warm waters, a volcano that projects above the ocean surface often acquires a fringing coral reef, which may develop into an atoll as the volcano becomes submerged.

CONTINENTAL-SHELF FLOOR

Bedrock exposed by tidal scour

Shoreline

Parallel strips of coarse material left by strong tidal currents

Sand deposited in wavy pattern by weaker currents

FEATURES OF THE OCEAN FLOOR

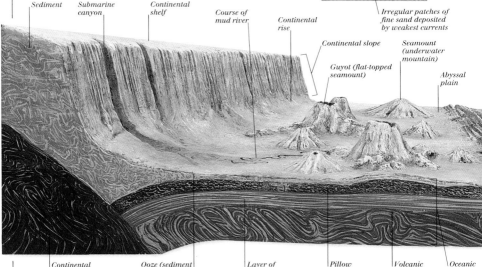

Sediment

Submarine canyon

Continental shelf

Course of mud river

Continental rise

Continental slope

Irregular patches of fine sand deposited by weakest currents

Seamount (underwater mountain)

Guyot (flat-topped seamount)

Abyssal plain

Continental crust

Ooze (sediment consisting of remains of tiny sea creatures)

Layer of volcanic rock

Pillow lava

Volcanic crystalline rock

Oceanic crust

KEY

☐ Calcareous ooze

☐ Pelagic clay

☐ Glacial sediments

☐ Siliceous ooze

☐ Terrigenous sediments

☐ Continental margin sediments

▨ Metalliferous muds

☐ Major nodule fields

DEEP-OCEAN FLOOR SEDIMENTS

ECHO-SOUND PROFILE OF OCEAN FLOOR

Sand wave

Event mark indicates synchronization of survey equipment

Minor oscillations caused by ship's movement

Sand wave

Seabed profile

22 1493   22

Velocity of sound in water (1,493 m/sec; 4,898 ft/sec)

Reference code

Midocean ridge

Ocean trench

Magma (molten rock)

Sediment

DEVELOPMENT OF AN ATOLL

Volcanic island

Coral grows on shoreline

Sea level

FRINGING REEF

Lagoon

Coral continues to grow, forming barrier reef

Eroded volcanic island subsides

BARRIER REEF

Coral continues to grow where waves bring food

Lagoon

Dead coral

Volcanic island becomes submerged

ATOLL

Coral submerged too deeply to grow

Volcanic island is submerged further

SUBMERGED ATOLL

The atmosphere

Exosphere
(altitude above
about 300 miles)

Corona

JET STREAM

THE EARTH IS SURROUNDED BY ITS ATMOSPHERE, a blanket of gases that enables life to exist on the planet. This layer has no definite outer edge, gradually becoming thinner until it merges into space, but over 80 percent of atmospheric gases are held by gravity within about 10 miles of the Earth's surface. The atmosphere blocks out much harmful ultraviolet solar radiation, and insulates the Earth against extremes of temperature by limiting both incoming solar radiation and the escape of re-radiated heat into space. This natural balance may be distorted by the greenhouse effect, as gases such as carbon dioxide have built up in the atmosphere, trapping more heat. Close to the Earth's surface, differences in air temperature and pressure cause air to circulate between the equator and poles. This circulation, together with the Coriolis force, gives rise to the prevailing surface winds and the high-level jet streams.

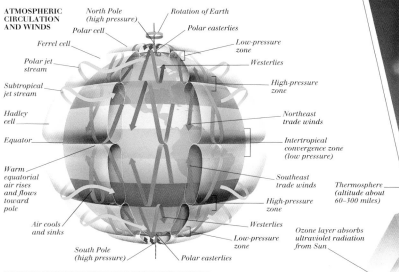

ATMOSPHERIC CIRCULATION AND WINDS

North Pole (high pressure)

Rotation of Earth

Polar cell

Polar easterlies

Ferrel cell

Low-pressure zone

Polar jet stream

Westerlies

Subtropical jet stream

High-pressure zone

Hadley cell

Northeast trade winds

Equator

Intertropical convergence zone (low pressure)

Warm equatorial air rises and flows toward pole

Southeast trade winds

Thermosphere (altitude about 60–300 miles)

High-pressure zone

Air cools and sinks

Westerlies

Ozone layer absorbs ultraviolet radiation from Sun

Low-pressure zone

South Pole (high pressure)

Polar easterlies

FORMATION OF ROSSBY WAVES IN THE JET STREAM

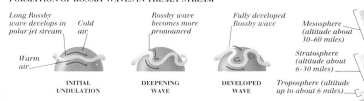

Long Rossby wave develops in polar jet stream

Cold air

Rossby wave becomes more pronounced

Fully developed Rossby wave

Mesosphere (altitude about 30–60 miles)

Warm air

Stratosphere (altitude about 6–30 miles)

INITIAL UNDULATION

DEEPENING WAVE

DEVELOPED WAVE

Troposphere (altitude up to about 6 miles)

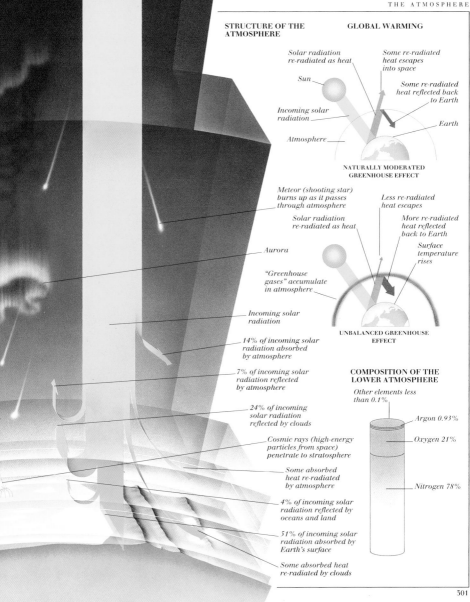

STRUCTURE OF THE ATMOSPHERE

GLOBAL WARMING

Solar radiation re-radiated as heat

Some re-radiated heat escapes into space

Sun

Some re-radiated heat reflected back to Earth

Incoming solar radiation

Earth

Atmosphere

NATURALLY MODERATED GREENHOUSE EFFECT

Meteor (shooting star) burns up as it passes through atmosphere

Less re-radiated heat escapes

Solar radiation re-radiated as heat

More re-radiated heat reflected back to Earth

Aurora

Surface temperature rises

"Greenhouse gases" accumulate in atmosphere

Incoming solar radiation

UNBALANCED GREENHOUSE EFFECT

14% of incoming solar radiation absorbed by atmosphere

7% of incoming solar radiation reflected by atmosphere

COMPOSITION OF THE LOWER ATMOSPHERE

Other elements less than 0.1%

24% of incoming solar radiation reflected by clouds

Argon 0.93%

Cosmic rays (high-energy particles from space) penetrate to stratosphere

Oxygen 21%

Some absorbed heat re-radiated by atmosphere

4% of incoming solar radiation reflected by oceans and land

Nitrogen 78%

51% of incoming solar radiation absorbed by Earth's surface

Some absorbed heat re-radiated by clouds

Weather

WEATHER IS DEFINED AS THE ATMOSPHERIC CONDITIONS at a particular time and place; climate is the average weather conditions for a given region over time. Weather conditions include temperature, wind, cloud cover, and precipitation, such as rain or snow. Good weather is associated with high-pressure areas, where air is sinking. Cloudy, wet, changeable weather is common in low-pressure zones with rising, unstable air. Such conditions occur at temperate latitudes, where warm air meets cool air along the polar fronts. Here, spiraling low-pressure cells known as depressions (mid-latitude cyclones) often form. A depression usually contains a sector of warmer air, beginning at a warm front and ending at a cold front. If the two fronts merge, forming an occluded front, the warm air is pushed upward. An extreme form of low-pressure cell is a hurricane (also called a typhoon or tropical cyclone), which brings torrential rain, and exceptionally strong winds.

TYPES OF OCCLUDED FRONT

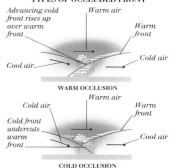

Advancing cold front rises up over warm front

Warm air

Warm front

Cool air

Cold air

WARM OCCLUSION

Cold air

Warm air

Warm front

Cold front undercuts warm front

Cool air

COLD OCCLUSION

FORMS OF PRECIPITATION

Water droplets less than 0.5 mm in diameter fall as drizzle

Water droplets coalesce to form raindrops 0.5–5.0 mm in diameter

Rising air

RAIN FROM CLOUDS NOT REACHING FREEZING LEVEL

TYPES OF CLOUD

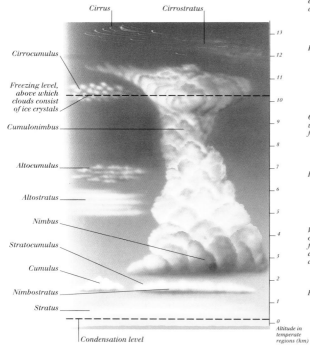

Cirrus

Cirrostratus

Cirrocumulus

Freezing level, above which clouds consist of ice crystals

Cumulonimbus

Altocumulus

Altostratus

Nimbus

Stratocumulus

Cumulus

Nimbostratus

Stratus

Condensation level

13
12
11
10
9
8
7
6
5
4
3
2
1
0
Altitude in temperate regions (km)

Ice crystal

Coalesced water droplets fall as rain

Snowflakes grown from ice crystals fall as snow

Snowflakes melt to fall as rain

Rising air

RAIN AND SNOW FROM CLOUDS REACHING FREEZING LEVEL

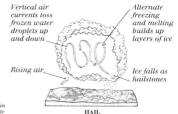

Vertical air currents toss frozen water droplets up and down

Alternate freezing and melting builds up layers of ice

Rising air

Ice falls as hailstones

HAIL

STRUCTURE OF A HURRICANE

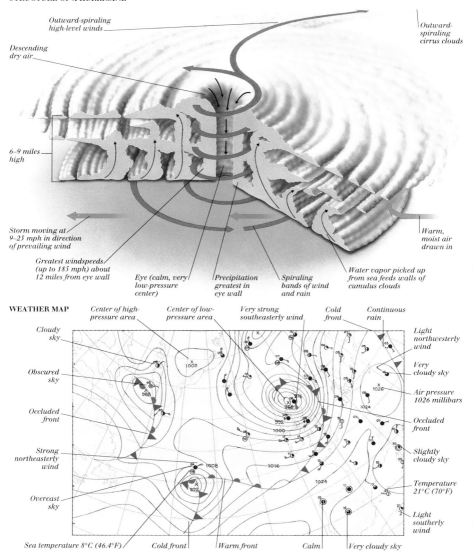

Outward-spiraling high-level winds

Outward-spiraling cirrus clouds

Descending dry air

6–9 miles high

Storm moving at 9–25 mph in direction of prevailing wind

Warm, moist air drawn in

Greatest windspeeds (up to 185 mph) about 12 miles from eye wall

Eye (calm, very low-pressure center)

Precipitation greatest in eye wall

Spiraling bands of wind and rain

Water vapor picked up from sea feeds walls of cumulus clouds

WEATHER MAP

Center of high-pressure area

Center of low-pressure area

Very strong southeasterly wind

Cold front

Continuous rain

Cloudy sky

Light northwesterly wind

Obscured sky

Very cloudy sky

Air pressure 1026 millibars

Occluded front

Occluded front

Strong northeasterly wind

Slightly cloudy sky

Overcast sky

Temperature 21°C (70°F)

Light southerly wind

Sea temperature 8°C (46.4°F)

Cold front

Warm front

Calm

Very cloudy sky

303

Physics and Chemistry

The variety of matter

**PLANT AND INSECT
(LIVING MATTER)**

MATTER IS ANYTHING THAT OCCUPIES SPACE. It includes
everything from natural substances, such as minerals or
living organisms, to synthetic materials. Matter can exist in
three distinct states—solid, liquid, and gas. A solid is rigid
and retains its shape. A liquid is fluid, has a definite shape,
and will take the shape of its container. A gas (also fluid) fills
a space, so its volume will be the same as the volume of its
container. Most substances can exist as a solid, a liquid, or
a gas: the state is determined by temperature. At very high temperatures,
matter becomes plasma, often considered to be a fourth state of matter. All
matter is composed of microscopic particles, such as atoms and molecules
(see pp. 308-309). The arrangement and interactions of these
particles give a substance its physical and chemical properties,
by which matter can be identified. There is a huge variety of
matter because particles can arrange themselves in countless
ways, in one substance or by mixing with others. Natural glass,
for example, seems to be a solid but is, in fact, a supercool
liquid: the atoms are not locked into a pattern and can flow.
Pure substances known as elements (see p. 310) combine to
form compounds or mixtures. Mixtures called colloids are made
up of larger particles of matter suspended in a solid, liquid, or
gas, while a solution is one substance dissolved in another.

TYPES OF COLLOID

HAIR GEL (SOLID IN LIQUID)

**SHAVING CREAM
(AIR IN LIQUID)**

**MIST
(LIQUID IN GAS)**

EXAMPLES OF MATTER

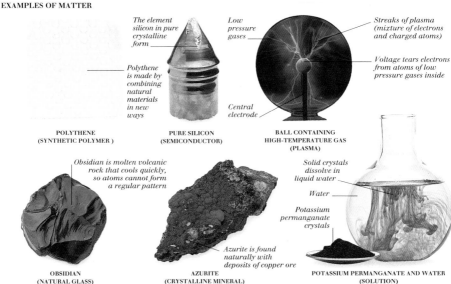

*The element
silicon in pure
crystalline
form*

*Polythene
is made by
combining
natural
materials
in new
ways*

*Low
pressure
gases*

*Streaks of plasma
(mixture of electrons
and charged atoms)*

*Voltage tears electrons
from atoms of low
pressure gases inside*

*Central
electrode*

**POLYTHENE
(SYNTHETIC POLYMER)**

**PURE SILICON
(SEMICONDUCTOR)**

**BALL CONTAINING
HIGH-TEMPERATURE GAS
(PLASMA)**

*Obsidian is molten volcanic
rock that cools quickly,
so atoms cannot form
a regular pattern*

*Solid crystals
dissolve in
liquid water*

Water

*Potassium
permanganate
crystals*

*Azurite is found
naturally with
deposits of copper ore*

**OBSIDIAN
(NATURAL GLASS)**

**AZURITE
(CRYSTALLINE MINERAL)**

**POTASSIUM PERMANGANATE AND WATER
(SOLUTION)**

STATES OF MATTER

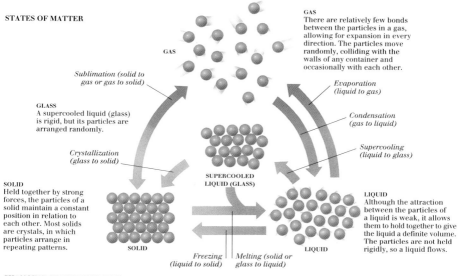

GAS
There are relatively few bonds between the particles in a gas, allowing for expansion in every direction. The particles move randomly, colliding with the walls of any container and occasionally with each other.

GAS

Sublimation (solid to gas or gas to solid)

Evaporation (liquid to gas)

GLASS
A supercooled liquid (glass) is rigid, but its particles are arranged randomly.

Condensation (gas to liquid)

Crystallization (glass to solid)

Supercooling (liquid to glass)

SUPERCOOLED LIQUID (GLASS)

SOLID
Held together by strong forces, the particles of a solid maintain a constant position in relation to each other. Most solids are crystals, in which particles arrange in repeating patterns.

SOLID

LIQUID
Although the attraction between the particles of a liquid is weak, it allows them to hold together to give the liquid a definite volume. The particles are not held rigidly, so a liquid flows.

LIQUID

Freezing (liquid to solid) | *Melting (solid or glass to liquid)*

CHANGING STATES OF WATER

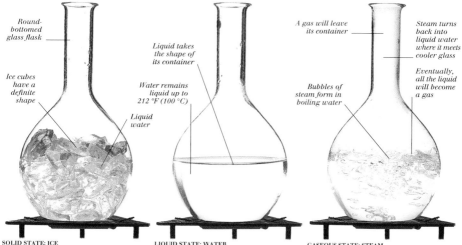

Round-bottomed glass flask

Ice cubes have a definite shape

Liquid water

Liquid takes the shape of its container

Water remains liquid up to 212 °F (100 °C)

A gas will leave its container

Bubbles of steam form in boiling water

Steam turns back into liquid water where it meets cooler glass

Eventually, all the liquid will become a gas

SOLID STATE: ICE
The solid state of water, ice, forms when liquid water is cooled sufficiently. Ice cubes are rigid, with a definite shape and volume.

LIQUID STATE: WATER
When the temperature of a substance rises above its freezing point, it melts to become a liquid. Ice changes to water.

GASEOUS STATE: STEAM
Above its boiling point, a substance will become a gas. When heated sufficiently, liquid water turns to steam, a colorless gas.

Atoms and molecules

FALSE-COLOR IMAGE
OF ACTUAL GOLD
ATOMS

ATOMS ARE THE smallest individual parts of an element (see pp. 310-311). They are tiny, with diameters in the order of one ten-thousand-millionth of a meter (10^{-10} m). Two or more atoms join together (bond) to form a molecule of a substance known as a compound. For example, when atoms of the elements hydrogen and fluorine join together, they form a molecule of the compound hydrogen fluoride. So molecules are the smallest individual parts of a compound. Atoms themselves are not indivisible —they possess an internal structure. At their center is a dense nucleus consisting of protons, which have a positive electric charge (see p. 316), and neutrons, which are uncharged. Around the nucleus are negatively charged electrons. It is the electrons that give a substance most of its physical and chemical properties. They do not follow definite paths around the nucleus. Instead, electrons are said to be found within certain regions, called orbitals. These are arranged around the nucleus in "shells," each containing electrons of a particular energy. For example, the first shell (1) can hold up to two electrons, in a so-called s-orbital (1s). The second shell (2) can hold up to eight electrons in s-orbitals (2s) and p-orbitals (2p). If an atom loses an electron, it becomes a positive ion (cation). If an electron is gained, an atom becomes a negative ion (anion). Ions of opposite charges will attract and join together in a type of bonding known as ionic bonding. In covalent bonding, the atoms bond by sharing their electrons in what become molecular orbitals.

ATOMIC ORBITALS

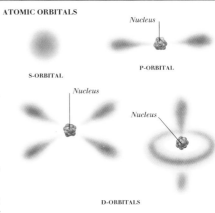

S-ORBITAL.

P-ORBITAL

D-ORBITALS

Nucleus

Nucleus

Nucleus

Nucleus

MOLECULAR ORBITALS

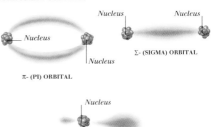

Nucleus

Nucleus

Nucleus

Σ- (SIGMA) ORBITAL

π- (PI) ORBITAL

Nucleus

SP³-HYBRID ORBITAL

EXAMPLE OF IONIC BONDING

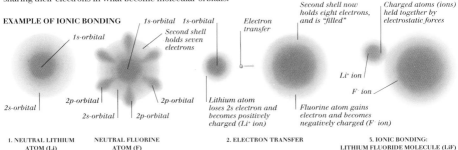

1s-orbital

2s-orbital

2p-orbital

2s-orbital

1. NEUTRAL LITHIUM
ATOM (Li)

1s-orbital   1s-orbital
Second shell
holds seven
electrons

2p-orbital   2p-orbital

NEUTRAL FLUORINE
ATOM (F)

Electron
transfer

Lithium atom
loses 2s electron and
becomes positively
charged (Li⁺ ion)

2. ELECTRON TRANSFER

Second shell now
holds eight electrons,
and is "filled"

Fluorine atom gains
electron and becomes
negatively charged (F⁻ ion)

Charged atoms (ions)
held together by
electrostatic forces

Li⁺ ion

F⁻ ion

5. IONIC BONDING:
LITHIUM FLUORIDE MOLECULE (LiF)

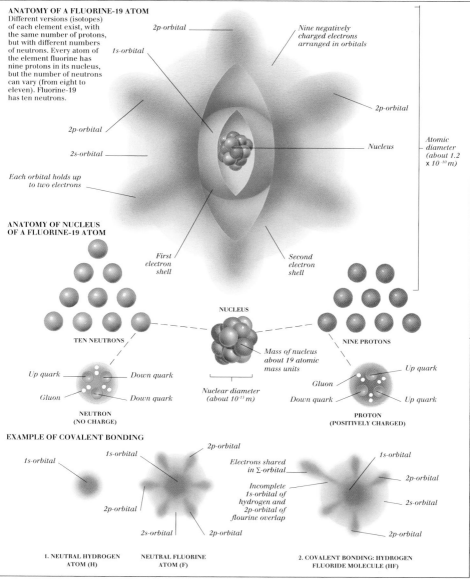

ANATOMY OF A FLUORINE-19 ATOM
Different versions (isotopes) of each element exist, with the same number of protons, but with different numbers of neutrons. Every atom of the element fluorine has nine protons in its nucleus, but the number of neutrons can vary (from eight to eleven). Fluorine-19 has ten neutrons.

2p-orbital

Nine negatively charged electrons arranged in orbitals

1s-orbital

2p-orbital

2s-orbital

Nucleus

Each orbital holds up to two electrons

Atomic diameter (about 1.2 × 10⁻¹⁰ m)

ANATOMY OF NUCLEUS OF A FLUORINE-19 ATOM

First electron shell

Second electron shell

NUCLEUS

TEN NEUTRONS

NINE PROTONS

Mass of nucleus about 19 atomic mass units

Nuclear diameter (about 10⁻¹⁵ m)

Up quark

Down quark

Gluon

Down quark

NEUTRON (NO CHARGE)

Up quark

Gluon

Down quark

Up quark

PROTON (POSITIVELY CHARGED)

EXAMPLE OF COVALENT BONDING

1s-orbital

1s-orbital

2p-orbital

2p-orbital

2s-orbital

2p-orbital

Electrons shared in Σ-orbital

Incomplete 1s-orbital of hydrogen and 2p-orbital of flourine overlap

1s-orbital

2p-orbital

2s-orbital

2p-orbital

1. NEUTRAL HYDROGEN ATOM (H)

NEUTRAL FLUORINE ATOM (F)

2. COVALENT BONDING: HYDROGEN FLUORIDE MOLECULE (HF)

309

The periodic table

AN ELEMENT is a substance that consists of atoms of one type only. The 92 elements that occur naturally, and the 17 elements created artificially, are often arranged into a chart called the periodic table. Each element is defined by its atomic number—the number of protons in the nucleus of each of its atoms (it is also the number of electrons present). Atomic numbers increase along each row (period) and down each column (group). The shape of the table is determined by the way in which electrons arrange themselves around the nucleus: the positioning of elements in order of increasing atomic number brings together atoms with a similar pattern of orbiting electrons (orbitals). These appear in blocks. Electrons occupy shells of a certain energy (see pp. 308-309). Periods are ordered according to the filling of successive shells with electrons, while groups reflect the number of electrons in the outer shell (valency electrons). These outer electrons are important—they decide the chemical properties of the atom. Elements that appear in the same group have similar properties because they have the same number of electrons in their outer shell. Elements in Group 0 have filled shells, where the outer shell holds its maximum number of electrons, and are stable. Atoms of Group I elements have just one electron in their outer shell. This makes them unstable—and ready to react with other substances.

METALS AND NON-METALS
Elements at the left-hand side of each period are metals. Metals easily lose electrons and form positive ions. Non-metals, on the right of a period, tend to become negative ions. Semi-metals, which have properties of both metals and non-metals, are between the two.

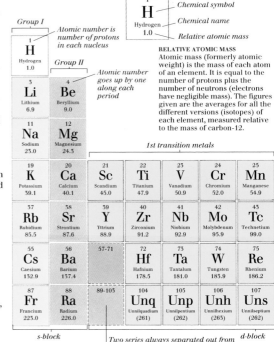

RELATIVE ATOMIC MASS
Atomic mass (formerly atomic weight) is the mass of each atom of an element. It is equal to the number of protons plus the number of neutrons (electrons have negligible mass). The figures given are the averages for all the different versions (isotopes) of each element, measured relative to the mass of carbon-12.

Atomic number
Chemical symbol
Chemical name
Relative atomic mass

| 1 |
| H |
| Hydrogen |
| 1.0 |

Group I
Atomic number is number of protons in each nucleus

| 1 |
| H |
| Hydrogen |
| 1.0 |

Group II
Atomic number goes up by one along each period

3	4
Li	Be
Lithium	Beryllium
6.9	9.0

11	12
Na	Mg
Sodium	Magnesium
23.0	24.3

1st transition metals

19	20	21	22	23	24	25
K	Ca	Sc	Ti	V	Cr	Mn
Potassium	Calcium	Scandium	Titanium	Vanadium	Chromium	Manganese
39.1	40.1	45.0	47.9	50.9	52.0	54.9

37	38	39	40	41	42	43
Rb	Sr	Y	Zr	Nb	Mo	Tc
Rubidium	Strontium	Yttrium	Zirconium	Niobium	Molybdenum	Technetium
85.5	87.6	88.9	91.2	92.9	95.9	99.0

55	56	57-71	72	73	74	75
Cs	Ba		Hf	Ta	W	Re
Caesium	Barium		Hafnium	Tantalum	Tungsten	Rhenium
132.9	137.4		178.5	181.0	185.9	186.2

87	88	89-103	104	105	106	107
Fr	Ra		Unq	Unp	Unh	Uns
Francium	Radium		Unnilquadium	Unnilpentium	Unnilhexium	Unnilseptium
223.0	226.0		(261)	(262)	(263)	(262)

s-block

Two series always separated out from the table to give it a coherent shape

d-block

Soft, silvery, and highly reactive metal

SODIUM:
GROUP 1 METAL

Silvery, reactive metal

MAGNESIUM:
GROUP 2 METAL

Hard, silvery metal

CHROMIUM:
1ST TRANSITION METAL

TYPES OF ELEMENT KEY:

- Alkali metals
- Alkaline earth metals
- Transition metals
- Lanthanides (rare earths)
- Actinides
- Poor metals
- Semi-metals
- Non-metals
- Noble gases

Radioactive metal

PLUTONIUM:
ACTINIDE SERIES METAL

57	58	59	60
La	Ce	Pr	Nd
Lanthanum	Cerium	Praseodymium	Neodymium
138.9	140.1	140.9	144.2

89	90	91	92
Ac	Th	Pa	U
Actinium	Thorium	Protactinium	Uranium
227.0	232.0	231.0	238.0

Bright yellow crystal

SULFUR:
GROUP 6 SOLID NON-METAL

Purple-black solid turns to gas easily

IODINE:
GROUP 7
SOLID NON-METAL

ALLOTROPES OF CARBON
Some elements exist in more than one form —these are known as allotropes. Carbon powder, graphite, and diamond are allotropes of carbon. They all consist of carbon atoms, but have very different physical properties.

DIAMOND

GRAPHITE

CARBON POWDER

					Group 0
					2 **He** Helium 4.0

Period

	Boron and carbon groups		Nitrogen and oxygen groups		Halogens	
	Group III	*Group IV*	*Group V*	*Group VI*	*Group VII*	

Group III	*Group IV*	*Group V*	*Group VI*	*Group VII*	Group 0
5 **B** Boron 10.8	6 **C** Carbon 12.0	7 **N** Nitrogen 14.0	8 **O** Oxygen 16.0	9 **F** Fluorine 19.0	10 **Ne** Neon 20.2
13 **Al** Aluminum 27.0	14 **Si** Silicon 28.1	15 **P** Phosphorus 31.0	16 **S** Sulfur 32.1	17 **Cl** Chlorine 35.5	18 **Ar** Argon 40.0

Short period

2nd transition metals   *3rd transition metals*

										Long period
26 **Fe** Iron 55.9	27 **Co** Cobalt 58.9	28 **Ni** Nickel 58.7	29 **Cu** Copper 63.5	30 **Zn** Zinc 65.4	31 **Ga** Gallium 69.7	32 **Ge** Germanium 72.6	33 **As** Arsenic 74.9	34 **Se** Selenium 79.0	35 **Br** Bromine 79.9	36 **Kr** Krypton 85.8
44 **Ru** Ruthenium 101.0	45 **Rh** Rhodium 102.9	46 **Pd** Palladium 106.4	47 **Ag** Silver 107.9	48 **Cd** Cadmium 112.4	49 **In** Indium 114.8	50 **Sn** Tin 118.7	51 **Sb** Antimony 121.8	52 **Te** Tellurium 127.6	53 **I** Iodine 126.9	54 **Xe** Xenon 151.3
76 **Os** Osmium 190.2	77 **Ir** Iridium 192.2	78 **Pt** Platinum 195.1	79 **Au** Gold 197.0	80 **Hg** Mercury 200.6	81 **Tl** Thallium 204.4	82 **Pb** Lead 207.2	83 **Bi** Bismuth 209.0	84 **Po** Polonium 210.0	85 **At** Astatine 210.0	86 **Rn** Radon 222.0
108 **Uno** Unniloctium (265)	109 **Une** Unnilennium (266)									

d-block

Atomic mass is estimated, as element exists fleetingly

p-block

Shiny semimetal

Unreactive, colorless gas glows red in discharge tube

NOBLE GASES
Group 0 contains elements that have a filled (complete) outer shell of electrons, which means the atoms do not need to lose or gain electrons by bonding with other atoms. This makes them stable and they do not easily form ions or react with other elements. Noble gases are also called rare or inert gases.

NEON:
GROUP 0
COLORLESS GAS

Yellow, unreactive precious metal

Soft, shiny, reactive metal

GOLD:
3RD TRANSITION METAL

TIN:
GROUP 4 POOR METAL

ANTIMONY:
GROUP 5 SEMI-METAL

61 **Pm** Promethium 147.0	62 **Sm** Samarium 150.4	63 **Eu** Europium 152.0	64 **Gd** Gadolinium 157.3	65 **Tb** Terbium 158.9	66 **Dy** Dysprosium 162.5	67 **Ho** Holmium 164.9	68 **Er** Erbium 167.5	69 **Tm** Thulium 168.9	70 **Yb** Ytterbium 175.0	71 **Lu** Lutetium 175.0
93 **Np** Neptunium 237.0	94 **Pu** Plutonium 242.0	95 **Am** Americium 243.0	96 **Cm** Curium 247.0	97 **Bk** Berkelium 247.0	98 **Cf** Californium 251.0	99 **Es** Einsteinium 254.0	100 **Fm** Fermium 253.0	101 **Md** Mendelevium 256.0	102 **No** Nobelium 254.0	105 **Lr** Lawrencium 257.0

f-block

Chemical reactions

A CHEMICAL REACTION TAKES PLACE whenever bonds between atoms are broken or made. In each case, atoms or groups of atoms rearrange, making new substances (products) from the original ones (reactants). Reactions happen naturally, or can be made to happen; they may take years, or only an instant. Some of the main types are shown here. A reaction usually involves a change in energy (see pp. 314-315). In a burning reaction, for example, the making of new bonds between atoms releases energy as heat and light. This type of reaction, in which heat is given off, is an exothermic reaction. Many reactions, like burning, are irreversible, but some can take place in either direction, and are said to be reversible. Reactions can be used to form solids from solutions: in a double decomposition reaction, two compounds in solution break down and re-form into two new substances, often creating a precipitate (insoluble solid); in displacement, an element (eg. copper) displaces another element (eg. silver) from a solution. The rate (speed) of a reaction is determined by many different factors, such as temperature, and the size and shape of the reactants. To describe and keep track of reactions, internationally recognized chemical symbols and equations are used. Reactions are also used in the laboratory to identify matter. An experiment with candle wax, for example, demonstrates that it contains carbon and hydrogen.

SALT FORMATION (ACID ON METAL)

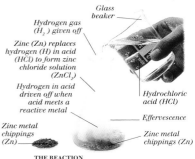

Glass beaker

Hydrogen gas (H_2) given off

Zinc (Zn) replaces hydrogen (H) in acid (HCl) to form zinc chloride solution ($ZnCl_2$)

Hydrogen in acid driven off when acid meets a reactive metal

Hydrochloric acid (HCl)

Effervescence

Zinc metal chippings (Zn)

Zinc metal chippings (Zn)

THE REACTION
Hydrochloric acid added to zinc produces zinc chloride and hydrogen.
$$Zn + 2HCl \rightarrow ZnCl_2 + H_2$$

DISPLACEMENT

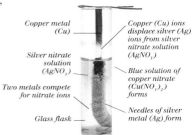

Copper metal (Cu)

Silver nitrate solution ($AgNO_3$)

Two metals compete for nitrate ions

Glass flask

Copper (Cu) ions displace silver (Ag) ions from silver nitrate solution ($AgNO_3$)

Blue solution of copper nitrate ($Cu(NO_3)_2$) forms

Needles of silver metal (Ag) form

THE REACTION
Copper metal added to silver nitrate solution produces copper nitrate and silver metal.
$$Cu + 2AgNO_3 \rightarrow Cu(NO_3)_2 + 2Ag$$

BURNING MATTER

Ammonium dichromate ($(NH_4)_2Cr_2O_7$)

Flame

In this burning reaction, atoms form simpler substances and give off heat and light

Ammonium dichromate ($(NH_4)_2Cr_2O_7$) converts to chromium oxide (Cr_2O_3)

Nitrogen monoxide (NO) and water vapor (H_2O) given off as colorless gases

THE REACTION
When lit, ammonium dichromate combines with oxygen from air.
$$(NH_4)_2Cr_2O_7 + O_2 \rightarrow Cr_2O_3 + 4H_2O + 2NO$$

A REVERSIBLE REACTION

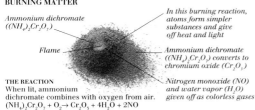

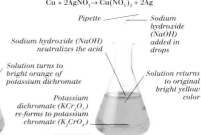

Flat-bottomed glass flask

Potassium chromate solution (K_2CrO_4)

Bright yellow solution contains potassium and chromate ions

Pipette

Hydrochloric acid (HCl) added in drops

Acid causes reaction to take place

Chromate ions converted to orange dichromate ions

Potassium dichromate (KCr_2O_7) forms

Sodium hydroxide (NaOH) neutralizes the acid

Solution turns to bright orange of potassium dichromate

Potassium dichromate (KCr_2O_7) re-forms to potassium chromate (K_2CrO_4)

Pipette

Sodium hydroxide (NaOH) added in drops

Solution returns to original bright yellow color

1. THE REACTANT
Potassium chromate dissolves in water to form potassium ions and chromate ions.
$$K_2CrO_4 \rightarrow 2K^+ + CrO_4^{2-}$$

2. THE REACTION
Addition of hydrochloric acid changes chromate ions into dichromate ions.
$$2CrO_4^{2-} \rightarrow Cr_2O_7^{2-}$$

3. REVERSING
Addition of sodium hydroxide changes dichromate ions back into chromate ions.
$$Cr_2O_7^{2-} \rightarrow 2CrO_4^{2-}$$

FERMENTATION

Yeast converts sugar into alcohol (C_2H_5OH) and carbon dioxide gas (CO_2)

Airtight stopper

Flat-bottomed glass flask

Yeast mixed with warm water and sugar $(C_6H_{12}O_6)$

Carbon dioxide bubbles (CO_2)

THE REACTION
Yeast converts sugar and warm water into alcohol and carbon dioxide.
$C_6H_{12}O_6 \rightarrow 2C_2H_5OH + 2CO_2$

DOUBLE DECOMPOSITION

Potassium iodide solution (KI)

Lead nitrate solution $(Pb(NO_3)_2)$

Two solutions swap partners

Potassium iodide solution added to lead nitrate solution

Lead iodide (PbI_2), a yellow solid, forms

Potassium nitrate solution (KNO_3) forms

1. THE REACTANTS
Potassium iodide in water (KI) and lead nitrate in water $(Pb(NO_3)_2)$ each form colorless solutions.

2. THE REACTION
When the solutions are mixed, lead iodide, a precipitate, and potassium nitrate solution are formed.
$2KI + Pb(NO_3)_2 \rightarrow PbI_2 + 2KNO_3$

TESTING CANDLE WAX, AN ORGANIC COMPOUND

Burning produces carbon dioxide gas (CO_2) and water vapor (H_2O)

Delivery tube

Clamp stand

Delivery tube

Gases are trapped in funnel

Unburned carbon forms soot particles

Stopper

Stopper

Tube connection to pump that sucks gases through

Flame

Thistle funnel

U-tube

Stopper

Burning candle wax

Water vapor condenses to form liquid water (H_2O)

Test tube

Clamp

Water vapor trapped by solid drying agent, anhydrous copper sulfate $(CuSO_4)$

Anhydrous copper sulfate $(CuSO_4)$

Carbon dioxide gas (CO_2) given off

Candle wax $(C_{18}H_{38})$, a hydrocarbon, contains the elements carbon and hydrogen

Anhydrous copper sulfate $(CuSO_4)$ crystals combine with water vapor (H_2O) to form darker blue hydrated copper sulfate $(CuSO_4 \cdot 10H_2O)$

Calcium hydroxide $(Ca(OH)_2)$ and carbon dioxide (CO_2) form insoluble calcium carbonate $(CaCO_3)$: lime water becomes milky

Calcium hydroxide solution (lime water, $Ca(OH)_2$)

1. THE BURNING REACTION
Burning wax produces carbon dioxide gas and water vapor.
$2C_{18}H_{38} + 55O_2 \rightarrow 36CO_2 + 38H_2O$

2. TESTING FOR WATER VAPOUR
A solid drying agent traps water vapor, proving the presence of hydrogen in the candle wax.
$CuSO_4 + 10H_2O \rightarrow CuSO_4 \cdot 10H_2O$

3. TESTING FOR CARBON DIOXIDE
Calcium hydroxide in solution reacts with carbon dioxide, forming a carbonate and turning milky.
$Ca(OH)_2 + CO_2 \rightarrow CaCO_3 + H_2O$

Energy

ANYTHING THAT HAPPENS—from a pin drop to an explosion
—requires energy. Energy is the capacity for doing work
(making something happen). Various forms of energy exist,
including light, heat, sound, electrical, chemical, nuclear,
kinetic, and potential energies. The Law of Conservation
of Energy states that the total amount of energy in the
Universe is fixed—energy cannot be created or destroyed,
it can only change from one form to another (energy
transfer). For example, potential energy is energy that
is stored, and can be used in the future. An object gains
potential energy when it is lifted; as the object is released,
potential energy changes into the energy of motion (kinetic
energy). During transference, some of the energy converts
into heat. A combined heat and power station can put some
of the "waste" heat to useful effect in local schools and
housing. Most of the Earth's energy is provided by the Sun,
in the form of electromagnetic radiation (see pp. 316-317).
Some of this energy transfers to plant and animal life, and
ultimately to fossil fuels, where it is stored in chemical
form. Our bodies obtain energy from the food we eat,
while energy needed for other tasks, such as heating and
transportation, can be obtained by burning fossil fuels
—or by harnessing natural forces like wind or moving
water—to generate electricity. Another source is nuclear
power, where energy is released by reactions in the nucleus
of an atom. All energy is measured by the international
unit, the joule (J). As a guide, one joule is about equal to
the amount of energy needed to lift an apple one yard.

SANKEY DIAGRAM SHOWING ENERGY FLOW IN A COAL-FIRED COMBINED HEAT AND POWER STATION

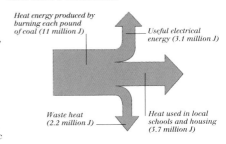

Heat energy produced by
burning each pound
of coal (11 million J)

Useful electrical
energy (3.1 million J)

Waste heat
(2.2 million J)

Heat used in local
schools and housing
(5.7 million J)

CROSS-SECTION OF HYDROELECTRIC POWER STATION WITH FRANCIS TURBINE

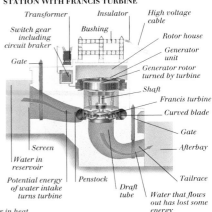

Transformer

Insulator

High voltage
cable

Switch gear
including
circuit braker

Bushing

Rotor house

Generator
unit

Gate

Generator rotor
turned by turbine

Shaft

Francis turbine

Curved blade

Gate

Afterbay

Screen

Water in
reservoir

Potential energy
of water intake
turns turbine

Penstock

Draft
tube

Tailrace

Water that flows
out has lost some
energy

CROSS-SECTION OF NUCLEAR POWER STATION WITH PRESSURIZED WATER REACTOR

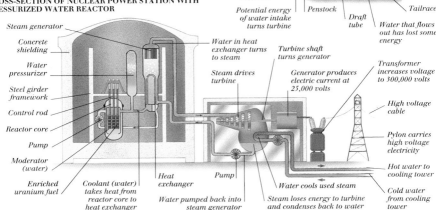

Steam generator

Concrete
shielding

Water
pressurizer

Steel girder
framework

Control rod

Reactor core

Pump

Moderator
(water)

Enriched
uranium fuel

Coolant (water)
takes heat from
reactor core to
heat exchanger

Heat
exchanger

Water in heat
exchanger turns
to steam

Steam drives
turbine

Water pumped back into
steam generator

Pump

Turbine shaft
turns generator

Generator produces
electric current at
25,000 volts

Water cools used steam

Steam loses energy to turbine
and condenses back to water

Transformer
increases voltage
to 300,000 volts

High voltage
cable

Pylon carries
high voltage
electricity

Hot water to
cooling tower

Cold water
from cooling
tower

ENERGY SYSTEMS

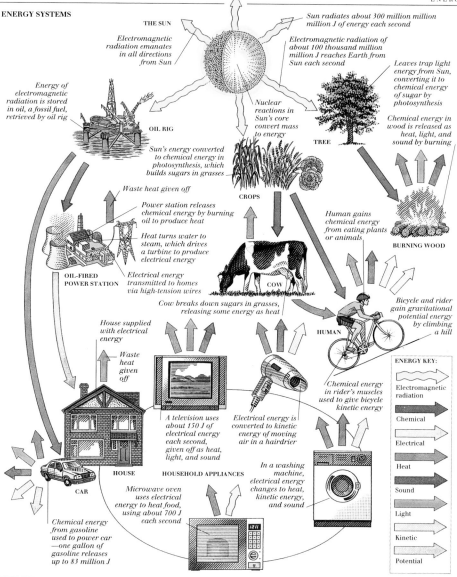

THE SUN

Electromagnetic radiation emanates in all directions from Sun

Sun radiates about 300 million million million J of energy each second

Electromagnetic radiation of about 100 thousand million million J reaches Earth from Sun each second

Leaves trap light energy from Sun, converting it to chemical energy of sugar by photosynthesis

Energy of electromagnetic radiation is stored in oil, a fossil fuel, retrieved by oil rig

OIL RIG

Nuclear reactions in Sun's core convert mass to energy

TREE

Chemical energy in wood is released as heat, light, and sound by burning

Sun's energy converted to chemical energy in photosynthesis, which builds sugars in grasses

CROPS

Waste heat given off

Power station releases chemical energy by burning oil to produce heat

Heat turns water to steam, which drives a turbine to produce electrical energy

OIL-FIRED POWER STATION

Electrical energy transmitted to homes via high-tension wires

Human gains chemical energy from eating plants or animals

BURNING WOOD

COW

Cow breaks down sugars in grasses, releasing some energy as heat

HUMAN

Bicycle and rider gain gravitational potential energy by climbing a hill

House supplied with electrical energy

Waste heat given off

A television uses about 150 J of electrical energy each second, given off as heat, light, and sound

Electrical energy is converted to kinetic energy of moving air in a hairdrier

Chemical energy in rider's muscles used to give bicycle kinetic energy

HOUSE

HOUSEHOLD APPLIANCES

CAR

Chemical energy from gasoline used to power car —one gallon of gasoline releases up to 83 million J

Microwave oven uses electrical energy to heat food, using about 700 J each second

In a washing machine, electrical energy changes to heat, kinetic energy, and sound

ENERGY KEY:

Electromagnetic radiation

Chemical

Electrical

Heat

Sound

Light

Kinetic

Potential

Electricity and magnetism

ELECTRICAL EFFECTS result from an imbalance of electric charge. There are two types of electric charge: positive (carried by protons) and negative (carried by electrons). If charges are opposite (unlike), they attract one another, while like charges repel. These forces of attraction and repulsion (electrostatic forces) exist between any two charged particles. Matter is normally uncharged, but if electrons are gained, an object will gain an overall negative charge; if they are removed, it becomes positive. Objects with an overall negative or positive charge are said to have an imbalance of charge, and exert the same forces as individual negative and positive charges. On this larger scale, the forces will always act to regain the balance of charge. This causes static electricity. Lightning, for example, is produced by clouds discharging a huge excess of negative electrons. If charges are free—in a wire or material that allows electrons to pass through it—the forces cause a flow of charge called an electric current. Some substances exhibit the strange phenomenon of magnetism—which also produces attractive and repulsive forces. Magnetic substances consist of small regions called domains. Normally unmagnetized, they can be magnetized by being placed in a magnetic field. Magnetism and electricity are inextricably linked, a fact put to use in motors and generators.

LIGHTNING

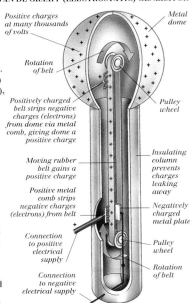

Positive charges at many thousands of volts

Metal dome

Rotation of belt

Positively charged belt strips negative charges (electrons) from dome via metal comb, giving dome a positive charge

Pulley wheel

Moving rubber belt gains a positive charge

Insulating column prevents charges leaking away

Positive metal comb strips negative charges (electrons) from belt

Negatively charged metal plate

Connection to positive electrical supply

Pulley wheel

Connection to negative electrical supply

Rotation of belt

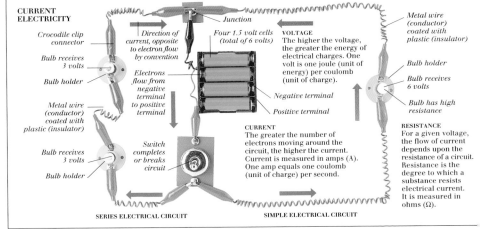

CURRENT ELECTRICITY

Crocodile clip connector

Bulb receives 3 volts

Bulb holder

Metal wire (conductor) coated with plastic (insulator)

Bulb receives 3 volts

Bulb holder

Junction

Direction of current, opposite to electron flow by convention

Electrons flow from negative terminal to positive terminal

Switch completes or breaks circuit

Four 1.5 volt cells (total of 6 volts)

VOLTAGE
The higher the voltage, the greater the energy of electrical charges. One volt is one joule (unit of energy) per coulomb (unit of charge).

Negative terminal

Positive terminal

CURRENT
The greater the number of electrons moving around the circuit, the higher the current. Current is measured in amps (A). One amp equals one coulomb (unit of charge) per second.

Metal wire (conductor) coated with plastic (insulator)

Bulb holder

Bulb receives 6 volts

Bulb has high resistance

RESISTANCE
For a given voltage, the flow of current depends upon the resistance of a circuit. Resistance is the degree to which a substance resists electrical current. It is measured in ohms (Ω).

SERIES ELECTRICAL CIRCUIT

SIMPLE ELECTRICAL CIRCUIT

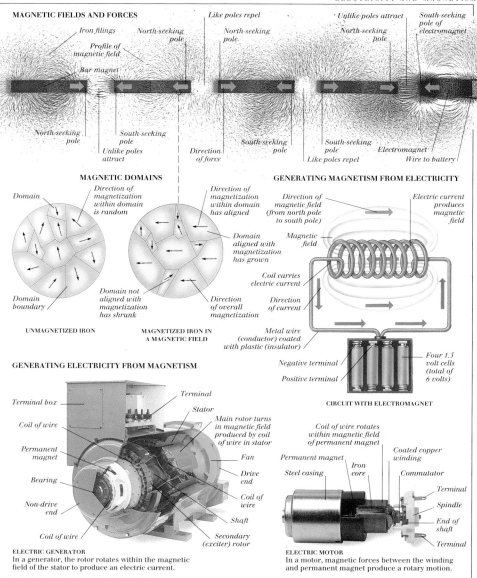

MAGNETIC FIELDS AND FORCES

Iron filings

Profile of magnetic field

Bar magnet

North-seeking pole

Like poles repel

North-seeking pole

Unlike poles attract

North-seeking pole

South-seeking pole of electromagnet

North-seeking pole

South-seeking pole

Unlike poles attract

Direction of force

South-seeking pole

South-seeking pole

Like poles repel

Electromagnet

Wire to battery

MAGNETIC DOMAINS

Domain

Direction of magnetization within domain is random

Direction of magnetization within domain has aligned

Domain aligned with magnetization has grown

Domain boundary

Domain not aligned with magnetization has shrunk

Direction of overall magnetization

UNMAGNETIZED IRON

MAGNETIZED IRON IN A MAGNETIC FIELD

GENERATING MAGNETISM FROM ELECTRICITY

Direction of magnetic field (from north pole to south pole)

Electric current produces magnetic field

Magnetic field

Coil carries electric current

Direction of current

Metal wire (conductor) coated with plastic (insulator)

Negative terminal

Positive terminal

Four 1.5 volt cells (total of 6 volts)

CIRCUIT WITH ELECTROMAGNET

GENERATING ELECTRICITY FROM MAGNETISM

Terminal box

Coil of wire

Permanent magnet

Bearing

Non-drive end

Coil of wire

Terminal

Stator

Main rotor turns in magnetic field produced by coil of wire in stator

Fan

Drive end

Coil of wire

Shaft

Secondary (exciter) rotor

ELECTRIC GENERATOR
In a generator, the rotor rotates within the magnetic field of the stator to produce an electric current.

Coil of wire rotates within magnetic field of permanent magnet

Permanent magnet

Iron core

Steel casing

Coated copper winding

Commutator

Terminal

Spindle

End of shaft

Terminal

ELECTRIC MOTOR
In a motor, magnetic forces between the winding and permanent magnet produce a rotary motion.

Light

LIGHT IS A FORM OF ENERGY. It is a type of electromagnetic radiation, like X rays or radio waves. All electromagnetic

INFRARED IMAGE
OF A HOUSE

radiation is produced by electric charges (see pp. 316–317): it is caused by the effects of oscillating electric and magnetic fields as they travel through space. Electromagnetic radiation is considered to have both wave and particle properties. It can be thought of as a wave of electricity and magnetism. In that case, the difference between the various forms of radiation is their wavelength. Radiation can also be said to consist of particles, or packets of energy, called photons. The difference between light and X rays, for instance, is the amount of energy that each photon carries. The complete range of radiation is referred to as the electromagnetic spectrum, extending from low energy, long wavelength radio waves to high energy, short wavelength gamma rays. Light is the only part of the electromagnetic spectrum that is visible. White light from the Sun is made up of all the visible wavelengths of radiation, which can be seen when it is separated by using a prism. Light, like all forms of electromagnetic radiation, can be reflected (bounced back) and refracted (bent). Different parts of the electromagnetic spectrum are produced in different ways. Sometimes visible light—and infrared radiation—is generated by the vibrating particles of warm or hot objects. The emission of light in this way is called incandescence. Light can also be produced by fluorescence, a phenomenon in which electrons gain and lose energy within atoms.

MAXWELLIAN DIAGRAM OF ELECTROMAGNETIC RADIATION AS WAVES

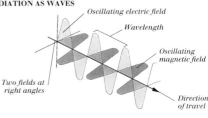

Oscillating electric field

Wavelength

Oscillating magnetic field

Two fields at right angles

Direction of travel

ELECTROMAGNETIC RADIATION AS PARTICLES

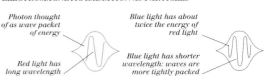

Photon thought of as wave packet of energy

Blue light has about twice the energy of red light

Red light has long wavelength

Blue light has shorter wavelength: waves are more tightly packed

PHOTON OF RED LIGHT   PHOTON OF BLUE LIGHT

SPLITTING WHITE LIGHT INTO THE SPECTRUM

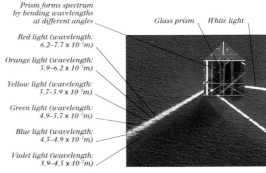

Prism forms spectrum by bending wavelengths at different angles

Glass prism   *White light*

Red light (wavelength: 6.2–7.7×10^{-7}m)

Orange light (wavelength: 5.9–6.2×10^{-7}m)

Yellow light (wavelength: 5.7–5.9×10^{-7}m)

Green light (wavelength: 4.9–5.7×10^{-7}m)

Blue light (wavelength: 4.5–4.9×10^{-7}m)

Violet light (wavelength: 3.9–4.5×10^{-7}m)

THE ELECTROMAGNETIC SPECTRUM

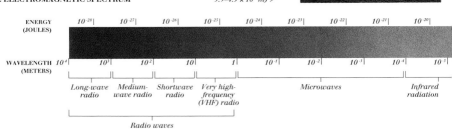

ENERGY (JOULES)	10^{-28}	10^{-27}	10^{-26}	10^{-25}	10^{-24}	10^{-23}	10^{-22}	10^{-21}	10^{-20}

WAVELENGTH (METERS)	10^{4}	10^{3}	10^{2}	10	1	10^{-1}	10^{-2}	10^{-3}	10^{-4}	10^{-5}

Long-wave radio *Medium-wave radio* *Shortwave radio* *Very high-frequency (VHF) radio* *Microwaves* *Infrared radiation*

Radio waves

ARTIFICIAL LIGHT SOURCES

FLUORESCENT TUBE

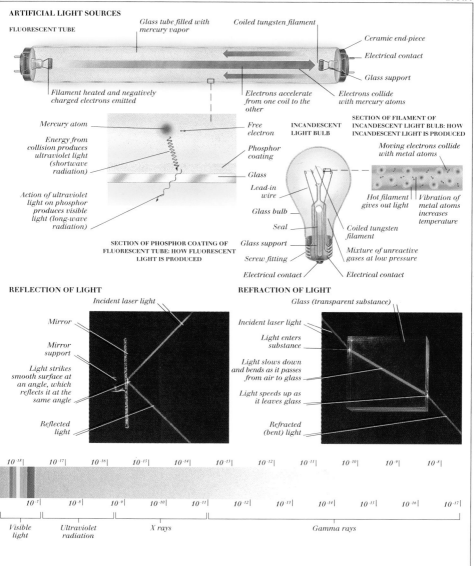

Glass tube filled with mercury vapor

Coiled tungsten filament

Ceramic end-piece

Electrical contact

Glass support

Filament heated and negatively charged electrons emitted

Electrons accelerate from one coil to the other

Electrons collide with mercury atoms

Mercury atom

Free electron

Energy from collision produces ultraviolet light (shortwave radiation)

Phosphor coating

Glass

Action of ultraviolet light on phosphor produces visible light (long-wave radiation)

INCANDESCENT LIGHT BULB

Lead-in wire

Glass bulb

Seal

Glass support

Screw fitting

Electrical contact

Coiled tungsten filament

Mixture of unreactive gases at low pressure

Electrical contact

SECTION OF PHOSPHOR COATING OF FLUORESCENT TUBE: HOW FLUORESCENT LIGHT IS PRODUCED

SECTION OF FILAMENT OF INCANDESCENT LIGHT BULB: HOW INCANDESCENT LIGHT IS PRODUCED

Moving electrons collide with metal atoms

Hot filament gives out light

Vibration of metal atoms increases temperature

REFLECTION OF LIGHT

Incident laser light

Mirror

Mirror support

Light strikes smooth surface at an angle, which reflects it at the same angle

Reflected light

REFRACTION OF LIGHT

Glass (transparent substance)

Incident laser light

Light enters substance

Light slows down and bends as it passes from air to glass

Light speeds up as it leaves glass

Refracted (bent) light

10^{-18} 10^{-17} 10^{-16} 10^{-15} 10^{-14} 10^{-13} 10^{-12} 10^{-11} 10^{-10} 10^{-9} 10^{-8}

10^{-7} 10^{-8} 10^{-9} 10^{-10} 10^{-11} 10^{-12} 10^{-13} 10^{-14} 10^{-15} 10^{-16} 10^{-17}

Visible light

Ultraviolet radiation

X rays

Gamma rays

319

Force and motion

FORCES ARE PUSHES OR PULLS that change the motion of objects. To make a stationary object move, or a moving object stop, a force is needed. A force is also required to change the speed or direction of an object. This change in speed or direction is known as acceleration. Acceleration depends on the size (magnitude) of the force, and on the mass of the object. The effects of forces were first summarized by Isaac Newton in his three laws of motion. The international unit of force, named after him, is the newton (N), which is approximately equal to the weight of one apple. Gravity—the force of attraction between any two masses—can be measured using a newton meter (spring balance). Forces are put to useful effect in machines. A simple machine, such as a wheel and axle, is a device that changes the size or direction of an applied force. It allows an applied force (the effort) to produce another force (the load). A lever uses a bar that turns on a fulcrum to exert force. In all simple machines, there is a relationship between force and distance. A small force (in a compound pulley, for instance) moves through a large distance to lift a heavy object a small distance. This is called the Law of Simple Machines.

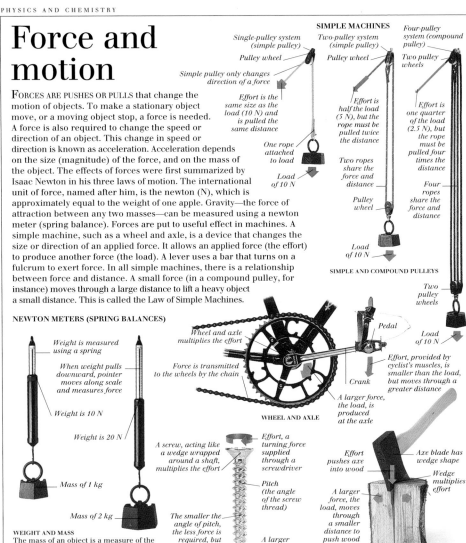

SIMPLE MACHINES

Single-pulley system (simple pulley)
Pulley wheel
Simple pulley only changes direction of a force
Effort is the same size as the load (10 N) and is pulled the same distance
One rope attached to load
Load of 10 N

Two-pulley system (simple pulley)
Pulley wheel
Effort is half the load (5 N), but the rope must be pulled twice the distance
Two ropes share the force and distance
Pulley wheel
Load of 10 N

Four-pulley system (compound pulley)
Two pulley wheels
Effort is one quarter of the load (2.5 N), but the rope must be pulled four times the distance
Four ropes share the force and distance
Two pulley wheels
Load of 10 N

SIMPLE AND COMPOUND PULLEYS

NEWTON METERS (SPRING BALANCES)

Weight is measured using a spring
When weight pulls downward, pointer moves along scale and measures force
Weight is 10 N
Weight is 20 N
Mass of 1 kg
Mass of 2 kg

WEIGHT AND MASS
The mass of an object is a measure of the quantity of matter that it possesses. Mass is usually measured in grams (g) or kilograms (kg). The weight of an object is the force exerted on the object's mass by gravity. Since weight is a force, its unit is the newton (N).

Wheel and axle multiplies the effort
Force is transmitted to the wheels by the chain
Pedal
Effort, provided by cyclist's muscles, is smaller than the load, but moves through a greater distance
Crank
A larger force, the load, is produced at the axle
WHEEL AND AXLE

A screw, acting like a wedge wrapped around a shaft, multiplies the effort
Effort, a turning force supplied through a screwdriver
Pitch (the angle of the screw thread)
The smaller the angle of pitch, the less force is required, but more turns are needed to move it through a greater distance
A larger force, the load, pulls the screw into wood
SCREW

Effort pushes axe into wood
Axe blade has wedge shape
Wedge multiplies effort
A larger force, the load, moves through a smaller distance to push wood apart
WEDGE

NEWTON'S THREE LAWS OF MOTION

NEWTON'S FIRST LAW
When no force acts on a body, it will continue in a state of rest or uniform motion.

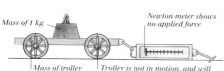

Mass of 1 kg

Newton meter shows no applied force

Mass of trolley is negligible

Trolley is not in motion, and will remain at rest until a force acts

NO FORCE, NO ACCELERATION: STATE OF REST

Constant speed

Newton meter shows no applied force

Mass of 1 kg

Trolley is in motion, and will continue at a constant speed in a straight line until a force acts

NO FORCE, NO ACCELERATION: UNIFORM MOTION

NEWTON'S SECOND LAW
When a force acts on a body, the motion of the body will change. The size of the change will depend upon the mass of the object and the magnitude of the applied force.

Acceleration is 2 ms^{-2}

Trolley and mass (1 kg) gain 2 meters per second of speed each second (2 ms^{-2})

Newton meter registers force of 2 N

Mass of 1 kg

Acceleration is 1 ms^{-2}

Trolley and mass (2 kg) gain 1 meter per second of speed each second (1 ms^{-2})

Newton meter registers force of 2 N

Mass of 2 kg

With the same applied force, an object with 2 kg mass accelerates at half the rate of object with 1 kg mass

FORCE AND ACCELERATION: SMALL MASS, LARGE ACCELERATION

FORCE AND ACCELERATION: LARGE MASS, SMALL ACCELERATION

NEWTON'S THIRD LAW
If one object exerts a force on another, an equal and opposite force, called the reaction force, is applied by the second object on the first.

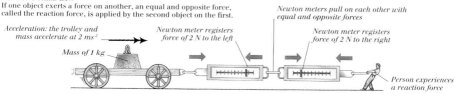

Newton meters pull on each other with equal and opposite forces

Acceleration: the trolley and mass accelerate at 2 ms^{-2}

Newton meter registers force of 2 N to the left

Newton meter registers force of 2 N to the right

Mass of 1 kg

Person experiences a reaction force

ACTION AND REACTION

THREE CLASSES OF LEVER

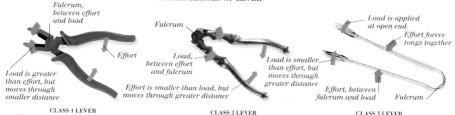

Fulcrum, between effort and load

Effort

Load is greater than effort, but moves through smaller distance

CLASS 1 LEVER
Pliers consist of two class 1 levers.

Fulcrum

Load, between effort and fulcrum

Effort is smaller than load, but moves through greater distance

CLASS 2 LEVER
Nutcrackers consist of two class 2 levers.

Load is applied at open end

Effort forces tongs together

Load is smaller than effort, but moves through greater distance

Effort, between fulcrum and load

Fulcrum

CLASS 3 LEVER
Tongs consist of two class 3 levers.

Rail and Road

Steam locomotives

<hr/>

WAGONS THAT ARE PULLED along tracks have been used to transport material since the 16th century, but these trains were drawn by men or horses until the invention of the steam locomotive. Steam locomotives enabled the basic railroad system to realize its true potential. In 1804, Richard Trevithick built the world's first working steam locomotive in South Wales. It was not entirely successful, but it encouraged others to develop new designs. By 1829, the British engineer Robert Stephenson had built the Rocket, considered to be the forerunner of the modern locomotive. The Rocket was a self-sufficient unit, carrying coal to heat the boiler and a water supply for generating steam. Steam passed from the boiler to force the pistons back and forth, and this movement turned the driving wheels, propelling the train forward. Used steam was then expelled in characteristic puffs. Later steam locomotives, like Ellerman Lines and the Mallard, worked in a similar way, but on a much larger scale. The simple design and reliability of steam locomotives ensured that they changed very little in 120 years of use, before being replaced in the 1950s by more efficient diesel and electric power (see pp. 326-329).

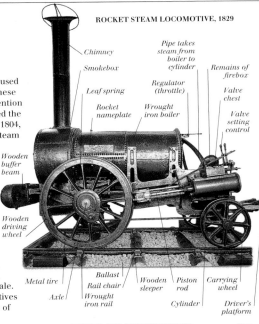

ROCKET STEAM LOCOMOTIVE, 1829

Chimney

Smokebox

Leaf spring

Rocket nameplate

Wooden buffer beam

Wooden driving wheel

Pipe takes steam from boiler to cylinder

Regulator (throttle)

Wrought iron boiler

Remains of firebox

Valve chest

Valve setting control

Metal tire

Axle

Ballast

Rail chair

Wrought iron rail

Wooden sleeper

Piston rod

Cylinder

Carrying wheel

Driver's platform

Stay

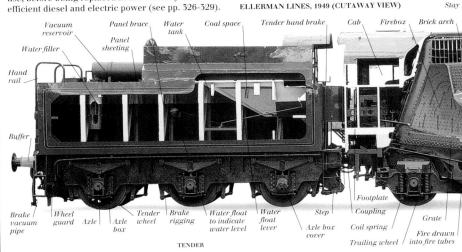

ELLERMAN LINES, 1949 (CUTAWAY VIEW)

Vacuum reservoir

Panel brace

Panel sheeting

Water tank

Coal space

Tender hand brake

Cab

Firebox

Brick arch

Water filler

Hand rail

Buffer

Brake vacuum pipe

Wheel guard

Axle

Axle box

Tender wheel

Brake rigging

Water float to indicate water level

Water float lever

Step

Axle box cover

Coupling

Coil spring

Footplate

Trailing wheel

Grate

Fire drawn into fire tubes

TENDER

CAB INTERIOR OF MALLARD EXPRESS STEAM LOCOMOTIVE, 1938

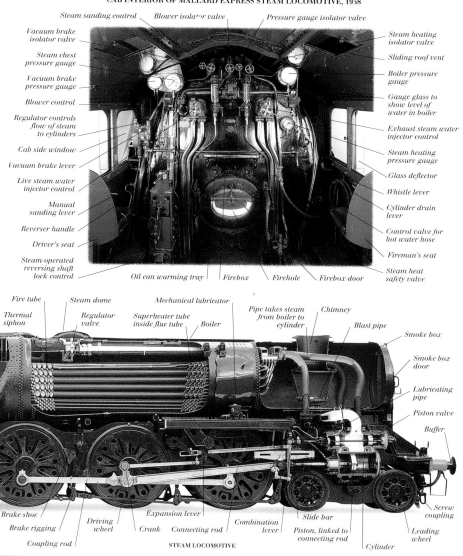

Steam sanding control
Blower isolator valve
Pressure gauge isolator valve
Steam heating isolator valve
Vacuum brake isolator valve
Sliding roof vent
Steam chest pressure gauge
Boiler pressure gauge
Vacuum brake pressure gauge
Gauge glass to show level of water in boiler
Blower control
Exhaust steam water injector control
Regulator controls flow of steam to cylinders
Steam heating pressure gauge
Cab side window
Glass deflector
Vacuum brake lever
Whistle lever
Live steam water injector control
Cylinder drain lever
Manual sanding lever
Control valve for hot water hose
Reverser handle
Fireman's seat
Driver's seat
Steam heat safety valve
Steam-operated reversing shaft lock control
Oil can warming tray
Firebox
Firehole
Firebox door

Fire tube
Steam dome
Mechanical lubricator
Pipe takes steam from boiler to cylinder
Chimney
Thermal siphon
Regulator valve
Superheater tube inside flue tube
Boiler
Blast pipe
Smoke box
Smoke box door
Lubricating pipe
Piston valve
Buffer
Brake shoe
Expansion lever
Slide bar
Screw coupling
Brake rigging
Driving wheel
Crank
Connecting rod
Combination lever
Piston, linked to connecting rod
Leading wheel
Coupling rod
Cylinder

STEAM LOCOMOTIVE

Diesel trains

RUDOLF DIESEL FIRST DEMONSTRATED the diesel engine in Germany in 1898, but it was not until the 1940s that diesel locomotives were successfully established on both passenger and freight services in the U.S. Early diesel locomotives like the Union Pacific were more expensive to build than steam locomotives, but were more efficient and cheaper to operate, especially where oil was plentiful. One feature of diesel engines is that the power output cannot be coupled directly to the wheels. To convert the mechanical energy produced by diesel engines, a transmission system is needed. Almost all diesel locomotives have electric transmissions, and are known as diesel-electric locomotives. The diesel engine works by drawing air into the cylinders and compressing it to increase its temperature; a small quantity of diesel fuel is then injected into it. The resulting combustion drives the generator (more recently an alternator) to produce electricity, which is fed to electric motors connected to the wheels. Diesel-electric locomotives are essentially electric locomotives that carry their own power plants, and are used worldwide today. The Deltic diesel-electric locomotive, similar to the one shown here, replaced classic express steam locomotives, and ran at speeds up to 100 mph.

FRONT VIEW OF UNION PACIFIC DIESEL-ELECTRIC LOCOMOTIVE, 1950s

Exhaust vent · Windshield wiper · Horn · Cab front window · Headlight · Cab door · Name of operating railroad · Illuminated locomotive unit number · Railroad crest · Cab step · Step · Motor-driven bogie axle · Air-brake coupling hose · Center buckeye coupler

PROTOTYPE DELTIC DIESEL-ELECTRIC LOCOMOTIVE, 1956

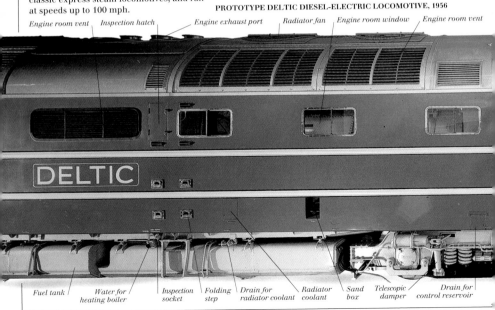

Engine room vent · Inspection hatch · Engine exhaust port · Radiator fan · Engine room window · Engine room vent

DELTIC

Fuel tank · Water for heating boiler · Inspection socket · Folding step · Drain for radiator coolant · Radiator coolant · Sand box · Telescopic damper · Drain for control reservoir

DIESEL ENGINE OF BRITISH RAIL CLASS 20
DIESEL-ELECTRIC LOCOMOTIVE

Exhaust vent

Cylinder head
(V-four configuration)

Turbo-charged diesel
engine drives generator

Generator
cooling fan

Generator
compartment
vent

Auxiliary
generator

Main generator
produces
electricity that
drives wheels

Main chassis
member

Innermost
wheel set on
cab-end bogie

Brake
rigging

Battery
box

Engine crankcase

Air reservoir and
isolator valves

Lubricating oil
primary pump and
fuel supply pump

Air brake pipe

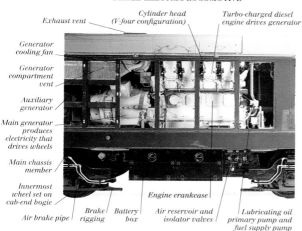

Cab
door

Driver's seat

Cab

Warning horn

Windshield

Windshield wiper

Cab window

Manufacturer's
logo

Cab vent

Indicator
light

Sand box

Buffer

Brake cylinder

Roller-bearing
axle box

Brake
shoe

Brake
actuating chain

Transverse leaf spring
secondary suspension

Coil spring primary
suspension

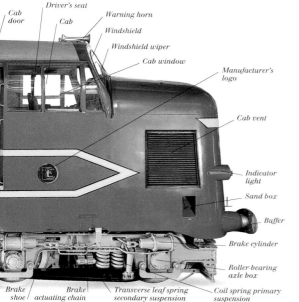

EXAMPLES OF FREIGHT CARS

BOX CAR

HOPPER CAR

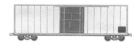

REFRIGERATOR CAR

LIVESTOCK CAR

FLAT CAR WITH BULKHEADS

AUTOMOBILE CAR

Electric and high-speed trains

THE FIRST ELECTRIC LOCOMOTIVE ran in 1879 in Berlin, Germany. In Europe, electric trains developed as a more efficient alternative to the steam locomotive and diesel-electric power. Like diesels, electric trains employ electric motors to drive the wheels but, unlike diesels, the electricity is generated externally at a power station. Electric current is picked up either from a catenary (overhead cable) via a pantograph, or from a third rail. Since it does not carry its own power-generating equipment, an electric locomotive has a better power-to-weight ratio and greater acceleration than its diesel-electric equivalent. This makes electric trains highly suitable for urban routes with many stops. They are also faster, quieter, and cause less pollution. The latest electric French TGV (Train à Grande Vitesse) reaches 186 mph; other trains, like the London to Paris and Brussels Eurostar, can run at several voltages and operate between different countries. Simpler electric trains perform special duties—the "People Mover" at Gatwick Airport, London, runs between terminals.

HOW ALTERNATING CURRENT (AC) ELECTRIC TRAINS WORK

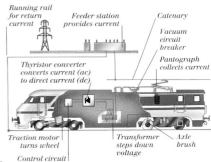

Running rail for return current

Feeder station provides current

Catenary

Vacuum circuit breaker

Pantograph collects current

Thyristor converter converts current (ac) to direct current (dc)

Traction motor turns wheel

Control circuit

Transformer steps down voltage

Axle brush

FRONT VIEW OF PARIS METRO

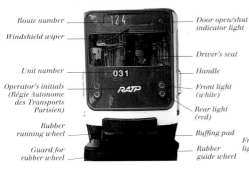

Route number

Windshield wiper

Unit number

Operator's initials (Régie Autonome des Transports Parisien)

Rubber running wheel

Guard for rubber wheel

Door open/shut indicator light

Driver's seat

Handle

Front light (white)

Rear light (red)

Buffing pad

Rubber guide wheel

FRONT VIEW OF ITALIAN STATE RAILWAYS CLASS 402 ELECTRIC LOCOMOTIVE

Collector strip for electric current

Double-arm pantograph

Headlight

Windshield wiper

Italian State Railways crest

Number of electric (E) locomotive (class 402 No. 5)

Buffer

Jumper cable

Conventional hook-screw coupling

Front light (white)

Rear light (red)

SIDE VIEW OF GATWICK EXPRESS "PEOPLE MOVER"

Pneumatic rubber wheel

Concrete track

Automatic door

No driver (train controlled by central computer)

EUROSTAR MULTI-VOLTAGE ELECTRIC TRAIN

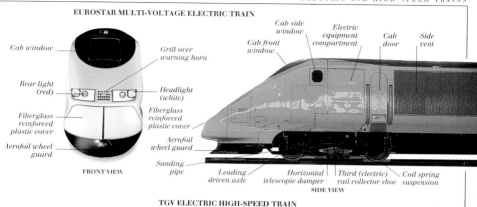

Cab window

Rear light (red)

Fiberglass reinforced plastic cover

Aerofoil wheel guard

FRONT VIEW

Grill over warning horn

Headlight (white)

Fiberglass reinforced plastic cover

Aerofoil wheel guard

Sanding pipe

Leading driven axle

Cab side window

Cab front window

Electric equipment compartment

Cab door

Side vent

Horizontal telescopic damper

Third (electric) rail collector shoe

Coil spring suspension

SIDE VIEW

TGV ELECTRIC HIGH-SPEED TRAIN

Luggage rack

Reading light

Double-glazed and tinted side window

Sliding curtain

Seat

Main overhead lighting

Automatic electric carriage end door

Antimacassar

Headrest

Armrest

Center gangway

INTERIOR OF TGV

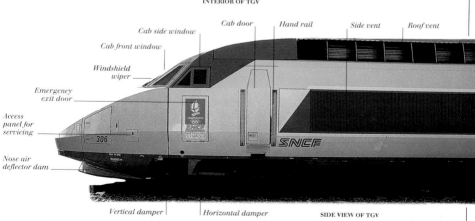

Cab side window

Cab front window

Windshield wiper

Emergency exit door

Access panel for servicing

Nose air deflector dam

Cab door

Hand rail

Side vent

Roof vent

306

SNCF

Vertical damper

Horizontal damper

SIDE VIEW OF TGV

329

Train equipment

MODERN RAILROAD TRACK consists of two parallel steel rails clipped onto a support called a sleeper. Sleepers are usually made of reinforced concrete, although wood and steel are still used. The distance between the inside edges of the rails is the track gauge. It evolved in Britain, which uses a gauge of 4 ft 8$\frac{1}{2}$ in (1,435 mm), known as the standard gauge. As engineering grew more sophisticated, narrower gauges were adopted because they cost less to build. The loading gauge, which is equally important, determines the size of the largest loaded vehicle that may pass through tunnels and under bridges with adequate clearance. Safe train operation relies on following a signaling system. At first, signaling was based on a simple time interval between trains, but it now depends on maintaining a safe distance between successive trains traveling in the same direction. Most modern signals are colored lights, but older mechanical semaphore signals are still used. On the latest high-speed lines, train drivers receive control instructions by electronic means. Signaling depends on reliable control of the train by effective braking. For fast, modern trains, which have considerable momentum, it is essential that each vehicle in the train can be braked by the driver or by a train control system, such as Automatic Train Protection (ATP). Braking is achieved by the brake shoe acting on the wheel rim (rim brakes), by disc brakes, or, increasingly, by electrical braking.

MECHANICAL SEMAPHORE SIGNAL

Red, square-ended arm in raised position means "all clear"

Red glass

Green glass

Actuating lever system

Motor operating "home" stop signal

Green glass

Yellow glass

Yellow, "distant" warning arm in horizontal position means "caution"

Tubular steel post

Ladder

Electrical relay box

FOUR-ASPECT COLORED LIGHT SIGNAL

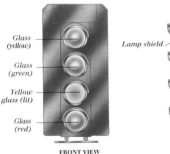

Glass (yellow)

Glass (green)

Yellow glass (lit)

Glass (red)

FRONT VIEW

Lifting lug

Lamp shield

Clip

Base

SIDE VIEW

HOW A MODERN MAIN-LINE SIGNALING SYSTEM WORKS

Red "stop" light instructs next train not to enter this section of track

Green "all clear" light instructs train B to proceed into this section of track

Green "all clear" light instructs train B to proceed into this section of track

Green "all clear" light instructs train B to proceed into this section of track

Pantograph

Catenary

Train B

Track

EXAMPLES OF INTERNATIONAL TRACK GAUGES

EXAMPLES OF INTERNATIONAL LOADING GAUGES

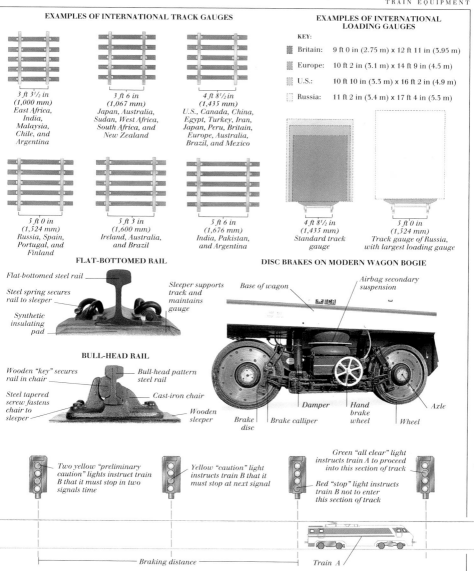

KEY:

Britain: 9 ft 0 in (2.75 m) x 12 ft 11 in (3.95 m)
Europe: 10 ft 2 in (3.1 m) x 14 ft 9 in (4.5 m)
U.S.: 10 ft 10 in (3.3 m) x 16 ft 2 in (4.9 m)
Russia: 11 ft 2 in (5.4 m) x 17 ft 4 in (5.3 m)

*3 ft 3½ in
(1,000 mm)
East Africa,
India,
Malaysia,
Chile, and
Argentina*

*3 ft 6 in
(1,067 mm)
Japan, Australia,
Sudan, West Africa,
South Africa, and
New Zealand*

*4 ft 8½ in
(1,435 mm)
U.S., Canada, China,
Egypt, Turkey, Iran,
Japan, Peru, Britain,
Europe, Australia,
Brazil, and Mexico*

*5 ft 0 in
(1,524 mm)
Russia, Spain,
Portugal, and
Finland*

*5 ft 3 in
(1,600 mm)
Ireland, Australia,
and Brazil*

*5 ft 6 in
(1,676 mm)
India, Pakistan,
and Argentina*

*4 ft 8½ in
(1,435 mm)
Standard track
gauge*

*5 ft 0 in
(1,524 mm)
Track gauge of Russia,
with largest loading gauge*

FLAT-BOTTOMED RAIL

Flat-bottomed steel rail

*Steel spring secures
rail to sleeper*

*Synthetic
insulating
pad*

*Sleeper supports
track and
maintains
gauge*

BULL-HEAD RAIL

*Wooden "key" secures
rail in chair*

*Steel tapered
screw fastens
chair to
sleeper*

*Bull-head pattern
steel rail*

Cast-iron chair

*Wooden
sleeper*

DISC BRAKES ON MODERN WAGON BOGIE

*Airbag secondary
suspension*

Base of wagon

Damper

*Hand
brake
wheel*

Axle

*Brake
disc*

Brake calliper

Wheel

*Two yellow "preliminary
caution" lights instruct train
B that it must stop in two
signals time*

*Yellow "caution" light
instructs train B that it
must stop at next signal*

*Green "all clear" light
instructs train A to proceed
into this section of track*

*Red "stop" light instructs
train B not to enter
this section of track*

Braking distance

Train A

Trolleys and buses

METROLINK TROLLEY, MANCHESTER, BRITAIN

WHEN CITY POPULATIONS exploded in the 1800s, there was an urgent need for mass transportation. Trolleys were an early solution. The first trolleys, like buses, were horse-drawn, but in 1881, electric streetcars appeared in Berlin, Germany. Electric trolleys soon became widespread throughout Europe and North America. Trolleys run on rails along a fixed route, using electric motors that receive power from overhead cables. As road networks developed, motorized buses offered a flexible alternative to trolleys. By the 1930s, they had replaced trolley systems in many cities. City buses typically have doors at both the front and rear to make loading and unloading easier. Double-decker designs are popular, occupying the same amount of street space as single-decker buses but able to transport twice the number of people. Buses are also commonly used for inter-city travel and touring. Tour buses have reclining seats, large windows, luggage space, and toilets. Recently, as city traffic has become increasingly congested, many city planners have designed new electric streetcar routes to run alongside bus routes as part of an integrated transport system.

EARLY TROLLEY, c.1900

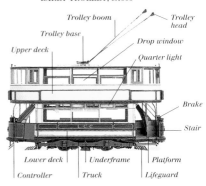

Labels: Trolley boom · Trolley head · Trolley base · Drop window · Upper deck · Quarter light · Brake · Stair · Lower deck · Underframe · Platform · Controller · Truck · Lifeguard

MCW METROBUS, LONDON, ENGLAND

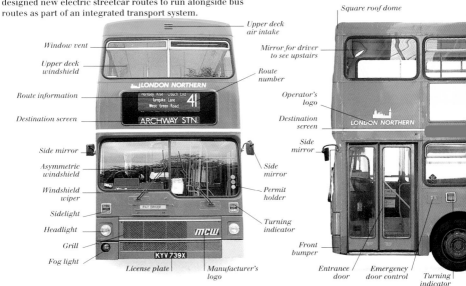

Labels: Square roof dome · Upper deck air intake · Mirror for driver to see upstairs · Window vent · Upper deck windshield · Route number · Operator's logo · Route information · Destination screen · Destination screen · Side mirror · Side mirror · Asymmetric windshield · Side mirror · Windshield wiper · Permit holder · Sidelight · Headlight · Turning indicator · Grill · Front bumper · Fog light · License plate · Manufacturer's logo · Entrance door · Emergency door control · Turning indicator

LONDON NORTHERN
Hornsey Rise Crouch End
Turnpike Lane
West Green Road
41
ARCHWAY STN.

PAY DRIVER

mcw

KYV 739X

LONDON NORTHERN

FRONT VIEW

SINGLE-DECKER BUS, NEW YORK CITY, NEW YORK

Wheelchair access
Sliding window
Sloped roof dome
Tinted glass
Air intake
Tire
Axle
Exit door
Access panel
Sidelight
Entrance door

SIDE VIEW

Marker light
Repeater indicator
Entrance door
Side mirror
Route number
Headlight
Bumper
Turning indicator
License plate
Bumper

FRONT VIEW

DOUBLE-DECKER TOUR BUS, PARIS, FRANCE

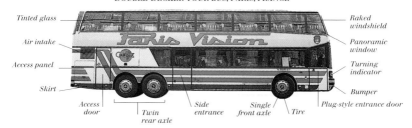

Tinted glass
Air intake
Access panel
Skirt
Access door
Twin rear axle
Side entrance
Single front axle
Tire

Raked windshield
Panoramic window
Turning indicator
Bumper
Plug-style entrance door

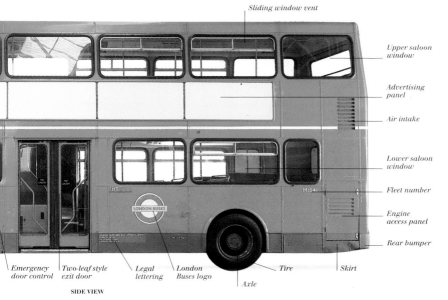

Sliding window vent

Upper saloon window
Advertising panel
Air intake
Lower saloon window
Fleet number
Engine access panel
Rear bumper

Emergency door control
Two-leaf style exit door
Legal lettering
London Buses logo
Tire
Skirt
Axle

SIDE VIEW

The first cars

THE EARLIEST ROAD VEHICLE powered by an engine, the Cugnot steam traction engine, was built in 1770. More practical steam carriages, such as the Bordino, were available in the early 19th century, but they were heavy and cumbersome. Restrictive laws and the introduction of railways, faster and able to carry more passengers, saw the decline of "cars" powered by steam. It was not until 1860 that the first practical power unit for road vehicles was developed with the invention of the internal combustion engine by the Belgian Étienne Lenoir. By around 1890, Karl Benz and Gottlieb Daimler in Germany and Albert de Dion and Armand Peugeot in France were building cars for sale to the public. These early cars, despite being primitive, expensive, and produced in limited numbers, heralded the age of the automobile.

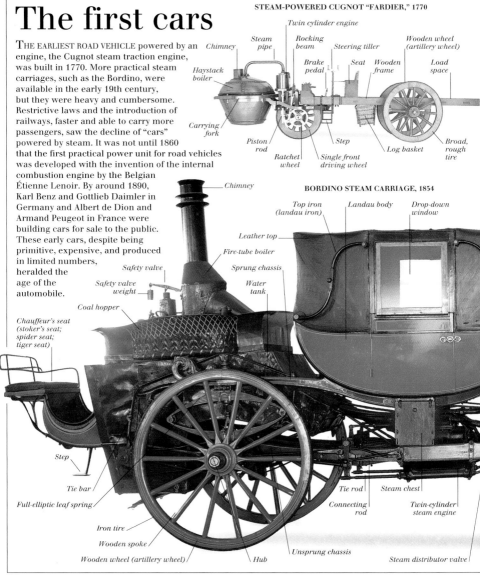

STEAM-POWERED CUGNOT "FARDIER," 1770

Twin cylinder engine
Chimney
Steam pipe
Rocking beam
Steering tiller
Wooden wheel (artillery wheel)
Brake pedal
Seat
Wooden frame
Load space
Haystack boiler
Carrying fork
Piston rod
Ratchet wheel
Single front driving wheel
Step
Log basket
Broad, rough tire

BORDINO STEAM CARRIAGE, 1854

Chimney
Top iron (landau iron)
Landau body
Drop-down window
Leather top
Fire-tube boiler
Sprung chassis
Water tank
Safety valve
Safety valve weight
Coal hopper
Chauffeur's seat (stoker's seat; spider seat; tiger seat)
Step
Tie bar
Full-elliptic leaf spring
Iron tire
Wooden spoke
Wooden wheel (artillery wheel)
Hub
Unsprung chassis
Tie rod
Steam chest
Connecting rod
Twin-cylinder steam engine
Steam distributor valve

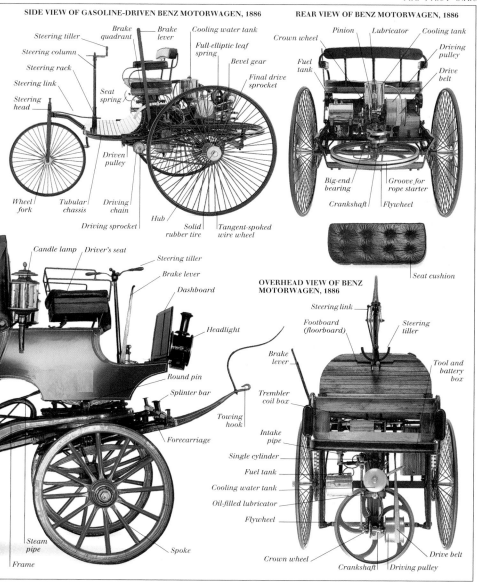

SIDE VIEW OF GASOLINE-DRIVEN BENZ MOTORWAGEN, 1886

Steering tiller
Steering column
Steering rack
Steering link
Steering head
Brake quadrant
Brake lever
Cooling water tank
Full-elliptic leaf spring
Bevel gear
Final drive sprocket
Seat spring
Driven pulley
Wheel fork
Tubular chassis
Driving chain
Hub
Driving sprocket
Solid rubber tire
Tangent-spoked wire wheel

REAR VIEW OF BENZ MOTORWAGEN, 1886

Crown wheel
Pinion
Lubricator
Cooling tank
Fuel tank
Driving pulley
Drive belt
Big-end bearing
Groove for rope starter
Crankshaft
Flywheel
Seat cushion

Candle lamp
Driver's seat
Steering tiller
Brake lever
Dashboard
Headlight
Round pin
Splinter bar
Towing hook
Forecarriage
Steam pipe
Frame
Spoke

OVERHEAD VIEW OF BENZ MOTORWAGEN, 1886

Steering link
Footboard (floorboard)
Steering tiller
Brake lever
Tool and battery box
Trembler coil box
Intake pipe
Single cylinder
Fuel tank
Cooling water tank
Oil-filled lubricator
Flywheel
Crown wheel
Crankshaft
Driving pulley
Drive belt

Elegance and utility

DURING THE FIRST DECADE OF THIS CENTURY, the motorist who could afford it had a choice of some of the finest cars ever made. These handbuilt cars were powerful and luxurious, using the finest wood, leather, and cloth, and bodywork made to the customer's individual requirements. Some had six-cylinder engines as big as 15 liters. The price of such cars was several times that of an average house, and their yearly running costs were also very high. As a result, basic, utilitarian cars became popular. Costing perhaps one-tenth of the price of a luxury car, these cars had very little trim and often had only single-cylinder engines.

1904 OLDSMOBILE SINGLE-CYLINDER ENGINE

Oil bottle dripfeed
Crankcase
Exhaust pipe
Starting handle bracket
Cylinder head
Cylinder
Starter cog
Carburetor
Engine timing gear
Crankshaft
Gear band
Flywheel

FRONT VIEW OF 1906 RENAULT

SIDE VIEW OF 1906 RENAULT

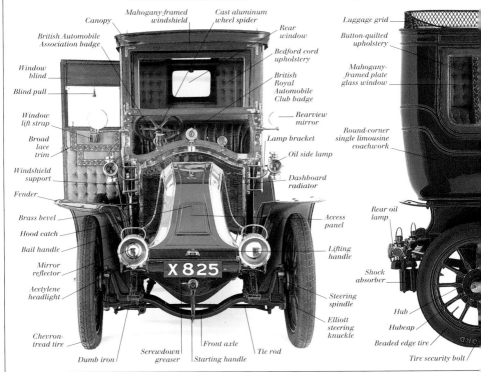

Canopy
Mahogany-framed windshield
Cast aluminum wheel spider
Rear window
British Automobile Association badge
Bedford cord upholstery
Window blind
British Royal Automobile Club badge
Blind pull
Window lift strap
Rearview mirror
Broad lace trim
Lamp bracket
Windshield support
Oil side lamp
Fender
Dashboard radiator
Brass bevel
Access panel
Hood catch
Lifting handle
Bail handle
Mirror reflector
Acetylene headlight
Steering spindle
Elliott steering knuckle
Chevron-tread tire
Dumb iron
Screwdown greaser
Front axle
Starting handle
Tie rod

Luggage grid
Button-quilted upholstery
Mahogany-framed plate glass window
Round-corner single limousine coachwork
Rear oil lamp
Shock absorber
Hub
Hubcap
Beaded edge tire
Tire security bolt

X 825

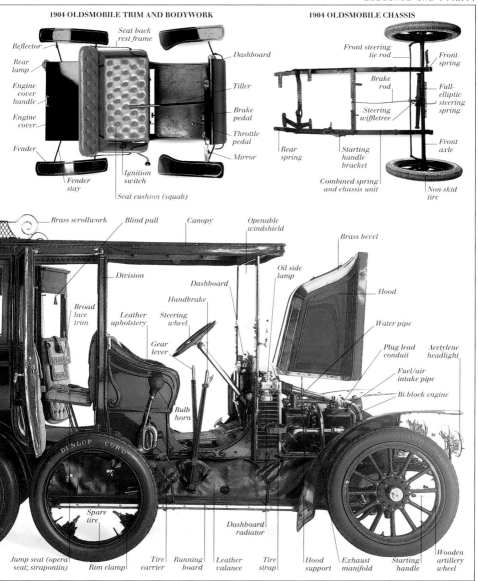

1904 OLDSMOBILE TRIM AND BODYWORK

Reflector
Rear lamp
Engine cover handle
Engine cover
Fender
Fender stay
Seat back rest frame
Dashboard
Tiller
Brake pedal
Throttle pedal
Mirror
Ignition switch
Seat cushion (squab)

1904 OLDSMOBILE CHASSIS

Front steering tie rod
Front spring
Brake rod
Full-elliptic steering spring
Steering wiffletree
Front axle
Rear spring
Starting handle bracket
Combined spring and chassis unit
Non-skid tire

Brass scrollwork
Blind pull
Canopy
Openable windshield
Brass bevel
Division
Oil side lamp
Hood
Broad lace trim
Dashboard
Handbrake
Leather upholstery
Steering wheel
Water pipe
Gear lever
Plug lead conduit
Acetylene headlight
Fuel/air intake pipe
Bi-block engine
Bulb horn
Spare tire
Dashboard radiator
Jump seat (opera seat; strapontin)
Rim clamp
Tire carrier
Running board
Leather valance
Tire strap
Hood support
Exhaust manifold
Starting handle
Wooden artillery wheel

DUNLOP CORD

Mass production

THE FIRST CARS WERE HAND-ASSEMBLED from individually built parts, a time-consuming procedure that required skilled mechanics and made cars very expensive. This problem was solved, in America, by a Detroit car manufacturer named Henry Ford. He introduced mass production by using standardized parts, and later combined these with a moving production line. The work was brought to the workers, each of whom performed one simple task in the construction process as the chassis moved along the line. The first mass-produced car, the Ford Model T, was launched in 1908. At first it was available in a limited range of body styles and colors. However, when the production line was introduced in 1914, the color range was cut back; the Model T became available, as Henry Ford said, in "any color you like, so long as it's black." Ford cut the production time for a car from several days to about 12 hours, and eventually to minutes, making cars much cheaper than before. As a result, half the cars in the world were Model T Fords by 1920.

FRONT VIEW OF 1913 FORD MODEL T

Throttle lever
Openable windshield
Steering wheel
Ignition lever
Windshield stay
Dashboard
Side lamp
Spring shock absorber
Bulb horn
Fender
Headlight
Radiator
Front transverse leaf spring
License plate
Starting handle
Steering knuckle
Front axle
Steering spindle connecting-rod

STAGES OF FORD MODEL T PRODUCTION

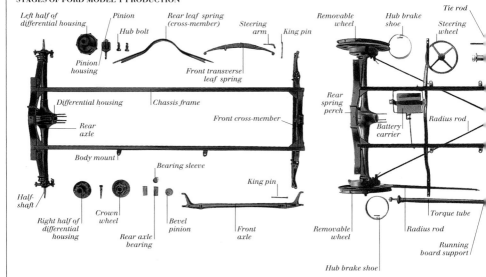

Left half of differential housing
Pinion
Rear leaf spring (cross-member)
Steering arm
King pin
Removable wheel
Hub brake shoe
Steering wheel
Tie rod
Hub bolt
Pinion housing
Front transverse leaf spring
Differential housing
Chassis frame
Rear spring perch
Radius rod
Front cross-member
Rear axle
Battery carrier
Body mount
Bearing sleeve
King pin
Half-shaft
Crown wheel
Bevel pinion
Front axle
Removable wheel
Radius rod
Torque tube
Right half of differential housing
Rear axle bearing
Running board support
Hub brake shoe

SIDE VIEW OF 1913 FORD MODEL T

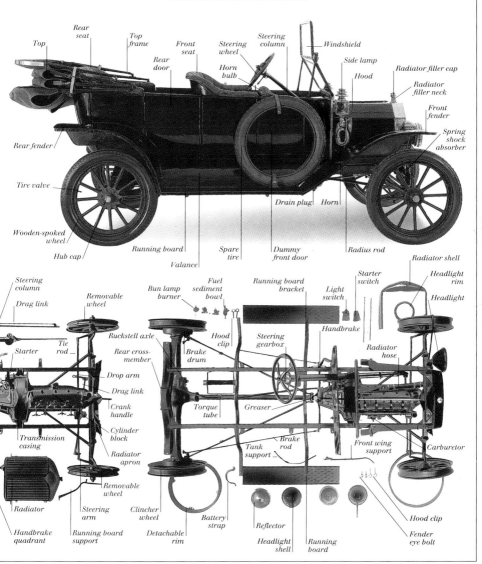

Top

Rear seat

Top frame

Rear door

Front seat

Steering wheel

Horn bulb

Steering column

Windshield

Side lamp

Hood

Radiator filler cap

Radiator filler neck

Front fender

Spring shock absorber

Rear fender

Tire valve

Wooden-spoked wheel

Hub cap

Running board

Valance

Spare tire

Drain plug

Horn

Dummy front door

Radius rod

Radiator shell

Steering column

Drag link

Removable wheel

Bun lamp burner

Fuel sediment bowl

Running board bracket

Light switch

Starter switch

Handbrake

Headlight rim

Headlight

Starter

Tie rod

Ruckstell axle

Rear cross-member

Drop arm

Drag link

Crank handle

Cylinder block

Radiator apron

Hood clip

Brake drum

Steering gearbox

Torque tube

Greaser

Radiator hose

Transmission casing

Tank support

Brake rod

Front wing support

Carburetor

Radiator

Steering arm

Removable wheel

Clincher wheel

Detachable rim

Battery strap

Reflector

Headlight shell

Running board

Hood clip

Fender eye bolt

Handbrake quadrant

Running board support

339

The "people's car"

THE MOST POPULAR CAR in the history of car manufacture is the Volkswagen Beetle, originally called the KdF Wagen. The car was developed in Germany in the 1930s by Dr. Ferdinand Porsche. At that time, Germany had only half the number of cars of Britain or France, and Adolf Hitler took a personal interest in the development of the Volkswagen ("people's car"). The intention was to provide a new industry, new jobs, and a car so inexpensive that anyone with a job could afford it. Dr. Porsche designed a car that was cheap to build and run; its rear-mounted, air-cooled engine cut down the number of parts needed and also reduced weight. However, few civilians managed to obtain the Beetle before the outbreak of the Second World War in 1939. After the war, the Beetle proved so popular that eventually more than 20 million were sold.

CUSTOMIZED VOLKSWAGEN BEETLE

FLAT-FOUR CYLINDER ARRANGEMENT

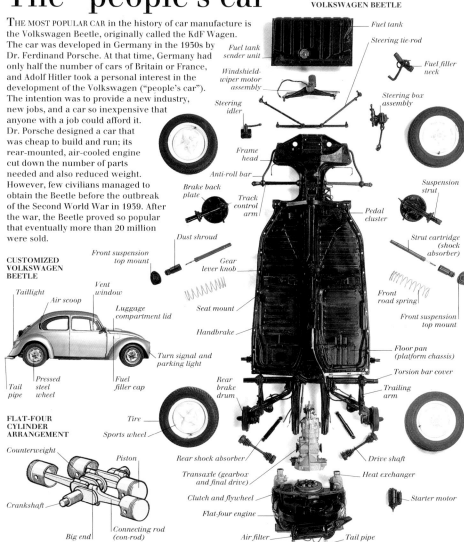

Fuel tank

Steering tie-rod

Fuel filler neck

Fuel tank sender unit

Windshield-wiper motor assembly

Steering box assembly

Steering idler

Suspension strut

Frame head

Anti-roll bar

Brake back plate

Track control arm

Pedal cluster

Strut cartridge (shock absorber)

Dust shroud

Front suspension top mount

Gear lever knob

Front road spring

Front suspension top mount

Taillight

Air scoop

Vent window

Luggage compartment lid

Seat mount

Handbrake

Floor pan (platform chassis)

Torsion bar cover

Trailing arm

Turn signal and parking light

Tail pipe

Pressed steel wheel

Fuel filler cap

Rear brake drum

Tire

Sports wheel

Rear shock absorber

Transaxle (gearbox and final drive)

Heat exchanger

Drive shaft

Starter motor

Counterweight

Piston

Clutch and flywheel

Flat-four engine

Crankshaft

Air filter

Tail pipe

Big end

Connecting rod (con-rod)

BODY SHELL OF
VOLKSWAGEN BEETLE

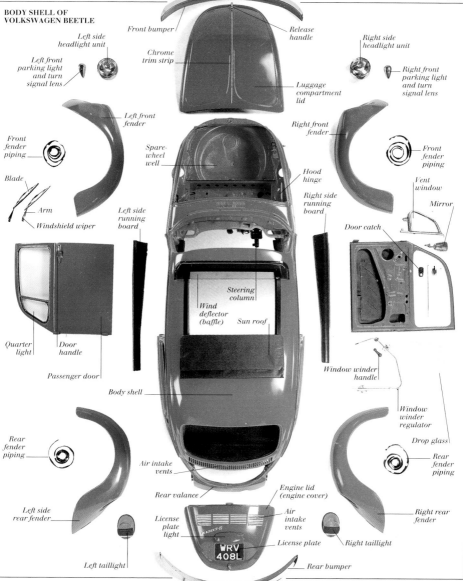

Front bumper

Release handle

Left side headlight unit

Right side headlight unit

Left front parking light and turn signal lens

Chrome trim strip

Right front parking light and turn signal lens

Luggage compartment lid

Left front fender

Right front fender

Front fender piping

Spare-wheel well

Front fender piping

Blade

Hood hinge

Vent window

Arm

Right side running board

Mirror

Windshield wiper

Left side running board

Door catch

Steering column

Wind deflector (baffle)

Sun roof

Quarter light

Door handle

Passenger door

Window winder handle

Body shell

Window winder regulator

Rear fender piping

Drop glass

Air intake vents

Rear fender piping

Left side rear fender

Rear valance

Engine lid (engine cover)

Right rear fender

License plate light

Air intake vents

License plate

WRV 408L

Left taillight

Right taillight

Rear bumper

Early engines

TROJAN TWO-STROKE ENGINE, 1927

STEAM AND ELECTRICITY were used to power cars until
early this century, but neither power source was ideal. Electric
cars had to stop frequently to recharge their heavy batteries, and
steam cars gave smooth power delivery but were too complicated
for the average motorist to use. A rival power source, the internal
combustion engine, was invented in 1860 by Étienne Lenoir
(see pp. 334-335). This engine converted the force of an explosion
into rotary motion to turn the wheels of a vehicle. Early variations
on this basic model included sleeve valves, separately cast
cylinders, and the two-stroke combustion cycle. Today, all

**BERSEY ELECTRIC
CAB, 1896**

combustion engines, including
the Wankel rotary and diesels
(see pp. 346-347), use the four-
stroke cycle, first demonstrated
by Nikolaus Otto in 1876. The
Otto cycle has proved the best
method of ensuring that the
engine turns over smoothly
and that exhaust emissions
are controllable.

Port linking combustion
chambers of upper
and lower cylinders

Water connection

Upper paired cylinder

Spark plug

Wide piston-ring

Transfer port

Wire gauze pad

Upper piston

Flywheel

Flexible,
forked
connecting-
rod

Mounting
for tray of
40 batteries

Housing for electric motors

Counterweight

Big end

Crankcase

SECTIONED WHITE STEAM CAR, 1903

Steering wheel

Throttle wheel

Brake
lever

Reverse
lever

Flash steam
generator

Automatic cylinder
lubricator

Lamp
bracket

High-pressure
cylinder

Rocking
lever

Exhaust
pipe

Water
pump

Condenser

Low-
pressure
cylinder

Fuel tank

Semi-elliptic
spring

Brake drum

Spiral
tubes

Steel-reinforced
wooden chassis

Steering
drop
arm

Water
tank

Drag link

Dumb iron

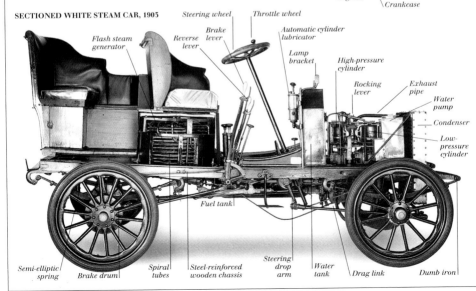

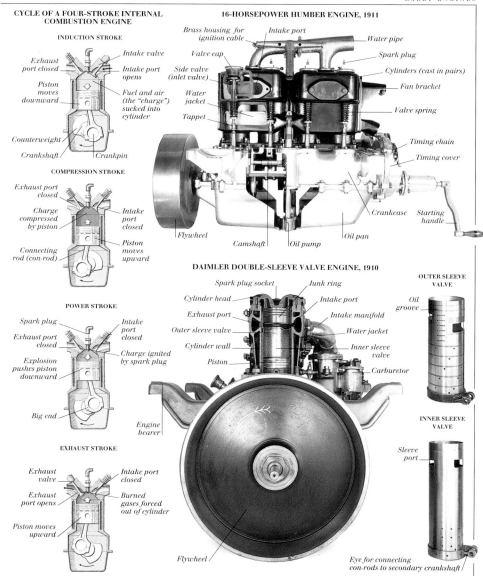

CYCLE OF A FOUR-STROKE INTERNAL COMBUSTION ENGINE

INDUCTION STROKE

Exhaust port closed

Piston moves downward

Counterweight

Crankshaft

Crankpin

Intake valve

Intake port opens

Fuel and air (the "charge") sucked into cylinder

COMPRESSION STROKE

Exhaust port closed

Charge compressed by piston

Connecting rod (con-rod)

Intake port closed

Piston moves upward

POWER STROKE

Spark plug

Exhaust port closed

Explosion pushes piston downward

Big end

Intake port closed

Charge ignited by spark plug

EXHAUST STROKE

Exhaust valve

Exhaust port opens

Piston moves upward

Intake port closed

Burned gases forced out of cylinder

16-HORSEPOWER HUMBER ENGINE, 1911

Brass housing for ignition cable

Valve cap

Side valve (inlet valve)

Water jacket

Tappet

Counterweight

Crankshaft

Flywheel

Camshaft

Oil pump

Intake port

Water pipe

Spark plug

Cylinders (cast in pairs)

Fan bracket

Valve spring

Timing chain

Timing cover

Crankcase

Starting handle

Oil pan

DAIMLER DOUBLE-SLEEVE VALVE ENGINE, 1910

Spark plug socket

Cylinder head

Exhaust port

Outer sleeve valve

Cylinder wall

Piston

Engine bearer

Flywheel

Junk ring

Intake port

Intake manifold

Water jacket

Inner sleeve valve

Carburetor

OUTER SLEEVE VALVE

Oil groove

INNER SLEEVE VALVE

Sleeve port

Eye for connecting con-rods to secondary crankshaft

Modern engines

TODAY'S GASOLINE ENGINE WORKS on the same basic principles as the first car engines of a century ago, although it has been greatly refined. Modern engines, often made from special metal alloys, are much lighter than earlier engines. Computerized ignition systems, fuel injectors, and multi-valve cylinder heads achieve a more efficient combustion of the fuel/air mixture (the charge) so that less fuel is wasted. As a result of this greater efficiency, the power and performance of a modern engine are increased, and the level of pollution in the exhaust gases is reduced. Exhaust pollution levels today are also lowered by the increasing use of special filters called catalytic converters, which absorb many exhaust pollutants. The need to produce ever more efficient engines means that it can take up to seven years to develop a new engine for a family car, at a cost of many millions of dollars.

FRONT VIEW OF A FORD COSWORTH V6 12-VALVE

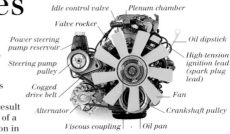

Idle control valve
Plenum chamber
Valve rocker
Power steering pump reservoir
Oil dipstick
High-tension ignition lead (spark plug lead)
Steering pump pulley
Cogged drive belt
Fan
Alternator
Crankshaft pulley
Viscous coupling
Oil pan

FRONT VIEW OF A FORD COSWORTH V6 24-VALVE

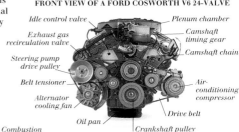

Idle control valve
Plenum chamber
Exhaust gas recirculation valve
Camshaft timing gear
Camshaft chain
Steering pump drive pulley
Belt tensioner
Air-conditioning compressor
Alternator cooling fan
Oil pan
Drive belt
Crankshaft pulley

SECTIONED VIEW OF A JAGUAR STRAIGHT 6

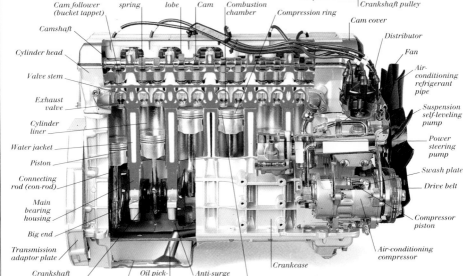

Valve spring
Cam lobe
Cam
Combustion chamber
Compression ring
Cam follower (bucket tappet)
Cam cover
Distributor
Camshaft
Fan
Cylinder head
Air-conditioning refrigerant pipe
Valve stem
Exhaust valve
Suspension self-leveling pump
Cylinder liner
Power steering pump
Water jacket
Swash plate
Piston
Drive belt
Connecting rod (con-rod)
Compressor piston
Main bearing housing
Big end
Air-conditioning compressor
Transmission adaptor plate
Crankshaft counterweight
Oil pan
Oil pick-up pipe
Anti-surge baffle
Crankcase
Oil-control ring (scraper ring)

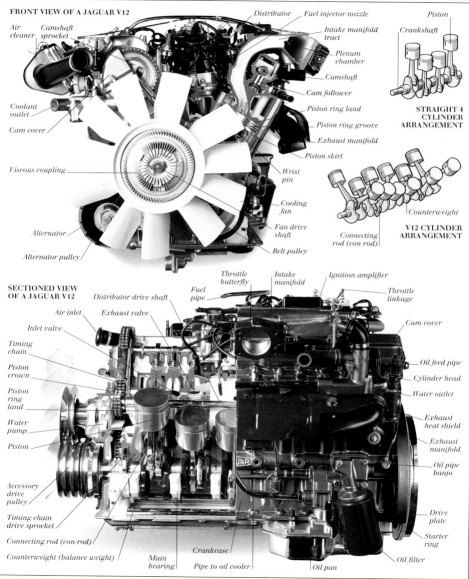

FRONT VIEW OF A JAGUAR V12

Distributor
Fuel injector nozzle
Piston
Crankshaft

Air cleaner
Camshaft sprocket
Intake manifold tract
Plenum chamber
Camshaft
Cam follower
Piston ring land
Piston ring groove
Exhaust manifold
Piston skirt

Coolant outlet
Cam cover

STRAIGHT 4 CYLINDER ARRANGEMENT

Viscous coupling

Wrist pin

Cooling fan
Fan drive shaft
Belt pulley

Counterweight
Connecting rod (con-rod)

V12 CYLINDER ARRANGEMENT

Alternator
Alternator pulley

SECTIONED VIEW OF A JAGUAR V12

Throttle butterfly
Intake manifold
Ignition amplifier
Fuel pipe
Throttle linkage

Distributor drive shaft
Exhaust valve
Cam cover

Air inlet
Inlet valve

Timing chain
Piston crown
Piston ring land
Water pump
Piston

Oil feed pipe
Cylinder head
Water outlet
Exhaust heat shield
Exhaust manifold
Oil pipe banjo

Accessory drive pulley
Timing chain drive sprocket
Connecting rod (con-rod)
Counterweight (balance weight)
Main bearing
Crankcase
Pipe to oil cooler
Oil pan
Oil filter

Drive plate
Starter ring

Alternative engines

THE MOST COMMON TYPE OF ALTERNATIVE ENGINE is the diesel engine. Instead of igniting the compressed fuel/air mixture with a spark, the diesel engine uses compression alone, which heats the mixture to the point where it explodes. A diesel engine's fuel consumption is low in comparison with similarly sized piston engines, despite its heavier, reinforced moving parts and cylinder block. Another type of engine is the rotary-combustion, first successfully developed by Felix Wankel in the 1950s. Its two trilobate (three-sided) rotors revolve in housings shaped in a fat figure eight. The four sequences of the four-stroke cycle, which occur consecutively in a piston engine, occur simultaneously in a rotary engine, producing power in a continuous stream.

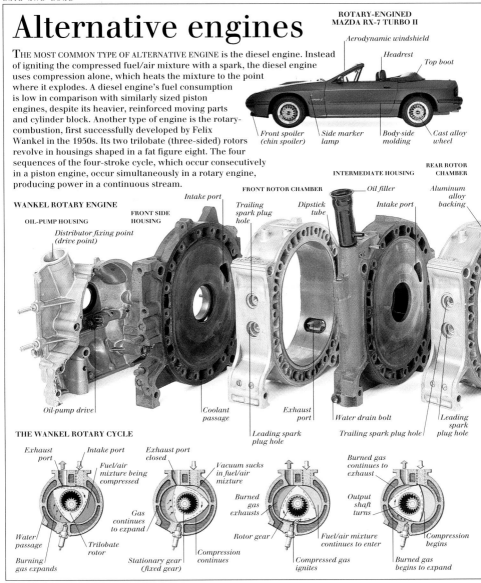

ROTARY-ENGINED MAZDA RX-7 TURBO II

Aerodynamic windshield
Headrest
Top boot
Front spoiler (chin spoiler)
Side marker lamp
Body-side molding
Cast alloy wheel

WANKEL ROTARY ENGINE

OIL-PUMP HOUSING
FRONT SIDE HOUSING
Distributor fixing point (drive point)
Intake port
FRONT ROTOR CHAMBER
Trailing spark plug hole
Dipstick tube
INTERMEDIATE HOUSING
Oil filler
Intake port
REAR ROTOR CHAMBER
Aluminum alloy backing

Oil-pump drive
Coolant passage
Exhaust port
Leading spark plug hole
Water drain bolt
Trailing spark plug hole
Leading spark plug hole

THE WANKEL ROTARY CYCLE

Exhaust port
Intake port
Fuel/air mixture being compressed
Exhaust port closed
Vacuum sucks in fuel/air mixture
Burned gas continues to exhaust
Water passage
Gas continues to expand
Burned gas exhausts
Output shaft turns
Compression begins
Burning gas expands
Trilobate rotor
Stationary gear (fixed gear)
Compression continues
Rotor gear
Compressed gas ignites
Fuel/air mixture continues to enter
Burned gas begins to expand

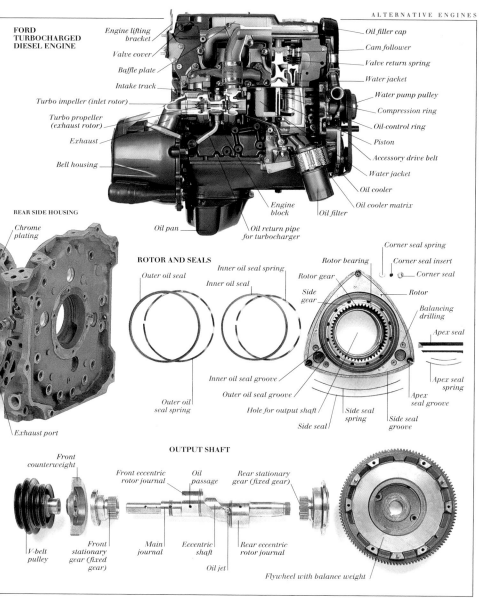

FORD TURBOCHARGED DIESEL ENGINE

Engine lifting bracket

Valve cover

Baffle plate

Intake track

Turbo impeller (inlet rotor)

Turbo propeller (exhaust rotor)

Exhaust

Bell housing

Oil filler cap

Cam follower

Valve return spring

Water jacket

Water pump pulley

Compression ring

Oil-control ring

Piston

Accessory drive belt

Water jacket

Oil cooler

Oil cooler matrix

Engine block

Oil filter

REAR SIDE HOUSING

Chrome plating

Oil pan

Oil return pipe for turbocharger

Exhaust port

ROTOR AND SEALS

Corner seal spring

Corner seal insert

Corner seal

Outer oil seal

Inner oil seal spring

Inner oil seal

Rotor bearing

Rotor gear

Side gear

Rotor

Balancing drilling

Apex seal

Apex seal spring

Inner oil seal groove

Outer oil seal groove

Outer oil seal spring

Hole for output shaft

Side seal

Side seal spring

Side seal groove

Apex seal groove

OUTPUT SHAFT

Front counterweight

Front eccentric rotor journal

Oil passage

Rear stationary gear (fixed gear)

V-belt pulley

Front stationary gear (fixed gear)

Main journal

Eccentric shaft

Oil jet

Rear eccentric rotor journal

Flywheel with balance weight

Modern bodywork

RENAULT LOGO

THE BODY OF A MODERN MASS-PRODUCED CAR is built on the monocoque (single-shell) principle, in which the roof, side panels, and floor are welded into a single integral unit. This bodyshell protects and supports the car's internal parts. Steel and glass are used to construct the bodyshell, creating a unit that is both light and strong. Its lightness helps to conserve energy, while its strength protects the occupants. Modern bodywork is designed with the aid of computers, which are used to predict factors such as aerodynamic efficiency and impact resistance. High technology is also employed on the production line, where robots are used to assemble, weld, and paint the body.

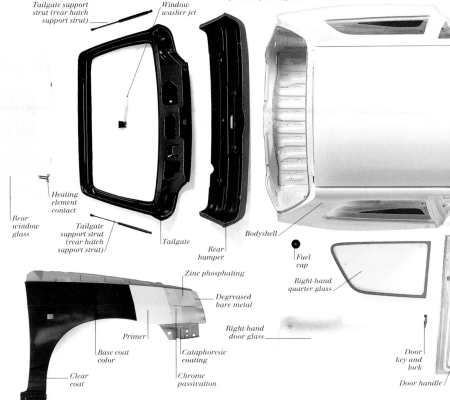

Door handle

Door lock

Left-hand door glass

Left-hand quarter glass

Tailgate support strut (rear hatch support strut)

Window washer jet

Heating element contact

Rear window glass

Tailgate support strut (rear hatch support strut)

Tailgate

Rear bumper

Bodyshell

Fuel cap

Right-hand quarter glass

Zinc phosphating

Degreased bare metal

Primer

Base coat color

Cataphoresic coating

Right-hand door glass

Clear coat

Chrome passivation

Door key and lock

Door handle

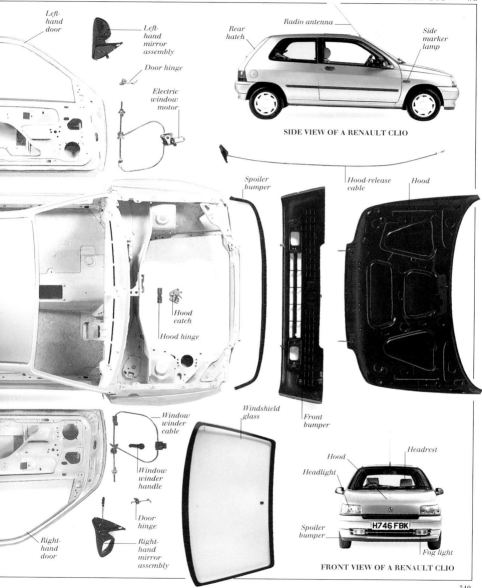

Left-hand door

Left-hand mirror assembly

Door hinge

Electric window motor

Radio antenna

Rear hatch

Side marker lamp

SIDE VIEW OF A RENAULT CLIO

Spoiler bumper

Hood-release cable

Hood

Hood catch

Hood hinge

Front bumper

Window winder cable

Windshield glass

Window winder handle

Door hinge

Right-hand door

Right-hand mirror assembly

Hood

Headrest

Headlight

Spoiler bumper

H746 FBK

Fog light

FRONT VIEW OF A RENAULT CLIO

Modern components

A TYPICAL MODERN CAR has several thousand individual mechanical components. These are assembled to form the car's various mechanical systems: engine and exhaust, transmission, steering, suspension, and brakes. To ensure that each system functions properly, components are manufactured to extremely fine tolerances—to within about one ten-thousandth of an inch in some cases.

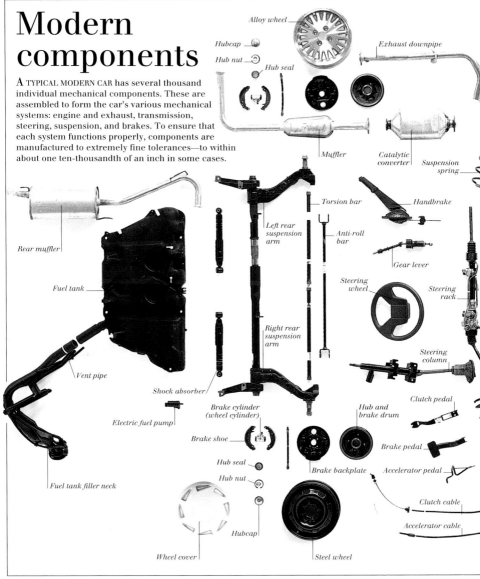

Alloy wheel

Hubcap

Hub nut

Hub seal

Exhaust downpipe

Muffler

Catalytic converter

Suspension spring

Rear muffler

Torsion bar

Handbrake

Left rear suspension arm

Anti-roll bar

Gear lever

Steering wheel

Steering rack

Fuel tank

Right rear suspension arm

Steering column

Vent pipe

Shock absorber

Clutch pedal

Brake cylinder (wheel cylinder)

Hub and brake drum

Electric fuel pump

Brake pedal

Brake shoe

Accelerator pedal

Hub seal

Brake backplate

Accelerator pedal

Hub nut

Fuel tank filler neck

Clutch cable

Accelerator cable

Hubcap

Wheel cover

Steel wheel

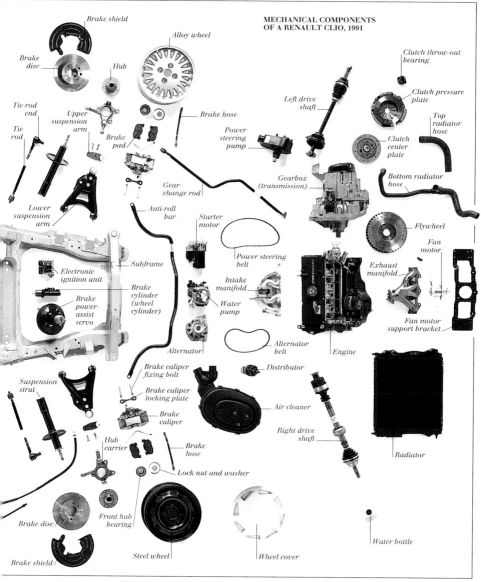

**MECHANICAL COMPONENTS
OF A RENAULT CLIO, 1991**

Brake shield

Alloy wheel

Clutch throw-out
bearing

Brake
disc

Hub

Clutch pressure
plate

Tie-rod
end

Upper
suspension
arm

Brake hose

Left drive
shaft

Top
radiator
hose

Tie
rod

Brake
pad

Power
steering
pump

Clutch
center
plate

Bottom radiator
hose

Gear-
change rod

Gearbox
(transmission)

Lower
suspension
arm

Anti-roll
bar

Starter
motor

Flywheel

Fan
motor

Electronic
ignition unit

Subframe

Power steering
belt

Exhaust
manifold

Brake
cylinder
(wheel
cylinder)

Intake
manifold

Brake
power-
assist
servo

Water
pump

Fan motor
support bracket

Alternator
belt

Engine

Alternator

Brake caliper
fixing bolt

Distributor

Suspension
strut

Brake caliper
locking plate

Air cleaner

Brake
caliper

Right drive
shaft

Hub
carrier

Brake
hose

Radiator

Lock nut and washer

Brake disc

Front hub
bearing

Water bottle

Brake shield

Steel wheel

Wheel cover

Modern trim

A MODERN CAR HAS TWO TYPES OF TRIM, according to the materials used: hard (chrome and plastics) and soft (upholstered materials). Safety and comfort are priorities in the trim's design: seats help the occupants maintain a comfortable posture, rubber seals keep out dirt and moisture, and headlights light the way. Older cars had interior or leather paneling cut and fitted by craftsmen; modern cars use precisely molded plastics and seat fabrics cut by robot-controlled lasers to reduce costs and production time. Doors are now assembled off the production line so that complex wiring can be built in.

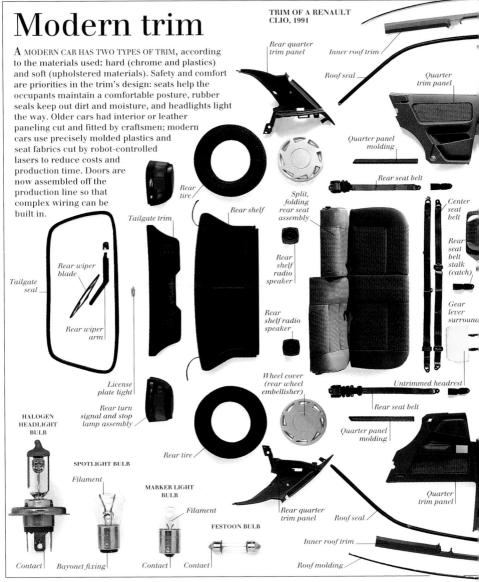

Rear quarter trim panel

Inner roof trim

Roof seal

Quarter trim panel

Quarter panel molding

Rear seat belt

Center seat belt

Rear seat belt stalk (catch)

Rear tire

Split, folding rear seat assembly

Rear shelf

Rear shelf radio speaker

Rear shelf radio speaker

Gear lever surround

Tailgate trim

Rear wiper blade

Tailgate seal

Rear wiper arm

License plate light

Wheel cover (rear wheel embellisher)

Untrimmed headrest

Rear seat belt

Rear turn signal and stop lamp assembly

HALOGEN HEADLIGHT BULB

Quarter panel molding

Rear tire

Quarter trim panel

SPOTLIGHT BULB

Filament

MARKER LIGHT BULB

Filament

FESTOON BULB

Rear quarter trim panel

Roof seal

Quarter trim panel

Contact

Bayonet fixing

Contact

Contact

Inner roof trim

Roof molding

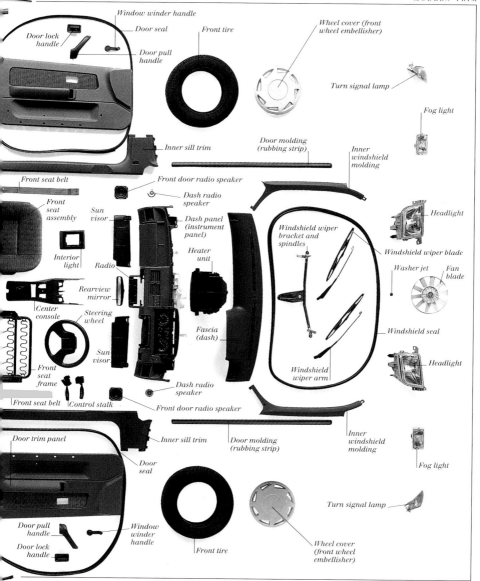

Window winder handle

Door lock handle

Door seal

Door pull handle

Front tire

Wheel cover (front wheel embellisher)

Turn signal lamp

Fog light

Inner sill trim

Door molding (rubbing strip)

Inner windshield molding

Front seat belt

Front door radio speaker

Dash radio speaker

Front seat assembly

Sun visor

Dash panel (instrument panel)

Headlight

Interior light

Heater unit

Windshield wiper bracket and spindles

Windshield wiper blade

Radio

Washer jet

Fan blade

Rearview mirror

Center console

Steering wheel

Fascia (dash)

Windshield seal

Front seat frame

Sun visor

Headlight

Front seat belt

Control stalk

Dash radio speaker

Windshield wiper arm

Front door radio speaker

Door trim panel

Inner sill trim

Door molding (rubbing strip)

Inner windshield molding

Door seal

Fog light

Door pull handle

Window winder handle

Turn signal lamp

Door lock handle

Front tire

Wheel cover (front wheel embellisher)

All-terrain vehicles

THE MODERN ALL-TERRAIN VEHICLE has its origins in the American military Jeep of the 1940s and the British Land Rover. Such vehicles have been used for a wide range of purposes, from safari travel to fire fighting. The principal special features of such cars—including four- or six-wheel drive, high ground clearance, and toughened braking, suspension, and transmission systems—are designed to enable driving under the most difficult off-road conditions. The vehicle shown here is equipped for safari travel and carries a comprehensive range of survival gear.

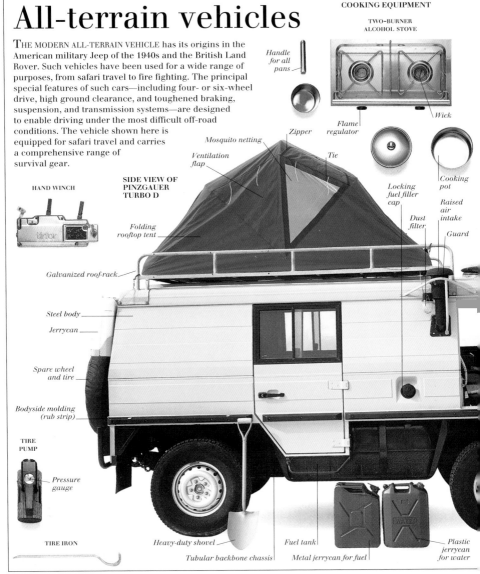

COOKING EQUIPMENT

TWO-BURNER ALCOHOL STOVE

Handle for all pans

Flame regulator

Wick

Cooking pot

Zipper

Tie

Mosquito netting

Ventilation flap

Locking fuel filler cap

Raised air intake

Dust filter

Guard

SIDE VIEW OF PINZGAUER TURBO D

HAND WINCH

Folding rooftop tent

Galvanized roof-rack

Steel body

Jerrycan

Spare wheel and tire

Bodyside molding (rub strip)

TIRE PUMP

Pressure gauge

TIRE IRON

Heavy-duty shovel

Tubular backbone chassis

Fuel tank

Metal jerrycan for fuel

Plastic jerrycan for water

LEFT-HAND TREAD PLATE

RIGHT-HAND TREAD PLATE

TOW STRAP

HEAVY-DUTY SHACKLE

SAFETY WINDSHIELD CLAMPS

Radio aerial

Observation roof hatch

WASHING BUCKET

Grab handle

Rearview mirror

Windshield washer bottle

Wrap-around bumper

Access step

SECURITY CHAIN

FRONT VIEW OF PINZGAUER TURBO D

Observation roof hatch

Radio aerial

Galvanized roof-rack

Laminated windshield

Rearview mirror

Air vent

Radiator grille

Indicator

Headlight guard

Headlight

External step

Independent swing axle

Locking differential

Towing loop

All-terrain tire

REAR VIEW OF PINZGAUER TURBO D

Roof-rack

Observation platform

External step for roof

Jerrycan

Jerrycan carrier

Spare wheel

Bodyside molding (rub strip)

Offset door hinge

Rear bumper

Rear light cluster

Mudflap

Door and wheel support frame

Off-road tire

Locking differential

Independent swing axle

Racing cars

SINCE MOTORING BEGAN, racing cars have been a major focus of innovation in car design. Features that are now commonplace, such as disc brakes, turbochargers, and even safety belts, were used first on competition cars. Research into racing cars has contributed to a new understanding of engine performance, aerodynamics, and tire adhesion, and has led to the development of ultra-light materials such as carbon-fiber for car bodies. Like the 1937 Bugatti Type 57S below, a modern Williams Formula One car has a low, streamlined body and an open cockpit. Unlike its forerunner, it also has a front wing that pushes the front wheels firmly onto the track, huge slick tires for extra grip, and electrical sensors that continually relay information to the pits about the car's performance.

Diffuser

Bodywork bracket

Heat shield

Forward radius arm

Rear wing upper mainplane

Slot

Upper flap

Half shaft

Rear radius arm

Temperature-sensitive sticker

Aeroquip pipe union

Oil tank

1937 BUGATTI TYPE 57S

Constant velocity joint cover

Rear wing end-plate

Diffuser

Rear brake duct

Fuel injection trumpet guard (debris guard)

Mounting point

Fuel injector

Cam cover

Cylinder head

Gearbox fixing stud

Electronic control-unit connector

Water outlet

Oil feed to engine

ENGINE COWLING

Dzus fastener

Tail pipe

Stressed cylinder block

Harmonically tuned exhaust pipe

RENAULT V10 RS1 ENGINE

SIDE FAIRING

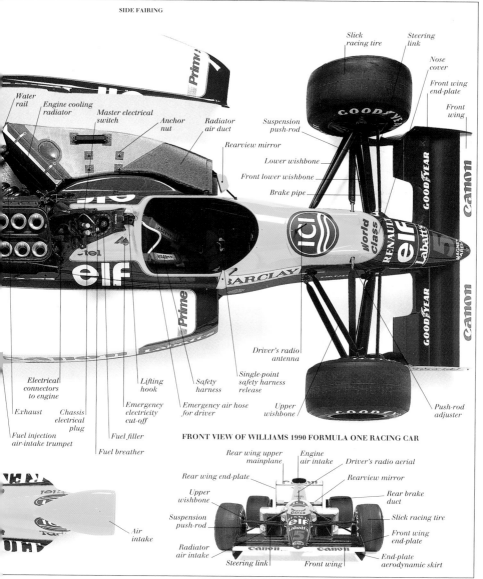

Slick racing tire

Steering link

Nose cover

Front wing end-plate

Front wing

Water rail

Engine cooling radiator

Master electrical switch

Anchor nut

Radiator air duct

Suspension push-rod

Rearview mirror

Lower wishbone

Front lower wishbone

Brake pipe

Driver's radio antenna

Electrical connectors to engine

Lifting hook

Safety harness

Single-point safety harness release

Exhaust

Chassis electrical plug

Emergency electricity cut-off

Emergency air hose for driver

Upper wishbone

Push-rod adjuster

Fuel injection air-intake trumpet

Fuel filler

Fuel breather

FRONT VIEW OF WILLIAMS 1990 FORMULA ONE RACING CAR

Rear wing upper mainplane

Engine air intake

Driver's radio aerial

Rear wing end-plate

Rearview mirror

Upper wishbone

Rear brake duct

Suspension push-rod

Slick racing tire

Radiator air intake

Front wing end-plate

Steering link

Front wing

End-plate aerodynamic skirt

Air intake

Bicycle anatomy

THE BICYCLE IS A TWO-WHEELED, lightweight machine, which is propelled by human power. It is efficient, cheap, easily manufactured, and one of the world's most popular forms of transportation. The first pedal-driven bicycle was built in Scotland in 1839. Since then the basic design—of a frame, wheels, brakes, handlebars, and a saddle—has been gradually improved, with the addition of a chain, gear system, and pneumatic tires (tires inflated with air). The recent invention of the mountain bike (all-terrain bike) has been an important development. With its strong, rugged frame, wide tires, and 21 gears, a mountain bike enables riders to reach rough and hilly areas that were previously inaccessible to cyclists.

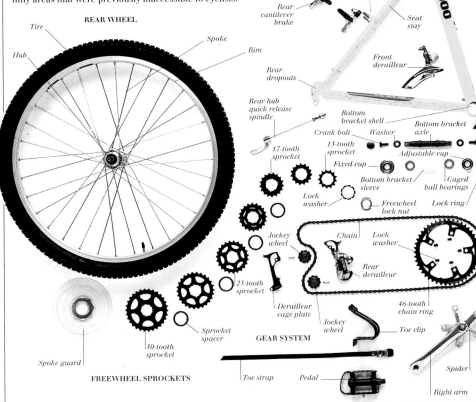

REAR WHEEL

Tire

Hub

Spoke

Rim

Saddle (seat)

Seat post

Seat post quick release bolt

Cable guide

Straddle wire

Seat tube

Rear cantilever brake

Seat stay

Front derailleur

Rear dropouts

Rear hub quick release spindle

Bottom bracket shell

Bottom bracket axle

Crank bolt

Washer

13-tooth sprocket

Adjustable cup

17-tooth sprocket

Fixed cup

Bottom bracket sleeve

Caged ball bearings

Lock washer

Freewheel lock nut

Lock ring

Jockey wheel

Chain

Lock washer

23-tooth sprocket

Rear derailleur

Derailleur cage plate

Jockey wheel

46-tooth chain ring

Toe clip

Spoke guard

30-tooth sprocket

Sprocket spacer

GEAR SYSTEM

Spider

FREEWHEEL SPROCKETS

Toe strap

Pedal

Right arm

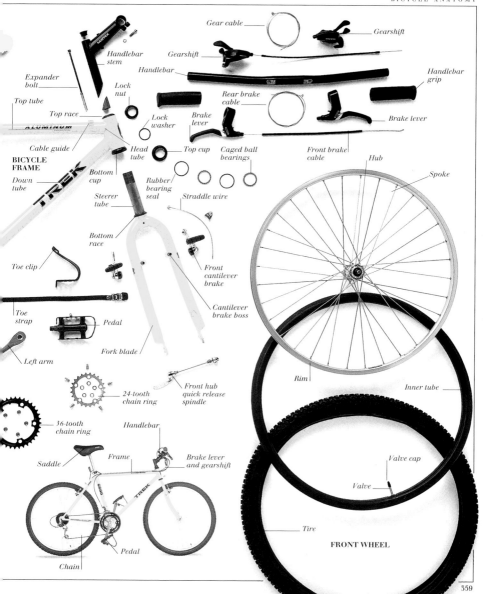

Gear cable

Gearshift

Gearshift

Handlebar stem

Handlebar

Handlebar grip

Expander bolt

Lock nut

Rear brake cable

Top tube

Top race

Lock washer

Brake lever

Brake lever

ALUMINUM

Cable guide

BICYCLE FRAME

Head tube

Top cup

Caged ball bearings

Front brake cable

Hub

Spoke

Bottom cup

Down tube

Rubber bearing seal

Straddle wire

Steerer tube

Bottom race

Front cantilever brake

Toe clip

Cantilever brake boss

Toe strap

Pedal

Left arm

Fork blade

Rim

Inner tube

24-tooth chain ring

Front hub quick release spindle

36-tooth chain ring

Handlebar

Saddle

Frame

Brake lever and gearshift

Valve cap

Pedal

Valve

Tire

FRONT WHEEL

Chain

Bicycles

ALTHOUGH ALL BICYCLES are made up of the same basic components, they can vary greatly in design. A racing bike, such as the Eddy Merckx model, with its light frame and steep head- and seat-angles, is built for speed. Its design forces the rider to adopt the aero tuck, a crouched, aerodynamic position. While a touring bike resembles a racing bike in many respects, it is designed for comfort and stability on long-distance journeys. Touring bikes are characterized by more relaxed frame angles, heavy chain stays that support the rear panniers, and a long wheelbase (the distance between the wheel axles) for reliable handling. All-purpose bicycles, known as hybrids, combine the light weight and speed of sports bikes with the rugged durability of mountain bikes (see pp. 358-359). Bicycles that are not designed for conventional road use include time-trial bikes, which have a short head tube, sloping top tube, aero handlebars, and aerodynamic tubing. Most Human Powered Vehicles (HPVs) are recumbents—the rider has a recumbent position—which maximize power output and minimize drag (resistance). Essential to the safety of all riders are helmets, and both front and rear lights; locks protect against theft.

FRONT AND REAR LIGHTS

HELMET

Hard outer shell

Red rear light

Air vent

White front light

Polystyrene padding

Quick-release strap

EDDY MERCKX RACING BICYCLE

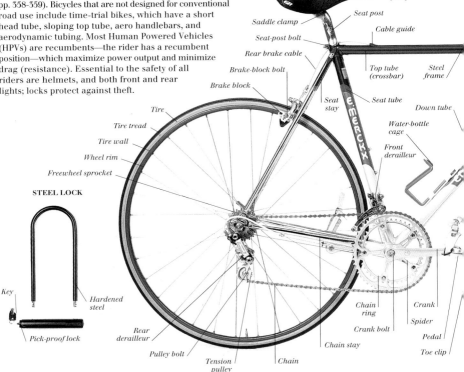

Saddle (seat)

Seat post

Saddle clamp

Cable guide

Seat-post bolt

Rear brake cable

Top tube (crossbar)

Steel frame

Brake-block bolt

Brake block

Seat stay

Seat tube

Down tube

Tire

Water-bottle cage

Tire tread

Tire wall

Front derailleur

Wheel rim

Freewheel sprocket

STEEL LOCK

Key

Hardened steel

Pick-proof lock

Rear derailleur

Pulley bolt

Tension pulley

Chain

Chain stay

Chain ring

Crank

Spider

Crank bolt

Pedal

Toe clip

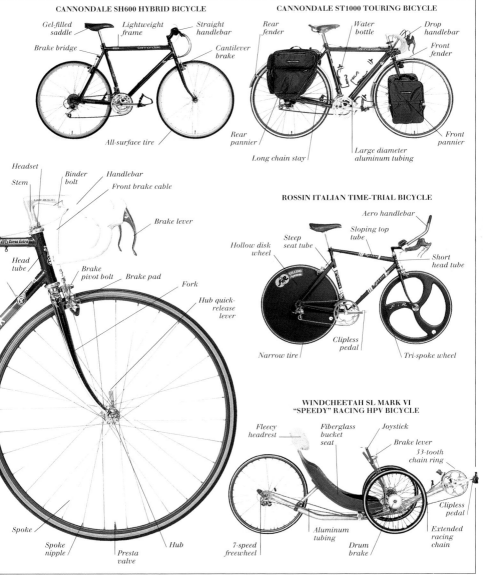

CANNONDALE SH600 HYBRID BICYCLE

Gel-filled saddle

Lightweight frame

Straight handlebar

Brake bridge

Cantilever brake

All-surface tire

CANNONDALE ST1000 TOURING BICYCLE

Rear fender

Water bottle

Drop handlebar

Front fender

Rear pannier

Front pannier

Long chain stay

Large diameter aluminum tubing

Headset

Stem

Binder bolt

Handlebar

Front brake cable

Brake lever

Head tube

Brake pivot bolt

Brake pad

Fork

Hub quick-release lever

Spoke

Spoke nipple

Presta valve

Hub

ROSSIN ITALIAN TIME-TRIAL BICYCLE

Aero handlebar

Sloping top tube

Steep seat tube

Hollow disk wheel

Short head tube

Clipless pedal

Narrow tire

Tri-spoke wheel

WINDCHEETAH SL MARK VI "SPEEDY" RACING HPV BICYCLE

Fleecy headrest

Fiberglass bucket seat

Joystick

Brake lever

53-tooth chain ring

Clipless pedal

Extended racing chain

7-speed freewheel

Aluminum tubing

Drum brake

The motorcycle

THE MOTORCYCLE HAS EVOLVED from a motorized cycle—a basic bicycle with an engine—into a sophisticated, high-performance machine. In 1901, the Werner brothers established the most viable location for the engine, positioning it low in the center of the chassis (see pp. 364-365): the new Werner became the basis for the modern motorcycle. Motorcycles are used for many purposes —for commuting, delivering messages, touring, and racing—and different machines have been developed to suit the demands of different types of riders. The Vespa scooter, for instance, which is small-wheeled, economical, and easy-to-ride, was designed to meet the needs of the commuter. Sidecars provided transportation for the family until the arrival of cheap cars caused their popularity to decline. Serious riders generally favor larger capacity machines that are capable of greater performance and offer more comfort. Four-cylinder machines have been common since the Honda CB750 appeared in 1969. Despite advances in motorcycle technology, many riders are attracted to the traditional look of motorcycles like the twin-cylinder Harley-Davidson. Harley-Davidson Glides exploit the style of the classic American V-twin engine, where the cylinders are placed in a V-formation.

1901 WERNER MOTORCYCLE

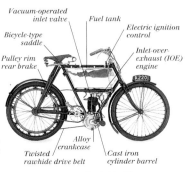

Vacuum-operated inlet valve
Fuel tank
Electric ignition control
Bicycle-type saddle
Inlet-over-exhaust (IOE) engine
Pulley rim rear brake
Twisted rawhide drive belt
Alloy crankcase
Cast iron cylinder barrel

1988 HARLEY-DAVIDSON FLHS ELECTRA GLIDE

1965 BMW R/60 WITH 1952 STEIB CHAIR

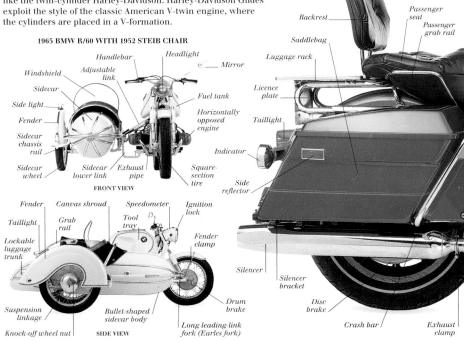

Backrest
Passenger seat
Passenger grab rail
Saddlebag
Luggage rack
Licence plate
Taillight
Indicator
Side reflector
Silencer
Silencer bracket
Disc brake
Crash bar
Exhaust clamp

Handlebar
Headlight
Windshield
Adjustable link
Mirror
Sidecar
Fuel tank
Side light
Horizontally opposed engine
Fender
Sidecar chassis rail
Sidecar wheel
Sidecar lower link
Exhaust pipe
Square-section tire
FRONT VIEW

Fender
Canvas shroud
Speedometer
Ignition lock
Taillight
Grab rail
Tool tray
Lockable luggage trunk
Fender clamp
Silencer
Suspension linkage
Bullet-shaped sidecar body
Drum brake
Knock-off wheel nut
SIDE VIEW
Long leading-link fork (Earles fork)

1969 HONDA CB750

1963 VESPA GRAND SPORT 160 MARK 1

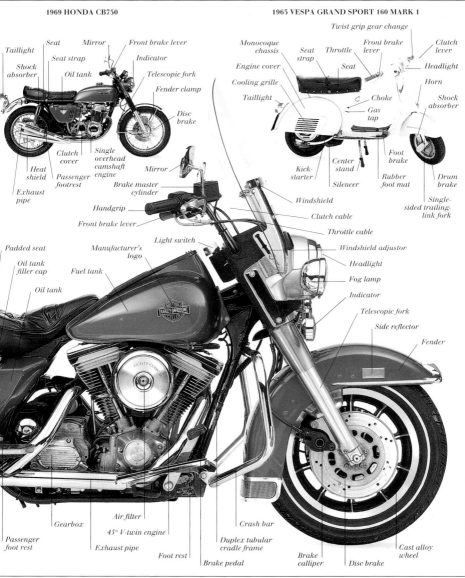

Taillight

Seat

Mirror

Front brake lever

Seat strap

Indicator

Shock absorber

Oil tank

Telescopic fork

Fender clamp

Disc brake

Clutch cover

Single overhead camshaft engine

Mirror

Heat shield

Passenger footrest

Exhaust pipe

Brake master cylinder

Handgrip

Front brake lever

Monocoque chassis

Engine cover

Cooling grille

Taillight

Seat strap

Throttle

Front brake lever

Clutch lever

Seat

Headlight

Horn

Choke

Shock absorber

Gas tap

Kick-starter

Center stand

Silencer

Foot brake

Rubber foot mat

Drum brake

Single-sided trailing-link fork

Windshield

Clutch cable

Throttle cable

Light switch

Manufacturer's logo

Padded seat

Fuel tank

Oil tank filler cap

Oil tank

Windshield adjustor

Headlight

Fog lamp

Indicator

Telescopic fork

Side reflector

Fender

Passenger foot rest

Gearbox

Air filter

45° V-twin engine

Exhaust pipe

Foot rest

Crash bar

Duplex tubular cradle frame

Brake pedal

Brake calliper

Disc brake

Cast alloy wheel

The motorcycle chassis

THE MOTORCYCLE CHASSIS is the main "body" of the motorcycle, to which the engine is attached. Consisting of the frame, wheels, suspension, and brakes, the chassis performs various functions. The frame, which is built from steel or alloy, keeps the wheels in line to maintain the handling of the motorcycle, and serves as a structure for mounting other components. The engine and gearbox unit is bolted into place, while items such as the seat, the fenders, and the fairing are more easily removable. Suspension cushions the rider from irregularities in the road surface. In most suspension systems, coil springs controlled by an oil damper separate the main mass of the motorcycle from the wheels. At the front, the spring and damper are usually incorporated in a telescopic fork; the rear employs a pivoted swing arm. The suspension also helps to retain maximum contact between the tires and the road, necessary to effective braking and steering. Drum brakes were common until the 1970s, but modern motorcycles use disc brakes, which are more powerful.

1985 HONDA VF750 WITH BODYWORK

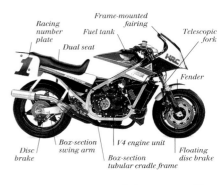

Racing number plate
Fuel tank
Dual seat
Frame-mounted fairing
Telescopic fork
Fender
Disc brake
Box-section swing arm
V4 engine unit
Box-section tubular cradle frame
Floating disc brake

1985 HONDA VF750 WITH BODYWORK REMOVED

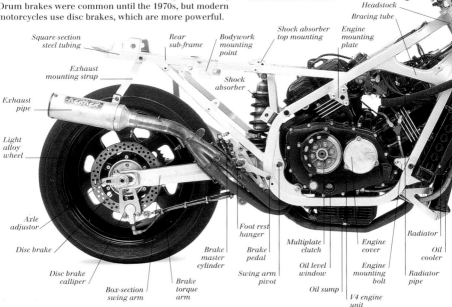

Brake master cylinder
Headstock
Bracing tube
Square-section steel tubing
Rear sub-frame
Bodywork mounting point
Shock absorber top mounting
Engine mounting plate
Exhaust mounting strap
Shock absorber
Exhaust pipe
Light alloy wheel
Axle adjustor
Disc brake
Disc brake calliper
Box-section swing arm
Brake torque arm
Brake master cylinder
Brake pedal
Foot rest hanger
Swing arm pivot
Multiplate clutch
Oil level window
Oil sump
Engine cover
Engine mounting bolt
V4 engine unit
Radiator
Oil cooler
Radiator pipe

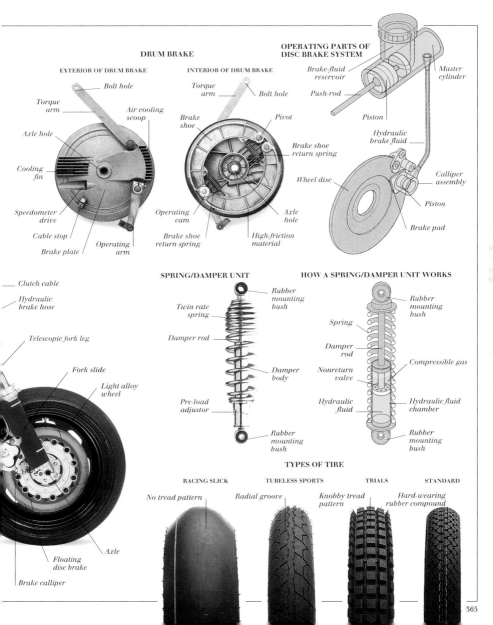

DRUM BRAKE

OPERATING PARTS OF DISC BRAKE SYSTEM

EXTERIOR OF DRUM BRAKE

Bolt hole

Torque arm

Air cooling scoop

Axle hole

Cooling fin

Speedometer drive

Cable stop

Brake plate

Operating arm

INTERIOR OF DRUM BRAKE

Torque arm

Bolt hole

Brake shoe

Pivot

Brake shoe return spring

Operating cam

Axle hole

Brake shoe return spring

High-friction material

Brake-fluid reservoir

Master cylinder

Push-rod

Piston

Hydraulic brake fluid

Wheel disc

Calliper assembly

Piston

Brake pad

Clutch cable

Hydraulic brake hose

Telescopic fork leg

Fork slide

Light alloy wheel

Axle

Floating disc brake

Brake calliper

SPRING/DAMPER UNIT

Rubber mounting bush

Twin rate spring

Damper rod

Damper body

Pre-load adjustor

Rubber mounting bush

HOW A SPRING/DAMPER UNIT WORKS

Rubber mounting bush

Spring

Damper rod

Nonreturn valve

Compressible gas

Hydraulic fluid

Hydraulic fluid chamber

Rubber mounting bush

TYPES OF TIRE

RACING SLICK

No tread pattern

TUBELESS SPORTS

Radial groove

TRIALS

Knobby tread pattern

STANDARD

Hard-wearing rubber compound

Motorcycle engines

MOTORCYCLE ENGINES must be lightweight and compact, and have a good power output. They have between one and six cylinders, can be cooled by air or water, and the capacity of the combustion chamber varies from 49cc (cubic centimeters) to 1500cc. Two types of internal combustion engine are common: the four-stroke, which is used in cars (see pp. 342-343), and the two-stroke. A basic two-stroke engine has only three moving parts—the crankshaft, the connecting rod, and the piston—but the power output is high. The engine fires every two strokes (rather than every four), giving a "power stroke" every revolution (see p. 343). Power is conveyed from the engine to the rear wheel by the transmission system. This usually consists of a clutch, a gearbox, and a final drive system. Clutches are multiplate devices, which run in oil. Gearboxes have five or six speeds and are operated by foot pedal. Shaft and belt drive systems are used in some cases, but chain drive to the rear wheel is most common.

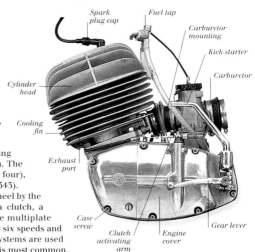

Spark plug cap
Fuel tap
Carburetor mounting
Kick-starter
Carburetor
Cylinder head
Cooling fin
Exhaust port
Case screw
Clutch activating arm
Engine cover
Gear lever

TRANSMISSION SYSTEM

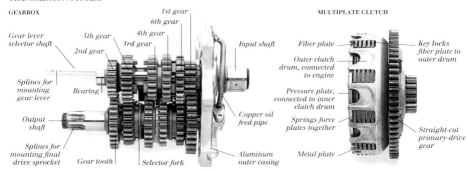

GEARBOX

Gear lever selector shaft
5th gear
2nd gear
1st gear
6th gear
4th gear
3rd gear
Input shaft
Splines for mounting gear lever
Bearing
Output shaft
Splines for mounting final drive sprocket
Gear tooth
Selector fork
Copper oil feed pipe
Aluminum outer casing

MULTIPLATE CLUTCH

Fiber plate
Outer clutch drum, connected to engine
Pressure plate, connected to inner clutch drum
Springs force plates together
Metal plate
Key locks fiber plate to outer drum
Straight-cut primary-drive gear

MODERN O-RING DRIVE CHAIN

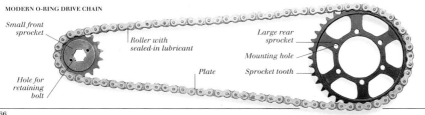

Small front sprocket
Roller with sealed-in lubricant
Large rear sprocket
Mounting hole
Hole for retaining bolt
Plate
Sprocket tooth

VELOCETTE OVERHEAD VALVE (OHV) ENGINE

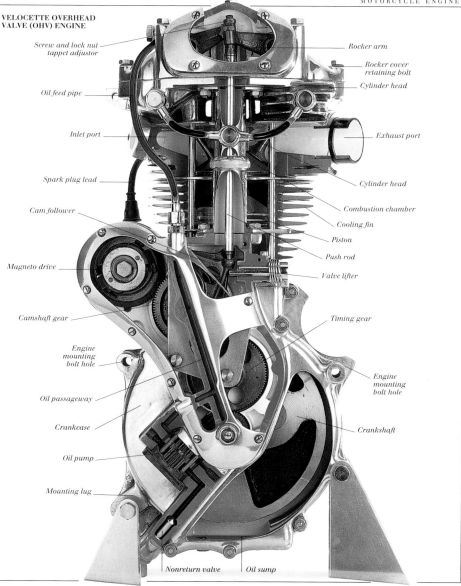

Screw and lock nut tappet adjustor

Oil feed pipe

Inlet port

Spark plug lead

Cam follower

Magneto drive

Camshaft gear

Engine mounting bolt hole

Oil passageway

Crankcase

Oil pump

Mounting lug

Rocker arm

Rocker cover retaining bolt

Cylinder head

Exhaust port

Cylinder head

Combustion chamber

Cooling fin

Piston

Push rod

Valve lifter

Timing gear

Engine mounting bolt hole

Crankshaft

Nonreturn valve

Oil sump

Competition motorcycles

THERE ARE MANY TYPES of motorcycle sports and in each, a special machine has evolved to perform to specific requirements. Races take place on roads or tracks or "off-road," in fields, dirt tracks, and even the desert. "Grand Prix" world championships in roadracing exist for 125cc, 250cc, and 500cc classes, as well as for sidecars. The latest racing sidecars have more in common with racing cars than motorcycles. The rider and passenger operate within an all-enclosing, aerodynamic fairing. The Suzuki RGV500 shown here, like other Grand Prix machines, carries advertising, which promotes the manufacturer and helps to cover the cost of developing motorcycle technology. In Speedway, which originated in the U.S. in 1902, motorcycles operate without brakes or a gearbox. Off-road competition motorcycles have less emphasis on high power output. In Motocross, for example, which is held on rough terrain, they must have high ground clearance, flexible long-travel suspension, and tires with a chunky tread pattern, to allow them to grip in sand or mud.

1992 HUSQVARNA MOTOCROSS TC610

Throttle cable
Hand protector
Flexible plastic fender
Handlebar brace
Long seat
Racing number
Radiator air vent
Telescopic fork
Plastic guard
Axle
Knobby tire
Disc brake
Brake calliper
Overhead camshaft engine
Gear lever
Shock absorber
Alloy swing arm
Lightweight exhaust system
Disc brake
Shock absorber linkage

1992 SUZUKI RGV500
SIDE VIEW

Exhaust pipe
Racing number
Air vent
One-piece seat and tail unit
Minimal seat padding
Shock absorber
Arched alloy swing arm

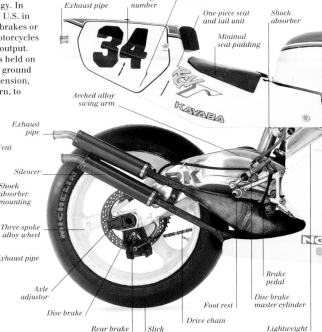

Exhaust pipe
Handlebar
Foot rest
Rear brake pedal
Drive chain
Wide, slick tire
REAR VIEW

Exhaust pipe
Vent
Silencer
Shock absorber mounting
Three-spoke alloy wheel
Exhaust pipe
Axle adjustor
Disc brake
Rear brake calliper
Slick racing tire
Drive chain
Foot rest
Brake pedal
Disc brake master cylinder
Lightweight alloy frame

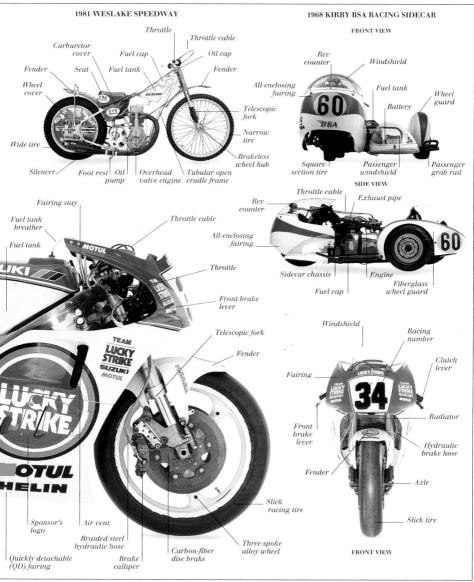

1981 WESLAKE SPEEDWAY

Throttle

Throttle cable

Carburetor cover

Fuel cap

Oil cap

Fender

Seat

Fuel tank

Fender

Wheel cover

Telescopic fork

Narrow tire

Wide tire

Brakeless wheel hub

Silencer

Foot rest

Oil pump

Overhead valve engine

Tubular open cradle frame

Fairing stay

Fuel tank breather

Throttle cable

Fuel tank

Throttle

Front brake lever

Telescopic fork

Fender

Sponsor's logo

Air vent

Braided steel hydraulic hose

Brake calliper

Carbon-fiber disc brake

Three-spoke alloy wheel

Slick racing tire

Quickly detachable (QD) fairing

1968 KIRBY BSA RACING SIDECAR

FRONT VIEW

Rev counter

Windshield

All-enclosing fairing

Fuel tank

Wheel guard

Battery

BSA

Square-section tire

Passenger windshield

Passenger grab rail

SIDE VIEW

Throttle cable

Exhaust pipe

Rev counter

All-enclosing fairing

Sidecar chassis

Engine

Fuel cap

Fiberglass wheel guard

Windshield

Racing number

Clutch lever

Fairing

Front brake lever

Radiator

Hydraulic brake hose

Fender

Axle

Slick tire

FRONT VIEW

369

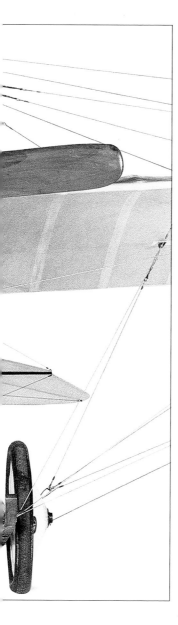

Sea and Air

Ships of Greece and Rome

ROMAN ANCHOR

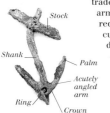

Stock

Shank

Palm

Acutely angled arm

Ring

Crown

IN THE EXPANSIVE EMPIRES OF GREECE AND ROME, powerful fleets were needed for battle, trade, and communication. Greek galleys were powered by a sail and many oars. A new armament, the embolos (ram), was fitted on to the galley bow. As ramming duels required fast and maneuverable boats, extra rows of oarsmen were added, culminating in the trireme. During the fifth and fourth centuries B.C., the trireme dominated the Mediterranean. It was powered by 170 oarsmen, each pulling one oar, and ranged on three levels, as the model opposite shows. The trireme also carried archers and soldiers for boarding enemy craft. Galleys were pulled out of the water when not in use, and were kept in dockyard ship-sheds. The merchant ships of the Greeks and Romans were mighty vessels, too. The full-bodied Roman corbita, for example, could hold up to 400 tons of cargo, such as spices, gems, silk, and animals. The construction of these boats was based on a stout hull with planking secured by mortice and tenon. Some of these ships made long trading voyages, sailing even as far as India. To make them easier to steer, corbitas set a foresail called an "artemon." It flew from a forward-leaning mast that was the forerunner of the long bowsprits carried by the great clipper ships of the 19th century.

ATTIC VASE SHOWING A GREEK GALLEY

Roband (rope band)

Ceruchi (lift)

Double halyard   **ROMAN CORBITA**

Bullseye

Fore mast

Heraldic device

Antenna (yard)

Buntline

Ring

Brace

Ruden (brail line)

Artemon (fore sail)

Fore stay

Oculus (eye)

Anchor

Tabling

Sheet

Bolt rope

Prow

Bronze mast truck

Windlass

Keraia (yard)

Scala (ladder)

Kalos (brailing rope)

Catena (riding bitt)

Ancorale (anchor rope; anchor rode)

Mast

Kubernetes (helmsman)

Embolos (ram; beak)

Sternpost

Hatch board

Pedalia (twin rudder)

Deck beam

Ophthalmos (eye)

Oar port sleeve

Zosteres (rubbing strake)

Kope (oar)

Cargo hold

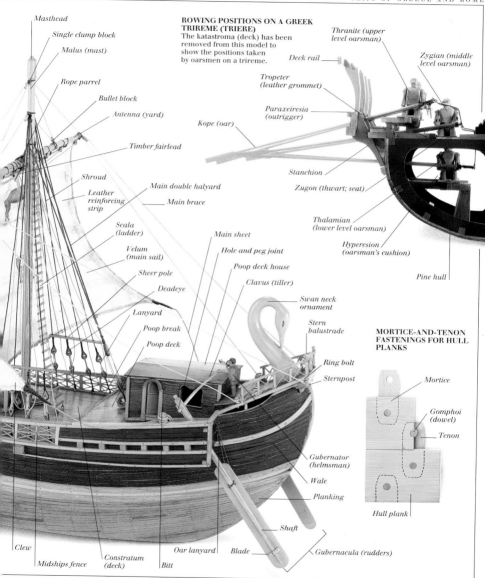

Masthead

Single clump block

Malus (mast)

Rope parrel

Bullet block

Antenna (yard)

Timber fairlead

Shroud

Leather reinforcing strip

Main double halyard

Main brace

Scala (ladder)

Velum (main sail)

Sheer pole

Deadeye

Lanyard

Poop break

Poop deck

Main sheet

Hole and peg joint

Poop deck house

Clavus (tiller)

Swan neck ornament

Stern balustrade

Ring bolt

Sternpost

Gubernator (helmsman)

Wale

Planking

Shaft

Blade

Gubernacula (rudders)

Clew

Midships fence

Constratum (deck)

Bitt

Oar lanyard

ROWING POSITIONS ON A GREEK TRIREME (TRIERE)
The katastroma (deck) has been removed from this model to show the positions taken by oarsmen on a trireme.

Thranite (upper level oarsman)

Zygian (middle level oarsman)

Deck rail

Tropeter (leather grommet)

Paraxeiresia (outrigger)

Kope (oar)

Stanchion

Zugon (thwart; seat)

Thalamian (lower level oarsman)

Hyperesion (oarsman's cushion)

Pine hull

MORTICE-AND-TENON FASTENINGS FOR HULL PLANKS

Mortice

Gomphoi (dowel)

Tenon

Hull plank

Viking ships

IN THE DARK AGES (roughly 500 A.D. to 1000 A.D.) the longships of Scandinavia were among the most feared sights for people of northern Europe. The Vikings launched raids from Scandinavia every summer in longships equipped with a single steering oar on the right, or "steerboard" side (hence, "starboard"). A longboat had one row of oars on each side and a single sail. The hull was clinker-built, with overlapping planks. Prowheads adorned fighting ships during war campaigns. The longship was also used for coastal travel. The karv below was probably built as transport for an important family, while the smaller faering was a rowing boat only. The fleet of William of Normandy that invaded England in 1066 owed much to the Viking boat building tradition, and has been depicted in the Bayeux Tapestry (right). Seals of port towns and royal courts through the ages provide a record of contemporary ship design. The seal opposite shows a European craft from somewhat later than the Viking period. Fighting platforms, or castles, and the addition of more masts and sails changed the character of the medieval ship. Note also that the steering oar has been replaced by a centered rudder.

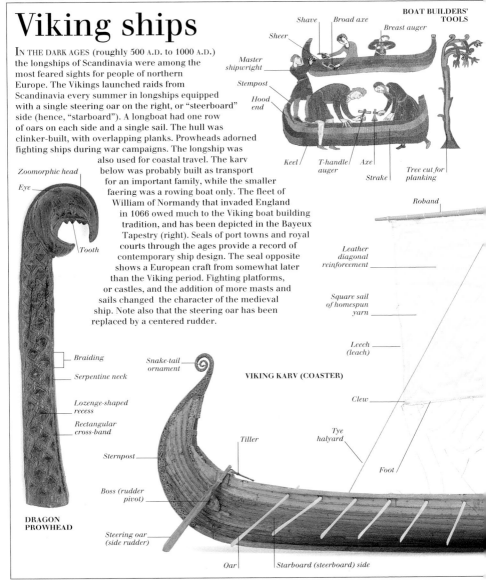

BOAT BUILDERS' TOOLS

Shave

Broad axe

Breast auger

Sheer

Master shipwright

Stempost

Hood end

Keel

T-handle auger

Axe

Strake

Tree cut for planking

Zoomorphic head

Eye

Tooth

Roband

Leather diagonal reinforcement

Square sail of homespun yarn

Leech (leach)

Braiding

Serpentine neck

Snake-tail ornament

VIKING KARV (COASTER)

Clew

Lozenge-shaped recess

Rectangular cross-band

Tiller

Tye halyard

Foot

Sternpost

Boss (rudder pivot)

DRAGON PROWHEAD

Steering oar (side rudder)

Oar

Starboard (steerboard) side

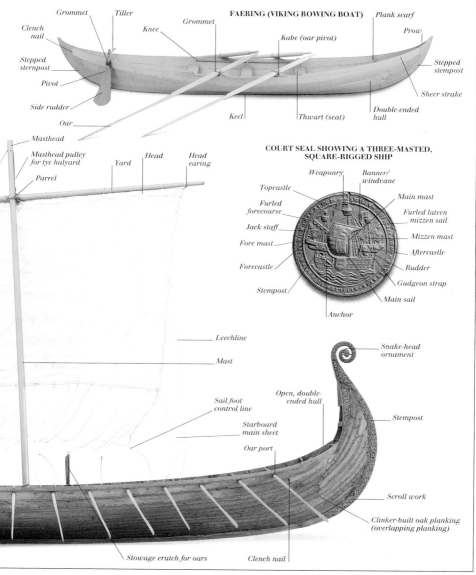

FAERING (VIKING ROWING BOAT)

Grommet

Tiller

Knee

Grommet

Kabe (oar pivot)

Plank scarf

Prow

Clench nail

Stepped sternpost

Pivot

Side rudder

Oar

Stepped stempost

Sheer strake

Double-ended hull

Keel

Thwart (seat)

COURT SEAL SHOWING A THREE-MASTED, SQUARE-RIGGED SHIP

Masthead

Masthead pulley for tye halyard

Parrel

Yard

Head

Head earing

Weaponry

Banner/ windvane

Topcastle

Furled forecourse

Jack staff

Fore mast

Forecastle

Stempost

Anchor

Main mast

Furled lateen mizzen sail

Mizzen mast

Aftercastle

Rudder

Gudgeon strap

Main sail

Leechline

Mast

Sail foot control line

Starboard main sheet

Oar port

Open, double-ended hull

Snake-head ornament

Stempost

Scroll work

Clinker-built oak planking (overlapping planking)

Stowage crutch for oars

Clench nail

Medieval warships and traders

FROM THE 16TH CENTURY, SHIPS WERE BUILT WITH A NEW FORM OF HULL, constructed with carvel (edge-to-edge) planking. Warships of the time, like King Henry VIII of England's Mary Rose, boasted awesome fire power. This ship carried both long-range bronze cannon, and short-range, anti personnel guns in iron. Elsewhere, ships took on a multiformity of shapes. Dhows transported slaves from East Africa to Arabia, their fore-and-aft rigged lateen sails allowing them to sail close to the wind around the lands of the Indian Ocean. The Chinese sailed to East Africa and Arabia in junks, trading goods that were carried in watertight compartments. New astronomical tools helped medieval sailors to find their way. Cross-staves and astrolabes were used to measure the altitude of the sun or stars. One of the cross-pieces was slid along the staff of the cross-stave—which was graduated in degrees of altitude—until its top aligned with the celestial body and its base with the horizon. The sighting rule of the astrolabe was simply lined up with a known body, and its altitude read from marks on the metal disk. Sundials used the shadow of the sun to show sailors the time of day.

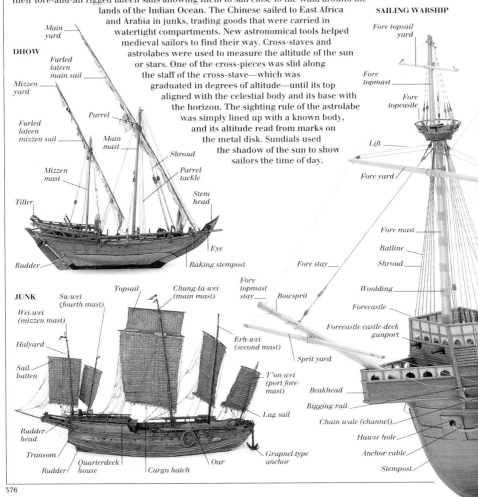

DHOW

Main yard

Furled lateen main sail

Mizzen yard

Parrel

Furled lateen mizzen sail

Main mast

Mizzen mast

Shroud

Parrel tackle

Tiller

Stem head

Rudder

Eye

Raking stempost

JUNK

Su-wei (fourth mast)

Wei-wei (mizzen mast)

Topsail

Chung-ta-wei (main mast)

Halyard

Sail batten

Erh-wei (second mast)

Sprit yard

T'on-wei (port fore-mast)

Rudder head

Lug sail

Transom

Quarterdeck house

Rudder

Cargo hatch

Oar

Grapnel-type anchor

Fore topmast stay

Bowsprit

Fore stay

SAILING WARSHIP

Fore topsail yard

Fore topmast

Fore topcastle

Lift

Fore yard

Fore mast

Ratline

Shroud

Woolding

Forecastle

Forecastle castle-deck gunport

Beakhead

Rigging rail

Chain wale (channel)

Hawse hole

Anchor cable

Stempost

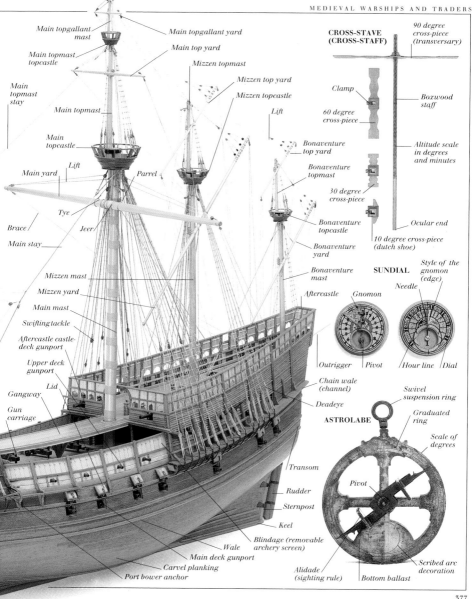

Main topgallant mast

Main topgallant yard

Main top yard

Main topmast topcastle

Mizzen topmast

Mizzen top yard

Mizzen topcastle

Main topmast stay

Lift

Main topmast

Bonaventure top yard

Main topcastle

Bonaventure topmast

Lift

Main yard

Parrel

Bonaventure topcastle

Tye

Bonaventure yard

Brace

Jeer

Bonaventure mast

Main stay

Mizzen mast

Aftercastle

Mizzen yard

Main mast

Swifting tackle

Aftercastle castle-deck gunport

Upper deck gunport

Outrigger

Pivot

Lid

Gangway

Chain wale (channel)

Gun carriage

Deadeye

Transom

Rudder

Sternpost

Keel

Blindage (removable archery screen)

Wale

Main deck gunport

Carvel planking

Port bower anchor

Alidade (sighting rule)

Bottom ballast

CROSS-STAVE (CROSS-STAFF)

90 degree cross-piece (transversary)

Clamp

Boxwood staff

60 degree cross-piece

Altitude scale in degrees and minutes

30 degree cross-piece

Ocular end

10 degree cross-piece (dutch shoe)

SUNDIAL

Style of the gnomon (edge)

Gnomon

Needle

Hour line

Dial

Swivel suspension ring

Graduated ring

ASTROLABE

Scale of degrees

Pivot

Scribed arc decoration

377

The expansion of sail

By THE 18TH CENTURY, SAILING SHIPS had become fast and effective floating fortresses. The navies of the north European powers competed with each other by building heavily-armed fighting ships called "men-of-war." The distinctive round stern of the ship below, with its open gallery, balcony, and elaborate wood carving is typical of the period. Hulls around this time were semicircular in cross section, although many boat designers were soon to return to the V-shaped hulls used by the Vikings. Ships of the period carried more sail than ever before. A labyrinth of rigging supported the masts and yards from which the profusion of square sails were set. Ships grew higher as extra masts were fitted above the lower masts, and the bowsprit became longer, to allow the ship to carry staysails, spritsails, and jibs. Ships went into battle in single file, so that broadsides from the multiple decks of guns would have maximum effect. Ships were classified by rates, the rating of a vessel depending on how many guns it had. A first rate ship had more than 100 guns. The guns fired solid round shot, usually made of iron.

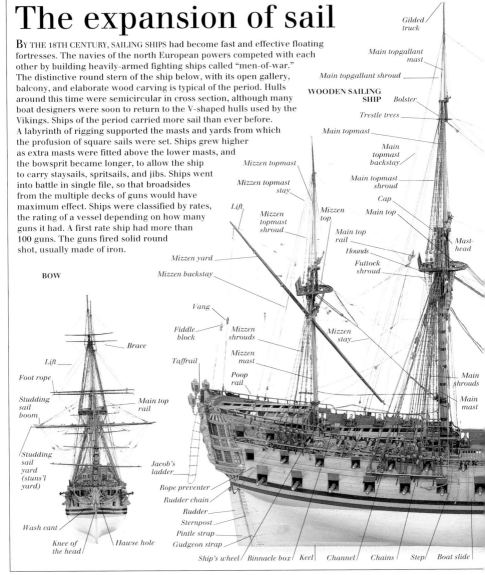

WOODEN SAILING SHIP

Gilded truck

Main topgallant mast

Main topgallant shroud

Bolster

Trestle trees

Main topmast

Main topmast backstay

Main topmast shroud

Cap

Main top

Mast-head

Main top rail

Hounds

Futtock shroud

Main shrouds

Main mast

Mizzen topmast

Mizzen topmast stay

Lift

Mizzen topmast shroud

Mizzen top

Mizzen yard

Mizzen backstay

Vang

Fiddle block

Mizzen shrouds

Mizzen mast

Mizzen stay

Poop rail

Taffrail

BOW

Brace

Lift

Foot rope

Studding sail boom

Main top rail

Studding sail yard (stuns'l yard)

Jacob's ladder

Rope preventer

Rudder chain

Rudder

Sternpost

Pintle strap

Gudgeon strap

Wash cant

Knee of the head

Hawse hole

Ship's wheel

Binnacle box

Keel

Channel

Chains

Step

Boat slide

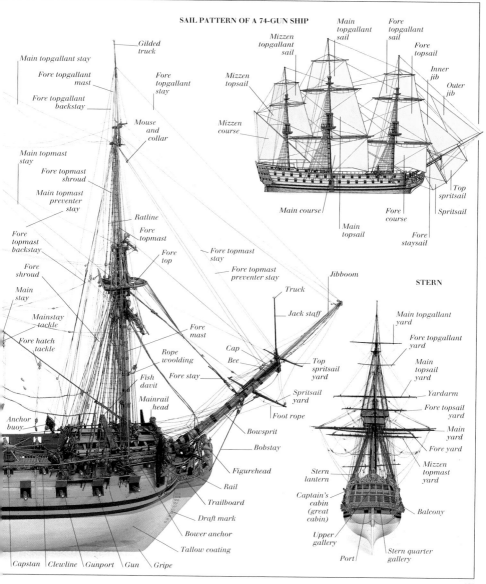

SAIL PATTERN OF A 74-GUN SHIP

Main topgallant stay

Gilded truck

Fore topgallant mast

Fore topgallant backstay

Fore topgallant stay

Mouse and collar

Main topmast stay

Fore topmast shroud

Main topmast preventer stay

Ratline

Fore topmast

Fore topmast backstay

Fore shroud

Fore top

Main stay

Fore topmast stay

Mainstay tackle

Fore topmast preventer stay

Fore hatch tackle

Fore mast

Rope woolding

Fish davit

Fore stay

Mainrail head

Anchor buoy

Bee

Cap

Foot rope

Mizzen topgallant sail

Main topgallant sail

Fore topgallant sail

Fore topsail

Mizzen topsail

Inner jib

Outer jib

Mizzen course

Main course

Main topsail

Fore course

Top spritsail

Spritsail

Fore staysail

Fore sail

STERN

Jibboom

Truck

Jack staff

Top spritsail yard

Spritsail yard

Bowsprit

Bobstay

Figurehead

Rail

Trailboard

Draft mark

Bower anchor

Tallow coating

Main topgallant yard

Fore topgallant yard

Main topsail yard

Yardarm

Fore topsail yard

Main yard

Fore yard

Mizzen topmast yard

Stern lantern

Captain's cabin (great cabin)

Upper gallery

Port

Balcony

Stern quarter gallery

Capstan

Clewline

Gunport

Gun

Gripe

A ship of the line

THE 74-GUN THIRD-RATER WAS A MAINSTAY of British and French battlefleets in the late 18th and early 19th centuries. (The biggest ships in the fledgling American navy of the time were 44-gun frigates.) The length of such a man-of-war was determined by the number of guns needed for each deck, allowing room for crews to man them. The gun deck of this vessel was about 170 ft (52 m) long. Her decks had to be strong to carry the weight of the guns. The deck planks have been removed in the model below to illustrate the number of beams needed to make the hull strong enough. Only timber with perfect grain was used. The upper deck was open at the waist, but forward and aft were officers' cabins. The forecastle (foc's'l) and quarterdeck carried light guns and provided platforms for handling the rigging and for reconnaissance. The ship's longboats, or launches, were carried on skids between the gangways.

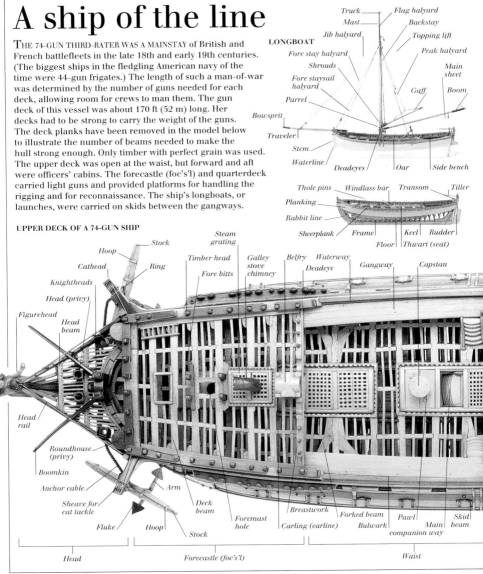

LONGBOAT

Truck · Flag halyard · Mast · Backstay · Jib halyard · Topping lift · Fore stay halyard · Peak halyard · Shrouds · Main sheet · Fore staysail halyard · Gaff · Boom · Parrel · Bowsprit · Traveler · Stem · Waterline · Deadeyes · Oar · Side bench

Thole pins · Windlass bar · Transom · Tiller · Planking · Rabbit line · Sheerplank · Frame · Keel · Rudder · Floor · Thwart (seat)

UPPER DECK OF A 74-GUN SHIP

Steam grating · Stock · Hoop · Timber head · Galley stove chimney · Belfry · Waterway · Gangway · Capstan · Cathead · Ring · Fore bits · Deadeye · Knightheads · Head (privy) · Figurehead · Head beam · Head rail · Roundhouse (privy) · Boomkin · Anchor cable · Arm · Deck beam · Foremast hole · Breastwork · Forked beam · Pawl · Skid beam · Sheave for cat tackle · Carling (carline) · Bulwark · Main companion way · Fluke · Hoop · Stock

Head · Forecastle (foc's'l) · Waist

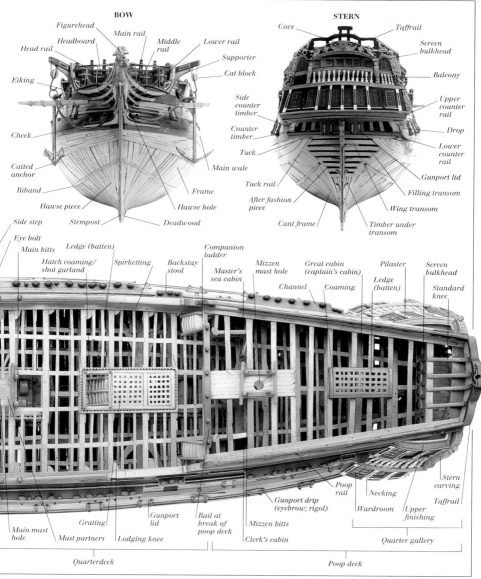

BOW

Figurehead
Main rail
Headboard
Head rail
Middle rail
Lower rail
Supporter
Cat block
Eiking
Cheek
Catted anchor
Riband
Hawse piece
Stempost
Deadwood
Main wale
Frame
Hawse hole

STERN

Cove
Taffrail
Screen bulkhead
Balcony
Upper counter rail
Drop
Lower counter rail
Gunport lid
Filling transom
Wing transom
Timber under transom
Side counter timber
Counter timber
Tuck
Tuck rail
After fashion piece
Cant frame

Side step
Eye bolt
Main bitts
Ledge (batten)
Hatch coaming/ shot garland
Spirketting
Backstay stool
Companion ladder
Master's sea cabin
Mizzen mast hole
Channel
Great cabin (captain's cabin)
Coaming
Pilaster
Ledge (batten)
Screen bulkhead
Standard knee

Main mast hole
Grating
Mast partners
Lodging knee
Gunport lid
Rail at break of poop deck
Mizzen bitts
Gunport drip (eyebrow; rigol)
Clerk's cabin
Poop rail
Necking
Wardroom
Stern carving
Taffrail
Upper finishing
Quarter gallery

Quarterdeck

Poop deck

Rigging

MOST SAILING SHIPS HAVE TWO TYPES OF RIGGING. Standing rigging—kept taut by turnbuckles or old-fashioned lanyards and deadeyes—refers to the ropes, wires, and chains that support the masts and yards (horizontal spars). Running rigging, which includes types of block and tackle, halyards, and sheets, is used to hoist, lower, or trim sails.

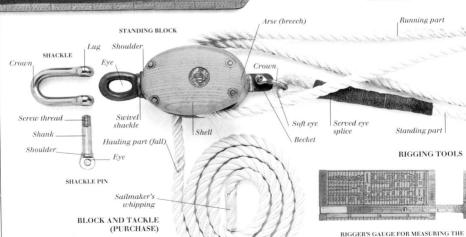

Outer jib stay

Inner jib stay

Inner jib tack

Fore topmast staysail tack

Bowsprit cap

Whisker boom

Fore stay

Jibboom

Bowsprit

Upper deadeye

Lower deadeye

Butterfly plate

Chain plate

Foot rope

Boom guy block

Spear

Martingale backrope

Martingale (dolphin striker)

Lizard

Chain bobstay

Handle

Lug

OTHER RIGGING FITTINGS

Shaft

BELAYING PIN

MAST BAND

STANDING BLOCK

Arse (breech)

Running part

Crown

SHACKLE

Lug

Shoulder

Eye

Crown

Screw thread

Shank

Shoulder

Eye

Swivel shackle

Hauling part (fall)

Shell

Soft eye

Becket

Served eye splice

Standing part

SHACKLE PIN

Sailmaker's whipping

RIGGING TOOLS

BLOCK AND TACKLE (PURCHASE)

Flemish coil (cheesing)

RIGGER'S GAUGE FOR MEASURING THE DIAMETER OF ROPE OR WIRE

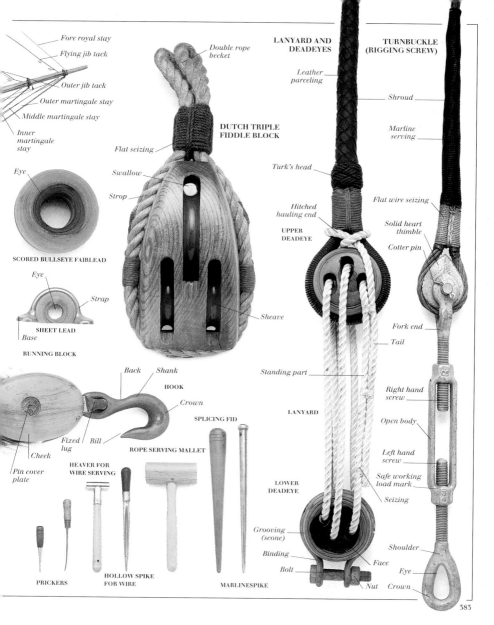

Fore royal stay

Flying jib tack

Outer jib tack

Outer martingale stay

Middle martingale stay

Inner martingale stay

Eye

SCORED BULLSEYE FAIRLEAD

Eye

Strap

SHEET LEAD

Base

RUNNING BLOCK

Cheek

Pin cover plate

Fixed lug

Bill

HOOK

Back

Shank

Crown

HEAVER FOR WIRE SERVING

ROPE SERVING MALLET

SPLICING FID

PRICKERS

HOLLOW SPIKE FOR WIRE

MARLINESPIKE

Double rope becket

Flat seizing

Swallow

Strop

DUTCH TRIPLE FIDDLE BLOCK

Sheave

LANYARD AND DEADEYES

Leather parceling

Turk's head

Hitched hauling end

UPPER DEADEYE

Standing part

LANYARD

LOWER DEADEYE

Grooving (scone)

Binding

Bolt

Face

Nut

TURNBUCKLE (RIGGING SCREW)

Shroud

Marline serving

Flat wire seizing

Solid heart thimble

Cotter pin

Fork end

Tail

Right hand screw

Open body

Left hand screw

Safe working load mark

Seizing

Shoulder

Eye

Crown

383

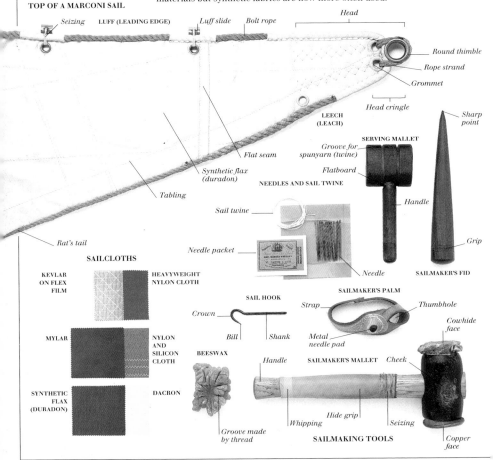

PARREL
BEADS

Sails

THERE ARE TWO MAIN TYPES OF SAILS: Old-fashioned square sails hang from yards at right angles to the mast, and are powerful drivers with following winds; fore-and-aft sails are set parallel to the length of the boat, with the luff (leading edge) of the sail attached to a mast or a stay. They are more efficient for all-round sailing, and almost all modern sailboats are rigged this way. Some fore-and-aft sails have a gaff at the head; Marconi-rig sails are pointed at the top (below). The bottom (foot) of the sail is on a boom. Sails are made of strips of cloth sewn together. Cotton and flax are traditional sail materials but synthetic fabrics are now more often used.

TOP OF A MARCONI SAIL

Seizing LUFF (LEADING EDGE) *Luff slide* *Bolt rope* *Head*

Round thimble

Rope strand

Grommet

Head cringle

LEECH (LEACH)

Sharp point

SERVING MALLET

Groove for spunyarn (twine)

Flat seam

Synthetic flax (duradon)

Flatboard

Handle

Tabling

Sail twine

Grip

Rat's tail

Needle packet

SAILMAKER'S FID

SAILCLOTHS

KEVLAR ON FLEX FILM

HEAVYWEIGHT NYLON CLOTH

Needle

MYLAR

NYLON AND SILICON CLOTH

SAIL HOOK

Crown

Bill *Shank*

SAILMAKER'S PALM

Strap

Thumbhole

Metal needle pad

Cowhide face

BEESWAX

SYNTHETIC FLAX (DURADON)

DACRON

Handle

SAILMAKER'S MALLET

Cheek

Whipping *Hide grip* *Seizing*

Copper face

Groove made by thread

SAILMAKING TOOLS

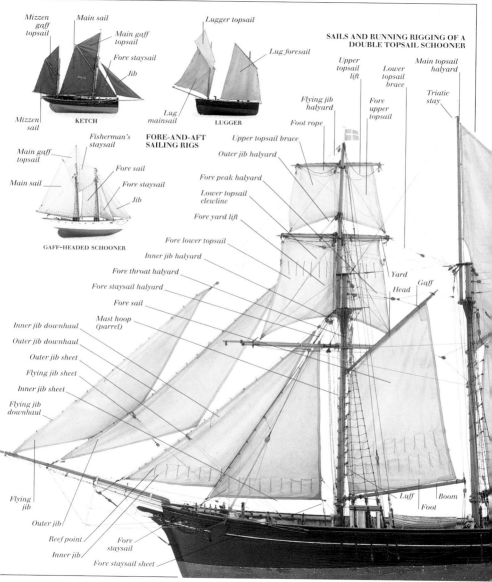

Mizzen gaff topsail

Main sail

Main gaff topsail

Fore staysail

Jib

Mizzen sail

KETCH

Lugger topsail

Lug foresail

Lug mainsail

LUGGER

FORE-AND-AFT SAILING RIGS

Fisherman's staysail

Main gaff topsail

Fore sail

Main sail

Fore staysail

Jib

GAFF-HEADED SCHOONER

SAILS AND RUNNING RIGGING OF A DOUBLE TOPSAIL SCHOONER

Upper topsail lift

Lower topsail brace

Main topsail halyard

Triatic stay

Flying jib halyard

Fore upper topsail

Foot rope

Upper topsail brace

Outer jib halyard

Fore peak halyard

Lower topsail clewline

Fore yard lift

Fore lower topsail

Inner jib halyard

Fore throat halyard

Fore staysail halyard

Fore sail

Mast hoop (parrel)

Inner jib downhaul

Outer jib downhaul

Outer jib sheet

Flying jib sheet

Inner jib sheet

Flying jib downhaul

Yard

Head

Gaff

Luff

Boom

Foot

Flying jib

Outer jib

Reef point

Fore staysail

Inner jib

Fore staysail sheet

Mooring and anchoring

IN MOST HARBORS AND PORTS, a ship can moor (tie up or "make fast") directly to a pier, wharf, or quay (pronounced "key"), using heavy hawsers and docking lines attached to bits or bollards. Hawsers are tied to each other with knots called bends. In open water, however, ships that are not under way must drop an anchor, which attaches the ship securely to the seabed. The earliest anchors were simply heavy stones. Later, various anchor designs were developed for different uses. Most small vessels today use Danforth or plow anchors, which dig deeply into the sea bottom. A permanent mooring is an anchor set in the bottom to which a ship can tie up without using its own anchor. On old sailing ships, anchors were pulled up, or "weighed," by sailors pushing against bars that turned a capstan, which wound up the anchor cable. Now, most capstans are powered by electricity.

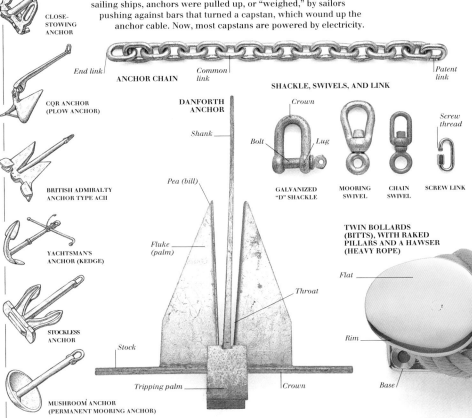

TYPES OF ANCHOR

CLOSE-STOWING ANCHOR

CQR ANCHOR (PLOW ANCHOR)

BRITISH ADMIRALTY ANCHOR TYPE ACII

YACHTSMAN'S ANCHOR (KEDGE)

STOCKLESS ANCHOR

MUSHROOM ANCHOR (PERMANENT MOORING ANCHOR)

STONE ANCHOR (KILLICK)
Rope hole

ANCHOR CHAIN
End link
Common link
Patent link

SHACKLE, SWIVELS, AND LINK

DANFORTH ANCHOR
Shank
Pea (bill)
Fluke (palm)
Throat
Stock
Tripping palm
Crown

Crown
Bolt
Lug
Screw thread

GALVANIZED "D" SHACKLE
MOORING SWIVEL
CHAIN SWIVEL
SCREW LINK

TWIN BOLLARDS (BITTS), WITH RAKED PILLARS AND A HAWSER (HEAVY ROPE)
Flat
Rim
Base

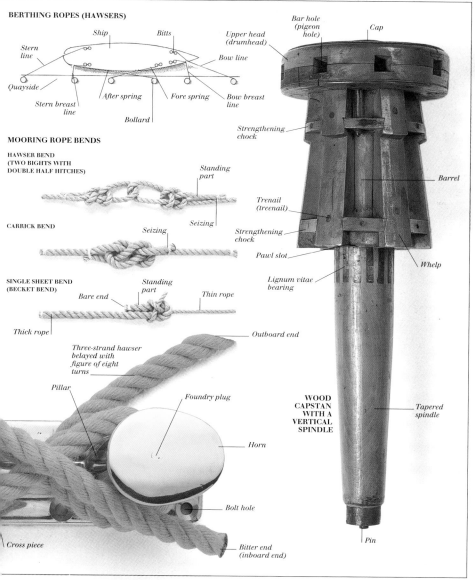

BERTHING ROPES (HAWSERS)

Stern line

Ship

Bitts

Upper head (drumhead)

Bow line

Quayside

Stern breast line

After spring

Fore spring

Bollard

Bow breast line

Bar hole (pigeon hole)

Cap

Strengthening chock

Barrel

Trenail (treenail)

Strengthening chock

Pawl slot

Whelp

Lignum vitae bearing

MOORING ROPE BENDS

**HAWSER BEND
(TWO BIGHTS WITH
DOUBLE HALF HITCHES)**

Standing part

Seizing

Seizing

CARRICK BEND

**SINGLE SHEET BEND
(BECKET BEND)**

Bare end

Standing part

Thin rope

Thick rope

Three-strand hawser belayed with figure of eight turns

Outboard end

Pillar

Foundry plug

Horn

Bolt hole

Cross piece

Bitter end (inboard end)

**WOOD
CAPSTAN
WITH A
VERTICAL
SPINDLE**

Tapered spindle

Pin

Ropes and knots

ALL KINDS OF ROPES ARE USED AT SEA, from thin twines and yarn to thick hawsers. Synthetic fibers are much in use today. Nylon ropes stretch, and so are ideal for anchoring; polyester (frequently called by the trade name Dacron) has little stretch and is used for halyards and sheets. Different knots have different uses. Knots that join two ropes are often called bends; hitches join a rope to another object. Ropes, usually called "lines" on board ship, can also be joined by seizing (lashing them together side by side) or splicing (unraveling the ends and weaving them together).

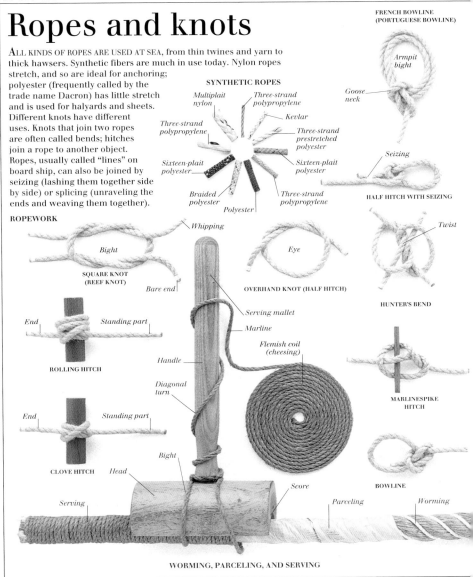

FRENCH BOWLINE (PORTUGUESE BOWLINE)

Armpit bight

Goose neck

Seizing

HALF HITCH WITH SEIZING

SYNTHETIC ROPES

Multiplait nylon

Three-strand polypropylene

Three-strand polypropylene

Kevlar

Three-strand prestretched polyester

Sixteen-plait polyester

Sixteen-plait polyester

Braided polyester

Three-strand polypropylene

Polyester

ROPEWORK

Whipping

Bight

SQUARE KNOT (REEF KNOT)

Bare end

Eye

OVERHAND KNOT (HALF HITCH)

Twist

HUNTER'S BEND

End   *Standing part*

ROLLING HITCH

Serving mallet

Marline

Flemish coil (cheesing)

Handle

Diagonal turn

End   *Standing part*

CLOVE HITCH   *Head*

Bight

MARLINESPIKE HITCH

Score

BOWLINE

Serving

Parceling

Worming

WORMING, PARCELING, AND SERVING

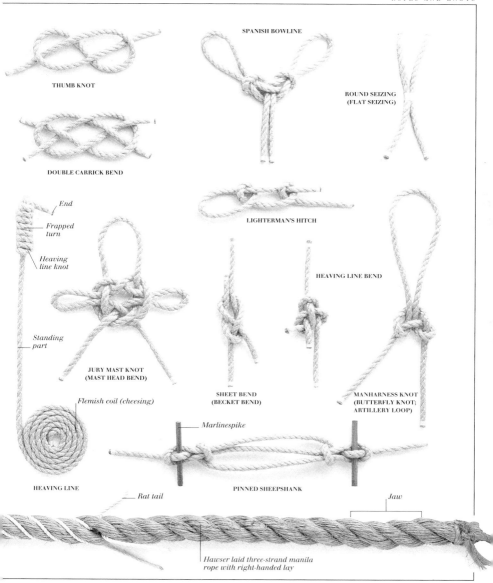

THUMB KNOT

SPANISH BOWLINE

ROUND SEIZING
(FLAT SEIZING)

DOUBLE CARRICK BEND

End

Frapped turn

Heaving line knot

LIGHTERMAN'S HITCH

HEAVING LINE BEND

Standing part

JURY MAST KNOT
(MAST HEAD BEND)

SHEET BEND
(BECKET BEND)

MANHARNESS KNOT
(BUTTERFLY KNOT;
ARTILLERY LOOP)

Flemish coil (cheesing)

Marlinespike

HEAVING LINE

PINNED SHEEPSHANK

Rat tail

Jaw

*Hawser laid three-strand manila
rope with right-handed lay*

Paddle wheels and propellers

THE INVENTION OF THE STEAM ENGINE IN THE 18TH CENTURY made mechanically driven ships fitted with paddle wheels or propellers a viable alternative to sails. Paddle wheels have fixed or feathered floats, and the model shown below features both types. Feathered floats give more propulsive power than fixed floats because they are almost upright at all times in the water. Paddle wheels were superseded by the propeller on oceangoing vessels in the mid-19th century. Propellers are more efficient, work better in rough water, and are less vulnerable in collisions. The first propellers were two-bladed, but later three- and four-bladed versions are more powerful; the shape and pitch of the blades have also been refined over the years. At the beginning of the 18th century, tillers were replaced on many larger ships by the ship's wheel as a means of steering.

SHIP'S WHEEL

King spoke handle

Handle

Spoke

Rim plate

Felloe (rim section)

Maker's name

Nave plate

Nave

PADDLE WHEEL WITH FIXED FLOATS

Wrist pin

Limb

Fixed float

Hub

Deck beam

OSCILLATING STEAM ENGINE

Slip eccentric for slide valve

Ahead/astern controls

Slide valve

Main crank

THREE-BLADED PROPELLER

Blade

Tapered shaft hole

Hub

Keyway

Strut

Frame

Piston rod (tail rod)

Stuffing box

Oscillating cylinder

Bottom plate (bedplate)

Slide valve rod

Control platform

PROPELLER ACTION

Propeller blade tip trace

Pitch

Blade

Propeller diameter

Hub

Propeller hub trace

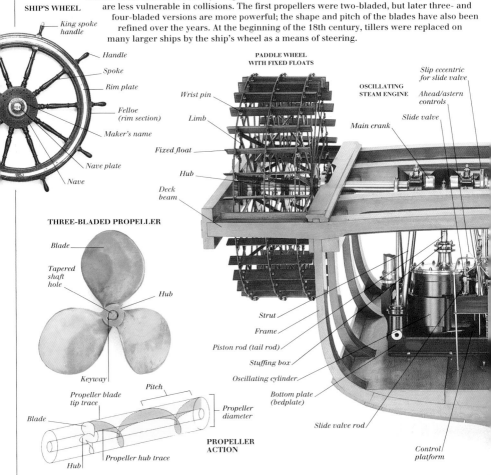

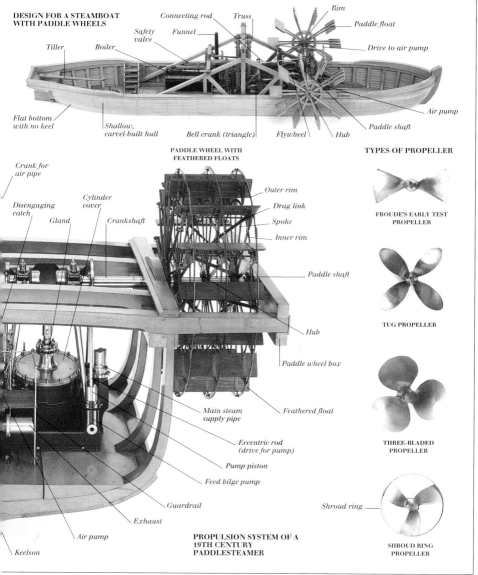

DESIGN FOR A STEAMBOAT WITH PADDLE WHEELS

Connecting rod
Truss
Rim
Paddle float
Safety valve
Funnel
Drive to air pump
Tiller
Boiler
Flat bottom with no keel
Shallow, carvel-built hull
Bell crank (triangle)
Flywheel
Hub
Paddle shaft
Air pump

PADDLE WHEEL WITH FEATHERED FLOATS

Crank for air pipe
Disengaging catch
Cylinder cover
Gland
Crankshaft
Outer rim
Drag link
Spoke
Inner rim
Paddle shaft
Hub
Paddle wheel box
Main steam supply pipe
Feathered float
Eccentric rod (drive for pump)
Pump piston
Feed bilge pump
Guardrail
Exhaust
Air pump
Keelson

TYPES OF PROPELLER

FROUDE'S EARLY TEST PROPELLER

TUG PROPELLER

THREE-BLADED PROPELLER

Shroud ring

SHROUD RING PROPELLER

PROPULSION SYSTEM OF A 19TH CENTURY PADDLESTEAMER

Anatomy of an iron ship

IRON PARTS WERE USED IN WOODEN SHIPS AS EARLY AS 1675, often in the same form as the wooden parts that they replaced. Eventually, as on the tea clipper Cutty Sark (below), iron standing rigging was found to be stronger than the traditional rope. The first "ironclads" were warships whose wooden hulls were protected by iron armor plates. Later ironclads actually had iron hulls. The model opposite is based on the British warship HMS Warrior, launched in 1860, the first battleship built entirely of iron. The plan of an iron paddlesteamer (bottom), built somewhat later, shows that the craft had the masts and bowsprit of a sailing ship; but it also boasted a steam propulsion plant amid ships that turned two side paddlewheels. Early iron plates were painstakingly riveted together (below), but by the 1940s, steel vessels were welded together, whole sections at a time. The Liberty ships built in America during World War II are prime examples of such "production-line" vessels.

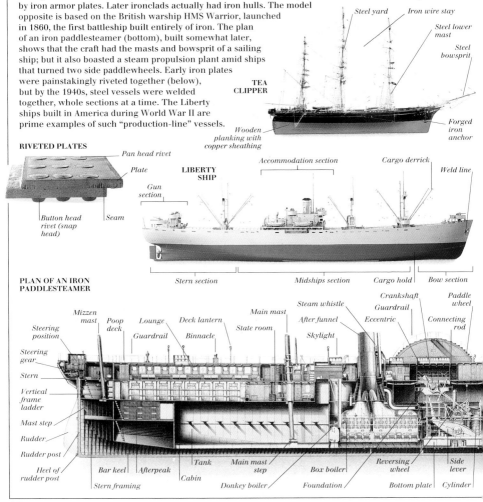

TEA CLIPPER

Steel yard
Iron wire stay
Steel lower mast
Steel bowsprit
Forged iron anchor
Wooden planking with copper sheathing

RIVETED PLATES

Pan head rivet
Plate
Button head rivet (snap head)
Seam

LIBERTY SHIP

Gun section
Accommodation section
Cargo derrick
Weld line
Stern section
Midships section
Cargo hold
Bow section

PLAN OF AN IRON PADDLESTEAMER

Mizzen mast
Poop deck
Lounge
Deck lantern
Main mast
Steam whistle
Crankshaft
Paddle wheel
Steering position
Guardrail
Binnacle
State room
After funnel
Eccentric
Guardrail
Connecting rod
Steering gear
Skylight
Stern
Vertical frame ladder
Mast step
Rudder
Rudder post
Heel of rudder post
Bar keel
Afterpeak
Tank
Main mast step
Box boiler
Reversing wheel
Side lever
Stern framing
Cabin
Donkey boiler
Foundation
Bottom plate
Cylinder

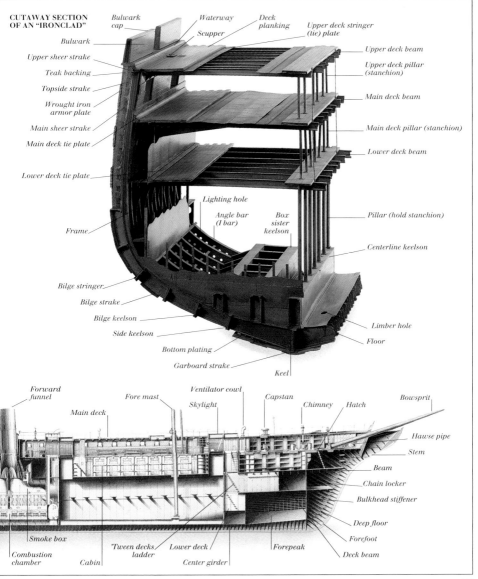

CUTAWAY SECTION OF AN "IRONCLAD"

Bulwark cap
Bulwark
Upper sheer strake
Teak backing
Topside strake
Wrought iron armor plate
Main sheer strake
Main deck tie plate
Lower deck tie plate
Frame
Bilge stringer
Bilge strake
Bilge keelson
Side keelson
Bottom plating
Garboard strake

Waterway
Scupper
Deck planking
Upper deck stringer (tie) plate

Lighting hole
Angle bar (I bar)
Box sister keelson

Keel

Upper deck beam
Upper deck pillar (stanchion)
Main deck beam
Main deck pillar (stanchion)
Lower deck beam
Pillar (hold stanchion)
Centerline keelson
Limber hole
Floor

Forward funnel
Main deck
Fore mast
Skylight
Ventilator cowl
Capstan
Chimney
Hatch
Bowsprit
Hawse pipe
Stem
Beam
Chain locker
Bulkhead stiffener
Deep floor
Forefoot
Deck beam

Smoke box
Combustion chamber
Cabin
'Tween decks ladder
Lower deck
Center girder
Forepeak

393

The battleship

IN THE EARLY YEARS OF THE 20TH CENTURY, sea warfare—
attacking enemy vessels or defending a ship—was
revolutionized by the introduction of Dreadnought-type
battleships like the Brazilian vessel below. These new
ships combined the latest advances in steam
propulsion, gunnery, and armor plating. Their gun
turrets, protected by armor up to 12 in (30 cm) thick,
were designed to fire shells over great distances.
The ship shown here, the Minas Geraes, was 500 ft
(152 m) long. It was built at Elswick, England, and
launched in 1908. Its chief armament was of 12 in (30 cm)
guns (firing shells with a 12 in diameter). Other naval
weapons developed in the 20th century include the torpedo—
as portrayed on the upper cigarette card (right). This was
a self-propelled underwater missile, often steered by
gyro-control. Depth charges were designed in the
First World War for use against submerged U-boats.
They are canisters filled with explosives that are
detonated by depth-sensitive pistols. The lower
cigarette card shows depth charges being
fired by a "thrower," fired from a
torpedo tube, and rolled from the
stern. Ship's shields were fitted to
warships from the late 19th century
onwards. The shield shown
opposite depicts a traditional
ship's cannon.

20TH CENTURY WEAPONRY

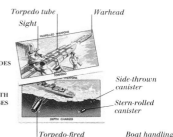

Torpedo tube   Warhead
Sight

TORPEDOES

Side-thrown
canister

DEPTH
CHARGES   Stern-rolled
canister

Torpedo-fired   Boat handling
canister   derrick

BRAZILIAN BATTLESHIP

Rangefinder   Forward   Gunnery
               funnel   spotting top
Light screen
               Lifeboat   Purchase wire
Compass
                              Searchlight
Compass and rangefinder
        platform   Searchlight
                              platform
Ship's wheel
                              Leading block
Navigating bridge
                              Tripod mast
Conning tower
                              Boat
Captain's shelter/   winch
chart house

Arms of
Brazil
               Weather shutter
                  for gun   "F" turret
Jack staff

        12 in (30 cm)
        gun

    Skylight

Stem   Porthole   Belt   Forward   Sighting "A" turret   Open gun mounting Steam launch
(false ram bow)   armor   accommodation hood
                              ladder   Turret barbette 4.7 in (12 cm) gun Guest boat boom

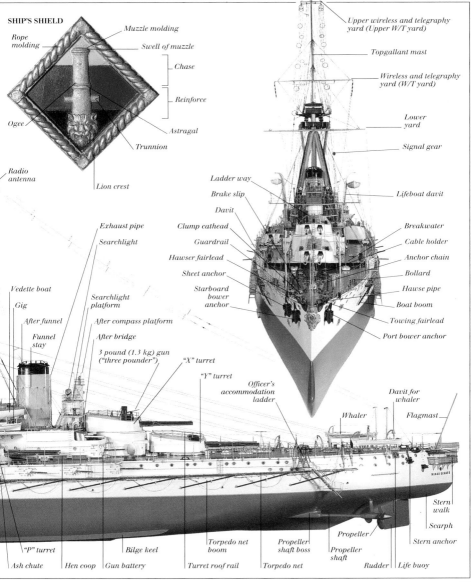

SHIP'S SHIELD

Rope molding

Muzzle molding

Swell of muzzle

Chase

Reinforce

Ogee

Astragal

Trunnion

Lion crest

Radio antenna

Upper wireless and telegraphy yard (Upper W/T yard)

Topgallant mast

Wireless and telegraphy yard (W/T yard)

Lower yard

Signal gear

Ladder way

Brake slip

Davit

Clump cathead

Guardrail

Hawser fairlead

Sheet anchor

Starboard bower anchor

Lifeboat davit

Breakwater

Cable holder

Anchor chain

Bollard

Hawse pipe

Boat boom

Towing fairlead

Port bower anchor

Exhaust pipe

Searchlight

Vedette boat

Gig

After funnel

Funnel stay

Searchlight platform

After compass platform

After bridge

3 pound (1.3 kg) gun ("three pounder")

"X" turret

"Y" turret

Officer's accommodation ladder

Davit for whaler

Whaler

Flagmast

"P" turret

Ash chute

Hen coop

Bilge keel

Gun battery

Torpedo net boom

Turret roof rail

Propeller shaft boss

Torpedo net

Propeller

Propeller shaft

Rudder

Life buoy

Stern anchor

Stern walk

Scarph

Frigates and submarines

From the mid-19th century, armored ships provided a new challenge to enemy craft. In response, huge revolving gun turrets were developed. These could shoot in any direction, were loaded quickly from the breech, and fired exploding shells. Today's fighting ships, like the Royal Navy frigate opposite, also carry missile launchers and helicopters. Submarines operate underwater, have great speed, and some can fire missiles while submerged. A nuclear sub can operate for several years without refueling.

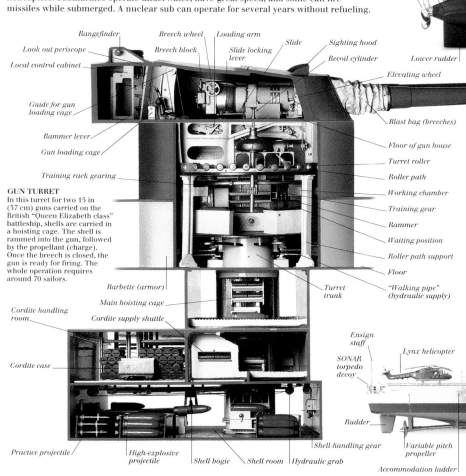

Stabilizer fin

Aft hydroplane

Propeller

Rangefinder

Look out periscope

Local control cabinet

Breech wheel

Breech block

Loading arm

Slide locking lever

Slide

Sighting hood

Recoil cylinder

Lower rudder

Elevating wheel

Guide for gun loading cage

Blast bag (breeches)

Rammer lever

Gun loading cage

Floor of gun house

Turret roller

Training rack gearing

Roller path

Working chamber

GUN TURRET
In this turret for two 15 in (37 cm) guns carried on the British "Queen Elizabeth class" battleship, shells are carried in a hoisting cage. The shell is rammed into the gun, followed by the propellant (charge). Once the breech is closed, the gun is ready for firing. The whole operation requires around 70 sailors.

Training gear

Rammer

Waiting position

Roller path support

Floor

Barbette (armor)

Main hoisting cage

Turret trunk

"Walking pipe" (hydraulic supply)

Cordite handling room

Cordite supply shuttle

Ensign staff

Lynx helicopter

SONAR torpedo decoy

Cordite case

Rudder

Variable pitch propeller

Practice projectile

High-explosive projectile

Shell bogie

Shell room

Hydraulic grab

Shell-handling gear

Accommodation ladder

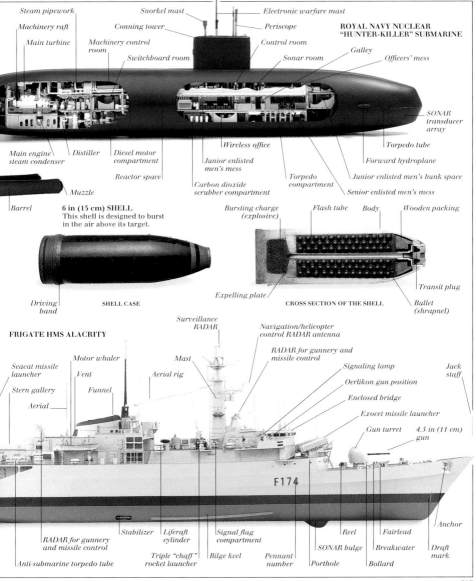

Steam pipework

Snorkel mast

Electronic warfare mast

Machinery raft

Conning tower

Periscope

ROYAL NAVY NUCLEAR
"HUNTER-KILLER" SUBMARINE

Main turbine

Machinery control
room

Control room

Main turbine

Switchboard room

Sonar room

Galley

Officers' mess

SONAR
transducer
array

Main engine
steam condenser

Distiller

Diesel motor
compartment

Wireless office

Torpedo tube

Reactor space

Junior enlisted
men's mess

Forward hydroplane

Muzzle

Carbon dioxide
scrubber compartment

Torpedo
compartment

Junior enlisted men's bunk space

Barrel

Senior enlisted men's mess

6 in (15 cm) SHELL
This shell is designed to burst
in the air above its target.

Bursting charge
(explosive)

Flash tube

Body

Wooden packing

Driving
band

SHELL CASE

Expelling plate

CROSS SECTION OF THE SHELL

Transit plug

Bullet
(shrapnel)

FRIGATE HMS ALACRITY

Surveillance
RADAR

Navigation/helicopter
control RADAR antenna

RADAR for gunnery and
missile control

Seacat missile
launcher

Motor whaler

Vent

Mast

Signaling lamp

Jack
staff

Stern gallery

Funnel

Aerial rig

Oerlikon gun position

Aerial

Enclosed bridge

Exocet missile launcher

Gun turret

4.5 in (11 cm)
gun

F174

RADAR for gunnery
and missile control

Stabilizer

Liferaft
cylinder

Signal flag
compartment

Reel

Fairlead

Anchor

Anti-submarine torpedo tube

Triple "chaff"
rocket launcher

Bilge keel

Pennant
number

Porthole

SONAR bulge

Bollard

Breakwater

Draft
mark

Pioneers of flight

FLIGHT HAS FASCINATED MANKIND for centuries, and countless unsuccessful flying machines have been designed. The first successful flight was made by the French Montgolfier brothers in 1783, when they flew a balloon over Paris. The next major advance was the development of gliders, notably by the Englishman Sir George Cayley, who in 1845 designed the first glider to make a sustained flight, and by the German Otto Lilienthal, who became known as the world's first pilot because he managed to achieve controlled flights. However, powered flight did not become a practical possibility until the invention of lightweight, gas-driven internal-combustion engines at the end of the 19th century. Then, in 1903, the American brothers Orville and Wilbur Wright made the first powered flight in their Wright Flyer biplane, which used a four-cylinder, gas-driven engine. Aircraft design advanced rapidly, and in 1909 the Frenchman Louis Blériot made his pioneering flight across the English Channel (see pp. 400-401). The American Glenn Curtiss also achieved several "firsts" in his Model-D Pusher and its variants, most notably winning the world's first competition for airspeed at Reims in 1909.

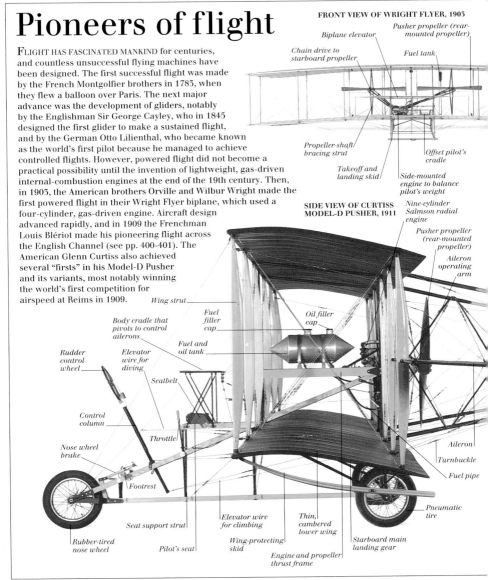

FRONT VIEW OF WRIGHT FLYER, 1903

Pusher propeller (rear-mounted propeller)

Biplane elevator

Chain drive to starboard propeller

Fuel tank

Propeller-shaft bracing strut

Offset pilot's cradle

Takeoff and landing skid

Side-mounted engine to balance pilot's weight

SIDE VIEW OF CURTISS MODEL-D PUSHER, 1911

Nine-cylinder Salmson radial engine

Pusher propeller (rear-mounted propeller)

Aileron operating arm

Wing strut

Fuel filler cap

Oil filler cap

Body cradle that pivots to control ailerons

Fuel and oil tank

Rudder control wheel

Elevator wire for diving

Seatbelt

Control column

Throttle

Nose wheel brake

Aileron

Turnbuckle

Fuel pipe

Footrest

Pneumatic tire

Seat support strut

Elevator wire for climbing

Thin, cambered lower wing

Starboard main landing gear

Rubber-tired nose wheel

Pilot's seat

Wing-protecting skid

Engine and propeller thrust frame

SIDE VIEW OF WRIGHT FLYER, 1903

Plain cotton fabric

Front diagonal strut

Elevator drive wheel

Interplane strut

Water-filled radiator

Wing warping wire

Chain drive

Pusher propeller (rear-mounted propeller)

Rigid leading edge

Steel hub

Steel propeller shaft

Water pipe

Front-mounted biplane elevator

Bracing wire

Rudder

Landing skid

Elevator control cable

Pilot's cradle

Magneto

Rudder control cable

Braced rudder strut

Warping connection strut

Four-cylinder 12-HP engine

Propeller-shaft bracing strut

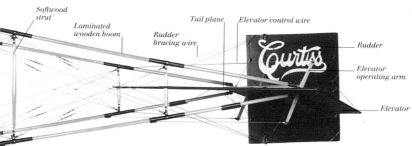

Softwood strut

Laminated wooden boom

Rudder bracing wire

Tail plane

Elevator control wire

Rudder

Elevator operating arm

Elevator

Curtiss

FRONT VIEW OF CURTISS MODEL-D PUSHER, 1911

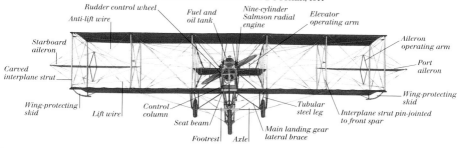

Rudder control wheel

Anti-lift wire

Fuel and oil tank

Nine-cylinder Salmson radial engine

Elevator operating arm

Starboard aileron

Aileron operating arm

Carved interplane strut

Port aileron

Wing-protecting skid

Lift wire

Control column

Seat beam

Footrest

Axle

Tubular steel leg

Main landing gear lateral brace

Interplane strut pin-jointed to front spar

Wing-protecting skid

Early monoplanes

RUMPLER MONOPLANE, 1908

MONOPLANES HAVE ONE WING on each side of the fuselage. The principal disadvantage of this arrangement in early wooden-framed aircraft was that single wings were weak. They required strong wires to brace them to king posts above and below the fuselage. However, single wings also had advantages: they experienced less drag than multiple wings, allowing greater speed; they also made aircraft more maneuverable because single wings were easier to warp (twist) than double wings, and warping the wings was how pilots controlled the roll of early aircraft. By 1912, the French pilot Louis Blériot had used a monoplane to make the first flight across the English Channel, and the Briton Robert Blackburn and the Frenchman Armand Deperdussin had proved the greater speed of monoplanes. However, a spate of crashes caused by broken wings discouraged monoplane production, except in Germany, where all-metal monoplanes were developed in 1917. The wings of all-metal monoplanes did not need strengthening by struts or bracing wires, but despite this, such planes were not widely adopted until the 1930s.

FRONT VIEW OF BLACKBURN MONOPLANE, 1912

Taut fabric

Carved wooden propeller

King post

Hub bolted to propeller

Nose ring

Pilot's viewing aperture

Exhaust valve push-rod

Gnome seven-cylinder rotary engine

Elevator hinge

Elevator

Landing gear rear cross-member

Wheel fairing

Rubber-sprung wheel

Tailskid

Landing gear front strut

Axle

Landing skid

Landing gear rear strut

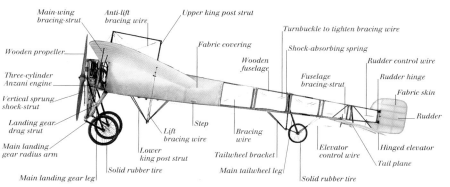

Main-wing bracing-strut

Anti-lift bracing wire

Upper king post strut

Fabric covering

Turnbuckle to tighten bracing wire

Shock-absorbing spring

Wooden propeller

Wooden fuselage

Rudder control wire

Rudder hinge

Three-cylinder Anzani engine

Fuselage bracing-strut

Fabric skin

Vertical sprung shock-strut

Rudder

Landing gear drag strut

Step

Lift bracing wire

Bracing wire

Hinged elevator

Main landing gear radius arm

Lower king post strut

Tailwheel bracket

Elevator control wire

Tail plane

Main landing gear leg

Solid rubber tire

Main tailwheel leg

Solid rubber tire

SIDE VIEW OF BLÉRIOT XI, 1909

Anti-lift bracing wire

Leading edge

Rib

Bracing wire anchor bolt

Concave undersurface

Lift bracing wire

Turnbuckle to tighten bracing wire

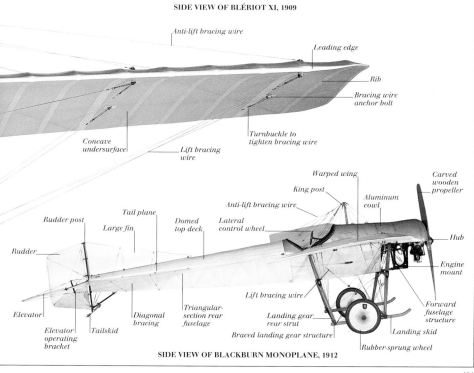

Warped wing

Carved wooden propeller

King post

Aluminum cowl

Anti-lift bracing wire

Rudder post

Tail plane

Domed top deck

Lateral control wheel

Large fin

Hub

Rudder

Engine mount

Elevator

Diagonal bracing

Triangular-section rear fuselage

Lift bracing wire

Forward fuselage structure

Elevator operating bracket

Tailskid

Landing gear rear strut

Braced landing gear structure

Landing skid

Rubber-sprung wheel

SIDE VIEW OF BLACKBURN MONOPLANE, 1912

Biplanes and triplanes

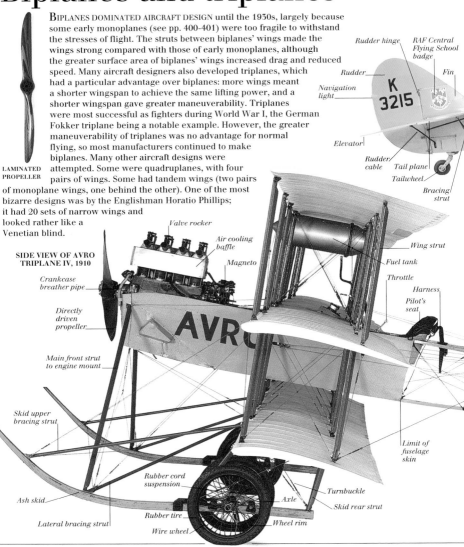

BIPLANES DOMINATED AIRCRAFT DESIGN until the 1930s, largely because some early monoplanes (see pp. 400-401) were too fragile to withstand the stresses of flight. The struts between biplanes' wings made the wings strong compared with those of early monoplanes, although the greater surface area of biplanes' wings increased drag and reduced speed. Many aircraft designers also developed triplanes, which had a particular advantage over biplanes: more wings meant a shorter wingspan to achieve the same lifting power, and a shorter wingspan gave greater maneuverability. Triplanes were most successful as fighters during World War I, the German Fokker triplane being a notable example. However, the greater maneuverability of triplanes was no advantage for normal flying, so most manufacturers continued to make biplanes. Many other aircraft designs were attempted. Some were quadruplanes, with four pairs of wings. Some had tandem wings (two pairs of monoplane wings, one behind the other). One of the most bizarre designs was by the Englishman Horatio Phillips; it had 20 sets of narrow wings and looked rather like a Venetian blind.

LAMINATED PROPELLER

Rudder hinge
RAF Central Flying School badge
Rudder
Fin
Navigation light
K 3215
Elevator
Rudder cable
Tail plane
Tailwheel
Bracing strut

SIDE VIEW OF AVRO TRIPLANE IV, 1910

Valve rocker
Air cooling baffle
Magneto
Crankcase breather pipe
Directly driven propeller
Wing strut
Fuel tank
Throttle
Harness
Pilot's seat
Main front strut to engine mount
AVRO
Skid upper bracing strut
Rubber cord suspension
Turnbuckle
Ash skid
Axle
Skid rear strut
Lateral bracing strut
Rubber tire
Wheel rim
Wire wheel
Limit of fuselage skin

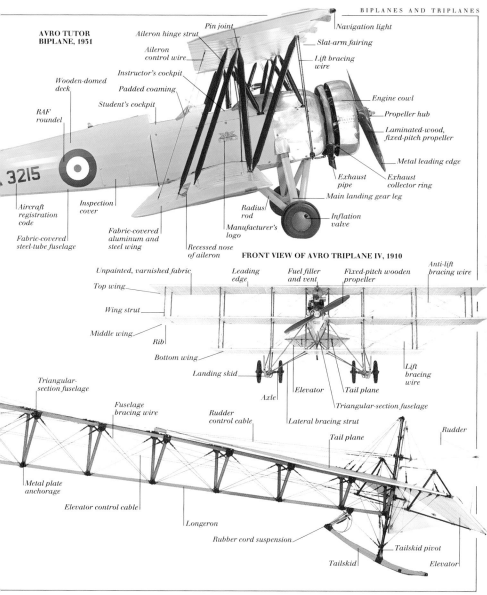

AVRO TUTOR BIPLANE, 1931

Pin joint

Aileron hinge strut

Navigation light

Aileron control wire

Slat-arm fairing

Instructor's cockpit

Lift bracing wire

Wooden-domed deck

Padded coaming

Engine cowl

Student's cockpit

Propeller hub

RAF roundel

Laminated-wood, fixed-pitch propeller

Metal leading edge

3215

Exhaust pipe

Exhaust collector ring

Aircraft registration code

Inspection cover

Main landing gear leg

Inflation valve

Fabric-covered steel-tube fuselage

Fabric-covered aluminum and steel wing

Radius rod

Manufacturer's logo

Recessed nose of aileron

FRONT VIEW OF AVRO TRIPLANE IV, 1910

Unpainted, varnished fabric

Leading edge

Fuel filler and vent

Fixed-pitch wooden propeller

Anti-lift bracing wire

Top wing

Wing strut

Middle wing

Rib

Bottom wing

Landing skid

Lift bracing wire

Axle

Elevator

Tail plane

Triangular-section fuselage

Fuselage bracing wire

Rudder control cable

Lateral bracing strut

Triangular-section fuselage

Tail plane

Rudder

Metal plate anchorage

Elevator control cable

Longeron

Rubber cord suspension

Tailskid pivot

Tailskid

Elevator

World War I aircraft

FLYING HELMET

W HEN WORLD WAR I STARTED in 1914, the main purpose of military aircraft was reconnaissance. The British-built BE 2, of which the BE 2B was a variant, was well suited to this duty; it was very stable in flight, allowing the occupants to study the terrain, take photographs, and make notes. The BE 2 was also one of the first aircraft to drop bombs. One of the biggest problems for aircraft designers during the war was mounting machine guns. On aircraft that had front-mounted propellers, the field of fire was restricted by the propeller and other parts of the aircraft. The problem was solved in 1915 by the Dutchman Anthony Fokker, who designed an interrupter gear that prevented a machine gun from firing when a propeller blade passed in front of the barrel. The German LVG CVI had a forward-firing gun to the right of the engine, as well as a rear-cockpit gun, and bombing capability. It was one of the most versatile aircraft of the war.

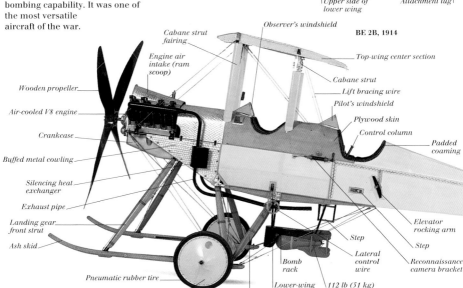

Interplane-strut attachment
Intermediate leading-edge rib
Airspeed-indicator tube
Leading edge
Wingtip
Airspeed-indicator tube
Main rib
Root
Airspeed indicator tube
Interplane strut
Trailing edge
Airspeed pitot tube
Interplane-strut attachment

Upper side of lower wing
Attachment lug

Observer's windshield
BE 2B, 1914

Cabane strut fairing
Engine air intake (ram scoop)
Top-wing center section
Cabane strut
Lift bracing wire
Wooden propeller
Pilot's windshield
Air-cooled V8 engine
Plywood skin
Control column
Crankcase
Padded coaming
Buffed metal cowling
Silencing heat exchanger
Exhaust pipe
Landing gear front strut
Elevator rocking arm
Ash skid
Step
Step
Lateral control wire
Reconnaissance camera bracket
Pneumatic rubber tire
Wheel cover
V-strut
Lower-wing attachment
Bomb rack
112 lb (51 kg) bomb

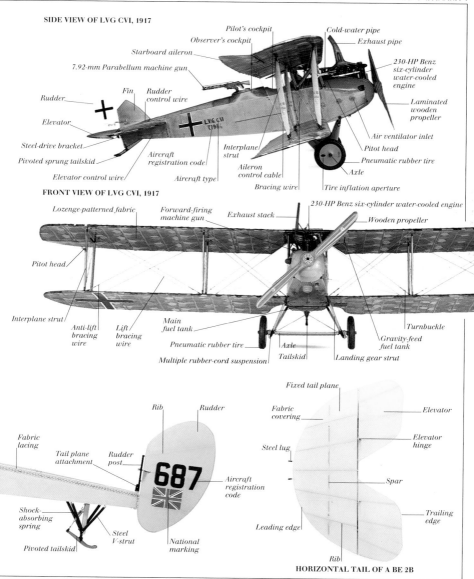

SIDE VIEW OF LVG CVI, 1917

Pilot's cockpit

Observer's cockpit

Cold-water pipe

Exhaust pipe

Starboard aileron

7.92-mm Parabellum machine gun

230-HP Benz six-cylinder water-cooled engine

Rudder

Fin

Rudder control wire

Laminated wooden propeller

Elevator

Air ventilator inlet

Steel-drive bracket

Pitot head

Pivoted sprung tailskid

Aircraft registration code

Interplane strut

Pneumatic rubber tire

Elevator control wire

Aircraft type

Aileron control cable

Axle

Bracing wire

Tire inflation aperture

FRONT VIEW OF LVG CVI, 1917

Lozenge-patterned fabric

Forward-firing machine gun

Exhaust stack

230-HP Benz six-cylinder water-cooled engine

Wooden propeller

Pitot head

Interplane strut

Anti-lift bracing wire

Lift bracing wire

Main fuel tank

Turnbuckle

Gravity-feed fuel tank

Pneumatic rubber tire

Axle

Tailskid

Landing gear strut

Multiple rubber-cord suspension

Fabric lacing

Rib

Rudder

Fixed tail plane

Fabric covering

Elevator

Tail plane attachment

Rudder post

Elevator hinge

Steel lug

Shock-absorbing spring

Steel V-strut

Aircraft registration code

Spar

Pivoted tailskid

National marking

Leading edge

Trailing edge

Rib

HORIZONTAL TAIL OF A BE 2B

687

Early passenger aircraft

FRONT VIEW OF LOCKHEED ELECTRA, 1954

U NTIL THE 1930s, most passenger aircraft were biplanes, with two pairs of wings and a wooden or metal framework covered with fabric or, sometimes, plywood. Such aircraft were restricted to low speeds and low altitudes because of the drag on their wings. Many had an open cockpit, situated behind or in front of an enclosed—but unpressurized—cabin that carried a maximum of 10 people. The passengers usually sat in wicker chairs that were not bolted to the floor, and the journey could be bumpy when flying through turbulence. Warm clothing, and earplugs to reduce the effects of prolonged noise, were often required. During the 1930s, powerful, streamlined, all-metal monoplanes, such as the Lockheed Electra shown here, became widespread. By 1939, the advent of pressurized cabins allowed fast flights at high altitudes, where there is less turbulence.

Flying boats were still necessary on many routes until 1945 because of inadequate runways and the frequency of emergency sea landings. World War II, however, resulted in enough good runways being built for land planes to become standard on all major airline routes.

Green starboard navigation light

Flush-riveted metal-skinned wing

Leading edge

Fuel-jettison valve

Static discharge wick

Split flap in landing position

PASSENGER CABIN TRIM PANELS

Roof trim panel

Forward bulkhead upper panel

Ashtray

Passenger service panel aperture

Starboard wall forward panel

Cockpit door panel

Forward bulkhead lower panel

Starboard wall mid-forward panel

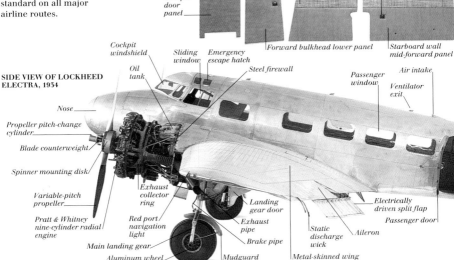

SIDE VIEW OF LOCKHEED ELECTRA, 1954

Cockpit windshield

Sliding window

Emergency escape hatch

Steel firewall

Passenger window

Air intake

Oil tank

Ventilator exit

Nose

Propeller pitch-change cylinder

Blade counterweight

Spinner mounting disk

Variable-pitch propeller

Pratt & Whitney nine-cylinder radial engine

Exhaust collector ring

Red port navigation light

Landing gear door

Exhaust pipe

Brake pipe

Static discharge wick

Electrically driven split flap

Passenger door

Aileron

Main landing gear

Aluminum wheel

Mudguard

Metal-skinned wing

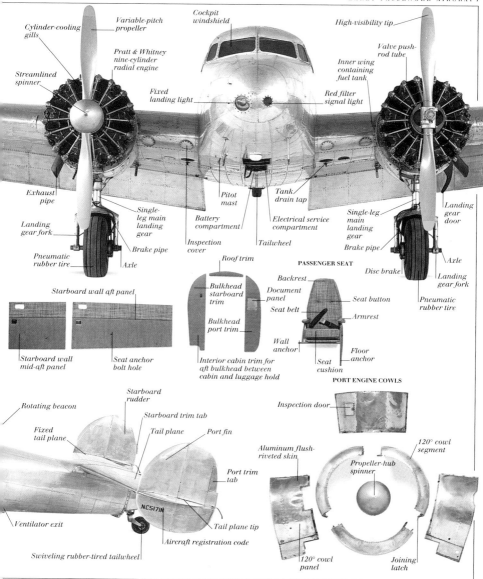

Cylinder-cooling gills

Variable-pitch propeller

Cockpit windshield

High-visibility tip

Pratt & Whitney nine-cylinder radial engine

Valve push-rod tube

Streamlined spinner

Inner wing containing fuel tank

Fixed landing light

Red filter signal light

Exhaust pipe

Single-leg main landing gear

Pitot mast

Tank drain tap

Single-leg main landing gear

Landing gear door

Landing gear fork

Battery compartment

Electrical service compartment

Brake pipe

Axle

Pneumatic rubber tire

Brake pipe

Inspection cover

Tailwheel

Disc brake

Landing gear fork

Axle

Pneumatic rubber tire

Roof trim

PASSENGER SEAT

Starboard wall aft panel

Bulkhead starboard trim

Backrest

Document panel

Seat button

Bulkhead port trim

Seat belt

Armrest

Starboard wall mid-aft panel

Seat anchor bolt hole

Interior cabin trim for aft bulkhead between cabin and luggage hold

Wall anchor

Seat cushion

Floor anchor

PORT ENGINE COWLS

Rotating beacon

Starboard rudder

Inspection door

Fixed tail plane

Starboard trim tab

Tail plane

Port fin

120° cowl segment

Aluminum flush-riveted skin

Propeller-hub spinner

Port trim tab

NC517IN

Ventilator exit

Tail plane tip

Swiveling rubber-tired tailwheel

Aircraft registration code

120° cowl panel

Joining latch

World War II aircraft

WHEN WORLD WAR II began in 1939, air forces had already replaced most of their fabric-skinned biplanes with all-metal stressed-skin monoplanes. Aircraft played a far greater role in military operations during World War II than ever before. The wide range of aircraft duties and the introduction of radar tracking and guidance systems put pressure on designers to improve aircraft performance. The main areas of improvement were speed, range, and engine power. Bombers became larger and more powerful—converting from two to four engines—in order to carry a heavier bomb load; the U.S. B-17 Flying Fortress could carry up to 6 tons of bombs over a distance of about 2,000 miles (3,200 km). Some aircraft increased their range by using drop tanks (fuel tanks that were jettisoned when empty to reduce drag). Fighters needed speed and maneuverability: the Hawker Tempest shown here had a maximum speed of 455 mph (700 kph) and was one of the few Allied aircraft capable of catching the German jet-powered V1 "flying bomb." By 1944, Britain had introduced its first turbojet-powered aircraft, the Gloster Meteor fighter, and Germany had introduced the fastest fighter in the world, the turbojet-powered Me 262, which had a maximum speed of 540 mph (868 kph).

STARBOARD ENGINE COWLINGS

Radiator-access cowling

Lower side cowling

Upper side cowling

Cowling fastener

PROPELLER

High-visibility yellow tip

Light-alloy propeller spinner

2,400-HP Napier Sabre 24-cylinder engine

Cartridge starter

Propeller governor

Radiator header tank

Propeller drive shaft

Distributor

Ejector exhaust

Magneto

Starter motor

Variable-pitch aluminum-alloy blade

COMPONENTS OF A HAWKER TEMPEST MARK V, c.1943

Engine top cowling

Upper side cowling

Lower side cowling

Cowling fastener

Radiator-access cowling

PORT ENGINE COWLINGS

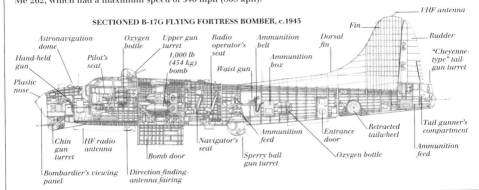

SECTIONED B-17G FLYING FORTRESS BOMBER, c.1943

Astronavigation dome

Oxygen bottle

Upper gun turret

Radio operator's seat

Ammunition belt

Dorsal fin

Fin

VHF antenna

Rudder

Hand-held gun

Pilot's seat

1,000 lb (454 kg) bomb

Ammunition box

Waist gun

"Cheyenne-type" tail-gun turret

Plastic nose

Chin gun turret

HF radio antenna

Bomb door

Navigator's seat

Direction-finding-antenna fairing

Ammunition feed

Sperry ball gun turret

Entrance door

Oxygen bottle

Retracted tailwheel

Tail gunner's compartment

Ammunition feed

Bombardier's viewing panel

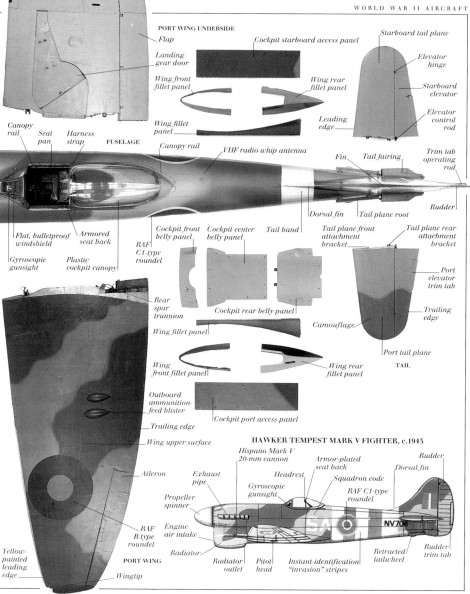

PORT WING UNDERSIDE

Flap

Cockpit starboard access panel

Starboard tail plane

Landing gear door

Elevator hinge

Wing front fillet panel

Wing rear fillet panel

Starboard elevator

Leading edge

Elevator control rod

Wing fillet panel

Canopy rail

Seat pan

Harness strap

FUSELAGE

Canopy rail

VHF radio whip antenna

Fin

Tail fairing

Trim tab operating rod

Rudder

Dorsal fin

Tail plane root

Tail band

Flat, bulletproof windshield

Armored seat back

Gyroscopic gunsight

Plastic cockpit canopy

Cockpit front belly panel

Cockpit center belly panel

RAF C1-type roundel

Tail plane front attachment bracket

Tail plane rear attachment bracket

Port elevator trim tab

Cockpit rear belly panel

Rear spar trunnion

Trailing edge

Wing fillet panel

Camouflage

Wing front fillet panel

Wing rear fillet panel

Port tail plane

TAIL

Outboard ammunition-feed blister

Cockpit port access panel

Trailing edge

HAWKER TEMPEST MARK V FIGHTER, c.1943

Wing upper surface

Hispano Mark V 20-mm cannon

Armor-plated seat back

Rudder

Aileron

Exhaust pipe

Headrest

Squadron code

Dorsal fin

Gyroscopic gunsight

Propeller spinner

RAF C1-type roundel

RAF B-type roundel

Engine air intake

NV70

Yellow-painted leading edge

Radiator

PORT WING

Radiator outlet

Pitot head

Instant-identification "invasion" stripes

Retracted tailwheel

Rudder trim tab

Wingtip

Modern piston aircraft engines

MID WEST TWO-STROKE, THREE-CYLINDER ENGINE

PISTON ENGINES today are used mainly to power the vast numbers of light aircraft and ultralights, as well as crop sprayers and crop dusters, small helicopters, and fire-bombers (which dump water on large fires). Virtually all heavier aircraft are now powered by jet engines. Modern piston aircraft engines work on the same basic principles as the engine used by the Wright brothers in the first powered flight in 1903. However, today's engines are more sophisticated than earlier engines. For example, modern aircraft engines may use a two-stroke or a four-stroke combustion cycle; they may have from one to nine air- or liquid-cooled cylinders, which may be arranged horizontally, in-line, in V formation, or radially; and they may drive the aircraft's propeller either directly or through a reduction gearbox. One of the more unconventional types of modern aircraft engine is the rotary engine shown here, which has a trilobate (three-sided) rotor spinning in a chamber shaped like a fat figure-eight.

MID WEST 75-HP TWO-STROKE, THREE-CYLINDER ENGINE

Spark plug
Coolant outlet
Cylinder head

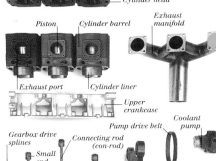

Piston
Cylinder barrel
Exhaust manifold
Exhaust port
Cylinder liner
Upper crankcase
Coolant pump
Pump drive belt

Reduction gearbox
Driven gear
Propeller drive flange
Torsional vibration damper
Sprag clutch

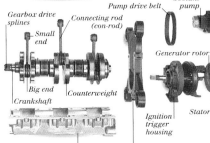

Gearbox drive splines
Connecting rod (con-rod)
Small end
Big end
Crankshaft
Counterweight
Generator rotor
Stator
Ignition trigger housing
Gearbox mounting plate
Lower crankcase
Engine mounting plate

ROTOR AND HOUSINGS OF A MID WEST SINGLE-ROTOR ENGINE

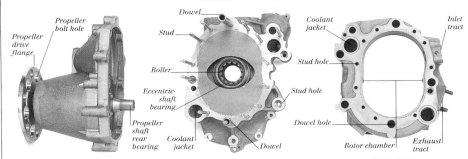

Propeller drive flange
Propeller bolt hole
Propeller shaft rear bearing

GEARBOX CASE

Dowel
Stud
Roller
Eccentric-shaft bearing
Propeller shaft rear bearing
Coolant jacket
Dowel

FRONT HOUSING (FRONT END PLATE)

Coolant jacket
Stud hole
Stud hole
Dowel hole
Rotor chamber

Inlet tract
Exhaust tract

TROCHOID HOUSING

MID WEST 90-HP TWIN-ROTOR ENGINE

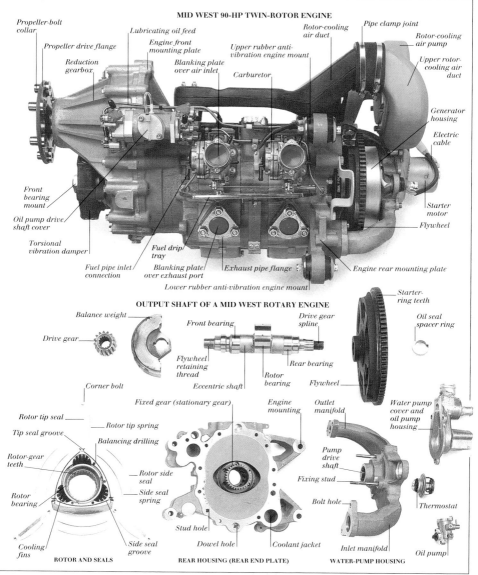

Propeller-bolt collar

Propeller drive flange

Reduction gearbox

Lubricating oil feed

Engine front mounting plate

Blanking plate over air inlet

Upper rubber anti-vibration engine mount

Carburetor

Rotor-cooling air duct

Pipe clamp joint

Rotor-cooling air pump

Upper rotor-cooling air duct

Generator housing

Electric cable

Starter motor

Flywheel

Front bearing mount

Oil pump drive shaft cover

Torsional vibration damper

Fuel pipe inlet connection

Fuel drip tray

Blanking plate over exhaust port

Exhaust pipe flange

Engine rear mounting plate

Lower rubber anti-vibration engine mount

OUTPUT SHAFT OF A MID WEST ROTARY ENGINE

Balance weight

Drive gear

Front bearing

Drive gear spline

Flywheel retaining thread

Eccentric shaft

Rotor bearing

Rear bearing

Flywheel

Starter-ring teeth

Oil seal spacer ring

Corner bolt

Rotor tip seal

Tip seal groove

Rotor-gear teeth

Rotor bearing

Rotor tip spring

Balancing drilling

Rotor side seal

Side seal spring

Cooling fins

Side seal groove

Stud hole

Dowel hole

Coolant jacket

Fixed gear (stationary gear)

Engine mounting

Outlet manifold

Pump drive shaft

Fixing stud

Bolt hole

Inlet manifold

Water pump cover and oil pump housing

Thermostat

Oil pump

ROTOR AND SEALS

REAR HOUSING (REAR END PLATE)

WATER-PUMP HOUSING

Modern jetliners 1

BAE 146 JETLINER

MODERN JETLINERS HAVE ENABLED ordinary people to travel to places where once only the wealthy could afford to go. Compared with the first jetliners (which were introduced in the 1940s), modern jetliners are much quieter, burn fuel more efficiently, and produce less air pollution. These advances are largely due to the replacement of turbojet engines with turbofan engines (see pp. 418-419). The greater power of turbofan engines at low speeds enables modern jetliners to carry more fuel and passengers than turbojet aircraft; a modern Boeing 747-400 (popularly known as a "jumbo jet") can fly 400 people for 8,500 miles (13,700 km) without needing to refuel. Jetliners fly at high altitudes, typically cruising at 26,000-36,000 ft (8,000-11,000 m), where they can use fuel efficiently and usually avoid bad weather. The pilot always controls the aircraft during takeoff and landing, but at other times the aircraft is usually controlled by an autopilot. Autopilots are complex onboard mechanisms that detect deviations from an aircraft's route and make appropriate adjustments to the flight controls. Flight decks are also equipped with radar that warns pilots of approaching hazards, such as mountain ranges, bad weather, and other aircraft.

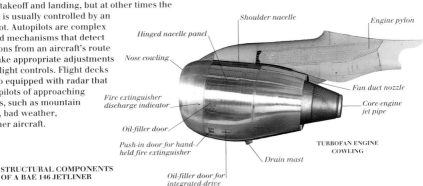

Shoulder nacelle

Engine pylon

Hinged nacelle panel

Nose cowling

Fan duct nozzle

Core-engine jet pipe

Fire extinguisher discharge indicator

Oil-filler door

Push-in door for hand-held fire extinguisher

Drain mast

TURBOFAN ENGINE COWLING

STRUCTURAL COMPONENTS OF A BAE 146 JETLINER

Oil-filler door for integrated-drive generator

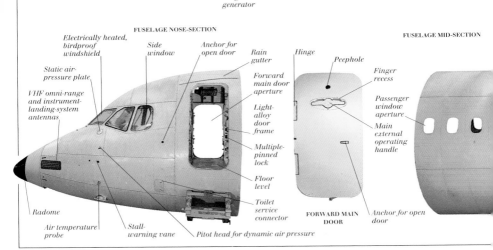

FUSELAGE NOSE-SECTION

FUSELAGE MID-SECTION

Electrically heated, birdproof windshield

Side window

Anchor for open door

Rain gutter

Hinge

Peephole

Finger recess

Static air-pressure plate

Forward main door aperture

Passenger window aperture

VHF omni-range and instrument-landing-system antennas

Light-alloy door frame

Main external operating handle

Multiple-pinned lock

Floor level

Toilet service connector

FORWARD MAIN DOOR

Anchor for open door

Radome

Air temperature probe

Stall-warning vane

Pitot head for dynamic air pressure

Overwing fuel-filler cap

Systems connector

Overwing fuel-filler cap

Fuel contents indicator

STARBOARD WING ASSEMBLY

Center-line (spine) of aircraft

Single-piece skin over inboard wing

Rubber sealing strip

Rubber sealing strip

Trailing edge

Trailing edge of fixed wing

Spoiler anchorage

Hydraulic actuator attachment

Pivot point

Flap-track fairing

Screw joint

Aft section

Hinge

INBOARD LIFT SPOILERS

Stainless-steel flap seal

MOVABLE FLAP TRACK AND FAIRING

Track roller

Upper carriage attached to flap

Tab hinge line

FOWLER FLAP

Leading edge

Anchor bearing

Track

Root

Gearbox mount

Bellcrank lever

Gearbox unit

Carriage drive nut

Flap drive screw

Lower carriage

Skin lap-joint

Leading edge

Main spar bridge

Root rib

Wing-root mount containing central fuel tank

Inboard tab

Attachment structure for wing-to-fuselage fillet

Cabin air-pressure discharge valve

Floor level

Fairing of landing gear bay

Fairing of landing gear pivot

Yellow anti-corrosion paint

Modern jetliners 2

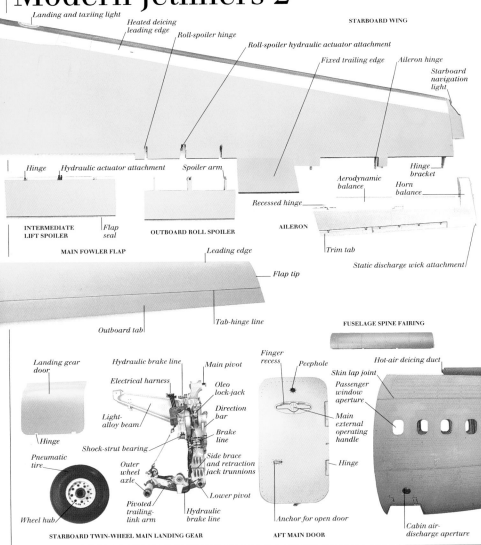

Landing and taxiing light

Heated deicing leading edge

Roll-spoiler hinge

STARBOARD WING

Roll-spoiler hydraulic actuator attachment

Fixed trailing edge

Aileron hinge

Starboard navigation light

Hinge

Hydraulic actuator attachment

Spoiler arm

Hinge bracket

Aerodynamic balance

Horn balance

Recessed hinge

INTERMEDIATE LIFT SPOILER

Flap seal

OUTBOARD ROLL SPOILER

AILERON

MAIN FOWLER FLAP

Leading edge

Trim tab

Static discharge wick attachment

Flap tip

Tab-hinge line

FUSELAGE SPINE FAIRING

Outboard tab

Landing gear door

Hydraulic brake line

Main pivot

Electrical harness

Finger recess

Peephole

Hot-air deicing duct

Skin lap joint

Oleo lock-jack

Passenger window aperture

Direction bar

Light-alloy beam

Main external operating handle

Brake line

Hinge

Shock-strut bearing

Pneumatic tire

Side brace and retraction jack trunnions

Outer wheel axle

Lower pivot

Hinge

Wheel hub

Pivoted trailing-link arm

Hydraulic brake line

Anchor for open door

Cabin air-discharge aperture

STARBOARD TWIN-WHEEL MAIN LANDING GEAR

AFT MAIN DOOR

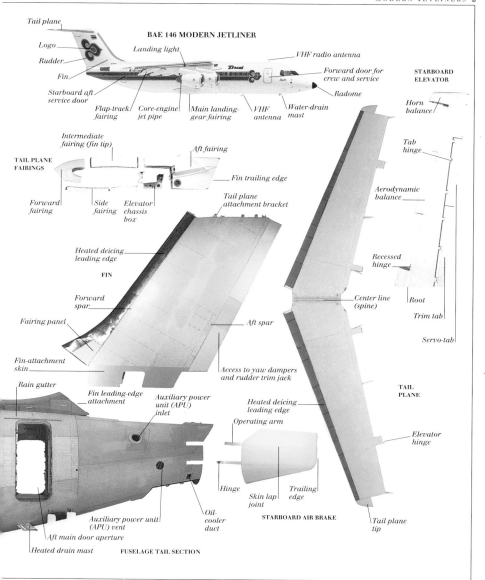

BAE 146 MODERN JETLINER

Tail plane

Logo

Rudder

Fin

Starboard aft
service door

Landing light

VHF radio antenna

Forward door for
crew and service

Radome

STARBOARD
ELEVATOR

Flap-track
fairing

Core-engine
jet pipe

Main landing-
gear fairing

VHF
antenna

Water-drain
mast

Horn
balance

TAIL PLANE
FAIRINGS

Intermediate
fairing (fin tip)

Aft fairing

Fin trailing edge

Tail plane
attachment bracket

Tab
hinge

Forward
fairing

Side
fairing

Elevator
chassis
box

Aerodynamic
balance

Heated deicing
leading edge

FIN

Recessed
hinge

Root

Forward
spar

Center line
(spine)

Trim tab

Fairing panel

Aft spar

Servo-tab

Fin-attachment
skin

Access to yaw dampers
and rudder trim jack

TAIL
PLANE

Rain gutter

Fin leading-edge
attachment

Auxiliary power
unit (APU)
inlet

Heated deicing
leading edge

Operating arm

Elevator
hinge

Auxiliary power unit
(APU) vent

Oil-
cooler
duct

Hinge

Skin lap
joint

Trailing
edge

STARBOARD AIR BRAKE

Tail plane
tip

Heated drain mast

FUSELAGE TAIL SECTION

Supersonic jetliners

COMPUTER-
DESIGNED SST

SUPERSONIC AIRCRAFT FLY FASTER than the speed of sound (Mach 1). There are many supersonic military aircraft, but only two supersonic passenger-carrying aircraft (also called SSTs, or supersonic transports) have been produced: the Russian Tu-144, and the Concorde, produced jointly by Britain and France. The Tu-144 had a greater maximum speed than the Concorde but was withdrawn in 1978, after only seven months in service. The Concorde has remained in service since 1976. It features many innovations, including a droop nose, which is lowered during takeoff and landing to aid visibility from the cockpit, and the pumping of fuel between forward and aft trim tanks to help stabilize the aircraft. The Concorde has a narrow fuselage and short-span wings to reduce drag during supersonic flight. Its noisy turbojet engines with afterburners enable it to carry 100 passengers at a cruising speed of Mach 2 at 50,000-60,000 ft (15,000-18,000 m). Once an aircraft is flying faster than Mach 1, it produces a continuous air-pressure wave, which is heard as a "sonic boom."

FRONT VIEW OF CONCORDE

Strake

Fin

Standby
pitot head

Inboard
elevon-
actuator
fairing

Nose
gear
leg

Starboard
outboard
engine air intake

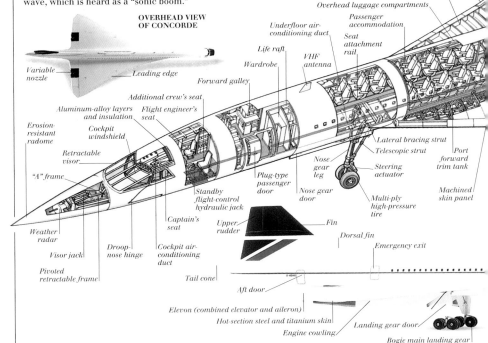

**OVERHEAD VIEW
OF CONCORDE**

Variable
nozzle

Leading edge

Underfloor air-
conditioning duct

Life raft

VHF
antenna

Wardrobe

Forward galley

Additional crew's seat

Flight engineer's
seat

Aluminum-alloy layers
and insulation

Erosion-
resistant
radome

Cockpit
windshield

Retractable
visor

"A" frame

Weather
radar

Visor jack

Droop-
nose hinge

Cockpit air-
conditioning
duct

Pivoted
retractable frame

Captain's
seat

Standby
flight-control
hydraulic jack

Plug-type
passenger
door

Nose
gear
leg

Nose gear
door

Tail cone

Upper
rudder

Fin

Aft door

Elevon (combined elevator and aileron)

Hot-section steel and titanium skin

Engine cowling

Dorsal fin

Emergency exit

Landing gear door

Bogie main landing gear

Steering
actuator

Multi-ply
high-pressure
tire

Lateral bracing strut

Telescopic strut

Port
forward
trim tank

Machined
skin panel

Toilets

Electrothermal
deicing panel

Starboard
forward trim tank

Overhead luggage compartments

Passenger
accommodation

Seat
attachment
rail

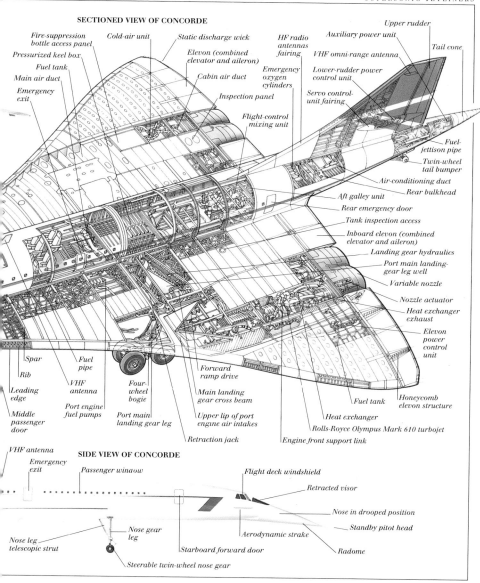

SECTIONED VIEW OF CONCORDE

Fire-suppression bottle access panel
Cold-air unit
Static discharge wick
HF radio antennas fairing
Auxiliary power unit
Upper rudder
Tail cone
Pressurized keel box
Elevon (combined elevator and aileron)
VHF omni-range antenna
Fuel tank
Cabin air duct
Emergency oxygen cylinders
Lower-rudder power control unit
Main air duct
Inspection panel
Servo control-unit fairing
Emergency exit
Flight-control mixing unit
Fuel-jettison pipe
Twin-wheel tail bumper
Air-conditioning duct
Rear bulkhead
Aft galley unit
Rear emergency door
Tank inspection access
Inboard elevon (combined elevator and aileron)
Landing gear hydraulics
Port main landing-gear leg well
Variable nozzle
Nozzle actuator
Heat exchanger exhaust
Elevon power control unit
Spar
Fuel pipe
Forward ramp drive
Rib
VHF antenna
Four-wheel bogie
Main landing gear cross beam
Leading edge
Port engine fuel pumps
Port main landing gear leg
Upper lip of port engine air intakes
Fuel tank
Honeycomb elevon structure
Middle passenger door
Heat exchanger
Rolls-Royce Olympus Mark 610 turbojet
Retraction jack
Engine front support link

VHF antenna
SIDE VIEW OF CONCORDE
Emergency exit
Passenger window
Flight deck windshield
Retracted visor
Nose in drooped position
Standby pitot head
Nose leg telescopic strut
Nose gear leg
Aerodynamic strake
Radome
Starboard forward door
Steerable twin-wheel nose gear

Jet engines

JET ENGINES ARE USED BY MOST MILITARY and heavy aircraft and by many helicopters. The simplest type of jet engine, or gas turbine, is the turbojet. It works by continuously burning a mixture of fuel and air in a combustion chamber to produce a jet of hot exhaust gas that is expelled through a nozzle to produce thrust. The hot gas also spins turbine blades which, in turn, spin the blades of an air compressor; the compressor forces air into the combustion chamber. Many of the fastest aircraft use turbojets, with additional booster units called afterburners, but their use is restricted by their high noise emission. Most jetliners use quieter turbofan jet engines. An enormous fan, driven by a low-pressure turbine, feeds some air into the compressor but feeds most of it through bypass ducts to join the exhaust jetstream in the tail cone. The bypass stream produces most of the thrust. Many smaller, propeller-driven aircraft use turboprop jet engines, in which the engine powers a propeller.

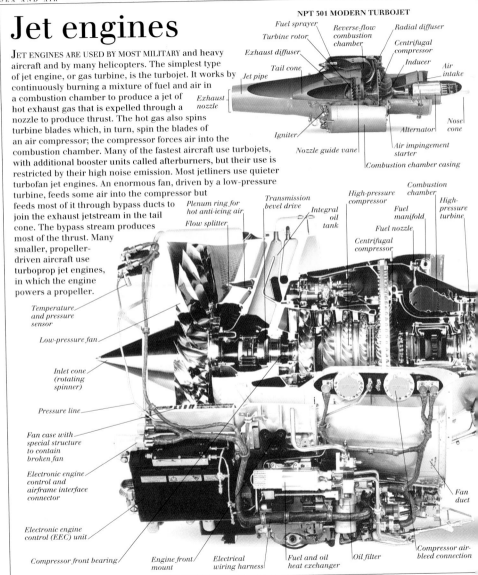

Fuel sprayer

Turbine rotor

Exhaust diffuser

Tail cone

Jet pipe

Exhaust nozzle

Reverse-flow combustion chamber

Radial diffuser

Centrifugal compressor

Inducer

Air intake

Nose cone

Alternator

Igniter

Nozzle guide vane

Air impingement starter

Combustion chamber casing

Plenum ring for hot anti-icing air

Flow splitter

Transmission bevel drive

Integral oil tank

Combustion chamber

High-pressure compressor

High-pressure turbine

Fuel manifold

Fuel nozzle

Centrifugal compressor

Temperature and pressure sensor

Low-pressure fan

Inlet cone (rotating spinner)

Pressure line

Fan case with special structure to contain broken fan

Electronic engine control and airframe interface connector

Electronic engine control (EEC) unit

Compressor front bearing

Engine front mount

Electrical wiring harness

Fuel and oil heat exchanger

Oil filter

Fan duct

Compressor air-bleed connection

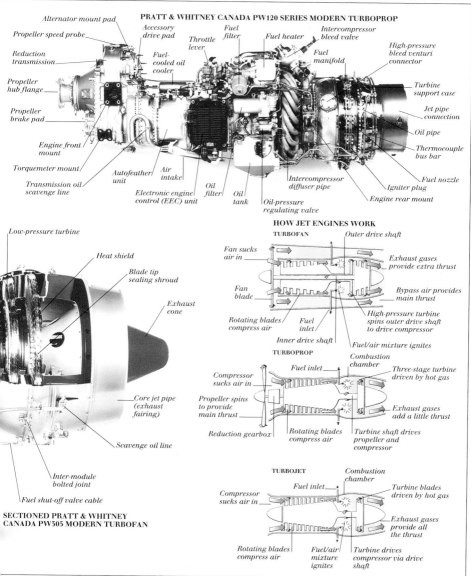

PRATT & WHITNEY CANADA PW120 SERIES MODERN TURBOPROP

Alternator mount pad

Propeller speed probe

Accessory drive pad

Throttle lever

Fuel filter

Fuel heater

Intercompressor bleed valve

High-pressure bleed venturi connector

Reduction transmission

Fuel-cooled oil cooler

Fuel manifold

Turbine support case

Propeller hub flange

Jet pipe connection

Oil pipe

Propeller brake pad

Thermocouple bus bar

Engine front mount

Fuel nozzle

Torquemeter mount

Air intake

Intercompressor diffuser pipe

Igniter plug

Engine rear mount

Autofeather unit

Transmission oil scavenge line

Electronic engine control (EEC) unit

Oil filter

Oil tank

Oil-pressure regulating valve

HOW JET ENGINES WORK

TURBOFAN

Fan sucks air in

Outer drive shaft

Exhaust gases provide extra thrust

Fan blade

Bypass air provides main thrust

Rotating blades compress air

Fuel inlet

High-pressure turbine spins outer drive shaft to drive compressor

Inner drive shaft

Fuel/air mixture ignites

TURBOPROP

Fuel inlet

Combustion chamber

Three-stage turbine driven by hot gas

Compressor sucks air in

Propeller spins to provide main thrust

Exhaust gases add a little thrust

Reduction gearbox

Rotating blades compress air

Turbine shaft drives propeller and compressor

TURBOJET

Fuel inlet

Combustion chamber

Turbine blades driven by hot gas

Compressor sucks air in

Exhaust gases provide all the thrust

Rotating blades compress air

Fuel/air mixture ignites

Turbine drives compressor via drive shaft

Low-pressure turbine

Heat shield

Blade tip sealing shroud

Exhaust cone

Core jet pipe (exhaust fairing)

Scavenge oil line

Inter-module bolted joint

Fuel shut-off valve cable

SECTIONED PRATT & WHITNEY CANADA PW305 MODERN TURBOFAN

Modern military aircraft

MODERN MILITARY AIRCRAFT ARE AMONG THE MOST SOPHISTICATED and expensive products of the 20th century. Fighters need computer-operated controls for maneuverability, powerful engines, and effective air-to-air weapons. Most modern fighters also have guided missiles, radar, and passive, infrared sensors. These developments enable today's fighters to engage in combat with adversaries who are outside visual range. Bombers carry a large weapon load and enough fuel for long-range flights. A few military aircraft, such as the Tornado and the F-14 Tomcat, have variable-sweep ("swing") wings. During takeoff and landing their wings are fully extended, but for high-speed flight and low-level attacks the wings are pivoted fully back. A recent development is the "stealth" bomber, which is designed to absorb or deflect enemy radar in order to remain undetected. Earlier bombers, such as the Tornado, use terrain-following radars to fly so close to the ground that they avoid enemy radar detection.

FRONT VIEW OF A PANAVIA TORNADO

Instrument landing system antenna

Birdproof windshield

Air data probe

Port variable-incidence air intake

Wing-root glove fairing

Starboard inboard stores pylon

Taileron

Starboard main landing-gear door

Main landing-gear leg

Laser ranger and marked-target seeker

Starboard nose gear door

Steerable twin-wheel nose gear

Radome containing ground-mapping, attack, and terrain-following radars

Taxiing light

Wing extended for takeoff and landing

Wing pivoted back for high-speed flight

SWING-WING F-14 TOMCAT FIGHTER

SIDE VIEW OF A PANAVIA TORNADO GR1A (RECONNAISSANCE VERSION), 1986

Pilot's cockpit

Navigator's instrument console

Navigator's cockpit

Single canopy over both cockpits

Engine air intake

Navigation light

Flat, birdproof windshield

High-velocity air duct to disperse rain

Upper "request identification" antenna

Air data probe

RESCUE

Radome containing ground-mapping, attack, and terrain-following radars

UHF antenna

Angle-of-attack probe

Tacan (tactical air navigation) antenna

Emergency canopy release handle

Nose gear door

Steerable nose gear leg

Pitot head

Twin nose-wheel

Hinged auxiliary air intake

Cold-air intake (ram scoop)

Heat exchanger exhaust duct

Window covering infrared reconnaissance camera

NORTHROP B-2 ("STEALTH" BOMBER), 1989

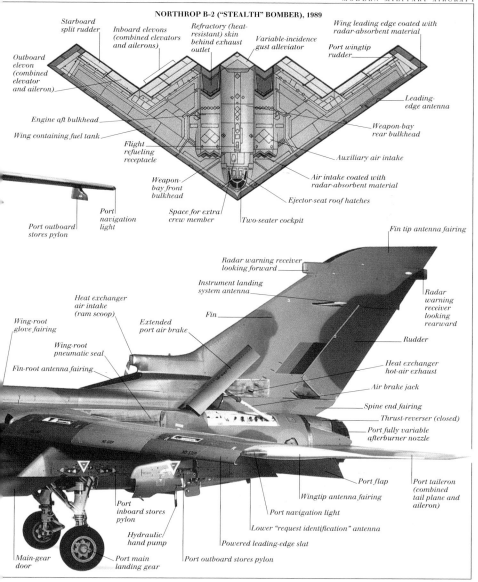

Starboard split rudder

Inboard elevons (combined elevators and ailerons)

Refractory (heat-resistant) skin behind exhaust outlet

Variable-incidence gust alleviator

Wing leading edge coated with radar-absorbent material

Port wingtip rudder

Outboard elevon (combined elevator and aileron)

Leading-edge antenna

Engine aft bulkhead

Wing containing fuel tank

Flight refueling receptacle

Weapon-bay rear bulkhead

Auxiliary air intake

Weapon-bay front bulkhead

Air intake coated with radar-absorbent material

Port outboard stores pylon

Port navigation light

Space for extra crew member

Ejector-seat roof hatches

Two-seater cockpit

Fin tip antenna fairing

Radar warning receiver looking forward

Instrument landing system antenna

Fin

Extended port air brake

Radar warning receiver looking rearward

Rudder

Heat exchanger air intake (ram scoop)

Wing-root glove fairing

Wing-root pneumatic seal

Fin-root antenna fairing

Heat exchanger hot-air exhaust

Air brake jack

Spine end fairing

Thrust-reverser (closed)

Port fully variable afterburner nozzle

Port flap

Port taileron (combined tail plane and aileron)

Wingtip antenna fairing

Port navigation light

Lower "request identification" antenna

Powered leading-edge slat

Port inboard stores pylon

Hydraulic/hand pump

Port outboard stores pylon

Main-gear door

Port main landing gear

Helicopters

HELICOPTERS USE ROTATING BLADES for lift, propulsion, and steering. The first machine to achieve sustained, controlled flight using rotating blades was the autogiro built in the 1920s by Juan de la Cierva of Spain. His machine had unpowered blades above the fuselage that relied on the flow of air to rotate them and provide lift while the autogiro was driven forward by a conventional propeller. Then, in 1939, the Russian-born American Igor Sikorsky produced his VS-300, the forerunner of the modern helicopter. Its engine-driven blades provided lift, propulsion, and steering. It could take off vertically, hover, and fly in any direction, and had a tail rotor to prevent the helicopter body from spinning. The introduction of gas turbine jet engines to helicopters in 1955 produced quieter, safer, and more powerful machines. Because of their versatility in flight, helicopters are used today for many purposes, including crop spraying, traffic surveillance, and transporting crews to deep-sea oil rigs, as well as acting as gunships, air ambulances, and air taxis.

BELL 47G-3B1

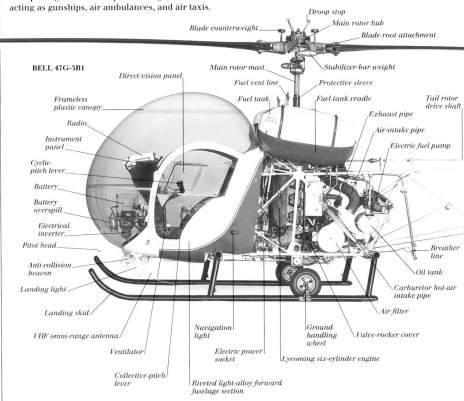

Droop stop
Blade counterweight
Main rotor hub
Blade-root attachment

BELL 47G-3B1

Direct-vision panel
Main rotor mast
Stabilizer-bar weight
Fuel vent line
Protective sleeve
Frameless plastic canopy
Fuel tank
Fuel-tank cradle
Tail rotor drive shaft
Radio
Exhaust pipe
Air-intake pipe
Instrument panel
Electric fuel pump
Cyclic-pitch lever
Battery
Battery overspill
Electrical inverter
Pitot head
Breather line
Anti-collision beacon
Oil tank
Landing light
Carburetor hot-air intake pipe
Landing skid
Air filter
VHF omni-range antenna
Navigation light
Ground-handling wheel
Valve-rocker cover
Ventilator
Electric power socket
Lycoming six-cylinder engine
Collective-pitch lever
Riveted light-alloy forward fuselage section

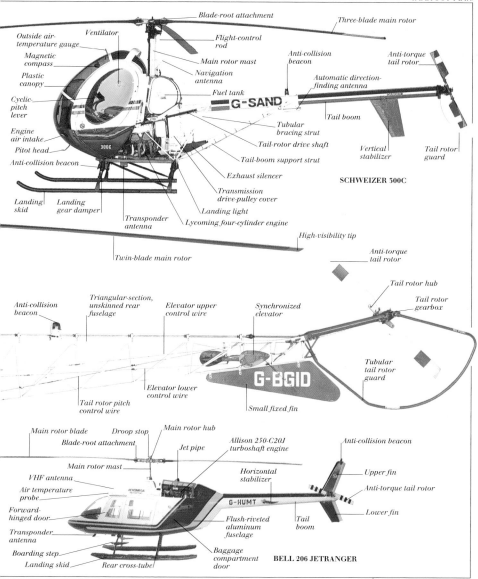

Blade-root attachment

Three-blade main rotor

Outside air-temperature gauge

Ventilator

Flight-control rod

Anti-collision beacon

Anti-torque tail rotor

Magnetic compass

Main rotor mast

Plastic canopy

Navigation antenna

Automatic direction-finding antenna

Fuel tank

Cyclic-pitch lever

G-SAND

Tail boom

Engine air intake

Tubular bracing strut

Pitot head

Tail-rotor drive shaft

300C

Vertical stabilizer

Tail rotor guard

Anti-collision beacon

Tail-boom support strut

Exhaust silencer

SCHWEIZER 300C

Landing skid

Landing gear damper

Transmission drive-pulley cover

Transponder antenna

Landing light

Lycoming four-cylinder engine

High-visibility tip

Twin-blade main rotor

Anti-torque tail rotor

Tail rotor hub

Tail rotor gearbox

Anti-collision beacon

Triangular-section, unskinned rear fuselage

Elevator upper control wire

Synchronized elevator

G-BGID

Tubular tail rotor guard

Elevator lower control wire

Tail rotor pitch control wire

Small fixed fin

Main rotor blade

Droop stop

Main rotor hub

Allison 250-C20J turboshaft engine

Anti-collision beacon

Blade-root attachment

Jet pipe

Main rotor mast

Horizontal stabilizer

Upper fin

VHF antenna

Anti-torque tail rotor

Air temperature probe

G-HUMT

Forward-hinged door

Flush-riveted aluminum fuselage

Lower fin

Transponder antenna

Tail boom

Boarding step

Baggage compartment door

Landing skid

Rear cross-tube

BELL 206 JETRANGER

423

Light aircraft

LIGHT AIRCRAFT, SUCH AS THE ARV SUPER 2 shown here, are small, lightweight, and of simple construction. More than a million have been built since World War I, mainly for recreational use by private owners. Virtually all light aircraft have piston engines, most of which are air-cooled, although some are liquid-cooled. Open cockpits, almost universal in the 1920s, have now been replaced by enclosed cabins. The cabins of high-wing aircraft have one or two doors, while those of low-wing aircraft usually have a sliding or hinged canopy. Most modern light aircraft are made of aluminum alloy, although some are made of wood or of fiber-reinforced materials. Light aircraft today also usually have navigational instruments, an electrical system, cabin heating, wheel brakes, and a two-way radio.

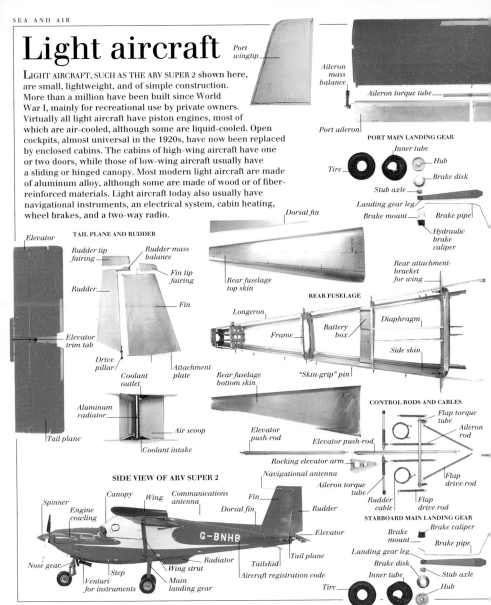

Port wingtip

Aileron mass balance

Aileron torque tube

Port aileron

PORT MAIN LANDING GEAR

Inner tube
Hub
Tire
Brake disk
Stub axle
Landing gear leg
Brake mount
Brake pipe
Hydraulic brake caliper
Rear attachment-bracket for wing

Dorsal fin

TAIL PLANE AND RUDDER

Elevator
Rudder tip fairing
Rudder mass balance
Fin tip fairing
Rudder
Fin
Elevator trim tab
Drive pillar
Coolant outlet
Attachment plate
Aluminum radiator
Air scoop
Tail plane
Coolant intake

Rear fuselage top skin

REAR FUSELAGE

Longeron
Battery box
Diaphragm
Frame
Side skin
Rear fuselage bottom skin
"Skin-grip" pin

Elevator push-rod
Elevator push-rod
Rocking elevator arm

CONTROL RODS AND CABLES

Flap torque tube
Aileron rod
Aileron torque tube
Rudder cable
Flap drive-rod
Flap drive-rod

SIDE VIEW OF ARV SUPER 2

Spinner
Engine cowling
Canopy
Wing
Communications antenna
Navigational antenna
Aileron torque tube
Fin
Dorsal fin
Rudder
Elevator
Nose gear
Step
Venturi for instruments
Radiator
Wing strut
Main landing gear
Tailskid
Tail plane
Aircraft registration code

G-BNHB

STARBOARD MAIN LANDING GEAR

Brake caliper
Brake mount
Brake pipe
Landing gear leg
Brake disk
Inner tube
Stub axle
Tire
Hub

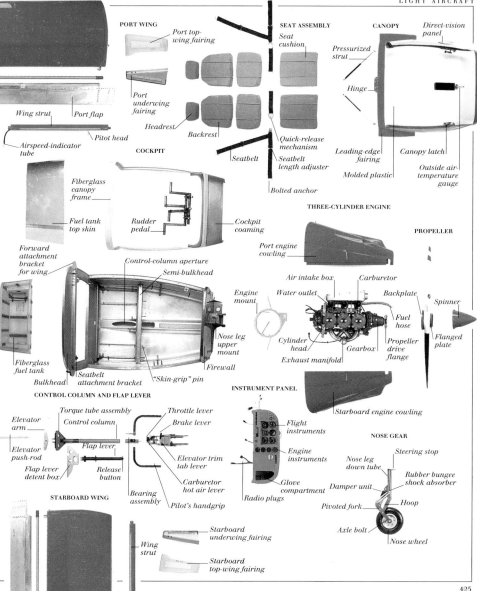

PORT WING

Port top-wing fairing

Port underwing fairing

Headrest

Wing strut

Port flap

Pitot head

Airspeed-indicator tube

SEAT ASSEMBLY

Seat cushion

Backrest

Seatbelt

Quick-release mechanism

Seatbelt length adjuster

Bolted anchor

CANOPY

Direct-vision panel

Pressurized strut

Hinge

Leading-edge fairing

Molded plastic

Canopy latch

Outside air-temperature gauge

COCKPIT

Fiberglass canopy frame

Fuel tank top skin

Rudder pedal

Cockpit coaming

Forward attachment bracket for wing

Control-column aperture

Semi-bulkhead

Engine mount

Nose leg upper mount

Fiberglass fuel tank

Bulkhead

Seatbelt attachment bracket

"Skin-grip" pin

Firewall

THREE-CYLINDER ENGINE

Port engine cowling

Air intake box

Carburetor

Water outlet

Backplate

Fuel hose

Cylinder head

Gearbox

Propeller drive flange

Exhaust manifold

PROPELLER

Spinner

Flanged plate

Starboard engine cowling

CONTROL COLUMN AND FLAP LEVER

Elevator arm

Torque tube assembly

Control column

Flap lever

Elevator push-rod

Flap lever detent box

Release button

Throttle lever

Brake lever

Elevator trim tab lever

Carburetor hot air lever

Bearing assembly

Pilot's handgrip

INSTRUMENT PANEL

Flight instruments

Engine instruments

Glove compartment

Radio plugs

NOSE GEAR

Steering stop

Nose leg down tube

Rubber bungee shock absorber

Damper unit

Hoop

Pivoted fork

Axle bolt

Nose wheel

STARBOARD WING

Wing strut

Starboard underwing fairing

Starboard top-wing fairing

Gliders, hang gliders, and ultralights

Grommet for front pylon strut

Instrument panel

MODERN GLIDERS ARE AMONG the most graceful and aerodynamically efficient of all aircraft. Unpowered but with a large wingspan (up to about 82 ft, or 25 m), gliders use currents of hot, rising air (thermals) to stay aloft, and a rudder, elevators, and ailerons for control. Modern gliders have achieved flights of more than 900 miles (1,450 km) and altitudes above 49,000 ft (15,000 m). Hang gliders consist of a simple frame across which rigid or flexible material is stretched to form the wings. The pilot is suspended below the wings in a harness or body bag and, gripping a triangular A-frame, steers by shifting weight from side to side. Like gliders, hang gliders rely on thermals for lift. Ultralights are basically powered hang gliders. A small engine and an open fiberglass car (trike), which can hold a crew of two, are suspended beneath a stronger version of a hang glider frame; the frame may have rigid or flexible wings. Ultralight pilots, like hang glider pilots, steer by shifting their weight against an A-frame. Ultralights can reach speeds of up to 100 mph (160 kph).

HANG GLIDER

King post

Apex

PEGASUS XL SE ULTRALIGHT

Stiffening rib

Center-line beam

Main suspension

Rear-mounted propeller (pusher propeller)

Fuel tank

Wheel part

Apex wire

Nose shell

Nose gear mount

Main wheel

Trike nacelle

Fixed nose wheel

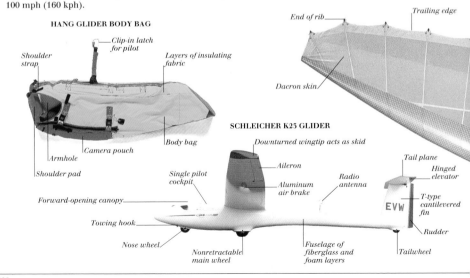

HANG GLIDER BODY BAG

Clip-in latch for pilot

Shoulder strap

Layers of insulating fabric

Camera pouch

Armhole

Shoulder pad

Body bag

End of rib

Trailing edge

Dacron skin

SCHLEICHER K23 GLIDER

Downturned wingtip acts as skid

Single pilot cockpit

Aileron

Aluminum air brake

Radio antenna

Tail plane

Hinged elevator

Forward-opening canopy

Towing hook

Nose wheel

Nonretractable main wheel

Fuselage of fiberglass and foam layers

T-type cantilevered fin

Rudder

Tailwheel

EVW

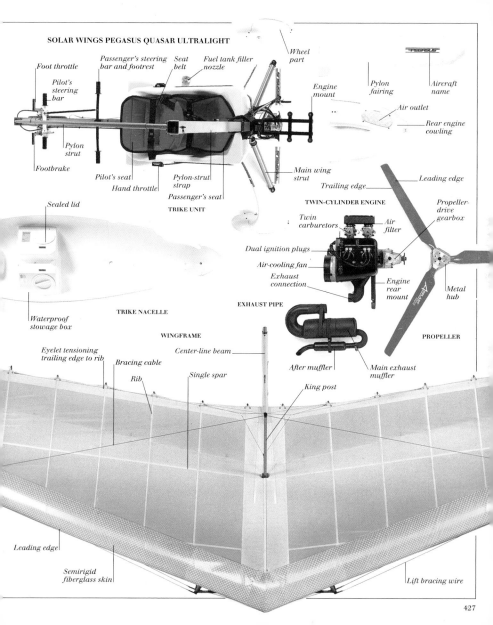

SOLAR WINGS PEGASUS QUASAR ULTRALIGHT

Foot throttle

Pilot's steering bar

Passenger's steering bar and footrest

Seat belt

Fuel tank filler nozzle

Wheel part

Engine mount

Pylon fairing

Aircraft name

Air outlet

Rear engine cowling

Pylon strut

Footbrake

Pilot's seat

Hand throttle

Pylon-strut strap

Passenger's seat

Main wing strut

Trailing edge

Leading edge

Propeller-drive gearbox

TRIKE UNIT

TWIN-CYLINDER ENGINE

Twin carburetors

Air filter

Dual ignition plugs

Air-cooling fan

Exhaust connection

Engine rear mount

Metal hub

PROPELLER

Sealed lid

Waterproof stowage box

TRIKE NACELLE

EXHAUST PIPE

WINGFRAME

Eyelet tensioning trailing edge to rib

Bracing cable

Rib

Center-line beam

Single spar

King post

After muffler

Main exhaust muffler

Leading edge

Semirigid fiberglass skin

Lift bracing wire

427

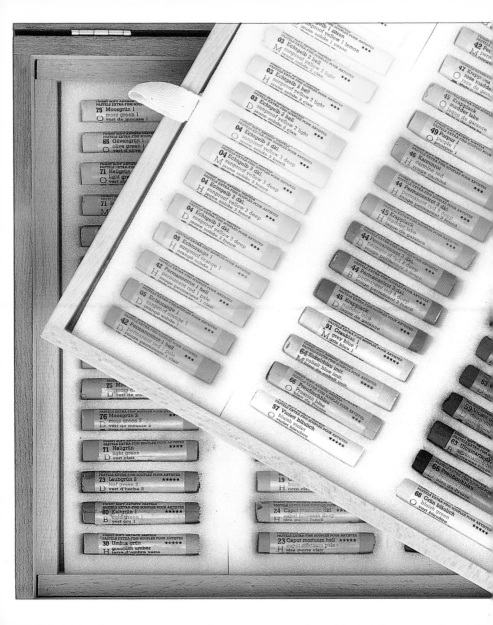

THE
VISUAL ARTS

Drawing

DRAWINGS CAN BE FINISHED WORKS OF ART, or preparatory studies for paintings and other visual arts. They can be made using a wide variety of drawing instruments such as pencils, graphite sticks, chalks, charcoal, pens and inks, and silver wires. The most common drawing instrument is the graphite pencil. A graphite pencil consists of a thin rod of graphite mixed with clay, encased in wood. Charcoal is one of the oldest drawing instruments. It is produced by firing twigs of willow, vine, or other woods at high temperatures in airtight containers. Erasers can be used to rub out marks made by drawing materials such as graphite pencils or charcoal, or to achieve a particular effect—such as smudging. Fixative is often applied—using a mouth diffuser or aerosol spray fixative—to prevent smudging once a drawing is finished. Silver lines can be produced by drawing silver wire across specially prepared paper— a technique known as silverpoint. The lines are permanent and cannot be erased. In time the silver lines oxidize and turn brown.

FIXATIVE AND MOUTH DIFFUSER

Hinge

Liquid fixative consisting of dissolved resin

Fixative is sucked into tube and sprayed onto drawing

CHALK, CRAYON, AND CHARCOAL

Calcite (calcium carbonate) mixed with pigment

BLUE CHALK

Iron oxide mixed with chalk

SANGUINE CRAYON

Carbonized wood

WILLOW CHARCOAL

ERASERS

Hard texture

Medium-soft, light line

PLASTIC ERASER

Soft texture

Very soft, dark line

KNEADED ERASER

DRAWING INSTRUMENTS

2B GRAPHITE PENCIL

8B GRAPHITE PENCIL

SILVER WIRE IN A METAL HOLDER

DRAWING BOARD

Drawing board

Paper

Drawing clip

DRAWING MATERIALS

Graphite stick

Colored pencil

Binder clip

Dip pen

Pencil sharpener

Sketch book

Ink bottle

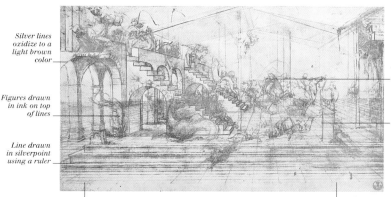

Silver lines
oxidize to a
light brown
color

Figures drawn
in ink on top
of lines

Line drawn
in silverpoint
using a ruler

Vanishing
point located
on head of
man riding
rearing horse

Lines of
squared
pavement slabs
recede toward
a single
vanishing
point

Complex perspective
drawing done as a
preparatory study
for a painting

Paper prepared
with size (glue)
and pigment

EXAMPLE OF A SILVERPOINT DRAWING
The Adoration of the Magi, Leonardo da Vinci, 1481
Pen and ink over silverpoint on paper
6½ x 11½ in (16.5 x 29.2 cm)

Handmade, tinted
paper

One of a series
of drawings
recording
London during
1944–1945

Charcoal lines
softened by
rubbing and
smudging

Charcoal
gives strong,
expressive lines

Broad charcoal
mark

Lines rapidly
drawn on site

EXAMPLE OF A CHARCOAL DRAWING
St. Paul's and the River, David Bomberg, 1945
Charcoal on paper
20 x 25⅛ in (50.8 x 65.8 cm)

Tempera

ILLUMINATED MANUSCRIPT

THE TERM TEMPERA is applied to any paint in which pigment is tempered (mixed) with a water-based binding medium—usually egg yolk. Egg tempera is applied to a smooth surface such as vellum (for illuminated manuscripts) or more commonly to hardwood panels prepared with gesso—a mixture of chalk and size (glue). Bristle brushes are used to apply the gesso. A layer of gesso grosso (coarse gesso) is followed by successive layers of gesso sotile (fine gesso) that are sanded between coats to provide a smooth, yet absorbent ground. The paint is applied with fine sable brushes in thin layers, using light brushstrokes. Tempera dries quickly to form a tough skin with a satin sheen. The luminous white surface of the gesso combined with the overlaid paint produces the brilliant crispness and rich colors particular to this medium. Egg tempera paintings are frequently gilded with gold. Leaves of finely beaten gold are applied to a bole (reddish-brown clay) base and polished by burnishing.

MATERIALS FOR GILDING

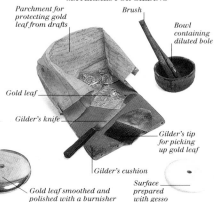

Parchment for protecting gold leaf from drafts

Brush

Bowl containing diluted bole

Gold leaf

Gilder's knife

Gilder's tip for picking up gold leaf

Gilder's cushion

Gold leaf smoothed and polished with a burnisher

Surface prepared with gesso

Gold leaf applied in overlapping layers

Bole brushed onto gesso

Burnisher

Agate tip

MATERIALS FOR TEMPERA PANEL PAINTING

Yolk

EGG

White

SIZE (GLUE)

GESSO

MORTAR AND PESTLE

Mortar

Lip

Pestle for crushing and grinding pigments

EGG YOLK BINDING MEDIUM

EXAMPLES OF BRUSHES

FLAT BRISTLE BRUSH

SABLE BRUSH NO. 6

SABLE BRUSH NO. 1

EXAMPLE OF A TEMPERA PAINTING
Presentation in the Temple, Ambrogio Lorenzetti, 1342
Tempera on wood, 8 ft 5⅛ in x 5 ft 6⅛ in (257 x 168 cm)

Altarpiece commissioned for Siena Cathedral, Italy

Textured gold ornament made by punching motifs into the gilded surface

The red tinge of the bole is just visible beneath the gold

Edge of a sheet of gold leaf

Crisp edge characteristic of tempera painting

Vine black used to create the dim cathedral interior

Highlights on the beard made by applying thin layers of white over dried paint

Red drapery painted in vermilion

Raised right hand and pointing finger is the gesture of prophecy

Receding floor tiles create the impression of depth

Patch of discolored varnish, left from last cleaning

VERDACCIO

**VERMILION AND
LEAD WHITE**

VERMILION

**RED EARTH
(IRON OXIDE)**

EXAMPLES OF PIGMENTS

MALACHITE

 **ULTRAMARINE
LAPIS LAZULI**

Warm flesh tones achieved by layering vermilion and white over an undercoat of verdaccio

Patterned gold halo glitters in candlelight

Ultramarine lapis lazuli, as costly as gold, was reserved for significant figures such as the Virgin Mary

Craquelure (pattern of cracks in the paint)

VINE BLACK

LEAD TIN YELLOW

**DETAIL FROM "PRESENTATION
IN THE TEMPLE"**

Fresco

FRESCO IS A METHOD OF WALL PAINTING. In buon fresco (true fresco), pigments are mixed with water and applied to an intonaco (layer of fresh, damp lime-plaster). The intonaco absorbs and binds the pigments as it dries making the picture a permanent part of the wall surface. The intonaco is applied in sections called giornate (daily sections). The size of each giornata depends on the artist's estimate of how much can be painted before the plaster sets. The junctions between giornate are sometimes visible on a finished fresco. The range of colors used in buon fresco are limited to lime-resistant pigments such as earth colors (below). Slaked lime (burnt lime mixed with water), bianco di San Giovanni (slaked lime that has been partly exposed to air), and chalk can be used to produce fresco whites. In fresco secco (dry fresco), pigments are mixed with a binding medium and applied to dry plaster. The pigments are not completely absorbed into the plaster and may flake off over time.

CROSS-SECTION SHOWING FRESCO LAYERS

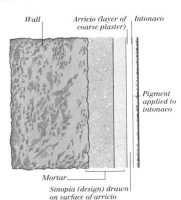

Wall

Arricio (layer of coarse plaster)

Intonaco

Pigment applied to intonaco

Mortar

Sinopia (design) drawn on surface of arricio

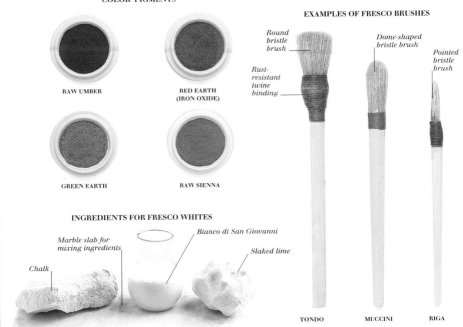

EXAMPLES OF EARTH COLOR PIGMENTS

RAW UMBER

RED EARTH (IRON OXIDE)

GREEN EARTH

RAW SIENNA

EXAMPLES OF FRESCO BRUSHES

Round bristle brush

Rust-resistant twine binding

Dome-shaped bristle brush

Pointed bristle brush

INGREDIENTS FOR FRESCO WHITES

Marble slab for mixing ingredients

Bianco di San Giovanni

Slaked lime

Chalk

TONDO

MUCCINI

RIGA

EXAMPLE OF A FRESCO
The Expulsion of the Merchants from the Temple, Giotto, c.1306
Fresco, 78 x 72 in (200 x 185 cm)

One of a series
of frescoes in the
Arena Chapel,
Padua, Italy

Temple acts as
a backdrop for
the action

Bianco di San
Giovanni often
used for fresco
whites

Patches of azurite
blue have turned
green due to
reaction with
carbon dioxide

Gold leaf applied
to apostle's halo

Green earth
pigment applied
to robe

Child painted
on top of
apostle's robe

Hairline junction
between giornate
is visible

Red earth
pigment applied
in buon fresco
has retained
rich hue

Azurite blue applied in fresco secco has
flaked off to reveal the plaster beneath

Dry, matt surface characteristic
of buon fresco

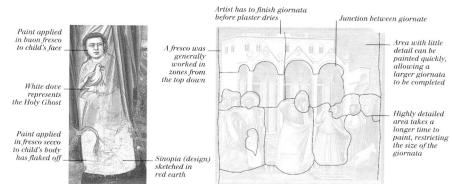

Paint applied
in buon fresco
to child's face

White dove
represents
the Holy Ghost

Paint applied
in fresco secco
to child's body
has flaked off

A fresco was
generally
worked in
zones from
the top down

Sinopia (design)
sketched in
red earth

Artist has to finish giornata
before plaster dries

Junction between giornate

Area with little
detail can be
painted quickly,
allowing a
larger giornata
to be completed

Highly detailed
area takes a
longer time to
paint, restricting
the size of the
giornata

**DETAIL FROM "THE
EXPULSION"**

GIORNATE (DAILY SECTIONS) IN "THE EXPULSION"

Oils

OIL PAINTS ARE MADE BY MIXING and grinding pigment with a drying vegetable oil such as linseed oil. The paint can be applied to many different surfaces and textures—the most common being canvas. Before painting, the canvas is stretched on a wooden frame and its surface is prepared with layers of size (glue) and primer. The two main types of brushes used in oil painting are stiff hog hair bristle brushes—generally used for covering large areas; and soft hair brushes made from sable or synthetic material—generally used for fine detail. Other tools, including painting knives, can also be used to achieve different effects. Oil paint can be applied thickly (a technique known as impasto), or can be thinned down using a solvent such as turpentine. Varnishes are sometimes applied to finished paintings to protect their surface and to give them a matt or gloss finish.

KIDNEY-
SHAPED
PALETTE

**DAMMAR RESIN
VARNISH**

*Crystals are
dissolved and
applied to
painting to
protect its
surface*

**COMMERCIAL
OIL PAINTS**

CADMIUM
RED

*Lightfast
opaque
color*

ULTRAMARINE

*Transparent
color*

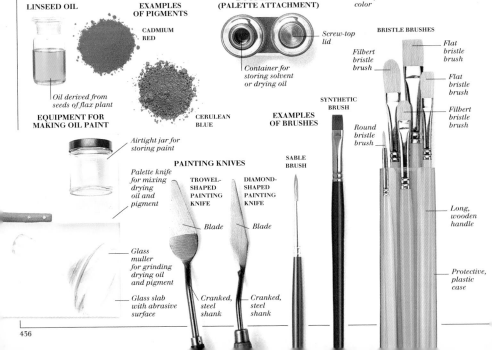

LINSEED OIL

*Oil derived from
seeds of flax plant*

**EQUIPMENT FOR
MAKING OIL PAINT**

**EXAMPLES
OF PIGMENTS**

CADMIUM
RED

CERULEAN
BLUE

*Airtight jar for
storing paint*

*Palette knife
for mixing
drying
oil and
pigment*

*Glass
muller
for grinding
drying oil
and pigment*

*Glass slab
with abrasive
surface*

**DOUBLE DIPPER
(PALETTE ATTACHMENT)**

*Screw-top
lid*

*Container for
storing solvent
or drying oil*

PAINTING KNIVES

**TROWEL-
SHAPED
PAINTING
KNIFE**

Blade

*Cranked,
steel
shank*

**DIAMOND-
SHAPED
PAINTING
KNIFE**

Blade

*Cranked,
steel
shank*

**EXAMPLES
OF BRUSHES**

**SABLE
BRUSH**

**SYNTHETIC
BRUSH**

*Round
bristle
brush*

BRISTLE BRUSHES

*Filbert
bristle
brush*

*Flat
bristle
brush*

*Flat
bristle
brush*

*Filbert
bristle
brush*

*Long,
wooden
handle*

*Protective,
plastic
case*

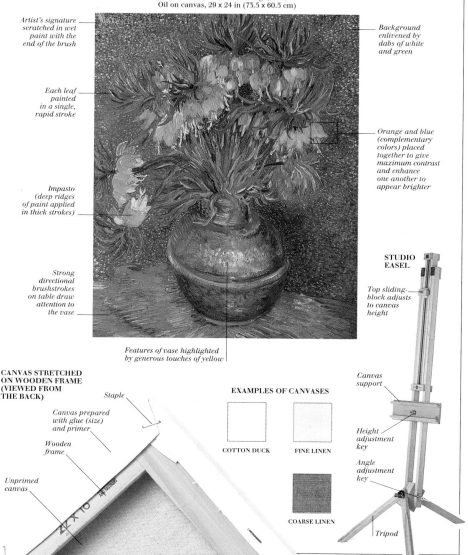

EXAMPLE OF AN OIL PAINTING
Fritillarias, Vincent van Gogh, 1886
Oil on canvas, 29 x 24 in (73.5 x 60.5 cm)

Artist's signature scratched in wet paint with the end of the brush

Background enlivened by dabs of white and green

Each leaf painted in a single, rapid stroke

Orange and blue (complementary colors) placed together to give maximum contrast and enhance one another to appear brighter

Impasto (deep ridges of paint applied in thick strokes)

Strong directional brushstrokes on table draw attention to the vase

Features of vase highlighted by generous touches of yellow

STUDIO EASEL

Top sliding-block adjusts to canvas height

Canvas support

Height adjustment key

Angle adjustment key

Tripod

CANVAS STRETCHED ON WOODEN FRAME (VIEWED FROM THE BACK)

Staple

Canvas prepared with glue (size) and primer

Wooden frame

Unprimed canvas

EXAMPLES OF CANVASES

COTTON DUCK

FINE LINEN

COARSE LINEN

Watercolor

GUM ARABIC

WATERCOLOR PAINT IS MADE OF GROUND PIGMENT mixed with a water-soluble binding medium, usually gum arabic. It is usually applied to paper using soft hair brushes such as sable, goat hair, squirrel, and synthetic brushes. Watercolors are often diluted and applied as overlaying washes (thin, transparent layers) to build up depth of color. Washes can be laid in a variety of ways to create a range of different effects. For example, a wet-in-wet wash can be achieved by laying a wash on top of another wet wash. The two washes blend together to give a fused effect. Sponges are used to modify washes by soaking up paint so that areas of pigment are lightened or removed from the paper. Watercolors can also be applied undiluted—a technique known as dry brush—to create a broken-color effect. Watercolors are generally transparent and allow light to reflect from the surface of the paper through the layers of paint to give a luminous effect. They can be thickened and made opaque by adding body color (Chinese white).

Natural sap from acacia tree

NATURAL SPONGE

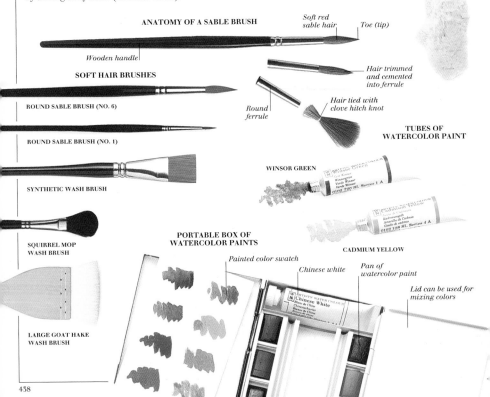

ANATOMY OF A SABLE BRUSH

Soft red sable hair　*Toe (tip)*

Wooden handle

SOFT HAIR BRUSHES

Hair trimmed and cemented into ferrule

ROUND SABLE BRUSH (NO. 6)

Round ferrule　*Hair tied with clove hitch knot*

ROUND SABLE BRUSH (NO. 1)

TUBES OF WATERCOLOR PAINT

SYNTHETIC WASH BRUSH

WINSOR GREEN

SQUIRREL MOP WASH BRUSH

PORTABLE BOX OF WATERCOLOR PAINTS

CADMIUM YELLOW

Painted color swatch

Chinese white　*Pan of watercolor paint*

Lid can be used for mixing colors

LARGE GOAT HAKE WASH BRUSH

EXAMPLE OF A WATERCOLOR
Burning of the Houses of Parliament, Turner, 1834
Watercolor on paper, 11½ x 17½ in (29.2 x 44.5 cm)

Transparent washes laid on top of each other to create tonal depth

Transparent washes allow light to reflect off the surface of the paper to give a luminous effect

Highlight scratched out with a scalpel

Paper shows through thin wash to give flames added highlight

Crowd painted with thin strokes laid over a pale wash

Undiluted paint applied, then partly washed out, to create the impression of water

EXAMPLES OF WATERCOLOR PAPERS

SMOOTH-TEXTURED PAPER

MEDIUM-TEXTURED PAPER

ROUGH-TEXTURED PAPER

EXAMPLES OF WASHES

WASH OVER DRY BRUSH
Wash laid over paint applied with dry brush gives two-tone effect

GRADED WASH
Strong wash applied to tilted paper gives graded effect

DRY BRUSH
Undiluted paint dragged across surface of paper gives broken effect

WET-IN-WET
Two diluted washes left to run together to give fused effect

COLOR WHEEL OF WATERCOLOR PAINTS

Yellow (primary color)

Secondary colors made by mixing yellow and blue

Secondary colors made by mixing red and yellow

Blue (primary color)

Red (primary color)

Secondary colors made by mixing blue and red

Pastels

PASTELS ARE STICKS OF PIGMENT made by mixing ground pigment with chalk and a binding medium, such as gum arabic. They vary in hardness depending on the proportion of the binding medium to the chalk. Soft pastel—the most common form of pastel—contains just enough binding medium to hold the pigment in stick form. Pastels can be applied directly to any support (surface) with sufficient tooth (texture). When a pastel is drawn over a textured surface, the pigment crumbles and lodges in the fibers of the support. Pastel marks have a particular soft, matt quality and are suitable for techniques such as blending, scumbling, and feathering. Blending is a technique of rubbing and fusing two or more colors on the support using fingers or various tools such as tortillons (paper stumps), soft hair brushes, kneaded erasers, and soft bread. Scumbling is a technique of building up layers of pastel colors. The side or blunted tip of a soft pastel is lightly drawn over an underpainted area so that patches of the color beneath show through. Feathering is a technique of applying parallel strokes of color with the point of a pastel, usually over an existing layer of pastel color. A thin spray of fixative can be applied—using a mouth diffuser (see pp. 430-431) or aerosol spray fixative—to a finished pastel painting, or in between layers of color, to prevent smudging.

EQUIPMENT FOR MAKING PASTELS

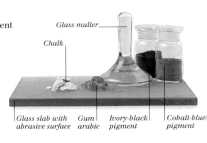

Glass muller

Chalk

Glass slab with abrasive surface | Gum arabic | Ivory-black pigment | Cobalt-blue pigment

EXAMPLES OF SOFT PASTELS

COBALT-BLUE HALF PASTEL

VERMILION HALF PASTEL

OLIVE-GREEN FULL PASTEL

MAUVE FULL PASTEL

EQUIPMENT USED WITH PASTELS

BOXED PASTEL SET

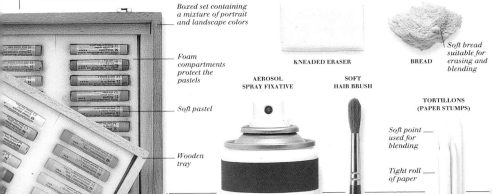

Boxed set containing a mixture of portrait and landscape colors

Foam compartments protect the pastels

Soft pastel

Wooden tray

KNEADED ERASER

AEROSOL SPRAY FIXATIVE

SOFT HAIR BRUSH

BREAD

Soft bread suitable for erasing and blending

TORTILLONS (PAPER STUMPS)

Soft point used for blending

Tight roll of paper

EXAMPLE OF A PASTEL PAINTING
Woman Drying her Neck, Edgar Degas, c.1898
Pastel on cardboard, 24½ x 25½ in (62.5 x 65.5 cm)

Pastels applied directly to support

Rich color of fabric created by overlaying yellows and oranges

Broken colors, characteristic of scumbling technique

Colors are blended together using fingers or tools such as tortillons

Built up layers of pastel

Toned color of paper visible beneath thinly applied pastels

Pure bright colors laid side by side produce strong contrasts

DETAIL FROM "WOMAN DRYING HER NECK"

Feathering technique used to produce skin tones

EXAMPLES OF TEXTURED PAPERS AND PASTEL BOARDS

WATERCOLOR PAPER (ROUGH TEXTURE)

GLASS PAPER

WATERCOLOR PAPER (MEDIUM TEXTURE)

INGRES PAPER

FLOCKED PASTEL BOARD

CANSON PAPER

EXAMPLES OF COLORED AND TINTED PAPERS

Acrylics

ACRYLIC PAINT IS MADE BY MIXING PIGMENT with a synthetic
resin. It can be thinned with water but dries to become water
insoluble. Acrylics are applied to many surfaces, such as
paper and acrylic-primed board and canvas. A variety of
brushes, painting knives, rollers, air-brushes, plastic
scrapers, and other tools are used in acrylic painting.
The versatility of acrylics makes them suitable for a wide
range of techniques. They can be used opaquely or—by
adding water—in a transparent, watercolor style. Acrylic
mediums can be added to the paint to adjust its consistency
for special effects such as glazing and impasto (ridges of paint
applied in thick strokes) or to make it more matt or glossy.
Acrylics are quick-drying, which allows layers of paint to be
applied on top of each other almost immediately.

EXAMPLES OF BRUSHES

Sable brush

Bristle sash brush

Synthetic bristle brush

Synthetic sable brush

Bristle brush

Goat hair brush

Synthetic wash brush

Ox hair brush

EXAMPLES OF PAINTS USED IN ACRYLICS

Azo yellow

Phthalo green

Cerulean blue

Phthalo blue

Quinacridone red

Titanium white

Pad of disposable paper palettes

Yellow ochre

Burnt umber

Burnt sienna

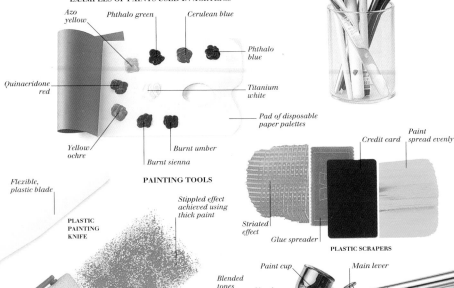

Credit card

Paint spread evenly

Flexible, plastic blade

PLASTIC PAINTING KNIFE

PAINTING TOOLS

Stippled effect achieved using thick paint

Striated effect

Glue spreader

PLASTIC SCRAPERS

Plastic handle

SPONGE ROLLER

Blended tones

Paint cup

Nozzle

Main lever

AIR-BRUSH

Uniform tone

Air hose

EXAMPLE OF AN ACRYLIC PAINTING
A Bigger Splash, David Hockney, 1967
Acrylic on canvas, 95½ x 96 in (242.5 x 243.8 cm)

Paint applied evenly using a roller

Cotton duck canvas support (surface)

Flatness of rollered areas enhanced by adding gel medium to the paint

Masking tape stuck onto canvas to define main shapes, and paint applied within these areas using a roller

Thin strip of pool edge left unpainted

Splash painted using thicker paint and small brush

Imprecise edge on end of spring board where paint has seeped under masking tape

EXAMPLES OF ACRYLIC PAINTS AND TECHNIQUES

Opaque effect

Extruded (squeezed) effect

Paint applied using painting knife

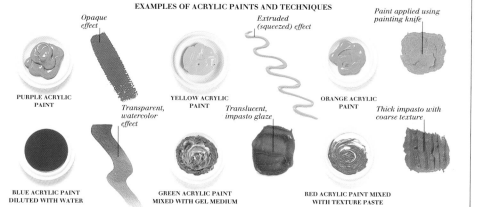

PURPLE ACRYLIC
PAINT

Transparent, watercolor effect

YELLOW ACRYLIC
PAINT

Translucent, impasto glaze

ORANGE ACRYLIC
PAINT

Thick impasto with coarse texture

BLUE ACRYLIC PAINT
DILUTED WITH WATER

GREEN ACRYLIC PAINT
MIXED WITH GEL MEDIUM

RED ACRYLIC PAINT MIXED
WITH TEXTURE PASTE

Calligraphy

CALLIGRAPHY IS BEAUTIFULLY FORMED LETTERING. The term applies to written text and illumination (the decoration of manuscripts using gold leaf and color). The essential materials needed to practice calligraphy are a writing tool, ink, and a writing surface. Quills are among the oldest writing tools. They are usually made from goose or turkey feathers, and are noted for their flexibility and ability to produce fine lines. A quill point, however, is not very durable and constant recutting and trimming is required. The most commonly used writing instrument in western calligraphy is a detachable, metal nib held in a penholder. The metal nib is very durable, and there are a wide range of different types. Particular types of nibs—such as copperplate, speedball, and round-hand nibs—are used for specific styles of lettering. Some nibs have integral ink reservoirs and others have reservoirs that are detachable. Brushes are also used for writing, and for filling in outlined letters and painting decoration. Other writing tools used in calligraphy are fountain pens, felt-tipped pens, rotring pens, and reed pens. Calligraphy inks may come in liquid form, or as a solid ink stick. Ink sticks are ground down in distilled water to form a liquid ink. The most common writing surfaces for calligraphy are good quality, smooth -surfaced papers. To achieve the best writing position, the calligrapher places the paper on a drawing board set at an angle.

EQUIPMENT USED IN BRUSH LETTERING

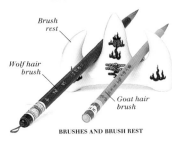

Brush rest

Wolf hair brush

Goat hair brush

BRUSHES AND BRUSH REST

Liquid ink made by grinding down ink stick in distilled water

Solid carbon ink stick

Ink stone

INK STICK AND STONE

PENS, NIBS, AND BRUSHES USED IN CALLIGRAPHY

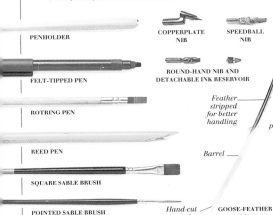

PENHOLDER

COPPERPLATE NIB

SPEEDBALL NIB

FELT-TIPPED PEN

ROUND-HAND NIB AND DETACHABLE INK RESERVOIR

ROTRING PEN

REED PEN

Feather

SQUARE SABLE BRUSH

Feather stripped for better handling

POINTED SABLE BRUSH

Barrel

Hand-cut point

GOOSE-FEATHER QUILL

GOAT HAIR BRUSH

WOLF HAIR BRUSH

FOUNTAIN PEN AND INK

Bottle of permanent black ink

Barrel

Clip

Nib

Outer cap

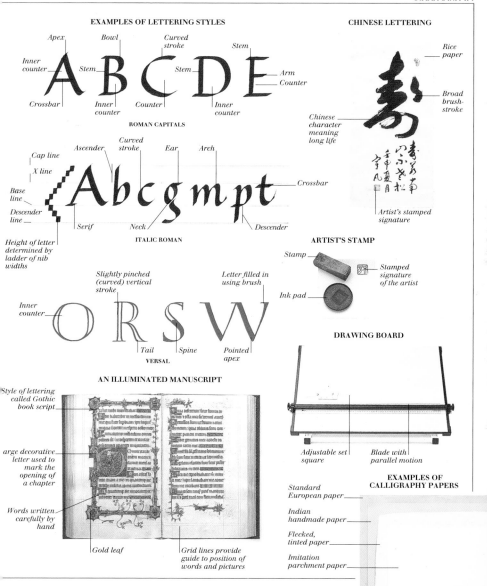

EXAMPLES OF LETTERING STYLES

Apex
Bowl
Curved stroke
Stem
Inner counter
Stem
Stem
Arm
Counter
Crossbar
Inner counter
Counter
Inner counter

ROMAN CAPITALS

Cap line
X line
Ascender
Curved stroke
Ear
Arch
Base line
Descender line
Crossbar
Height of letter determined by ladder of nib widths
Serif
Neck
Descender

ITALIC ROMAN

Slightly pinched (curved) vertical stroke
Letter filled in using brush
Inner counter
Tail
Spine
Pointed apex

VERSAL

AN ILLUMINATED MANUSCRIPT

Style of lettering called Gothic book script
Large decorative letter used to mark the opening of a chapter
Words written carefully by hand
Gold leaf
Grid lines provide guide to position of words and pictures

CHINESE LETTERING

Rice paper
Broad brush-stroke
Chinese character meaning long life
Artist's stamped signature

ARTIST'S STAMP

Stamp
Stamped signature of the artist
Ink pad

DRAWING BOARD

Adjustable set square
Blade with parallel motion

EXAMPLES OF CALLIGRAPHY PAPERS

Standard European paper
Indian handmade paper
Flecked, tinted paper
Imitation parchment paper

Printmaking 1

PRINTS ARE MADE BY FOUR BASIC printing processes – intaglio, lithographic, relief, and screen. In intaglio printing, lines are engraved or etched onto the surface of a metal plate. Lines are engraved using sharp metal tools. They are etched by corroding the metal plate with acid, using acid-resistant ground to protect the areas not to be etched. The plate is then inked and wiped, leaving the grooves filled with ink and the surface clean. Dampened paper is laid over the plate, and both paper and plate are passed through the rollers of an etching press. The pressure of the rollers forces the paper into the grooves, so that it takes up the ink, leaving an impression on the paper. Lithographic printing is based on the antipathy between grease and water. An image is drawn on a surface—usually a stone or metal plate—with a greasy medium, such as tusche (lihographic ink). The greasy drawing is fixed onto the plate by applying an acidic solution, such as gum arabic. The surface is then dampened and rolled with ink. The ink adheres only to the greasy areas and is repelled by the water. Paper is laid on the plate and pressure is applied by means of a press. In relief printing, the non-printing areas of a wood or linoleum block are cut away using gouges, knives, and other tools. The printing areas are left raised in relief and are rolled with ink. Paper is laid on the inked block and pressure is applied by means of a press or by burnishing (rubbing) the back of the paper. The most common forms of relief printing are woodcut, wood engraving, and linocut. In screen printing, the printing surface is a mesh stretched across a wooden frame. A stencil is applied to the mesh to seal the non-printing areas and ink is scraped through the mesh to produce an image.

THE FOUR MAIN PRINTING PROCESSES

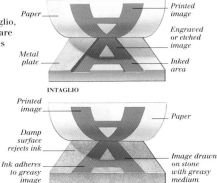

Paper
Printed image
Engraved or etched image
Metal plate
Inked area

INTAGLIO

Printed image
Paper
Damp surface rejects ink
Ink adheres to greasy image
Image drawn on stone with greasy medium

LITHOGRAPHIC

Paper
Printed image
Raised figure
Inked surface
Wood block

RELIEF

Wooden frame
Stencil
Ink forced through mesh
Printed image
Paper

SCREEN

LEATHER INK DABBER

EQUIPMENT USED IN INTAGLIO PRINTING

ROCKER **SCRIBER** **ROULETTE** **SCRAPER** **BURNISHER** **CLAMP**

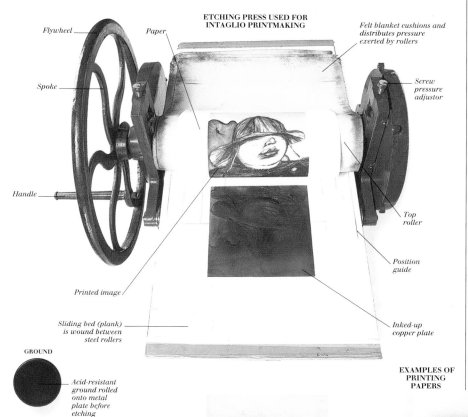

ETCHING PRESS USED FOR INTAGLIO PRINTMAKING

Flywheel

Paper

Felt blanket cushions and distributes pressure exerted by rollers

Spoke

Screw pressure adjustor

Handle

Top roller

Printed image

Position guide

Sliding bed (plank) is wound between steel rollers

Inked-up copper plate

GROUND

Acid-resistant ground rolled onto metal plate before etching

EXAMPLES OF PRINTING PAPERS

GROUND ROLLER

Gelatine roller

Wooden handle

EXAMPLE OF AN INTAGLIO PRINT
Annie with a Sun Hat, Jock McFadyen, 1993
Etched copper plate, 16 x 15¾ in (41 x 40 cm)

Printmaking 2

EXAMPLE OF A LITHOGRAPHIC STONE AND PRINT
Crown Gateway 2, Mandy Bonnell, 1987
Lithograph, 19½ x 15¾ in (50 x 40 cm)

IMAGE DRAWN ON STONE

LITHOGRAPIC PRINT

EXAMPLE OF A SCREEN PRINT
Sea Change, Patrick Hughes, 1992
Screen print, 30 x 37 in (77 x 94.5 cm)

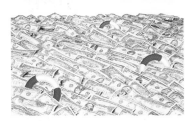

SCREEN AND SQUEEGEE

Squeegee

Rubber blade

Mesh

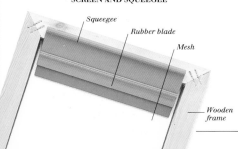

Wooden frame

EQUIPMENT USED IN LITHOGRAPHIC PRINTING

CRAYON AND HOLDER

LITHOGRAPHIC PENCIL

TUSCHE (LITHOGRAPHIC INK) PEN

ERASING STICK

EXPANDABLE SPONGE

TUSCHE (LITHOGRAPHIC INK) STICK

RUBBING INK

INK ROLLER

MILD ACIDIC SOLUTION

GUM ARABIC SOLUTION

WATER-BASED SCREEN PRINTING INKS

BLUE ACRYLIC INK

RED ACRYLIC INK

BROWN TEXTILE INK

EQUIPMENT USED IN RELIEF PRINTING

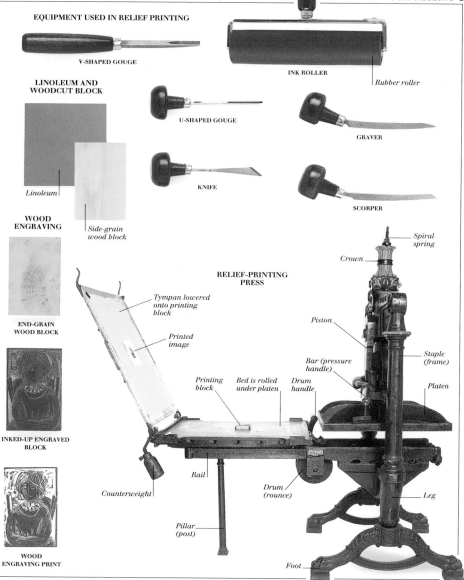

V-SHAPED GOUGE

INK ROLLER

Rubber roller

LINOLEUM AND WOODCUT BLOCK

U-SHAPED GOUGE

GRAVER

Linoleum

KNIFE

SCORPER

WOOD ENGRAVING

Side-grain wood block

END-GRAIN WOOD BLOCK

INKED-UP ENGRAVED BLOCK

WOOD ENGRAVING PRINT

RELIEF-PRINTING PRESS

Spiral spring

Crown

Tympan lowered onto printing block

Piston

Printed image

Bar (pressure handle)

Staple (frame)

Printing block

Bed is rolled under platen

Drum handle

Platen

Counterweight

Rail

Drum (rounce)

Leg

Pillar (post)

Foot

Mosaic

MOSAIC IS THE ART OF MAKING patterns and pictures from tesserae (small, colored pieces of glass, marble, and other materials). Different materials are cut into tesserae using different tools. Smalti (glass enamel) and marble are cut into pieces using a hammer and a hardy (a pointed blade) embedded in a log. Vitreous glass is cut into pieces using a pair of pliers. Mosaics can be made using a direct or indirect method. In the direct method, the tesserae are laid directly into a bed of cement–based adhesive. In the indirect method, the design is drawn in reverse on paper or cloth. The tesserae are then stuck face down on the paper or cloth using water-soluble glue. Adhesive is spread with a trowel onto a solid surface—such as a wall—and the back of the mosaic is laid into the adhesive. Finally, the paper or cloth is soaked off to reveal the mosaic. Gaps between tesserae can be filled with grout. Grout is forced into gaps by dragging a grouting squeegee across the face of the mosaic. Mosaics are usually used to decorate walls and floors, but they can also be applied to smaller objects.

EQUIPMENT FOR BREAKING MARBLE

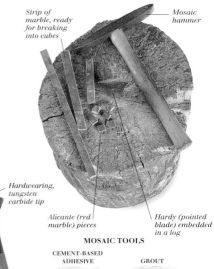

Strip of marble, ready for breaking into cubes

Mosaic hammer

Alicante (red marble) pieces

Hardy (pointed blade) embedded in a log

PLIERS

Hardwearing, tungsten carbide tip

Handle with rubber grip

MOSAIC TOOLS

CEMENT-BASED ADHESIVE   GROUT

SMALTI (GLASS ENAMEL)

EXAMPLE OF A MOSAIC (DIRECT METHOD)
Seascape, Tessa Hunkin, 1993
Smalti mosaic on board
31½ in (80 cm) diameter

RED SMALTI

YELLOW SMALTI

BLUE SMALTI

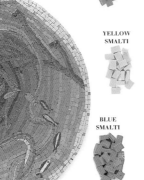

Gold-leaf smalti

TROWEL   *Notch*

Wooden handle

Steel blade

Wooden handle

GROUTING SQUEEGEE

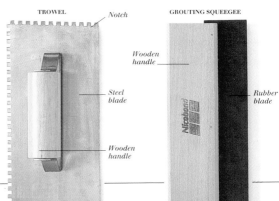

Wooden handle

Rubber blade

Nicobond

STAGES IN THE CREATION OF A MOSAIC (INDIRECT METHOD)

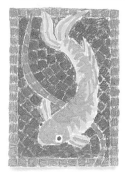

COLOR SKETCH
A color sketch is drawn in oil pastel to give a clear impression of how the finished mosaic will look.

REVERSE IMAGE
Tesserae are glued face down on reverse image on paper. Mosaic is then attached to solid surface and paper is removed.

MOSAIC POT

Geometric design

Grout

MOSAIC MOSQUE DESIGN

Floral design

Geometric border

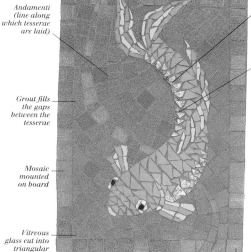

Andamenti (line along which tesserae are laid)

Grout fills the gaps between the tesserae

Mosaic mounted on board

Vitreous glass cut into triangular shape with pliers

Gold tessera with ripple finish

Gold tessera placed upside-down

FINISHED MOSAIC
Goldfish, Tessa Hunkin, 1993
Vitreous glass mosaic on board
14 x 10 in (35.5 x 25.5 cm)

Border of square vitreous glass

VITREOUS GLASS

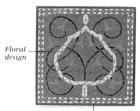

GREEN VITREOUS GLASS WITH GOLD LEAF

RED VITREOUS GLASS

Plain finish

Ripple finish

BLUE VITREOUS GLASS

SHEETS OF VITREOUS GLASS

Sculpture 1

THE TWO TRADITIONAL SCULPTURE METHODS are carving and modeling. A carved sculpture is made by cutting away the surplus from a block of hard material such as stone, marble, or wood. The tools used for carving vary according to the material being carved. Heavy steel points, claws, and chisels that are struck with a lump hammer are generally used for stone and marble. Sharp gouges and chisels that are struck with a wooden mallet are used for wood. Sculptures formed from hard materials are generally finished by filing with rasps, rifflers, and other abrasive implements. Modeling is a process by which shapes are built up, using malleable materials such as clay, plaster, and wax. The material is cut with wire-ended tools and modeled with the fingers or a variety of hardwood and metal implements. For large or intricate modeled sculptures an armature (frame), made from metal or wood, is used to provide internal support. Sculptures formed in soft materials may harden naturally or can be made more durable by firing in a kiln. Modeled sculptures are often first designed in wax or another material to be cast later in a metal (see pp. 454-455) such as bronze. The development of many new materials in the 20th century has enabled sculptors to experiment with new techniques such as construction (joining preformed pieces of material such as machine components, mirrors, and furniture) and kinetic (mobile) sculpture.

EXAMPLES OF MARBLE-CARVING TOOLS

2½ lb (1.1 kg) iron head

Ash handle

LUMP HAMMER

EXAMPLES OF WOOD-CARVING TOOLS

CABINET RASP

STRAIGHT GOUGE

SALMON BEND GOUGE

CHISEL

Stone for sharpening wood-carving tools

Cedar box

ARKANSAS HONE-STONE

CARVING MALLET

CALLIPERS

Curved leg

Gap measures distance between two points on a sculpture

Wing nut

WIDE MARBLE CLAW **NARROW MARBLE CLAW**

POINT

FLAT CHISEL

BULLNOSE CHISEL

EXAMPLES OF RIFFLERS (FOR STONE, MARBLE, AND WOOD)

12 IN (50 CM) RIFFLER

6 IN (15 CM) RIFFLER

Surface for sharpening stone-carving tools

DIAMOND WHETSTONE

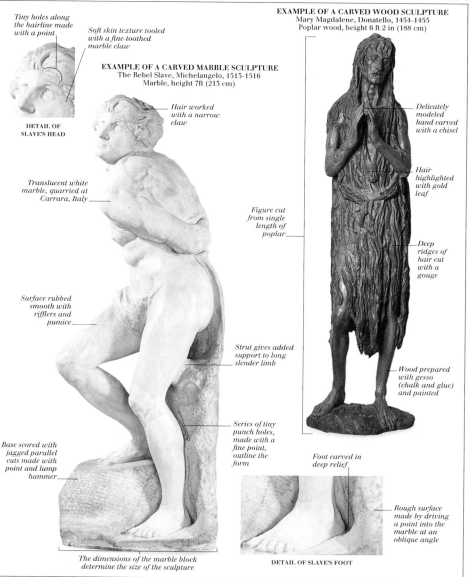

Tiny holes along the hairline made with a point

Soft skin texture tooled with a fine-toothed marble claw

DETAIL OF SLAVE'S HEAD

EXAMPLE OF A CARVED WOOD SCULPTURE
Mary Magdalene, Donatello, 1454-1455
Poplar wood, height 6 ft 2 in (188 cm)

EXAMPLE OF A CARVED MARBLE SCULPTURE
The Rebel Slave, Michelangelo, 1513-1516
Marble, height 7ft (213 cm)

Hair worked with a narrow claw

Translucent white marble, quarried at Carrara, Italy

Figure cut from single length of poplar

Surface rubbed smooth with rifflers and pumice

Strut gives added support to long slender limb

Series of tiny punch holes, made with a fine point, outline the form

Base scored with jagged parallel cuts made with point and lump hammer

Delicately modeled hand carved with a chisel

Hair highlighted with gold leaf

Deep ridges of hair cut with a gouge

Wood prepared with gesso (chalk and glue) and painted

Foot carved in deep relief

Rough surface made by driving a point into the marble at an oblique angle

The dimensions of the marble block determine the size of the sculpture

DETAIL OF SLAVE'S FOOT

Sculpture 2

EXAMPLES OF MODELING TOOLS

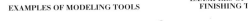

WIRE-ENDED CUTTING TOOL

CURVED MOLDING TOOL

SPATULA-ENDED WAX MODELING TOOL

ROUNDED WAX MODELING TOOL

EXAMPLES OF BRONZE FINISHING TOOLS

HOOKED RIFFLER   POINTED RIFFLER

ALCOHOL BURNER (FOR HEATING WAX MODELING TOOLS)

Wick

Brass holder

Glass bowl

Denatured alcohol

STAGES IN THE LOST-WAX METHOD OF CASTING
Based on Mars, Giambologna, c.1546

Wax-covered wire armature

ORIGINAL MODEL
An original, solid wax model is made and preserved so that numerous replicas can be cast.

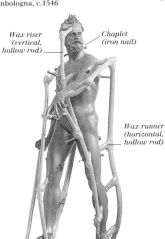

Wax riser (vertical, hollow rod)

Chaplet (iron nail)

Wax runner (horizontal, hollow rod)

HOLLOW WAX FIGURE IS CAST
A new, hollow wax model is cast from the original model. It is filled with a plaster core that is held in place with nails. Wax runners and risers are attached.

Fire-resistant clay

FIGURE IS BAKED IN CASTING MOLD
The model is encased in clay and baked. The wax melts away (through the channels made by the wax rods) and is replaced by molten bronze.

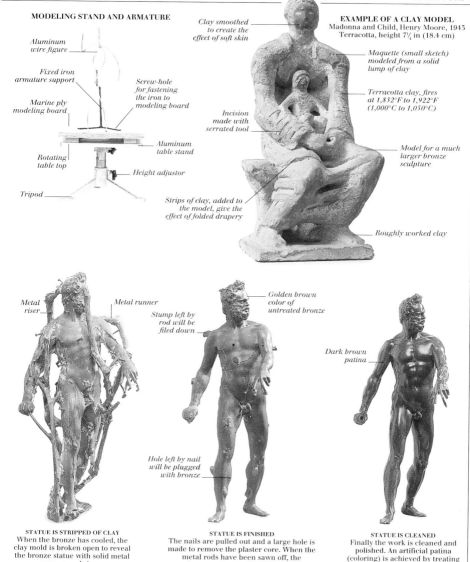

MODELING STAND AND ARMATURE

Aluminum wire figure

Fixed iron armature support

Marine ply modeling board

Screw-hole for fastening the iron to modeling board

Rotating table top

Aluminum table stand

Height adjustor

Tripod

EXAMPLE OF A CLAY MODEL
Madonna and Child, Henry Moore, 1943
Terracotta, height 7¼ in (18.4 cm)

Clay smoothed to create the effect of soft skin

Maquette (small sketch) modeled from a solid lump of clay

Terracotta clay, fires at 1,832°F to 1,922°F (1,000°C to 1,050°C)

Incision made with serrated tool

Model for a much larger bronze sculpture

Strips of clay, added to the model, give the effect of folded drapery

Roughly worked clay

Metal riser

Metal runner

Stump left by rod will be filed down

Golden brown color of untreated bronze

Dark brown patina

Hole left by nail will be plugged with bronze

STATUE IS STRIPPED OF CLAY
When the bronze has cooled, the clay mold is broken open to reveal the bronze statue with solid metal runners and risers.

STATUE IS FINISHED
The nails are pulled out and a large hole is made to remove the plaster core. When the metal rods have been sawn off, the sculpture is filed to refine the surface.

STATUE IS CLEANED
Finally the work is cleaned and polished. An artificial patina (coloring) is achieved by treating the surface with chemicals.

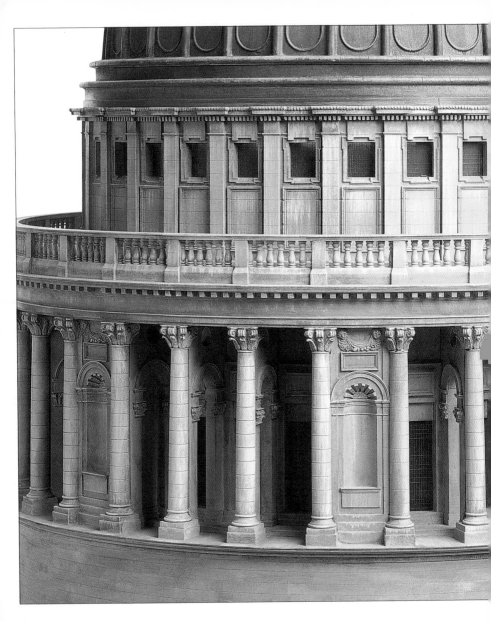

ARCHITECTURE

Ancient Egypt

THE CIVILIZATION OF THE ANCIENT EGYPTIANS (which lasted from about 3100 BC until it was finally absorbed into the Roman empire in 30 BC) is famous for its temples and tombs. Egyptian temples were often huge and geometric, like the Temple of Amon-Re (below and right). They were usually decorated with hieroglyphs (sacred characters used for picture writing) and painted reliefs depicting gods, Pharaohs (kings), and queens. Tombs were particularly important to the Egyptians, who believed that the dead were resurrected in the afterlife. The tombs were often decorated—for example, the surround of the false door opposite— in order to give comfort to the dead. The best-known ancient Egyptian tombs are the pyramids, which were designed to symbolize the rays of the sun. Many of the architectural forms used by the ancient Egyptians were later adopted by other civilizations. For example, columns and capitals were later used by the ancient Greeks (see pp. 460-461) and ancient Romans (see pp. 462-465).

FRONT VIEW OF HYPOSTYLE HALL, TEMPLE OF AMON-RE

Cornice decorated with cavetto molding

Campaniform (open papyrus) capital

Architrave

Papyrus-bud capital

Socle

Side aisle　*Central nave*　*Side aisle*

SIDE VIEW OF HYPOSTYLE HALL, TEMPLE OF AMON-RE, KARNAK, EGYPT, c.1290 BC

Horus, the sun-god　*Architrave*　*Stone slab forming flat roof of side aisle*

Kepresh crown with disc

Chons, the moon-god　*Amon-Re, king of the gods*　*Hathor, the sky-goddess*　*Papyrus motif*　*Cartouche (oval border) containing the titles of the Pharaoh (king)*　*Socle*　*Aisle running north–south*

LIMESTONE FALSE DOOR WITH HIEROGLYPHS, TOMB OF KING TJETJI, GIZA, EGYPT, c.2400 BC

Lintel

Hieroglyph representing a house

Disc representing sun or light

Eroded image of Tjetji

Limestone stela (slab)

Hoe-shaped hieroglyph representing "mr" sound

Head of false door

Image of Tjetji's wife

Image of Tjetji's daughter

PLANT CAPITAL OF THE PTOLEMAIC-ROMAN PERIOD, EGYPT, 332-30 BC

Palm leaf

Papyrus flower

Papyrus leaf

Papyrus stem

Lotus bud

Lotus stem

Cornice decorated with cavetto molding

Bead molding

Trellis window

Rectangular pier decorated with hieroglyphs

Elevated roof of central nave

Clerestory

Disc representing sun or light

Architrave

Square abacus

Papyrus-bud capital

Papyriform column

Shaft

Scene depicting a Pharaoh (king) paying homage to the god Amon-Re

Central nave

ANCIENT EGYPTIAN BUILDING DECORATION

DECORATED WINDOW, MEDINET HABU, EGYPT, C.1198 BC

ROPE AND PATERAE DECORATION

CAPITAL WITH THE HEAD OF THE SKY-GODDESS HATHOR, TEMPLE OF ISIS, PHILAE, EGYPT, 285-47 BC

LOTUS AND PAPYRUS FRIEZE DECORATION

Ancient Greece

THE CLASSICAL TEMPLES OF ANCIENT GREECE were built according to the belief that certain forms and proportions were pleasing to the gods. There were three main ancient Greek architectural orders (styles), which can be distinguished by the decoration and proportions of their columns, capitals (column tops), and entablatures (structures resting on the capitals). The oldest is the Doric order, which dates from the seventh century BC and was used mainly on the Greek mainland and in the western colonies, such as Sicily and southern Italy. The Temple of Neptune, shown here, is a classic example of this order. It is hypaethral (roofless) and peripteral (surrounded by a single row of columns). About a century later, the more decorative Ionic order developed on the Aegean Islands. Features of this order include volutes (spiral scrolls) on capitals and acroteria (pediment ornaments). The Corinthian order was invented in Athens in the fifth century BC and is typically identified by an acanthus leaf on the capitals. This order was later widely used in ancient Roman architecture.

CAPITALS OF THE THREE ORDERS OF ANCIENT GREEK ARCHITECTURE

Abacus
Echinus
Annulet
Trachelion (neck)

DORIC CAPITAL, THE PROPYLAEUM (GATEWAY), THE ACROPOLIS, ATHENS, GREECE, 449 BC

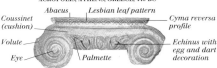

Coussinet (cushion)
Abacus
Lesbian leaf pattern
Cyma reversa profile
Volute
Echinus with egg and dart decoration
Eye
Palmette

IONIC CAPITAL, THE PROPYLAEUM (GATEWAY), TEMPLE OF ATHENA POLIAS, PRIENE, GREECE, c.554 BC

Mask
Abacus
Volute
Cauliculus
Acanthus leaf
Bell-shaped core

CORINTHIAN CAPITAL FROM A STOA (PORTICO), PROBABLY FROM ASIA MINOR

TEMPLE OF NEPTUNE, PAESTUM, ITALY, c.460 BC

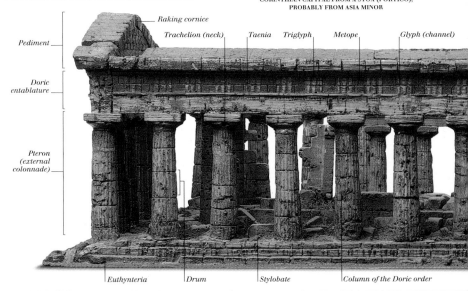

Pediment
Raking cornice
Trachelion (neck)
Taenia
Triglyph
Metope
Glyph (channel)
Doric entablature
Pteron (external colonnade)
Euthynteria
Drum
Stylobate
Column of the Doric order

PLAN OF THE TEMPLE OF NEPTUNE, PAESTUM

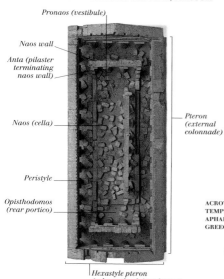

Pronaos (vestibule)

Naos wall

Anta (pilaster terminating naos wall)

Naos (cella)

Peristyle

Opisthodomos (rear portico)

Pteron (external colonnade)

Hexastyle pteron (colonnade of six columns)

ANCIENT GREEK BUILDING DECORATION

Volute

FACADE, TREASURY OF ATREUS, MYCENAE, GREECE, 1350-1250 BC

Meander

FRETWORK, PARTHENON, ATHENS, GREECE, 447-456 BC

ACROTERION, TEMPLE OF APHAIA, AEGINA, GREECE, 490 BC

Griffon (gryphon)

Raking cornice

ANTEFIXA, TEMPLE OF APHAIA, AEGINA, GREECE, 490 BC

Palmette

Volute

Regula (short fillet beneath taenia)

Eaves

Cornice

Frieze

Architrave

Capital

Shaft

Crepidoma (stepped base)

Entasis (slight curve of a column)

Intercolumniation

Fluting

461

Ancient Rome 1

IN THE EARLY PERIOD OF THE ROMAN EMPIRE extensive use
was made of ancient Greek architectural ideas, particularly
those of the Corinthian order (see pp. 460-461). As a result,
many early Roman buildings—such as the Temple of Vesta
(opposite)—closely resemble ancient Greek buildings. A
distinctive Roman style began to evolve in the first century
AD. This style developed the interiors of buildings (the Greeks
had concentrated on the exterior) by wing arches, vaults, and
domes inside the buildings and by ornamenting internal walls;
many of these features can be seen in the Pantheon. Exterior
columns were often used for decorative rather than structural
purposes, as in the Colosseum and the Porta Nigra (see
pp. 464-465). Smaller buildings had timber frames with
wattle-and-daub walls, as in the mill (see pp. 464-465).
Roman architecture remained influential for many centuries,
with some of its principles being used in the 11th century in
Romanesque buildings (see pp. 468-469) and also in the 15th
and 16th centuries in Renaissance buildings (see pp. 474-477).

ANCIENT ROMAN BUILDING DECORATION

FESTOON, TEMPLE OF VESTA,
TIVOLI, ITALY, C.80 BC

RICHLY DECORATED
ROMAN OVUM

INTERIOR OF THE PANTHEON, ROME, ITALY, 118-c.128

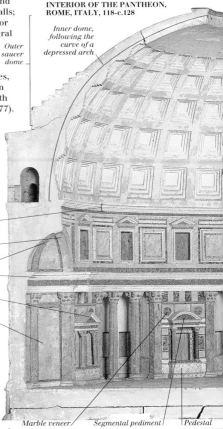

Inner dome,
following the
curve of a
depressed arch

Outer
saucer
dome

Entablature

Curved
cornice

Lesene

Cornice

Triangular
pediment

Concave
niche

Relieving
arch

Opening for
ventilation

Cornice

Marble veneer · Segmental pediment · Pedestal

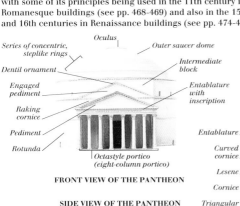

Oculus

Series of concentric,
steplike rings

Outer saucer dome

Dentil ornament

Intermediate
block

Engaged
pediment

Entablature
with
inscription

Raking
cornice

Pediment

Rotunda

Octastyle portico
(eight-column portico)

FRONT VIEW OF THE PANTHEON

SIDE VIEW OF THE PANTHEON

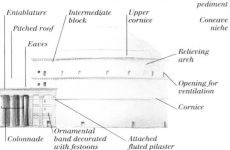

Entablature

Pitched roof

Eaves

Intermediate
block

Upper
cornice

Colonnade

Ornamental
band decorated
with festoons

Attached
fluted pilaster

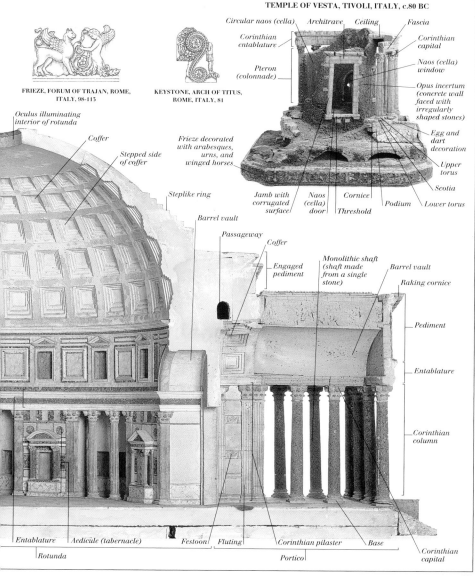

TEMPLE OF VESTA, TIVOLI, ITALY, c.80 BC

Circular naos (cella)

Architrave

Ceiling

Fascia

Corinthian entablature

Corinthian capital

Pteron (colonnade)

Naos (cella) window

Opus incertum (concrete wall faced with irregularly shaped stones)

FRIEZE, FORUM OF TRAJAN, ROME, ITALY, 98-113

KEYSTONE, ARCH OF TITUS, ROME, ITALY, 81

Oculus illuminating interior of rotunda

Coffer

Stepped side of coffer

Frieze decorated with arabesques, urns, and winged horses

Steplike ring

Egg and dart decoration

Upper torus

Scotia

Lower torus

Jamb with corrugated surface

Naos (cella) door

Cornice

Threshold

Podium

Barrel vault

Passageway

Coffer

Engaged pediment

Monolithic shaft (shaft made from a single stone)

Barrel vault

Raking cornice

Pediment

Entablature

Corinthian column

Entablature

Aedicule (tabernacle)

Festoon

Fluting

Corinthian pilaster

Base

Rotunda

Portico

Corinthian capital

Ancient Rome 2

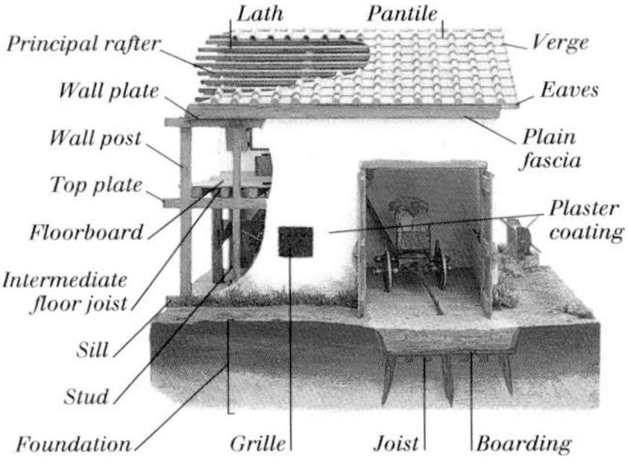

FRONT VIEW OF A ROMAN MILL, 1ST CENTURY BC

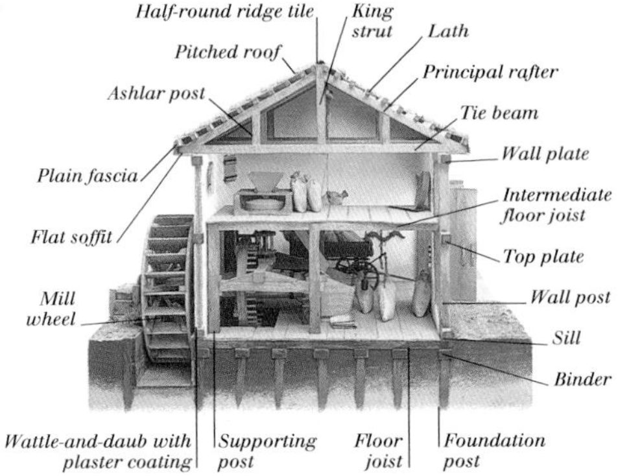

SIDE VIEW OF A ROMAN MILL

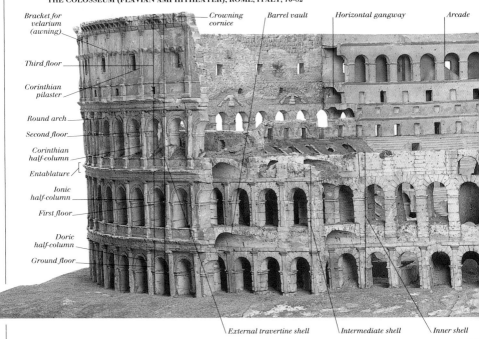

Side view labels:
Principal rafter · Lath · Pantile · Verge
Wall plate · Eaves
Wall post · Plain fascia
Top plate
Floorboard · Plaster coating
Intermediate floor joist
Sill
Stud
Foundation · Grille · Joist · Boarding

Front view labels:
Half-round ridge tile · King strut · Lath
Pitched roof · Principal rafter
Ashlar post · Tie beam
Plain fascia · Wall plate
Flat soffit · Intermediate floor joist
Top plate
Mill wheel · Wall post
Sill
Binder
Wattle-and-daub with plaster coating · Supporting post · Floor joist · Foundation post

THE COLOSSEUM (FLAVIAN AMPHITHEATER), ROME, ITALY, 70-82

Colosseum labels:
Bracket for velarium (awning) · Crowning cornice · Barrel vault · Horizontal gangway · Arcade
Third floor
Corinthian pilaster
Round arch
Second floor
Corinthian half-column
Entablature
Ionic half-column
First floor
Doric half-column
Ground floor
External travertine shell · Intermediate shell · Inner shell

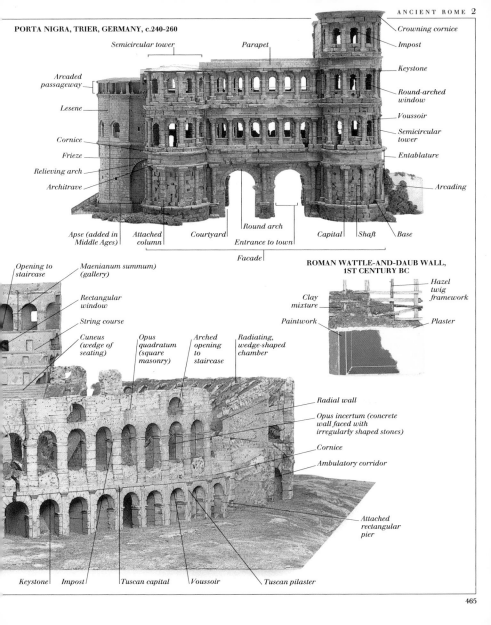

PORTA NIGRA, TRIER, GERMANY, c.240-260

Semicircular tower

Parapet

Crowning cornice

Impost

Arcaded passageway

Keystone

Lesene

Round-arched window

Cornice

Voussoir

Frieze

Semicircular tower

Relieving arch

Entablature

Architrave

Arcading

Apse (added in Middle Ages)

Attached column

Courtyard

Round arch

Entrance to town

Capital

Shaft

Base

Facade

Opening to staircase

Maenianum summum) (gallery)

ROMAN WATTLE-AND-DAUB WALL, 1ST CENTURY BC

Hazel twig framework

Rectangular window

Clay mixture

String course

Paintwork

Plaster

Cuneus (wedge of seating)

Opus quadratum (square masonry)

Arched opening to staircase

Radiating, wedge-shaped chamber

Radial wall

Opus incertum (concrete wall faced with irregularly shaped stones)

Cornice

Ambulatory corridor

Attached rectangular pier

Keystone

Impost

Tuscan capital

Voussoir

Tuscan pilaster

Medieval castles and houses

WARFARE WAS COMMON IN EUROPE in the Middle Ages, and many monarchs and nobles built castles as a form of defense. Typical medieval castles have outer walls surrounding a moat. Inside the moat is a bailey (courtyard), protected by a chemise (jacket wall). The innermost and strongest part of a medieval castle is the keep. There are two main types of keep: towers called donjons, such as the Tour de César and Coucy-le-Château in France, and rectangular keeps ("hall-keeps"), such as the Tower of London. Castles were often guarded by salients (projecting fortifications), like those of the Bastille. Medieval houses typically had timber cruck (tent-like) frames, wattle-and-daub walls, and pitched roofs, like those on medieval London Bridge (opposite).

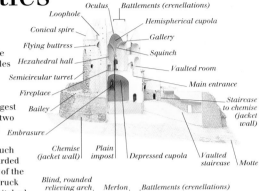

DONJON, TOUR DE CESAR, PROVINS, FRANCE, 12TH CENTURY

Oculus
Loophole
Conical spire
Hexahedral hall
Semicircular turret
Fireplace
Bailey
Embrasure
Flying buttress
Chemise (jacket wall)
Plain impost
Battlements (crenellations)
Hemispherical cupola
Gallery
Squinch
Vaulted room
Main entrance
Staircase to chemise (jacket wall)
Depressed cupola
Vaulted staircase
Motte

Loophole

SALIENT, CAERNARVON CASTLE, BRITAIN, 1283-1323

Timber cruck frame

CRUCK-FRAMED HOUSE, BRITAIN, c.1200

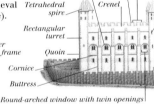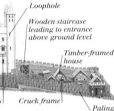

Blind, rounded relieving arch
Tetrahedral spire
Rectangular turret
Quoin
Cornice
Buttress
Round-arched window with twin openings
Merlon
Crenel
Battlements (crenellations)
Loophole
Wooden staircase leading to entrance above ground level
Timber-framed house
Cruck frame
Paling

TOWER OF LONDON, BRITAIN, FROM 1070

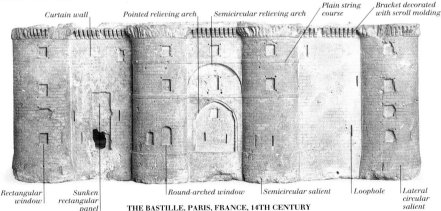

Curtain wall
Pointed relieving arch
Semicircular relieving arch
Plain string course
Bracket decorated with scroll molding
Rectangular window
Sunken rectangular panel
Round-arched window
Semicircular salient
Loophole
Lateral circular salient

THE BASTILLE, PARIS, FRANCE, 14TH CENTURY

MEDIEVAL LONDON BRIDGE, BRITAIN, 1176 (WITH 14TH-CENTURY BATTLEMENTED BUILDING, NONESUCH HOUSE, AND TWO-TOWERED GATE)

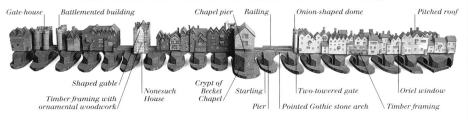

Gate-house
Battlemented building
Chapel pier
Railing
Onion-shaped dome
Pitched roof
Shaped gable
Nonesuch House
Crypt of Becket Chapel
Starling
Two-towered gate
Oriel window
Timber framing with ornamental woodwork
Pier
Pointed Gothic stone arch
Timber framing

DONJON, COUCY-LE-CHATEAU, AISNE, FRANCE, 1225-1245

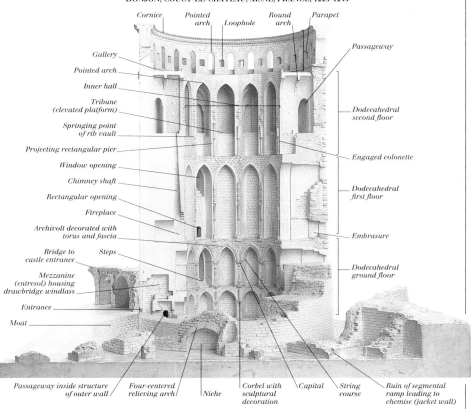

Cornice
Pointed arch
Loophole
Round arch
Parapet
Passageway
Gallery
Pointed arch
Inner hall
Tribune (elevated platform)
Springing point of rib vault
Projecting rectangular pier
Window opening
Chimney shaft
Rectangular opening
Fireplace
Archivolt decorated with torus and fascia
Bridge to castle entrance
Steps
Mezzanine (entresol) housing drawbridge windlass
Entrance
Moat
Dodecahedral second floor
Engaged colonette
Dodecahedral first floor
Embrasure
Dodecahedral ground floor
Passageway inside structure of outer wall
Four-centered relieving arch
Niche
Corbel with sculptural decoration
Capital
String course
Ruin of segmental ramp leading to chemise (jacket wall)

Medieval churches

ABBEY OF ST. FOI, CONQUES, FRANCE, c.1050–c.1150

LARGE NUMBERS OF CHURCHES were built in Europe in the Middle Ages. European churches of this period typically have high vaults supported by massive piers and columns. In the 10th century, the Romanesque style developed. Romanesque architects adopted many Roman or early Christian architectural ideas, such as cross-shaped ground plans—like that of Angoulême Cathedral (opposite)—and the basilican system of a nave with a central vessel and side aisles. In the mid-12th century, flying buttresses and pointed vaults appeared. These features later became widely used in Gothic architecture (see pp. 470-471). Bagneux Church (opposite) has both styles: a Romanesque tower and a Gothic nave and choir.

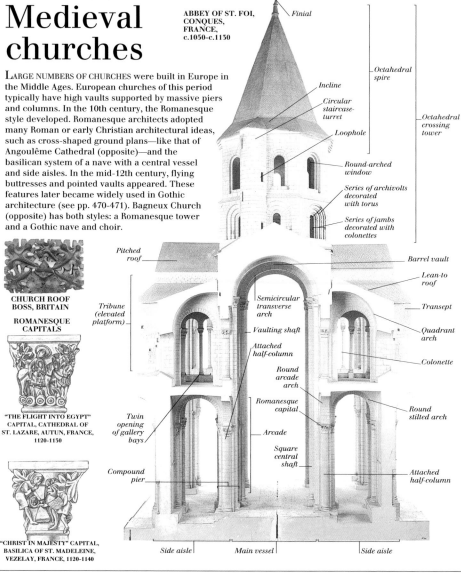

Finial

Incline

Circular staircase-turret

Loophole

Octahedral spire

Octahedral crossing tower

Round-arched window

Series of archivolts decorated with torus

Series of jambs decorated with colonettes

Pitched roof

Barrel vault

Lean-to roof

Transept

Quadrant arch

Colonette

Semicircular transverse arch

Vaulting shaft

Attached half-column

Round arcade arch

Romanesque capital

Tribune (elevated platform)

Twin opening of gallery bays

Arcade

Square central shaft

Compound pier

Round stilted arch

Attached half-column

CHURCH ROOF BOSS, BRITAIN

ROMANESQUE CAPITALS

"THE FLIGHT INTO EGYPT" CAPITAL, CATHEDRAL OF ST. LAZARE, AUTUN, FRANCE, 1120-1150

"CHRIST IN MAJESTY" CAPITAL, BASILICA OF ST. MADELEINE, VEZELAY, FRANCE, 1120-1140

Side aisle   *Main vessel*   *Side aisle*

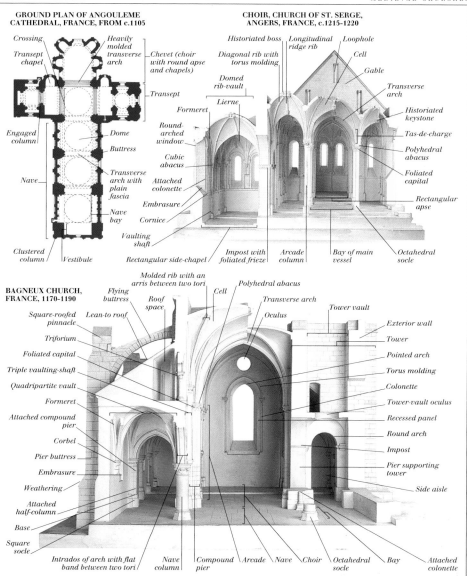

GROUND PLAN OF ANGOULEME CATHEDRAL, FRANCE, FROM c.1105

Crossing
Transept chapel
Heavily molded transverse arch
Chevet (choir with round apse and chapels)
Transept
Engaged column
Dome
Buttress
Nave
Transverse arch with plain fascia
Nave bay
Clustered column
Vestibule

CHOIR, CHURCH OF ST. SERGE, ANGERS, FRANCE, c.1215-1220

Historiated boss
Longitudinal ridge rib
Loophole
Cell
Gable
Diagonal rib with torus molding
Domed rib-vault
Transverse arch
Lierne
Historiated keystone
Formeret
Round-arched window
Tas-de-charge
Polyhedral abacus
Cubic abacus
Foliated capital
Attached colonette
Embrasure
Cornice
Rectangular apse
Vaulting shaft
Rectangular side-chapel
Impost with foliated frieze
Arcade column
Bay of main vessel
Octahedral socle

BAGNEUX CHURCH, FRANCE, 1170-1190

Molded rib with an arris between two tori
Cell
Polyhedral abacus
Flying buttress
Roof space
Transverse arch
Tower vault
Square-roofed pinnacle
Lean-to roof
Oculus
Exterior wall
Triforium
Tower
Foliated capital
Pointed arch
Triple vaulting-shaft
Torus molding
Quadripartite vault
Colonette
Formeret
Tower-vault oculus
Attached compound pier
Recessed panel
Corbel
Round arch
Pier buttress
Impost
Embrasure
Pier supporting tower
Weathering
Side aisle
Attached half-column
Base
Square socle
Intrados of arch with flat band between two tori
Nave column
Compound pier
Arcade
Nave
Choir
Octahedral socle
Bay
Attached colonette

Gothic 1

GOTHIC STAINED GLASS WITH FOLIATED SCROLL MOTIF, ON WOODEN FORM

GOTHIC BUILDINGS are characterized by rib vaults, pointed or lancet arches, flying buttresses, decorative tracery and gables, and stained-glass windows. Typical Gothic buildings include the Cathedrals of Salisbury and old St. Paul's in England, and Notre Dame de Paris in France (see pp. 472-473). The Gothic style developed out of Romanesque architecture in France (see pp. 468-469) in the mid-12th century and then spread throughout Europe. The decorative elements of Gothic architecture became highly developed in buildings of the English Decorated style (late 13th-14th century) and the French Flamboyant style (15th-16th century). These styles are exemplified by the tower of Salisbury Cathedral and by the staircase in the Church of St. Maclou (see pp. 472-473), respectively. In both of these styles, embellishments such as ballflowers and curvilinear (flowing) tracery were used liberally. The English Perpendicular style (late 14th-15th century), which followed the Decorated style, emphasized the vertical and horizontal elements of a building. A notable feature of this style is the hammer-beam roof.

GROUND PLAN OF SALISBURY CATHEDRAL

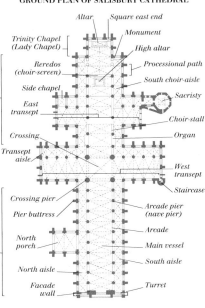

Altar
Square east end
Trinity Chapel (Lady Chapel)
Monument
High altar
Reredos (choir-screen)
Processional path
Side chapel
South choir-aisle
Choir
East transept
Sacristy
Choir-stall
Crossing
Organ
Transept aisle
West transept
Crossing pier
Staircase
Pier buttress
Arcade pier (nave pier)
Arcade
North porch
Main vessel
Nave
South aisle
North aisle
Facade wall
Turret

GOTHIC TORUS WITH BALLFLOWERS

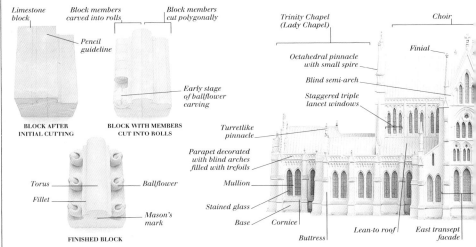

Limestone block
Block members carved into rolls
Block members cut polygonally
Pencil guideline
Early stage of ballflower carving

BLOCK AFTER INITIAL CUTTING

BLOCK WITH MEMBERS CUT INTO ROLLS

Torus
Ballflower
Fillet
Mason's mark

FINISHED BLOCK

Trinity Chapel (Lady Chapel)
Choir
Octahedral pinnacle with small spire
Finial
Blind semi-arch
Staggered triple lancet windows
Turretlike pinnacle
Parapet decorated with blind arches filled with trefoils
Mullion
Stained glass
Base
Cornice
Buttress
Lean-to roof
East transept facade

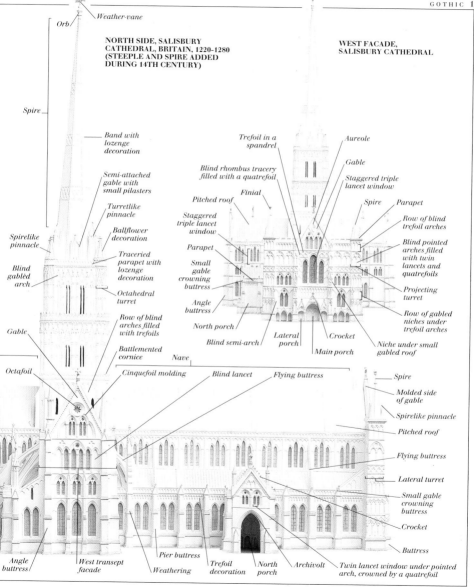

NORTH SIDE, SALISBURY CATHEDRAL, BRITAIN, 1220-1280 (STEEPLE AND SPIRE ADDED DURING 14TH CENTURY)

WEST FACADE, SALISBURY CATHEDRAL

Orb

Weather-vane

Spire

Band with lozenge decoration

Semi-attached gable with small pilasters

Turretlike pinnacle

Ballflower decoration

Spirelike pinnacle

Traceried parapet with lozenge decoration

Blind gabled arch

Octahedral turret

Gable

Row of blind arches filled with trefoils

Octafoil

Battlemented cornice

Cinquefoil molding

Trefoil in a spandrel

Aureole

Gable

Blind rhombus tracery filled with a quatrefoil

Staggered triple lancet window

Finial

Pitched roof

Spire

Parapet

Staggered triple lancet window

Row of blind trefoil arches

Parapet

Blind pointed arches filled with twin lancets and quatrefoils

Small gable crowning buttress

Projecting turret

Angle buttress

Row of gabled niches under trefoil arches

North porch

Lateral porch

Crocket

Niche under small gabled roof

Blind semi-arch

Main porch

Nave

Blind lancet

Flying buttress

Spire

Molded side of gable

Spirelike pinnacle

Pitched roof

Flying buttress

Lateral turret

Small gable crowning buttress

Crocket

Buttress

Angle buttress

West transept facade

Weathering

Pier buttress

Trefoil decoration

North porch

Archivolt

Twin lancet window under pointed arch, crowned by a quatrefoil

Gothic 2

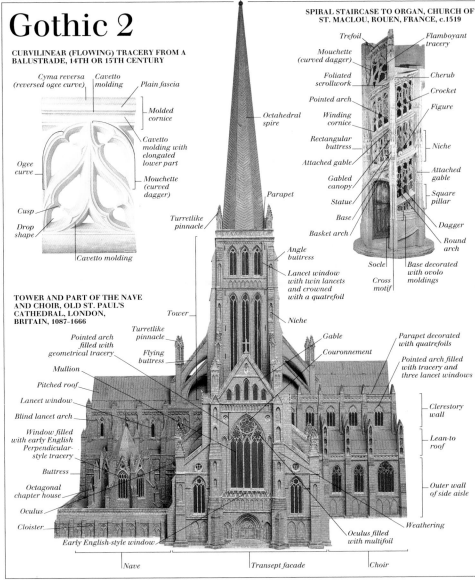

CURVILINEAR (FLOWING) TRACERY FROM A BALUSTRADE, 14TH OR 15TH CENTURY

Cyma reversa (reversed ogee curve)

Cavetto molding

Plain fascia

Molded cornice

Cavetto molding with elongated lower part

Mouchette (curved dagger)

Ogee curve

Cusp

Drop shape

Cavetto molding

SPIRAL STAIRCASE TO ORGAN, CHURCH OF ST. MACLOU, ROUEN, FRANCE, c.1519

Trefoil

Mouchette (curved dagger)

Foliated scrollwork

Pointed arch

Winding cornice

Rectangular buttress

Attached gable

Gabled canopy

Statue

Base

Basket arch

Flamboyant tracery

Cherub

Crocket

Figure

Niche

Attached gable

Square pillar

Dagger

Round arch

Socle

Cross motif

Base decorated with ovolo moldings

Octahedral spire

Parapet

Turretlike pinnacle

Angle buttress

Lancet window with twin lancets and crowned with a quatrefoil

Niche

TOWER AND PART OF THE NAVE AND CHOIR, OLD ST. PAUL'S CATHEDRAL, LONDON, BRITAIN, 1087-1666

Tower

Pointed arch filled with geometrical tracery

Turretlike pinnacle

Flying buttress

Mullion

Pitched roof

Lancet window

Blind lancet arch

Window filled with early English Perpendicular-style tracery

Buttress

Octagonal chapter house

Oculus

Cloister

Early English-style window

Gable

Couronnement

Parapet decorated with quatrefoils

Pointed arch filled with tracery and three lancet windows

Clerestory wall

Lean-to roof

Outer wall of side aisle

Weathering

Oculus filled with multifoil

Nave

Transept facade

Choir

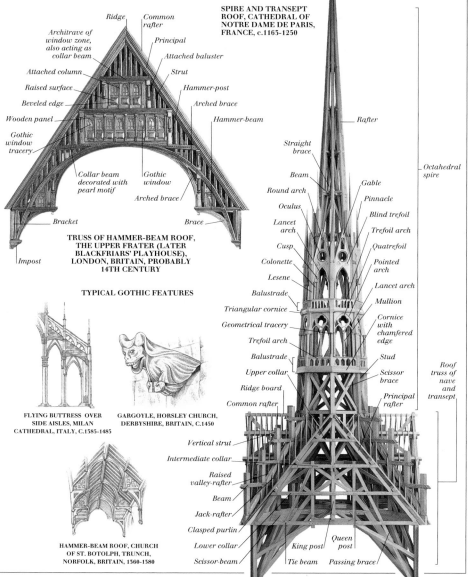

Ridge

Common rafter

Architrave of window zone, also acting as collar beam

Principal

Attached baluster

Attached column

Strut

Raised surface

Hammer-post

Beveled edge

Arched brace

Wooden panel

Hammer-beam

Gothic window tracery

Collar beam decorated with pearl motif

Gothic window

Arched brace

Bracket

Brace

Impost

SPIRE AND TRANSEPT ROOF, CATHEDRAL OF NOTRE DAME DE PARIS, FRANCE, c.1163-1250

TRUSS OF HAMMER-BEAM ROOF, THE UPPER FRATER (LATER BLACKFRIARS' PLAYHOUSE), LONDON, BRITAIN, PROBABLY 14TH CENTURY

TYPICAL GOTHIC FEATURES

FLYING BUTTRESS OVER SIDE AISLES, MILAN CATHEDRAL, ITALY, C.1385-1485

GARGOYLE, HORSLEY CHURCH, DERBYSHIRE, BRITAIN, C.1450

HAMMER-BEAM ROOF, CHURCH OF ST. BOTOLPH, TRUNCH, NORFOLK, BRITAIN, 1360-1580

Rafter

Straight brace

Beam

Gable

Round arch

Pinnacle

Oculus

Blind trefoil

Lancet arch

Trefoil arch

Cusp

Quatrefoil

Colonette

Pointed arch

Lesene

Lancet arch

Balustrade

Mullion

Triangular cornice

Geometrical tracery

Cornice with chamfered edge

Trefoil arch

Balustrade

Stud

Upper collar

Scissor brace

Ridge board

Principal rafter

Common rafter

Octahedral spire

Roof truss of nave and transept

Vertical strut

Intermediate collar

Raised valley-rafter

Beam

Jack-rafter

Clasped purlin

Lower collar

Queen post

Scissor-beam

King post

Tie beam

Passing brace

Renaissance 1

FACADE ON TO PIAZZA, PALAZZO STROZZI

THE RENAISSANCE was a period in European history—lasting roughly from the 14th century to the mid-17th century—during which the arts and sciences underwent great changes. In architecture, these changes were marked by a return to the classical forms and proportions of ancient Roman buildings. The Renaissance originated in Italy, and the buildings most characteristic of its style can be found there, such as the Palazzo Strozzi shown here. Mannerism is a branch of the Renaissance style that distorts the classical forms; an example is the Laurentian Library staircase. As the Renaissance style spread to other European countries, many of its features were incorporated into the local architecture. For example, the Château de Montal in France (see pp. 476-477) incorporates aedicules (tabernacles).

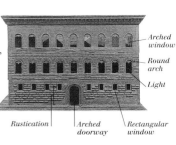

Crowning cornice

Arched window

Round arch

Light

Rustication

Arched doorway

Rectangular window

SIDE VIEW OF PALAZZO STROZZI, FLORENCE, ITALY, 1489 (BY G. DA SANGALLO, B. DA MAIANO, AND CRONACA)

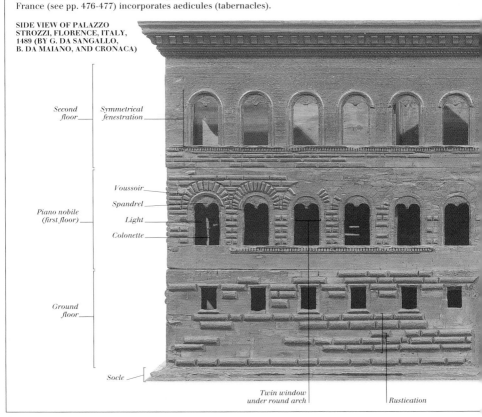

Second floor

Symmetrical fenestration

Voussoir

Spandrel

Piano nobile (first floor)

Light

Colonette

Ground floor

Socle

Twin window under round arch

Rustication

DETAILS FROM ITALIAN RENAISSANCE BUILDINGS

**PANEL FROM DRUM OF DOME,
FLORENCE CATHEDRAL, 1420-1456**

**COFFERING IN DOME,
PAZZI CHAPEL,
FLORENCE, 1429-1461**

**STAIRCASE,
LAURENTIAN LIBRARY,
FLORENCE, 1559**

**PORTICO, VILLA ROTUNDA,
VICENZA, 1567-1569**

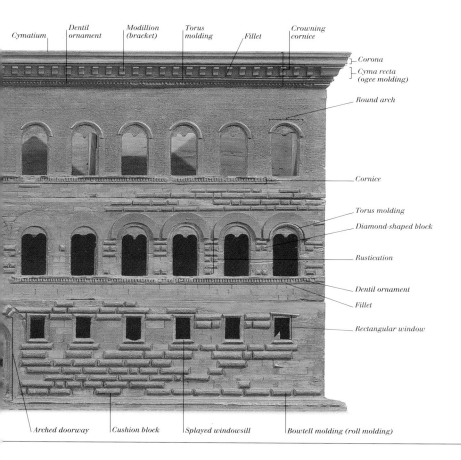

Cymatium

Dentil ornament

Modillion (bracket)

Torus molding

Fillet

Crowning cornice

Corona

Cyma recta (ogee molding)

Round arch

Cornice

Torus molding

Diamond-shaped block

Rustication

Dentil ornament

Fillet

Rectangular window

Arched doorway

Cushion block

Splayed windowsill

Bowtell molding (roll molding)

Renaissance 2

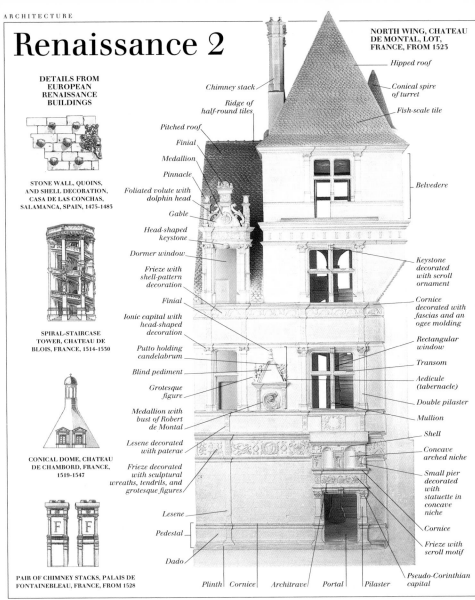

NORTH WING, CHATEAU DE MONTAL, LOT, FRANCE, FROM 1523

DETAILS FROM EUROPEAN RENAISSANCE BUILDINGS

STONE WALL, QUOINS, AND SHELL DECORATION, CASA DE LAS CONCHAS, SALAMANCA, SPAIN, 1475-1483

SPIRAL-STAIRCASE TOWER, CHATEAU DE BLOIS, FRANCE, 1514-1550

CONICAL DOME, CHATEAU DE CHAMBORD, FRANCE, 1519-1547

PAIR OF CHIMNEY STACKS, PALAIS DE FONTAINEBLEAU, FRANCE, FROM 1528

Chimney stack
Ridge of half-round tiles
Pitched roof
Finial
Medallion
Pinnacle
Foliated volute with dolphin head
Gable
Head-shaped keystone
Dormer window
Frieze with shell-pattern decoration
Finial
Ionic capital with head-shaped decoration
Putto holding candelabrum
Blind pediment
Grotesque figure
Medallion with bust of Robert de Montal
Lesene decorated with paterae
Frieze decorated with sculptural wreaths, tendrils, and grotesque figures
Lesene
Pedestal
Dado

Hipped roof
Conical spire of turret
Fish-scale tile
Belvedere
Keystone decorated with scroll ornament
Cornice decorated with fascias and an ogee molding
Rectangular window
Transom
Aedicule (tabernacle)
Double pilaster
Mullion
Shell
Concave arched niche
Small pier decorated with statuette in concave niche
Cornice
Frieze with scroll motif
Pseudo-Corinthian capital

Plinth   Cornice   Architrave   Portal   Pilaster

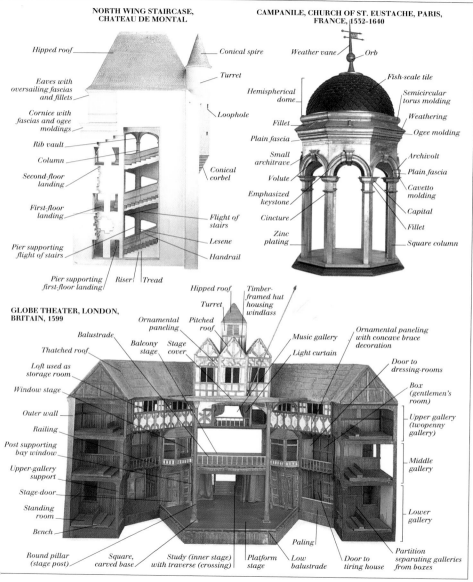

NORTH WING STAIRCASE, CHATEAU DE MONTAL

Hipped roof

Eaves with oversailing fascias and fillets

Cornice with fascias and ogee moldings

Rib vault

Column

Second-floor landing

First-floor landing

Pier supporting flight of stairs

Pier supporting first-floor landing

Riser

Tread

Conical spire

Turret

Loophole

Conical corbel

Flight of stairs

Lesene

Handrail

CAMPANILE, CHURCH OF ST. EUSTACHE, PARIS, FRANCE, 1532-1640

Weather vane

Orb

Hemispherical dome

Fillet

Plain fascia

Small architrave

Volute

Emphasized keystone

Cincture

Zinc plating

Fish-scale tile

Semicircular torus molding

Weathering

Ogee molding

Archivolt

Plain fascia

Cavetto molding

Capital

Fillet

Square column

GLOBE THEATER, LONDON, BRITAIN, 1599

Balustrade

Thatched roof

Loft used as storage room

Window stage

Outer wall

Railing

Post supporting bay window

Upper-gallery support

Stage-door

Standing room

Bench

Round pillar (stage post)

Square, carved base

Study (inner stage) with traverse (crossing)

Hipped roof

Turret

Ornamental paneling

Balcony stage

Pitched roof

Stage cover

Timber-framed hut housing windlass

Music gallery

Light curtain

Ornamental paneling with concave brace decoration

Door to dressing-rooms

Box (gentlemen's room)

Upper gallery (twopenny gallery)

Middle gallery

Lower gallery

Partition separating galleries from boxes

Platform stage

Low balustrade

Door to tiring house

Paling

Baroque and neoclassical 1

THE BAROQUE STYLE EVOLVED IN THE EARLY 17TH CENTURY in Rome. It is characterized by curved outlines and ostentatious decoration, as can be seen in the Italian church details (right). The baroque style was particularly widely favored in Italy, Spain, and Germany. It was also adopted in Britain and France, but with adaptations. The British architects Sir Christopher Wren and Nicholas Hawksmoor, for example, used baroque features—such as the concave walls of St. Paul's Cathedral and the curved buttresses of the Church of St. George in the East (see pp. 480-481)—but they did so with restraint. Similarly, the curved buttresses and volutes of the Parisian Church of St. Paul-St. Louis are relatively plain. In the second half of the 17th century, a distinct classical style (known as neoclassicism) developed in northern Europe as a reaction to the excesses of baroque. Typical of this new style were churches such as the Madeleine (a proposed facade is shown below), as well as secular buildings such as the Cirque Napoleon (opposite) and the buildings of the British architect Sir John Soane (see pp. 482-483). In early 18th century France, an extremely lavish form of baroque developed, known as rococo. The balcony from Nantes (see pp. 482-483) with its twisted ironwork and head-shaped corbels is typical of this style.

DETAILS FROM ITALIAN BAROQUE CHURCHES

SCROLLED BUTTRESS, CHURCH OF ST. MARIA DELLA SALUTE, VENICE, 1631-1682

STATUE OF THE ECSTASY OF ST. THERESA, CHURCH OF ST. MARIA DELLA VITTORIA, ROME, 1645-1652

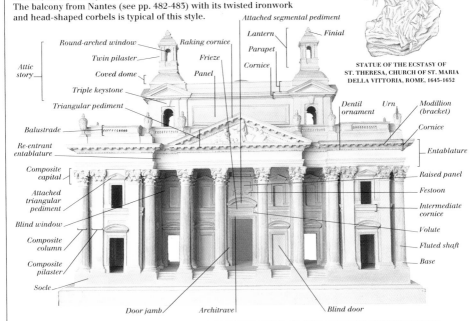

PROPOSED FACADE, THE MADELEINE (NEOCLASSICAL), PARIS, FRANCE, 1764 (BY P. CONTANT D'IVRY)

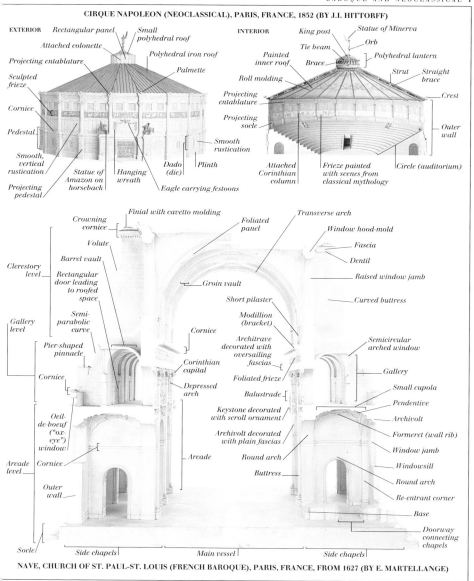

CIRQUE NAPOLEON (NEOCLASSICAL), PARIS, FRANCE, 1852 (BY J.I. HITTORFF)

EXTERIOR

Rectangular panel
Small polyhedral roof
Attached colonette
Projecting entablature
Polyhedral iron roof
Palmette
Sculpted frieze
Cornice
Pedestal
Smooth, vertical rustication
Statue of Amazon on horseback
Hanging wreath
Dado (die)
Plinth
Smooth rustication
Eagle carrying festoons
Projecting pedestal

INTERIOR

King post
Statue of Minerva
Tie beam
Orb
Painted inner roof
Brace
Polyhedral lantern
Roll molding
Strut
Straight brace
Projecting entablature
Crest
Projecting socle
Outer wall
Attached Corinthian column
Frieze painted with scenes from classical mythology
Circle (auditorium)

Finial with cavetto molding
Foliated panel
Transverse arch
Window hood-mold
Crowning cornice
Fascia
Volute
Dentil
Barrel vault
Clerestory level
Rectangular door leading to roofed space
Raised window jamb
Groin vault
Short pilaster
Curved buttress
Semi-parabolic curve
Gallery level
Modillion (bracket)
Cornice
Pier-shaped pinnacle
Semicircular arched window
Architrave decorated with oversailing fascias
Corinthian capital
Gallery
Cornice
Depressed arch
Foliated frieze
Small cupola
Balustrade
Pendentive
Oeil-de-boeuf ("ox-eye") window
Keystone decorated with scroll ornament
Archivolt
Archivolt decorated with plain fascias
Formeret (wall rib)
Cornice
Arcade
Window jamb
Arcade level
Round arch
Windowsill
Outer wall
Buttress
Round arch
Re-entrant corner
Base
Socle
Doorway connecting chapels
Side chapels
Main vessel
Side chapels

NAVE, CHURCH OF ST. PAUL-ST. LOUIS (FRENCH BAROQUE), PARIS, FRANCE, FROM 1627 (BY E. MARTELLANGE)

Baroque and neoclassical 2

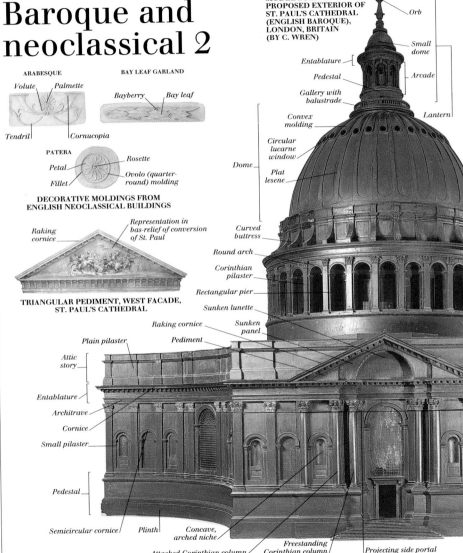

ARABESQUE

Volute
Palmette
Tendril
Cornucopia

BAY LEAF GARLAND

Bayberry
Bay leaf

PATERA

Petal
Rosette
Fillet
Ovolo (quarter-round) molding

DECORATIVE MOLDINGS FROM ENGLISH NEOCLASSICAL BUILDINGS

Raking cornice
Representation in bas-relief of conversion of St. Paul

TRIANGULAR PEDIMENT, WEST FACADE, ST. PAUL'S CATHEDRAL

MODEL BUILT IN 1674 OF PROPOSED EXTERIOR OF ST. PAUL'S CATHEDRAL (ENGLISH BAROQUE), LONDON, BRITAIN (BY C. WREN)

Cross
Orb
Small dome
Entablature
Pedestal
Arcade
Gallery with balustrade
Lantern
Convex molding
Circular lucarne window
Dome
Plat lesene
Curved buttress
Round arch
Corinthian pilaster
Rectangular pier
Sunken lunette
Sunken panel
Raking cornice
Pediment
Plain pilaster
Attic story
Entablature
Architrave
Cornice
Small pilaster
Pedestal
Semicircular cornice
Plinth
Concave, arched niche
Attached Corinthian column
Freestanding Corinthian column
Projecting side portal

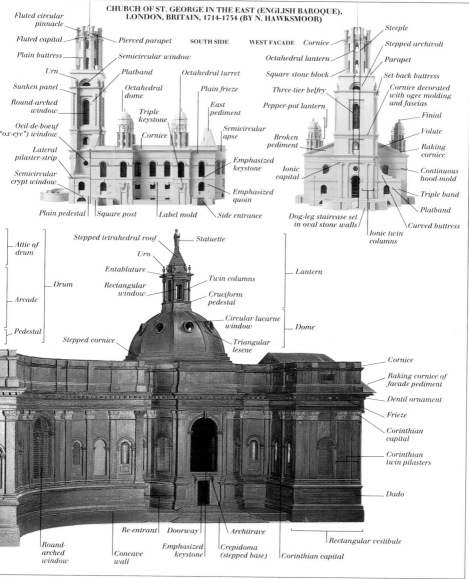

CHURCH OF ST. GEORGE IN THE EAST (ENGLISH BAROQUE), LONDON, BRITAIN, 1714-1734 (BY N. HAWKSMOOR)

SOUTH SIDE

WEST FACADE

Fluted circular pinnacle

Fluted capital

Pierced parapet

Plain buttress

Semicircular window

Urn

Platband

Sunken panel

Octahedral dome

Round-arched window

Octahedral turret

Triple keystone

Octahedral turret

Plain frieze

Oeil-de-boeuf ("ox-eye") window

Cornice

East pediment

Lateral pilaster-strip

Semicircular apse

Semicircular crypt window

Emphasized keystone

Plain pedestal

Square post

Label mold

Side entrance

Emphasized quoin

Steeple

Cornice

Stepped archivolt

Octahedral lantern

Parapet

Square stone block

Set-back buttress

Three-tier belfry

Cornice decorated with ogee molding and fascias

Pepper-pot lantern

Finial

Broken pediment

Volute

Ionic capital

Raking cornice

Continuous hood-mold

Triple band

Platband

Dog-leg staircase set in oval stone walls

Curved buttress

Ionic twin columns

Attic of drum

Stepped tetrahedral roof

Statuette

Urn

Entablature

Twin columns

Drum

Rectangular window

Cruciform pedestal

Lantern

Arcade

Circular lucarne window

Dome

Pedestal

Stepped cornice

Triangular lesene

Cornice

Raking cornice of facade pediment

Dentil ornament

Frieze

Corinthian capital

Corinthian twin pilasters

Dado

Round-arched window

Re-entrant

Doorway

Architrave

Concave wall

Emphasized keystone

Crepidoma (stepped base)

Corinthian capital

Rectangular vestibule

Baroque and neoclassical 3

DETAILS FROM BAROQUE, NEOCLASSICAL, AND ROCOCO BUILDINGS

CORNER OF THE NEW STATE PAPER OFFICE (NEOCLASSICAL), LONDON, BRITAIN, 1830-1831 (BY J. SOANE)

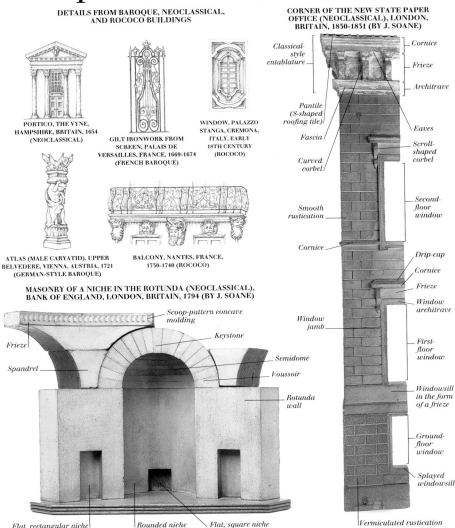

PORTICO, THE VYNE, HAMPSHIRE, BRITAIN, 1654 (NEOCLASSICAL)

GILT IRONWORK FROM SCREEN, PALAIS DE VERSAILLES, FRANCE, 1669-1674 (FRENCH BAROQUE)

WINDOW, PALAZZO STANGA, CREMONA, ITALY, EARLY 18TH CENTURY (ROCOCO)

ATLAS (MALE CARYATID), UPPER BELVEDERE, VIENNA, AUSTRIA, 1721 (GERMAN-STYLE BAROQUE)

BALCONY, NANTES, FRANCE, 1750-1740 (ROCOCO)

MASONRY OF A NICHE IN THE ROTUNDA (NEOCLASSICAL), BANK OF ENGLAND, LONDON, BRITAIN, 1794 (BY J. SOANE)

Classical-style entablature

Cornice

Frieze

Architrave

Pantile (S-shaped roofing tile)

Fascia

Eaves

Scroll-shaped corbel

Curved corbel

Smooth rustication

Second-floor window

Cornice

Drip-cap

Cornice

Frieze

Window architrave

Window jamb

First-floor window

Windowsill in the form of a frieze

Ground-floor window

Splayed windowsill

Vermiculated rustication

Scoop-pattern concave molding

Keystone

Frieze

Semidome

Spandrel

Voussoir

Rotunda wall

Flat, rectangular niche

Rounded niche

Flat, square niche

TYRINGHAM HOUSE (NEOCLASSICAL), BUCKINGHAMSHIRE, BRITAIN, 1793-1797 (BY J. SOANE)

**ROOF LEVEL
(ATTIC LEVEL)**

Space for illumination above unroofed central hall

Chimney stack

Space above unroofed main staircase

Flat roof

Oculus illuminating secondary staircase

Parapet rail

Balustrade

Baluster

Cornice

Attic story of convex portico

Cornice

**FIRST-FLOOR LEVEL
(CHAMBER FLOOR)**

Upper level of central hall, open to floor below

Main staircase

Secondary staircase

Abacus

Triangular pilaster

Pilaster capital

Attached Tuscan twin pilasters

First-floor story of convex portico

Windowsill

Bow front

**GROUND-FLOOR LEVEL
(PRINCIPAL FLOOR)**

Withdrawing room

Central hall

Library and breakfast room

Main staircase

Eating room

Water closet (toilet)

Secondary staircase

Segmented lintel course

Windowsill

Band incised with Greek-style fret ornament

Window architrave

Window jamb

Base

Basement

Plinth

Horizontal rustication

Vestibule (entrance hall)

Ground-floor storey of convex portico

**FACADE OF
TYRINGHAM HOUSE**

Chimney stack

Voussoir

Rail

Baluster

Parapet

Balustrade

Cornice

Entablature

Basement window

Capital

Shaft

Ionic column

Circular entrance steps

Base

Entrance door

PROSTYLE COLONNADE

Arches and vaults

ARCHES ARE CURVED STRUCTURES used to bridge spans and to support the weight of upper parts of buildings, such as domes, as in St. Paul's Cathedral (below) and the historical temple (opposite). The voussoirs (wedge-shaped blocks) that form an arch (right) support each other and convert the downward force of the weight of the building into an outward force. This outward force is in turn transferred to buttresses, piers, or abutments. A vault is an arched roof or ceiling. There are four main types of vault (opposite). A barrel vault is a single vault, semicircular in cross-section; a groin vault consists of two barrel vaults intersecting at right angles; a rib vault is a groin vault reinforced by ribs; and a fan vault is a rib vault in which the ribs radiate from the springing point (where the arch begins) like a fan.

PARTS OF AN ARCH

Voussoir — Keystone — Crown — Abutment
Keystone
Extrados
Abutment
Intrados (soffit) — Haunch
Impost — Intrados (soffit)
Springing point
Abutment
Span — Abutment

FRONT   SIDE

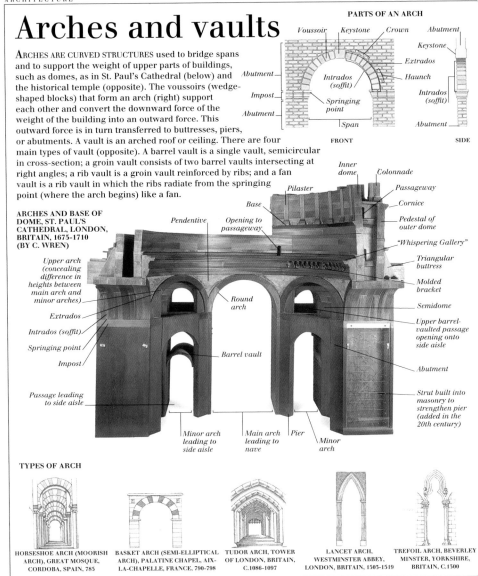

ARCHES AND BASE OF DOME, ST. PAUL'S CATHEDRAL, LONDON, BRITAIN, 1675-1710 (BY C. WREN)

Pendentive
Opening to passageway
Base
Pilaster
Inner dome
Colonnade
Passageway
Cornice
Pedestal of outer dome
"Whispering Gallery"
Triangular buttress
Molded bracket
Semidome
Upper barrel-vaulted passage opening onto side aisle
Abutment
Strut built into masonry to strengthen pier (added in the 20th century)

Upper arch (concealing difference in heights between main arch and minor arches)
Extrados
Intrados (soffit)
Springing point
Impost
Round arch
Barrel vault
Passage leading to side aisle
Minor arch leading to side aisle
Main arch leading to nave
Pier
Minor arch

TYPES OF ARCH

HORSESHOE ARCH (MOORISH ARCH), GREAT MOSQUE, CORDOBA, SPAIN, 785

BASKET ARCH (SEMI-ELLIPTICAL ARCH), PALATINE CHAPEL, AIX-LA-CHAPELLE, FRANCE, 790-798

TUDOR ARCH, TOWER OF LONDON, BRITAIN, C.1086-1097

LANCET ARCH, WESTMINSTER ABBEY, LONDON, BRITAIN, 1503-1519

TREFOIL ARCH, BEVERLEY MINSTER, YORKSHIRE, BRITAIN, C.1300

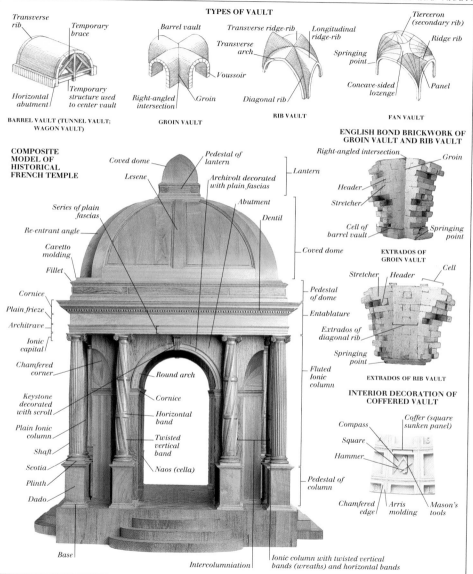

TYPES OF VAULT

Transverse rib
Temporary brace
Horizontal abutment
Temporary structure used to center vault

BARREL VAULT (TUNNEL VAULT; WAGON VAULT)

Barrel vault
Voussoir
Right-angled intersection
Groin

GROIN VAULT

Transverse ridge-rib
Longitudinal ridge-rib
Transverse arch
Diagonal rib

RIB VAULT

Tierceron (secondary rib)
Ridge rib
Springing point
Concave-sided lozenge
Panel

FAN VAULT

ENGLISH BOND BRICKWORK OF GROIN VAULT AND RIB VAULT

Right-angled intersection
Groin
Header
Stretcher
Cell of barrel vault
Springing point

EXTRADOS OF GROIN VAULT

Stretcher
Header
Cell
Extrados of diagonal rib
Springing point

EXTRADOS OF RIB VAULT

COMPOSITE MODEL OF HISTORICAL FRENCH TEMPLE

Coved dome
Lesene
Series of plain fascias
Re-entrant angle
Cavetto molding
Fillet
Cornice
Plain frieze
Architrave
Ionic capital
Chamfered corner
Keystone decorated with scroll
Plain Ionic column
Shaft
Scotia
Plinth
Dado
Base

Pedestal of lantern
Archivolt decorated with plain fascias
Abutment
Dentil

Lantern

Coved dome

Pedestal of dome
Entablature
Fluted Ionic column

Round arch
Cornice
Horizontal band
Twisted vertical band
Naos (cella)

Pedestal of column

Intercolumniation
Ionic column with twisted vertical bands (wreaths) and horizontal bands

INTERIOR DECORATION OF COFFERED VAULT

Compass
Square
Hammer
Coffer (square sunken panel)
Chamfered edge
Arris molding
Mason's tools

Domes

A DOME IS A CONVEX ROOF. Domes are categorized according to the shapes of both the base and the section through the center of the dome. The base may be circular, square, or polygonal (many-sided), depending on the plan of the drum (the walls on which the dome rests). The section of a dome may be the same shape as any arch (see pp. 484-485). Various types of dome are illustrated here: a hemispherical dome, which has a circular base and a semicircular section; a saucer dome, which has a circular base and a segmental (less than a semicircle) section; a polyhedral dome, which is a dome on a polygonal base whose sides meet at the top of the dome; and an onion dome, which has a circular or polygonal base and an ogee-shaped section. Many domes have a lantern (a turret with windows) to provide light inside.

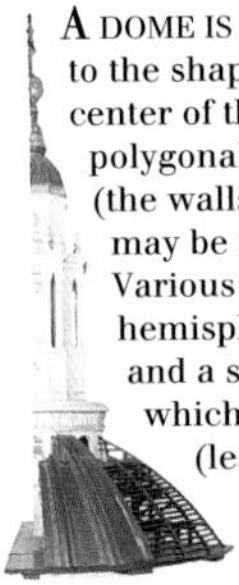

LANTERN AND UPPER DOME TIMBERING, ST. PAUL'S CATHEDRAL

DOME TIMBERING, CHURCH OF THE SORBONNE, PARIS, FRANCE, 1635-1642 (BY J. LEMERCIER)

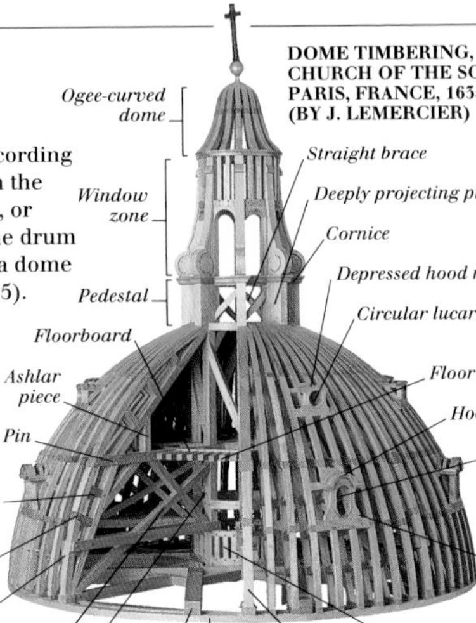

Ogee-curved dome
Straight brace
Window zone
Deeply projecting pier buttress
Cornice
Depressed hood mold
Pedestal
Circular lucarne window
Floorboard
Ashlar piece
Floor joist
Pin
Hood mold
Short strut
Waisted-oval lucarne window
Mortise and tenon joint
Ogee-curved window frame
Principal rafter
Straight brace
Vertical post
Tie beam
Circular baseplate
Common rafter
Shaft connecting lantern and church interior

ROOF WITH LANTERN AND ONION DOME

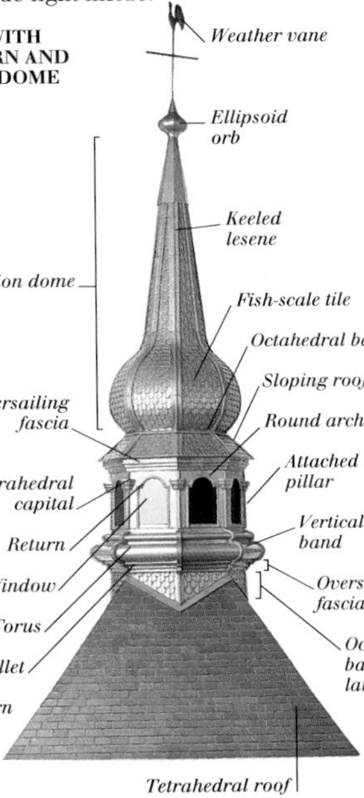

Weather vane
Ellipsoid orb
Keeled lesene
Onion dome
Fish-scale tile
Octahedral base
Sloping roof
Oversailing fascia
Round arch
Tetrahedral capital
Attached pillar
Return
Vertical band
Window
Oversailing fascia
Torus
Octahedral base of lantern
Fillet
Lantern
Tetrahedral roof

REPRESENTATION OF DOME METALING, CHURCH OF THE SORBONNE

Cross
Orb
Square rib
Inverted ovolo (quarter-round)
Astragal
Volute
Fillet
Roll molding
Plain fascia
Buttress
Round-arched window
Volute
Ovolo (quarter-round)
Cornice
Fillet
Projecting pier buttress
Lantern
Dome on a circular base
Fish-scale tile
Inverted demi-heart torus molding
Hood mold
Waisted-oval lucarne window
Small volute
Gutter
Parapet
Small roll
Fillet
Plain fascia
Triple lesene
Semicircular torus molding

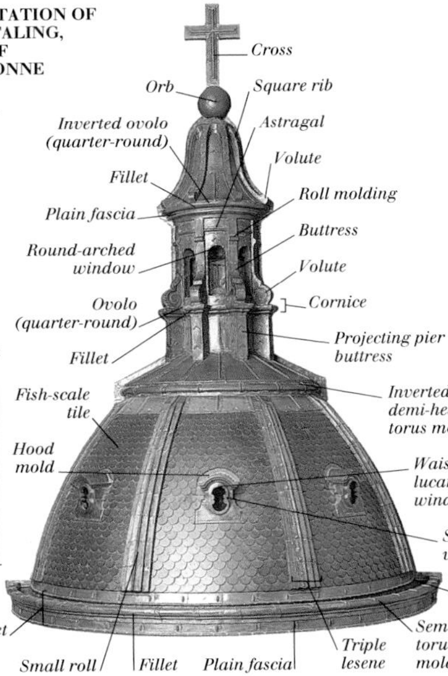

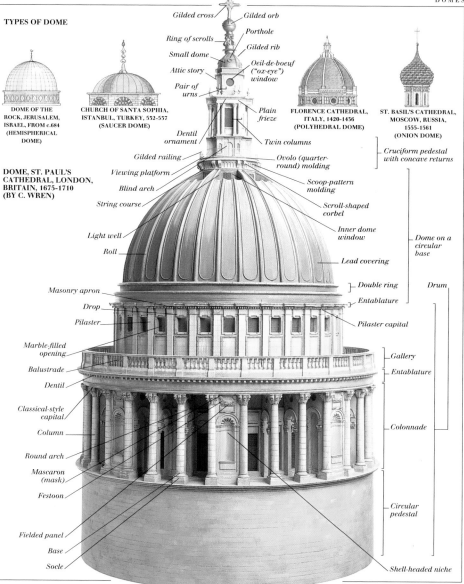

TYPES OF DOME

Gilded cross

Gilded orb

Ring of scrolls

Porthole

Small dome

Gilded rib

Attic story

Oeil-de-boeuf ("ox-eye") window

Pair of urns

Plain frieze

DOME OF THE ROCK, JERUSALEM, ISRAEL, FROM c.684 (HEMISPHERICAL DOME)

CHURCH OF SANTA SOPHIA, ISTANBUL, TURKEY, 552-557 (SAUCER DOME)

FLORENCE CATHEDRAL, ITALY, 1420-1456 (POLYHEDRAL DOME)

ST. BASIL'S CATHEDRAL, MOSCOW, RUSSIA, 1555-1561 (ONION DOME)

Dentil ornament

Twin columns

Gilded railing

Ovolo (quarter-round) molding

Viewing platform

Scoop-pattern molding

DOME, ST. PAUL'S CATHEDRAL, LONDON, BRITAIN, 1675-1710 (BY C. WREN)

Cruciform pedestal with concave returns

Blind arch

Scroll-shaped corbel

String course

Inner dome window

Light well

Dome on a circular base

Roll

Lead covering

Masonry apron

Double ring

Drum

Drop

Entablature

Pilaster

Pilaster capital

Marble-filled opening

Gallery

Balustrade

Entablature

Dentil

Classical-style capital

Column

Colonnade

Round arch

Mascaron (mask)

Festoon

Circular pedestal

Fielded panel

Base

Socle

Shell-headed niche

Islamic buildings

**OPUS SECTILE
MOSAIC DESIGN**

THE ISLAMIC RELIGION was founded by the prophet Mohammed, who was born in Mecca (in present-day Saudi Arabia) about 570 AD. During the next three centuries, Islam spread from Arabia to North Africa and Spain, as well as into India and much of the rest of Asia. The worldwide influence of Islam remains strong today. Common characteristics of Islamic buildings include ogee arches and roofs, onion domes, and walls decorated with carved stone, paintings, inlays, or mosaics. The most important type of Islamic building is the mosque—the place of worship—which generally has a minaret (tower) from which the muezzin (official crier) calls Muslims to prayer. Most mosques have a mihrab (decorative niche) that indicates the direction of Mecca. As figurative art is not allowed in Islam, buildings are ornamented with geometric and arabesque motifs and inscriptions (frequently Koranic verses).

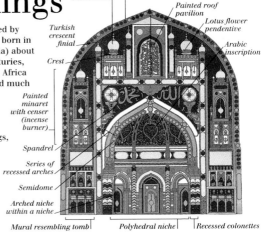

Budlike onion dome
Depressed arch surrounding mihrab
Painted roof pavilion
Lotus flower pendentive
Turkish crescent finial
Arabic inscription
Crest
Painted minaret with censer (incense burner)
Spandrel
Series of recessed arches
Semidome
Arched niche within a niche
Mural resembling tomb
Polyhedral niche
Recessed colonettes

MIHRAB, JAMI MASJID (PRINCIPAL OR CONGREGATIONAL MOSQUE), BIJAPUR, INDIA, c.1636

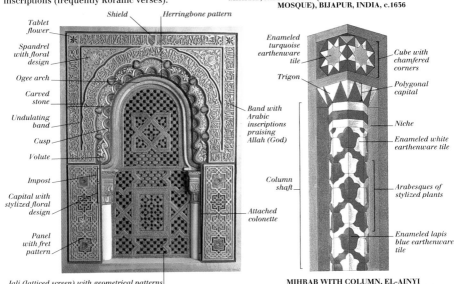

Tablet flower
Shield
Herringbone pattern
Spandrel with floral design
Ogee arch
Carved stone
Undulating band
Cusp
Volute
Impost
Capital with stylized floral design
Panel with fret pattern
Band with Arabic inscriptions praising Allah (God)
Attached colonette

Jali (latticed screen) with geometrical patterns

ARCH, THE ALHAMBRA, GRANADA, SPAIN, 1333-1354

Enameled turquoise earthenware tile
Cube with chamfered corners
Trigon
Polygonal capital
Niche
Enameled white earthenware tile
Column shaft
Arabesques of stylized plants
Enameled lapis blue earthenware tile

MIHRAB WITH COLUMN, EL-AINYI MOSQUE, CAIRO, EGYPT, 15TH CENTURY

EXAMPLES OF ISLAMIC MOSAICS, EGYPT AND SYRIA

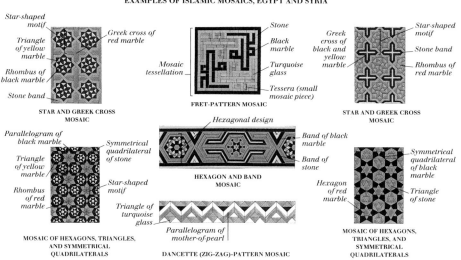

Star-shaped motif
Triangle of yellow marble
Greek cross of red marble
Rhombus of black marble
Stone band

STAR AND GREEK CROSS MOSAIC

Mosaic tessellation
Stone
Black marble
Turquoise glass
Tessera (small mosaic piece)

FRET-PATTERN MOSAIC

Greek cross of black and yellow marble
Star-shaped motif
Stone band
Rhombus of red marble

STAR AND GREEK CROSS MOSAIC

Parallelogram of black marble
Triangle of yellow marble
Rhombus of red marble
Symmetrical quadrilateral of stone
Star-shaped motif

MOSAIC OF HEXAGONS, TRIANGLES, AND SYMMETRICAL QUADRILATERALS

Hexagonal design
Band of black marble
Band of stone

HEXAGON AND BAND MOSAIC

Triangle of turquoise glass
Parallelogram of mother-of-pearl

DANCETTE (ZIG-ZAG)-PATTERN MOSAIC

Symmetrical quadrilateral of black marble
Hexagon of red marble
Triangle of stone

MOSAIC OF HEXAGONS, TRIANGLES, AND SYMMETRICAL QUADRILATERALS

MARBLE TOMB OF ITIMAD-UD-DAULA, AGRA, INDIA, c.1622-1628

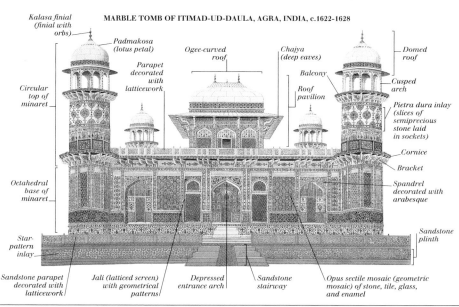

Kalasa finial (finial with orbs)
Padmakosa (lotus petal)
Ogee-curved roof
Chajya (deep eaves)
Domed roof
Parapet decorated with latticework
Balcony
Cusped arch
Roof pavilion
Circular top of minaret
Pietra dura inlay (slices of semiprecious stone laid in sockets)
Cornice
Bracket
Spandrel decorated with arabesque
Octahedral base of minaret
Star-pattern inlay
Sandstone plinth
Sandstone parapet decorated with latticework
Jali (latticed screen) with geometrical patterns
Depressed entrance arch
Sandstone stairway
Opus sectile mosaic (geometric mosaic) of stone, tile, glass, and enamel

South and east Asia

THE TRADITIONAL ARCHITECTURE of south and east Asia has been profoundly influenced by the spread from India of Buddhism and Hinduism. This influence is shown by both the abundance and by the architectural styles of temples and shrines in the region. Many early Hindu temples consist of rooms carved from solid rock faces. However, freestanding structures began to be built in southern India from about the eighth century AD. Many were built in the Dravidian style, like the Temple of Virupaksha (opposite), with its characteristic antarala (terraced tower), perforated windows, and numerous arches, pilasters, and carvings. The earliest Buddhist religious monuments were Indian stupas, which consisted of a single hemispherical dome surmounted by a chattravali (shaft) and surrounded by railings with ornate gates. Later Indian stupas and those built elsewhere were sometimes modified. For example, in Sri Lanka, the dome became bell-shaped, and was called a dagoba. Buddhist pagodas, such as the Burmese example (right), are multistoried temples, each story having a projecting roof. The form of these buildings probably derived from the yasti (pointed spire) of the stupa. Another feature of many traditional Asian buildings is their imaginative roof forms, such as gambrel (mansard) roofs, and roofs with angle rafters (below).

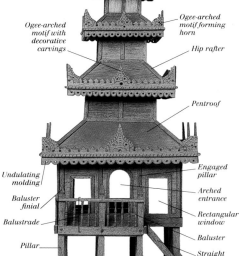

SEVEN-STORIED PAGODA IN BURMESE STYLE, c.9TH-10TH CENTURY

Gilded band
Gilded iron hti (crown)
Dubika (mast)
Arrow motif
Torus molding with spiral carving
Decorative eaves board
Ogee-arched motif with decorative carvings
Ogee-arched motif forming horn
Hip rafter
Pentroof
Engaged pillar
Undulating molding
Arched entrance
Baluster finial
Rectangular window
Balustrade
Baluster
Pillar
Straight brace

DETAILS FROM EAST ASIAN BUILDINGS

KASUGA-STYLE ROOF WITH SUMIGI (ANGLE RAFTERS), KASUGADO SHRINE OF ENJOJI, NARA, JAPAN, 12TH-14TH CENTURY

TERRACES, TEMPLE OF HEAVEN, BEIJING, CHINA, 15TH CENTURY

GAMBREL (MANSARD) ROOF WITH UPSWEPT EAVES AND UNDULATING GABLES, HIMEJI CASTLE, HIMEJI, JAPAN, 1608-1609

CORNER CAPITAL WITH ROOF BEAMS, POPCHU-SA TEMPLE, POPCHU-SA, SOUTH KOREA, 17TH CENTURY

SOUTH AND EAST ASIA

PERFORATED STONE WINDOWS, TEMPLES OF VIRUPAKSHA
AND MALLIKARJUNA, PATTADAKAL, INDIA, 8TH CENTURY

Tablet
flower

Fret
motif

Chain
motif

Floral
pattern

Leaf

Scroll
motif

Sickle
motif

Semicircle

DAGOBA STUPA,
KANDY, SRI LANKA,
c.2ND CENTURY BC–
7TH CENTURY AD

Chattra
(umbrella)

Hanging
ornament

Chattravali (shaft)

Ring with
indentations
symbolizing
chattras

Ornamental
metalwork

Yasti (tee;
pointed spire)

Harmika (stylized
square railing)

Auda
(bell-shaped
dome)

Trimala
(series of
three circular
courses)

Circular
base

SIDE VIEW AND
PLAN VIEW,
TEMPLE OF
VIRUPAKSHA,
PATTADAKAL,
INDIA, c.746

Stupica (small stupa) of
the Dravidian order

Dravidian
finial

Blind
chataya
arch

Perforated
window

Gopuram finial
(wagonlike finial)

Bracketed
capital

Small
gopuram
(gate head)

Parapet

Roll
cornice

Antarala
(terraced
tower)

Niche
with
statue

Plan
view

Twin
pilasters

Pradakshina
(circumambulatory
passage around
shrine)

Shrine

Shrine
chamber

Niche

Gate

Mandapa
(pillared hall)

Pillar

Panel with
bas-relief
carving

Gate

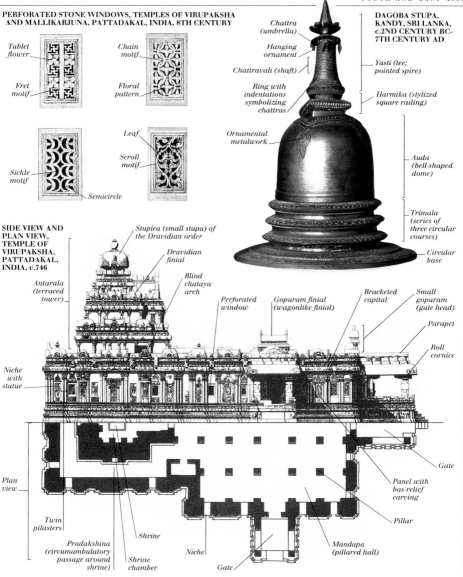

The 19th century

BUILDINGS OF THE 19TH CENTURY are characterized by the use of new materials and by a great diversity of architectural styles. From the end of the 18th century, iron and steel became widely used as alternatives to wood for the framework of buildings, as in the flax-spinning mill shown here. Built in Britain in 1796, this mill exemplifies an architectural style that became common throughout the industrialized world for more than a century. The Industrial Revolution also brought mass production of building parts—a development that enabled the British architect Sir Joseph Paxton to erect London's Crystal Palace (a building made entirely of iron and glass) in only nine months, ready for the Great Exhibition of 1851. The 19th century saw a widespread revival of older architectural styles. For example, in the United States and Germany, Neo-Greek architecture was fashionable; in Britain and France, Neo-Baroque, Neo-Byzantine, and Neo-Gothic styles (as seen in the Palace of Westminster and Tower Bridge, London) were dominant.

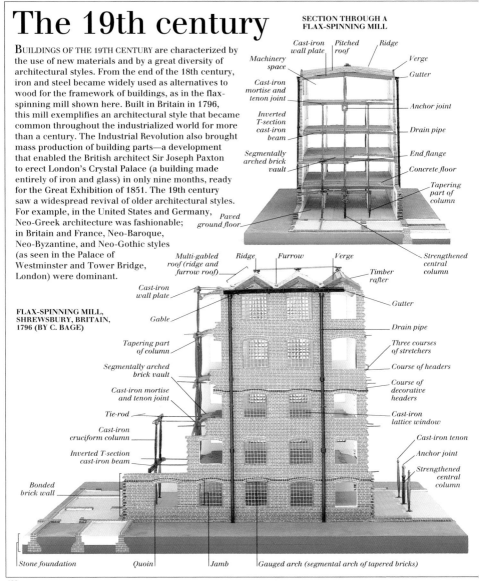

Cast-iron wall plate
Pitched roof
Ridge
Verge
Machinery space
Gutter
Cast-iron mortise and tenon joint
Anchor joint
Inverted T-section cast-iron beam
Drain pipe
Segmentally arched brick vault
End flange
Concrete floor
Tapering part of column
Paved ground floor
Strengthened central column

FLAX-SPINNING MILL, SHREWSBURY, BRITAIN, 1796 (BY C. BAGE)

Multi-gabled roof (ridge and furrow roof)
Ridge
Furrow
Verge
Timber rafter
Cast-iron wall plate
Gutter
Gable
Drain pipe
Tapering part of column
Three courses of stretchers
Segmentally arched brick vault
Course of headers
Cast-iron mortise and tenon joint
Course of decorative headers
Tie-rod
Cast-iron lattice window
Cast-iron cruciform column
Cast-iron tenon
Inverted T-section cast-iron beam
Anchor joint
Strengthened central column
Bonded brick wall
Stone foundation
Quoin
Jamb
Gauged arch (segmental arch of tapered bricks)

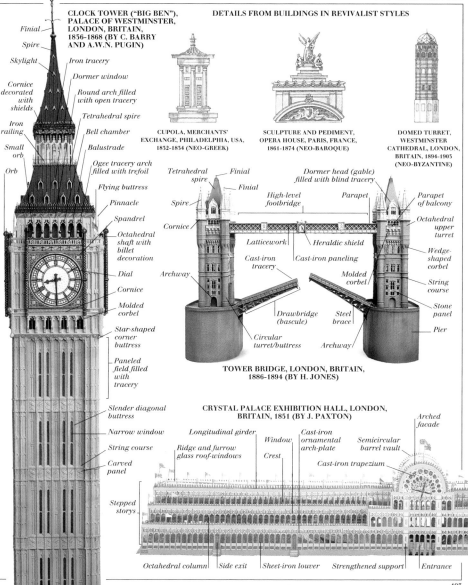

CLOCK TOWER ("BIG BEN"), PALACE OF WESTMINSTER, LONDON, BRITAIN, 1836-1868 (BY C. BARRY AND A.W.N. PUGIN)

- Finial
- Spire
- Skylight
- Cornice decorated with shields
- Iron railing
- Small orb
- Orb
- Iron tracery
- Dormer window
- Round arch filled with open tracery
- Tetrahedral spire
- Bell chamber
- Balustrade
- Ogee tracery arch filled with trefoil
- Flying buttress
- Pinnacle
- Spandrel
- Octahedral shaft with billet decoration
- Dial
- Cornice
- Molded corbel
- Star-shaped corner buttress
- Paneled field filled with tracery
- Slender diagonal buttress
- Narrow window
- String course
- Carved panel
- Stepped storys

DETAILS FROM BUILDINGS IN REVIVALIST STYLES

CUPOLA, MERCHANTS' EXCHANGE, PHILADELPHIA, USA, 1832-1834 (NEO-GREEK)

SCULPTURE AND PEDIMENT, OPERA HOUSE, PARIS, FRANCE, 1861-1874 (NEO-BAROQUE)

DOMED TURRET, WESTMINSTER CATHEDRAL, LONDON, BRITAIN, 1894-1903 (NEO-BYZANTINE)

- Tetrahedral spire
- Finial
- Spire
- Cornice
- Finial
- High-level footbridge
- Dormer head (gable) filled with blind tracery
- Parapet
- Latticework
- Heraldic shield
- Cast-iron paneling
- Cast-iron tracery
- Archway
- Drawbridge (bascule)
- Steel brace
- Molded corbel
- Circular turret/buttress
- Archway
- Parapet of balcony
- Octahedral upper turret
- Wedge-shaped corbel
- String course
- Stone panel
- Pier

TOWER BRIDGE, LONDON, BRITAIN, 1886-1894 (BY H. JONES)

CRYSTAL PALACE EXHIBITION HALL, LONDON, BRITAIN, 1851 (BY J. PAXTON)

- Longitudinal girder
- Ridge and furrow glass roof-windows
- Window
- Crest
- Cast-iron ornamental arch-plate
- Semicircular barrel vault
- Cast-iron trapezium
- Arched facade
- Octahedral column
- Side exit
- Sheet-iron louver
- Strengthened support
- Entrance

The early 20th century

ARCHITECTURE OF THE EARLY 20TH CENTURY is notable for radical new types of steel and glass buildings—particularly skyscrapers—and the widespread use of steel-reinforced concrete. The steel-framed skyscraper was pioneered in Chicago in the 1880s but did not become widespread until the first decades of the 20th century. As construction techniques were refined, skyscrapers became higher and higher. For example, the Empire State Building (right) of 1929-1931 has 102 storys. Many buildings of this period were constructed from lightweight concrete slabs that could be supported by cantilever beams or by pilotis (stilts), as in the Villa Savoye (below). The early 20th century also produced a great variety of architectural styles, some of which are illustrated opposite. Despite their diversity, the styles of this period generally had one thing in common: they were completely new, with few links to past architectural styles. This originality is in marked contrast to 19th-century architecture (see pp. 492-493), much of which was revivalist.

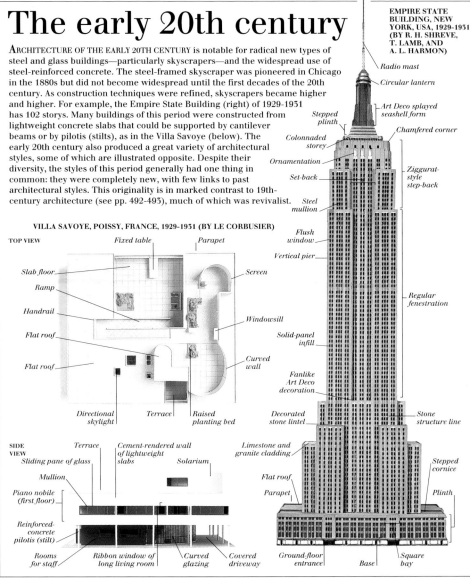

EMPIRE STATE BUILDING, NEW YORK, USA, 1929-1931 (BY R. H. SHREVE, T. LAMB, AND A. L. HARMON)

- Radio mast
- Circular lantern
- Art Deco splayed seashell form
- Chamfered corner
- Stepped plinth
- Colonnaded storey
- Ornamentation
- Set-back
- Ziggurat-style step-back
- Steel mullion
- Flush window
- Vertical pier
- Regular fenestration
- Solid-panel infill
- Fanlike Art Deco decoration
- Decorated stone lintel
- Stone structure line
- Limestone and granite cladding
- Stepped cornice
- Flat roof
- Parapet
- Plinth
- Ground-floor entrance
- Base
- Square bay

VILLA SAVOYE, POISSY, FRANCE, 1929-1931 (BY LE CORBUSIER)

TOP VIEW
- Fixed table
- Parapet
- Slab floor
- Ramp
- Handrail
- Flat roof
- Flat roof
- Screen
- Windowsill
- Curved wall
- Directional skylight
- Terrace
- Raised planting bed

SIDE VIEW
- Terrace
- Cement-rendered wall of lightweight slabs
- Solarium
- Sliding pane of glass
- Mullion
- Piano nobile (first floor)
- Reinforced-concrete pilotis (stilt)
- Rooms for staff
- Ribbon window of long living room
- Curved glazing
- Covered driveway

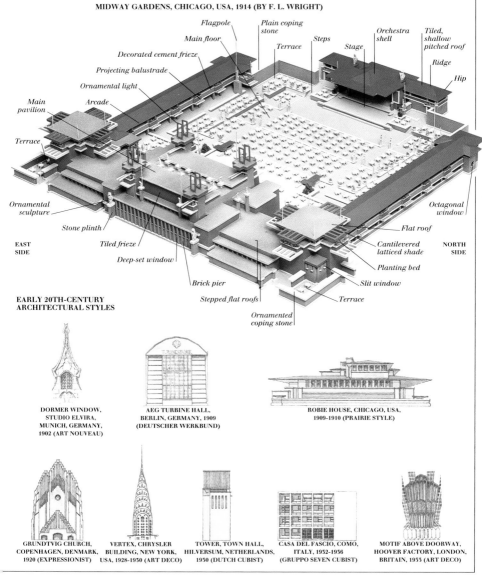

MIDWAY GARDENS, CHICAGO, USA, 1914 (BY F. L. WRIGHT)

Flagpole
Plain coping stone
Main floor
Terrace
Steps
Stage
Orchestra shell
Tiled, shallow pitched roof
Decorated cement frieze
Projecting balustrade
Ornamental light
Arcade
Ridge
Hip
Main pavilion
Terrace
Ornamental sculpture
Stone plinth
Tiled frieze
Deep-set window
Brick pier
Stepped flat roofs
Ornamented coping stone
Octagonal window
Flat roof
Cantilevered latticed shade
Planting bed
Slit window
Terrace

EAST SIDE

NORTH SIDE

EARLY 20TH-CENTURY ARCHITECTURAL STYLES

DORMER WINDOW, STUDIO ELVIRA, MUNICH, GERMANY, 1902 (ART NOUVEAU)

AEG TURBINE HALL, BERLIN, GERMANY, 1909 (DEUTSCHER WERKBUND)

ROBIE HOUSE, CHICAGO, USA, 1909-1910 (PRAIRIE STYLE)

GRUNDTVIG CHURCH, COPENHAGEN, DENMARK, 1920 (EXPRESSIONIST)

VERTEX, CHRYSLER BUILDING, NEW YORK, USA, 1928-1930 (ART DECO)

TOWER, TOWN HALL, HILVERSUM, NETHERLANDS, 1930 (DUTCH CUBIST)

CASA DEL FASCIO, COMO, ITALY, 1932-1936 (GRUPPO SEVEN CUBIST)

MOTIF ABOVE DOORWAY, HOOVER FACTORY, LONDON, BRITAIN, 1933 (ART DECO)

Modern buildings 1

ARCHITECTURE SINCE ABOUT THE 1950s is generally known as modern architecture. One of its main influences has been functionalism—a belief that a building's function should be apparent in its design. Both the Centre Georges Pompidou (below and opposite) and the Hong Kong and Shanghai Bank (see pp. 498-499) are functionalist buildings. On each, elements of engineering and the building's services are clearly visible on the outside. In the 1980s, some architects rejected functionalism in favor of postmodernism, in which historical styles—particularly neoclassicism—were revived, using modern building materials and techniques. In many modern buildings, walls are made of glass or concrete hung from a frame, as in the Kawana House (right); this type of wall construction is known as curtain walling. Other modern construction techniques include the intricate interlocking of concrete vaults—as in the Sydney Opera House (see pp. 498-499)—and the use of high-tension beams to create complex roof shapes, such as the paraboloid roof of the Church of St. Pierre de Libreville (see pp. 498-499).

Solar panel

Concrete frame

Pile foundation

Raft   Composite cladding panel

SIDE VIEW

Rocker beam

Curtain walling

Lattice beam

Floor-beam connection   Floor

FRONT VIEW

SERVICES FACADE, CENTRE GEORGES POMPIDOU, PARIS, FRANCE, 1977 (BY R. PIANO AND R. ROGERS)

Metal-faced fire-resistant panel

Air-conditioning duct

Cooling tower

Water pipe

Grand gallery level

Main gallery levels

Library level

Administrative level

Mezzanine gallery level

Reception level

Staircase to grand hall

Electrical plant

Water-cooled fire-resistant column

Continuous glazing

Tinted glass

Services entrance

PRINCIPAL FACADE, CENTRE GEORGES POMPIDOU

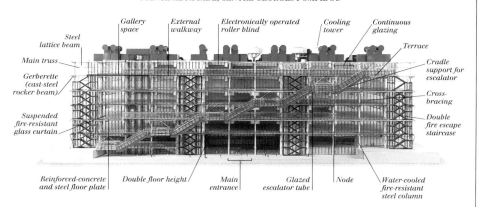

Gallery space

External walkway

Electronically operated roller blind

Cooling tower

Continuous glazing

Steel lattice beam

Main truss

Gerberette (cast-steel rocker beam)

Suspended fire-resistant glass curtain

Terrace

Cradle support for escalator

Cross-bracing

Double fire escape staircase

Reinforced-concrete and steel floor plate

Double floor height

Main entrance

Glazed escalator tube

Node

Water-cooled fire-resistant steel column

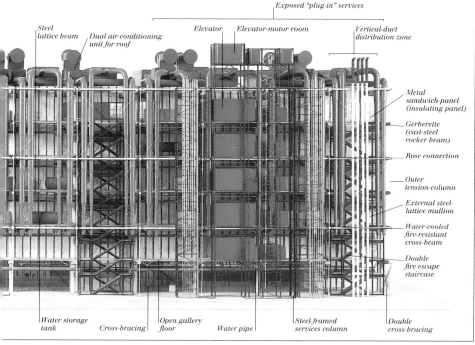

Exposed "plug-in" services

Steel lattice beam

Dual air-conditioning unit for roof

Elevator

Elevator-motor room

Vertical-duct distribution zone

Metal sandwich-panel (insulating panel)

Gerberette (cast-steel rocker beam)

Rose connection

Outer tension-column

External steel-lattice mullion

Water-cooled fire-resistant cross-beam

Double fire escape staircase

Water storage tank

Cross-bracing

Open gallery floor

Water pipe

Steel-framed services column

Double cross-bracing

Modern buildings 2

HONG KONG AND SHANGHAI BANK, HONG KONG, 1981-1985 (BY N. FOSTER)

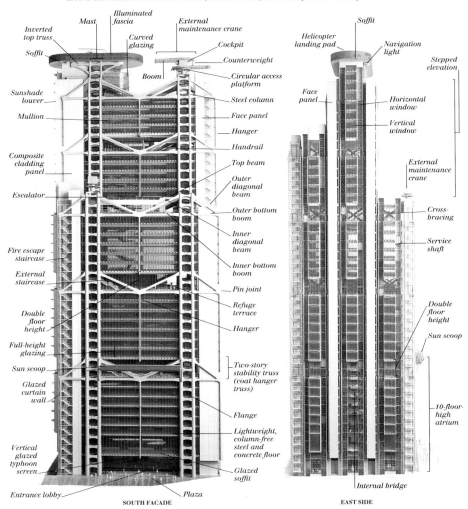

Inverted top truss
Mast
Illuminated fascia
Curved glazing
External maintenance crane
Cockpit
Soffit
Counterweight
Boom
Circular access platform
Steel column
Sunshade louver
Face panel
Mullion
Hanger
Handrail
Composite cladding panel
Top beam
Outer diagonal beam
Escalator
Outer bottom boom
Inner diagonal beam
Fire escape staircase
Inner bottom boom
External staircase
Pin joint
Refuge terrace
Double floor height
Hanger
Full-height glazing
Sun scoop
Two-story stability truss (coat hanger truss)
Glazed curtain wall
Flange
Lightweight, column-free steel and concrete floor
Vertical glazed typhoon screen
Glazed soffit
Entrance lobby
Plaza

SOUTH FACADE

Soffit
Helicopter landing pad
Navigation light
Stepped elevation
Face panel
Horizontal window
Vertical window
External maintenance crane
Cross-bracing
Service shaft
Double floor height
Sun scoop
10-floor-high atrium
Internal bridge

EAST SIDE

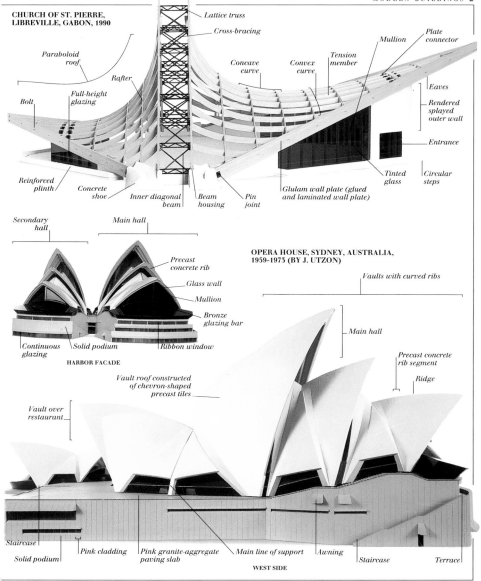

CHURCH OF ST. PIERRE, LIBREVILLE, GABON, 1990

Lattice truss

Cross-bracing

Paraboloid roof

Rafter

Concave curve

Convex curve

Tension member

Mullion

Plate connector

Eaves

Full-height glazing

Rendered splayed outer wall

Bolt

Entrance

Reinforced plinth

Concrete shoe

Inner diagonal beam

Beam housing

Pin joint

Tinted glass

Circular steps

Glulam wall plate (glued and laminated wall plate)

Secondary hall

Main hall

OPERA HOUSE, SYDNEY, AUSTRALIA, 1959-1973 (BY J. UTZON)

Vaults with curved ribs

Precast concrete rib

Glass wall

Mullion

Bronze glazing bar

Main hall

Precast concrete rib segment

Ridge

Continuous glazing

Solid podium

Ribbon window

HARBOR FACADE

Vault roof constructed of chevron-shaped precast tiles

Vault over restaurant

Staircase

Solid podium

Pink cladding

Pink granite-aggregate paving slab

Main line of support

Awning

Staircase

Terrace

WEST SIDE

MUSIC

Musical notation

MUSICAL NOTATION IS ANY METHOD by which sounds are written down so that they can be read and performed by others. The present-day conventional system of notation uses a five-line stave (staff)—divided by vertical lines into sections known as bars—on which notes, rests, clefs, key signatures, time signatures, accidentals, and other symbols are written. A note indicates the duration of a sound and, according to its position on the stave, its pitch. Notes can be arranged on the stave in order of pitch to form a scale. A silence in the music is indicated by a rest. The clef, which is placed at the beginning of a stave, fixes the pitch. The key signature, which is placed after the clef, indicates the key. The time signature, placed after the key signature, shows the number of beats in a bar. Accidentals are used to indicate the raising or lowering of the pitch of a note.

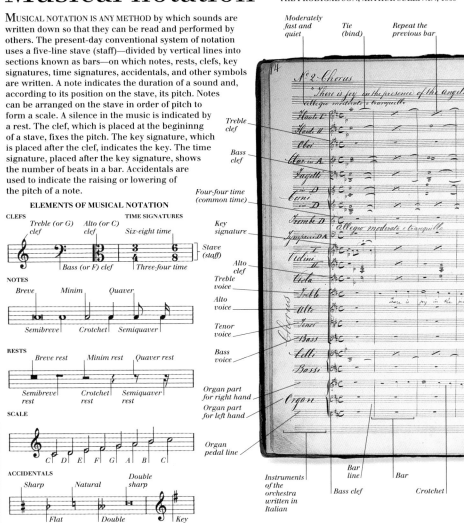

ELEMENTS OF MUSICAL NOTATION

CLEFS

Treble (or G) clef Alto (or C) clef

Bass (or F) clef

TIME SIGNATURES

Six-eight time

Three-four time

NOTES

Breve Minim Quaver

Semibreve Crotchet Semiquaver

RESTS

Breve rest Minim rest Quaver rest

Semibreve rest Crotchet rest Semiquaver rest

SCALE

C D E F G A B C

ACCIDENTALS

Sharp Natural Double sharp

Flat Double flat Key signature

Moderately fast and quiet Tie (bind) Repeat the previous bar

Treble clef

Bass clef

Four-four time (common time)

Key signature

Stave (staff)

Alto clef

Treble voice

Alto voice

Tenor voice

Bass voice

Organ part for right hand

Organ part for left hand

Organ pedal line

Instruments of the orchestra written in Italian

Bass clef

Bar line

Bar

Crotchet

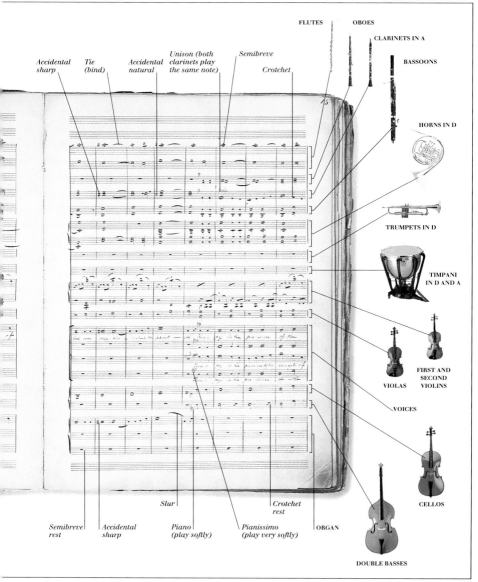

FLUTES

OBOES

CLARINETS IN A

BASSOONS

HORNS IN D

TRUMPETS IN D

TIMPANI
IN D AND A

FIRST AND
SECOND
VIOLINS

VIOLAS

VOICES

CELLOS

ORGAN

DOUBLE BASSES

Accidental
sharp

Tie
(bind)

Accidental
natural

Unison (both
clarinets play
the same note)

Semibreve

Crotchet

Semibreve
rest

Accidental
sharp

Slur

Piano
(play softly)

Pianissimo
(play very softly)

Crotchet
rest

Orchestras

AN ORCHESTRA IS A GROUP of musicians that
plays music written for a specific combination of
instruments. The number and type of instruments
included in the orchestra depends on the style of
music being played. The modern orchestra (also
known as a symphony orchestra) is made up
of four sections of instruments—stringed,
woodwind, brass, and percussion. The
stringed section consists of violins, violas,
cellos (violoncellos), double basses, and
sometimes a harp (see pp. 510-511). The main
instruments of the woodwind section are flutes,
oboes, clarinets, and bassoons—the piccolo, cor
anglais, bass clarinet, saxophone, and double
bassoon (contrabassoon) can also be included
if the music requires them (see pp. 508-509).
The brass section usually consists of horns,
trumpets, trombones, and the tuba (see
pp. 506-507). The main instruments of
the percussion section are the timpani
(see pp. 518-519). The snare drum,
bass drum, cymbals, tambourine,
triangle, tubular bells, xylophone,
vibraphone, gong (tam-tam),
castanets, and maracas can
also be included in the
percussion section (see
pp. 516-517). The musicians
are usually arranged in a semi-
circle—strings spread along the
front, woodwind and brass in the
center, and percussion at the back.
A conductor stands in front of the
musicians and controls the tempo
(speed) of the music and the overall
balance of the sound, ensuring
that no instruments are too
loud or too soft in relation
to the others.

XYLOPHONE

VIBRAPHONE

TAM-TAM
(GONG)

TUBULAR
BELLS

CASTANETS

TAMBOURINE

MARACAS

TRIANGLE

TRUMPETS

HORNS

CLARINETS

BASS
CLARINET

HARP

SAXOPHONE

PICCOLO

SECOND VIOLINS

FIRST VIOLINS

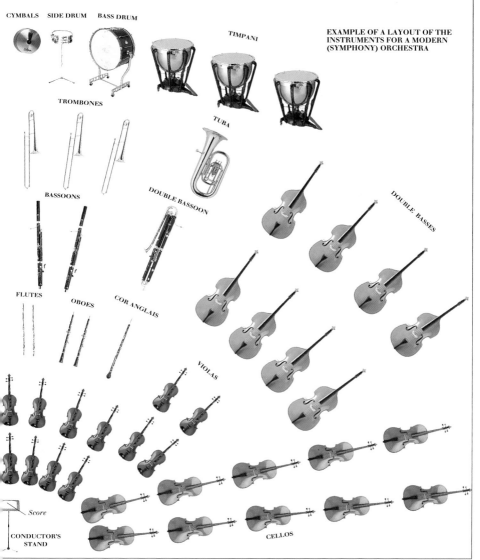

CYMBALS SIDE DRUM BASS DRUM

TIMPANI

**EXAMPLE OF A LAYOUT OF THE
INSTRUMENTS FOR A MODERN
(SYMPHONY) ORCHESTRA**

TROMBONES

TUBA

BASSOONS

DOUBLE BASSOON

DOUBLE BASSES

FLUTES

OBOES

COR ANGLAIS

VIOLAS

Score

CONDUCTOR'S
STAND

CELLOS

Brass instruments

BUGLE

BRASS INSTRUMENTS ARE WIND INSTRUMENTS that are made of metal, usually brass. Although they appear in many different shapes and sizes, all brass instruments have a mouthpiece, a length of hollow tube, and a flared bell. The mouthpiece of a brass instrument may be cup-shaped, as in the cornet, or cone-shaped, as in the horn. The tube may be wide or narrow, mainly conical, as in the horn and tuba, or mainly cylindrical, as in the trumpet and trombone. The sound of a brass instrument is made by the player's lips vibrating against the mouthpiece, so that the air vibrates in the tube. By changing lip tension, the player can vary the vibrations and produce notes of different pitches. The range of notes produced by a brass instrument can be extended by means of a valve system. Most brass instruments, such as the trumpet, have piston valves that divert the air in the instrument along an extra piece of tubing (known as a valve slide) when pressed down. The total length of the tube is increased and the pitch of the note produced is lowered. Instead of valves, the trombone has a movable slide that can be pushed away from or drawn toward the player. The sound of a brass instrument can also be changed by inserting a mute into the bell of the instrument.

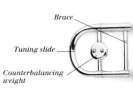

Brace

Tuning slide

Counterbalancing weight

SIMPLIFIED DIAGRAM SHOWING HOW A PISTON VALVE SYSTEM WORKS

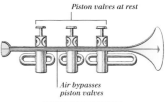

Piston valves at rest

Air bypasses piston valves

PISTON VALVES AT REST

First piston valve pressed down

Second and third piston valves at rest

Air diverted through first valve slide

PISTON VALVE PRESSED DOWN

TRUMPET

Finger button

First piston valve

Spring returns piston valve to rest position

Second piston valve

Third piston valve

Holes divert air into valve slides

Little finger support

Music stand holder

Narrow, cylindrical tube

Flared bell

Cup-shaped mouthpiece

Mouthpiece receiver

Tuning slide

Tuning slide water key

First valve slide

First valve slide thumb hook

Second valve slide

Third valve slide finger ring

Third valve slide

Third valve slide water key

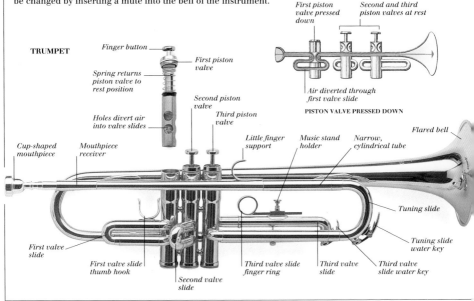

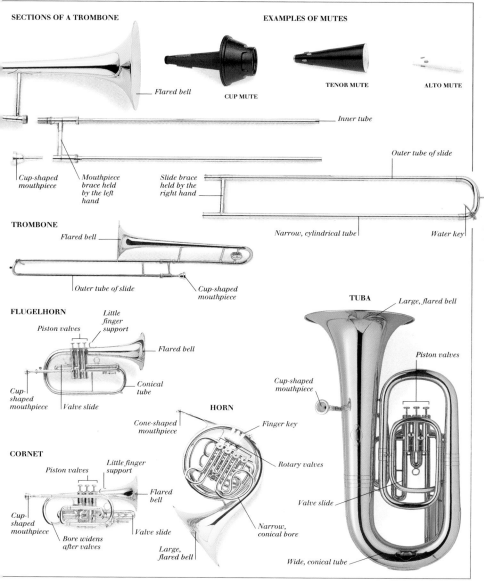

SECTIONS OF A TROMBONE

EXAMPLES OF MUTES

Flared bell

CUP MUTE

TENOR MUTE

ALTO MUTE

Inner tube

Outer tube of slide

Cup-shaped mouthpiece

Mouthpiece brace held by the left hand

Slide brace held by the right hand

Narrow, cylindrical tube

Water key

TROMBONE

Flared bell

Outer tube of slide

Cup-shaped mouthpiece

TUBA

Large, flared bell

FLUGELHORN

Piston valves

Little finger support

Flared bell

Piston valves

Cup-shaped mouthpiece

Valve slide

Conical tube

Cup-shaped mouthpiece

HORN

Cone-shaped mouthpiece

Finger key

Rotary valves

Valve slide

CORNET

Piston valves

Little finger support

Flared bell

Cup-shaped mouthpiece

Bore widens after valves

Valve slide

Narrow, conical bore

Large, flared bell

Wide, conical tube

Woodwind instruments

WOODWIND INSTRUMENTS ARE wind instruments that are generally made of wood, although some are made of metal or plastic. The sound of a woodwind instrument is produced by the vibration of air in a hollow tube. The air is made to vibrate by blowing across a blow hole—as in the flute and piccolo— or by blowing through a single reed— as in the clarinet and saxophone— or a double reed—as in the bassoon, cor anglais, and oboe. The pitch of a woodwind instrument can be changed by opening or closing holes cut into the tube of the instrument.

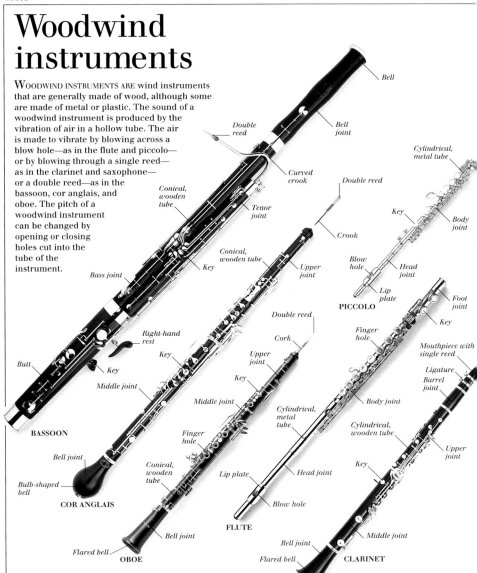

Bell

Double reed

Bell joint

Cylindrical, metal tube

Conical, wooden tube

Curved crook

Double reed

Key

Tenor joint

Body joint

Conical, wooden tube

Crook

Upper joint

Blow hole

Head joint

Key

Bass joint

Lip plate

PICCOLO

Double reed

Foot joint

Right-hand rest

Cork

Finger hole

Key

Upper joint

Mouthpiece with single reed

Butt

Key

Key

Ligature

Barrel joint

Middle joint

Key

Middle joint

Cylindrical, metal tube

Body joint

Cylindrical, wooden tube

BASSOON

Finger hole

Key

Upper joint

Bell joint

Conical, wooden tube

Lip plate

Head joint

Bulb-shaped bell

COR ANGLAIS

Blow hole

FLUTE

Bell joint

Middle joint

Flared bell

Bell joint

OBOE

Flared bell

CLARINET

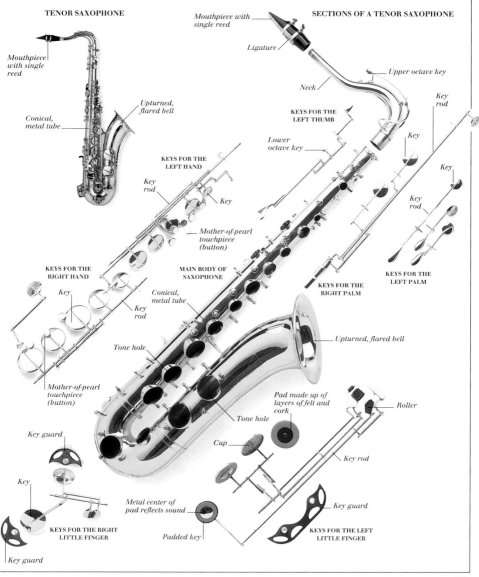

TENOR SAXOPHONE

Mouthpiece with single reed

Conical, metal tube

Upturned, flared bell

SECTIONS OF A TENOR SAXOPHONE

Mouthpiece with single reed

Ligature

Neck

Upper octave key

Key rod

KEYS FOR THE LEFT THUMB

Lower octave key

Key

Key

Key rod

KEYS FOR THE LEFT PALM

KEYS FOR THE LEFT HAND

Key rod

Key

Mother-of-pearl touchpiece (button)

KEYS FOR THE RIGHT HAND

Key

Key rod

MAIN BODY OF SAXOPHONE

Conical, metal tube

Tone hole

KEYS FOR THE RIGHT PALM

Mother-of-pearl touchpiece (button)

Upturned, flared bell

Tone hole

Pad made up of layers of felt and cork

Roller

Cup

Key guard

Key rod

Key

Metal center of pad reflects sound

KEYS FOR THE RIGHT LITTLE FINGER

Padded key

Key guard

KEYS FOR THE LEFT LITTLE FINGER

Key guard

Stringed instruments

STRINGED INSTRUMENTS PRODUCE SOUND by the vibration of stretched strings. This may be done by drawing a bow across the strings, as in the violin; or by plucking the strings, as in the harp and guitar (see pp. 512-513). The four modern members of the bowed string family are the violin, viola, cello (violoncello), and double bass. Each consists of a hollow, wooden body, a long neck, and four strings. The bow is a wooden stick with horsehair stretched across its length. The vibrations made by drawing the bow across the strings are transmitted to the hollow body, and this itself vibrates, amplifying and enriching the sound produced. The harp consists of a set of strings of different lengths stretched across a wooden frame. The strings are plucked by the player's thumbs and fingers—except the little finger of each hand—which produces vibrations that are amplified by the harp's sound board. The pitch of the note produced by any stringed instrument depends on the length, weight, and tension of the string. A shorter, lighter, or tighter string gives a higher note.

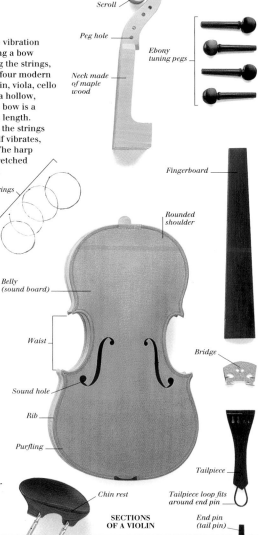

Scroll eye

Scroll

Peg hole

Ebony tuning pegs

Neck made of maple wood

Fingerboard

Rounded shoulder

Strings

Belly (sound board)

Waist

Bridge

Sound hole

Rib

Purfling

Head

Point

Stick

Scroll

Scroll eye

Horsehair

Peg box

Tuning peg

Nut

String

Fingerboard

Rounded shoulder

Belly (sound board)

Purfling

Waist

Sound hole

Bridge

Tuning adjustor

Frog

Tailpiece

Screw

Chin rest

Tailpiece loop fits around end pin

Chin rest

VIOLIN BOW

VIOLIN

SECTIONS OF A VIOLIN

End pin (tail pin)

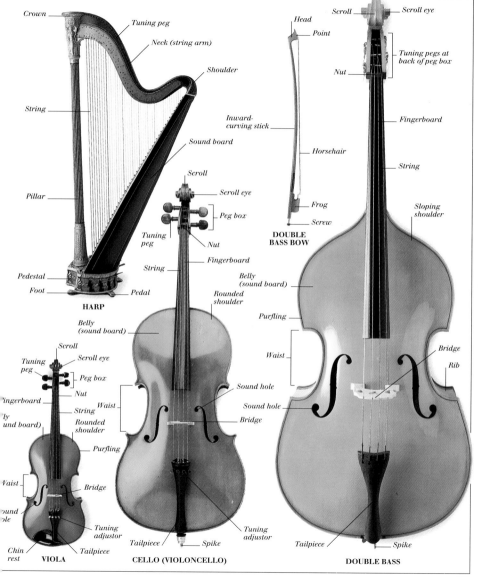

Crown
Tuning peg
Neck (string arm)
Shoulder
String
Sound board
Pillar
Pedestal
Foot
Pedal

HARP

Head
Point
Inward-curving stick
Horsehair
Frog
Screw

DOUBLE BASS BOW

Scroll
Scroll eye
Tuning pegs at back of peg box
Nut
Fingerboard
String
Sloping shoulder

Scroll
Scroll eye
Peg box
Tuning peg
Nut
Fingerboard
String
Belly (sound board)
Rounded shoulder
Belly (sound board)
Waist
Sound hole
Bridge
Tuning adjustor
Tailpiece
Spike

CELLO (VIOLONCELLO)

Scroll
Tuning peg
Scroll eye
Peg box
Nut
Fingerboard
String
Belly (sound board)
Rounded shoulder
Purfling
Waist
Bridge
Tuning adjustor
Chin rest
Tailpiece
Sound hole
Waist

VIOLA

Purfling
Waist
Sound hole
Sound hole
Bridge
Bridge
Rib
Tailpiece
Spike

DOUBLE BASS

Guitars

THE GUITAR IS A PLUCKED stringed instrument
(see pp. 510-511). There are two types of guitar—
acoustic and electric. Acoustic guitars have hollow
bodies and six or twelve strings. Plucking or strumming
the strings produces vibrations that are amplified by their
hollow bodies. Electric guitars usually have solid bodies
and six strings. Pick-ups placed under the strings convert
vibrations into electronic signals that are magnified by
an amplifier, and sent to a loudspeaker where they are
converted into sounds (see pp. 520-521). Electric bass
guitars are very similar in structure to electric guitars,
and produce sound in the same way, but have four
heavier-gage strings and play lower pitched notes.

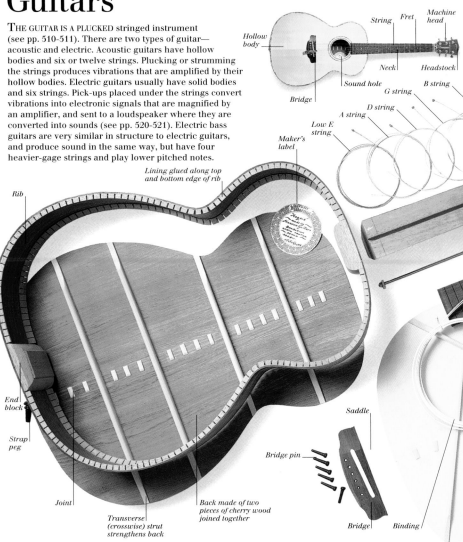

String · Fret · Machine head

Hollow body

Neck · Headstock

Sound hole · B string

G string

Bridge

D string

A string

Low E string

Maker's label

Lining glued along top and bottom edge of rib

Rib

End block

Strap peg

Saddle

Joint

Bridge pin

Back made of two pieces of cherry wood joined together

Transverse (crosswise) strut strengthens back

Bridge · Binding

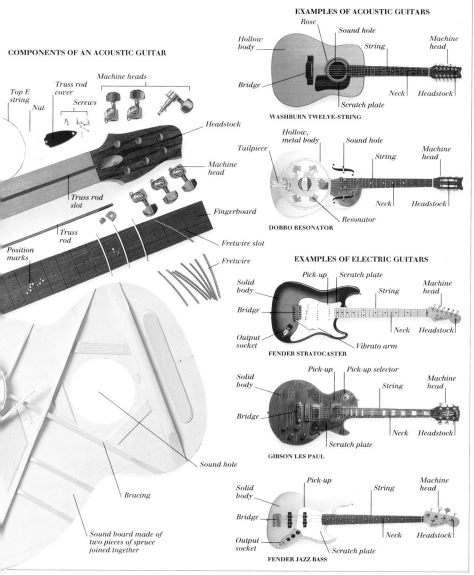

COMPONENTS OF AN ACOUSTIC GUITAR

Top E string
Nut
Truss rod cover
Screws
Machine heads
Headstock
Machine head
Truss rod slot
Truss rod
Fingerboard
Position marks
Fretwire slot
Fretwire
Sound hole
Bracing
Sound board made of two pieces of spruce joined together

EXAMPLES OF ACOUSTIC GUITARS

Rose
Sound hole
Hollow body
String
Machine head
Bridge
Neck
Headstock
Scratch plate

WASHBURN TWELVE-STRING

Hollow, metal body
Sound hole
Tailpiece
String
Machine head
Neck
Headstock
Resonator

DOBRO RESONATOR

EXAMPLES OF ELECTRIC GUITARS

Pick-up
Scratch plate
Solid body
String
Machine head
Bridge
Neck
Headstock
Output socket
Vibrato arm

FENDER STRATOCASTER

Pick-up
Pick-up selector
Solid body
String
Machine head
Bridge
Neck
Headstock
Scratch plate

GIBSON LES PAUL

Pick-up
String
Machine head
Solid body
Bridge
Neck
Headstock
Output socket
Scratch plate

FENDER JAZZ BASS

Keyboard instruments

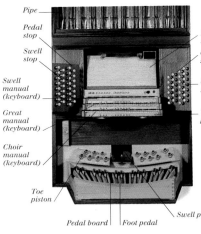

KEYBOARD INSTRUMENTS are instruments that are sounded by means of a keyboard. The organ and piano are two of the principal members of the keyboard family. The organ consists of pipes which are operated by one or more keyboards and foot pedals. The pipes are lined up in rows (known as ranks or registers) on top of a wind chest. The sound of the organ is made when air is admitted into a pipe by pressing a key or pedal. The piano consists of wire strings stretched over a metal frame, and a keyboard and pedals that operate hammers and dampers. The piano frame is either vertical—as in the upright piano—or horizontal—as in the grand piano. When a key is at rest, a damper lies against the string to keep it from vibrating. When a key is pressed down, the damper moves away from the string as the hammer strikes it, causing the string to vibrate and sound a note.

ORGAN PIPE

UPRIGHT PIANO

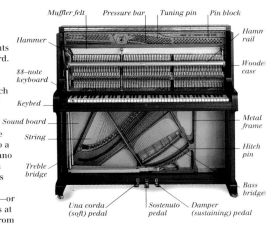

Muffler felt · Pressure bar · Tuning pin · Pin block

Hammer

Hammer rail

88–note keyboard

Wooden case

Keybed

Sound board

Metal frame

String

Hitch pin

Treble bridge

Bass bridge

Una corda (soft) pedal · Sostenuto pedal · Damper (sustaining) pedal

ORGAN CONSOLE

Pipe

Pedal stop

Swell stop

Swell manual (keyboard)

Great manual (keyboard)

Choir manual (keyboard)

Music stand

Choir stop

Great stop

Thumb piston

Toe piston

Pedal board | Foot pedal

Swell pedal

UPRIGHT PIANO ACTION

KEY AT REST

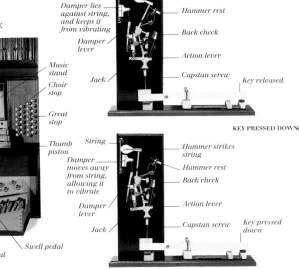

String

Damper lies against string, and keeps it from vibrating

Hammer

Hammer rest

Back check

Damper lever

Jack

Action lever

Capstan screw

Key released

KEY PRESSED DOWN

String

Damper moves away from string, allowing it to vibrate

Hammer strikes string

Hammer rest

Back check

Damper lever

Jack

Action lever

Capstan screw

Key pressed down

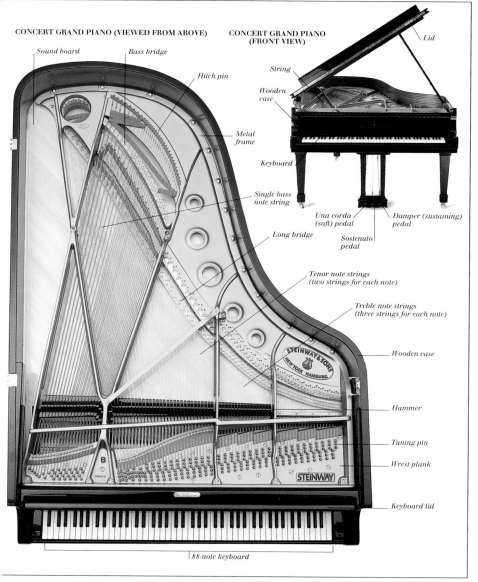

CONCERT GRAND PIANO (VIEWED FROM ABOVE)

CONCERT GRAND PIANO (FRONT VIEW)

Sound board

Bass bridge

Hitch pin

Metal frame

Single bass note string

Long bridge

Tenor note strings (two strings for each note)

Treble note strings (three strings for each note)

Lid

String

Wooden case

Keyboard

Una corda (soft) pedal

Sostenuto pedal

Damper (sustaining) pedal

Wooden case

Hammer

Tuning pin

Wrest plank

Keyboard lid

88-note keyboard

STEINWAY & SONS
NEW YORK HAMBURG

STEINWAY

B
S18422

Percussion instruments

TEMPLE BLOCKS

PERCUSSION INSTRUMENTS are a large group of instruments that produce sound by being struck, shaken, scraped, or clashed together. Some percussion instruments—such as the gong (tam-tam), cymbals, and maracas—do not have a definite pitch and are used for rhythm and impact, and the distinctive timber (color) of their sound. Other percussion instruments—such as the xylophone, vibraphone, and tubular bells—are tuned to a definite pitch and can play melody, harmony, and rhythms. The xylophone and vibraphone each have two rows of bars that are arranged in a similar way to the black and white keys of a piano. Metal tubes are suspended below the bars to amplify the sound. The vibraphone has electrically operated fans that rotate in the tubes and produce a vibrato (wavering pitch) effect.

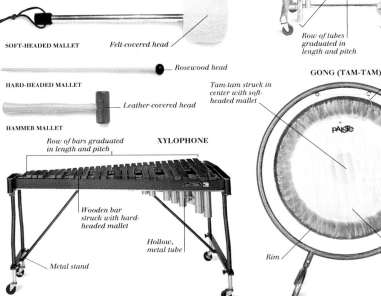

TUBULAR BELLS

Tube struck with mallet

Hollow, metal tube

Damper bar

Metal frame

Mechanism linking pedal and damper bar

Row of tubes graduated in length and pitch

Damper pedal

EXAMPLES OF MALLETS

SOFT-HEADED MALLET   Felt-covered head

HARD-HEADED MALLET   Rosewood head

Leather-covered head

HAMMER MALLET

Row of bars graduated in length and pitch   **XYLOPHONE**

Wooden bar struck with hard-headed mallet

Hollow, metal tube

Metal stand

GONG (TAM-TAM)

Tam-tam struck in center with soft-headed mallet

Cord

Metal frame

PAISTE

Rim

Large, metal disk

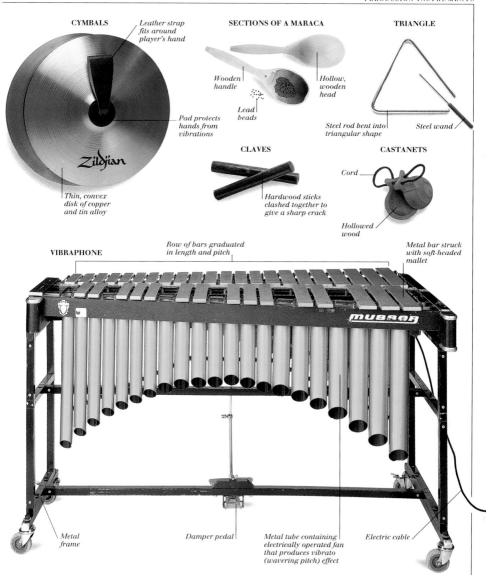

CYMBALS

Leather strap fits around player's hand

Pad protects hands from vibrations

Zildjian

Thin, convex disk of copper and tin alloy

SECTIONS OF A MARACA

Wooden handle

Lead beads

Hollow, wooden head

TRIANGLE

Steel rod bent into triangular shape

Steel wand

CLAVES

Hardwood sticks clashed together to give a sharp crack

CASTANETS

Cord

Hollowed wood

VIBRAPHONE

Row of bars graduated in length and pitch

Metal bar struck with soft-headed mallet

MUSSER

Metal frame

Damper pedal

Metal tube containing electrically operated fan that produces vibrato (wavering pitch) effect

Electric cable

Drums

A DRUM IS A percussion instrument that consists of a drumhead, made of skin or plastic, stretched over one or both ends of a hollow vessel (the body shell). Drums are played in most parts of the world and are made in a number of different shapes and sizes. They can be divided into three groups according to the shape of the body shell: frame drums (e.g., tambourines), bowl-shaped drums (e.g., timpani), and tubular drums (e.g., congas). Drums are usually sounded by striking the drumhead with the hands or with mallets, such as a hard-headed stick. The drumhead vibrates, and its vibrations are amplified by the hollow body shell. The snare drum has wires—known as snares—stretched across the lower drumhead; the snares vibrate against the lower drumhead when the drum is played. Most drums, such as congas, do not have a definite pitch and can play only rhythms (see pp. 516-517). Other drums, such as timpani, have a definite pitch and can play melody, harmony, and rhythms. They can be tuned by adjusting the tension of the drumhead. Different types of drum can be combined together with other percussion instruments to form a drum kit. The basic components of the drum kit are bass drum, tom-toms, floor tom (tenor drum), snare drum, and cymbals.

TAMBOURINE

DRUM KIT

Crash cymbal

Tension key

Tension rod

Tom-tom

Lug

Hi-hat cymbal

Snare drum

Tripod stand

Chain

Tension screw

Felt-covered mallet

Pedal

Pedal

SNARE DRUM (VIEWED FROM BELOW)

Snare mounting

Adjustable damper

Lug

Transparent lower drumhead

Snare

Upper drumhead

Stick

Snare release lever

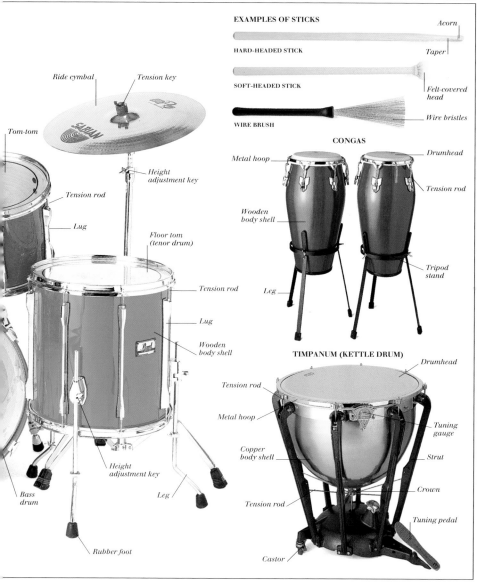

EXAMPLES OF STICKS

Acorn

HARD-HEADED STICK

Taper

SOFT-HEADED STICK

Felt-covered head

WIRE BRUSH

Wire bristles

Ride cymbal

Tension key

Tom-tom

Height adjustment key

Tension rod

Lug

Floor tom (tenor drum)

Tension rod

Lug

Wooden body shell

Height adjustment key

Leg

Bass drum

Rubber foot

CONGAS

Metal hoop

Drumhead

Tension rod

Wooden body shell

Leg

Tripod stand

TIMPANUM (KETTLE DRUM)

Drumhead

Tension rod

Metal hoop

Tuning gauge

Strut

Copper body shell

Crown

Tension rod

Tuning pedal

Castor

Electronic instruments

ELECTRONIC DRUMS

ELECTRONIC INSTRUMENTS generate electronic signals
that are magnified by an amplifier, and sent to a loudspeaker
where they are converted into sounds. Synthesizers, and other
electronic instruments, simulate the characteristic sounds of
conventional instruments, and also create entirely new sounds.
Most electronic instruments are keyboard instruments, but electronic
wind and percussion instruments are also popular. A digital sampler
records and stores sounds from musical instruments or other sources.
When the sound is played back, the pitch of the original sound can be
altered. A keyboard can be connected to the sampler so that a tune can
be played using the sampled sounds. With a MIDI (Musical Instrument
Digital Interface) system, a computer can be linked with other electronic
instruments, such as keyboards and electronic drums, to make sounds
together or in sequence. It is also possible, using music software, to
compose and play music on a home computer.

Drum pad

Height adjustment key

Tripod

HOME KEYBOARD

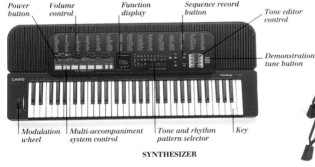

Power button | *Volume control* | *Function display* | *Sequence record button* | *Tone editor control*

Demonstration tune button

Modulation wheel | *Multi-accompaniment system control* | *Tone and rhythm pattern selector* | *Key*

SYNTHESIZER

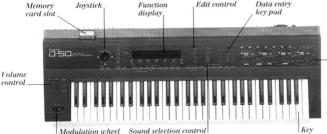

Memory card slot | *Joystick* | *Function display* | *Edit control* | *Data entry key pad*

Sound waveform selection guide

Volume control

Modulation wheel | *Sound selection control* | *Key*

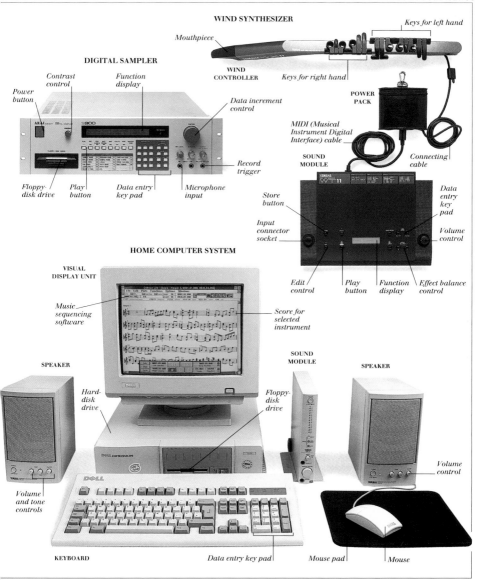

WIND SYNTHESIZER

Keys for left hand

Mouthpiece

DIGITAL SAMPLER

WIND
CONTROLLER

Keys for right hand

Contrast
control

Function
display

Power
button

Data increment
control

POWER
PACK

MIDI (Musical
Instrument Digital
Interface) cable

SOUND
MODULE

Connecting
cable

Record
trigger

Floppy-
disk drive

Play
button

Data entry
key pad

Microphone
input

Store
button

Data
entry
key
pad

Input
connector
socket

Volume
control

HOME COMPUTER SYSTEM

VISUAL
DISPLAY UNIT

Edit
control

Play
button

Function
display

Effect balance
control

Music
sequencing
software

Score for
selected
instrument

SOUND
MODULE

SPEAKER

SPEAKER

Hard-
disk
drive

Floppy-
disk
drive

Volume
control

Volume
and tone
controls

KEYBOARD

Data entry key pad

Mouse pad

Mouse

521

Sports

Soccer

GAMES INVOLVING KICKING A BALL have a long history and were recorded in China as early as 300 BC; in medieval Europe, street football was banned as a menace to the public; only in 1863 were the rules established, specifically banning carrying the ball for all players except the goalkeeper, and separating rugby from soccer. Soccer, also known as association football, is a team sport in which players attempt to score goals by passing and dribbling the ball down the field past opposing defenders, and kicking or heading the ball into the goal net, outwitting the defending goalkeeper or "goalie." Each team consists of ten outfield players (defenders, midfielders, and strikers) and a goalkeeper. Players from the opposing team may challenge the player in possession of the ball, but an illegal or foul tackle results in a penalty if a foul occurs inside the penalty area or a free kick if outside the penalty area. The round ball used in soccer is more easily controlled than the oval balls used in American, Canadian, and Australian rules football and in rugby. The result is a more "open" or flowing game which is played and watched by millions of people worldwide.

LINESMAN'S FLAG

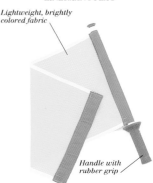

Lightweight, brightly colored fabric

Handle with rubber grip

REFEREE'S EQUIPMENT

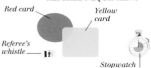

Red card

Yellow card

Referee's whistle

Stopwatch

FIELD MARKINGS

Halfway line

5 ft (1.5 m)

HALFWAY-LINE FLAG

Corner arc

CORNER FLAG

24 ft (7.3 m)

Goal line

GOAL

SOCCER FIELD

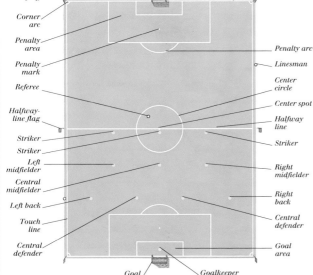

150–300 ft (46–91 m)

Corner flag

Goal line

Corner arc

Penalty area

Penalty arc

Penalty mark

Linesman

Referee

Center circle

Center spot

Halfway-line flag

Halfway line

Striker

Striker

Striker

Left midfielder

Right midfielder

Central midfielder

Left back

Right back

Touch line

Central defender

Central defender

Goal area

Goal

Goalkeeper

GOALKEEPER

Goalkeeper's shirt

Glove

Shin guard

Shorts

Sock

Soccer shoe

SOCCER UNIFORM

Open-neck collar

Lightweight, man-made fabric team shirt

Team logo

Manufacturer's logo

Ribbed welt

Sponsor's logo

Manufacturer's name

Ball size number

Edge cut to fit perfectly

MAKING A SOCCER BALL

Hole punched in panel for stitching

Mitre

MULTIPLEX

Waxed thread

8½–9 in (22–23 cm)

Needle

Bladder valve

Bladder made from latex rubber

Panels sewn together with ball inside out

Laminated panel

Long cotton sock

Club crest

Team shorts

Synthetic shoelace

Interchangeable nylon stud

SOCCER SHOE

Football

IN AMERICAN AND CANADIAN FOOTBALL, the object of the game is to get the ball across the opponent's goal line, either by passing or carrying it across (a touchdown), or by kicking it between their goalposts (a field goal). An American football team has 11 players on the field at a time, although up to 40 players can appear for each side in a single game. The agile offense tries to score points, and the heavy hitting defense holds back the opposition. When in possession of the ball, a team has four chances (downs), to move it at least ten yards up the field to make a first down. The opposition gains possession if they fail, or by tackling and intercepting the ball. Canadian football is played on a larger field, with 12 men on each side. A team has only three chances, instead of four, to achieve a first down. Otherwise, the game is very similar to American football. Helmets, face masks, and layers of body padding are worn by the players for protection.

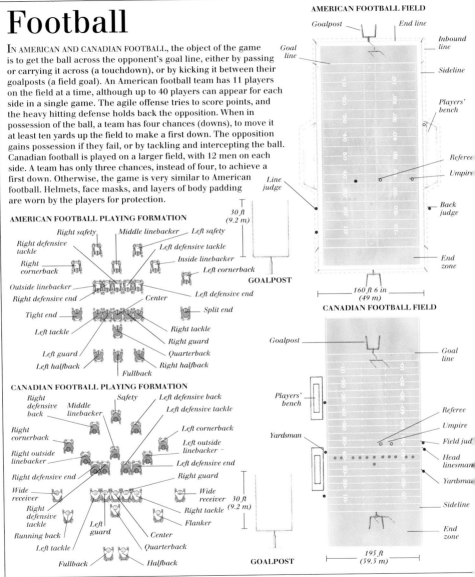

AMERICAN FOOTBALL FIELD

- Goalpost
- End line
- Goal line
- Inbound line
- Sideline
- Players' bench
- Referee
- Umpire
- Back judge
- End zone

160 ft 6 in
(49 m)

AMERICAN FOOTBALL PLAYING FORMATION

- Right safety
- Middle linebacker
- Left safety
- Right defensive tackle
- Left defensive tackle
- Inside linebacker
- Right cornerback
- Left cornerback
- Outside linebacker
- Right defensive end
- Center
- Left defensive end
- Tight end
- Split end
- Left tackle
- Right tackle
- Right guard
- Left guard
- Quarterback
- Left halfback
- Right halfback
- Fullback

Line judge

30 ft
(9.2 m)

GOALPOST

CANADIAN FOOTBALL PLAYING FORMATION

- Right defensive back
- Middle linebacker
- Safety
- Left defensive back
- Left defensive tackle
- Right cornerback
- Left cornerback
- Left outside linebacker
- Right outside linebacker
- Left defensive end
- Right defensive end
- Right guard
- Wide receiver
- Wide receiver
- Right defensive tackle
- Right tackle
- Flanker
- Running back
- Left guard
- Center
- Left tackle
- Quarterback
- Fullback
- Halfback

30 ft
(9.2 m)

GOALPOST

CANADIAN FOOTBALL FIELD

- Goalpost
- Goal line
- Players' bench
- Referee
- Umpire
- Field judge
- Yardsman
- Head linesman
- Yardsman
- Sideline
- End zone

195 ft
(59.5 m)

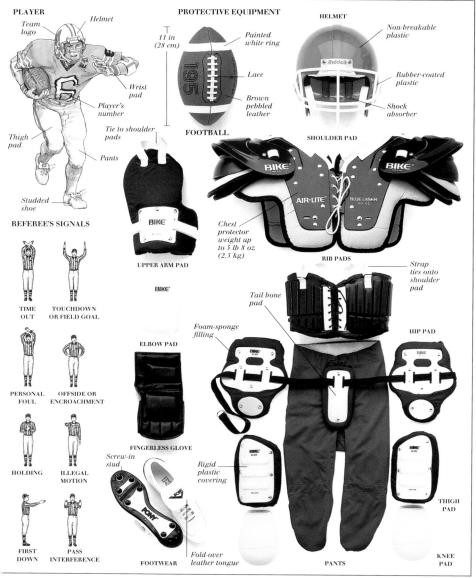

PLAYER

Team logo
Helmet
Wrist pad
Player's number
Thigh pad
Pants
Studded shoe

PROTECTIVE EQUIPMENT

11 in (28 cm)
Painted white ring
Lace
Brown pebbled leather
FOOTBALL

HELMET

Non-breakable plastic
Rubber-coated plastic
Shock absorber
Riddell

Tie to shoulder pads
UPPER ARM PAD
BIKE

SHOULDER PAD
BIKE
BIKE
AIR·LITE
BLUE LASER 40-42
Chest protector weight up to 5 lb 8 oz (2.5 kg)

RIB PADS
Strap ties onto shoulder pad

Tail bone pad
Foam-sponge filling

HIP PAD
BIKE

ELBOW PAD
BIKE

FINGERLESS GLOVE

Screw-in stud
Rigid plastic covering

THIGH PAD
BIKE AL02

FOOTWEAR
PONY
Fold-over leather tongue

PANTS

KNEE PAD

REFEREE'S SIGNALS

TIME OUT

TOUCHDOWN OR FIELD GOAL

PERSONAL FOUL

OFFSIDE OR ENCROACHMENT

HOLDING

ILLEGAL MOTION

FIRST DOWN

PASS INTERFERENCE

Australian rules and Gaelic football

VARIETIES OF FOOTBALL have developed all over the world and Australian rules football is considered to be one of the roughest versions, allowing full body tackles although participants wear no protective padding. Two teams of 18 players play on a large, oval pitch. Players can kick or punch the ball, which is shaped like a rugby ball, but cannot throw it. Running with the ball is permitted, as long as the ball touches the ground at least once every ten meters. The full backs defend two sets of posts. Teams try to score goals (six points) between the inner posts or behinds (one point) inside the outer posts. Each game has four quarters of 25 minutes, and the team with the most points at the end of the allotted time is the winner. In Gaelic football, an Irish version of soccer (see pp. 524–525), a size 5 association football is used. Each team can have 15 players on the field at a time. Players are allowed to catch, fist, and kick the ball, or dribble it using their hands or feet, but cannot throw it. Teams are awarded three points for getting the ball into the net, and one point for getting it through the posts above the crossbar. Gaelic football is rarely played outside of Ireland.

START OF PLAY

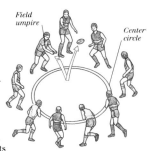

Field umpire

Center circle

SCORING

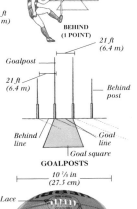

GOAL
(6 POINTS)

BEHIND
(1 POINT)

21 ft
(6.4 m)

Goalpost

21 ft
(6.4 m)

Behind post

Behind line

Goal line

Goal square

GOALPOSTS

10 ⅞ in
(27.5 cm)

Lace

Leather covering

AUSTRALIAN RULES FOOTBALL

AUSTRALIAN RULES FOOTBALL FIELD

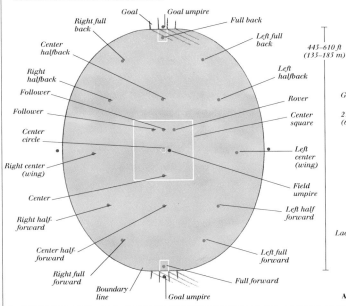

Goal

Goal umpire

Right full back

Full back

Center halfback

Left full back

Right halfback

Left halfback

Follower

Follower

Rover

Center circle

Center square

Right center (wing)

Left center (wing)

Center

Field umpire

Right half-forward

Left half forward

Center half-forward

Left full forward

Right full forward

Full forward

Boundary line

Goal umpire

445–610 ft
(135–185 m)

AUSTRALIAN RULES FOOTBALL SKILLS

RUNNING WITH THE BALL

KICKING

TACKLING

TAKING A MARK

PASSING THE BALL

AUSTRALIAN RULES FOOTBALL UNIFORM

Australian Football League logo

Team colors

Sleeveless team guernsey

Sock

Shorts

GAELIC FOOTBALL PITCH

Corner flag

Goalkeeper

Goal umpire

Goal area

Right fullback

Left fullback

Fullback

Right halfback

Left halfback

Center halfback

Center flag

Linesman

Linesman

Left midfielder

Right midfielder

Midfield line

Referee

Left half-forward

Right half-forward

Center half-forward

Right full-forward

Left full-forward

Full forward

260–295 ft
(80–90 m)

CONTROLLING THE BALL

SCORING IN GAELIC FOOTBALL

GOAL (3 POINTS)

POINT (1 POINT)

8 ¹/₂–9 in
(22–23 cm)

21ft
(6.4 m)

Goalpost

Crossbar

Parallelogram

GOAL

oneills
all-ireland

GAELIC FOOTBALL

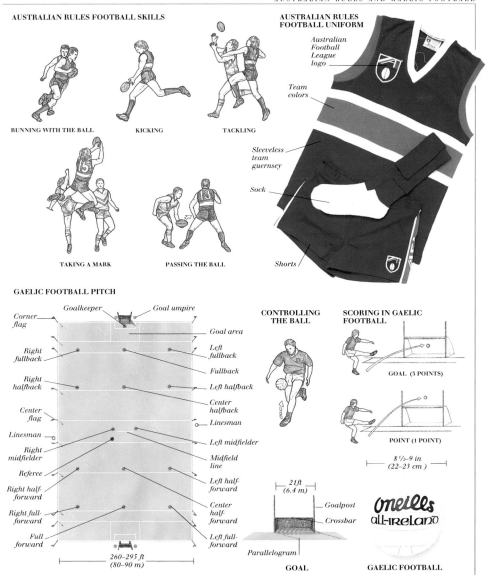

529

Rugby

RUGBY IS PLAYED WITH AN OVAL BALL which may be carried, thrown, or kicked. There are two types of rugby. Rugby Union is an amateur game played by two teams of 15 players. Players can score points in two ways: by placing the ball behind the opponents' goal line (a try, scoring four points) or by kicking it over the crossbar of the opponent's goal (a conversion, scoring two points; a penalty kick, scoring three points; or a drop-kick, scoring three points). Rugby League developed from the Union game but is played by 13 players at amateur and professional levels. In League games, a try scores four points; a conversion scores two points; a drop goal scores three points, and a penalty kick scores two points. In both forms of the game, whenever a rule is broken, play is resumed with a scrum. In a scrum, each team's forwards bind together facing each other and fight for possession of the ball.

RUGBY UNION FIELD

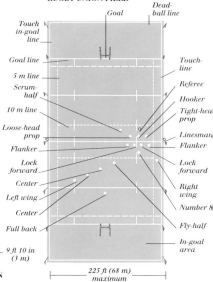

Touch in-goal line
Goal line
5 m line
Scrum-half
10 m line
Loose-head prop
Flanker
Lock forward
Center
Left wing
Center
Full back

Goal
Dead-ball line
Touch-line
Referee
Hooker
Tight-head prop
Linesman
Flanker
Lock forward
Right wing
Number 8
Fly-half
In-goal area

225 ft (68 m) maximum

RUGBY UNION SCRUM

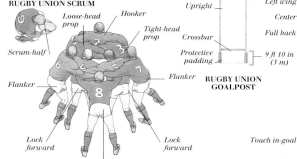

Loose-head prop
Hooker
Tight-head prop
Scrum-half
Flanker
Flanker
Lock forward
Lock forward
Number 8

RUGBY UNION GOALPOST

18 ft (5.5 m)
Upright
Crossbar
Protective padding
9 ft 10 in (3 m)

RUGBY LEAGUE SCRUM

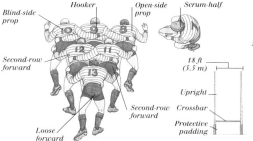

Blind-side prop
Hooker
Open-side prop
Scrum-half
Second-row forward
Second-row forward
Second-row forward
Loose forward

RUGBY LEAGUE GOALPOST

18 ft (5.5 m)
Upright
Crossbar
Protective padding

RUGBY LEAGUE FIELD

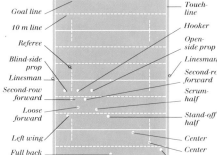

Touch in-goal
Goal line
10 m line
Referee
Blind-side prop
Linesman
Second-row forward
Loose forward
Left wing
Full back

Goal
Dead-ball line
Touch in-goal line
Touch-line
Hooker
Open-side prop
Linesman
Second-row forward
Scrum-half
Stand-off half
Center
Center
Right wing

225 ft (68 m) maximum

RUGBY SCORING AND SKILLS

GOAL

Goal line

TRY

PASS

PLACE KICK

FLYING TACKLE

RUGBY UNION PLAYER

Shirt in team color

Knee-high sock

Team shorts

Studded boot

RUGBY UNION BALL

Four-panel construction

Laminated leather panel covered with textured plastic

Mitre MULTIPLEX

11–12 in (28–30 cm)

RUGBY LEAGUE BALL

Four-panel construction

Laminated leather panel covered with smooth plastic

Mitre MULTIPLEX 13

11 in (28 cm)

RUGBY LEAGUE SHIRT

Team crest

Official logo of the British Rugby Football League

Three-quarter sleeve

UMBRO

Team crest

Button-up collar

RUGBY UNION SHIRT

Ankle support

Mizuno ALL

Circular stud

RUGBY SHOE

Team color

RUGBY SHIRTS

Long sleeve

Team crest

531

Basketball

BASKETBALL IS A BALL GAME for two teams of five players, originally devised in 1890 by James Naismith for the Y.M.C.A. in Springfield, Massachusetts. The object of the game is to take possession of the ball and score points by throwing the ball into the opposing team's basket. A player moves the ball up and down the court by bouncing it along the ground or "dribbling"; the ball may be passed between players by throwing, bouncing, or rolling. Players may not run with or kick the ball, although pivoting on one foot is allowed. The game begins with the referee throwing the ball into the air and a player from each team jumping up to try and "tip" the ball to a teammate. The length of the game and the number of periods played varies at different levels. There are amateur, professional, and international rules. No game ends in a draw. As many extra periods as necessary are played to break the tie. In addition to the five players on court, each team has up to seven substitutes, but players may only leave the court with the permission of the referee. Basketball is a noncontact sport and fouls on other players are penalized by a throw-in awarded against the offending team; a free throw at the basket is awarded when a player is fouled in the act of shooting. Basketball is a fast-moving game, requiring both physical and mental coordination. Skillful tactical play matters more than simple physical strength and the agility of the players makes the game an excellent spectator sport.

CHEST PASS

DRIBBLE

OVERHEAD PASS

INTERNATIONAL BASKETBALL COURT

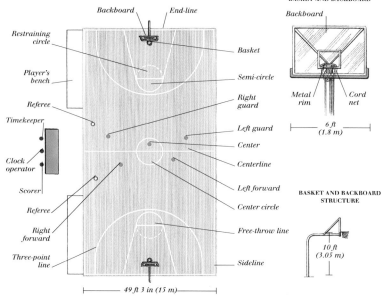

Backboard

End-line

Restraining circle

Player's bench

Referee

Timekeeper

Clock operator

Scorer

Referee

Right forward

Three-point line

Basket

Semi-circle

Right guard

Left guard

Center

Centerline

Left forward

Center circle

Free-throw line

Sideline

49 ft 3 in (15 m)

BASKET AND BACKBOARD

Backboard

Metal rim

Cord net

6 ft (1.8 m)

BASKET AND BACKBOARD STRUCTURE

10 ft (3.05 m)

LAY-UP SHOT

JUMP SHOT

LONG PASS

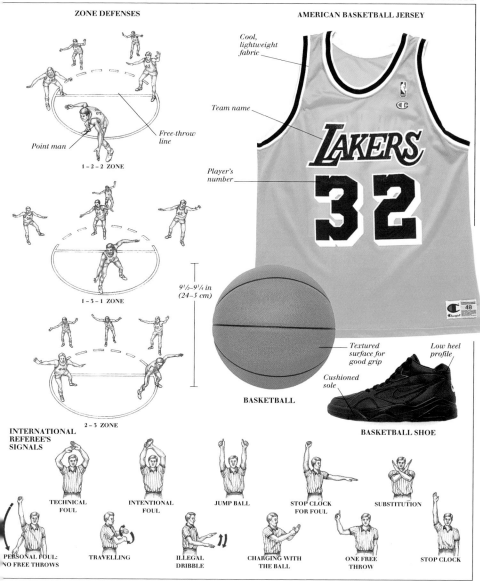

ZONE DEFENSES

Point man

Free-throw line

1 – 2 – 2 ZONE

1 – 3 – 1 ZONE

2 – 3 ZONE

9½–9¾ in
(24–5 cm)

AMERICAN BASKETBALL JERSEY

Cool, lightweight fabric

Team name

Player's number

LAKERS

32

48

Textured surface for good grip

BASKETBALL

Low heel profile

Cushioned sole

BASKETBALL SHOE

INTERNATIONAL REFEREE'S SIGNALS

TECHNICAL FOUL

INTENTIONAL FOUL

JUMP BALL

STOP CLOCK FOR FOUL

SUBSTITUTION

PERSONAL FOUL: NO FREE THROWS

TRAVELLING

ILLEGAL DRIBBLE

CHARGING WITH THE BALL

ONE FREE THROW

STOP CLOCK

Volleyball, netball, and handball

OVERHAND SERVE   **SPIKE (SMASH)**

VOLLEYBALL, NETBALL, AND HANDBALL are fast-moving team sports played with balls, usually on courts with a hard surface. In volleyball, the object of the game is to hit the ball over a net strung across the center of the court so that it touches the ground on the opponent's side. The team of six players can take three hits to direct the ball over the net, although the same player cannot hit the ball twice in a row. Players can hit the ball with their arms, hands or any other part of their upper body. Teams score points only while serving. The first team to score 15 points, with a two-point margin over their opponent, wins the game. Netball is similar to basketball (see pp. 532–533), but is played on a slightly larger court with seven players instead of five. A team moves the ball toward the goal by throwing, passing, and catching it with the aim of throwing the ball through the opponents' goal net. Players are confined by their playing position to specific areas of the court. Team handball is one of the world's fastest games. Each side has seven players. A team moves the ball by dribbling, passing, or bouncing it as they run. Players may stop, catch, throw, bounce, or strike the ball with any part of the body above the knees. Each team tries to score goals by directing the ball past the opposition's goalkeeper into the net, which is similar to a soccer goal net (see pp. 524–525).

UNDERHAND SERVE   **FOREARM PASS (DIG)**

VOLLEYBALL KIT

Team colors

VOLLEYBALL COURT

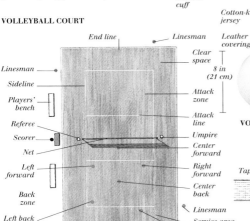

- End line
- Linesman
- Linesman
- Sideline
- Players' bench
- Referee
- Scorer
- Net
- Left forward
- Back zone
- Left back
- Linesman
- 29 ft 6 in (9 m)
- Clear space
- Attack zone
- Attack line
- Umpire
- Center forward
- Right forward
- Center back
- Linesman
- Service area
- Server

Ribbed cuff

Cotton-knit jersey

Elastic waist

Leather covering

8 in (21 cm)

VOLLEYBALL

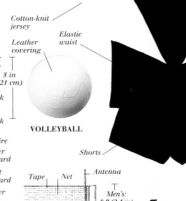

Shorts

Elastic knit fabric

Injected molded padding

VOLLEYBALL NET

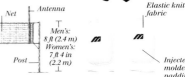

Tape   Net   Antenna

Men's: 8 ft (2.4 m)
Women's: 7 ft 4 in (2.2 m)

Post

KNEE PADS

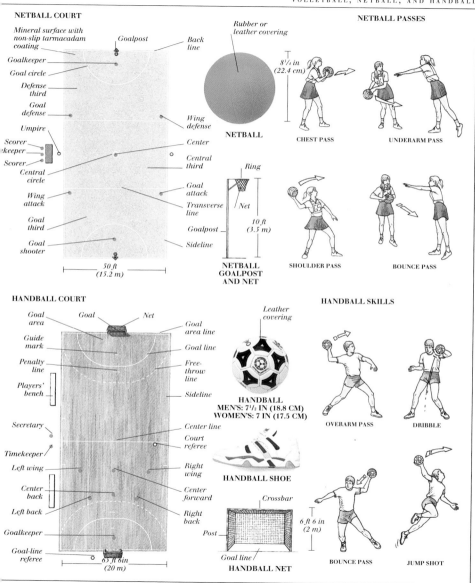

NETBALL COURT

Mineral surface with non-slip tarmacadam coating

Goalpost

Back line

Goalkeeper

Goal circle

Defense third

Goal defense

Umpire

Scorer keeper

Scorer

Central circle

Wing attack

Goal third

Goal shooter

Wing defense

Center

Central third

Goal attack

Transverse line

Goalpost

Sideline

50 ft (15.2 m)

NETBALL PASSES

Rubber or leather covering

NETBALL

8¼ in (22.4 cm)

CHEST PASS

UNDERARM PASS

Ring

Net

10 ft (3.5 m)

NETBALL GOALPOST AND NET

SHOULDER PASS

BOUNCE PASS

HANDBALL COURT

Goal area

Goal

Net

Guide mark

Penalty line

Players' bench

Secretary

Timekeeper

Left wing

Center back

Left back

Goalkeeper

Goal-line referee

Goal area line

Goal line

Free-throw line

Sideline

Center line

Court referee

Right wing

Center forward

Right back

65 ft 6 in (20 m)

HANDBALL SKILLS

Leather covering

HANDBALL
MEN'S: 7½ IN (18.8 CM)
WOMEN'S: 7 IN (17.5 CM)

OVERARM PASS

DRIBBLE

HANDBALL SHOE

Crossbar

6 ft 6 in (2 m)

Post

Goal line

HANDBALL NET

BOUNCE PASS

JUMP SHOT

Baseball

BASEBALL IS A BALL GAME for two teams of nine players. The batter hits the ball thrown by the opposing team's pitcher, into the area between the foul lines. He then runs round all four fixed bases in order to score a run, touching or "tagging" each base in turn. The pitcher must throw the ball at a height between the batter's armpits and knees, a height which is called the strike zone. A ball pitched in this area that crosses over the home plate is called a "strike" and the batter has three strikes in which to try to hit the ball (otherwise he has "struck out"). The fielding team tries to get the batting team out by catching the ball before it bounces, tagging a player of the batting team who is running between bases with the ball, or by tagging a base before the player has reached it. Members of the batting team may stop safely at a base as long as it is not occupied by another member of their team. When the batter runs to first base, his teammate at first base must run onto second – this is called a force play. A game consists of nine innings and each team will bat once during an inning. When three members of the batting team are out, the teams swap roles. The team with the most runs wins the game.

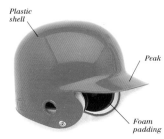

BATTER'S HELMET

Plastic shell

Peak

Foam padding

Wire coated in strong nylon

Plastic-coated foam padding

CATCHER'S MASK

BASEBALL FIELD

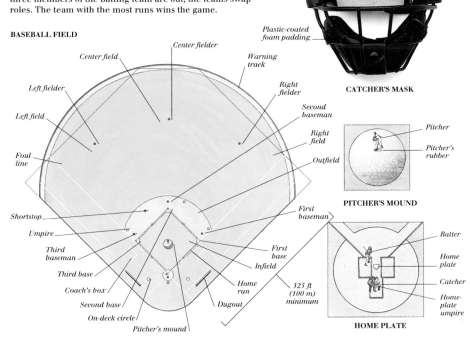

Center fielder

Center field

Warning track

Left fielder

Right fielder

Left field

Second baseman

Foul line

Right field

Outfield

Shortstop

First baseman

Umpire

First base

Third baseman

Infield

Third base

Home run

Coach's box

325 ft (100 m) minimum

Second base

Dugout

On-deck circle

Pitcher's mound

Pitcher

Pitcher's rubber

PITCHER'S MOUND

Batter

Home plate

Catcher

Home-plate umpire

HOME PLATE

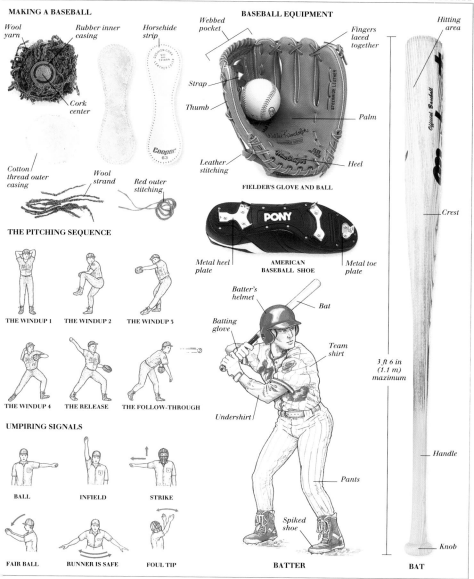

MAKING A BASEBALL

Wool yarn

Rubber inner casing

Horsehide strip

Cork center

Cotton thread outer casing

Wool strand

Red outer stitching

BASEBALL EQUIPMENT

Webbed pocket

Fingers laced together

Strap

Thumb

Palm

Leather stitching

Heel

FIELDER'S GLOVE AND BALL

Metal heel plate

Metal toe plate

AMERICAN BASEBALL SHOE

THE PITCHING SEQUENCE

THE WINDUP 1

THE WINDUP 2

THE WINDUP 3

THE WINDUP 4

THE RELEASE

THE FOLLOW-THROUGH

UMPIRING SIGNALS

BALL

INFIELD

STRIKE

FAIR BALL

RUNNER IS SAFE

FOUL TIP

Batter's helmet

Bat

Batting glove

Team shirt

Undershirt

Pants

Spiked shoe

BATTER

Hitting area

Crest

3 ft 6 in (1.1 m) maximum

Handle

Knob

BAT

Cricket

CRICKET IS A BALL GAME PLAYED by two teams of eleven players on a pitch with two sets of three stumps (wickets). The bowler bowls the ball down the pitch to the batsman of the opposing team, who must defend the wicket in front of which he stands. The object of the game is to score as many runs as possible. Runs can be scored individually by running the length of the playing strip, or by hitting a ball which lands outside the boundary (six), or which lands inside the boundary but bounces or rolls outside (four); the opposing team will bowl and field, attempting to dismiss the batsmen. A batsman can be dismissed in one of several ways: by the bowler hitting the wicket with the ball ("bowled"); by a fielder catching the ball hit by the batsman before it touches the ground ("caught"); by the wicket-keeper or another fielder breaking the wicket while the batsman is attempting a run and is therefore out of his ground ("stumped" or "run out"); by the batsman breaking the wicket with his own bat or body ("hit wicket"); by a part of the batsman's body being hit by a ball that would otherwise have hit the wicket ("leg before wicket" ["lbw"]). A match consists of one or two innings and each innings ends when the tenth batsman of the batting team is out, when a certain number of overs (a series of six balls bowled) have been played, or when the captain of the batting team "declares" ending the innings voluntarily.

FORWARD DEFENSIVE STROKE

BACKWARD DEFENSIVE STROKE

ON-DRIVE

OFF-DRIVE

PULL

HOOK

SQUARE CUT

LEG GLANCE

POSSIBLE FIELD POSITIONS FOR AN AWAY SWING BOWLER TO A RIGHT-HANDED BATSMAN (IN RED) AND OTHER FIELD POSITIONS

Long on
Long off
Umpire
Bowler
Boundary line
Non-striking batsman
Deep mid-wicket
Extra cover
Mid-on
Silly mid-on
Mid-off
Forward short leg
Silly mid-off
Square leg
Cover
Deep square leg
Point
Square-leg umpire
Gulley
Batsman
Third man
Long leg
Second slip
Leg slip
Bowler
Wicket-keeper
Return crease
First slip
Fine leg
Sight screen
Umpire
Non-striking batsman

CRICKET PITCH

Wicket-keeper
Batsman
Wicket
Bowling crease
66 ft (20 m)

CRICKET BALL AND WICKE

Leather skin
Seam
BALL
Bail
WICKET
Stump

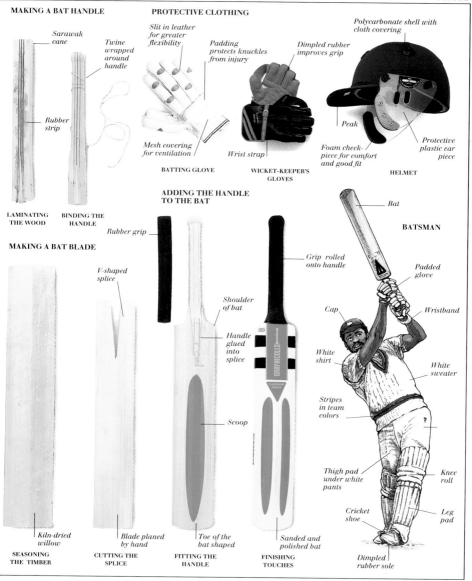

MAKING A BAT HANDLE

Sarawak cane

Twine wrapped around handle

Rubber strip

LAMINATING THE WOOD

BINDING THE HANDLE

PROTECTIVE CLOTHING

Slit in leather for greater flexibility

Padding protects knuckles from injury

Mesh covering for ventilation

BATTING GLOVE

Dimpled rubber improves grip

Wrist strap

WICKET-KEEPER'S GLOVES

Polycarbonate shell with cloth covering

Peak

Foam cheek-piece for comfort and good fit

Protective plastic ear piece

HELMET

ADDING THE HANDLE TO THE BAT

Rubber grip

MAKING A BAT BLADE

V-shaped splice

Grip rolled onto handle

Shoulder of bat

Handle glued into splice

Scoop

Kiln-dried willow

SEASONING THE TIMBER

Blade planed by hand

CUTTING THE SPLICE

Toe of the bat shaped

FITTING THE HANDLE

Sanded and polished bat

FINISHING TOUCHES

Bat

BATSMAN

Padded glove

Cap

Wristband

White shirt

White sweater

Stripes in team colors

Thigh pad under white pants

Knee roll

Cricket shoe

Leg pad

Dimpled rubber sole

Field hockey, lacrosse, and hurling

ALL OVER THE WORLD, TEAM GAMES have evolved which require that a ball be struck or carried, and tossed at the end of a stick. Early forms of these games include hurling, shinty, bandy, and pelota. Field hockey is played by men and women: two teams of eleven players try to gain and keep possession of the ball and score goals by using the hockey stick to propel the ball into their opponents' goal net. Skills such as passing, pushing, or hitting the ball by slapping or lifting it in a flicking movement, and shooting at the goal are crucial. Field hockey is played indoors and outdoors on grass or synthetic fields. Lacrosse is played internationally as a 12-a-side game for women and as 10-a-side game for men. The women's field has no absolute boundaries but the men's has clearly defined sidelines and end lines. The ball is kept in play by being carried, thrown or batted with the crosse, and rolled or kicked in any direction. In men's and women's lacrosse, play can continue behind the marked goal areas. Similar skills are required in hurling – a Gaelic field game played on the same pitch as Gaelic football (see pp. 528–529), using the same goalposts and net. In hurling, the ball may be struck with or carried on the hurley and, when off the ground, may be struck with the hand or kicked. Goals (three points) are scored when the ball passes between the posts and under the crossbar; one point is scored when the ball passes between the posts and over the crossbar.

GOALKEEPER'S EQUIPMENT

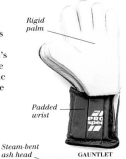

Air vent

Hard shell

Face mask

HELMET

Strap

Rigid palm

Padded wrist

GAUNTLET

FIELD HOCKEY STICK AND BALL

STICK

Handle *Tape* *Blade*

Slazenger FLEXI

3 ft (91 cm)

Steam-bent ash head

Stitched seam

$2^{1}/_{4}–3$ in (7–7.5 cm)

BALL

FIELD HOCKEY FIELD

Center forward *Inside right* *Right wing* *Right half* *Right back*

Sideline

Corner flag

Shooting circle

Goal

Penalty spot

Five yard mark

Goal line

180 ft (55 m)

Inside left *Left wing* *Umpire* *Center half* *Left half* *Left back* *Goalkeeper*

Protective overshoe

Padding protects toes against the hard ball

Strap

GOALKEEPER'S BOOT

7 ft (2.1 m)

FIELD HOCKEY GOAL

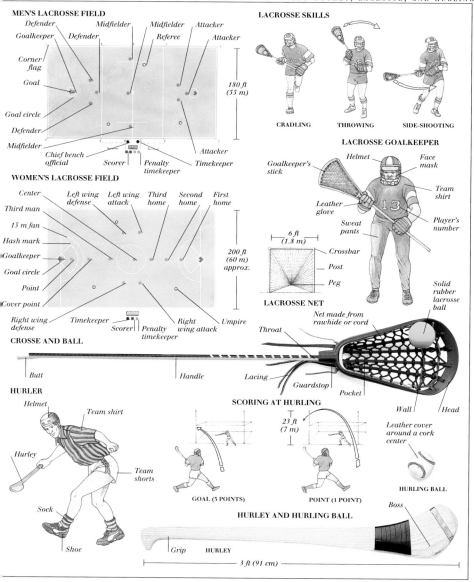

MEN'S LACROSSE FIELD

Defender
Goalkeeper
Defender
Midfielder
Midfielder
Referee
Attacker
Attacker

Corner flag

Goal

180 ft (55 m)

Goal circle

Defender

Midfielder

Chief bench official
Scorer
Penalty timekeeper
Attacker
Timekeeper

WOMEN'S LACROSSE FIELD

Center
Left wing defense
Left wing attack
Third home
Second home
First home

Third man

15 m fan

Hash mark

Goalkeeper

200 ft (60 m) approx.

Goal circle

Point

Cover point

Right wing defense
Timekeeper
Scorer
Penalty timekeeper
Right wing attack
Umpire

CROSSE AND BALL

Butt

Handle

HURLER

Helmet

Team shirt

Hurley

Team shorts

Sock

Shoe

Grip   HURLEY

LACROSSE SKILLS

CRADLING   THROWING   SIDE-SHOOTING

LACROSSE GOALKEEPER

Goalkeeper's stick
Helmet
Face mask
Team shirt
Leather glove
Sweat pants
Player's number

6 ft (1.8 m)
Crossbar
Post
Peg

Solid rubber lacrosse ball

LACROSSE NET

Net made from rawhide or cord

Throat

Lacing
Guardstop
Pocket

Wall   Head

Leather cover around a cork center

HURLING BALL

SCORING AT HURLING

23 ft (7 m)

GOAL (5 POINTS)   POINT (1 POINT)

HURLEY AND HURLING BALL

Boss

3 ft (91 cm)

Track and field

THE SPORTS that make up athletics are divided into two main groups: track events – which include sprinting, middle, and long distance running, relay running, hurdling, and walking – and field events which require jumping and throwing skills. Contests designed to test the speed, strength, agility, and stamina of athletes were held by the ancient Greeks over 4,000 years ago. However, the abolition of the Olympic Games in 393 AD meant that track and field events were neglected until the revival of large-scale competitions in the mid-nineteenth century. Modern stadiums offer areas reserved for the long jump, triple jump, and pole vault usually situated outside the running track. The javelin, shot, hammer, and discus are thrown within the track area. Most athletes specialize in one or two events but, in the heptathlon, women compete in seven events, held over two days: 200 m and 800 m races, 100 m hurdles, javelin, shot put, high jump, and long jump. In the decathlon, men compete in ten events over two days: 100 m, 400 m, and 1,500 m races, 110 m hurdles, javelin, discus, shot put, pole vault, high jump, and long jump.

Steel wire

Head

Body

Swivel

Metal rim

Center weight

Hammer handle

DISCUS
MEN'S: 4 LB 7 OZ (2 KG)
WOMEN'S: 2 LB 3 OZ (1 KG)

HAMMER
16 LB (7 KG)

Rubber coating

Shot pellet filling

5 in (12.7 cm)

4 in (10 cm)

MEN'S SHOT
16 LB (7 KG)

WOMEN'S SHOT
8 LB 12 OZ (4 KG)

JAVELIN Cord grip Shaft Tip

Men: 8 ft 6 in (2.6 m)
Women: 7 ft 6 in (2.3 m)

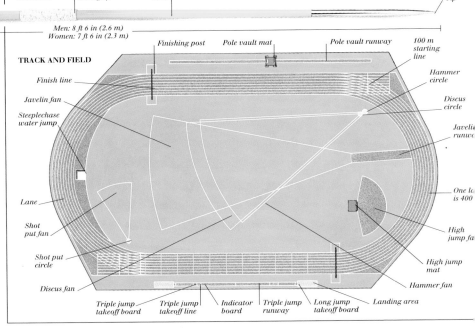

TRACK AND FIELD

Finishing post
Pole vault mat
Pole vault runway
100 m starting line
Hammer circle
Finish line
Discus circle
Javelin fan
Javeli runwa
Steeplechase water jump
One l is 400
Lane
High jump fa
Shot put fan
High jump mat
Shot put circle
Hammer fan
Discus fan
Triple jump takeoff board
Triple jump takeoff line
Indicator board
Triple jump runway
Long jump takeoff board
Landing area

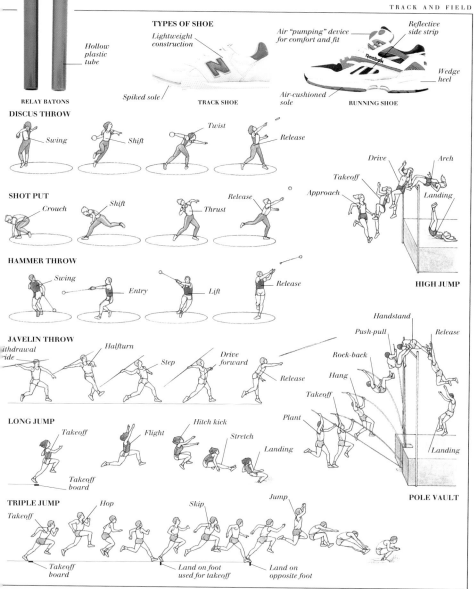

RELAY BATONS

Hollow plastic tube

TYPES OF SHOE

Lightweight construction

Spiked sole

TRACK SHOE

Air "pumping" device for comfort and fit

Reflective side strip

Wedge heel

Air-cushioned sole

RUNNING SHOE

DISCUS THROW

Swing — Shift — Twist — Release

SHOT PUT

Crouch — Shift — Thrust — Release

HAMMER THROW

Swing — Entry — Lift — Release

JAVELIN THROW

Withdrawal ride — Halfturn — Step — Drive forward — Release

LONG JUMP

Takeoff — Flight — Hitch kick — Stretch — Landing

Takeoff board

TRIPLE JUMP

Takeoff — Hop — Skip — Jump

Takeoff board — Land on foot used for takeoff — Land on opposite foot

HIGH JUMP

Approach — Takeoff — Drive — Arch — Landing

POLE VAULT

Plant — Takeoff — Hang — Rock-back — Push-pull — Handstand — Release — Landing

543

Racket sports

PROTECTIVE EYEWEAR

THE OBJECT OF ALL RACKET SPORTS is to make shots the opponent cannot return. Games are played by two players (singles) or four players (doubles). Racket shape and size is tailored to each sport, but all rackets are constructed of wood, plastic, aluminum, or high-performance materials such as fiberglass and carbon graphite. Racket strings are usually synthetic, although natural gut is still used. Tennis is played on a court divided by a low net. Opposing players alternate games. At least six games must be won to gain a set, and two or sometimes three sets are needed to win a match. Tennis courts may be concrete, grass, clay, or synthetic, each surface requiring a different style of play. Badminton is an indoor sport that is played with light, flexible rackets and a birdie on a court with a high net. Players can score points only on their serve. The first to reach 15 points (11 points for women's singles) wins the game. Two games are needed to win a match. Squash and racketball are both played in enclosed courts. One player hits the ball against the front wall, and the other tries to return it before it bounces on the floor more than once. Squash rackets have smaller, rounder heads and stiffer frames than badminton rackets. International courts are wider than those in the U.S., where a much harder ball is used. Squash games are played to nine points (international) or 15 points (U.S.). In racketball, players use a ball that is larger and bouncier than a squash ball. The racketball racket is thick and sturdy, with a large head, short handle, and a strap that loops around the wrist. Points can be won only when serving, and the first player to reach 21 points wins.

TENNIS RACKET

Synthetic string

Frame

Head

Logo

Throat

Grip

Butt

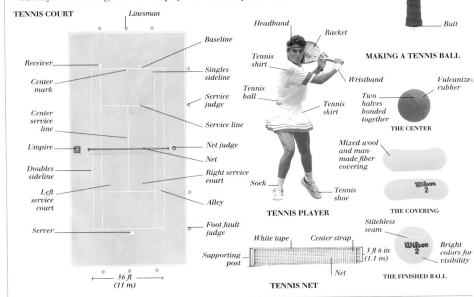

TENNIS COURT

Linesman

Baseline

Receiver

Center mark

Singles sideline

Center service line

Service judge

Service line

Umpire

Net judge

Net

Doubles sideline

Right service court

Left service court

Alley

Server

Foot fault judge

36 ft
(11 m)

TENNIS PLAYER

Headband

Racket

Tennis shirt

Wristband

Tennis ball

Tennis skirt

Sock

Tennis shoe

MAKING A TENNIS BALL

Vulcanized rubber

Two halves bonded together

THE CENTER

Mixed wool and man-made fiber covering

Wilson 2

THE COVERING

Stitchless seam

Wilson 2

Bright colors for visibility

THE FINISHED BALL

TENNIS NET

White tape

Center strap

3 ft 6 in
(1.1 m)

Supporting post

Net

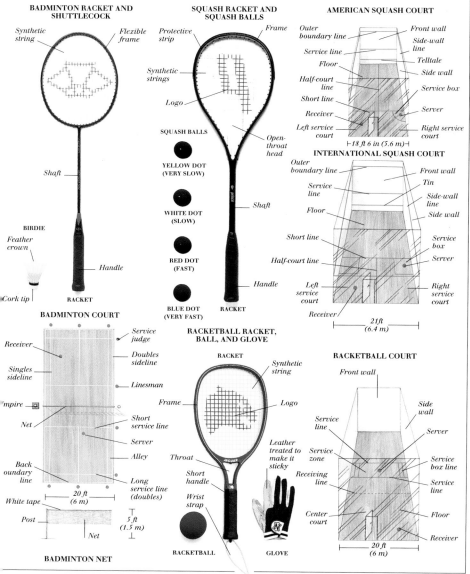

BADMINTON RACKET AND SHUTTLECOCK

Synthetic string

Flexible frame

Shaft

BIRDIE

Feather crown

Handle

Cork tip

RACKET

SQUASH RACKET AND SQUASH BALLS

Protective strip

Frame

Synthetic strings

Logo

Open-throat head

Shaft

Handle

RACKET

SQUASH BALLS

YELLOW DOT (VERY SLOW)

WHITE DOT (SLOW)

RED DOT (FAST)

BLUE DOT (VERY FAST)

AMERICAN SQUASH COURT

Outer boundary line

Front wall

Side-wall line

Service line

Telltale

Floor

Side wall

Half-court line

Service box

Short line

Server

Receiver

Left service court

Right service court

├─18 ft 6 in (5.6 m)─┤

INTERNATIONAL SQUASH COURT

Outer boundary line

Front wall

Tin

Service line

Side-wall line

Floor

Side wall

Short line

Service box

Half-court line

Server

Left service court

Right service court

Receiver

21ft (6.4 m)

BADMINTON COURT

Receiver

Service judge

Doubles sideline

Singles sideline

Linesman

Umpire

Net

Short service line

Server

Back boundary line

Alley

Long service line (doubles)

20 ft (6 m)

White tape

Post

5 ft (1.5 m)

Net

BADMINTON NET

RACKETBALL RACKET, BALL, AND GLOVE

RACKET

Synthetic string

Frame

Logo

Leather treated to make it sticky

Throat

Short handle

Wrist strap

RACKETBALL

GLOVE

RACKETBALL COURT

Front wall

Side wall

Service line

Server

Service zone

Service box line

Receiving line

Service line

Center court

Floor

Receiver

20 ft (6 m)

545

Golf

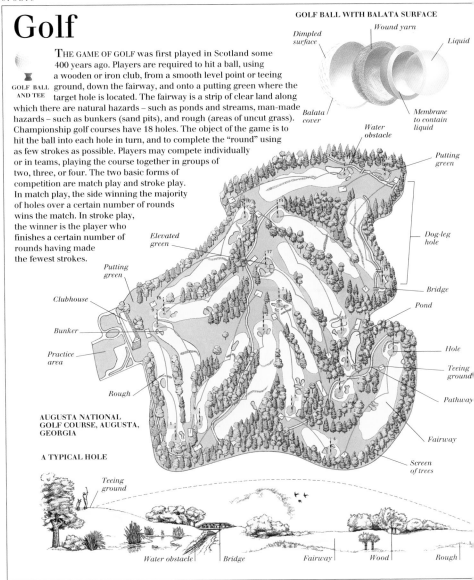

GOLF BALL AND TEE

THE GAME OF GOLF was first played in Scotland some 400 years ago. Players are required to hit a ball, using a wooden or iron club, from a smooth level point or teeing ground, down the fairway, and onto a putting green where the target hole is located. The fairway is a strip of clear land along which there are natural hazards – such as ponds and streams, man-made hazards – such as bunkers (sand pits), and rough (areas of uncut grass). Championship golf courses have 18 holes. The object of the game is to hit the ball into each hole in turn, and to complete the "round" using as few strokes as possible. Players may compete individually or in teams, playing the course together in groups of two, three, or four. The two basic forms of competition are match play and stroke play. In match play, the side winning the majority of holes over a certain number of rounds wins the match. In stroke play, the winner is the player who finishes a certain number of rounds having made the fewest strokes.

GOLF BALL WITH BALATA SURFACE

Dimpled surface

Wound yarn

Liquid

Balata cover

Membrane to contain liquid

Water obstacle

Putting green

Dog-leg hole

Bridge

Pond

Hole

Teeing ground

Pathway

Fairway

Screen of trees

Elevated green

Putting green

Clubhouse

Bunker

Practice area

Rough

AUGUSTA NATIONAL GOLF COURSE, AUGUSTA, GEORGIA

A TYPICAL HOLE

Teeing ground

Water obstacle

Bridge

Fairway

Wood

Rough

MAKING A WOODEN CLUB

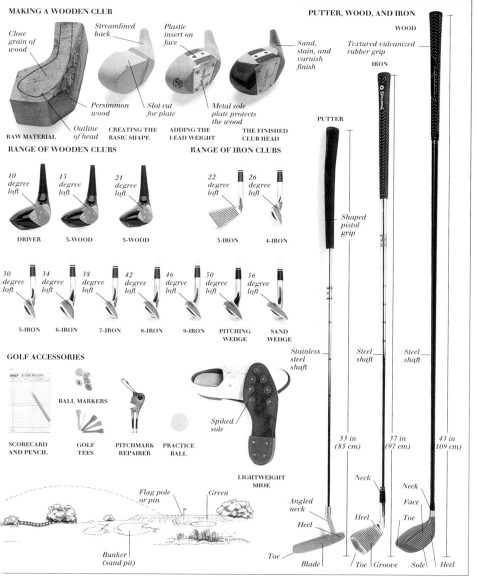

Close grain of wood

Streamlined back

Plastic insert on face

Sand, stain, and varnish finish

Persimmon wood

Slot cut for plate

Metal sole plate protects the wood

Outline of head

RAW MATERIAL

CREATING THE BASIC SHAPE

ADDING THE LEAD WEIGHT

THE FINISHED CLUB HEAD

PUTTER, WOOD, AND IRON

WOOD

Textured vulcanized rubber grip

IRON

PUTTER

Shaped pistol grip

Stainless steel shaft

Steel shaft

Steel shaft

33 in (85 cm)

37 in (97 cm)

43 in (109 cm)

Neck

Neck

Angled neck

Face

Heel

Toe

Heel

Blade

Toe Groove

Sole Heel

Toe

RANGE OF WOODEN CLUBS

10 degree loft

DRIVER

15 degree loft

5-WOOD

21 degree loft

5-WOOD

30 degree loft

5-IRON

34 degree loft

6-IRON

38 degree loft

7-IRON

42 degree loft

8-IRON

46 degree loft

9-IRON

50 degree loft

PITCHING WEDGE

56 degree loft

SAND WEDGE

RANGE OF IRON CLUBS

22 degree loft

5-IRON

26 degree loft

4-IRON

GOLF ACCESSORIES

GOLF SCORE RECORD

BALL MARKERS

SCORECARD AND PENCIL

GOLF TEES

PITCHMARK REPAIRER

PRACTICE BALL

Spiked sole

LIGHTWEIGHT SHOE

Flag pole or pin

Green

Bunker (sand pit)

547

Archery and shooting

TARGET SHOOTING AND ARCHERY EVOLVED as practice for hunting and battle skills. Modern bows, although designed according to the principles of early hunting bows, use laminates, fiberglass, dacron, and carbon, and are equipped with sights and stabilizers. Competitors in target archery shoot over distances of 100 ft (30 m), 165 ft (50 m), 230 ft (70 m), and 300 ft (90 m) for men, and 100 ft (30 m), 165 ft (50 m), 200 ft (60 m), and 230 ft (70 m) for women. The closer the shot is to the center of the target, the higher the score. The individual scores are added up, and the archer with the highest total wins the competition. Crossbows are used in match competitions over 33 ft (10 m), and 100 ft (30 m). Rifle shooting is divided into three categories: smallbore, bigbore, and air rifle. Contests take place over a variety of distances and further subdivisions are based on the type of shooting position used; prone, kneeling, or standing. The Olympic biathlon combines cross-country skiing and rifle shooting over a course of approximately $12\frac{1}{2}$ miles (20 km). Additional magazines of ammunition are carried in the butt of the rifles. Bigbore rifles fitted with a telescopic sight can be used for hunting and running game target shooting. Pistol shooting events, using rapid-fire pistols, target pistols, and air pistols, take place over 33 ft (10 m), 82 ft (25 m), and 165 ft (50 m) distances. In rapid-fire pistol shooting, a total of 60 shots are fired from a distance of 82 ft (25 m).

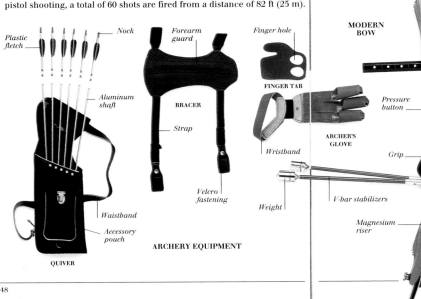

CROSSBOW AND BOLT

Laminated fiberglass bow

Bolt

Bolt rest

$1\frac{1}{4}$ in (45 mm)

CROSSBOW TARGET

Stirrup held between feet when drawing bow

Sight

Hardwood laminate limb

Dacron string

Sight

MODERN BOW

Plastic fletch

Nock

Forearm guard

Finger hole

Aluminum shaft

BRACER

FINGER TAB

Strap

Pressure button

ARCHER'S GLOVE

Wristband

Grip

Velcro fastening

Weight

V-bar stabilizers

Waistband

Accessory pouch

Magnesium riser

ARCHERY EQUIPMENT

QUIVER

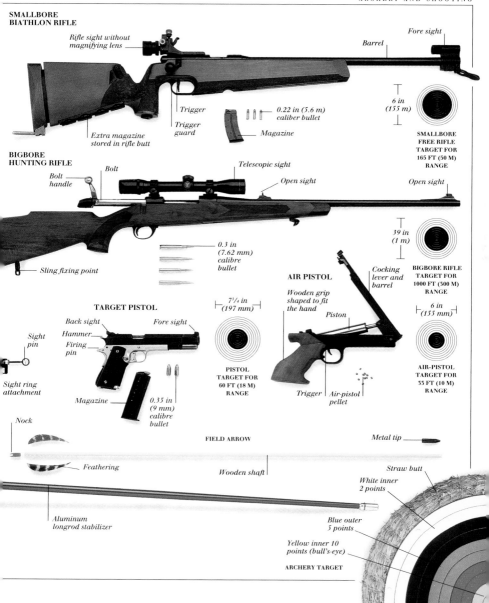

SMALLBORE BIATHLON RIFLE

Rifle sight without magnifying lens

Fore sight

Barrel

Trigger

Trigger guard

0.22 in (5.6 m) caliber bullet

Magazine

Extra magazine stored in rifle butt

6 in (155 m)

SMALLBORE FREE RIFLE TARGET FOR 165 FT (50 M) RANGE

BIGBORE HUNTING RIFLE

Bolt handle

Bolt

Telescopic sight

Open sight

Open sight

0.3 in (7.62 mm) calibre bullet

39 in (1 m)

BIGBORE RIFLE TARGET FOR 1000 FT (500 M) RANGE

Sling fixing point

Cocking lever and barrel

6 in (155 mm)

AIR PISTOL

Wooden grip shaped to fit the hand

Piston

TARGET PISTOL

Back sight

Fore sight

7¼ in (197 mm)

Hammer

Firing pin

Sight pin

Sight ring attachment

Magazine

0.35 in (9 mm) calibre bullet

PISTOL TARGET FOR 60 FT (18 M) RANGE

Trigger

Air-pistol pellet

AIR-PISTOL TARGET FOR 33 FT (10 M) RANGE

Nock

FIELD ARROW

Metal tip

Feathering

Wooden shaft

Straw butt

White inner 2 points

Aluminum longrod stabilizer

Blue outer 5 points

Yellow inner 10 points (bull's-eye)

ARCHERY TARGET

Ice hockey

ICE HOCKEY IS PLAYED by two teams of six players on
an ice rink, with a goal net at each end. The object of this
fast, and often dangerous, game is to hit a frozen rubber
puck into the opposing team's net with an ice hockey stick.
The game begins when the referee drops the puck between
the sticks of two players from opposing teams, who face
off. The rink is divided into three areas: defending, neutral,
and attacking zones. Players may move with the puck and
pass it to one another along the ice, but the puck should
not travel more than two zones across the rink markings.
A goal is scored when the puck entirely crosses the goal-
line between the posts and under the crossbar of the goal.
A team may field up to 20 players although only six players
are allowed on the ice at one time; substitutions occur
frequently. Each game consists of three periods of
20 minutes, divided by breaks of 15 minutes.

GOALKEEPER

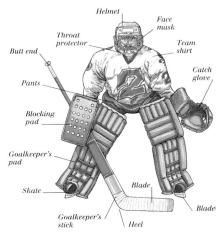

Helmet
Face mask
Throat protector
Team shirt
Butt end
Catch glove
Pants
Blocking pad
Goalkeeper's pad
Blade
Skate
Blade
Goalkeeper's stick
Heel

ICE HOCKEY RINK

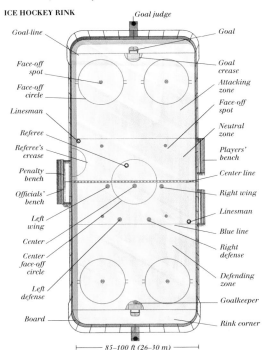

Goal judge
Goal-line
Goal
Face-off spot
Goal crease
Face-off circle
Attacking zone
Linesman
Face-off spot
Referee
Neutral zone
Referee's crease
Players' bench
Penalty bench
Center line
Officials' bench
Right wing
Left wing
Linesman
Center
Blue line
Center face-off circle
Right defense
Left defense
Defending zone
Board
Goalkeeper
Rink corner

85–100 ft (26–30 m)

THE FACE OFF

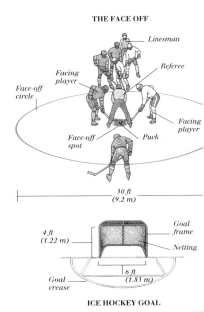

Linesman
Referee
Facing player
Face-off circle
Facing player
Face-off spot
Puck

30 ft
(9.2 m)

4 ft
(1.22 m)
Goal frame
Netting
Goal crease
6 ft
(1.83 m)

ICE HOCKEY GOAL

GOALKEEPER'S HELMET

Customized paint

Face guard

Chin protection

Shoulder padding

ELBOW PADS

PLAYER'S BODY ARMOR

Air vents

Rigid plastic shell

Manufacturer's logo

Chin strap

Foam padding

PLAYER'S HELMET

SHOULDER AND CHEST PADDING

ICE HOCKEY STICKS

MADE IN FINLAND

GOALKEEPER'S STICK

OUTFIELD PLAYER'S STICK

TORSPO

Pro 5000

TORSPO

Pro 500

4 ft 9 in (147 cm)

Thin shaft

Wide lower shaft

DR
Daignault · Rolland
4355 M
DÉFENSE · PRO · DEFENCE

Strap

Chest padding

Wrist protection

DR
IGNAULT
LAND
3075N

Heavy padding

Flexible gusset

Rigid finger cap

GLOVE

TORSPO
20

LEG PROTECTOR

Rigid plastic casing

DR
Daignault · Rolland
CENTURION

Knee protection

Thick foam backing

Leg pad

Vulcanized rubber

3 in (7.62 cm)

FROZEN PUCK

TORSPO

TORSPO

15 in (39 cm)

12½ in (32 cm)

Thick blade

Heel

Ankle support

501

Safety heel tip

Blade **SKATE**

Puck stopper

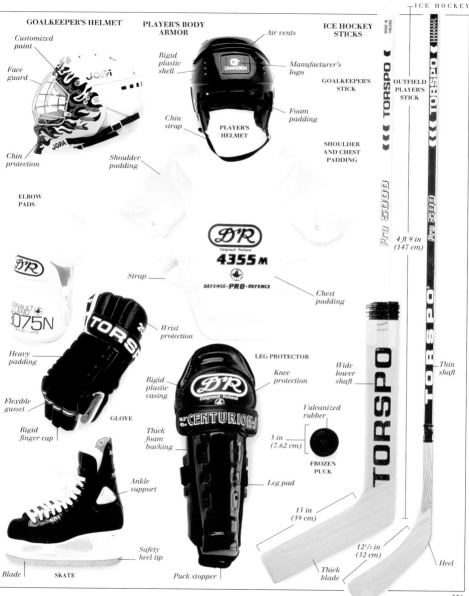

Alpine skiing

COMPETITIVE ALPINE SKIING is divided into four disciplines: downhill, slalom, giant slalom, and super-giant slalom (Super-G). Each one tests different skills. In downhill skiing, competitors race down a slope marked out by control flags, known as "gates," and are timed on a single run only. Competitors wear crash helmets, one-piece Lycra suits, and long skis with flattened tips to minimize air resistance. Slalom and giant slalom skiers negotiate a twisting course requiring balance, agility, and quick reactions. Courses are defined by pairs of gates. Racers must pass through each pair of gates to complete the course successfully. Competitors are timed on two runs over different courses, and the skier who completes the courses in the shortest time wins. The equipment and protective guards used by slalom skiers are shown opposite. In Super-G races, competitors ski a single run that combines the technical challenge of slalom with the speed of downhill. The course requires skiers to complete medium-to-long radius turns at high speed, and contain up to two jumps. Clothing is the same as for downhill, but slightly shorter skis are used.

DOWNHILL SKIER

Ski goggles
Helmet
One-piece lycra ski suit
Wrist strap
Ski pole
Basket
Ski boot
Safety binding
Tail
Ski glove

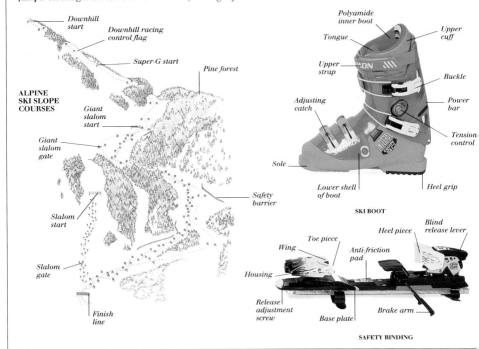

Downhill start
Downhill racing control flag
Super-G start
Pine forest

ALPINE SKI SLOPE COURSES

Giant slalom start
Giant slalom gate
Slalom start
Slalom gate
Finish line
Safety barrier

Polyamide inner boot
Tongue
Upper cuff
Upper strap
Buckle
Adjusting catch
Power bar
Tension control
Sole
Lower shell of boot
Heel grip

SKI BOOT

Wing
Toe piece
Anti-friction pad
Heel piece
Blind release lever
Housing
Release adjustment screw
Base plate
Brake arm

SAFETY BINDING

SLALOM CLOTHING AND EQUIPMENT

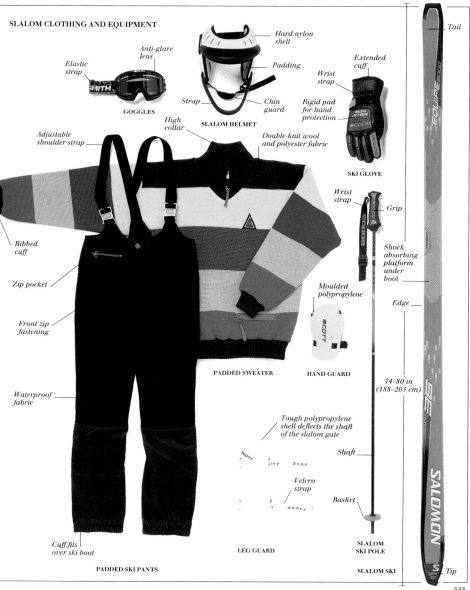

GOGGLES
- Elastic strap
- Anti-glare lens

SLALOM HELMET
- Hard nylon shell
- Padding
- Strap
- Chin guard

SKI GLOVE
- Extended cuff
- Wrist strap
- Rigid pad for hand protection

PADDED SWEATER
- High collar
- Double-knit wool and polyester fabric
- Adjustable shoulder strap
- Ribbed cuff
- Zip pocket
- Front zip fastening

HAND GUARD
- Moulded polypropylene

PADDED SKI PANTS
- Waterproof fabric
- Cuff fits over ski boot

LEG GUARD
- Tough polypropylene shell deflects the shaft of the slalom gate
- Velcro strap

SLALOM SKI POLE
- Wrist strap
- Grip
- Shock-absorbing platform under boot
- Shaft
- Basket
- 74–80 in (188–203 cm)

SLALOM SKI
- Tail
- Edge
- Tip

553

Equestrian sports

Eᴏᴜᴇsᴛʀɪᴀɴ sᴘᴏʀᴛs ʜᴀᴠᴇ ᴛᴀᴋᴇɴ place throughout the world for centuries: events involving mounted horses were recorded in the Olympic Games of 642 ʙᴄ. Show jumping, however, is a much more recent innovation, and the first competitions were held at the beginning of the 1900s. In this sport, horse and rider must negotiate a course of variable, unfixed obstacles, making as few mistakes as possible. Show-jumping fences consist of wooden stands, known as standards or wings, that support planks or poles. Parts of the fence are designed to collapse on impact, preventing injury to the horse and rider. Judges penalize competitors for errors, such as knocking down obstacles, refusing jumps, or deviating from the course. Depending on the type of competition, the rider with the fewest faults, most points, or fastest time wins. There are two basic forms of horse racing – flat races and races with jumps, such as steeplechase or hurdle races. Thoroughbred horses are used in this sport, because they have great strength and stamina and can achieve speeds of up to 40 mph (65 kph). Jockeys wear silks – caps and jackets designed in distinctive colors and patterns which help identify the horses. In harness racing, the horse is driven from a light, two-wheeled carriage called a sulky. Horses are trained to trot and to pace, and different races are held for each of these types of gait. In pacing races, the horses wear hobbles to prevent them from breaking into a trot or gallop. Breeds such as the Standard-bred and the French Trotter have been developed especially for this sport.

SHOW-JUMPING SADDLE

High cantle

Deep seat

Pommel

Forward-cut flap

Knee roll

SHOW-JUMPING FENCES

Standard   Foot

Plank

UPRIGHT PLANKS

Standard   Foot

Pole

UPRIGHT POLES

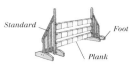

Back pole

Standard

Foot   Pole

TRIPLE BAR (STAIRCASE)

Standard

Foot   Pole

HOG'S-BACK

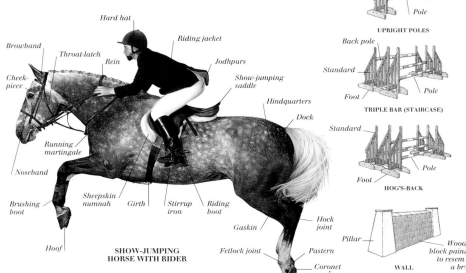

Hard hat

Riding jacket

Browband

Throat-latch

Rein

Jodhpurs

Cheek-piece

Show-jumping saddle

Hindquarters

Dock

Running martingale

Noseband

Brushing boot

Sheepskin numnah   Girth   Stirrup iron   Riding boot

Gaskin

Hoof

SHOW-JUMPING HORSE WITH RIDER

Fetlock joint   Pastern

Hock joint

Coronet

Pillar

Wood block pain to resem a br

WALL

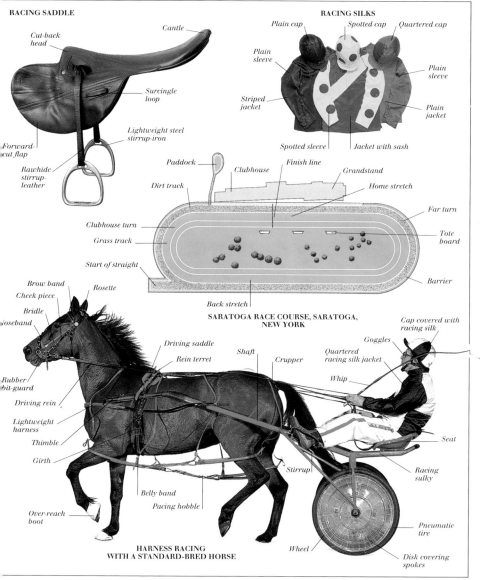

RACING SADDLE

Cut-back head

Cantle

Surcingle loop

Lightweight steel stirrup-iron

Forward-cut flap

Rawhide stirrup-leather

RACING SILKS

Plain cap

Spotted cap

Quartered cap

Plain sleeve

Plain sleeve

Striped jacket

Plain jacket

Spotted sleeve

Jacket with sash

Paddock

Clubhouse

Finish line

Grandstand

Dirt track

Home stretch

Far turn

Clubhouse turn

Grass track

Tote board

Start of straight

Barrier

Back stretch

SARATOGA RACE COURSE, SARATOGA, NEW YORK

Brow band

Cheek piece

Rosette

Bridle

Noseband

Rubber bit-guard

Driving rein

Lightweight harness

Thimble

Girth

Over-reach boot

Driving saddle

Rein terret

Shaft

Crupper

Belly band

Pacing hobble

Stirrup

Cap covered with racing silk

Goggles

Quartered racing silk jacket

Whip

Seat

Racing sulky

Pneumatic tire

Wheel

Disk covering spokes

HARNESS RACING WITH A STANDARD-BRED HORSE

Judo and fencing

COMBAT SPORTS ARE BASED ON THE SKILLS used in fighting. In these sports, the competitors may be unarmed – as in judo and boxing – or armed – as in fencing and kendo. Judo is a system of unarmed combat developed in the East. Translated from the Japanese the name means "the gentle way." Students learn how to turn an opponent's force to their own advantage. The usual uniform is loose white pants and a jacket, fastened with a cloth belt. The color of belt indicates the student's level of expertise, from white-belted novices to the expert black belts. Competitions take place on a mat or "shiaijo," 30 or 33 ft (9 or 10 m) square in size, bounded by "danger" and "safety" areas to prevent injury. Competitors try to throw, pin, or master their opponent by applying pressure to the arm joints or neck. Judo matches are strictly monitored, and competitors receive points for superior technique, not for injuring their opponent. Fencing is a combat sport using swords, which takes place on a narrow piste or strip 46 ft (14 m) long. Competitors try to hit specific target areas on their opponent with their sword or foil while avoiding being touched themselves. The winner is the one who scores the greatest number of hits. Fencers wear uniforms made from strong white material, which affords maximum protection while allowing freedom of movement, steel mesh masks with padded bibs to protect the fencer's neck, and a long white glove on their sword hand. Fencing foils do not have sharpened blades, and their tips end in a blunt button to prevent injuries. Three types of swords are used – foils, épées, and sabres. Official foil and épée competitions always use an electric scoring system. The sword tips are connected to lights by a long wire that passes underneath each fencer's jacket. A bulb flashes when a hit is made.

JUDO HOLDS AND THROWS

SIDE FOUR QUARTER HOLD

SINGLE WING

BODY DROP

ONE ARM SHOULDER THROW

SHOULDER WHEEL

SWEEPING LOW THROW

STOMACH THROW

KNEE WHEEL

JUDO KIT

JUDO MAT

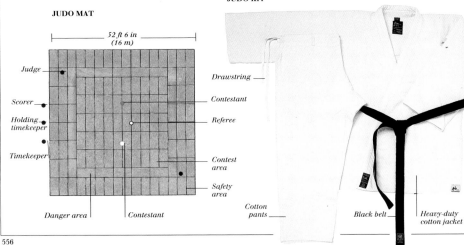

52 ft 6 in
(16 m)

Judge

Scorer

Holding timekeeper

Timekeeper

Danger area

Contestant

Drawstring

Contestant

Referee

Contest area

Safety area

Cotton pants

Black belt

Heavy-duty cotton jacket

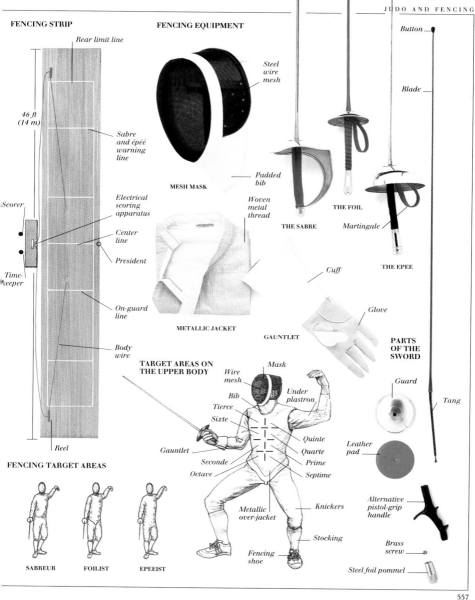

FENCING STRIP

Rear limit line

46 ft
(14 m)

Sabre
and épéé
warning
line

Scorer

Electrical
scoring
apparatus

Center
line

President

Time-
keeper

On-guard
line

Body
wire

Reel

FENCING TARGET AREAS

SABREUR   FOILIST   EPEEIST

FENCING EQUIPMENT

Steel
wire
mesh

MESH MASK

Padded
bib

Woven
metal
thread

METALLIC JACKET

Cuff

Glove

GAUNTLET

**TARGET AREAS ON
THE UPPER BODY**

Mask

Wire
mesh

Bib

Tierce

Sixte

Gauntlet

Seconde

Octave

Under
plastron

Quinte

Quarte

Prime

Septime

Metallic
over-jacket

Knickers

Stocking

Fencing
shoe

Button

Blade

THE FOIL

THE SABRE

Martingale

THE EPEE

**PARTS
OF THE
SWORD**

Guard

Tang

Leather
pad

Alternative
pistol-grip
handle

Brass
screw

Steel foil pommel

557

Swimming and diving

SWIMMING GOGGLES

SWIMMING WAS INCLUDED in the first modern Olympic Games in 1896 and diving events were added in 1904. Swimming is both an individual and a team sport and races take place over a predetermined distance in one of the four major categories of stroke – freestyle (usually front crawl), butterfly, breaststroke, and backstroke. Competition pools are clearly marked for racing and anti-turbulence lane lines are used to separate the swimmers and help keep the water calm. The first team or individual to finish the race is the winner. Competitive diving is divided into men's and women's springboard and platform (highboard) events. There are six official groups of dives: forward dives, backward dives, armstand dives, twist dives, reverse dives, and inward dives. Competitors perform a set number of dives and after each one a panel of judges awards marks according to the quality of execution and the degree of difficulty.

STYLES OF DIVES

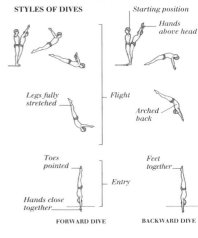

Starting position

Hands above head

Legs fully stretched

Flight

Arched back

Toes pointed

Entry

Feet together

Hands close together

FORWARD DIVE

BACKWARD DIVE

SWIMMING POOL

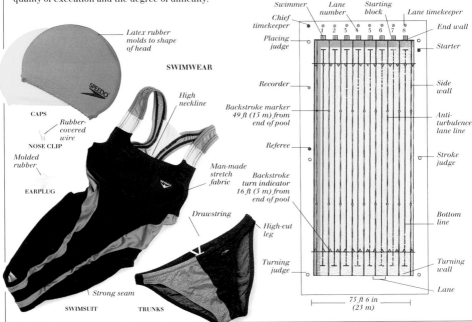

Latex rubber molds to shape of head

CAPS

SWIMWEAR

Rubber-covered wire

NOSE CLIP

High neckline

Molded rubber

EARPLUG

Man-made stretch fabric

Drawstring

High-cut leg

Strong seam

SWIMSUIT   **TRUNKS**

Swimmer

Chief timekeeper

Lane number

Starting block

Lane timekeeper

Placing judge

End wall

Starter

Recorder

Side wall

Backstroke marker 49 ft (15 m) from end of pool

Anti-turbulence lane line

Referee

Stroke judge

Backstroke turn indicator 16 ft (5 m) from end of pool

Bottom line

Turning judge

Turning wall

Lane

75 ft 6 in (23 m)

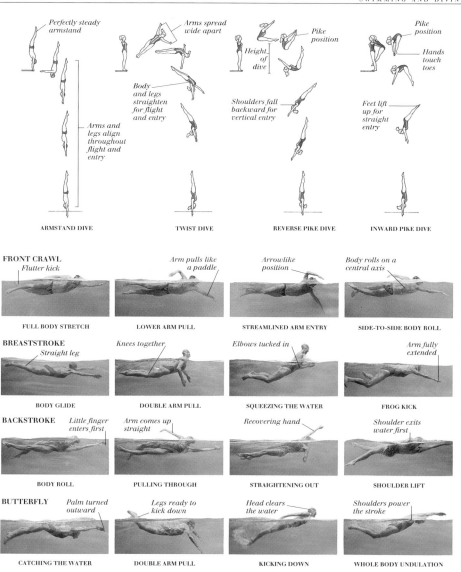

Perfectly steady armstand

Arms and legs align throughout flight and entry

ARMSTAND DIVE

Arms spread wide apart

Body and legs straighten for flight and entry

TWIST DIVE

Pike position

Height of dive

Shoulders fall backward for vertical entry

REVERSE PIKE DIVE

Pike position

Hands touch toes

Feet lift up for straight entry

INWARD PIKE DIVE

FRONT CRAWL
Flutter kick

FULL BODY STRETCH

Arm pulls like a paddle

LOWER ARM PULL

Arrowlike position

STREAMLINED ARM ENTRY

Body rolls on a central axis

SIDE-TO-SIDE BODY ROLL

BREASTSTROKE
Straight leg

BODY GLIDE

Knees together

DOUBLE ARM PULL

Elbows tucked in

SQUEEZING THE WATER

Arm fully extended

FROG KICK

BACKSTROKE
Little finger enters first

BODY ROLL

Arm comes up straight

PULLING THROUGH

Recovering hand

STRAIGHTENING OUT

Shoulder exits water first

SHOULDER LIFT

BUTTERFLY
Palm turned outward

CATCHING THE WATER

Legs ready to kick down

DOUBLE ARM PULL

Head clears the water

KICKING DOWN

Shoulders power the stroke

WHOLE BODY UNDULATION

Kayaking, rowing, and sailing

WATERBORNE SPORTS are as varied as the crafts used. There are two disciplines in rowing; sweep rowing, in which each rower has one oar, and sculling, in which rowers use two oars. There are a number of different Olympic and competitive rowing events for both men and women. The number of rowers and weight classes vary. Some rowing events use a coxswain; a steersman who does not row but directs the crew. Kayaks are used in straight sprint and slalom races. Slalom races take place over a course consisting of 20 to 25 gates, including at least six upstream gates. In yacht racing, competitors must complete prescribed courses, organized by the race committees, in the shortest possible time, using sail power only. Olympic events include classes for keel boats, dinghies, catamarans, and windsurfers.

SAILING GEAR

Person flotati device

Sleeveless long johns

Long-sleeved jacket

Neoprene material

Belt

GLOVE

Bootla

Ribbed top

Non-slip sole

BOOT

High density polythene

ONE-PERSON KAYAK AND PADDLE

Blade

Rim

Shaft

Nose cone

Right rail

Cockpit

Back strap

Stern

Grab loop

Bow

Left rail

Seat

Cockpit rim

**SINGLE SCULL AND OARS
(WITH CLOTH DECKING REMOVED)**

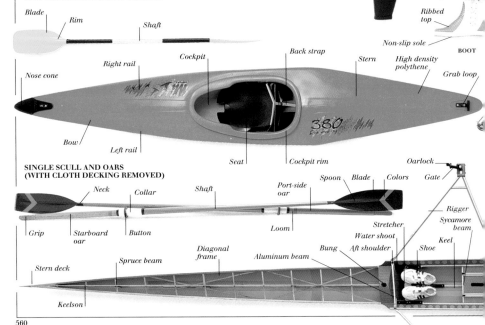

Oarlock

Neck

Collar

Shaft

Port-side oar

Spoon

Blade

Colors

Gate

Rigger

Grip

Starboard oar

Button

Loom

Stretcher

Water shoot

Sycamore beam

Keel

Diagonal frame

Bung

Aft shoulder

Shoe

Stern deck

Spruce beam

Aluminum beam

Keelson

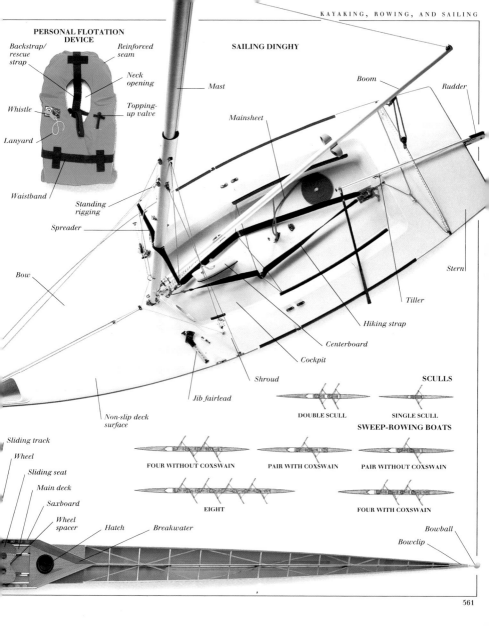

PERSONAL FLOTATION DEVICE

Backstrap/ rescue strap

Reinforced seam

Neck opening

Whistle

Topping-up valve

Lanyard

Waistband

Standing rigging

Spreader

Bow

Non-slip deck surface

Jib fairlead

Shroud

Cockpit

Centerboard

Hiking strap

Tiller

Stern

SAILING DINGHY

Mast

Boom

Rudder

Mainsheet

SCULLS

DOUBLE SCULL

SINGLE SCULL

SWEEP-ROWING BOATS

FOUR WITHOUT COXSWAIN

PAIR WITH COXSWAIN

PAIR WITHOUT COXSWAIN

EIGHT

FOUR WITH COXSWAIN

Sliding track

Wheel

Sliding seat

Main deck

Saxboard

Wheel spacer

Hatch

Breakwater

Bowball

Bowclip

561

Angling

ANGLING MEANS FISHING WITH A ROD, reel, line, and lure. There are several different types of angling: freshwater coarse angling, for members of the carp family and pike; freshwater game angling, for salmon and trout; and sea angling, for sea fish such as flatfish, bass, and mackerel. Anglers use a variety of methods of catching fish. These include bait fishing, in which bait (food to allure the fish) is placed on a hook and cast into the water; fly fishing, in which a natural or artificial fly is used to lure the fish; and spinning, in which a lure that looks like a small fish revolves as it is pulled through the water. The angler uses the rod, reel, and line to cast the lure over the water. The reel controls the line as it spills off the spool and as it is wound back. Weights may be fixed to the line so that it will sink. Swivels are attached to prevent the line from twisting. When a fish bites, the hook must become embedded in its mouth and remain there while the catch is reeled in.

BUTT SECTION

Keeper ring

Handgrip

Drag spindle

Drag washer

Disk drag

Disk spring

Gear retainer

Dual click gear

Retaining screw

Check slide

Check pawl cover

Check pawl

Check spring

REELS

Plate-nut

Spool-release button

Reel foot (reel scoop)

Click mechanism

Mechanical brake

Side plate

Centrifugal brake

Spool

Handle

Star drag

Level-wind system

BAITCASTER

Line

Unskirted spool

Reel foot (reel scoop)

Handle

Tension nut (drag adjustment)

Ratchet (anti-reverse device)

Handgrip

Reel

Bail arm

SPINNING REEL

HOOKS, SWIVELS, AND WEIGHTS

Eye

Shank

Gap

ANATOMY OF A HOOK

Bend

Throat

Point

Barb

TREBLE HOOK

ABERDEEN HOOK

REVERSED BEND HOOK

EXAMPLES OF BARREL SWIVELS

HILLMAN ANTI-KINK WEIGHT

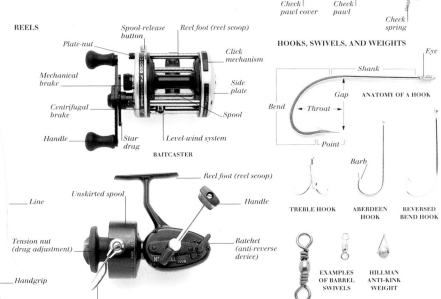

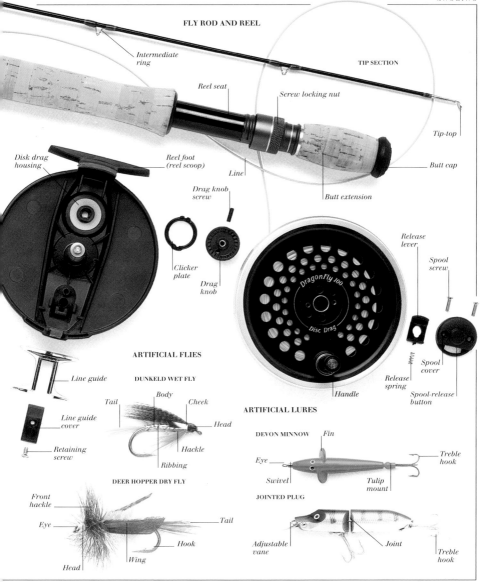

FLY ROD AND REEL

Intermediate ring

TIP SECTION

Reel seat

Screw locking nut

Tip-top

Disk drag housing

Reel foot (reel scoop)

Line

Butt cap

Butt extension

Drag knob screw

Release lever

Spool screw

Clicker plate

Drag knob

Spool cover

Release spring

Spool-release button

Handle

Line guide

ARTIFICIAL FLIES

DUNKELD WET FLY

Tail

Body

Cheek

Head

Line guide cover

Hackle

Retaining screw

Ribbing

ARTIFICIAL LURES

DEVON MINNOW

Fin

Eye

Treble hook

Swivel

Tulip mount

DEER HOPPER DRY FLY

Front hackle

Eye

Tail

Hook

Head

Wing

JOINTED PLUG

Adjustable vane

Joint

Treble hook

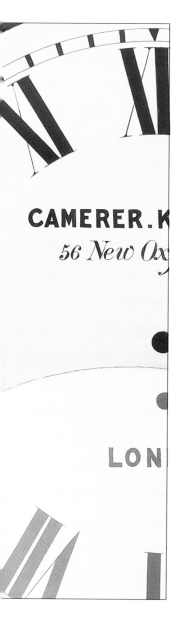

EVERYDAY THINGS

Drills

THE ELECTRICALLY POWERED MOTOR OF A POWER DRILL, cooled by a fan, turns a shaft at high speed. The shaft connects, in turn, to a system of gears that rotates a chuck even faster. Clamped by the chuck, a sharp drill bit cuts out the hole, and at the same time the bit's screw-shaped grooves channel the waste out of the hole. For drilling hard materials, many power drills have a hammer mechanism; when this is operated a ratchet in the gearcase causes the chuck and bit to pound in and out as they drill. A hand drill, although slower and less forceful than a power drill, is easier to control. For cutting wide holes, carpenters often prefer a brace-and-bit. This acts like a lever: the bowed handle of the brace moves a larger distance than the bit, turning the bit with extra force.

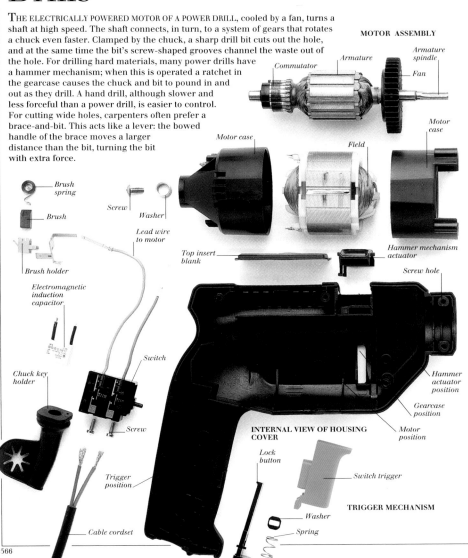

MOTOR ASSEMBLY

Commutator

Armature

Armature spindle

Fan

Motor case

Motor case

Field

Brush spring

Screw

Washer

Brush

Lead wire to motor

Brush holder

Electromagnetic induction capacitor

Top insert blank

Hammer mechanism actuator

Screw hole

Switch

Chuck key holder

Screw

Hammer actuator position

Gearcase position

Motor position

INTERNAL VIEW OF HOUSING COVER

Lock button

Switch trigger

Trigger position

TRIGGER MECHANISM

Washer

Spring

Cable cordset

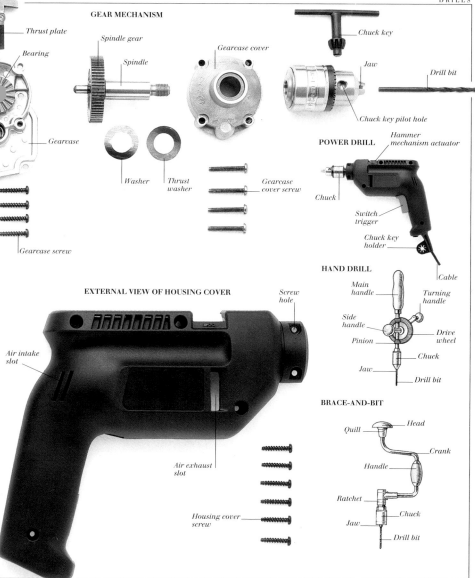

GEAR MECHANISM

Thrust plate

Bearing

Gearcase

Gearcase screw

Spindle gear

Spindle

Washer

Thrust washer

Gearcase cover

Gearcase cover screw

Chuck key

Jaw

Chuck key pilot hole

Drill bit

POWER DRILL

Hammer mechanism actuator

Chuck

Switch trigger

Chuck key holder

Cable

HAND DRILL

Main handle

Side handle

Pinion

Jaw

Turning handle

Drive wheel

Chuck

Drill bit

EXTERNAL VIEW OF HOUSING COVER

Screw hole

Air intake slot

Air exhaust slot

Housing cover screw

BRACE-AND-BIT

Quill

Head

Crank

Handle

Ratchet

Chuck

Jaw

Drill bit

567

Shoes

WELL MADE SHOES PROTECT THE FEET and are also comfortable and long lasting. The best shoemakers use a wood or plastic mold, called a last, which matches the shape of the customer's foot. The different parts of a shoe are stitched and glued together around the last; rivets and nails are used only in the heel, which is built up from layers of leather and rubber. The steel shank gives support to the arch of the foot and, with the seat lift, helps the wearer maintain posture. The layers of the sole give strength, while the soft insole cushions the foot. The leather welt sewn between the leather uppers and the sole ensures a strong join.

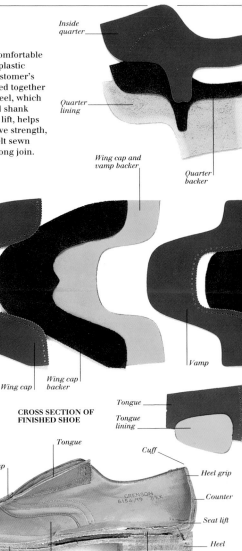

Inside quarter

Quarter lining

Wing cap and vamp backer

Quarter backer

Inner sock

Counter

Tongue

Shoelace

Outside quarter

Vamp

Box toe

Punchhole

Wing cap

Welt

Welt

Perforated wing cap

Wing cap

Wing cap backer

Vamp

CROSS SECTION OF FINISHED SHOE

Tongue

Tongue lining

Tongue

Cuff

Heel grip

Counter

Seat lift

Heel

Vamp

Insole

Bottom filler

Outsole

Lining

Steel shank

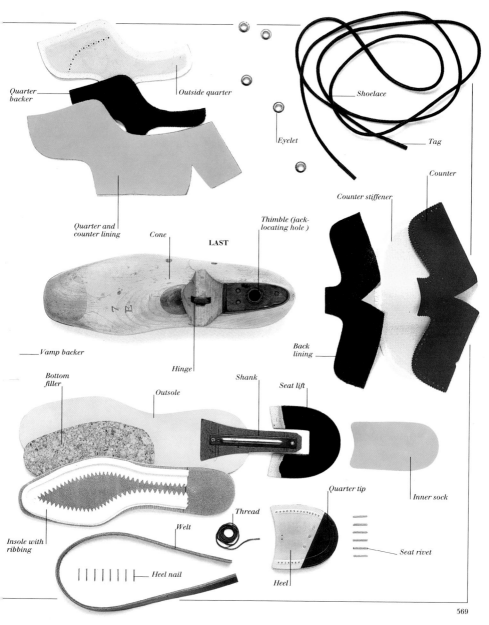

Quarter backer

Outside quarter

Shoelace

Eyelet

Tag

Counter

Counter stiffener

Quarter and counter lining

Cone

LAST

Thimble (jack-locating hole)

Vamp backer

Back lining

Hinge

Bottom filler

Outsole

Shank

Seat lift

Quarter tip

Inner sock

Insole with ribbing

Thread

Welt

Seat rivet

Heel nail

Heel

569

Clock

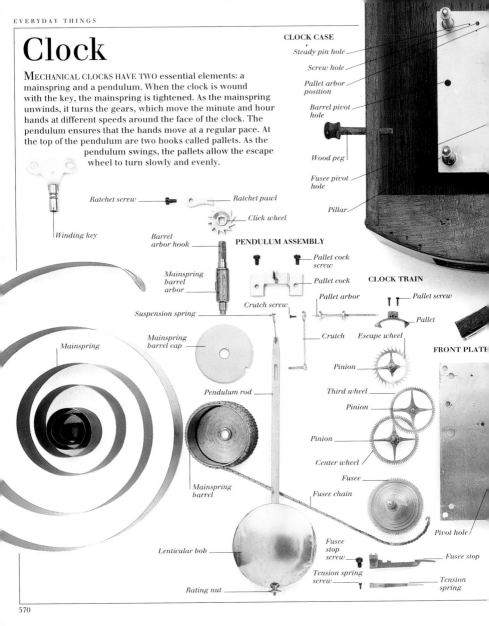

MECHANICAL CLOCKS HAVE TWO essential elements: a
mainspring and a pendulum. When the clock is wound
with the key, the mainspring is tightened. As the mainspring
unwinds, it turns the gears, which move the minute and hour
hands at different speeds around the face of the clock. The
pendulum ensures that the hands move at a regular pace. At
the top of the pendulum are two hooks called pallets. As the
pendulum swings, the pallets allow the escape
wheel to turn slowly and evenly.

CLOCK CASE

Steady pin hole

Screw hole

Pallet arbor
position

Barrel pivot
hole

Wood peg

Fusee pivot
hole

Pillar

Winding key

Ratchet screw

Ratchet pawl

Click wheel

Barrel
arbor hook

PENDULUM ASSEMBLY

Pallet cock
screw

Mainspring
barrel
arbor

Pallet cock

CLOCK TRAIN

Pallet arbor

Pallet screw

Pallet

Suspension spring

Crutch screw

Escape wheel

Mainspring

Mainspring
barrel cap

Crutch

FRONT PLATE

Pinion

Pendulum rod

Third wheel

Pinion

Pinion

Center wheel

Mainspring
barrel

Fusee

Fusee chain

Pivot hole

Lenticular bob

Fusee
stop
screw

Fusee stop

Tension spring
screw

Tension
spring

Rating nut

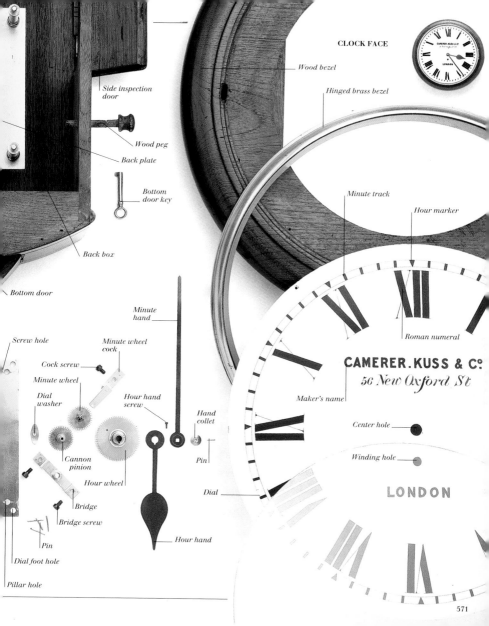

CLOCK FACE

Wood bezel

Hinged brass bezel

Side inspection door

Wood peg

Back plate

Bottom door key

Minute track

Hour marker

Back box

Bottom door

Minute hand

Screw hole

Minute wheel cock

Cock screw

Minute wheel

Dial washer

Hour hand screw

Hand collet

Maker's name

Cannon pinion

Pin

Hour wheel

Bridge

Bridge screw

Pin

Dial foot hole

Pillar hole

Hour hand

Dial

Roman numeral

CAMERER. KUSS & C°.
56 New Oxford St

Center hole

Winding hole

LONDON

Lamp

THE FIRST SPRING-TENSIONED, adjustable work lamp was designed in 1934 by George Carwardine. This type of lamp imitates the human arm in the way that it can be kept in a fixed position or moved easily and precisely. In the arm, such control is achieved by coordinating the opposing action of paired muscles (e.g., when the biceps contracts, the triceps relaxes and the arm bends). In the work lamp, one muscle of a pair is represented by the springs that pull on the rigid bars of the lamp; the other muscle is represented by the nuts, bolts, screws, and washers in the lamp's joints that resist the pull of the springs. By balancing the pull of the springs against the resistance in the joints, the lamp's height and angle can be adjusted with minimal pressure.

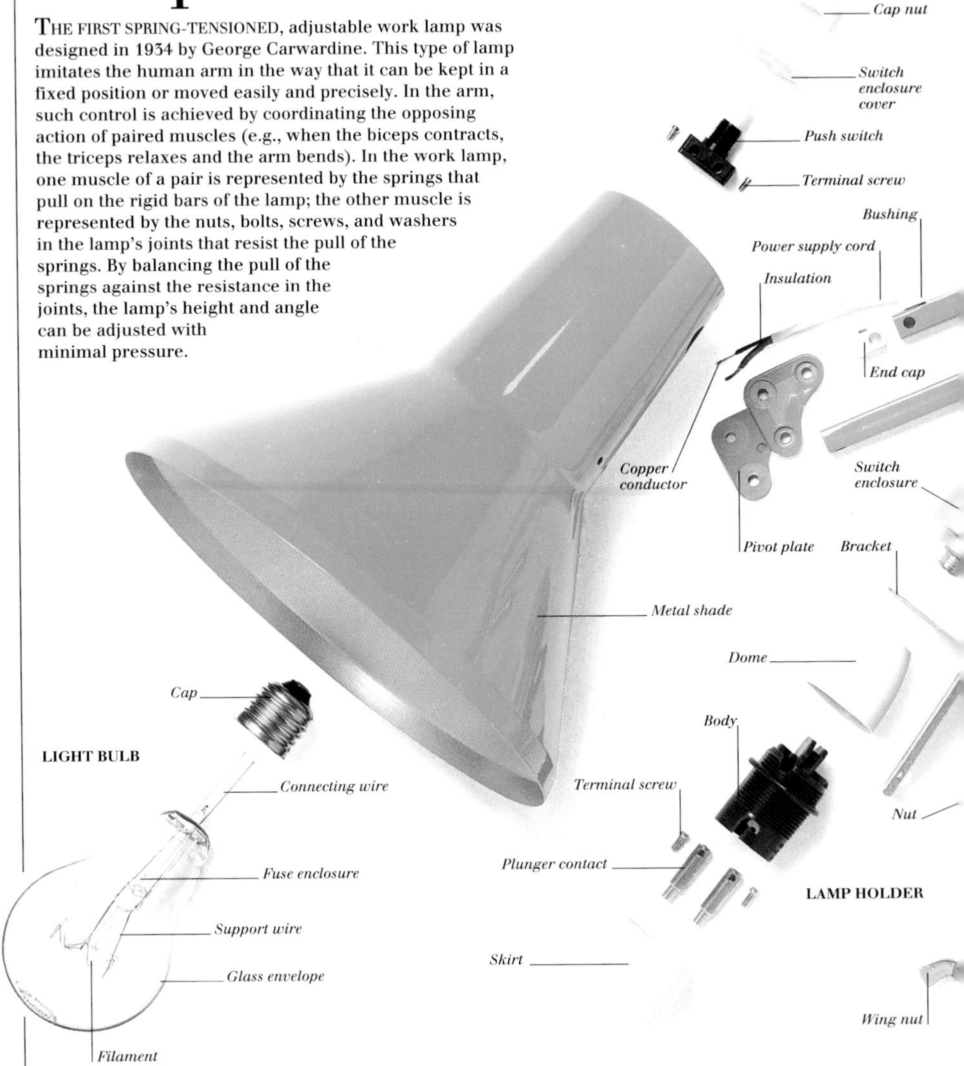

Cap nut

Switch enclosure cover

Push switch

Terminal screw

Bushing

Power supply cord

Insulation

End cap

Copper conductor

Switch enclosure

Pivot plate   Bracket

Metal shade

Dome

Cap

Body

LIGHT BULB

Connecting wire

Terminal screw

Nut

Fuse enclosure

Plunger contact

LAMP HOLDER

Support wire

Glass envelope

Skirt

Filament

Wing nut

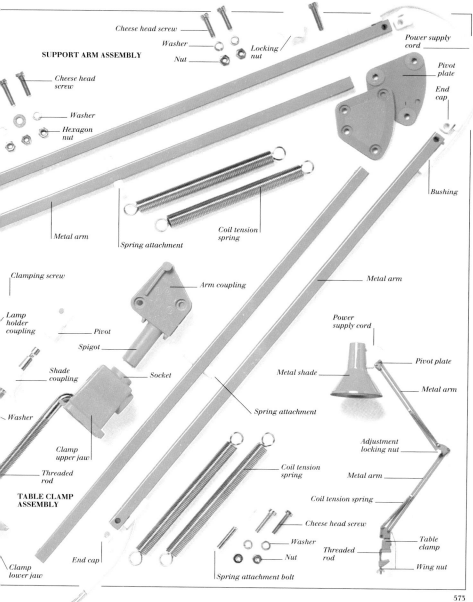

Cheese head screw

Washer

Nut

Locking nut

Power supply cord

SUPPORT ARM ASSEMBLY

Pivot plate

End cap

Cheese head screw

Washer

Hexagon nut

Bushing

Metal arm

Coil tension spring

Spring attachment

Clamping screw

Arm coupling

Metal arm

Lamp holder coupling

Pivot

Power supply cord

Pivot plate

Spigot

Metal shade

Metal arm

Shade coupling

Socket

Spring attachment

Washer

Adjustment locking nut

Metal arm

Clamp upper jaw

Coil tension spring

Coil tension spring

Threaded rod

TABLE CLAMP ASSEMBLY

Cheese head screw

Table clamp

Washer

Threaded rod

Nut

Wing nut

Clamp lower jaw

End cap

Spring attachment bolt

Mini television

MINIATURIZED TELEVISION SETS are small enough to be held in the hand while being watched. A signal sent by a broadcast transmitter is picked up by the television antenna and passed to an electron gun at the back of the television set. In response to the signal this gun produces an electron beam that is passed through a deflection yoke. The yoke contains magnets and coils that cause the beam to scan across the screen in a series of lines. The screen is coated with phosphor, which glows when hit by the beam. As the beam scans the screen, its strength is varied so that the phosphor glows with different intensities in different parts of the screen. A continuous sequence of 25 black-and-white pictures per second appears on the screen so rapidly that the illusion of a moving picture is created.

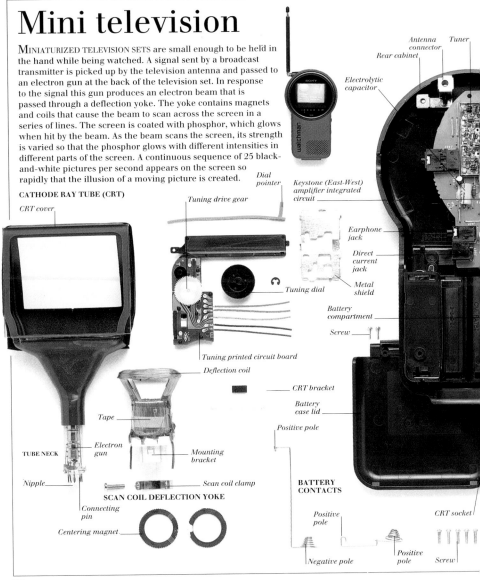

CATHODE RAY TUBE (CRT)

CRT cover

Antenna connector
Tuner
Rear cabinet
Electrolytic capacitor

Dial pointer
Keystone (East-West) amplifier integrated circuit

Tuning drive gear

Earphone jack

Direct current jack

Metal shield

Tuning dial

Battery compartment

Screw

Tuning printed circuit board

Deflection coil

CRT bracket

Battery case lid

Positive pole

Tape

Electron gun

Mounting bracket

TUBE NECK

Nipple

Scan coil clamp

SCAN COIL DEFLECTION YOKE

BATTERY CONTACTS

Connecting pin

Centering magnet

Positive pole

Negative pole

Positive pole

CRT socket

Screw

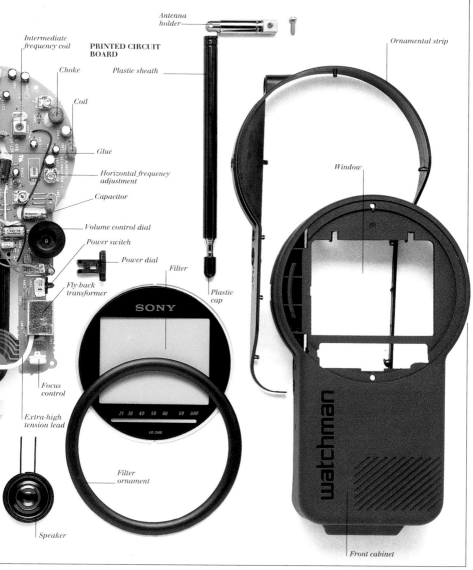

Intermediate
frequency coil

**PRINTED CIRCUIT
BOARD**

Antenna
holder

Choke

Plastic sheath

Coil

Ornamental strip

Glue

Horizontal frequency
adjustment

Capacitor

Window

Volume control dial

Power switch

Power dial

Filter

Fly-back
transformer

Plastic
cap

SONY

Focus
control

Extra-high
tension lead

21 30 40 50 60 68 UHF

FD-250B

Filter
ornament

watchman

Speaker

Front cabinet

Chair

A TRADITIONALLY MADE DINING CHAIR, such as the Regency-style carver shown here, is held together, not by nails or bolts, but by snugly fitting joints, screws, dowels, and glue. Its curved arms and top splats, as well as its tapering legs, are cut from seasoned—that is, dried—mahogany. Mortice slots in the back legs receive the tenon tongues of the top and bottom splats; angled grooves at the top of the back legs, called rebates, take the curved arm rail. Though the various joints are so tight-fitting that they could produce a solid frame on their own, screws and glue are used to give the joints added strength. The comfortable, upholstered seat pad shown here consists of a patterned cover, calico lining, and foam padding that has been treated for fire safety; it is supported by webbing stretched across a wood frame.

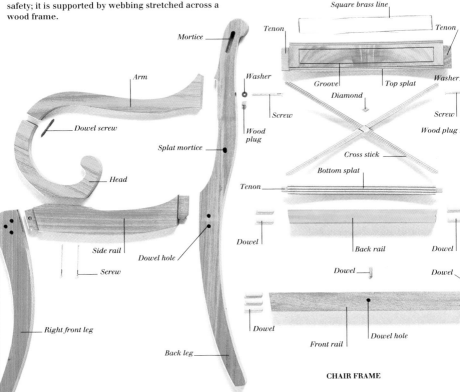

Cross stick

Top splat

Bottom splat

Arm

Head

Seat pad

Front rail

Back leg

Left front leg

Square brass line

Mortice

Tenon

Tenon

Washer

Groove

Top splat

Washer

Arm

Diamond

Screw

Screw

Dowel screw

Wood plug

Wood plug

Splat mortice

Cross stick

Head

Bottom splat

Tenon

Side rail

Back rail

Dowel

Dowel hole

Dowel

Dowel

Screw

Dowel

Dowel

Right front leg

Dowel

Front rail

Dowel hole

Back leg

CHAIR FRAME

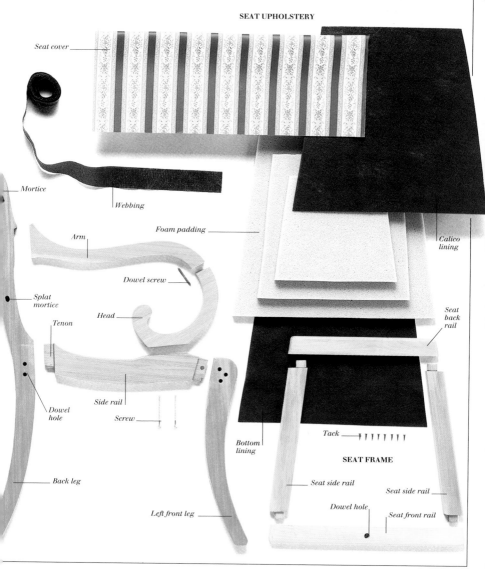

SEAT UPHOLSTERY

Seat cover

Mortice

Webbing

Foam padding

Calico lining

Arm

Dowel screw

Splat mortice

Head

Seat back rail

Tenon

Side rail

Screw

Dowel hole

Back leg

Bottom lining

Tack

SEAT FRAME

Left front leg

Seat side rail

Seat side rail

Dowel hole

Seat front rail

Toaster

MOST ELECTRIC TOASTERS NOT ONLY GRILL slices of bread, they also pop them up when ready. While the slices rest on a spring-loaded rack, electric heating elements toast the bread. At the same time, a bimetallic strip heats and expands. One of the two metals in this strip expands more quickly than the other, causing the strip to curve. As it bends, it completes an electrical circuit and activates an electromagnet. The magnet attracts a catch, releasing the spring that holds the rack down in the toaster. The elements switch off, and the toasted slices pop up.

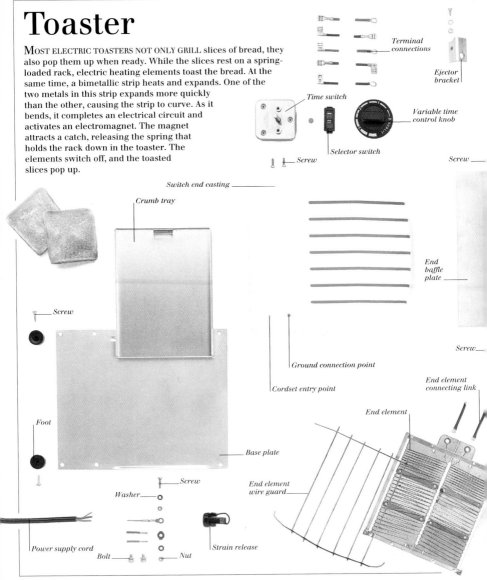

Terminal connections

Ejector bracket

Time switch

Variable time control knob

Selector switch

Screw

Screw

Switch end casting

Crumb tray

End baffle plate

Screw

Screw

Ground connection point

Cordset entry point

End element connecting link

End element

Foot

Base plate

Screw

End element wire guard

Washer

Power supply cord

Bolt

Nut

Strain release

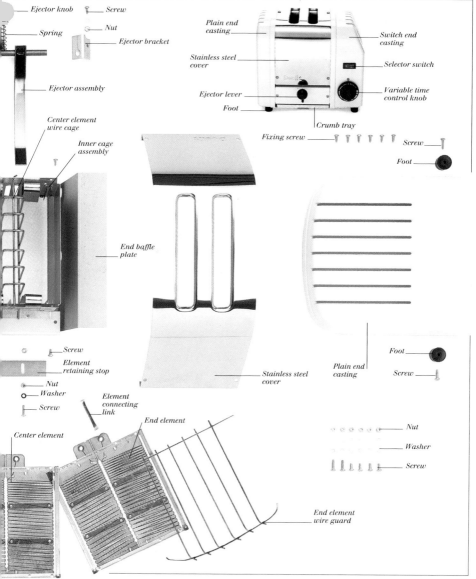

Ejector knob

Screw

Nut

Spring

Ejector bracket

Ejector assembly

Plain end casting

Switch end casting

Stainless steel cover

Selector switch

Ejector lever

Variable time control knob

Foot

Crumb tray

Fixing screw

Screw

Foot

Center element wire cage

Inner cage assembly

End baffle plate

Screw

Element retaining stop

Foot

Plain end casting

Screw

Nut

Washer

Screw

Stainless steel cover

Element connecting link

End element

Nut

Washer

Screw

Center element

End element wire guard

Lawnmower

THE SHARP BLADES OF A LAWNMOWER—whether driven by electrical, gasoline, or human power—shave grass close to the ground. The gasoline-powered type shown here has a small engine that is electrically ignited by a battery and spark plug. This engine rotates a horizontal blade at the base of the lawnmower, which then slices the grass against a fixed blade. A grass bag at the back of the machine collects the cuttings. As the engine rotates the blades, it also turns the rear wheels, moving the lawnmower forward. Gears ensure that the horizontal blade spins faster than the wheels so that all of the grass is cut neatly before the lawnmower moves on.

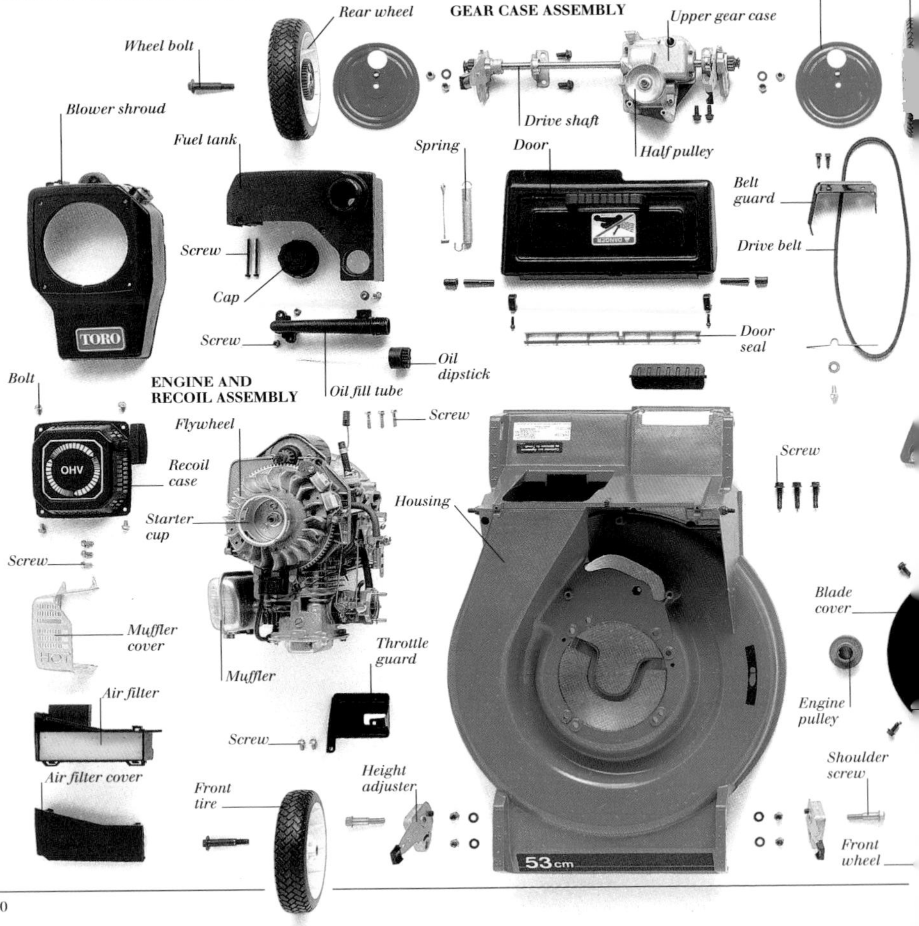

Rear tire

Wheel cover

GEAR CASE ASSEMBLY

Rear wheel

Upper gear case

Wheel bolt

Blower shroud

Fuel tank

Drive shaft

Spring

Door

Half pulley

Belt guard

Screw

Drive belt

Cap

Door seal

Screw

Oil dipstick

Bolt

ENGINE AND RECOIL ASSEMBLY

Oil fill tube

Screw

Flywheel

Screw

Recoil case

Housing

Screw

Starter cup

TORO

OHV

Screw

Blade cover

Muffler cover

Throttle guard

Air filter

Muffler

Engine pulley

Screw

Air filter cover

Front tire

Height adjuster

Shoulder screw

53 cm

Front wheel

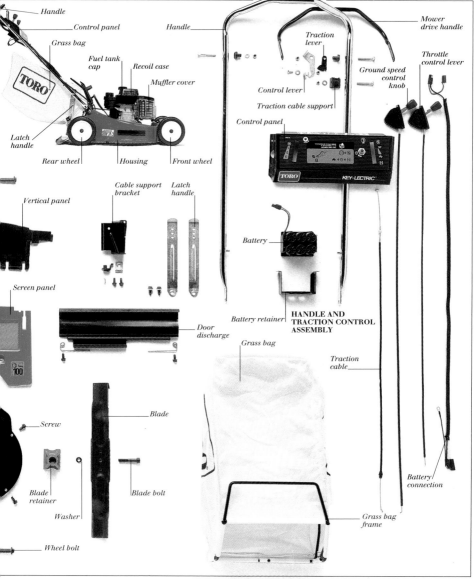

Handle

Control panel

Grass bag

Fuel tank cap

Recoil case

Muffler cover

TORO

Latch handle

Rear wheel

Housing

Front wheel

Handle

Mower drive handle

Traction lever

Ground speed control knob

Throttle control lever

Control lever

Traction cable support

Control panel

TORO   KEY-LECTRIC

Battery

Vertical panel

Cable support bracket

Latch handle

Screen panel

Battery retainer

Door discharge

Grass bag

HANDLE AND TRACTION CONTROL ASSEMBLY

Traction cable

Screw

Blade

Blade retainer

Washer

Blade bolt

Grass bag frame

Battery connection

Wheel bolt

Saddle

THE FIRST HORSEBACK RIDERS HAD NO SADDLES; they sat bareback, clinging to the animal's mane. Next came a simple cloth saddle. The leather saddle, which was invented about 2,000 years ago by the warriors of the Asian steppes, revolutionized horseback riding. On this saddle, horsemen could gallop toward the enemy, fire arrows in all directions, and stay on their horses. Modern saddles are of two main types. The Western saddle is a heavy, working saddle used mainly by ranch hands in the United States. It has a metal horn at the front for securing a lasso and a high cantle at the back to keep the rider on the horse. The English saddle is much lighter. Designed for sport, it allows the horse to gallop fast. Its drawback is that it provides less stability; to stay on the horse, the rider must grip the animal with the knees.

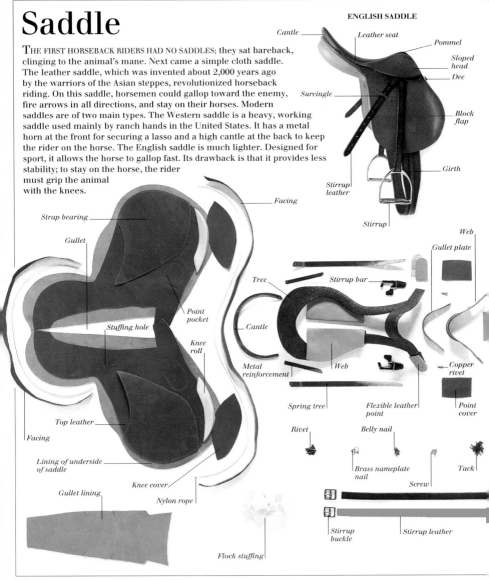

Cantle

Leather seat

Pommel

Sloped head

Dee

Surcingle

Block flap

Girth

Stirrup leather

Stirrup

Web

Gullet plate

Facing

Strap bearing

Gullet

Tree

Stirrup bar

Point pocket

Stuffing hole

Cantle

Web

Copper rivet

Knee roll

Metal reinforcement

Top leather

Spring tree

Flexible leather point

Point cover

Facing

Rivet

Belly nail

Lining of underside of saddle

Knee cover

Brass nameplate nail

Tack

Gullet lining

Nylon rope

Screw

Stirrup buckle

Stirrup leather

Flock stuffing

SHAPED GIRTH

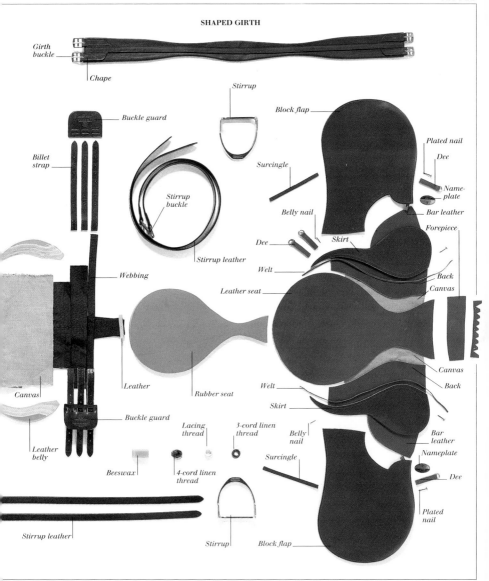

Girth buckle

Chape

Stirrup

Block flap

Plated nail

Dee

Buckle guard

Nameplate

Billet strap

Surcingle

Bar leather

Stirrup buckle

Belly nail

Forepiece

Dee

Skirt

Welt

Back

Canvas

Stirrup leather

Webbing

Leather seat

Canvas

Leather

Back

Rubber seat

Welt

Skirt

Canvas

Buckle guard

Lacing thread

3-cord linen thread

Belly nail

Bar leather

Leather belly

Beeswax

4-cord linen thread

Surcingle

Nameplate

Dee

Stirrup leather

Stirrup

Block flap

Plated nail

CD-ROM

CD-ROM ————
drive

A CD-ROM IS A TYPE OF COMPACT DISC (CD) that can be used to produce images on a computer screen. ROM stands for Read Only Memory, which means that the digitally recorded data registered in pits on the surface of the disc is fixed and cannot be altered or replaced. The CD is loaded into the CD-ROM player, where the data on the spinning disc is read by a laser. CD-ROMs are different from vinyl records in that they are not read along a spiral groove, from outer circumference to inner edge: instead each image or piece of information has a coordinate on the disc, which is located by the laser. Information picked up by the laser is relayed to the computer, where it is translated into the text and images that appear on screen. The information is relayed through a SCSI (Small Computer System Interface), which processes the electronic impulses between the disc drive and the computer system. The user can move around the program by clicking on different parts of the screen with a mouse (a hand-held tool with a clicking button whose movement on its pad is mimicked by an icon on the screen). The image in the viewing area (see opposite) can be changed by clicking on the active scrolling button: this moves a rectangular panel down the scrolling figure in the navigational panel. Clicking on active text will provide a new screen with more information, either in the form of text and diagrams, or as narrated animated sequences.

CD
loading
tray

Caddy
cover flap

Front bezel

Push
button

CD-ROM CASING

CD-ROM
drive motor

Film strip
connector

Laser

Roller
bearing

Guide post

Insulating
grommet

Power connector
to CD-ROM

SCSI connectors

Connector

Ground
connection to case

Connector clasp

SCSI selector switch

Power
switch

Washer

Washer

Gearing
mechanism

Ground
wire

Spring

Surface-
mounted
integrated
circuit

Power
supply
screening
cover

Mounting
rail

Screws

Transistor

CD-ROM disc

CD-ROM disc

Power on/off LED
(Light Emitting Diode)

CD-ROM DISC DRIVE

CD-ROM LOADING MECHANISM

CONTENTS PAGE

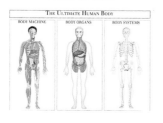

THE ULTIMATE HUMAN BODY

BODY MACHINE | BODY ORGANS | BODY SYSTEMS

External speaker

Disc

Keyboard

Display monitor

Mouse

CD-ROM PLAYER

COMPUTER HARDWARE

Mouse pad

SCREEN FROM A CD-ROM PROGRAM

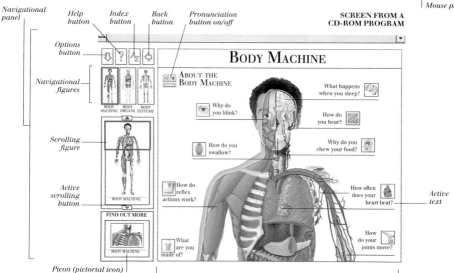

Navigational panel

Help button

Index button

Back button

Pronunciation button on/off

Options button

Navigational figures

BODY MACHINE | BODY ORGANS | BODY SYSTEMS

Scrolling figure

Active scrolling button

BODY MACHINE

FIND OUT MORE

BODY MACHINE

Picon (pictorial icon)

BODY MACHINE

ABOUT THE BODY MACHINE

What happens when you sleep?

Why do you blink?

How do you hear?

How do you swallow?

Why do you chew your food?

How do reflex actions work?

How often does your heart beat?

Active text

What are you made of?

How do your joints move?

Viewing area

ZOOMING INTO MULTI-LAYERED INFORMATION

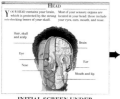

HEAD

YOUR HEAD contains your brain, which is protected by the strong interlocking bones of your skull. Most of your sensory organs are located in your head; these include your eyes, ears, mouth, and nose.

Hair, skull and scalp

Brain

Eye

Ear

Nose

Mouth and lip

INITIAL SCREEN UNDER BODY ORGANS MENU

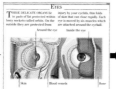

EYES

THESE DELICATE ORGANS lie in pads of fat protected within bony sockets called orbits. On the outside they are protected from injury by your eyelids, thin folds of skin that can close rapidly. Each eye is moved by six muscles which are attached around the eyeball.

Around the eye | Inside the eye

Skin | Blood vessels | Bone

CLICKING ON "EYES" LABEL PRODUCES MORE INFORMATION

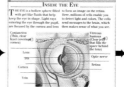

INSIDE THE EYE

THE EYE is a hollow sphere filled with gel-like fluids that help keep the eye in shape. Light rays entering the eye through the pupil, are focused by the cornea and lens to form an image on the retina. Here, millions of cells enable you to detect light and colors. The cells send messages to the brain, which then makes sense of what you see.

Conjunctiva (Thin, clear layer covering cornea)

Vitreous humour (Clear jelly that fills the space behind the lens)

Lens

Iris

Optic nerve

Cornea

Retina

Vein

EACH LABEL PRODUCES A FURTHER SCREEN

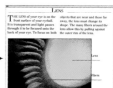

LENS

THE LENS of your eye is on the front surface of your eyeball. It is transparent and light passes through it to be focused onto the back of your eye. To focus on both objects that are near and those far away, the lens must change its shape. The many fibers around the lens allow this by pulling against the outer rim of the lens.

Lens

Fibers

THE FINAL IMAGE SHOWS MICROSCOPIC DETAIL

Books

THOUGH THE PROCESS OF BOOKBINDING today is usually mechanized, some books are still bound by hand. The pages of a book are printed on large sheets of paper called sections, or signatures. When folded, sections usually make 8, 16, or 32 pages. To assemble a hand-bound hardback book, the binder first places the folded sections in the correct order within the endpapers. Next, he or she sews the sections together along the spine edge using strong thread and then pastes them with glue for extra strength. After trimming the pages, the binder puts the book in a press and hammers the spine to shape it. The binder then glues one or more linings on the spine. The cover, or case, comes last. To make this, the bookbinder sticks cover boards to the endpapers, front and back, and then covers them with cloth or leather.

HALF-BOUND BOOK

LEATHER-BOUND BOOK

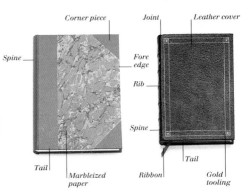

Corner piece

Joint

Leather cover

Spine

Fore edge

Rib

Spine

Tail

Tail

Marbleized paper

Ribbon

Gold tooling

HALF-BOUND BOOK

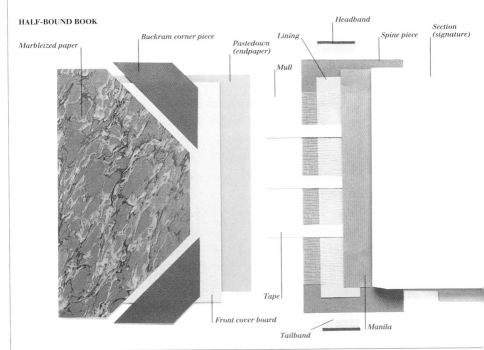

Marbleized paper

Buckram corner piece

Pastedown (endpaper)

Lining

Headband

Spine piece

Section (signature)

Mull

Tape

Front cover board

Tailband

Manila

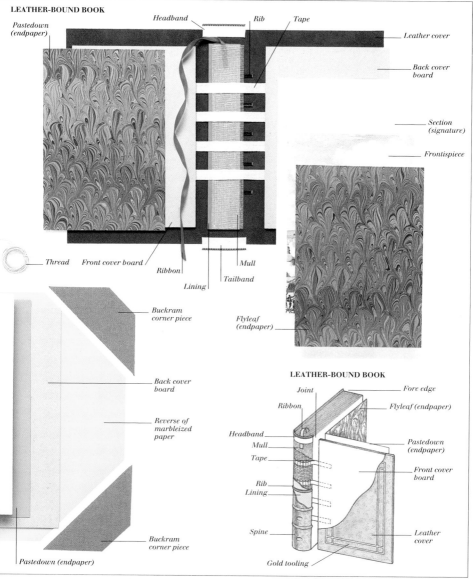

LEATHER-BOUND BOOK

Pastedown (endpaper)

Headband

Rib

Tape

Leather cover

Back cover board

Section (signature)

Frontispiece

Thread

Front cover board

Ribbon

Mull

Lining

Tailband

Flyleaf (endpaper)

Buckram corner piece

Back cover board

Reverse of marbleized paper

Buckram corner piece

Pastedown (endpaper)

LEATHER-BOUND BOOK

Joint

Ribbon

Headband

Mull

Tape

Rib

Lining

Spine

Gold tooling

Fore edge

Flyleaf (endpaper)

Pastedown (endpaper)

Front cover board

Leather cover

Camera

A CAMERA IS AN INSTRUMENT used for recording images on photographic film. It consists of a light-tight box with a shutter, a lens containing a diaphragm, and a viewing system. When the shutter is released, the film is exposed to light from the subject that is being photographed. Adjusting the shutter speed alters the time for which the film is exposed to light. The diaphragm, by altering the aperture of the lens, controls the intensity of light entering the camera. The total amount of light entering the camera is called the exposure. The lens focuses the light onto the film. When there is insufficient light to produce an adequate image, a flashgun may be used to give extra light.

FRONT VIEW OF CAMERA

Shutter speed dial
Film rewind/back cover release knob
Shutter release button
Exposure counter
Strap lug
Lens lock release lever
X-flash sync terminal

FRONT BOARD ASSEMBLY

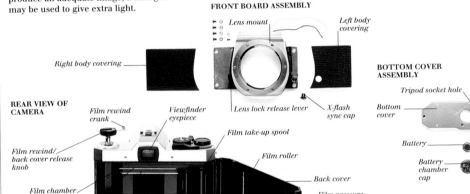

Lens mount
Left body covering
Right body covering
Lens lock release lever
X-flash sync cap

BOTTOM COVER ASSEMBLY

Tripod socket hole
Bottom cover
Battery
Battery chamber cap

REAR VIEW OF CAMERA

Film rewind crank
Viewfinder eyepiece
Film take-up spool
Film roller
Film rewind/back cover release knob
Back cover
Film pressure plate
Film chamber
Film rail
Film sprocket spool
Film guide rail
Shutter curtain

LENS BARREL ASSEMBLY

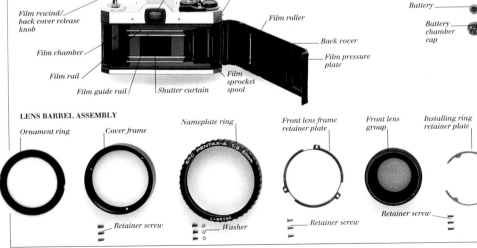

Ornament ring
Cover frame
Nameplate ring
Front lens frame retainer plate
Front lens group
Installing ring retainer plate
Retainer screw
Washer
Retainer screw
Retainer screw

TOP COVER ASSEMBLY

Shutter dial knob spring

Film speed indicator

Counter dial housing

Film wind lever

Speed dial knob

Shutter speed dial

Retainer screw

Counter dial cover

Exposure counter dial

Wind lever install spring

Wind lever collar

Top cover

X-contact

Hot shoe

Rewind shaft

Film rewind/ back cover release knob

Retainer screw

Washer

Rewind shaft bushing

Window

Prism retainer plate

Shutter release button

Shutter speed index

Film rewind crank

MAIN BODY

Prism retainer spring

Strap lug

Viewfinder eyepiece

Pentaprism

Cover frame

Retainer screw

TOP VIEW OF CAMERA

Focusing ring

Aperture/distance index

Subject distance scale

Depth-of-field guide

Lens alignment node

Aperture auto-lock button

Lens lock release lever

Shutter release button

Hole for film rewind button

Shutter cocked indicator

Exposure counter

Retainer screw

Film rewind crank

Film rewind/back cover release knob

Hot shoe

X-contact

Shutter speed index

Film speed indicator

Shutter speed dial

Film wind lever

Supporter ring retainer plate

Supporter ring

Diaphragm blade

Installing ring

Main barrel assembly

Rear lens group

Opening and closing plate

Appendix: useful data

UNITS OF MEASUREMENT

U.S. unit	Equivalent
Length	
1 foot (ft)	12 inches (in)
1 yard (yd)	3 feet
1 rod (rd)	5.5 yards
1 mile (mi)	1,760 yards
Mass	
1 dram (dr)	27.344 grains (gr)
1 ounce (oz)	16 drams
1 pound (lb)	16 ounces
1 hundredweight (cwt) (long)	112 pounds
1 hundredweight (cwt) (short)	100 pounds
1 ton (long)	2,240 pounds
1 ton (short)	2,000 pounds
Area	
1 square foot (ft²)	144 square inches (in²)
1 square yard (yd²)	9 square feet
1 acre	4,840 square yards
1 square mile	640 acres
Volume	
1 cubic foot	1,728 cubic inches
1 cubic yard	27 cubic feet
Capacity (liquid and dry measures)	
1 fluidram (fl dr)	60 minims (min)
1 fluid ounce (fl oz)	8 fluidrams
1 gill (gi)	4 fluid ounces
1 pint (pt)	4 gills
1 quart (qt)	2 pints
1 gallon (gal)	4 quarts
1 peck (pk)	2 gallons
1 bushel (bu)	4 pecks

Metric unit	Equivalent
Length	
1 centimeter (cm)	10 millimeters (mm)
1 meter (m)	100 centimeters
1 kilometer (km)	1,000 meters
Mass	
1 kilogram (kg)	1,000 grams (g)
1 tonne (t)	1,000 kilograms
Area	
1 square centimeter (cm²)	100 square millimeters (mm²)
1 square meter (m²)	10,000 square centimeters
1 hectare	10,000 square meters
1 square kilometer (km²)	1,000,000 square meters
Volume	
1 cubic centimeter (cc)	1 milliliter (ml)
1 liter (l)	1,000 milliliters
1 cubic meter (m³)	1,000 liters
Capacity (liquid and dry measures)	
1 centiliter (cl)	10 milliliters (ml)
1 deciliter (dl)	10 centiliters
1 liter (l)	10 deciliters
1 decaliter (dal)	10 liters
1 hectoliter (hl)	10 decaliters
1 kiloliter (kl)	10 hectoliters

AREAS AND VOLUMES

CIRCLE
Radius r
Diameter $d = 2 \times r$
Circumference $= 2 \times \pi \times r$
Area $= \pi \times r^2$
($\pi = 3.1416$)

TRIANGLE
Height h
Sides a, b, c
Perimeter $= a + b + c$
Area $= \frac{1}{2} \times b \times h$

RECTANGLE
Sides a, b
Perimeter $= 2 \times (a + b)$
Area $= a \times b$

CYLINDER
Height h
Radius r
Surface area $= 2 \times \pi \times r \times h$
(excluding ends)
Volume $= \pi \times r^2 \times h$

CONE
Height h
Radius r
Side l
Surface area $= \pi \times r \times l$ (excluding base)
Volume $= \frac{1}{3} \times \pi \times r^2 \times l$

RECTANGULAR BLOCK
Sides a, b, c
Surface area $= 2 \times (a \times b + b \times c + a \times c)$
Volume $= a \times b \times c$

TEMPERATURE SCALES

To convert from Celsius (C) to Fahrenheit (F): $F = (C \times 9 \div 5) + 32$
To convert from Fahrenheit to Celsius: $C = (F - 32) \times 5 \div 9$
To convert from Celsius to Kelvin (K): $K = C + 273$
To convert from Kelvin to Celsius: $C = K - 273$

Celsius	-20	-10	0	10	20	30	40	50	60	70	80	90	100
Fahrenheit	-4	14	32	50	68	86	104	122	140	158	176	194	212
Kelvin	253	263	273	283	293	303	313	323	333	343	353	363	373

U.S. – METRIC CONVERSIONS

To convert	Into	Multiply by
Length		
Inches	centimeters	2.5400
Feet	meters	0.3048
Miles	kilometers	1.6090
Yards	meters	0.9144
Mass		
Ounces	grams	28.3500
Pounds	kilograms	0.4536
Long tons	tonnes	1.0160
Short tons	tonnes	0.9070
Area		
Square inches	square centimeters	6.4520
Square feet	square meters	0.0929
Acres	hectares	0.4047
Square miles	square kilometers	2.5900
Square yards	square meters	0.8361
Volume		
Cubic inches	cubic centimeters	16.3900
Cubic feet	cubic meters	0.0283
Capacity		
Pints (liquid)	liters	0.4730
Gallons (liquid)	liters	3.7850

METRIC – U.S. CONVERSIONS

To convert	Into	Multiply by
Length		
Centimeters	inches	0.3937
Meters	feet	3.2810
Kilometers	miles	0.6214
Meters	yards	1.0940
Mass		
Grams	ounces	0.0352
Kilograms	pounds	2.2050
Tonnes	long tons	0.9843
Tonnes	short tons	1.1025
Area		
Square centimeters	square inches	0.1550
Square meters	square feet	10.7600
Hectares	acres	2.4710
Square kilometers	square miles	0.3861
Square meters	square yards	1.1960
Volume		
Cubic centimeters	cubic inches	0.0610
Cubic meters	cubic feet	35.3100
Capacity		
Liters	pints (liquid)	2.1142
Liters	gallons (liquid)	0.2642

NUMBER SYSTEMS

Roman	Arabic
I	1
II	2
III	3
IV	4
V	5
VI	6
VII	7
VIII	8
IX	9
X	10
XI	11
XII	12
XIII	13
XIV	14
XV	15
XX	20
XXI	21
XXX	30
XL	40
L	50
LX	60
LXX	70
LXXX	80
XC	90
C	100
CI	101
CC	200
CCC	300
CD	400
D	500
DC	600
DCC	700
DCCC	800
CM	900
M	1,000
MM	2,000

PHYSICS SYMBOLS

Symbol	Meaning
α	alpha particle
β	beta ray
γ	gamma ray; photon
ε	electromotive force
η	efficiency; viscosity
λ	wavelength
μ	micro-; permeability
ν	frequency; neutrino
ρ	density; resistivity
σ	conductivity
c	velocity of light
e	electronic charge

MATHEMATICS SYMBOLS

Symbol	Meaning
$+$	plus
$-$	minus
$\pm$	plus or minus
$\times$	multiplied by
$\div$	divided by
$=$	equals
$>$	is greater than
$<$	is less than
$\geq$	is greater than or equal to
$\leq$	is less than or equal to
$\%$	per cent
$\sqrt{}$	root
π	pi (3.1416)
°	degree
∞	infinity
$\approx$	is approximately equal to
$\angle$	angle

CHEMISTRY SYMBOLS

Symbol	Meaning
+	plus; together with
−	single bond
•	single bond; single unpaired electron; two separate parts or compounds regarded as loosely joined
=	double bond
≡	triple bond
R	group
X	halogen atom
Z	atomic number

BIOLOGY SYMBOLS

Symbol	Meaning
○	female individual (used in inheritance charts)
□	male individual (used in inheritance charts)
♀	female
♂	male
×	crossed with; hybrid
+	wild type
F_1	offspring of the first generation
F_2	offspring of the second generation

POWERS OF TEN USED WITH SCIENTIFIC UNITS

Factor	Name	Prefix	Symbol
10^{18}	quintillion	exa-	E
10^{15}	quadrillion	peta-	P
10^{12}	trillion	tera-	T
10^9	billion	giga-	G
10^6	million	mega-	M
10^3	thousand	kilo-	k
10^2	hundred	hecto-	h
10^1	ten	deca-	da
10^{-1}	one tenth	deci-	d
10^{-2}	one hundredth	centi-	c
10^{-3}	one thousandth	milli-	m
10^{-6}	one millionth	micro-	μ
10^{-9}	one billionth	nano-	n
10^{-12}	one trillionth	pico-	p
10^{-15}	one quadrillionth	femto-	f
10^{-18}	one quintillionth	atto-	a

Index

606

628

Acknowledgments

Dorling Kindersley would like to thank
(in order of sections):

The Universe
(consultant editors – Sue Becklake, Gevorkyan
Tatyana Alekseyevna):
John Becklake; the Memorial Museum of
Cosmonautics, Moscow; The Cosmos Pavilion,
Moscow; The United States Space and Rocket
Center, Alabama; Broadhurst, Clarkson and
Fuller Ltd; Susannah Massey

Prehistoric Earth
(consultant editors – William Lindsay, Martyn
Bramwell, Dr. Ralph E. Molnar, David
Lambert):
Dr. Monty Reid, Andrew Neuman, and the staff of the
Royal Tyrrell Museum of Palaeontology, Drumheller,
Alberta; Dr. Angela Milner and the staff of the
Department of Palaeontology, the Natural History
Museum, London; Professor W. Ziegler and the
staff, in particular Michael Loderstaedt, of the
Naturmuseum Senckenburg, Frankfurt; Dr.
Alexander Liebau, Axel Hunghrebüller, Reiner
Schoch, and the staff of the Institut und Museum
für Geologie und Paläontologie der Universität,
Tübingen; Rupert Wild of the Institut für
Paläontologie, Staatliches Museum für Naturkunde,
Stuttgart; Dr. Scheiber of the Stadtmuseum,
Nördlingen; Professor Dr. Dietrich Herm of
Staatssammlung für Paläontologie und Historische
Geologie, München; Dr. Michael Keith-Lucas of
the Department of Botany, University of Reading;
Richard Walker; American Museum of Natural
History, New York

Plants
(consultant editor – Richard Walker):
Diana Miller; Lawrie Springate; Karen Sidwell; Chris
Thody; Michelle End; Susan Barnes and Chris Jones
of the EMU Unit of the Natural History Museum,
London; Jenny Evans of Kew Gardens, London;
Kate Biggs of the Royal Horticultural Society Gardens,
Wisley, Surrey; Spike Walker of Microworld Services;
Neil Fletcher; John Bryant of Bedgebury Pinetum,
Kent; Dean Franklin

Animals
(consultant editor – Richard Walker):
David Manning's Animal Ark; Intellectual Animals;
Howletts Zoo, Canterbury; John Dunlop; Alexander
O'Donnell; Sue Evans of the Royal Veterinary
College, London; Dr. Geoff Potts and Fred Frettsome
of the Marine Biological Association of the United
Kingdom, Plymouth; Jeremy Adams of the Booth
Museum of Natural History, Brighton; Derek Telling
of the Department of Anatomy, University of Bristol;
the Natural History Museum, London; Andy Highfield
of the Tortoise Trust; Brian Harris of the Aquarium,
London Zoo; the Invertebrate Department, London
Zoo; Dr. Harold McClure of the Yerkes Regional
Primate Research Center, Emory University, Atlanta,
Georgia; Nielson Lausen of the Harvard Medical

School, New England Regional Primates Research
Center, Southborough, Massachusetts; Dr. Paul
Hopwood of the Department of Veterinary Anatomy,
University of Sydney; Dean Franklin

The Human Body
(consultant editors – Dr. Frances Williams,
Dr. Fiona Payne, Richard Cummins FRCS):
Derek Edwards and Dr Martin Collins, British School
of Osteopathy; Dr. M.C.E. Hutchinson of the
Department of Anatomy, United Medical and Dental
Schools of Guy's and St. Thomas' Hospitals, London.
Models – Barry O'Rorke (Bodyline Agency) and
Pauline Swaine (MOT Model Agency)

Geology, Geography, and Meteorology
(consultant editor – Martyn Bramwell):
Dr. John Nudds of the Manchester Museum,
Manchester; Dr. Alan Wooley and Dr. Andrew Clark
of the Natural History Museum, London; Graham
Bartlett of the National Meteorological Library and
Archive, Bracknell; Tony Drake of BP Exploration,
Uxbridge; Jane Davies of the Royal Society of
Chemistry, Cambridge; Dr. Tony Waltham of
Nottingham Trent University, Nottingham; staff of the
Smithsonian Institute, Washington; staff of the United
States Geological Survey, Washington; staff of the
National Geographic Society, Washington; staff of
Edward Lawrence Associates (Export Ltd), Midhurst;
John Farndon; David Lambert

Rail and Road
Rail (consultant editor – John Coiley)
Michael Ashworth of the London Transport Museum

Road (consultant editors – David Burgess-Wise,
Hugo Wilson):
The National Motor Museum, Beaulieu; Alf Newell of
Renault UK Ltd; David Suter of Cheltenham Cutaway
Exhibits Ltd; Francesca Riccini of the Science
Museum, London. Signore Amadelli of the Museo
dell' Automobile Carlo Biscaretti di Ruffia; Paul
Bolton of the Mazda MCL Group; Duncan Bradford
of Reg Mills Wire Wheels; John and Leslie Brewster
of Autocavan; David Burgess-Wise; Trevor Cass of
Garrett Turbo Service; John Corbett of The Patrick
Collection; Gary Crumpler of Williams Grand Prix
Engineering Ltd; Mollie Easterbrooke and Duncan
Gough of Overland Ltd; Arthur Fairley of the
Vauxhall Motor Co; Paul Foulkes-Halbard of Filching
Manor Motor Museum; Frank Gilbert of I. Wilkinson
and Son Ltd; Paolo Gratton of Gratton Museum;
Colvin Gunn of Gunn and Son; Judy Hogg of Ecurie
Bertelli; Milton Holman of Dream Cars; Ian Matthews
of IMAT Electronics; Eric Neal of Jaguar Cars Ltd;
Paul Niblett, Keith Davidson, Mark Reumel, and
David Woolf of Michelin Tyre plc; Doug Nye;
Kevin O'Keefe of O'Keefe Cars; Seat UK; Roger Smith;
Jim Stirling of Ironbridge Gorge Museum, Stafford-
shire; Jon Taylor; Doug Thompson; Martyn Watkins
of Ford Motor Co Ltd; John Cattermole, Customer
Services Manager, at London Northern Buses;
F. W. Evans Cycles Ltd; Trek UK Ltd (Bicycle);
Sam Grimmer

Physics and Chemistry
(consultant editor – Jack Challoner)

Sea and Air
Sea (consultant editors – Geoff Hales and
Harvey B. Loomis):
David Spence, Gillian Hutchinson, David Topliss,
Simon Stephens, Robert Baldwin, Jonathan Betts, all
of the National Maritime Museum, London; Ian Friel;
Simon Turnage of Captain O.M. Watts of London Ltd;
Davey and Co Ltd, Great Dunmow; Avon Inflatables
Ltd, Llanelli; Musto Ltd, Benfleet; Peter Martin of
Spencer Rigging Ltd, Southampton; Peter Rowson of
Ratseys Sailmakers, Southampton; Swiftech Ltd,
Wallingford; Colin Scattergood of the Barrow Boat Co
Ltd, Colchester; Professor J.S. Morrison of the
Trireme Trust, Cambridge; The Cutty Sark Maritime
Trust; Adrian Daniels of Kelvin Hughes Marine
Instruments, London; Arthur Credland of Hull City
Council Museums and Art Galleries; The Hull
Maritime Society; Gerald Clark; Peter Fitzgerald of
the Science Museum, London; Alec Michael of HMB
Subwork Ltd, Great Yarmouth, and Ray Ward of the
OSEL Group, Great Yarmouth; Richard Bird of UWI,
Weybridge; Walker Marine Instruments,
Birmingham; The International Sailing Craft
Association; The Exeter Maritime Museum; Jane
Wilson of the Trinity Lighthouse Co, London; The
Imperial War Museum Collections; Thorn Security
Ltd; Michael Bach

Air (consultant editor – Bill Gunston):
Aeromega Helicopters, Stapleford; Aero Shopping,
London; Avionics Mobile Services Ltd, Watford;
Roy Barber and John Chapman of the RAF Museum,
Hendon; Mitch Barnes Aviation, London; Mike Beach;
British Caledonian Flight Training Ltd; Fred Coates
of Helitech (Luton) Ltd; Michael Cuttell and CSE
Aviation Ltd, Oxford; Dowty Aerospace Landing Gear,
Gloucester; Guy Hartcup of the Airship Association;
Anthony Hooley, Chris Walsh, and David Cord of
British Aerospace Regional Aircraft Ltd; Ken Huntley
of Mid-West Aero Engines Ltd; Imperial War
Museum, Duxford; The London Gliding Club,
Dunstable; Musée des Ballons, Calvados; Noel Penny
Turbines Ltd; Andy Pavey of Aviation Scotland Ltd;
Tony Pavey of Thermal Aircraft Developments,
London; the Commanding Officer and personnel
of RAF St Athan; the Commanding Officer and
personnel of RAF Wittering; The Science Museum,
London; Ross Sharp of the Science Museum,
Wroughton; The Shuttleworth Collection; Skysport
Engineering; Mike Smith; Solar Wings Ltd,
Marlborough; Julian Temple of Brooklands Museum
Trust Ltd; Kelvin Wilson of Flying Start

Architecture
(consultant editor – Alexandra Kennedy):
Stephen Cutler for advice and text; Gavin Morgan of
the Museum of London, London; Chris Zeuner of the
Weald and Downland Museum, Singleton, Sussex;
Alan Hills and James Putnam of the British Museum,
London; Dr. Simon Penn and Michael Thomas of the
Avoncroft Museum of Buildings, Bromsgrove,

Worcestershire; Christina Scull of Sir John Soane's Museum, London; Paul Kennedy and John Williamson of the London Door Co, London; Lou Davis of The Original Box Sash Window Co, Windsor; Goddard and Gibbs Studios Ltd, London, for access to stained glass windows; The Royal Courts of Justice, Strand, London; Charles Brooking and Peter Dalton for access to the doors and windows in the Charles Brooking Collection, University of Greenwich, Dartford, Kent; Clare O'Brien of the Shakespeare Globe Trust, Shakespeare's Globe Museum, Bear Gardens, Southwark, London; Ken Teague of the Horniman Museum, London; Canon Haliburton, Mike Payton, Ken Stones, and Anthony Webb of St. Paul's Cathedral, London; Roy Spring of Salisbury Cathedral; Reverend Gillean Craig of the Church of St. George in the East, London; the Science Museum, London; Dr. Neil Bingham; Lin Kennedy of Historic Royal Palaces; Katy Harris of Sir Norman Foster and Partners; Production Design, Thames Television plc, London, for supplying models; Dominique Reynier of Le Centre Georges Pompidou, Paris; Denis Roche of Le Musée National des Monuments Français, Paris; Franck Gioria and students of Les Compagnons du Devoir, Paris, for access to construction models; Frank Folliot of Le Musée Carnavalet, Paris; Dr Martina Harms of Hessische Landesmuseums, Darmstadt; Jefferson Chapman of the University of Tennessee, Knoxville, for access to the model of the Hypostyle Hall, Temple of Amon-Re; staff of the Palazzo Strozzi, Florence; staff of the Sydney Opera House, Sydney; staff of the Empire State Building, New York; Nick Jackson; Ann Terrell

The Visual Arts
(consultant editor – Pip Seymour):
Rosemary Simmons; Michael Taylor of Paupers Press, London; Tessa Hunkin and Emma Biggs of Mosaic Workshop, London; John Tiranti, Jonathan Lyons of Alec Tiranti Ltd, London; Chris Hough; Dr. Ashok Roy; Satwinder Sehmi of Alphabet Soup, London; Phillip Poole of Cornelissens, London; George Weil and Sons Ltd, London; The National Gallery, London; Chris Webster of the Tate Gallery, London; China Art Cultural Centre, London; London Graphic Centre, London; A.P. Fitzpatrick, London; Flowers Graphics, London; Intaglio Printmaker, London; Falkiner Papers, London; Edgar Udny and Co, London; John Green

Music
(consultant editor – Susan Sturrock):
Boosey and Hawkes Music Publishers Ltd, London, for permission to reproduce extract from The Prodigal Son by Arthur Sullivan; The Bass and Drum Cellar, London; Empire Drums and Percussion, London; Argents (part of World of Music), London; Bill Lewington Ltd, London; Frobenius organ at Kingston Parish Church, Kingston-upon-Thames, Surrey; Yamaha-Kemble Music (UK) Ltd, Tilbrook, Milton Keynes; Yamaha Atelier, London; Akai (UK) Ltd, Hounslow, Middlesex; Casio Electronics Co Ltd, London; Roland (UK) Ltd, Fleet, Hampshire; Richard Schulman

Sports
The Sports Council Information Centre, London; The British Olympic Games Committee; Brian Crennell of Black's Leisure Group (First Sport); Lillywhites of Piccadilly, London; Mitre Sports International Ltd, Huddersfield; David Bloomfield of the Football Association; Denver Athletics Ltd, Norfolk; Greg Everest and Keith Birley of the British League of Australian Rules Football; Peter McNally of the Gaelic Athletic Association; Rex King of the Rugby Football Union, Twickenham; Neil Tunnicliffe of the Rugby Football League, Leeds; Wayne Patterson of the Basketball Hall of Fame, Springfield, Connecticut; Brian Coleman of the English Basketball Association; All American Imports, Northampton; George Bulman of the English Volleyball Association; Julie Longdon of Mizuno Mallory (UK) Ltd; Juliet Stanford of the All-England Netball Association; Jeff Rowland of the British Handball Association; Cally Melin of Adidas UK Ltd; Patrick Donnely of the Baseball Hall of Fame, Cooperstown, New York; Ian Lepage and Stephen Barlow of the Hockey Association, Milton Keynes; Alison Taylor and Anita Mason of the All England Women's Lacrosse Association, Birmingham; David Shuttleworth of the English Lacrosse Union; Les Barnett and Jock Bentley of the British Athletic Federation Ltd, Birmingham; Mike Gilks of the Badminton Association of England; Gurinder Purewall for advice on archery; Chris McCartney of the US Archery Association; Geoff Doe of the National Smallbore Rifle Association, Bisley, Surrey, for information and reference material on shooting; Fagan Sports Goods Distributors, Surrey; Konrad Bartelski for advice on skiing; The British Ski Federation, Edinburgh; Mike Barnett of Snow and Rock of London; Sally Spurway of Mast-Co. Ltd, Reading; Sarah Morgan for advice on equestrian sports; Steve Brown and the New York Racing Association Inc, New York; Danrho of London; Alan Skipp and James Chambers of the Amateur Fencing Association, London; Carla Richards of the US Fencing Association; Hamilton Bland and John Dryer of the Amateur Swimming Association, Loughborough; Cotswold Camping Ltd, London; Tim Spalton of Glyn Locke (Racing Shells) Ltd, Chalgrove; Terry Friel of the US Rowing Association; House of Hardy; Leeda Fishing Tackle

Everyday Things
City Clocks (Clocks); Christopher Cullen of Babber Electronics; Sony UK Ltd (Mini-television); Black and Decker Ltd (Drills); British Footwear Manufacturing Federation; Grenson Shoes Ltd (Shoes); The Folio Society; R S Bookbinders (Books); Pentax UK Ltd (Camera); F E Murdin of the Decorative Lighting Association; Habitat (Lamp); Chingford Reproductions Ltd (Chair); Dualit Ltd (Toaster); J B Dove; Toro Wheelhorse UK Ltd (Lawnmower); WandH Gidden Ltd (Saddle)

PHOTOGRAPHY:
M. Alexander; Peter Anderson; Charles Brooks; Jane Burton; Peter Chadwick; Simon Clay; John Coiley; Andy Crawford; Geoff Dann; Philip Dowell; John Downs; Mike Dunning; Torla Evans; David Exton; Robert and Anthony Fretwell of Fretwell Photography Ltd.; Philip Gatward; Anna Hodgson; Gary Kevin; J. Heseltine; Cyril Laubscher; John Lepine; Lynton Gardiner (American Museum of Natural History, New York); Steve Gorton; Michelangelo Gratton; Judith Harrington; Peter Hayman; Anna Hodgson; Colin Keates; Gary Kevin; Dave King; Bob Langrish; Brian D.Morgan; Nick Nicholls; Nick Parfitt; Tim Parmenter and Colin Keates (Natural History Museum, London); Tim Ridley; Dave Rudkin; Philippe Sebert; James Stevenson; Clive Streeter; Harry Taylor; Matthew Ward; Jerry Young

PHOTOGRAPHIC ASSISTANCE:
Kevin Zak; Gary Ombler

ILLUSTRATORS:
Julian Baum; Rick Blakeley; Kuo Kang Chen; Karen Cochrane; Simone End; Ian Fleming; Roy Flooks; Mark Franklin; David Gardner; Will Giles; Mick Gillah; David Hopkins; Selwyn Hutchinson; Mei Lim; Linden Artists; Nick Loates; Chris Lyon; Kathleen McDougall; Coral Mula; Sandra Pond; Dave Pugh; Colin Rose; Graham Rosewarne; John Temperton; John Woodcock; Chris Woolmer

MODEL MAKERS:
Roby Braun; David Donkin; Morrison Frederick; Gordon Models; John Holmes; Graham High and Jeremy Hunt of Centaur Studios; Richard Kemp; Kelvin Thatcher; Paul Wilkinson

ADDITIONAL DESIGN ASSISTANCE:
Stefan Morris; Ulysses Santos; Suchada Smith

ADDITIONAL EDITORIAL ASSISTANCE:
Helen Castle; Colette Connolly; Camela Decaire; Nick Harris; Andrea Horth; Stewart McEwen; Damien Moore; Melanie Tham;

INDEX: Kay Wright

Picture credits:

Action Plus 550tc; Anglo Australian Telescope Board 11cl, 11cra, 11cbl, 12tr, 12bc, 13tl, 13bl, 14tl, 16b, 17tc, 17bl, 22tl/D.Malin 16tl, 26tr, 27tl; Austin Brown and the Aviation Picture Library 426tl; Baptistery, Florence/Alison Harris 453r; Biophoto Associates 217ca, 217cra, 228cbc, 228cbc 230tr; Paul Brierley 311bra; British Aerospace/Anthony Hooley 412tl, 415tl; British Aerospace (Commercial Aircraft) Ltd 416tl; by permission of the British Library 432tl; British Museum 459tl, 459tr, 460tr, 460tc, 460tb, 489b; BP Exploration 299; Duncan Brown 25tl; Frank Lloyd Wright, American, 1867-1959, Model of Midway Gardens, 1914, executed by Richard Tickner, mixed media, 1987, 41.9 x 81.3 x 76.2, 1989.48. view 1. Photography courtesy of the Art Intitute of Chicago 495t; J.A. Coiley 331cr; Bruce Coleman Ltd/Andy Price 272tl; Courtesy of the Board of Trustees of the Victoria and Albert Museum, London 454-455b; European Passenger Services 529tl; ESA /PLV 11bl; French Railways 329c; Geoscience Features 311cla; Robert Harding Picture Library 62tl; Michael Holford /British Museum 372bl, Michael Holford 374tr; Hutchison Picture Library 60cl; The Image Bank/Edward Bower 306tr; Jet Propulsion Laboratory 11cbr; 30bc; 31bc; 31bcr; 58tl; 42crb; 44cb; 44cbr; 44bc; 44br; 46tl; 46cr; 46cb; 46bc; 46br; 50tl; 50cra; 50cl; 50c; 50cr; 50br; KeyMed Ltd 248bl, 249bl, 249bcl; Department of Prints and Drawings, Uffizi, Florence/Philip Gatward 451tlc/Uffizi, Florence/Philip Gatward 453tl; Dr. D.N. Landon (Institute of Neurology) 228bl,br; Life Science Images/Ron Boardman 244bl, 244br; The Lund Observatory 15bc; Brian Morrison 329tl, 329tr;

© The Henry Moore Foundation 455tl, 455tr; Musée d'Orsay, Paris/Philippe Sebert 457tc, 441tc; Musée du Louvre, Paris/Philippe Sebert 453tl, 453r; NASA/AUI 13tr; NASA/JPL 11 cbr, 11br, 50tl, 50bl, 50br, 50bc, 51bc, 51bcr, 51bl, 54cr, 38tl, 40tl, 40cr, 42cr, 44tl, 44cb, 44cbr, 44bc, 44br, 44cr, 46crb, 46tl, 46cr, 46cb, 46bc, 46br, 48tl, 48cra, 48bc, 48br, 50tl, 50bc, 50bc, 50cbr, 50br, 50cr, 52cr; National Maritime Museum 575br, 592-593b; National Medical Slide Bank 217cr; Nature Photographers/Paul Sterry 286tl; Newage International 317bl; Oxford Scientific Films/Breck P. Kent 166tl; Planet Earth 274tr; Quadrant 526tr; Margaret Robinson 532tl, 453br; Giotto The Expulsion of the Merchants from the Temple Scala 455tc, 455bl, 455br; Science Photo Library 10bl, 13tr, 28tr, 214bcr, 214bl, 256tr/Michael Abbey 225tc/Agema Infrared Systems 318tl/AGFA 220tl/Biophoto Associates: 217crb/Dr. Jeremy Burgess/Science Photo Library 132tr; Dr. Jeremy Burgess 255bcl/CNRI 214tl, 214cl, 214c, 214cr, 214bl, 214clb, 214crb, 214blc, 214br, 217cb, 255bcr, 258tl, 249bcr, 253tr, 253cra, 256tl; Science Photo library /Earth Satellite Corporation 288cl, 293br/Dr. Brian Eyden 228cbr/Professor C. Ferlaud 245bl/Vaughan Fleming 51ttl/Simon Fraser/U.S. Dept.of Energy 214bcl, 266tl/Eric Grave 217br/Hale Observatories 32br/Max Planck Institute for Radio Astronomy 15tl/Jan Hinsch 225tc/Jodrell Bank 11 tr, 13c /Manfred Kage 217c, 255br, 237br/Dr. William C. Keel 13br/Keith Kent 516tl/Russ Lappa 510bra/Astrid & Hans-Freider Michler 217tr/Dennis Milon 52bl/NASA 11cla, 12tl, 15tr, 30c, 31br, 32tl, 35tl, 36tl, 36cl, 36cr, 36bc, 42br, 42tr, 44tl 52tl, 291tr, 300tl/National Optical Astro Observatory 52tr/NIBSC 253crb/

Novosti Press Agency 42bc/Omikron 244bc/ David Parker 63bl, 304-305, 308br/Philippe Plailly 308tl, Roussel-UCLAF/CNRI 217tc/Rev Ronald Royer 32cr/Royal Observatory, Edinburgh/D Malin 11 tl, 11cr,12c, 16cl, 16cr, 17br/David Scharf 255bl/Dr. Kaus Schiller 248bcl, 248bcr, 248br/Secchi-Lecaque/Roussel-UCLAF/CNRI 253br/H. Sochurek 214cb/Stammers/Thompson 230tl/Sheila Terry 254tl/US Department of Energy 510bc/US Geological Survey/Science Photo Library 8-9, 50bcr, 42tl, 42bl/Tom Van Sant/Geosphere Project, Santa Monica/Science Photo Library 273tr, 281tr, 296tr, 297tl/Dr. Christopher B. Williams/(Saint Marks Hospital)249br; Oxford Scientific Films/Animals Animals/Breck P. Kent 167tl; Pratt & Whitney Canada 418-419b, 419t; Science Museum 306bl, 306bcl, 306 bcr, 524t, 326-527b, 330tr, 331cl, 331 cb; Sporting Pictures 524tl, 544cr; Tony Stone Worldwide 280tl; David Bomberg St. Pauls and River 1945/Dinora Davies-Rees/Tate Gallery 431bc; David Hockney A Bigger Splash 1967/ © David Hockney/Tate Gallery 443tc; J.M.W. Turner The Burning of the Houses of Parliament Tate Gallery 439tc; Vision 26tr, 27c; Jerry Young 506tl; Dr. Robert Youngson 241cr; Zefa 217bc/Janicek 276tl/H. Sochurek 210tl, 250tl, 254tl,/G. Steenmans 292tl

(t=top, b=bottom, a=above, l-left, r=right, c=center)

Every effort has been made to trace the copyright holders. Dorling Kindersley apologises for any unintentional omissions and would be pleased, in any such cases, to add an acknowledgment in future editions.

Some pages in this book previously appeared in the *Visual Dictionary* series published by Dorling Kindersley. Contributors to this series include:

Project Art Editors:
Duncan Brown, Ross George, Nicola Liddiard, Andrew Nash, Clare Shedden, Bryn Walls

Designers:
Lesley Betts, Paul Calver, Simone End, Ellen Woodward

Additional design assistance:
Sandra Archer, Christina Betts, Alexandra Brown, Nick Jackson, Susan Knight

Project Editors:
Fiona Courtney-Thompson, Paul Docherty, Tim Fraser, Stephanie Jackson, Mary Lindsay

Editorial Assistant:
Emily Hill

Additional editorial assistance:
Susan Bosanko, Edward Bunting, Candace Burch, Deirdre Clark, Jeanette Cossar, Danièle Guitton, Jacqui Hand, David Harding, Nicholas Jackson, Edwina Johnson, David Lambert, Gail Lawther, David Learmount, Paul Jackson, Christine Murdock, Bob Ogden, Cathy Rubinstein, Louise Tucker, Dr. Robert Youngson

Picture Researchers:
Vere Dodds, Danièle Guitton, Anna Lord, Catherine O'Rourke, Christine Rista, Sandra Schneider, Vanessa Smith, Clive Webster

Series Editor:
Martyn Page

Series Art Editor:
Paul Wilkinson

Managing Art Editors
Philip Gilderdale, Steve Knowlden

Art Director
Chez Picthall

Managing Editor
Ruth Midgley

Production:
Jayne Simpson